# North Carolina Hiking Trails

# Trail Books by the Author

*Hiking and Backpacking* (1979, 1983)

*North Carolina Hiking Trails* (1982, 1988)

*Hiking the Old Dominion:*
*The Trails of Virginia* (1984)

*South Carolina Hiking Trails* (1984)

*Hiking and Backpacking Basics* (1985)

*Hiking the Mountain State:*
*The Trails of West Virginia* (1986)

*Monongahela National Forest*
*Hiking Guide,* with Bruce
Sundquist (1988)

# North Carolina Hiking Trails

## Second Edition

Allen de Hart

APPALACHIAN MOUNTAIN CLUB BOOKS
Boston, Massachusetts

Cover design/Paula Bowers Moran

SECOND EDITION

*Library of Congress Cataloging-in-Publication Data*
De Hart, Allen.
    North Carolina hiking trails/by Allen de Hart.—2nd ed. p. cm.
    Includes index.
    ISBN 0-910146-69-1 (alk. paper)
    1. Hiking—North Carolina—Guide-books. 2. Trails—North Carolina—Guide-books. 3. North Carolina—Description and travel—1981–    —Guide-books. I. Title.
GV199.42.N66D4 1988
917.56—dc19                                         87-31848CIP

The paper used in this publication meets the minimum requirements of the American National Standard for Information Sciences—Permanence of Paper for Printed Library Materials, ANSI Z39.48-1984. ∞

**Due to changes in conditions, use of the
information in this book is at the sole risk
of the user.**

Printed in the United States of America

10 9 8 7 6

*To the volunteers who design, construct, and maintain the hiking trails in North Carolina.*

# Photo Credits

# Contents

# Foreword

It would be difficult, indeed, to find an author as well quali-
fied as Allen de Hart to write this comprehensive guide to the
vast system of trails in North Carolina. Who else has walked *all*
of the trails in our state, to become acquainted with everything
an interested hiker would benefit by knowing before choosing
and embarking on a hiking trip? In addition to providing the
logistics for hiking the trails, De Hart ferrets out and describes
plants and animals, other special features, and interesting history, dating back to the aborigines, related to the trails.

Hiking on trails everywhere in our nation is becoming an
ever-increasing form of recreation. In North Carolina, new
hiking clubs have appeared, old clubs have doubled or tripled
their membership, and the number of hikers has greatly increased in recent years. This expanded interest has created a
pressing need for a comprehensive guide to available trails in
our state. The first edition of *North Carolina Hiking Trails*, which
was published in 1982, organized for the first time all the trails
in North Carolina in a handy form, with concise directions on
how to choose a hiking trail, how to plan for a hiking trip, and
how to locate and enjoy hiking particular trails. Before writing
the second edition, De Hart rewalked and checked the trails
continuously, and he listened to many hikers' suggestions and
requests. The book has been totally revised based on this information. It has been reorganized to present its great number of
trails (over 750) in a manner that enables users to find the trails
they may be interested in within groups of trails: national, state,

municipal and county, and private and commercial. The trails are numbered, and there is an index showing the page number(s) for each trail. Although the Mountains-to-Sea Trail in North Carolina is far from completed, De Hart has reviewed the entire route from Clingmans Dome in the Smokies to Nags Head on the Outer Banks.

*North Carolina Hiking Trails* also gives a fascinating overview of the topography of North Carolina. Its trails offer an excellent variety of geography, geology, vegetation, and animal life. From the North Carolina coast to the summit of Mt. Mitchell there is a difference in elevation of 6,684 feet. The state can be divided by elevation into three major ecosystems: the coastal plain, extending inland to approximately 500 feet in elevation near the Chapel Hill area; the Piedmont region, extending to around 1,500 feet at the foothills of the Blue Ridge; and the mountain area beyond. In the short distance of less than forty miles from the foothills to the higher mountain peaks of the Smoky Mountain and Black Mountain ranges, the great variety of wild flowers and trees is especially noteworthy—almost as many kinds of native species as in all of Europe. The change in elevation permits the hiker to experience an interesting transition in climate and wildlife as well as vegetation.

*North Carolina Hiking Trails* is a prodigious work of pertinent information on the trails in our state. I can certainly recommend the guide for all who want to know about North Carolina's unusually varied and rewarding trails.

*Arch Nichols*
*Asheville, North Carolina*

# Acknowledgments

It is with gratitude that I acknowledge the many resource personnel and hikers whose assistance made this second edition possible. The logistics, the research, the relentless field work, all required dedicated teamwork. One avid hiker, Alan Householder (Weaverville), volunteered to assist in the mountain region. Without his service in planning, shuttle service, and double-checking my original work, we could not have met a publication deadline. "Hiking makes my mind and body one," was his reply to questions on the value of hiking. Todd Shearon (Wilsons Mill) faithfully assisted in the piedmont and coastal regions. Thankfully, our work was mitigated by having our original research material from the 1980–1981 assistance of Kay Scott, a former state trails coordinator of the Division of Parks and Recreation.

National forest personnel who gave support and information were George Olson, supervisor of the state's national forests; David Hammond, forester; and Richard Gueho and Melinda Waldrep, landscape architects, all from the headquarters office (Asheville). "Hiking gives me an opportunity to exercise my body and rest my mind," said Waldrep, whose work is also that of forest trails coordinator. Assistance in the ranger districts came from Paul Bullard, district ranger of the Croatan National Forest (New Bern), and in the Nantahala National Forest from Stephen Rickerson, district ranger, and Donnie Richardson, supervisory forester in the Cheoah district (Robbinsville). Others in the Nantahala were Ronald Raum, district ranger, and

Bruce Bayle in the Highlands district (Highlands); Terry Pierce, supervisory forester in the Tusquitee district (Murphy); and Lewis Kearney, district ranger, and James Hunnicutt, forestry technician, in the Wayah district (Franklin). In the Pisgah National Forest were Charles Miller, district ranger in the French Broad district (Hot Springs); Pat Cook, district ranger, and James Blevins, forestry technician, in the Grandfather district (Marion); Art Rowe, district ranger, Paul Wright, resource assistant, and Susan Oderwald, forester, in the Pisgah district (Pisgah Forest); and from the Toecane district (Burnsville), Richard Preston, supervisory forester. From the Uwharrie National Forest (Troy) were Eurial Turner, district ranger, and Bill Culpepper, assistant ranger.

Harry Baker, landscape architect for the Blue Ridge Parkway (Asheville), provided a continuous flow of maps on the development of the *Tanawha Trail* and the *Mountains-to-Sea Trail*. And the major resource assistance from the Great Smoky Mountains National Park came from Joseph Smith, assistant chief ranger for North Carolina (Cherokee); Pat Deason, ranger at Deep Creek ranger station (Bryson City); Mark Motsko, ranger at 20-Mile ranger station (Fontana); and Keith Nelson, park ranger (Gatlinburg).

Assistants from the state offices, particularly the Division of Parks and Recreation, were Jim Hallsey, chief of operations, and his staff. In his foreword to the first edition of this guide he wrote, "It is difficult to perceive the character of an area from the windshield of an automobile speeding along an interstate highway. And it is just as difficult to know anything about the farmer in the field we just passed in 8.3 seconds. We need to slow down. We need to look around. We need to walk! Happily, this guidebook offers a practical, economical, and healthy way to regain our sense of perspective and appreciation to know again, or perhaps for the first time, North Carolina and her people." Other staff were Susan Currie, trails coordinator; Bynum Riggsbee, visitor services director; and Mike Dunn, interpretation and education director. Rebecca Richards, public information officer for the Division of Forest Resources, provided information on the state forests.

The list of families and friends who provided food and shelter during the years of both editions is too numerous for this space, but among those who provided a consistent home away from home were Drs. Frank and Doris Hammett (Waynesville); Dr. and Mrs. Lee Copple (Highlands); and Mr. and Mrs. Barry (Kay Scott) Rosen (Morganton). I am also indebted to many hikers and backpackers who were part of a continuous chain of strength in snow and ice, summer heat and storm, long hours, and the discomforts of bugs, blisters, and nettles. In recognition, they are Hill Allen, Robert Ballance, Frank Barringer, Mike Batts, Mike Beaman, Richard Byrd, Kevin Bighannitti, Tom Boles, Tom Bond, Peyton Bonner, John Borum, Jimmy Boyette, Chris Bracknell, Andy Britt, Cathy Carter, Dean Carter, Richard Caviness, Kim Caudle, John Chess, John Chesson, Sherry Clark, Gale Clayton, Joe Cohn, Steve Cosby, Paula Crenshaw, John Culbertson, Susan Currie, Mike Daley, Tony Droppleman, Greg Fredrick, Bill Flournoy, Larry Gibbons, Dave Giesen, Fess Green, Todd Gregory, Jim Hallsey, Heath Hamrich, Robert Hall, Rusty Hamilton, Tom Harris, Bill Hatch, Rudy Hauser, Tate Hayman, Lisa Helm, David Hicks, Patrick Hobin, Van Hockett, Alan Householder, Bryan Jackson, Lloyd Jacobs, Tim Jenkins, Joel Johnson, Randy Johnson, Billy Jones, Jeff Jones, Tom Key, Steve King, Hans Kirsch, Sherri Lanier, John LeMay, John Lentz, Jack Lewis, Darin Matthews, John Matthews, Ray Matthews, Taylor Mayo, Hazel Monroe, Charles Moore, Roger Moore, Lenny Murdock, Lisa Myers, Billy Norris, Les Parks, Reggie Ponder, Jay Price, Fletcher Raiford, Georgette Ray, Mark Roberts, Mike Sanderson, Chuck Satterwhite, Brooks Savage, Kay Scott, Ed Seagroves, Greg Seamster, Todd Shearon, John Shelton, Brad Shuler, Alison Sipfle, Brad Smith, Joe Smith, Scott Smith, Eddie Sori, Steve Strader, Gigi Sugg, Kenneth Tippette, Doug Wassum, Mark Waters, Buster White, Travis Winn, and Kevin Zoltek.

Also, thanks to Arlyn Powell, former editor and publisher at the AMC, for requesting this book in the first place, and to his successor, Michael Cirone, for his continued encouragement and support. Generous thanks to my family who supported my work and tolerated a house full of maps, and to my friend and neighbor, Jeannette Lord, who volunteered her time as proofreader.

# Introduction

*North Carolina trails are the gateways to Nature's gardens.*
                                                    —Lisa Atwood

The purpose of this book is to describe the hiking trails of North Carolina—where the footpaths begin and end and what you can discover on them. "All walking is discovery," wrote naturalist Hal Borland in the *New York Times.* "On foot we take the time to see things whole." On foot you can take the time to discover the state's natural beauty, from the aerial mists of the Great Smoky Mountains to the golden sands of Atlantic islands. On foot you can touch the tussocks of carpet moss on the *Linville Gorge Trail,* smell the sweet fragrance of *arborescens* azalea on the *Pink Beds Trail,* and listen to scarlet tanagers on the *Joyce Kilmer Memorial Trail.* Your discoveries are unlimited among the state's nearly 760 trails—about 2,400 miles in all.

Immensely diverse, there is a trail to suit every preference. There are long backcountry trails in the wilderness for mystery, "silence and whispers," "sudden radiances," and "idle aires," as Fiona MacLeod wrote in *Where the Forest Murmurs.* Or you can take short walks for magnificent views of sunsets over the Smokies on the *Waterrock Knob Trail,* or in the "land of waterfalls" follow the *Whitewater Falls Trail,* or listen to the "talking trees" on the Holmes State Forest trails, or walk an estuarian boardwalk on the *Cedar Point Tidewater Trail,* or appreciate the *Walden Nature Trail* for the handicapped at Tanglewood Park. Each of the state's trails is distinctive, unique, with its own ambience, almost a personality. They all deserve superlatives, but I have restrained my descriptions to invite your judgments so that you may have plenty of surprises. I have hiked all these trails at least once, some of them many times, and the *Greencroft Gardens Trail* more than once a week since 1963. Rehiking always brings a new experience. John Burroughs, a hiking friend of John Muir, said, "Follow the path you took yesterday to find new things." I have found many new things in observing the process of succession, in the changes of the seasons, and wildlife habitats. I found trails that were manicured, neatly blazed, frequently used, remote and wild, or clean but natural. In contrast some were eroded, neglected, mutilated by dirt bikes and ATVs, or covered with USFS timbering slash. In addition to the natural forest duff, there are trails with soft grass, pea gravel, wood chips, clay, sand, sawdust, rocks, brick, asphalt, and cement. To walk these trails I learned about their history, about the people who constructed them, the animal and plant life, and the cities and towns and countryside around them. For me it was an extraordinary field trip, a valuable natural history classroom. It was a long journey of reality, like the state's motto, *Esse quam videri* (to be, rather than to seem).

Some of the trails have more distinctive features than others. For example the five longest singular trails are the *Appalachian Trail* (301.9 mi), the *Bartram Trail* (81 mi), the *Cape Hatteras Beach Trail* (75.8 mi), the *Buckhorn Trail* (45.4 mi), and the *Lakeshore Trail* (42.7 mi). The *Mountains-to-Sea Trail*, when completed, will be the state's longest. In contrast the three shortest trails are *Black Camp Gap Trail* (66 yd), on the Heintooga Rd, 3.6 mi off the Blue Ridge Parkway at mp 458.2; *Shot Pouch Trail* (75 yd), an access route to the *Appalachian Trail* off Wayah Bald Rd; and *Gwyn Memorial Trail* (91 yd) at mp 298.6 on the Blue Ridge Parkway. The highest trail is *Mt Mitchell Summit Trail,* and the highest changes in elevation are the *Noland Divide Trail* (4,155 ft) and the *Baxter Creek Trail* (4,142 ft), both in the Smokies. The trail with the views of all 49 mountain peaks over 6,000 ft or more in the state is on the *Crabtree Bald Trail.* The lowest trail elevation is the *Cape Hatteras Beach Trail,* and the trail with the most insectivorous plants is the *Sheep Ridge Trail.*

### The First Trails

Some archeologists claim that American Indians were living in the area that is now North Carolina as long ago as 5000 B.C. during the Archaic Period. They base their claim on excavations in Rowan, Stanly, Montgomery, and Orange counties. The Woodland Period, the first 1500 years A.D., shows the development of pottery, agriculture, and burial ceremonies. By the time of Spanish and English explorations, it is estimated the region had about 25 tribes in an aboriginal population of 30,000. The tribes constituted three major linguistic families: the Algonquin in the coastal area of the Albermarle and Pamlico sounds (which included the Hatteras Indians); the Iroquoian, including tribes east of Raleigh to Beaufort County and all of the Cherokee in the mountains; and the Siouan tribes, including such groups as Catawba, Occaneechi, Keyauwee, and Waxhaw in the central area of the state.

The Indian trails developed from the paths made by animals to their food and water sources. As nomadic life changed to more permanent settlements with the advent of agriculture, the trails became major routes between communities for communication and trade. These trails were also used for warfare between the tribes and exploration by the Europeans, and later some trails became colonial roads. The 1928 trail map by W. E. Myer shows a remarkable similarity in trail location to some of the current superhighways. For example, I-85 follows part of the *Lower Cherokee Trading Path* in South Carolina and the *Occaneechi Path* from Charlotte to Petersburg. The *Saponi Trail* was a route much like the US-29 route from Greensboro to Charlottesville and I-77 from Charlotte to Columbia on the *Occaneechi Path*. The *Catawba Trail* went NW from near Spartanburg, through Asheville, and on to Kentucky to join what became the *Daniel Boone Trail* (that was from the Yadkin River Trading Fort near Salisbury to Boonesborough, Kentucky). From an area near Lake Keowee in South Carolina, the *Tuckaleechee Trail* wove through the mountains to the Tennessee River and into Tennessee. A multiple trail intersection was at Wilkesboro. The *Occoneechi Path* on its route from the *Old Cherokee Path* passed near Morganton to the *Occoneechi Path* near Hillsborough; the *New River Trail* went N into Virginia and West Virginia; the *Northern Trail* went S to join the *Cherokee Trading Path* near Spartanburg; and the trail that became the *Daniel Boone Trail* passed through from Salisbury on its route to the Cumberland Gap at the boundary of Tennessee, Virginia and Kentucky. (Here it joined what was earlier called the *Warrior's Path* and later the *Wilderness Trail*).

The first known contact of Europeans with the Indians was in 1524 when Giovanni da Verrazzano, in the service of France, explored the coastline between areas now known as Wilmington and Kitty Hawk. In 1540 the daring Spanish explorer Hernando de Soto left Florida on his long march to the Mississippi. It was May 21, when he arrived in Xualla, a large village inhabited by the Saura tribe between the Saluda and Broad rivers in what is now South Carolina. De Soto's route across the Appalachians has been disputed, but most studies indicate that he followed a trail across the Blue Ridge Mountains near present-day Highlands and Franklin and to Guasili (the mouth of Peachtree Creek at the Hiwassee River, 3 mi E of what is now Murphy). The Saura tribe must have had a trail from Xualla (in what is now Greenville County, South Carolina) to what is now the Asheville area, because the Cherokee name for Swannanoa means "trail of the Saura" or Suali (pronounced "Shualla" by the Spaniards). In 1566 another Spanish exploratory force, led by Juan Pardo, followed the trail that de Soto had traveled from Charleston to Xualla (called Joaro by Pardo), where they built a fort to make their excursions into the hills and mountains of the Appalachians.

English exploration on the Indian paths began in early July 1584 when captains Philip Amandas and Arthur Barlowe went ashore in the Pamlico Sound (about 20 mi from an island called Roanoak). They stayed two months with friendly Indians who fed them fruits and white corn and "braces of fat bucks, conies, hares, fish, the best in the world." A year later, almost to the day, another English expedition of 108 arrived with Thomas Hariot, the first scientist-historian to visit the Indians. They stayed for nearly a year and in the process followed numerous trails and rivers. One trail led to a "great lake," Paquipe (Lake Mattamuskeet). But the year ended in warfare with the natives. The next expedition, July 22, 1587, became the historic "Lost Colony" of Roanoke Island. Following the English establishment of Jamestown in 1607, the trails into North Carolina began with John Pory in 1622. He made a 60-mi "fruitful and pleasant" overland journey to the Chowan River. In 1650 Edward Bland went to the Roanoke River, and in 1654, Nathaniel Batts established a permanent residence by the Chowan River (near present-day Winton).

Another explorer ("father of piedmont explorers") was a German physician from Virginia, John Lederer, who in 1670 was sent by Sir William Berkeley into the heart of the Carolinas. Riding a horse, he and his Indian guide followed the "Trading Path" (*Occaneechi Path*) to Suala (mentioned by de Soto). Lederer followed an eastern return route on his two-month excursion. He kept a detailed diary of his journey (much like current *Appalachian Trail* hikers, with the exception that it was written in Latin). In 1671 Thomas Batts followed a trail to the headwaters of the New River from the *Occaneechi Path*, and in May 1673 James Needham, Gabriel Arthur, and an Indian guide, left Petersburg, followed the *Occaneechi Path* to the Catawba River, and journeyed west on a trail to Hickory Nut Gap by Chimney Rock. (Needham was slain by Indians on his second journey.)

In 1700, John Lawson, surveyor general for the North Carolina colony, began a 1,000-mi journey on the trails from Charleston, South Carolina, into the piedmont and out to the coast of North Carolina. He kept a lengthy diary that was published in England as *Lawson's History of Carolina*. Understanding and generally sympathetic to the natives, he and his friend Baron Christoph von Graffenried (founder of New Bern) were captured upstream on the Neuse River by the Tuscarora in 1711. A few days after Lawson's torture and execution, the baron's ransom offer was accepted for his freedom. He was led "two hours" from the village (near Contentnea Creek, E of present-day Snow Hill) and sent home on foot (about 40 mi). Of all hikes home, could there be a hike with greater solace?

Other colonial trailblazers were pioneer explorer Daniel

Boone, Methodist circuit rider Bishop Francis Asbury, and naturalist William Bartram. Boone, who lived near the Trading Fork of the Yadkin River (N of Salisbury), began an expedition with a party of six in 1767 to explore Kentucky. Twice captured and twice escaped, he returned in 1771, but started on another expedition in 1773 (see Chapter 10, Section 3). From 1771 to 1816 Bishop Asbury was the champion of equestrians. He covered 275,000 mi over the pioneer trails from New England to South Carolina, and his circuit included 60 trips across the Appalachians. On November 29, 1810, he wrote in his famous diary that "our troubles began at the foaming, roaring stream (Cataloochee Creek) and losing ourselves in the wood," but they arrived safely at their destination in present-day Clyde (See Chapter 7, *Asbury Trail*). In 1775, when Bartram was on his 2,500-mi journey from Pennsylvania to Florida and back, he followed a "trading path" into the Cherokee territory on "serpentine paths of verdant swelling knolls . . . and fragrant strawberries, their rich juice dying my horse's feet." (See *Bartram Trail,* Chapter 2.)

### *How to Use This Book*

This completely revised second edition is divided into 16 chapters that cover the national forests (Croatan, Nantahala, Pisgah, and Uwharrie); the national parks and refuges; the state parks, forests, and historic sites; city and county parks, private and college properties; and a progress report on the *Mountains-to-Sea Trail.* Each chapter and section has an introduction to acquaint you with the location of and access to the properties, addresses and telehone numbers for information, and the nearest support services. If not in the main introduction, this information will be shown in a specific area or park where trails are concentrated. An appendix provides you with names and addresses of clubs and organizations and trail-supply stores that can assist you in your planning. It is recommended that allied maps be secured in your advance planning and that some familiarity be developed with the topography of the area to which you are going. This will enable you to plan better for your transportation, seasonal needs, and hiking and camping supplies. This book is designed to be carried in a jacket pocket or your pack, and the pocket map is outlined for a general location of where the trails are located.

• FORMAT FOR TRAIL DESCRIPTIONS: The trails are described either numerically (all USFS trails are described from the lowest to the highest number, the official method of USFS inventories) or alphabetically (for all other trails). Exceptions are made when trail proximity or connections are an advantage to your planning options.

• TITLE AND NUMBER: The trail name is from the most current source, but references may indicate that it was formerly known by another name. Some trails will carry a double name because they run jointly for a distance. An example is where the *Mountains-to-Sea Trail* runs jointly with an original trail. The first number nearest the title is the USFS trail number, listed in parentheses, the official number assigned by the USFS on its trail inventories and maps. It is significant because it is on all the U.S. Geological Survey maps modified for USFS use—the topo map you should use in the national forests. This is the same number that you will see on special maps (examples are the Linville Wilderness or Joyce Kilmer/Slickrock Wilderness) created by the USFS. Additionally, you may see the trail number on commercial maps. If the number is absent, the USFS has not assigned a number or the number may have been deleted from its inventories. Each district or national forest should have its own group of numbers, but unfortunately you will find that the assignments in North Carolina are set at random (with trail inventories from 1 to 400 and a jump to 1000). The exception is the Croatan National Forest with all numbers in the 500 range. A few major or interstate trails will carry the same number through all districts, regardless of the national forest. Examples are the *Appalachian Trail* (#1); the *Bartram Trail* (#67); and the *Overmountain Victory Trail* (#308). The second number on the page, at the right margin in bold type, is a numeric assignment by the publishers of this book for the purpose of matching trails in the book to the pocket maps. These numbers are also listed in the Index to serve as an easy locator reference.

• MILEAGE: The trail length is always within the nearest 0.1 of a mile (with the exception of short trails that may be described in yards or feet). All numbers followed by *mi* (mile/s) indicate the distance from one trailhead to another. If the mileage is followed by *round-trip* or *backtrack*, it means the distance is a loop (perhaps using a road route) or doubled by returning on the same route. When a group of trails is used for a combined or connecting mileage, the length will be followed by *combined* to indicate the total mileage of multiple routes. I used a 400 Rola-tape measuring wheel (which registers each foot) on all the trails.

• CONNECTING TRAILS: Where a single trail is listed with a number of connecting trails, some of the trails may be covered in more detail under another heading. If so, they will be enclosed in parentheses. Although reading about a connecting trail may create a temporary break in your chain of thought, a return to the main description usually will start with the words "to continue" or "continuing ahead." The objective is to give you an option on how far you wish to hike before backtracking, making a loop, or staying on the main trail. If continuing, you can ignore the paragraphs in parentheses, but the information will be available if you change your mind.

• DIFFICULTY: Trails are described as *easy* (meaning the trail has a gentle grade, may be short, and does not require a rest stop); *moderate* (with a greater change in elevation or rough treadway that requires some exertion and likely rest stops); and *strenuous* (with the need for some skill over rough treadway, high or steep elevation change, exertion, and perhaps frequent rest stops). Elevation changes on strenuous trails are usually listed.

• SPECIAL FEATURES: Some of the trails have features that are more distinctive, unique, unusual, rare, or outstanding than trails in general. This listing will follow "Length and Difficulty" or "Connecting Trail" and will precede "Trailhead and Description." The word "scenic" is frequently used as synonymous with impressive, bucolic, unspoiled, panoramic, or pleasant to experience. I have made an effort to avoid using superlatives for every trail, even when I may have felt it was deserving. I found beauty in all the trails; you probably will also, but I have left some mystery for your judgment.

• TRAILHEAD: Where possible, access to a trailhead is described from the North Carolina official highway map. More specifically I have used county and city maps. Because the USGS or the USGS-FS (Forest Service) topographic maps are not as easily or quickly attainable, they are not emphasized but are listed either after the introductory paragraphs or at the end of the trail description. The nearest city, town, or community is usually cited, otherwise roads by title and number and their junctions are listed. If the trailhead has more than one access option, the easiest and nearest is described first.

• DESCRIPTION: Trail descriptions are determined by trail length, usage, features, history, connective value, difficulty, and book space. Most of the trails are described as *main* or *primary* (blazed, marked, or maintained). Some are *primitive* (the opposite of primary), and others are as follows: *side* or *spur* (a shorter route or to a point of interest); *multiple* (used by horses, people, or vehicles); *jeep* (mainly old forest or hunting roads); *manway* or *wilderness* (exceptionally primitive, grown up, or obscure); *special* (used for special populations, such as the physically handicapped). A *gated* trail may be a foot trail for pedestrians during a protective season for wildlife that is open to both hikers and vehicles at other times and a *seeded* trail is usually a former logging road planted with grass for soil stabilization. There are numerous paths used by hunters and fishermen that may be called a *fisherman's* trail or *hunter's* trail in both public and private game lands. Some of the mountain trails are used as *ski* trails in wintertime. Other trails may be described as *recreational* (jogging, exercise, fitness); *historic* (emphasizing heritage, historic districts, historic sites); and *nature* (interpretive, botanical, kiosk displays).

• ADDRESS AND ACCESS: The addresses and telephone numbers are your most immediate source of additional information about the trail area and trail conditions. They are listed at the end of an introduction or description. The access either explains how to arrive at the address or at campgrounds, parks, or special places administered by the address source.

• SUPPORT FACILITIES: To assist you in planning for your food supply, gasoline and vehicle services, and accommodations, the nearest stores are listed at large or major groupings of trails. The nearest (or most amenable to hikers) commercial campgrounds are listed, particularly in areas where public campgrounds do not have full service or hot showers.

• MAPS: An official North Carolina highway map is essential. Although you may be familiar with the area, you may need to give someone clear directions about where you will be or how you are to be picked up after a long hike. The map is available at service stations, Chambers of Commerce, and free from the North Carolina Department of Transportation, PO Box 25201, Raleigh, NC 27611, tel: 919-733-7600. Detailed county maps are available from county courthouses, local Chambers of Commerce, and statewide from the N.C. Dept of Transportation for a nominal cost. City maps are available from city newsstands and bookstores and Chambers of Commerce for a small charge. Additionally you may wish to contact the state's Division of Travel and Tourism, N.C. Dept of Commerce, 430 N. Salisbury St, Raleigh, NC 27611, tel: 919-733-4171 (in Raleigh) or 1-800-847-4862 (toll-free elsewhere), for information on county or city vacation attractions and services. If you plan to hike in a wilderness area, a topographic map and compass are necessary. They could save your life in a crisis or if you are lost. (See the Index for a dealer listing. Or, if you plan to order topo maps, the address is Branch of Distribution, USGS, Box 25286 Federal Center, Denver, CO 80225. Because you must pay in advance, write for a free N.C. Map Index and order form. Expect two to four weeks delivery.) The best source for acquiring the USGS-FS maps (which show the forest boundaries and the trails with numbers) is to contact National Forests of North Carolina, Post and Otis Sts, PO Box 2750, Asheville, NC 28802, tel: 704-257-4200. Also ask for a revised list (most recent dates of publication) of the USFS forest and wilderness maps. State parks and county and city parks also have maps of their areas. Contact the main offices (addresses in Chapters 9, 10, 11, 12, and 13). For a map of the Great Smoky Mountains National Park, contact the main office address in Chapter 7.

• SIGNS, BLAZES, AND MARKERS: It would be ideal if all trails were signed and blazed. Because they are not, it is suggested that you carefully follow the directions in this book. If there are signs, they are usually at the trailheads, and blazes are usually painted on the trees at eye level at irregular intervals. An exceptionally large number of trails in the national forests have neither. One district, Grandfather, in the Pisgah forest has 200 mi of trails, none of which (except the *MST*) is blazed. As a result I have described the trails with other emphasis—rock formations, flora, bridges, streams, unique points of interest, for example. (Do not expect to see signs or markers in any of the wilderness areas. That is in keeping with the wilderness milieu.) Vandalism results in the loss of numerous signs. You will find more signs in the Great Smoky Mountains National Park (GSMNP) and state parks than in the national forests, but many of the trail distance signs in the GSMNP are not correct. The USFS trail numbers and the assigned numbers in this book for the map references will not be seen on trail posts, trees, or other markers. The *AT* blaze is a white 2x6-inch vertical bar with the same size blue blazes indicating a spur (often to water) or an alternate route. The *Bartram Trail* blaze is yellow, the same size of the *AT*, and the *MST* blaze is a white dot, three inches in diameter. You will see a wide range of other colors where there is a color-coded trail system (one county park has black and brown in addition to bright colors). The USFS boundary line has bright red markings, and some trees for timbering may have blue, white, green, or yellow markings.

• PLANTS AND ANIMALS: North Carolina has 89 species of ferns and over 3,500 species and varieties of other vascular plants. Flowering plants account for nearly 3,000, with 313 species native only to the mountains; 183 species in the piedmont; and 469 species in the coastal plains. Many others grow in two or all the regions. A recommended sourcebook for the botany-oriented hiker is *Manual of the Vascular Flora of the Carolinas* by Radford, Ahles, and Bell. Another book is *Wild Flowers of North Carolina* by Justice and Bell. Two pocket-size books on trees are *Common Forest Trees of North Carolina* by the North Carolina Department of Natural Resources, Division of Forest Resources, and *Important Trees of Eastern Forests* by the USFS. There are some exceptionally beautiful areas of gardenlike displays in all the national forests and in the GSMNP. I have described their locations throughout this book, but I have avoided a description of areas with the most rare species. The *USFS Land and Resource Management Plan (1986-2000)* lists 31 endangered species that are in the Nantahala and Pisgah forests and 13 in the Croatan and Uwharrie forests. Some emphasis has been given some plants with the botanical name in parentheses. After the first mention of the botanical name, it is not used again. The most common rhododendron (one of nearly 20 species) is the *Rhododendron maximum,* called rosebay or great laurel with light pink and whitish blossoms. It is the source of massive thickets or slicks in the mountains. *Rhododendron catawbiense,* called mountain rosebay or purple laurel, is seen both in the mountains and a few scattered counties in the piedmont. Craggy Gardens on the Blue Ridge Parkway and Roan Mountain have superb examples. Most of the other species are called azalea, and I have made that distinction where they appear prominent. My listing is according to what I saw at a particular time of the season. Your hike will offer others.

Wildlife is likely to be seen on any day's hike, particularly in parks, refuges, and forests where wildlife is protected and hunting forbidden. Your best chance is to know the animals' watering and feeding places and look for them early or late in the day. Also, walk softly, talk at low decibels, and leave the dogs at home. In the Nantahala and Pisgah forests alone, there are about 400 vertebrate species. There are 138 species of reptiles and amphibians, 442 species of mollusks, and 418 species of fish. There are 12,000 species of *Arthropods,* some of which (such as mosquitoes, "no-seeums," chiggers, mites, ticks, and flies) welcome your visit on the trails. Your chance of hearing, or perhaps seeing, birds is good. A recommended book is *Birds of the Carolinas* by Potter, Parnell, and Teulings. Other books are *Amphibians and Reptiles in the Carolinas and Virginia* by Martof, Palmer, Bailey, Harrison, and Dermid; *Mammals of North Carolina* by Brimley; *Amphibians and Reptiles of the GSMNP* by Huheey and Stupka; and the Golden Press pocket-size guidebooks on butterflies and moths, spiders, and fishes.

### Health and Safety

Accidents happen to the most cautious hiker, and even a minor mishap can ruin an otherwise pleasant journey. To minimize risk and to maintain good health, some suggestions (more critical in the backpacking backcountry) are listed below. Although you may wish to hike alone, the park and forest officials (who must make plans for a rescue) encourage you to have one or more companions to reduce the danger of hypothermia, poisonous snake bites, injury from a fall, and being lost or sick. Someone in the group should carry a first-aid kit with water purifier, moleskin, assorted band-aids, *Neomycin* or other antibiotic, *Bactrain* or other disinfectant ointment, prescription pills for severe pain, aspirin or other simple pain killer, gauze pads, adhesive tape, tweezers, biodegradable soap, sunburn ointment, insect repellent, knife, snakebite kit if in snake territory, Pepto-Bismol tablets or other brand, and your personal medical needs. A basic safety package would include waterproof matches, maps, compass, emergency freeze-dried food, a whistle, a 75-ft rope, a knife (preferably *Swiss*), flashlight (preferably one with krypton bulbs), and a windproof hooded jacket. Your guide or outdoor store consultant may recommend more or less. You may wish to read *Medicine for the Outdoors* by Auerbach during your planning. Another book is *Wilderness Survival* by Shanks.

Hypothermia, the number-one cause of death for outdoor recreationalists, is caused by the lowering of body heat. It can be fatal even in the summertime. Sweaty and wet clothes lose about 90 percent of their dry insulating value, and wind chill increases the danger. The best lines of defense are to stay dry, get out of the wind, rain, or snow to avoid exhaustion, and know the symptoms and treatment. The symptoms are uncontrollable shivering; vague, incoherent speech; frequent stumbling; and drowsiness. The victim may be unaware of all of these. Treatment for mild impairment is to place the victim in a dry place, in dry clothes, and in a warm sleeping bag and give warm drinks; try to keep semiconscious victims awake and provide person-to-person skin contact in a warm sleeping bag.

If you become lost use the universal distress signal of three of anything—shouts, whistles, light flashes, or smoke signals. Do not panic, stay in one place, make a fire and stay warm, conserve your food, drink plenty of water, and climb a tree if it will help determine your location. After a reasonable time without rescue, find a valley and follow its water sources downstream. Someone has said that to be safe in the forest "use your head first and if things go wrong remember to keep it."

Lightning is another danger. Some precautions are to stay off sharp prominent peaks, avoid standing under a cliff or in a cave entrance, avoid seams or crevices on rocks, and avoid standing under prominent trees or other tall objects. Squat down and insulate yourself from the ground if possible. Also do not stay on a beach or in a boat or cross a stream or marsh. Anything metal, including your pack frame, should be removed from your body.

Some precautions to take when crossing a stream include unfastening your backpack belly band, keeping your boots on (or using your spare pair), always facing upstream, keeping your balance with a steady pole, and avoiding rapids.

You should carry pure drinking water and use only water officially designated safe by the forest or park. My listing of springs and clear streams in this book does not mean the water has been tested. Properly boiling the water remains one of the best ways to be safe, or use Globaline or Potable-Aqua purifiers or other brands. For the health of you and others, particularly downstream, camp at least 50 ft away from streams. Human waste should be 300 ft away from a campsite or stream and should be buried if vault toilets are not available. Another rule is to carry out all trash. A few other suggestions are not to hike at night, be sure your boots fit to avoid blisters, and use care with fires, knives, or firearms if hunting (firearms are prohibited in state and national parks).

### Planning the Trip

When the explorer John Muir (1838–1914) was asked about how he prepared for a hiking trip, he replied, "I throw a loaf of bread and a pound of tea in an old sack and jump over the back fence." That was before the 1960s when millions of Americans entered the forests and parks with freeze-dried foods, instant drinks, non-rash underwear, contoured packs, nonblister boots, and space blankets. By the 1970s the marketplace was a hiker's delight, and magazines such as *Backpacker* (which began in 1972) and *Outside* (which began in 1977) carried stories and advertisements about the ultimate adventures of adventurous people and equipment in the "age of Gore-Tex." Thus when you go shopping for hiking gear, expect the best. If you are not an experienced hiker, my first suggestion is for you to acquire a guidebook on backpacking and camping. Examples are *The Complete Walker* by Colin Fletcher and *Walk Softly in the Wilderness* by John Hart.

Your checklist for getting started should include the choice of dependable companions and trail selections; choice and purchase of your equipment, maps, food, gear, and supplies; contacts with the forest or park headquarters for weather conditions and safety hazards, or permits (if required); plans for daily or roundtrip mileage, campsites, and vehicle parking or shuttles. After parking your vehicle at the trailhead, be sure it is locked and that all valuables are stored in the trunk (better yet, left at home). Mountain shuttle information to trailheads is available from Appalachian Trail Shuttle Service, Rte 6, Box 889, Franklin, NC 28734, tel: 704-524-5369, and Mountain Trails Shuttle Service, Box 145, Fontana Village, Fontana, NC 28733, tel: 704-488-2305/498-2337. Descriptions of where to park at the trailheads are included in this book. Also, throughout the book I have indicated what areas require permits for camping and have explained how the permits can be acquired.

Ostensibly you wish for the trail and the campsites to be natural and clean. You can help in keeping them desirable by avoiding impact. That means no-trace camping—removing all litter, trash, and garbage, erasing evidence of campfires, never digging trenches, refraining from using over-used campsites, and avoiding shortcutting switchbacks.

In planning your trip you may wish to include other outdoor sports. For whitewater sports and mountain climbing contact the Nantahala Outdoors Center, US-19 W, Box 41, Bryson City, NC 28713, tel: 704-488-2175. For horseback riding trails and camps contact Extension Horse Specialist, Department of Animal Husbandry, North Carolina State University, Box 7621, Raleigh, NC 27695, tel: 919-737-2761. Cross-country skiing information is available from the National Ski Patrol, Cataloochee Ski Area, Maggie Valley, NC 28751, tel: 704-926-0285.

Concerning emergencies, the following numbers are in addition to a call to the local operator: the N.C. Wildlife Resources Commission for boating accidents, missing persons, fishing and game laws, tel: 1-800-662-7137; Poison Control, tel: 1-800-672-1697; GSMNP, tel: 615-436-1231; BRP, tel: 1-800-727-5929 or 704-259-0701; national forests, tel: 1-800-222-1155 for fires, crime, vandalism, missing persons.

To assist you in your planning, I have listed in the Appendix information on the state's *AT* clubs, the addresses of other clubs, some U.S. and state government agencies, state citizens' groups, college and university clubs, and trail suppliers.

Many hikers before you have described their hiking experiences as a time to "hear myself think," "get acquainted with my soul," "have a psychological holiday." Henry David Thoreau said "for absolute freedom and wildness." The American Hiking Society describes it as "brushing past a thousand life forms, beckoning,/ leading you onward to new sensations and discoveries around the bend./ In that moment when you are on a trail,/ your mind is free to roam,/ to observe, to daydream./ All extraneous concerns drop away. . . . "

Now that you have this guidebook in hand and are preparing for the trails, I hope you will also become active in preserving the natural resources by joining an organization whose mission it is to protect and maintain the trails. And, I hope that you enjoy hiking the trails as much as I have enjoyed hiking and describing them. Welcome to the trails of North Carolina.

# Abbreviations

In an effort to save space in this book, abbreviations are used wherever possible. The majority are part of everyday usage.

| | |
|---|---|
| AMC | Appalachian Mountain Club |
| AT | Appalachian National Scenic Trail |
| ATC | Appalachian Trail Conference |
| ATV | all-terrain vehicle |
| BRP | Blue Ridge Parkway |
| BT | Bartram Trail |
| ca | circa |
| CCC | Civilian Conservation Corps |
| CMC | Carolina Mountain Club |
| DNRCD | Department of Natural Resources and Community Development |
| E | east |
| elev | elevation |
| fac | facilities |
| FR | forest road |
| FS | forest service |
| ft | foot/feet |
| GSMNP | Great Smoky Mountains National Park |
| I | interstate highway |
| jct | junction or intersection |
| L | left |
| mi | mile/s |
| mil | million |

| | |
|---|---|
| mp | milepost (usually on the BRP) |
| MST | Mountains-to-Sea Trail |
| Mt | Mount (used in proper names) |
| Mtn, | mtn/s Mountain, mountain/s |
| N | north |
| NC | state primary road |
| NE | northeast |
| NF | National Forest |
| NP | National Park |
| NPS | National Park Service |
| NW | northwest |
| ORV | off-road vehicle |
| R | right |
| Rd | Road (used in proper names) |
| rec | recreation/al |
| RR | railroad |
| RS | ranger station |
| rte | route |
| S | south |
| SC | South Carolina primary road |
| sec | section |
| SR | state secondary road |
| sta | station |
| svc | service/s |
| tel | telephone |
| topo | topographic map |
| TVA | Tennessee Valley Authority |
| US | federal highway |
| USFS | United States Forest Service |
| USGS | United States Geological Survey |
| USGS-FS | United States Geological Survey-Forest Service |
| W | west |
| YACC | Young Adult Conservation Corps |
| YCC | Youth Conservation Corps |
| yd | yard/s |
| 4WD | four-wheel drive |

# PART I

# Trails in the National Forests

*National Forests exist today because the people want them. To make them accomplish the most good the people themselves must make clear how they want them run.*

—Gifford Pinchot, June 14, 1907

North Carolina has four national forests with a total of 1,217,357 acres: Nantahala (517,436); Pisgah (495,979); Croatan (157,054); and Uwharrie (46,888). Within the forests are 180 developed recreational areas, 40 special-interest areas, and 11 wilderness areas. There are 1,885 identified plant species and 645 species of vertebrates, including fish species. An average of 65 mmbf (million board feet) of timber is harvested annually. There are 1,627 miles of trails (1,480 of which are hiking trails).

The state is the birthplace of professional forestry management because in 1892 George Vanderbilt employed Gifford Pinchot (1865-1946) to manage the Vanderbilt Forest at Biltmore in Asheville. Pinchot (born in Simsbury, Connecticut) graduated from Yale in 1889 and studied forestry at the *Ecole Nationale Forestiere* in France. His success prompted Vanderbilt to purchase an additional 120,000 acres, a section of which later became part of the Pisgah National Forest. In 1895 Carl Schenck, a renowned German forester, succeeded Pinchot, and Pinchot was made a member of the National Forest Commission to work out the plans of the U.S. Forest Reserve Act authorized by Congress in 1891. Pinchot headed the Department of

Agriculture's Forestry Division from 1898 to 1910 (under three U.S. presidents) while holding a professorship of forestry at Yale University. During this period he was influential in the establishment of the U.S. Forest Service (USFS) in 1905 and by 1908 had become chairman of the National Conservation Commission. Although his stay in North Carolina was only a few years, his pioneering philosophy of forestry laid the foundation not only for Dr. Schenck's first forestry school in America, but also for the shaping of USFS policy since. His statement quoted at the beginning of this chapter has proven true many times, both in Congress (25 acts) and on the state level.

Among the Congressional acts that affect North Carolina's national forests are the Weeks Law (1911) that authorized the purchase of lands for timber production; the Multiple Use-Sustained Yield Act (1960) that reemphasized the basic purposes of forests for outdoor recreation, watershed, range, mineral resources, wildlife and fish, as well as timber production; the Wilderness Act (1964) that established a system of preserving areas from all timber cutting and mining and development; the National Trails System Act (1968) that established a protective system of national recreational and scenic trails (such as the *Appalachian Trail*); the National Environmental Policy Act (1970) that required all federal agencies to prepare reports on the environmental impact of all planned programs and actions in formal Environmental Impact Statements (hereafter referred to as EIS); the Forest and Rangeland Renewable Resources Planning Act (RPA) (1974) that required the USFS to prepare long-range programs of forest administration, roads and trails, research, and cooperative programs; and the National Forest Management Act (NFMA) (1976) that required full public participation in the development and revision of land management plans and periodic proposal of a Land and Resource Management Plan (hereafter referred to as the Plan) by the national forests.

The first Plan in 1985 proposed a 50-year management process that would have tripled the mileage of timber roads and nearly doubled timber harvesting. (Already the nation had 343,000 mi of timber roads, eight times the spread of the U.S.

Interstate Highway System.) The Plan would have drained 60,000 acres of precious pocosin in the Croatan for timber management and allowed 6,000 acres for peat mining. There was low priority in the Plan for wildlife and fish protection with zero increase in wildlife habitat capability. There was an unrealistic estimate of recreation supply and demand, and the astonishing proposal of only 2.2 mi annual increase in trail construction (from the current 6.2 mi). Furthermore the Plan for the Nantahala and Pisgah forests recommended only one of five wilderness study areas be suggested to Congress. Once the public was aware of these proposals, it vigorously objected. The state's USFS headquarters in Asheville responded with a second Plan.

In the second Plan the USFS personnel proposed a shorter period. Instead of 50 years, it would extend from 1986 to 2000. It reduced timber roads from the current level and barely increased timber harvesting. Wildlife and fish habitat improvement was increased 100 percent in the Nantahala and Pisgah forests and 200 percent in the Croatan and Uwharrie Plan. A slight increase in recreation development was proposed, and trail construction was increased from 4 mi to 24 mi annually in the Nantahala and Pisgah. In the Croatan and Uwharrie it was increased from 2.2 to 7 mi. (Because the trail construction and reconstruction included ORV trails, it was an irresolute commitment to either user.)

The Croatan and Uwharrie Final Plan and EIS were approved by the regional forester in Atlanta in May 1986. The Plan covered eight public issues and management concerns of transportation, land, pocosins, wildlife and fish, vegetation, recreation, ORVs, and fire management. Its preparers stated it was designed "to achieve a high level of diversity of plant and animal communities of species." The Nantahala and Pisgah Final Plan and EIS were approved in April 1987. (It was delayed six months because George S. Dunlop, the Assistant Secretary of the U.S. Department of Agriculture for Natural Resources and Environment requested a review before its publication.) The Plan covered 11 public issues and management concerns of fire management, land ownership and special uses, minerals and mining, recreation, social and economic considerations, transportation, vegetation, visual quality, water, wilderness, and wildlife and fish. Its preparers stated that it was designed to "provide for multiple use and sustained yield of goods and services." It further stated that "emphasis will be placed on converting existing trails into loop trail systems . . . and any management activity adjacent to a trail will be considered for its impact on the trail." Although the Plan was considered an improvement by the public, it was not accepted by a number of organizations because it required a new timber demand analysis. "There is absolutely no basis for yet another timber demand study," said Ron Tipton, Southeast Regional Director of the Wilderness Society. The Society, joined by the Sierra Club and the North Carolina Wildlife Federation, appealed the Plan and were represented by the Southern Environmental Law Center based in Charlottesville, Virginia. The center filed a legal challenge in September 1987.

Meanwhile, the USFS subsidy to private timber companies in North Carolina was costing the taxpayers $4.77 million annually because timber was sold below cost (a Congressional report also showed that a loss nationwide was $621 million). While the money was available for new timber roads, recreation trails (cited as "non-revenue producing" by the USFS) were overgrown and being abandoned. "For the fiscal year 1987, the districts received an average of $6,000 to maintain approximately 30 mi of trails," said George Olson, former forest supervisor of the national forests in North Carolina. "Each district ranger determines on what trails his allocation will be spent," he said. George (Pat) Cook, former district ranger for the Grandfather Ranger District, said that he received only $2,000 for the 201 mi of trails in his district. "Most of the money goes into maintenance by our YCC, the balance to buy tools and to pay for supervision of volunteer groups," said Cook. Olson stated that budget cuts and lack of personnel were the cause of inadequate trail maintenance. "Basically, the entire job of maintaining trails is done by volunteers or volunteer organizations," he said.

Because 60 percent of the state's trail mileage is in the national forests, it is of vital concern to hikers that funds be allocated for adequate trail maintenance. (Trail maintenance guidelines are in Appendix G of the Final Plan. Maintenance schedules are proposed for two or three times annually to once every two years.) Some exceptions to regular maintenance are the national recreation trails that have preservation contracts and wilderness trails where any type of maintenance may have ceased. There are 11 wilderness areas—six in the mountains, one in the piedmont, and four in the coastal area—for a total of 101,303 acres. (Those with trails are described singularly in the next four chapters.) Two wilderness study areas with trails (Lost Cove and Harper Creek) are covered in the Grandfather Ranger District.

Camping permits are not required except in the Linville Gorge Wilderness Area (see details in Chapter 3, Section 2). Wilderness trails are remote, usually unblazed and unmarked. Motorized vehicles are not permitted; there are not any shelters or campgrounds or restrooms. The hiker must prepare for and meet nature on its terms. This is reason enough for the hiker to have special guidelines to safely encounter the "wilderness experience": Be in good physical health. Plan and prepare well in advance. Avoid holidays or popular weekends. Secure and carry a topo map(s) (named at the end of each trail description in this book) and a wilderness map (if such exists) from the ranger's office. Choose a companion, but confine the group to six or less. File a trip plan to leave with your family or with the ranger in case of an emergency. Complete a checklist of backpacking gear, clothing, food, medication, snakebite and first-aid kit, compass, flashlight, waterproof matches, and other essentials. Do not smoke while hiking. Be weather-wise, but do not carry a radio. Walk softly and quietly to prevent disturbing the wildlife. Carry a stove and use foods that require less cooking. Boil and treat all water. Keep fires small. Camp at least 100 ft from springs and other water sources. Never cut standing trees. Use only biodegradable soap. Carry out all refuse. Know the symptoms of and how to treat hypothermia (see Health and Safety in the introduction). Practice no-trace camping (such as spreading duff or twigs over the vacated campsite). Do not feed the bears or other wildlife. Collect native fruits, nuts, and berries only for personal consumption. The USFS advises not leaving trails for cross-country or bushwhacking trips unless you are experienced and have wilderness survival skills.

Hunting and fishing are allowed in the national forests, including wilderness areas, but are restricted in recreational areas and some special areas. Licenses are required by the North Carolina Wildlife Resources Commission, which determines and sets seasons, bag limits, and other regulations for wildlife and fish management. The Commission also regulates private game lands that have been leased for public use. For information or to make a report about licenses, game laws, boating, violations of the laws, hunting or fishing accidents, or the disappearance of a person, call toll free 1–800-662-7137 (a 24-hour service every day of the year). Address: North Carolina Wildlife Resources Commission, 512 N Salisbury Street, Raleigh, NC 27611.

• INFORMATION: Forest Supervisor, National Forests of North Carolina, Post Office Bldg, Post and Otis Streets (PO Box 2750), Asheville, NC 28802, tel: 704-257-4200.

# 1.

## Croatan National Forest

*Cypress knees are the swamp's natural footbridge.*
—Todd Shearon

The history of the Croatan National Forest, the most coastal of North Carolina's four national forests, began in 1933 when a purchase unit was established. In 1935 77,000 acres were acquired. Today it encompasses 157,054 acres. The forest is almost totally surrounded by the Neuse, Trent, White Oak, and Newport rivers. Bogue Sound and Bogue Banks separate its southern border from the Atlantic Ocean.

The name of Croatan comes from the Algonquin Indian word for "council town." Today, however, its coastal environment is used for year-round recreation. Within the forest are 95,000 acres of pocosin, which is an Indian word meaning "swamp on a hill." Actually, pocosin is a layer of organic topsoil that has resulted from a series of physiographic and biological changes occurring within the last 9,000 years. A wet upland bog with black organic muck, pocosin varies in depth from inches at the edge to several feet in the central area. It has high acidity, dense vegetation, and no drainage pattern in low sections. In 1984, 30,009 acres of pocosin were designated by Congress as four roadless areas that represent a unique estuarian ecosystem. The largest of these is Pocosin (11,000 acres), a tract between NC-58 and Ellis Lake area. Others are Sheep Ridge (9,549 acres), bordered on the SE by beautiful Great Lake and Long Lake; Pond Pine (1,860 acres), between the Pocosin and

9

Sheep Ridge areas; and Catfish Lake South (7,600 acres), between Maysville on NC-58 and Catfish Lake.

In the Land Resource Management Plan (1986–2000) of June 1986, Regional Forester John E. Alcock approved Alternative E, which promised protection of the entire pocosin from drainage or peat-moss mining. But less than six months later in November 1986, the tranquility of these wilderness areas was threatened when Major Dennis Brooks, director of the U.S. Marine Corps (USMC) Cherry Point Public Affairs Office, stated that plans were proposed for constructing a $9.8 million combat-training air base near the edge of the wilderness by 1991. "Everybody is competing for space. We are going to be doubling (to 120) our numbers of Harriers." This proposal came a week after the Federal Highway Administration presented a plan for a $10.4 million project to pave a 15-mi secondary road between two of the wilderness areas. Although Federal officers said the project would have little impact on the forest, representatives of the Sierra Club, the North Carolina Wildlife Federation, the National Wildlife Federation, and the North Carolina Trails Committee disagreed. A local citizen, Edwin Edmondson, said that roads cut in the forest had endangered the black bear. "In 30 years I've seen the black bear population go from a nuisance to nothing." The two projects appeared to be related, but the district ranger, Paul Bullard, said, "The USMC is not a party to the road project." On March 31, 1987, Col. K. D. Holland, Director of Operations at Cherry Point, admitted that there was "substantial opposition," that at least four other sites existed outside the Croatan, and that plans had been dropped for a landing strip in the Croatan.

Hunting (both big and small game), fishing (both salt and freshwater), boating, swimming, water skiing, camping, picnicking, and hiking are popular in the Croatan. There are at least 106 species of fish, including pickerel, perch, bass, sunfish, and bluegill, in the 4,300 acres of five spring-fed freshwater lakes. Although lake fishing is usually poor because of high acidity, the saltwater fishing is popular at the lower end of the Neuse River and in the saltwater marshes. Unique activities include oystering, crabbing, and flounder gigging.

More than 90 species of reptiles and amphibians have been discovered in the forest. Among them are the spotted turtle (*Clemmys guttata*); Mabee's salamander (*Ambystoma mabeei*); the more rare tiger salamander (*Ambystoma tigrinum*); and the longest snake in the forest, the eastern coachwhip (*Masticophis flagellum*). Poisonous reptiles are the cottonmouth moccasin, eastern diamondback rattlesnake, timber rattlesnake, pigmy rattlesnake (*Sistrurus miliarius*), and copperhead. The bays, swamps, marshes, and creeks provide a haven for migratory ducks and geese. Such birds as egrets, including the snowy egret; flycatchers; woodpeckers; woodcocks; hawks, including the marsh hawk; osprey, and owls are plentiful, too. Among the threatened or endangered species are the red-cockaded woodpecker (*Picoides borealis*), American alligator (*Alligator mississipiensis*), and the bald eagle (*Haliaeetus leucocephalis*).

Large stands of pines—virgin pond, loblolly, and long leaf—are in the forest. Common hardwoods are oaks (including laurel [*Quercus laurifolia*], bluejack, and blackjack), yellow poplar, sweet and tupelo gums, swamp cypress (*Taxodium distichum*), American holly, and maple. Wildflowers—bright red pine lily (*Lilium catesbaei*), orchids, gaillaria, and nine species of insectivorous plants—are profuse. Shrubs include titi, fetterbush, gallberry, wax myrtle, and honeycup.

Recreational areas (open March 1 through November 30) are located at Brice Creek, Cahooque Creek, Fishers Landing, Haywood Landing, and Pinecliff. Two campgrounds, Cedar Point and Neuse River, are described below. In addition to trails included below, there are numerous unnamed fishermen's trails and backcountry roads for hiking.

• ADDRESS AND ACCESS: Maps and additional information are available from the District Ranger, Croatan National Forest, 435 Thurmond Rd, New Bern, NC 28560, tel: 919-638-5628. Access is 4 mi SE of New Bern on US-70, at the jct with Thurmond Rd, L.

• SUPPORT FACILITIES: There are facilities for camping and other activities in the Croatan National Forest at the Neuse River Recreation Area and the Cedar Point Campground; there are no hook-ups. Access to the Neuse River Recreation Area from the Ranger's office is 3 mi SE on US-70 to Riverdale Mini-Mart, and L on SR-1107 and FR-141 to Fishers Landing. On the S side of the NF is Cedar Point Campground near Swansboro. From the jct of NC-58/24, go N on NC-58 for 0.6 mi, and L onto FR-153. A nearby commercial campground is the Neuse River Campground. From the city of New Bern go 3 mi N on US-17; full svc, rec fac; open year-round; address is Rte 6, Box 190, New Bern, NC 28560, tel: 638-2556. Another camping area is Pender Park Campground: From the jct of US-70 and NC-24, go W 10 mi on NC-24 (near the community of Ocean); full svc, rec fac; open year-round; address is 1 Pender Park South, Newport, NC 28570, tel: 919-726-4902.

## ▶ CEDAR POINT RECREATION AREA
### (Carteret County)

The Cedar Point Recreation Area has facilities for boating, camping (without hookups but with trailer space), drinking water, fishing, nature study trails, picnicking, and sanitary facilities.

• ACCESS: From the jct of NC-58/24 E of Swansboro, go 0.6 mi N on NC-58 to the entrance to Cedar Point, L, on FR-153. Go 0.4 mi and bear L at a fork on FR-153A to the parking area near White Oak River.

### *Cedar Point Tideland Trail (USFS #502)*                    1

• LENGTH AND DIFFICULTY: 1.4 mi, easy

• SPECIAL FEATURES: viewing blinds for shorebirds

• TRAILHEAD AND DESCRIPTION: From the parking area follow the trail signs and cross the first of six boardwalks at 0.1 mi. Pass the first of two blinds for viewing birds and other wildlife at 0.4 mi. The second viewing blind is at 0.6 mi. Cross fire road, the last boardwalk at 1.1 mi, and return on a loop trail to the parking lot at 1.4 mi. The trail is well-graded through pine and hardwoods and includes 0.3 mi of cypress boardwalks in a marshland estuary. The trail is a national recreation trail, initially listed as the *Chautauqua Trail*. (*USGS-FS Map:* Swansboro)

## ▶ PINECLIFF RECREATION AREA
### (Craven County)

The Pinecliff Recreation Area is on the S side of the Neuse River (within sight of the ferry to Minnesott Beach). It has facilities for drinking water, fishing, picnicking, and sanitary stations. It is the N trailhead for the *Neusiok Trail* that extends 21.7 mi S to the Newport River in Carteret County. If hiking the trail when the Pinecliff entrance gate is closed, park and walk 0.2 mi to the picnic area.

• ACCESS: From the jct of US-70 and NC-101 in Havelock turn L on NC-101 and go 5.3 mi to the jct of NC-101 and NC-306. Turn L on NC-306, Neuse River Ferry Rd, and go 3.3 mi to FR-132. Turn L on an unpaved road and go 1.7 mi to Pinecliff Recreation Area.

### *Neusiok Trail* (*USFS #503*)                    2

• LENGTH AND DIFFICULTY: 21.7 mi, moderate

• SPECIAL FEATURES: Neuse River beach, estuaries

• TRAILHEAD AND DESCRIPTION: The best sections for backpacking and primitive camping on the *Neusiok Trail* are between the Neuse River and NC-306, between NC-101 and Bellfinger Rd, and S of the Alligator Tram Rd. Camping is not allowed on the Weyerhaeuser property between the gated areas described below, and camping is impossible in the dense vegetation along Deep Creek Rd. Hiking is preferable in the winter months to avoid insects, heat, and snakes. Insect repellent is recommended. All water for drinking and cooking must be carried. Long trousers, high boots, watchful eyes, staying on the trail, and sleeping in tents are precautions against poisonous snakes. All trash must be packed out.

From the parking area enter the picnic area, pass L of the picnic shelter, and follow white blazes to a boardwalk at 0.3 mi. If the boardwalk is under water, go R to the beach and continue upstream. Follow up the Neuse River beach among scenic swamp cypress groves and Spanish moss. (The private Cahooque Hunting Club camp is L in the forest.) Ahead can be seen the Cherry Point U.S. Marine Corps Air Station. At 1.4 mi leave the beach, ascend the steps, and follow an erratic path through hardwoods and pine. Glimpses of Hancock Creek can be seen through the trees, R, at 2 mi. Pass L of a bog cove at 2.3 mi, cross a swamp with prominent cypress knees at 2.5 mi, and another swamp at 2.7 mi. Pass R of a private road for Weyerhaeuser Paper Company at 2.9 mi. Wade through another swamp among palmetto (*Sabal minor*) at 3.1 mi. Make a sharp L at 3.6 mi to avoid a wide swamp, but wade it and a tributary to Cahooque Creek at 4.4 mi. Turn R on an old field road bordered with loblolly pine at 4.5 mi and enter a swamp with a boardwalk at 5.3 mi. Follow the edge of a hardwood timber cut and cross two boardwalks at 4.6 mi and 5.7 mi. At 6 mi is a grove of large beech and holly. For the remainder of this section follow an old road through pines and reach a gated road at NC-306. (NC-101 is 2 mi R; on NC-306 and FR-132, L, it is 2.7 mi for a return to the Pinecliff Picnic area.)

Cross the road and follow a footpath through dense undergrowth and tall pine. At 6.9 mi cross a boardwalk and follow an old field road bordered with loblolly and pond pine. At 8 mi turn sharply R onto an old forest road. Cross FR-136 (which goes 1 mi out to NC-101) and continue through the forest. At 8.6 mi begin an 0.8-mi section of tall oak and pine and patches of sensitive fern (*Onoclea sensibilis*). Reach NC-101 at 9.4 mi (R: 6.8 mi back to the Pinecliff Picnic area on NC-101 and NC-306. L: 2.1 mi to North Harlowe store with groceries, gasoline, and telephone).

Cross NC-101 and enter a beautiful open forest of long-leaf pine. Scattered undergrowth is yaupon, bracken, beard grass, blueberry, and Christmas fern. Cross a 300-ft boardwalk at 10.2 mi to a hardwood forest. A 150-ft boardwalk is at 10.7 mi. (Here is a jct where the trail continues L through a pine forest, a timber cut area, a section of dense undergrowth, and scattered insect eating plants. The blazes are faint or non-existent in sections. Exit at Bellfinger Rd [FR-147] after 2 mi.) A better route from the boardwalk is straight for 0.1 mi to Bellfinger Rd. Turn L and follow it for 1.4 mi to jct with the route mentioned above. Go 0.2 mi farther on Bellfinger Rd to jct with Deep Creek Rd (FR-169) at 12.4 mi. (L for 1.1 mi on Deep Creek Rd is North Harlowe store.)

Turn R on Deep Creek Rd (FR-169) and hike S to a gated private road at the edge of the Croatan National Forest at 14.8 mi. (Hiking is allowed without permit through the Weyerhaeuser Paper Company property, but vehicular traffic is not allowed except for members of the Riverside Hunting Club.) Follow the sandy road, avoiding all R jct; turn on the first L, Alligator Tram Rd (FR-124), and arrive at another locked road gate at 16.5 mi for re-entrance to the Croatan National Forest. Continue ahead for 0.5 mi and turn R sharply over a canal footbridge to enter a dense area of undergrowth. At 17.6 mi the trail enters an open long-leaf pine forest on a hunter's road. Follow the old road in sections of switch cane and bracken, cross a small stream at 18.6 mi, pass a trash dump, leave the old road at 19.1 mi, and arrive at Mill Creek Road (SR-1154) at 20.1 mi. (It is 0.2 mi L to E-Z Chek store with groceries, gasoline, and telephone. The owner allows hikers to park vehicles here while on the trail.)

Cross Mill Creek Rd (also called Newport Rd or Orange Street) and follow blazes through hardwoods and softwoods for 1.6 mi; reach the Newport River parking area and S terminus of the trail at 21.7 mi. (It is 1.1 mi on FR-181 back to Mill Creek Rd [SR-1154], and 5.5 mi L on Mill Creek Rd to Newport.) (*USGS-FS Maps:* Cherry Point, Newport)

▶ **ISLAND CREEK AREA**
   **(Jones County)**

• ACCESS: In a separate N tract of the forest, this area can be reached from Pollocksville, jct of US-17 and Island Creek Rd

(SR-1004). Drive E on Island Creek Rd for 5.5 mi to the Island Creek parking area, L. Or, from business US-70/Island Creek Rd jct at the Trent River bridge in New Bern, go W on Island Creek Rd for 8 mi to the parking area, R.

### Island Creek Trail (USFS #509)                                    3

* LENGTH AND DIFFICULTY: 0.6 mi, easy

* SPECIAL FEATURES: climax forest, limestone base

* TRAILHEAD AND DESCRIPTION: From the parking area follow the sign into a picturesque and unusual natural history area in a virgin forest that has progressed through plant succession stages to a beech climax forest. On a base of limestone the flora and fauna are unique to eastern North Carolina. Large beds of Christmas fern form a ground cover with tall oaks, hickories, pines, and cucumber trees. The Trent Woods Garden Club of New Bern has assisted the USFS in developing the trail, and its 8 sq mi have been registered as a natural area by the N.C. Natural Heritage Program. (*USGS-FS Map:* Pollocksville)

## ▶GREAT LAKE AREA
### (Craven, Jones, and Carteret Counties)

Great Lake is in the center of the Croatan National Forest. It is the largest of five lakes—Great, Catfish, Long, Little, and Ellis—the last two being on private property. Two wilderness areas adjoin the lake, Sheep Ridge on the N side and Pond Pine on the S side.

* ACCESS: Vehicle access to the lake is possible only on a primitive road (FR-126) for 7 mi from NC-58 in the community of Kuhns. In Kuhns go N 0.7 mi on Young Rd (SR-1103) (Kuhns Rd or Black Swamp Rd [SR-1100] in Jones County). Turn R on Hill Rd (SR-1101), which becomes FR-126 after 1 mi. A trail to the lake is described below.

### Sheep Ridge Trail (USFS #513)  **4**

- LENGTH AND DIFFICULTY: 3.5 mi, strenuous

- SPECIAL FEATURES: remote pocosin, insectivorous plants

- TRAILHEAD AND DESCRIPTION: This is the only trail of its kind in the state; it is located entirely in a pocosin. Access to the NW trailhead is from the jct of NC-58 and Catfish Lake Rd (SR-1105), 1.5 mi SE from the town of Maysville. On SR-1105 go 2 mi on a paved road that becomes a dirt road at the forest boundary. Continue another 4.4 mi and turn R on FR-152, but immediately turn L on FR-173. An access from US-70 is a turn on Catfish Lake Rd (SR-1100) at the Croatan Presbyterian Church in Croatan, and 7.7 mi straight to FR-152; turn L. The first 0.5 mi is accessible by passenger car, but the next 1 mi may require either 4WD or hiking. At the end of FR-173 (and jct with FR-3103, L) is the trailhead. High rubber boots will be necessary, except in parts near the Great Lake. A topo map and a compass should also be carried because if you get lost the risk of not being found is high. Cottonmouth moccasins inhabit the area.

Cross a canal either by jumping, pole vaulting, or making a bridge (the hiker would need to carry in an 8-ft pole or strong 8-ft boards for a footbridge). After crossing the canal, enter the trail on a straight line that appears to have once been the route of a vehicle or tractor, but whose lead is not always dependable. The trail is consistently covered with spongy compacted sphagnum moss, insectivorous plants, cotton grass, pleea, (*Pleea tenuifolia*), and entangling greenbrier in titi (*Cyrilla racemiflora*) and zenobia (*Zenobia pulverulenta*). Two species of pitcher plants are prevalent, the red-leaved parrot (*Sarracenia purpurea*) that blooms in April and May and the green-leaved trumpet (*Sarracenia flava*) that blooms from April to September. More open areas have round-leaved sundews, butterworts, and the Venus' flytrap that is protected by law. Underneath is a black organic muck with a web of roots that makes the treadway unstable and absorbent. After 0.7 mi the pond pines become taller. At 1.6 mi arrive at the Great Lake area and curve R to follow sections of taller pond pine, scattered hardwoods, and less dense undergrowth. Reach FR-126 at 3.5 mi. Backtrack or use a vehicle shuttle on FR-126 as described above. (*USGS-FS Maps:* Catfish Lake, Hadnot Creek)

### *Hunter Creek Trail* (*USFS #505*)       5
### (Carteret County)

• LENGTH AND DIFFICULTY: 2 mi round-trip; easy

• TRAILHEAD AND DESCRIPTION: For access to *Hunter Creek Trail* turn off NC-58 1 mi S of Kuhns (near old RR crossing) and go 3.6 mi on FR-144 to the trailhead, L. Because the road continues R in a crescent and meets the NE end of the trail, the hike can be made in a loop of 2.9 mi. Begin the trail through hardwoods and pond pine with Hunters Creek on the L. Ahead and N is the edge of Pond Pine Wilderness. Reach the NE trailhead at 1 mi. (*USGS-FS Map*: Hadnot Creek)

# 2.

## Nantahala National Forest

*I think that I shall never see*
*A poem as lovely as a tree.*

—Alfred Joyce Kilmer

The Nantahala National Forest, the state's largest (517,436 acres), is a vast area of mountain ranges, waterfalls, lakes, and rivers in the southwest corner of the state. In 1981 the Balsam-Bonas Defeat Land Purchase added 40,000 acres in Jackson County. Congress declared in Public Law 98–11 that the area would be designated the Roy Taylor Forest in recognition of Congressman Taylor's affection and respect for the mountains, forests, and streams of Western North Carolina and for his "sustained efforts to protect areas especially suited to outdoor recreation and the enjoyment of nature and to assure public access thereto." While serving 16 years as a Congressman, Taylor was a member of the Committee on Interior and Insular Affairs and chairman of the Subcommittee on National Parks and Recreation.

There are three Wilderness Areas in the Nantahala National Forest: Joyce Kilmer/Slickrock (13,132 acres) in the Cheoah District, Southern Nantahala (12,076 acres) in the Wayah District, and Ellicott Rock (3,930 acres) in the Highlands District. Within the Joyce Kilmer/Slickrock area is the Joyce Kilmer Memorial Forest, a 3,800-acre sanctuary of virgin timber and pristine wilderness splendor. No other forest in the state can compare to its large groves of tulip trees (yellow poplar).

Established in 1920, the Nantahala National Forest received

its name from a Cherokee Indian word meaning "Land of the Noonday Sun," an appropriate description for the many narrow gorges that receive the sun's direct rays only at midday. In the eight-mile-long Nantahala Gorge, mostly in Swain County, the precipitous gorge walls tower 2,000 feet. Other deep chasms are Tuskasegee, Wolf Creek, Cullasaja, Chattooga, and scores of deep north-side coves.

Nantahala is also a land of hundreds of waterfalls. Whitewater Falls, south of Sapphire, is considered to be the highest cascading river (411 feet) in eastern America. Cullasaja Falls, west of Highlands, is similar to Whitewater Falls, with cascades thundering 250 feet into the gorge. Other spectacular falls are Dry Falls, Bridal Veil Falls, and Glen Falls near Highlands, Rainbow Falls south of Sapphire, and Toxaway Falls near Sapphire. Ten major rivers flow through the forest. The turbulent Chattooga is a National Wild and Scenic River, with headwaters in the Highlands Ranger District, and a 4.5-mile section of the Horsepasture River near Sapphire has also been made a part of the National Wild and Scenic Rivers System.

The Nantahala region is also a land of precious stones—ruby, sapphire, garnet, and amythest. Wildlife roams its forest— deer, wild boar, foxes, bear, mink, and raccoon. It is home for at least 38 species of birds, including grouse, turkey, hawks, and owls. First investigated by William Bartram in 1776, its plant life is a botanist's dream. All the hardwoods and conifers common to the southern Appalachians are found here. Rare and endangered species of flowering plants are hidden in countless vales and rock crevices or can be found blooming on fertile slopes.

Previous to the coming of the white man, the forests of the Nantahala were the home of the Cherokee Indian Nation whose domain was mainly from western Virginia to Alabama. Their famous Chief Junaluska was born and lies buried in the Nantahala. During different periods the Cherokee were both enemy and ally of the early settlers. For example, the Cherokees fought side by side with the troops of Gen. Andrew Jackson against the Creek Indians at the Battle of Horseshoe Bend in 1814. Chief Junaluska later said, "If I had known that Jackson [U.S. president, 1829–1837] would drive us from our homes, I would have killed him that day at the Horseshoe." When the Supreme Court upheld the rights of the Indians after Georgia attempted to evict them, President Jackson is reported to have remarked, "John Marshall has made his decision; now let him enforce it." In 1838 President Jackson's successor, President Martin Van Buren, ordered Gen. Winfield Scott to enforce the provision of a fraudulent 1836 government treaty the Cherokees signed for a move west of the Mississippi (now Oklahoma). The removal in the winter of 1838–39 of approximately 17,000 Cherokees was a shameful "Trail of Tears," and 25 percent died during the march. The Reverend Evan Jones of South Carolina described the exodus as "multitudes . . . allowed no time to take anything with them . . . their houses were left prey to plunder."

It is estimated that 1,000 Cherokees fled to the mountains, mainly in the area of Swain, Jackson, and Haywood counties. One of those who fled was Tsali, who accidentally killed a soldier on the march. General Scott promised that all the other Indians in the mountains would be permitted to remain if Tsali and two family escapees would surrender and be executed for the soldier's death. The military kept its promise and the Cherokee descendants today are part of the Qualla Reservation, the largest Indian reservation east of the Mississippi. (See *Tsali Trail* in this chapter, the Great Smoky Mountains National Park in Chapter 7, and the Cherokee Arboretum in Chapter 14.)

The history of the Cherokee is vividly portrayed in the summer outdoor drama "Unto These Hills" in the Mountainside Theatre in Cherokee, late June to late August. For information contact Cherokee Tribal Travel and Promotion, PO Box 465, Cherokee, NC 28719, tel: 704-497-9195.

The four districts of the Nantahala National Forest are as follow:

*Cheoah Ranger District,* USFS, Rte 1, Box 16-A, Robbinsville, NC 28711, tel: 704-479-6431. (From Robbinsville go 1 mi W on US-129; turn L on SR-1116.)

*Highlands Ranger District,* USFS, Rte 2, Box 385, Highlands, NC 28741, tel: 704-526-3765. (From Highlands go 4 mi E on US-64.)

*Tusquitee Ranger District,* USFS, 201 Woodland Drive, Murphy, NC 28906, tel: 704-837-5152. (Across the Hiwassee River at the first traffic light L from jct of US-19/219 and US-64.)

*Wayah Ranger District,* USFS, Rte 10, Box 210, Franklin, NC 28734, tel: 704-524-4410. (Turn at first R off US-64 W from US-64 and US-441/23 S jct.)

Because the *Bartram Trail* traverses all four districts, it is described first.

### Bartram Trail *(81 mi; USFS #67)*      **6–10**

(Sections 1 and 2 are in Macon County; Sections 3 and 4 are in Graham and Cherokee Counties.)

* CONNECTING TRAILS:
  *(Hurrah Ridge Trail)*
  *(West Fork Trail)*
  *(Trimont Trail)*
  *(Appalachian Trail)*
  *(Laurel Creek Trail)*

The *Bartram Trail* is named in honor of William Bartram (1739–1823), the first American-born naturalist to receive international fame for his botanical research. Born in Philadelphia, Bartram's expeditions in the southeastern states traversed at least 28 counties in North Carolina, three of which are Macon, Cherokee, and Graham. The exact route of his expedition is not known, but the North Carolina Bartram Trail Society and the Nantahala National Forest staff have jointly planned the trail to run as close to the original area he explored as is feasible in the Nantahala Forest. Crossed in places by private property, the trail is not continuous and hiking it requires considerable vehicle switching. Generally running E to W, it provides some remote areas where may be seen bear, deer, turkey, grouse, and numerous song birds such as tanagers, towhees, and the Carolina junco.

From Oconee State Park in South Carolina the *Bartram Trail* traverses NW over Long Mountain, turning SW as it crosses the

Chattooga River into Georgia's Chattahoochee National Forest near Earl's Ford for a 37.4-mi route to North Carolina. At Warwoman Dell near Clayton it goes N to Rabun Bald (4,696 ft). From there it is 4.2 mi to FR-7, near the North Carolina state line and the southern entrance into the Nantahala National Forest. It is at this point that the description of the trail begins. Some suggested campsites and water sources are described along the trail, and support systems are listed at the end of each section. Contact the North Carolina Bartram Trail Society for assistance with vehicle shuttles. For information on the *Bartram Trail* in South Carolina see *South Carolina Hiking Trails* by Allen de Hart, Globe Pequot Press, Old Chester Rd, Box Q, Chester, CT 06412, tel: 1–800-243-0495; and for Georgia see *Hiking Trails of North Georgia* by Tim Homan, Peachtree Publishers, Ltd, 494 Armour Circle NE, Atlanta, GA 30324, tel: 404-876-8761. Other information is available from the Bartram Trail Conference, 3815 Interstate Court, Suite 202A, Montgomery, AL 36109, tel: 205-277-7050, and the North Carolina Bartram Trail Society, Rte 3, Box 406, Sylva, NC 28723, tel: 704-293-9661.

### *1: Chattahoochee National Forest to Franklin*

• LENGTH AND DIFFICULTY: 23.3 mi, moderate to strenuous (elev change, 1,244 ft)

• SPECIAL FEATURES: vistas from Scaly Mtn, Jones Knob, and Whiterock Mtn

• TRAILHEAD AND DESCRIPTION: This section is in the Highlands District of the Nantahala National Forest. From the jct of NC-106 and US-64/NC-28 in Highlands, go S on NC-106 for 6.8 mi to Scaly Mtn jct with Hale Ridge Rd (SR-1625) and turn L. Proceed for 2.6 mi and turn L on Chattahoochee FR-7. After 1.1 mi park near the trailhead sign.

Ascend N through hardwoods, buckberry, and rosebay rhododendron on a well-graded trail built by the YCC and blazed yellow. Cross log bridges at 0.1 mi and 0.6 mi, and skirt a timbered area. Skirt E of Osage Mtn at 0.9 mi and cross a ridge at 1.1 mi. Ascend and descend on the graded trail between coves and streams that are tributaries of Overflow Creek, crossing footbridges at 1.5 mi, 1.7 mi, 2.1 mi, and 2.4 mi. (At 2.5 mi pass jct with *Hurrah Ridge Trail,* R. It goes for 0.6 mi, leading to Blue Valley Rd, FR-79.) Continue under a heavy canopy of rosebay rhododendron, large oaks, and white pines. (At 2.9 mi pass jct of *West Fork Trail,* R; it travels for 1 mi, leading to Blue Valley Rd, FR-79.) Begin ascent to NC-106 at 3.1 mi, and reach the Osage Mtn Overlook at 3.6 mi. Cross the highway, climb steeply at a power line and through open woods of oak and locust damaged by fire. At 4 mi is a small waterfall, a natural shower, 35 yd L. Rock-hop a cascading stream above the falls, pass through rhododendron thickets, ascend steeply, and turn sharply R onto a fire road at 4.4 mi. Continue the ascent for scenic views of Georgia, Osage Mtn, Blue Valley, and Little Scaly Mtn. At 5 mi jct with the *Scaly Mtn Trail* (USFS #67A), L, a spur trail that ascends 0.5 mi to scenic Scaly Mtn (4,804 ft). Follow the old fire and timber road around the mtn into a timber clearcut and a garden of flame azalea, rhododendron, laurel, and wildflowers that reaches a peak of color the second week in June. At a road jct, keep L (R is to a TV relay station). At 6.2 mi jct with Hickory Gap Rd (SR-1621); turn L. (It is 1.1 mi, R, on Hickory Gap Rd to Broadway Gap and Turtle Pond Rd [SR-1620] for a jct with NC-106. On NC-106 it is 1.5 mi R to the Osage Mtn Overlook described above; on NC-106 L it is 2.4 mi to Glen Falls and the town of Highlands.)

Hike the Hickory Gap Rd for 2.5 mi, past an open area named Lickskillet, and reach Hickory Gap at 8.7 mi. The road is rough and passes through private properties. From Hickory Gap descend L on the road to the NF boundary and then climb steeply to a ridgetop and rock outcrop for E views of the Turtle Creek area and, on clear days, views of Whiteside Mtn, Shortoff Mtn, and Balsam Mtn. Reach a clearcut area of Jones Gap at 9.7 mi; here are panoramic views of Balsam Mtn (E), Plott Balsams (NE), Smoky Mtns (N), and Blue Ridge Mtns (S), particularly on clear days. Continue on a seeded trail, pass outcroppings, and take the E slope of Jones Knob (4,622) where a blue-blazed spur, *Jones Knob Trail* (USFS #67B), L, leads to the top for 0.3

mi. Arrive at Whiterock Gap at 10.5 mi. Here are good camp-sites and a spring is nearby. Skirt E of Whiterock Mtn, but a blue-blazed spur, *Whiterock Mtn Trail* (USFS #67C), L, ascends 0.3 mi to the top for vistas. Cliffsides, three species of rhodo-dendron, laurel, orchids and other wildflowers, and a combina-tion of conifers and hardwoods make this area incredibly scenic. Proceed to the ridge and skirt W of Little Fishhawk Mtn to the ridge base of Fishhawk Mtn (4,748 ft) at 11.7 mi. The trail is under construction beyond this point to Hickory Knoll Rd, but an estimated direction and distance are described below. From Fishhawk Mtn go NW to Wolf Rock for 0.7 mi and turn W on the ridge. Reach Doubletop Fields (an orchard) after another 1.2 mi. (It is 0.6 mi ahead, SW, to the first of two peaks at Cedar Cliff.) Turn R in the orchard and descend on a rough road that parallels Possum Creek part of the distance. Reach Hickory Knoll Rd (SR-1642) after another 1.5 mi; turn L. (From here to Franklin, the trail is on paved roads.) Follow the road past Hickory Knoll Church and make a sharp R at the jct with Clarks Chapel Rd (SR-1646). Follow SR-1646 for 2.6 mi to the commu-nity of Prentiss and jct with Teague Rd (SR-1651). Turn L, cross Little Tennessee River bridge and after 0.3 mi turn R on SR-1651. After 0.6 mi it becomes Wide Horizon Rd (SR-1652). After another 2.6 mi jct with US-23/441 and turn R. Go 0.8 mi (past a shopping center, L) and jct with US-64. (Ahead US-441 business goes 1 mi to downtown Franklin). Follow US-64 W for 1 mi and turn R on White Rd (SR-1153) for another 0.3 mi to the Wayah Ranger District office for a total distance of 11.6 mi from Fishhawk Mtn and 23.3 mi from the beginning of this section. (*USGS-FS Maps:* Scaly Mtn, Rabun Bald, Prentiss, Franklin)

• SUPPORT FACILITIES: Highlands: groceries, svc sta, tel, restau-rants, sport supplies; Town House (hotel), Main St, open June-October, tel: 704-526-2790. Franklin: shopping centers and supply stores; Franklin Hotel, 223 W Palmer St, 1 block W on US-23/64/441/NC-28, open May-October, tel: 704-524-4431. The Pines Campground, 6 mi W on US-64 from jct of US-441/64 in Franklin, full svc, including laundry; open year-round, 590 Hayesville Hwy, Franklin, NC 28734, tel: 704-524-4490.

### 2: Franklin to Beechertown

• LENGTH AND DIFFICULTY: 35.7 mi, moderate to strenuous (elev change, 2,333 ft)

• SPECIAL FEATURES: Wayah Bald, Nantahala Lake, surge chamber area

• TRAILHEAD AND DESCRIPTION: This section is in the Wayah District of the Nantahala National Forest and is a National Recreation Trail for the first 17.6 mi (dedicated May 18, 1985). To approach the trailhead from the Franklin Bypass (US-64), go S of Franklin to the jct of US-441/23 and US-64. Proceed W on US-64 to the Wayah District sign at 1 mi, and turn R on SR-1153. Go 0.3 mi (Wayah District Office, R) to jct with old US-64 and Pressley Rd (SR-1315). Cross old US-64 and drive 1.7 mi on Pressley Rd to its end and park at the Wallace Branch parking area. Cross the stream on a footbridge and hike through a young forest with scattered mature poplars and oaks. Cross a cascading stream R at 0.1 mi and cascades L on Wallace Branch at 0.3 mi. Enter a white pine stand at 0.4 mi and cross an old road at 0.5 mi. (The former *Bartram Trail* turned R and followed through a white pine forest, a good campsite area, for 0.7 mi to the *Trimont-Bartram Trail* on the Trimont Ridge. Motorcyclists now use this trail extensively and the yellow blazes have been painted black. Nevertheless, it is a more open and scenic trail than the current well-graded trail built by the YCC and YACC.) Cross a small stream and ascend on the NE side of the ridge. Reach the ridgecrest at 0.8 mi, and continue on the slope to jct with the old *Trimont-Bartram Trail* at 1.3 mi. Turn L and follow the ridge W. (To the R it is 0.4 mi to the jct of the former *Bartram Trail,* R, and the old *Trimont Trail* that leads to a residential area in Franklin to the E at 4.1 mi. Motorcyclists, ATVs, and horseback riders use the trail in this area. For hikers who wish to hike the old *Trimont-Bartram Trail,* request permission on an individual basis from Henry Walls, tel: 704-524-5568 or

704-424-2314, in Franklin. His property adjoins the old trail route off the Trimont Trail street in West Franklin. The trail runs 13.1 mi from the Amoco Station on Harrison St to Wayah Bald. It includes 4.1 mi of old roads marked with faded blue and yellow blazes.) At 1.6 mi pass S of Bruce Knob, turn sharply R and reach a gap at 1.8 mi. Begin a long ascent, steep in spots, along the ridge spine. Reach the crest at 2.3 mi, then descend to Locust Tree Gap at 2.5 mi. Traverse a large black cohosh (*Cimicifuga racemosa*) garden. Ascend and skirt S of Wilkes Knob (3,800 ft) at 3.2 mi. Descend and ascend over knobs for 2.1 mi, and reach a gravel road at 5.3 mi. Continue on the ridge, skirt N side of the knob, descend and ascend over knobs for another 2.2 mi; reach a grazing road at 7.5 mi. Follow the grazing road for 0.1 mi, then turn L and leave the old road at 7.7 mi; ascend at a sharp R. Along the ascent are trillium, doll's eyes (*Actaea pachypoda*), maidenhair fern (*Adiantum pedatum*), wild orchids, and bee balm (*Monarda didyma*). Hardwoods include hickory, locust, and oak. At 8 mi skirt the S side of a knob in a horseshoe shape and ascend from a plateau at 8.6 mi. A deep rock fissure is found at 9.2 mi, near a sharp R. Reach an old lodge and a grassy field at 9.6 mi. Follow an old road to jct with the *AT* at 10 mi. Turn L, follow the *AT* through chestnut oak, laurel, and azalea to Wayah Bald observation tower (5,342 ft) at 10.2 mi. Views are outstanding, particularly E. (Wayah is an Indian word for "wolf".) It is 4.3 mi on the gravel road to Wayah Gap and paved SR-1310.

Follow the yellow and white blazes into the forest, R, and descend through yellow birch, conifers, and rhododendron, with Canadian violets and other wildflowers. At 11.9 mi pass the old jct of the *AT* and *Bartram Trail*. A campsite area and spring are on the R at 12 mi. Turn R off the *AT* at 12.1 mi onto McDonald Ridge W of Wine Spring Bald. Enter an open grazing field of orchard grass and clover at 12.4 mi. Blazes are infrequent. Follow a seeded road through two more grazing fields for 1.7 mi, and then reach Sawmill Gap and FR-711 at 14.1 mi. Turn L from the gate, go 30 yd, turn R on a seeded road, and ascend. At 14.6 mi turn L on a bank and follow to the crest of a rocky ridge. Follow the ridge up and down from cols for 1.8 mi. There are partial views of Nantahala Lake. Descend; at 17.6 mi, near a small stream, R, reach paved SR-1310 at the lakeside (L it is 7.1 mi to Wayah Gap and the *AT*).

Turn R on SR-1310; arrive at the Lake Side Camp Store at 18.2 mi. (The store has groceries, sports supplies, snack shop, gasoline, telephone; open year-round.) Continue on the road for another 0.3 mi and turn off the road, L, by abandoned cars. Descend on a dirt driveway and cross Lee Branch into a young poplar forest. Reach an old woods road, fork R, and enter a white pine grove at 18.7 mi. Leave the old road at 19.3 mi onto a foot trail among loosestrife (*Lysimachia lanceolata*) and white snakeroot (*Eupatorium rugosum*). Cross a ridge, return to old road, and enter a stand of white pine at 19.5 mi. Leave old road on a footpath that curves around the ridge on a level contour; lake views, L, are through the trees. At 20.3 mi turn sharply L by tall poplar and descend on an old woods road. Pass through a rhododendron grove and through a patch of colicroot (*Aletris farinosa*). Pass a view of the Nantahala Lake Dam at 20.7 mi and enter another old road for a view of a deep chasm, L. Bear L at a road fork, pass an abandoned dump truck, descend on three switchbacks, pass under a powerline, and arrive at a gravel road at 21.2 mi (road R goes 0.9 mi to SR-1401). Ahead, follow an old road across the Nantahala River (low flow here), and turn R at a locked cable gate. Follow the private road downstream, pass cascading stream in Lambert Cove at 21.4 mi and a spring, L, at 22.4 mi. Pass under a large penstock from Whiteoak Dam at 23.3 mi, cross a wood bridge over Dicks Creek to SR-1401, and cross the road to the entrance of Appletree Group Camp at 23.4 mi. (To reach Beechertown by vehicle, from this point, drive E on SR-1401 across the bridge and immediately turn L on FR-308. Go 3.2 mi to jct with SR-1310; turn L and arrive at US-19 after another 4.1 mi.)

Continuing on the *Bartram Trail*, cross the rail fence near the Appletree Group Camp sign and go 0.2 mi to the old Piercy Creek Rd. Turn R, follow downstream, pass campsites C and D. (Sections of the *Bartram Trail* now follow the old *Nantahala Trail*.) At 25.3 mi cross Walnut Creek and Poplar Creek at 25.7 mi. (R it is 0.2 mi to the Nantahala River and FR-308). Ascend on a S slope, cross a ridge, and follow a N slope around Turkey Pen Cove at 27 mi. At 27.9 mi turn R, downstream, and reach the confluence with Piercy Creek at 28.1 mi. Cross the stream, turn L, and follow an old road through a white pine forest and good campsites. Reach jct, L, with *Laurel Creek Trail* at 28.4 mi. (*Laurel Creek Trail* goes 1.5 mi to jct with *Appletree Trail* where a L turn provides a return to Appletree Group Camp after another 1.1 mi. See Section 4 of this chapter.) Continue upstream in a white pine forest on a pleasant old road with switchbacks. At 28.8 mi cross a small stream where trail is arbored with rhododendron. At 29.4 mi turn sharply R on a footpath. (Ahead the *Nantahala Trail* continues 0.5 mi to Sutherland Gap and jct with the *London Bald Trail*, another loop option for a return to Appletree Group Camp.) On the footpath follow along the slope and curve around spur ridges. Pass a spring at 29.8 mi, ascend, and curve around another spur ridge E of Rattlesnake Knob (4,052 ft) at 30.2 mi. Slopes have hot-tempered yellow jackets and plenty of rattlesnake orchids. Other wildflowers on the banks of rich soil are meadow rue (*Thalictrum clavatum*), galax (*Galax aphlla*), flowering raspberry (*Rubus odoratus*), blue-bead (*Clintonia borealis*), sweet Cicely (*Osmorhoza claytonii*), and Indian pipe (*Monotropa uniflora*). Some of the trees are oak, birch, white pine, rhododendron, basswood and butternut (*Juglans cinerea*). Shrubs include bladdernut (*Staphylea trifolia*), rhododendron, and laurel. At 30.8 mi follow an old woods road for 0.3 mi. At 31.4 mi reach the crest of the ridge and the boundary of the Nantahala Power and Light Company (NPLC). Spectacular views are to the Snowbird Mtns and the Nantahala Gorge and N toward Cheoah Bald. Descend on 10 switchbacks to the NPLC surge chamber at 31.8 mi. Descend on the well-graded NPLC access road for 1.9 mi to a locked gate. Turn sharply L down an embankment to a paved driveway at the NPLC entrance road. Turn L on the entrance road and reach the Nantahala River launch site in Beechertown and jct with US-19 at 34 mi. Here is drinking water, comfort station, and a good location for vehicle shuttle, but camping is not allowed. Support facilities are described below. This is the end of Section 2 of the *Bartram Trail*, which has 1.7 mi on roads from the Wayah Ranger Station to the Wallace Branch Parking area, 17.6 mi to Nantahala Lake, and another 14.7 mi to Beechertown for a total of 35.7 mi. (*USGS-FS Maps:* Franklin, Wayah Bald, Topton, Hewitt)

• SUPPORT FACILITIES: On US-19 L (SW) it is 1.5 mi to Brookside Campground with full svc (including hot showers, laundry, and grocery store), rec fac, open all year, fully operational May 1 through October 1. Address: Box 93, Topton, NC 28781, tel: 704-321-5209. On US-19 R (NE) it is 8.5 mi to Wesser and the Nantahala Outdoor Center for hiking and outdoor sports supplies, restaurant, groceries, motel. Address: US-19 W, Box 41, Bryson City, NC 28713, tel: 704-488-2175.

### 3: Beechertown to Tatham Gap

• LENGTH AND DIFFICULTY: 11.5 mi, moderate to strenuous (elev change, 2,116 ft)

• SPECIAL FEATURES: Johanna Bald, remoteness

• TRAILHEAD AND DESCRIPTION: This section is in the Cheoah District of the Nantahala National Forest. It officially begins at Tulula Gap on US-129. A vehicle approach from Beechertown is to take US-19 S for 2.5 mi to Topton and turn R on US-129 for 2.1 mi to the trailhead, L, across the road jct with Campbell Rd (SR-1200). However, a bushwacking foot route is described below that involves private property. Until the official route of the *Bartram Trail* is constructed, hikers are advised to respect the private-property signs. Cross US-19 between two power lines, visible from the Nantahala River launch site. At 0.1 mi cross the Southern RR and ascend steeply (over 500 ft elev gain in 0.3 mi) in a hollow. Reach an abandoned Graham County RR and platform at 0.4 mi with outstanding views of the Nantahala Gorge. Reach a gravel road that leads to paved Campbell Rd (SR-1200); turn L and reach US-129 at 0.6 mi. Parking space is severely limited on US-129 in a dangerous curve. (It is 11 mi W on US-129 and 1.1 mi on SR-1116 to the Cheoah Ranger District headquarters.)

Begin at the *Bartram Trail* sign at a manicured trailhead (S side of US-129). Ascend gradually and at 0.3 mi enter a burned open slope with new growth, berries, and wildflowers. Cross a footbridge at 0.4 mi, reenter the young forest, and reach Snowbird Mtn on the ridgecrest at 0.7 mi. Curve around a knoll at 1.3 mi, and return to the ridge at 1.6 mi. At 2 mi follow the Graham-Cherokee county line. (For the next 5 mi there are long sections of the trail where timber cutting has destroyed the trail, and trees with blazes are missing. Where in doubt, stay on the major ridge line. There are not any good campsites on the ridge.) Reach Jutts Gap (3,700 ft) at 5.1 mi, ascend on switchbacks S of a knob, and skirt the S side of Little Bald (4,300 ft) at 6.3 mi. At 8.5 mi reach Teyahalee Bald (Johanna Bald) lookout tower (4,716 ft), with TV and radio transmitting stations. From Johanna Bald hike on FR-423B, rough and rocky in places, as it winds down the mtn for 3 mi to Tatham Gap (3,645 ft) at 11.5 mi. To the L is Andrews and to the R is Robbinsville. Descending to Robbinsville it is 3.3 mi on gravel FR-423 before Long Creek Rd (SR-1110). It is another 2.5 mi to the jct of Kilmer Rd (SR-1127) near the large lumber company in Robbinsville. A turn R through the town on SR-1127 is an additional 1.5 mi to US-129. Some of the vegetation in this section includes oak, birch, red maple, hemlock, wild cherry, sourwood, dogwood, azalea, rhododendron, chestnut sprouts, pine, hickory, striped maple, locust, and a wide variety of wildflowers. (*USGS-FS Maps:* Hewitt, Robbinsville, Andrews)

• SUPPORT FACILITIES: In Robbinsville there are shopping centers, restaurants, supply and service stores, PO, motel, and medical personnel.

### 4: Tatham Gap to Porterfield Gap

• LENGTH AND DIFFICULTY: 10.5 mi, moderate to strenuous

• SPECIAL FEATURES: wild, rugged, isolated

• TRAILHEAD AND DESCRIPTION: This section is in the Tusquitee Ranger District of the Nantahala National Forest. It is strenuous not because of high elev gains on the ridgeline, but because of obscure routing, summer growth, and difficult routes up the

Snowbird Mtns to Porterfield Gap. Plans by the N.C. Bartram Trail Society are to improve the treadway and to increase the number of blazes. Also, the Society plans to eventually route the trail to connect with trails in the Cherokee National Forest in Tennessee. Access is across the road from the ending of Section 3 in Tatham Gap, described above. The trail crosses a number of significant points of flat areas and near high peaks along the main ridge. Forest trees are chiefly hardwoods of oak, birch, beech, and maple. Wildflowers are prominent; deer and grouse are the major wildlife. At 3 mi reach Walker Field (4,015 ft). Skirt S of Old Billy Top (4,120 ft) at 4.6 mi and reach Cozad Gap (3,360 ft) at 7 mi. At 10.1 mi ascend to skirt S of Rocky Spring Top (3,791 ft) and descend on a rough treadway to Porterfield Gap (3,462 ft) at 10.5 mi. For hikers who do not wish to backtrack to Tatham Gap, the two exits from Porterfield Gap are described below.

The N exit, down the mtn and partially by Wolfpen Branch, is 1 mi on an old jeep road to Little Snowbird Creek, where it jcts with a rough road used by owners of private summer homes in Long Bottoms. Follow the road for 2.3 mi downstream where it becomes Little Snowbird Rd (SR-1115). Here the road is gravel for 4.9 mi, and paved for another 5 mi to jct with Kilmer Rd (SR-1127). A turn R (E) is another 5.2 mi to downtown Robbinsville on SR-1127. Another exit from Porterfield Gap is down the mtn, S, on old logging roads mainly on USFS property along Allman Creek for 2.8 mi to jct with Allman Creek Rd (SR-1378). After 0.6 mi jct with Hyatt Creek Rd (SR-1379), a paved road, for 0.8 mi into the town of Marble and US-19/129. Before either route is chosen, it is recommended that the hiker carry USGS-FS topo maps of Marble and Santeetlah Creek and a compass. (*USGS-FS Maps:* Andrews, Marble, Robbinsville, Santeetlah Creek)

• SUPPORT FACILITIES: (See information above in Section 3.)

---

## ▶ SECTION 1: CHEOAH RANGER DISTRICT

The Cheoah Ranger District has 120,110 acres with Lake Santeetlah in the center. On the N boundary is the Little Tennessee River that is also the S boundary of Great Smoky Mountains National Park, but the river is dammed for the entire distance by Calderwood Lake, Lake Cheoah, and Fontana Lake. The S boundary is rimmed by the remote Snowbird Mountains, and its W border is more remote along the Tennessee line that fronts the Cherokee National Forest. Also in the W is the 14,900-acre Joyce Kilmer/Slickrock Wilderness Area, with its NW corner in Tennessee. Some of the most spectacular mountain views are in this district, particularly from the *AT* that ascends to Cheoah Bald (5,062 ft) from Wesser and crosses the Fontana Dam after 25.2 mi. Other panoramic views are from Wauchecha Bald (4,368 ft), Joanna Bald (4,716 ft), and Hangover Mtn (4,170 ft).

There are five recreational areas, all of which provide developed family campgrounds, except the Joyce Kilmer Memorial Forest (but Horse Cove is nearby). The Tsali area is described under *Tsali Trail,* and Cheoah Point and Horse Cove are described under the Kilmer/Slickrock trails. Cable Cove is near Fontana Lake, 4.5 mi E on NC-28 from Fontana Village. Rattler Ford Group Campground (reservations required) is by Santeetlah Creek near the entrance to the Kilmer Memorial Forest. The national forest outside the campgrounds is also available for "primitive camping" unless the area is posted closed (such as for boating, picnicking, trailheads, or administrative sites). The Kilmer/Slickrock Wilderness Area is protected by regulations and general etiquette as described in the introduction to this chapter.

The construction of the Tellico-Robbinsville Scenic Highway, under the direction of the Federal Highway Administration, will provide paved-road access from Santeetlah Gap jct with SR-1127 to Tellico Plains in Tennessee. The highway dramatically affects the trail system in the area. For example, district ranger Stephen Rickerson has stated that *Cedar Top Trail* #61 and *Hooper Bald Trail* #60 are "both impacted heavily." Maintenance has ceased on the remaining sections of the trails and their descriptions are omitted. The new road will provide fast access to *King Meadows Trail* at Hooper Bald and to *Big Snowbird Trail* from Big Junction. There will be an improved access route to Strawberry Knob and the *Fodderstack Trail* #94 (TN) once the highway is completed. But the road has mutilated and scarred the mountains with some artificial walls where grass or trees can never grow, and where the wilderness qualities are destroyed forever. Conservationists tried for many years to prevent its construction.

There are two special-interest trails at the Cheoah Ranger Station. The *Camp Santeetlah Historic Trail* (USFS #152) begins at the parking area. Follow the signs on the paved trail that switchbacks up the hillside into a forest of hemlock, pitch pine, poplar, hickory, ferns, laurel, and trailing arbutus. Along the way are history markers, one of which indicates that the trail was dedicated August 13, 1983, "in honor of the men who served the Civilian Conservation Corps (CCC) and their lasting contributions to our nation's national forests," specifically Camp NCF-24, Co 3447, that opened here in 1934 and closed in 1941. Reach an observation deck at 0.4 mi; backtrack. Or, continue ahead on the *Cheoah Trail* (USFS #143). It is a 2.3-mi loop, timber-management interpretive trail with signed timber stands and examples of timber management. Timber cuts and silvicultural work are demonstrated on the slopes facing Santeetlah Lake. Another trail, the *Massey Branch Fitness Trail,* is 0.5 mi E of the ranger station on Massey Branch Rd (SR-1116). The loop trail is 0.7 mi with 14 exercise stations on a wood-chip treadway under white pine, oak, and maple. It has an excellent view of part of Santeetlah Lake after the 120-yd climb to an easy route.                                                           **11–13**

• ADDRESS AND ACCESS: District Ranger, Cheoah Ranger District, Rte 1, Box 16-A, Robbinsville, NC 28711, tel: 704-479-6431. From Robbinsville go 1 mi W on US-129 and turn L on Massey Branch Rd (SR-1116) for 1.1 mi to the ranger station. District Ranger, Tellico Ranger District, Cherokee National Forest, Ball Play Rd, Tellico Plains, TN 37385, tel: 615-253-3094.

# ► TSALI RECREATION AREA
## (Graham and Swain Counties)

The Tsali Campground and Fishing Access Area provides a ramp for boating, fishing in Fontana Lake, water skiing, camping (with showers and flush toilets), horseback riding, picnicking, nature study, and hiking. From the Tsali Campground to the Lake is a 0.5-mi footpath, *Mouse Branch Trail* (USFS #153). The area is named in honor of the Cherokee Indian, Tsali (Charlie), who escaped with his family from the "Trail of Tears" (see introduction to this chapter) to the Smoky Mountains. In the escape a U.S. Army soldier was accidentally killed. Gen. Winfield Scott asked Will Thomas, a Cherokee friend, to find Tsali and tell him that if he would surrender and pay the penalty of death, all the other Cherokee who had escaped the march to Oklahoma (approximately 1,000) would be permitted to remain. Tsali replied, "I will come. If I must die, let it be by our own people." Tsali, his oldest son, and his son-in-law were executed by a three-member Cherokee firing squad here at the old stockade.                                                                14

• ACCESS: From the jct of NC-28 and US-19 in Lauada, go W on NC-28 for 6.6 mi to the Tsali Campground sign, R, and on FR-521 go 1.6 mi to the parking area.

## *Tsali Trail* (USFS #38)                                                          15

• LENGTH AND DIFFICULTY: 17.4 mi, easy to moderate

• TRAILHEAD AND DESCRIPTION: The *Tsali Trail* has also been designated the *Tsali Horse Trail*; it consists of well-graded treadway by the campground, hitching racks, and observation points halfway along the trail near the Graham and Swain county line. From the parking area take either the R or L loop; they circle the peninsula with dips or curves at more than 40 coves. Vegetation is that of the lower-slope (less than 2,000 ft elev) Appalachian hardwood forest. Most of the forest is open with light understory, but often there are small patches of berries, sumac, sourwood, and laurel. There are scattered hemlock, scrub and white pine, and poplar. Wildflowers include sunflower, cone flower (*Rudbeckia hirta*), downy false foxglove (*Aureolaria virginica*), horsemint (*Collinsonia canadensis*), wild phlox, soapwort, gentian, orchids, henbit, and violets. (*USGS-FS Map:* Noland Creek)

### *Grassy Gap Trail* (5 mi round-trip; USFS #66); *Panther Creek Trail* (7.2 mi round-trip; USFS #68); *Reid Branch Trail* (0.5 mi; USFS #155)                                      16–18

* LENGTH AND DIFFICULTY: 12.7 mi combined, easy to strenuous

* TRAILHEAD AND DESCRIPTION: From the jct of NC-28 and Panther Creek Rd (SR-1232) at Panther Creek Bridge and backwater of Fontana Lake (2 mi W of Tsali Campground on NC-28), drive up SR-1232 beside Panther Creek for 2.3 mi to the parking area. *Panther Creek Trail* forks R and *Grassy Gap Trail* forks L. On *Grassy Gap Trail* follow up Rock Creek, bearing L of woods road that goes up Cook Branch. Continue to follow Rock Creek in a hardwood forest with rhododendron, and bear L at 1 mi at the confluence of Rock Creek and an unnamed stream. Follow the unnamed stream past a number of cascading streams and at 2 mi begin a steep 0.5-mi climb to the *AT* at Grassy Gap (3,050 ft). Backtrack or follow L on the *AT* for 2.9 mi to the Nantahala River and Wesser. Or, follow R (W) for 4 mi to Sassafras Gap on the *AT* and make a connection with *Bear Creek-Ledbetter Trail.*
  Panther Creek Trail forks R (as described above) and follows Shell Stand Creek, crossing Whiteoak Branch at 1.4 mi and approaching Reid Branch at 1.8 mi. Jct with *Reid Branch Trail* (USFS #155) is on the R. (The *Reid Branch Trail* ascends N for 0.5 mi to FR-410, which exits to Panther Creek Rd.) Continue on *Panther Creek Trail,* L, up Shell Stand Creek in a forest of oak, maple, birch, rhododendron, and scattered hemlock. Reach the trail's terminus at 3.6 mi near the confluence of Deep Creek and Whiteoak Creek, an excellent area for backpack camping. Backtrack. (*USGS-FS Maps:* Hewitt, Wesser)

* SUPPORT FACILITIES: One of the nearest commercial campgrounds is Lost Mine Campground, 8 mi SW on US-19 from

the jct of US-19 and NC-28. Turn off at the sign and proceed for 1 mi L up Silver Creek. Full svc, rec fac. Open March 15 through October 31, tel: 704-488-6445. Bryson City, with restaurants, motels, and shopping areas, is 12 mi E of Tsali.

▶ **FONTANA VILLAGE AREA**
**(Graham County)**

*Look Rock Trail* *(USFS #40)*                                    **19**

• LENGTH AND DIFFICULTY: 2 mi round-trip, moderate

• TRAILHEAD AND DESCRIPTION: From the SW end of Fontana Village on SR-1246, near the last cottages, look for Look Rock signs across a "T" intersection. Ascend gradually up a slope on the R side of a stream. Cross the stream at 0.5 mi and reach by switchbacks the former *AT* at 1 mi. The trail is now the *Yellow Creek Mtn Trail* from Tapoco W to Walker Gap E. (A loop hike could be made here by following *Yellow Creek Mtn Trail* L for 1.6 mi to Walker Gap [3,450 ft] and the current *AT*. Turn L on the *AT* and descend for 2.7 mi to NC-28, near Fontana Lake Dock. Turn L on NC-28 and go 2.5 mi to Fontana Village for a complete loop of 7.8 mi.) (*USGS-FS Map:* Fontana Dam)

*Lewellyn Cove Nature Trail* *(0.7 mi; USFS #50);* *Fontana Village Trail* *(0.9 mi; USFS #157)*                          **20–21**

• LENGTH AND DIFFICULTY: 1.6 mi combined, easy

• TRAILHEAD AND DESCRIPTION: From Fontana Village entrance road and Fontana Texaco sta, drive 1.4 mi E on NC-28 to the parking area. A well-graded and heavily used loop trail is across the highway. Fifty indigenous trees and shrubs are labeled with botanical and common names. A visitor's trail connecting with Fontana Village, the *Fontana Village Trail*, runs from the stream in Lewellyn Cove for 0.9 mi. (Other planned connections will run to the golf course and swimming pool area.) (*USGS-FS Map:* Fontana Dam)

## ▶ YELLOW CREEK MOUNTAIN AREA
### (Graham County)

*Yellow Creek Mountain Trail (USFS #48)*                           **22**

- LENGTH AND DIFFICULTY: 9.3 mi, strenuous (elev change 2,350 ft)

- CONNECTING TRAILS:
  *(Look Rock Trail)*
  *(AT)*

- TRAILHEAD AND DESCRIPTION: In Tapoco (14.5 mi W from Robbinsville on US-129) at the jct of US-129 and Rhymers Ferry Rd (SR-1247) (which leads 8.5 mi to NC-28 in Fontana Village), park in a small area on US-129. Walk 30 yd on SR-1247 and cross Meadow Branch on a footbridge. (This blue-blazed trail is infrequently hiked, but because of its scenic beauty, it deserves more attention. One disadvantage is its lack of water sources. Until 1947 it was the circuitous route followed by the *AT* between the Smokies and the Cheoah mtns. It was re-opened in 1971 by the Boy Scouts of Tapoco, Troop 415.) Climb steeply up the switchbacks through rhododendron, scrub pine, white pine, dogwood, laurel, and witch-hazel (*Hamamelis virginiana*). Follow the ridge for 0.6 mi and a burned S slope to reach Bearpen Gap at 1.4 mi under a powerline. Along the route are splendid views of the Cheoah River Valley and Hangover Lead. Banks of wildflowers are profuse—trailing arbutus, coral bell, goldenrod, and Devil's shoestrings (*Tephrosia virginiana*) in clusters of pink wings and yellow standards (the latter plant contains rotenone, an insecticide ingredient). (At Bearpen Gap a loop trail can be made by following an unnamed trail L to Rhymers Ferry Rd, SR-1274, at Jenkins Grocery. Turn L and follow the road to the trailhead at 3 mi.) Continue on the *Yellow Creek Mtn Trail* up the mtn, using care to avoid other trails and woods roads, to Old Yellow Creek Rd (also called Oldfield Gap Rd, SR-1249) at 1.8 mi. Cross the road, L, and ascend an embankment to follow a ridge of oak, pine, sourwood, and laurel. Continue on the ridge, ascending and descending over knolls to a steep climb at 3.1 mi. Reach Kirkland Gap (2,800 ft) at 5.6 mi, and Green Gap (3,455 ft) at 7.8 mi. *Look Rock Trail* is L of the Gap. (It descends 1 mi to the SW corner of Fontana Village, connecting with SR-1246.) Arrive at Walker Gap (3,450 ft) at 9.3 mi to join the current route of the *AT*. Backtrack or take the *AT* N for 2.7 mi to NC-28. Another route would be to take the AT S to Yellow Creek Gap at Tuskeegee Rd (SR-1242) for 3.7 mi. Vehicle switching would be necessary. (*USGS-FS Maps:* Fontana Dam, Tapoco)

## ▶ JOYCE KILMER/SLICKROCK WILDERNESS AREA (Graham County, North Carolina; Monroe County, Tennessee)

The Joyce Kilmer Memorial Forest, of which 3,840 acres are in the Little Santeetlah Creek watershed, and the Slickrock Creek watershed, with 11,060 acres, together form two basins separated by a ridge between Stratton Bald and Haoe Lookout. The Smokies are north across the Little Tennessee River, and the Cherokee National Forest in Tennessee is to the west. Filled with virgin timber, the Kilmer Memorial was established by Congress in 1936 to honor the famous author of "Trees," Alfred Joyce Kilmer, a soldier who was killed in World War I at the Battle of Ovreq. The Belton Lumber Company started cutting the virgin timber up the Little Santeetlah Creek in 1890, but before it reached the huge trees in what is now the Kilmer Memorial Forest, the company went bankrupt and the trees were spared. In 1936 the USFS also purchased the Slickrock Creek basin from the Babcock Lumber Company of Pennsylvania, which had cut more than 70 percent of the timber in the watershed.

This wilderness is rich in both flora and fauna. Hundreds of species of shrubs, wildflowers, vines, ferns, mosses, lichens, and herbaceous plants form the understory. Rhododendron, laurel, and flame azalea are also abundant. Trees include poplar, hemlock, sycamore, basswood, oak, maple, birch, and beech. Animal life includes boar, fox, bear, deer, raccoon, mink, and other smaller mammals. Two species of poisonous snakes—the copperhead and the timber rattler—are in the area. In addition to the song birds, the wilderness has grouse, wild turkey, owls, hawks, and raven. Under specific state laws, hunting and fishing are allowed in the wilderness by the North Carolina Wildlife Resources Commission, Division of Game, as described in the introduction to this chapter.

• SUPPORT FACILITIES: For the Slickrock Creek Wilderness Area, the closest USFS campground is Cheoah Point on Santeetlah Lake, 8.6 mi E on US-129 from the Cheoah Dam bridge and *Slickrock Creek Trail* parking area in Tapoco. Enter the campground on Old US-129 (SR-1146). Facilities include campsites, tables, grills, drinking water, comfort stations, and picnic area. (From the campground it is 7 mi E on US-129 to Robbinsville.) From the Cheoah Dam bridge it is 2.2 mi N on US-129 to a motel, restaurant (with mountain recipes), groceries, gasoline, and telephone. Address: Crossroads of Time, Deals Gap, Tapoco, NC 28780, tel: 704-498-2231. Also, from the Cheoah Dam bridge 0.4 mi E on US-129 turn L on Rhymers Ferry Rd (SR-1247) for 1.3 mi to Jenkins Grocery. A USFS campground for the Kilmer Wilderness Area is Horse Cove, 0.2 mi on FR-416 across Kilmer Rd (SR-1127) from the Kilmer Memorial Forest and picnic area entrance. Facilities at Horse Cove are the same as for Cheoah Point. Groceries, motel, and shopping centers are 13.4 mi E on Kilmer Rd (SR-1127) to Robbinsville.

• SLICKROCK ACCESS: There are two road access points for the Slickrock Wilderness Area trails. One is at the S side of the US-129 bridge over Calderwood Lake, below Cheoah Dam, and the other is at Big Fat Gap, via FR-62, 7 mi from US-219 and 2.2 mi SE from the Cheoah Dam bridge. FR-62 is closed to vehicles from late December to mid- or late March because of weather conditions.

*Slickrock Creek Trail* (13 mi; USFS #42); *Hangover Lead Trail* (5.2 mi; USFS #43)                    **23–31**

- CONNECTING TRAILS:
  *Ike Branch Trail* (2.1 mi; USFS #45)
  *Nichols Cove Trail* (2.9 mi; USFS #44)
  *Yellowhammer Gap Trail* (1.7 mi; USFS #49)
  *Big Fat Trail* (1.5 mi; USFS #41)
  *(Haoe Lead Trail)*

- TOTAL LENGTH AND DIFFICULTY: 26.4 mi combined, moderate to strenuous (elev change 4,150 ft)

- SPECIAL FEATURES: fishing, Lower Falls, Hangover outcroppings

- TRAILHEAD AND DESCRIPTION: The greatly contrasting *Slickrock Creek Trail* and the *Hangover Lead Trail* run N-S and can easily be connected with short trails at either end to form a major loop into the Slickrock Wilderness Area basin and E rim. Additional trail loops are possible into the Tennessee section of the wilderness for the W rim to make a complete rim loop of approx 26.6 mi. Sections of the wilderness are rugged and remote with minimum trail signing and generally without blazes. Hikers are advised to take adequate food and clothing, raingear (there are thunderstorms almost daily in the summer), tent, stove (frequently the wood is wet), topo maps, and compass. Although there are plenty of water sources on all the basin and mountainside trails, water is absent or intermittent on the rim trails. (Drinking water from Slickrock Creek should be boiled or treated.) Wilderness rules and regulations apply on all the trails, and hikers are reminded to follow the "no-trace" policy of hiking and camping. Slickrock Creek is an excellent brown-trout stream.

From the parking area at the S side of the Cheoah Dam bridge follow the *Slickrock Creek Trail* sign into the woods and parallel Calderwood Lake on a wide scenic trail. At 0.7 mi jct with *Ike Branch Trail*, L (described on the return route). Plant life in the vicinity includes poplar, birch, maple, hemlock, fetterbush, jewel weed (*Impatiens capensis and pallida*), sweet Cicily, and wild hydrangea (*Hydrangea arborescens*). At 0.8 mi cross a footbridge; and at 1 and 1.4 mi cross boardwalks over a precipice. A pink rhododendron (*Rhododendron minus*) grows here and frequently (with other species) in the entire Slickrock basin. At 1.6 mi cross another bridge over a precipice and turn L to the mouth of Slickrock Creek. Pass the edge of the lake backwater and arrive beside the pools and cascades of Slickrock Creek at 1.9 mi. Follow upstream on sections of an old RR grade. (This was the access route of the Babcock Lumber Company of Pittsburgh that cut 70 percent of the virgin forest in the gorge between 1915 and 1922. It had to cease logging when Calderwood Lake was constructed.) Rocky treadways, rock walls, wildflowers, and cascades make this section of the trail scenic. Rockhop or wade the creek at 2.7 mi into Tennessee and reach the Lower Falls at 3 mi. Continue upstream and cross the creek again at 3.5 mi to a jct with *Ike Branch Trail* at 3.7 mi. Good campsites are in this area. To complete this first loop turn L on *Ike Branch Trail* up Yellowhammer Creek in a forest of poplar, sycamore, basswood, rhododendron, and ferns. Ascend; at 4.2 mi jct with *Yellowhammer Gap Trail* (which leads to *Nichols Cove Trail*, R, at 4.3 mi.) (The *Hangover Lead Trail* is described on the longer return loops.) Pass through an area of oak, pine, buckberry, flame azalea, and huckleberry on a dry ridge at 4.6 mi. Cross another ridge at 4.9 mi and descend into a deep hollow of hemlock, poplar, and rhododendron. Cross a stream four times and descend on an exceptionally steep slope by a ravine. Reach the N terminus of *Ike Branch Trail* and jct with *Slickrock Creek Trail* at 5.8 mi; turn R and return to the parking area for a total of 6.5 mi.

For a second and longer loop continue upstream on the *Slickrock Creek Trail* from the jct with the *Ike Branch Trail* at 3.7 mi. Cross a small tributary before fording Slickrock Creek into Tennessee at 4 mi. At 4.2 mi reach the jct with *Stiffknee Trail* (USFS #106) at the state line. (*Stiffknee Trail* goes W up Little Slickrock Creek for 3.3 mi to Farr Gap and jct with *Fodderstack Trail* [USFS #95]. The *Stiffknee Trail* could be a route to *Fodderstack Trail* for a complete hike of the rim by using *Fodderstack, Stratton Bald, Haoe,* and *Hangover Lead* trails for approx 26.6 mi. A major problem with such a loop is the lack of water on the basin's rim.) Continue upstream for 0.2 mi to jct with *Nichols Cove Trail*, L, after fording Slickrock Creek in the process. Here the hiker has a choice of following *Nichols Cove Trail* to rejoin the *Slickrock Creek Trail* after 2.8 mi to *Big Fat Trail*, or follow *Yellowhammer Trail* off *Nichols Cove Trail* to *Ike Branch Trail* and return for a loop of lesser distance. If *Nichols Cove Trail* is chosen, ascend in a narrow scenic passage of waterfalls and cascades, hemlocks, ferns, and rhododendron. Cross the stream six times and at 0.9 mi jct with *Yellowhammer Gap Trail*, L. The 1.7-mi *Yellowhammer Trail* ascends gently NW and crosses a number of small drains from the Hangover Lead. The trail weaves in and out of coves in a forest predominated by oak, poplar, birch, and rhododendron. At 1.8 mi jct with *Ike Branch Trail* and the *Hangover Lead Trail*. A turn R on the *Ike Branch Trail* continues NW for a return to US-129 and a loop of 9.5 mi.) Continue ahead on the *Nichols Cove Trail*, pass signs of former human habitation at rock piles and terraces, tombstones, and once cleared fields at 1.3 mi. Begin a steep ascent at 1.8 mi to reach a ridge nose where a L curve goes to the ridgecrest. Cross two more ridges and begin to descend at 2.4 mi. After 0.3 mi of a steep descent, reach a level area, cross Big Fat Branch, and jct with *Big Fat Trail* at 2.9 mi. There are good campsites here. To the R it is 150 yd to *Slickrock Creek Trail,* and to the L on *Big Fat Trail* it is 1.5 mi up to *Big Fat Gap*. (The *Big Fat Trail* ascends to switchbacks at 0.2 mi and follows mainly on the S side of the stream, steeply in sections. Cross the stream at 0.9 mi, shift S to cross a tributary, and follow switchbacks to reach Big Fat Gap parking area and FR-62 at 1.5 mi. At the Fat Gap parking area, a L turn on the *Hangover Lead Trail* for 2.4 mi for a jct with *Ike Branch Trail,* R, will lead back to US-129 in Tapoco for a loop of 11.6 mi.

If choosing to hike the *Slickrock Creek Trail* instead of the *Nichols Cove Trail*, continue upstream on remnant sections of the old RR grade and cross the stream to the Tennessee side at 4.7 mi. Enter a rocky section at 5.2 mi and pass through a narrow canyon at 5.4 mi. Cross Wildcat Branch, a tributary, curve around the nose of two spur ridges, and cross back into North Carolina at 6.2 mi. (For the next 0.2 mi the area is good for camping.) Cross the creek again at 6.4 mi and at 6.6 mi (the last crossing from Tennessee) below Wildcat Falls. Cross Slickrock Creek and reach the confluence of Slickrock Creek and Big Stack Gap Branch and *Big Stack Gap Trail* (USFS #139), R, at 7.3 mi. (The *Big Stack Gap Branch Trail* goes 1.8 mi upstream to a crosstrail with *Fodderstack Trail* and *Crowder Creek Trail* #48 in Cherokee National Forest.) Cross a tributary at 7.5 mi and Slickrock Creek again to reach the jct with *Nichols Cove Trail* at 7.9 mi. A third loop option can be made here by returning to US-129 on either *Nichols Cove, Yellowhammer,* and *Ike Branch* trails for a total of 13.8 mi or climbing the *Big Fat Trail* to jct with *Hangover Lead* and *Ike Branch* trails N for a total of 14.1 mi.

For the fourth and final loop option, continue upstream and ascend to the nose of a spur ridge to cross Buckeye Branch at 8.2 mi. Ascend gradually, cross two more drains before crossing Hangover Creek at 9 mi, the last generally level area for camping within the next 4 mi. At 9.6 mi the trail forks. (Ahead is a 0.7-mi dead-end trail to the cascading confluence of Slickrock Creek and Naked Ground Branch.) At the fork, turn sharply L on a W slope and curve around the ridge to cross a tributary that flows into Hangover Creek. For the next 2.9 mi ascend on switchbacks (where some sections are overgrown) on a steep ridgeline, but cross a tributary four times before reaching the major ridge knoll. The forest in this area is mixed hardwoods, rhododendron, and scattered conifers. Reach a trail crossroads at 13 mi with *Haoe Lead Trail* and *Naked Ground Trail* (4,850 ft). (With a vehicle shuttle, trail connections can be made to all trails described below in the Kilmer basin. The *Haoe Lead Trail* connects R, 0.5 mi, with the *Stratton Bald Trail*.) Follow the *Haoe Lead Trail* L for 0.8 mi along the ridgeline to jct with a shortcut R of the *Haoe Lead Trail* and 0.1 mi farther for another jct of the *Haoe Lead Trail*, R, and the beginning of the *Hangover Lead Trail*, L, at Haoe Lookout (5,249 ft) at 13.9 mi. (Here the *Haoe Lead Trail* goes down the mtn for 5.1 mi to Kilmer Rd.) The Hangover Lookout (the site of a former fire tower) has limited vistas. Proceed on the *Hangover Lead Trail,* descend easily to Saddle Tree Gap, and jct with the *Deep Creek Trail*, R, at 14.1 mi. (The *Deep Creek Trail* descends to join the *Haoe Lead Trail* described below.) Ahead at this point is a 0.2-mi dead-end spur to prominent rocks and cliffs for the most panoramic and spectac-

ular viewing of the Slickrock Wilderness Area. Dense rhododendron landscapes the rocks. Back on the *Hangover Lead
Trail* descend in a forest of beech and birch. At 14.6 mi in a
rhododendron slick is another good view E. Begin steep descent
and enter a virgin hemlock forest at 15.1 mi. (Damp, often
foggy, and dark serpentine-shaped roots in rhododendron
thickets may offer the fantasy of a descent into the land of *The
Hobbit*.) Begin a gradual descent at 15.3 mi and follow the trail
through oak, red- and green-striped maple, birch, sassafras,
hemlock, and flame azalea to the edge of the ridge. Descend
steeply on six switchbacks at 16.5 mi and reach Big Fat Gap
parking area at 16.7 mi. (The large public parking area is popular both for hikers and hunters.) To the L the 1.5 mi *Big Fat
Trail* descends to connect with the *Slickrock Creek Trail*, and to
the R FR-62 winds down the mtn for 7 mi to US-129, 2.2 mi SE
of Tapoco. Cross the parking area, ascend steeply on an old
woods road into a hardwood forest with scattered conifers to
the summit of Cold Spring Knob (3,480 ft) at 17.1 mi. Follow
the dry ridge on a moderate and gradual descent to the summit
of Caney Ridge (2,800 ft) that rises from the E, at 18.2 mi.
Among hardwoods, huckleberry, and buckberry descend to
Yellowhammer Gap (2,520 ft) and jct with *Ike Branch Trail* at
19.1 mi. Turn R, descend to jct with *Slickrock Creek Trail*, turn R,
and return to the parking area at US-129 at the Cheoah Dam
bridge for a total loop of 21.4 mi. (*USGS-FS Maps:* Tapoco,
Whiteoak Flats)

• KILMER ACCESS: There are two road routes to the Kilmer section of the Kilmer/Slickrock Wilderness Area. One paved road
entrance is from Robbinsville. Drive 1 mi W of Robbinsville on
US-129, turn L on Massey Branch Rd (SR-1116) toward the RS.
At 4.3 mi turn R on Kilmer Rd (SR-1127), pass the jct with the
new Tellico-Robbinsville Scenic Highway, and descend to a
crossroads with Santeetlah Rd (FR-416) at 13.4 mi. The Kilmer
Picnic Area and Memorial Forest entrance road is L for 0.6 mi.
The other route, 7.2 mi E of Tapoco on US-129, begins at the
jct with Old US-129 (SR-1147). Drive 0.5 mi to Santeetlah Rd
(SR-1134), which becomes FR-416 on a gravel road, and reach

the crossroads with SR-1127 at the entrance to the Kilmer Picnic Area after 6 mi.

### Haoe Lead Trail *(6.5 mi; USFS #53)*                                    **32–35**

* CONNECTING TRAILS:
  *Deep Creek Trail (3.9 mi; USFS #46)*
  *Jenkins Meadow Trail (1.8 mi; USFS #53A)*
  *(Hangover Lead Trail)*
  *(Slickrock Creek Trail)*
  *(Naked Ground Trail)*
  *(Stratton Bald Trail)*

* TOTAL LENGTH AND DIFFICULTY: 12.2 mi combined, moderate to strenuous

* SPECIAL FEATURES: Deep Creek cascades, Haoe Lookout area

* TRAILHEAD AND DESCRIPTION: From the crossroads of Kilmer Rd and Santeetlah Rd, described above, drive up (W) Kilmer Rd (also called "Wagon Train Road," SR-1127) for 5.4 mi to a large parking area, R. Park here for entrance across the road to the *Haoe Lead Trail*. (Up the road it is 0.2 mi to the Maple Springs Observation area and the cul-de-sac end of this previously controversial road that conservationists stopped from penetrating the Slickrock area. The *Maple Springs Observation Trail* is a 220-yd paved scenic loop [designed for wheelchair access] that provides N views of the Cheoah River Valley, Yellow Creek Mtn, and the Great Smoky Mtns.) Ascend the graded *Haoe Lead Trail* (constructed by the YACC in 1979) in a forest of hardwoods and white pine. At 0.5 mi reach a ridgeline and cross to the N slope in a rocky area. At 0.8 mi is water, L. Jct R at 1.1 mi with *Deep Creek Trail*.

(*Deep Creek Trail* begins in a rocky area. Ferns are prominent with wildflowers that include umbrella-leaf [*Diphylleia cymosa*], crested dwarf iris, black and blue cohosh, and twisted stalk [*Streptopus roseus*]. Trees include basswood, hemlock, birch, and buckeye. Cross small streamlets, pass large rock formations at 0.7 mi and 1.1 mi. Pass a second-growth forest at 1.6 mi and reach cascading Deep Creek at 2.1 mi. Cross a footbridge to an old timber road and turn L. [To the R is the former entrance to the *Deep Creek Trail,* 2.5 mi downstream to FR-445 that forks from FR-62, the route to Big Fat Gap. Entrance remains possible on this route though sections are overgrown.] Ascend steadily into the Hudson Deaden Branch area through rhododendron, hemlock and hardwoods, and more steeply on switchbacks to jct at 3.9 mi with the *Hangover Lead Trail* in Saddle Tree Gap [5,120 ft], the boundary of the Kilmer/Slickrock Wilderness Area.) (To the R it is 90 yd to the fork where the *Hangover Lead Trail* goes L and a 0.2-mi spur route, R, ascends to panoramic views at Hangover Mountain. The L fork of *Hangover Lead Trail* ascends 0.2 mi to the Haoe Lookout [5,249 ft] and jct L with *Haoe Lead Trail.* A return can be made here on the *Haoe Lead Trail* for a total loop of 9.2 mi.)

To continue on the *Haoe Lead Trail* from the NE jct with the *Deep Creek Trail,* ascend steadily to Rock Creek Knob and follow W on the main ridgeline. Turn on a S slope and at 3.3 mi cross the Kilmer/Slickrock Wilderness boundary and jct with the N trailhead of *Jenkins Meadow Trail* at 3.6 mi.

(The *Jenkins Meadow Trail,* #54A, descends SE on a slope to join a ridgeline and wilderness boundary at 0.7 mi, and at 1.8 mi ends at a jct with *Naked Ground Trail.* It is another 0.9 mi L on the *Naked Ground Trail* to SR-1127.)

Continue on the *Haoe Lead Trail* up the slope and to the main ridgeline to a more level area known as Jenkins Meadow. Pass through dense groves of rhododendron and ascend steeply to Haoe lookout at 5.1 mi and jct with the *Hangover Lead Trail,* R. (From here a loop of 9.2 mi can be made by reversing the route described above for the *Deep Creek Trail.*) Continue L from the Lookout, descend, follow narrow ridgecrest at 5.6 mi, and at 6 mi arrive at the jct with *Slickrock Creek Trail,* R, and *Naked Ground Trail,* L. Ahead the *Haoe Lead Trail* ascends its final 0.5 mi to a jct with the *Stratton Bald Trail* and the boundary of the wilderness area at 6.5 mi. (To the R the *Stratton Bald Trail* goes 1.8 mi to the *Fodderstack Trail,* #95, in the Cherokee National Forest, and L it descends for 6.7 mi to SR-1127.) Backtrack, or use a connecting trail. (*USGS-FS Maps:* Big Junction, Santeetlah, Tapoco)

**Naked Ground Trail** *(5.7 mi; USFS #55);* **Stratton Bald Trail**
*(8.5 mi; USFS #54)*                                    **36–37**

* CONNECTING TRAILS:
*(Jenkins Meadow Trail)*
*(Haoe Lead Trail)*
*(Slickrock Creek Trail)*

* TOTAL LENGTH AND DIFFICULTY: 14.2 mi combined, strenuous (elev change 3,220 ft)

* SPECIAL FEATURES: wildlife and wildflowers on Horse Cove Ridge

* TRAILHEAD AND DESCRIPTION: These two trails can make a 13.2-mi loop: the first provides a study of the Little Santeetlah Creek drainage, and the second provides a major observation of Horse Cove Ridge high above the eastern flow of both the Little Santeetlah and Santeetlah creeks. Park at either the space assigned at the Kilmer Picnic area entrance on SR-1127 and *Naked Ground Trail* E trailhead or at the Rattler Ford Group Campground entrance across the bridge S of *Stratton Bald Trail* on SR-1127. It is 0.4 mi between the two parking options.

If beginning on the *Naked Ground Trail*, ascend on switchbacks to the ridgecrest and jct with *Jenkins Meadow Trail*, R, near a spring. (*Jenkins Meadow Trail* is a 1.8-mi connector that ascends from here to *Haoe Lead Trail* described above.) Follow the slope, L, cross a small stream at 1.4 mi and at 1.7 mi. At 1.8 mi is the old trail that connected with the Kilmer Picnic Area, a route that is now closed. At 1.9 mi jct with an alternate trail. The L route crosses the Little Santeetlah and follows through a damp and dense forest of rhododendron, tall hemlock, and tulip poplar. It rejoins the R alternate after 0.6 mi. Cross Adamcamp Branch at 2.9 mi on a footbridge, and cross five more streams before beginning the final ascent; last dependable water is at 4.8 mi. Begin the first of 14 switchbacks at 4.9 mi in a forest of oak, yellow birch, and flame azalea. Arrive at Naked Ground Gap and end of *Naked Ground Trail* at 5.7 mi, and jct with *Haoe Lead Trail*, R and L. Here is a popular campsite and outstanding views of the Little Santeetlah Creek Drainage. Across the gap is the S trailhead of the *Slickrock Creek Trail*.

To continue the loop, turn L and ascend 0.5 mi on the *Haoe Lead Trail* at 6.2 mi. (To the R the *Stratton Bald Trail* goes 1.8 mi to its W-end jct with *Fodderstack Trail*, #95, in the Cherokee National Forest.) Turn L and descend on a ridge with four switchbacks. Among the oaks and yellow birch are flame azaleas (which usually bloom here in late July), blue beads, Indian cucumber-root (*Medeola virginians*), and moosewood (*Viburnum alnifolium*). At 6.8 mi jct with blue-blazed 0.6-mi *Wolf Laurel Trail*, R. (It descends gradually to FR-81F in a level area of Wolf Laurel Basin. To reach this trail by road, take SR-1127 E from the Kilmer entrance road for 2.3 mi to Santeetlah Gap. Turn R and go 6.7 mi to Fork Ridge Rd, R, [FR-81F] for another 3 mi on a narrow 4WD road.) At 7.5 mi is a timber road, R, that leads to FR-81F. Wildlife is often seen here. Continue on ridge through sections of open forest. Some of the understory vegetation includes flame azalea, huckleberry, bladdernut, and mountain laurel. At 8.9 mi are scenic views E and S. Pass a large rock overhang at 9.8 mi. At 11.4 mi pass ruins of an old cabin, and at 11.5 mi a scenic forest slope, L. At 11.7 mi leave the wilderness boundary; at 12.4 mi cross a number of small streams with footbridges and descend into a grove of hemlock, white pine, great laurel, rhododendron (*Rhododendron arborescens*), and white honeysuckle to parallel Santeetlah Creek. Reach SR-1127 at 12.9 mi and turn L to follow SR-1127 for 0.3 mi to the parking area (or R 0.1 mi to Rattler Ford Group Campground parking area). (*USGS-FS Maps:* Big Junction, Santeetlah Creek, Tapoco)

### *Joyce Kilmer Memorial Trail (1.2 mi; USFS #56); Poplar Cove Loop Trail (0.7 mi; USFS #58)* 38–39

- LENGTH AND DIFFICULTY: 1.9 mi combined, easy

- SPECIAL FEATURES: virgin forest, historic memorial

- TRAILHEAD AND DESCRIPTION: From the parking area of the Joyce Kilmer Memorial Forest and picnic area at the end of FR-

416, follow the trail signs and ascend alongside cascading Little Santeetlah Creek to cross a footbridge. Log seats for rest and contemplation are along the trail in this primeval forest of mosses, rhododendron, hemlock, yellow poplar, fetterbush, trillium, cohosh, wood sorrel, and crested dwarf iris. At the jct with *Poplar Cove Trail* is a sign that indicates Alfred Joyce Kilmer was born in New Brunswick, New Jersey, December 6, 1886, and killed in action in France, July 30, 1918. The grove of yellow poplar is the most spectacular feature on the trails; many are 16 to 21 ft in circumference and over 100 ft tall. Cross another footbridge over Little Santeetlah Creek on the return loop to the parking lot. (*USGS-FS Map:* Santeetlah Creek)

## ▶SNOWBIRD MOUNTAIN AREA
### (Graham County)

### *Snowbird Loop Nature Trail* (USFS #39)     40

• LENGTH AND DIFFICULTY: 0.5 mi, easy

• TRAILHEAD AND DESCRIPTION: From Cheoah RS go SW on Massey Branch Rd (SR-1116) for 2.3 mi to jct with Kilmer Rd (SR-1127) and turn R sharply on SR-1127. Go 1.3 mi to Snowbird picnic area before crossing Snowbird Creek bridge for parking. A well-graded nature trail follows Snowbird Creek upstream, across the road. Circle up the slope for a return in a beautiful forest of hemlock, holly, rhododendron, cucumber tree, oak, maple, and extra-large sassafras trees. (*USGS-FS Map:* Robbinsville)

### *Big Snowbird Trail* (*10.7 mi; USFS #64*)     41–45

• CONNECTING TRAILS:
*Snowbird Mountain Trail* (10.6 mi; USFS #415)
*Sassafras Creek Trail* (2.5 mi; USFS #65)
*Middle Falls Trail* (1.0 mi; USFS #64A)
*Mitchell Lick Trail* (1.5 mi; USFS #154)

• TOTAL LENGTH AND DIFFICULTY: 26.3 mi combined, moderate to strenuous (elev change 2,739 ft)

• SPECIAL FEATURES: RR history, remote, waterfalls

• TRAILHEAD AND DESCRIPTION: Three major trails begin at Junction, the end of FR-75, deep in the enchanting back-country of the Snowbird Mountains. The *Big Snowbird Trail* follows Snowbird Creek up and through the watershed for a gain of 2,600 ft to Big Junction at the Tennessee state line. The *Snowbird Mountain Trail* rejoins the *Big Snowbird Trail* near the top of the basin but follows a high ridge route on the S. *King Meadows Trail* also follows a high ridge route but is N of the basin; it ends at Hooper Bald after a 2,700-ft elev gain, and can be connected with the other two trails by the 1.5-mi *Mitchell Lick Trail*. These trails provide loop options, but scarce water sources on the ridges limit convenient campsites. A rugged and remote area, it was once the home of the Cherokee who found security here from the "Trail of Tears." Early white pioneers prospected for minerals and set up scattered grazing farms, but it was the timbering of the virgin forests of chestnut, poplar, and hemlock from 1928 to 1942 that severely altered the environment. Now healing from the scars of the Buffalo-Snowbird RR, you will see historic signs of both the old RR and pioneer life on the high plateaus. Access is as follows:

From the jct of US-129 and Kilmer Rd SR-1127 in Robbinsville, go 3.3 mi to jct with Massey Branch Rd (SR-1116), from which it is 2.3 mi R to Cheoah RS, and bear L at the fork on SR-1127 for 2.2 mi to jct with Little Snowbird Rd (SR-1115). Turn L on SR-1115 and go another 2.2 mi to jct with Hard Slate Rd (SR-1121). Turn a sharp L at jct and continue for 1 mi to a bridge over Snowbird Creek. Look for "Dead End" sign and "One Way" sign on R at bridge over Little Snowbird Creek. This is Big Snowbird Rd (SR-1120), which becomes FR-75. Proceed on this gravel road for 6 mi to the Junction parking area, a total of 13.7 mi from Robbinsville and 12.7 mi from Cheoah RS.

Begin the trail on an old RR grade that crosses a number of earthen hummocks and goes under large poplars and maples.

At 0.2 mi *Snowbird Mountain Trail* begins on the L. Continue on the *Big Snowbird Trail* on the old RR grade and L of cascading Snowbird Creek. The understory is composed of rhododendron, wild hydrangea, and sweet pepperbush; the forest trees are hemlock, birch, basswood, poplar, and cucumber tree. At 2.8 mi reach the jct of *Sassafras Creek Trail*, L, 250 yd beyond Sassafras Creek. (This trail is an alternate to the *Big Snowbird Trail*. If you choose this trail, ascend on an old RR grade for 0.7 mi to Sassafras Falls. After 0.1 mi beyond the falls, leave the old RR grade and turn R [an old trail continues upstream and forks after 0.1 mi, the L going up Fall Branch for 1 mi, the other up Sassafras Creek for 2.2 mi, and both to jct with the *Snowbird Mountain Trail*]. Climb steeply to Burnt Rock Ridge at 2 mi, descend to the mouth of Littleflat Branch, and rejoin *Big Snowbird Trail* at 2.5 mi.)

Continue on an old RR grade and pass L of Big Falls at 3.9 mi. Reach an alternate trail, *Middle Falls Trail*, at 4 mi. (This trail, R, near Mouse Knob Branch, ascends steeply for 0.2 mi, and then descends gradually to the *Big Snowbird Trail* after 1 mi. It is an alternate that avoids 11 fordings of Snowbird Creek, which may be impossible to cross during high water.) If continuing on the *Big Snowbird Trail*, cross the creek frequently and arrive at beautiful Middle Falls and its large pool at 5.1 mi. At 5.3 mi the *Sassafras Creek Trail* jct is L, at the mouth of Littleflat Branch.

After a few yd *Middle Falls Trail* rejoins, R. The *Big Snowbird Trail* continues to Upper Falls at 6.3 mi. Follow the trail past Meadow Branch, Rockbar Branch, a number of unnamed tributaries, Bearpen Branch, and two more tributaries before leaving the main stream, L, at 8.7 mi. Ascend steeply to jct with *Mitchell Lick Trail* at 9 mi. (*Mitchell Lick Trail* is a 1.5-mi connector to *King Meadows Trail* described below.) Follow the *Big Snowbird Trail* L, and at 9.3 mi jct with *Snowbird Mountain Trail*, L. (The *Snowbird Mountain Trail* is described below.) Continue the ascent along the Graham/Cherokee county line to the ridgetop, the boundary of Tennessee-North Carolina, and turn R at 9.8 mi. Follow the ridge NE, ascend to a knob and then to scenic Laurel Top (5,317 ft) at 10.3 mi. At 10.7 mi reach the end of the trail at Big Junction. Backtrack, or return on one of the other two major trails, or arrange a vehicle switch to the Tellico-Robbinsville Scenic Highway at Big Junction.

To hike the green-blazed *Snowbird Mountain Trail*, begin at the *Big Snowbird Trail*, L, 0.2 mi from Junction (as described above). On a graded trail cross two streams lined with birch, poplar, sassafras, spice bush (*Linders benzoin*), hemlock, rhododendron, and violets. Pass Wildcat Branch cove amd reach Deep Gap (3,340 ft) at 1.3 mi. Turn R, ascend to Wildcat Knob on Sassafras Ridge at 2.5 mi, and continue to descend and ascend over and around knolls. At 3.2 mi is a USGS benchmark on a knoll (3,830 ft) and an old trail intersection (R to Snowbird Creek and L to Juanita Branch). At 5 mi reach Bee Gap (4,040 ft), where a faint trail, R, descends along Falls Branch to Sassafras Falls and the *Sassafras Creek Trail*. Continue traversing on gradual and sometimes steep grades through scattered grassy fields, hardwoods, laurel, flame azalea, and rhododendron. At 6.7 mi pass an old trail R that leads 2.2 mi down Sassafras Creek to *Sassafras Creek Trail*. Ascend to Pantherflat Top (4,680 ft) at 8.5 mi and dip to a gap before ascending Dillard Top (4,680 ft) at 9 mi. The trail's end and jct with *Big Snowbird Trail* is at 10.6 mi. Return options include backtracking or descending on *Big Snowbird Trail* for 9.3 mi to make a 20-mi loop to Junction parking area or taking *Mitchell Lick Trail* to jct with *King Meadows Trail* for 1.8 mi and a loop back to Junction for 18.4 mi. (*USGS-FS Maps*: Big Junction, Marble, McDaniel Bald, Santeetlah Creek)

### King Meadows Trail *(USFS #63)*                 46–47

- LENGTH AND DIFFICULTY: 6 mi, strenuous (elev change, 2,700 ft)

- CONNECTING TRAIL:
  *(Mitchell Lick Trail)*

- TRAILHEAD AND DESCRIPTION: This yellow-blazed trail is overgrown for the first 2.5 mi. At the end of FR-75, at Junction, follow the *Big Snowbird Trail*, pass the jct with the *Snowbird Mountain Trail*, L, at 0.2 mi, and go upstream for another 0.2 mi to jct with the *King Meadows Trail*, R. Cross Snowbird Creek and begin the ascent of Firescald Ridge (L of Owlcamp Branch). At 0.8 mi reach the ridge of the Snowbird Creek Divide in a hardwood forest. Continue the ascent, and at 1.7 mi make a long curve around a high knoll to reach Deep Gap (also known as Twin Oaks Gap) at 2.5 mi. Intersect with an old sled road, R and ahead, that was used by early settlers of the mountain plateaus. Continue ahead, ascend steeply, curve around Bee Knob and arrive at King Meadows at 3.3 mi. Pass through a partially grassy area formerly cleared of trees by early settlers. Ascend for 1.1 mi, leave the ridge, and pass over a saddle in the main curve around Queen Ridge at 4.9 mi. Enter a small gap and ascend to a more level area and jct with *Mitchell Lick Trail* at 5.6 mi. (The *Mitchell Lick Trail*, an old jeep road, connects to the Snowbird trails described above. It descends to cross Sarvis Branch at 0.4 mi, follows Flat Ridge before descending to cross Snowbird Creek in a forest of hemlock and hardwoods, and reaches *Big Snowbird Trail* at 1.5 mi.) Ahead, on the *King Meadows Trail* it is 0.4 mi to Hooper Bald (5,429 ft), the trail's end, and former jct with *Hooper Bald Trail*. Exit at the Tellico-Robbinsville Scenic Highway with a vehicle shuttle, or backtrack. (*USGS-FS Maps:* Santeetlah Creek, Big Junction)

• SUPPORT FACILITIES: The nearest USFS campground (no hook-ups) is Horse Cove across from the entrance to the Joyce Kilmer Memorial Forest. It is 7.2 mi W on Kilmer Rd (SR-1127) from the jct with Little Snowbird Rd (SR-1115). Motels, shopping centers, restaurants, and other services are available in Robbinsville.

▶ **NOLTON RIDGE AREA**
**(Graham and Swain Counties)**

*Bear Creek-Ledbetter Trail (USFS #62)*                              **48**

• LENGTH AND DIFFICULTY: 8 mi, moderate to strenuous (elev change 1,820 ft)

• TRAILHEAD AND DESCRIPTION: This is a 16-mi round-trip trail or a minimum of 13.4 mi using alternate trails. From the jct of US-129 and 19 in Topton, take US-129 W for 4.1 mi to Bear Creek Rd (SR-1201) and turn R. (It is 7.6 mi ahead on US-129 to Robbinsville.) Cross over an old railroad, pass a log cottage and mobile home on the L, enter the edge of the forest and park. Follow the road through a young forest of mixed hardwoods, hemlock, poplar, rhododendron, tag alder, laurel, yellow root, and a wide variety of ferns and flowers along the creek. At 0.3 mi cross an old bridge onto a seeded road. At 0.7 mi cross Dee Branch, and cross Bear Creek at 0.9 mi. From this point on, the trail is on the R side of Bear Creek, but it crosses Cherry Branch at 1.7 mi. Ruins of a few old houses are near the trail. Cross from Graham into Swain County at 3.5 mi and reach the Ledbetter jeep road, R, at 3.7 mi. (This jeep road ascends and descends on Nolton Ridge to Campbell Rd [SR-1200]). Skirt Little Bald on an even contour at 4 mi, curving R at the headwaters of Ledbetter Creek. Continue skirting around the ridges and coves, cross Mudcut Branch at 6.2 mi and then a number of unnamed streams flowing SE from Cheoah Bald mountain range. At 8 mi a service road leads L up to the Sassafras Gap Lean-to, 120 yds SE of the *AT*. (On the *AT* it is 5.4 mi NW to Stekoah Gap and Johnson Gap Rd SR-1211; L is to Robbinsville and R is to Fontana Village. On the *AT*, R [SE], it is 7 mi to the Nantahala River and Wesser. The route is scenic for viewing the Nantahala Gorge. A relocation of the *AT* around the Jump-up affords an optional route.) Cheoah Bald (5,062 ft) is on the *AT*, 1.1 mi L from Sassafras Gap. (*USGS-FS Map*: Hewitt)


▶**CHEOAH MOUNTAIN AREA**
   **(Graham County)**


*Wauchecha Bald Trail (8.3 mi; USFS #69/47); Cody Gap Trail (0.4 mi; USFS #156)*                          **49–50**

- LENGTH AND DIFFICULTY: 8.7 mi combined, strenuous (elev change 2,425 ft)

- SPECIAL FEATURES: rugged and remote

- TRAILHEAD AND DESCRIPTION: From Robbinsville, jct of US-129 and NC-143, go W on US-129 for 7 mi and turn L on SR-1146 at Cheoah Point Campground. Follow a sign for 0.7 mi to the campground and park near the entrance where a blue-blazed trail begins at a telephone pole. Go up the ridge through white pines for 0.2 mi to US-129. Cross the highway, climb steeply under a powerline, and reach Cheoah Mtn ridge at 0.7 mi. Leave the ridge at 1.8 mi, cross a stream at 2.2 mi, and return to the ridge at 2.7 mi. Cross an old road at 2.8 mi. Vegetation is mixed hardwoods, rhododendron, hemlock, and laurel. Formerly called *Old Roughy Trail*, it lives up to its name in some of the knoll climbs. Descend slightly from the ridge and cross Hazelnut Spring at 4.2 mi. Continue to ascend and follow the S slope of the ridge at a number of points. Reach Locust Licklog Gap at 5.2 mi, and Haw Gap at 6.2 mi. At 6.9 mi there is a jct with a partially used FR, L. (It descends 4 mi to Yellow Creek Gap at Tuskeegee Rd [SR-1242] and jct with the *AT*.) Continue ahead to Wauchecha Bald (4,385 ft), the site of a former fire tower, at 7.1 mi. Here is a jct with the original *Wauchecha Bald Trail* (USFS #47). Follow the trail for another 0.7 mi to a fork. The trail bears R for 0.5 mi to the *AT*, S, and at the fork the *Cody Gap Trail* bears L for 0.4 mi to the *AT*, N. (It is 2.4 mi N on the *AT* from Cody Gap to Yellow Creek Gap and SR-1242.) (*USGS-FS Maps*: Robbinsville, Fontana Dam)

## ▶ SECTION 2: HIGHLANDS RANGER DISTRICT

The Highlands Ranger District almost doubled its size when the 40,000-acre Balsam-Bonas Defeat lands (now the Roy Taylor Forest) were acquired in 1981. Congress appropriated $13.4 million for the purchase, identified by the USFS as probably the largest single holding suitable for the forest system in the eastern part of the nation. The new property, all in Jackson County, adjoins the Blue Ridge Parkway on the N boundary of the district. Mead Lake and Wolf Creek Lake, 90 mi of streams, and eight waterfalls are in the tract. Headwaters of Tanasee Creek, Wolf Creek, Caney Fork, and Moses Creek drain into the scenic Tuckasegee River from high ridges such as Rich Mtn and Coward Mtn. Among the peaks that are about a mile high are Coward Bald, Chestnut Knob, Gage Bald, Charley Bald, and Rocky Knob.

A wider range of the district's 105,084 acres is in the SE corner of Macon County. Its boundaries extend to the Georgia state line and the Chattahoochee National Forest, and the South Carolina state line and the Sumter National Forest. Its western border is with the Wayah District, but E of Franklin. A wilderness area, the 3,030-acre Ellicott Rock Wilderness Area covers a rugged and beautiful area of the Chattooga River in a tri-state tract. Some of the state's major waterfalls are in the district. They include the highest, 411-ft Whitewater Falls; Dry Falls; Cullasaja Falls; Rainbow Falls; and Flat Creek Falls. A major mountain attraction is Whiteside Mtn (4,930 ft) 5 mi E of Highlands. Its sheer rock face is considered to be among the highest in eastern America. Another scenic mtn is Yellow Mtn (5,127 ft) with abundant wildflowers and blueberries. The district's major trail is the Bartram, which enters from Georgia S of Osage Mtn and ascends to the high country of Scaly Mtn, Whiterock Mtn, and Fishhawk Mtn before descending to Hickory Knoll Creek. The district's major recreational areas are Cliffside Lake and Vanhook Glade, 4.5 mi W of Highlands on US-64.

• ADDRESS AND ACCESS: District Ranger, Highlands Ranger District, USFS, Rt 2, Box 385, Highlands, NC 28741, tel: 704-526-3765, 4 mi E of Highlands on US-64.

## ▶CLIFFSIDE LAKE AND VANHOOK GLADE RECREATION AREAS
### (Macon County)

Cliffside Lake and Vanhook Glade recreation areas provide camping, picnicking, fishing, swimming, boating, nature study, and hiking on interconnecting trails. Service facilities do not include hook-up sites for campers. Vegetation in the area includes a mature forest of hemlock, white pine, oak, maple, rhododendron, buckberry, and numerous species of wildflowers. Fish are chiefly rainbow and brook trout. (*USGS-FS Map:* Highlands)

• ACCESS: In Highlands at the jct of US-64 and NC-28, proceed N on US-64 and NC-28 for 4.4 mi to the Cliffside entrance. Go 1.4 mi on FR-57. The Vanhook Glade Campground is on the highway 0.2 mi before the Cliffside entrance.

*Clifftop Vista Trail (1.5 mi; USFS #2A); Potts Memorial Trail (0.5 mi; USFS #2B); Clifftop Nature Trail (1.1 mi; USFS #2F); Vanhook Trail (0.3 mi; USFS #2C)*　　　　　　　**51–54**

• LENGTH AND DIFFICULTY: 3.4 mi combined, easy to moderate

• TRAILHEAD AND DESCRIPTION: From the parking area at Cliffside Lake go W on the road across Skitty Creek for a few yd, where the *Clifftop Vista Trail* begins at a sign. Go either R or L to the summit of the ridge. If R, pass or take as a side trail the *Potts Memorial Trail* to a white pine plantation. Continue in a circular direction and reach a gazebo at 1.8 mi, where scenic views are provided of Flat Mtn and the Cullasaja River basin. Here is a jct with the *Clifftop Nature Trail* that goes R or L. To the R, the trail ends at FR-57, 0.4 mi from the Vanhook Glade Campground. To the L, it winds down the mtn on switchbacks to the point of origin at the parking area. The trail provides descriptions of the trees and shrubs in a mixed hardwood forest with an understory of sourwood, buckberry, sweet pepperbush (*Clethra acuminata*), and dogwood. The *Vanhook Trail* is a connector trail from the Vanhook Glade Campground for 0.3 mi NW to FR-57 and another 0.6 mi on the road to Cliffside Lake.

*Cliffside Loop Trail (0.8 mi; USFS #2); Homesite Road Trail (1.4 mi; USFS #2E); Skitty Creek Trail (0.3 mi; USFS #9)*
**55–57**

• LENGTH AND DIFFICULTY: 2.5 mi combined, easy

• TRAILHEAD AND DESCRIPTION: From the parking area at Cliffside Lake walk to the loop on the road and circle the lake, or join the Homesite Road Trail for a longer hike. At the Cliffside Lake Dam follow Skitty Creek for a few yd before turning E through a hardwood forest. At an old road on which there are private homes, turn R and reach a gate at 1.4 mi at US-64. Dry Falls is R, 0.4 mi on US-64, and Bridal Veil Falls is L, 0.4 mi on US-64. Backtrack, or follow US-64, R (NW) for 0.2 mi to *Skitty Creek Trail*, R, and return via FR-57 to the lake area.

*Dry Falls Trail (USFS #2D)* **58**

• LENGTH AND DIFFICULTY: 0.1 mi, easy

• TRAILHEAD AND DESCRIPTION: From the parking area on US-64/NC-28 (1 mi E of the Cliffside Lake entrance) follow the signs and descend to the 70-ft waterfall with a trail running underneath. Rare plants are in the area, watered by a constant mist from the updraft in the Cullasaja Gorge (in Cherokee "Cullasaja" means honey or sugar water). The surrounding stone is schist and gneiss, between 500 and 800 million years old.

## ▶ CHINQUAPIN MOUNTAIN AND GLEN FALLS AREA (Macon County)

*Chinquapin Mountain Trail (3.2 mi round-trip; USFS #3); Glen Falls Trail (2.8 mi round-trip; USFS #8)* **59–60**

• LENGTH AND DIFFICULTY: 6 mi combined, moderate to strenuous

• TRAILHEAD AND DESCRIPTION: From the jct of US-64 and NC-28/106 in Highlands, go SW on NC-106 for 1.7 mi to a sign for

Glen Falls Scenic Area. Turn L and proceed on a gravel road for 1 mi to the parking area. Follow the trail sign, bear R at the fork with *Glen Falls Trail*. Descend, cross East Fork a number of times and pass through hardwoods, conifers, and rhododendron. Rock-hopping is necessary at some of the stream crossings. At 0.5 mi reach a jct with other access points from NC-106. Ascend gradually on switchbacks, pass a spur trail to views of Blue Valley, and reach the summit of Chinquapin Mtn (4,160 ft) at 1.6 mi. Backtrack.

For the *Glen Falls Trail* follow the same directions as above to the parking area. Enter the trail by following gray blazes and bear L. (To the R is the *Chinquapin Mtn Trail*.) Descend steeply through mixed hardwoods past three major cascades. Spur trails lead to impressive views from the main trail. Descend to FR-79C, Blue Valley Rd, at 1.4 mi. Return by the same route, or use a vehicle shuttle placed on Blue Valley Rd, off NC-28, near the Georgia state line. (It is SR-1618 before it becomes FR-79C). (*USGS-FS Map:* Highlands)

## ▶ CHATTOOGA RIVER AREA
### (Jackson and Macon Counties)

***Bad Creek Trail*** (*3.1 mi; USFS #6*); ***Fork Mountain Trail*** (*6.4 mi*)                **61–63**

- LENGTH AND DIFFICULTY: 12.6 mi round-trip; combined, easy to strenuous

- CONNECTING TRAILS:
  (*Ellicott Rock Trail*)
  (*Chattooga Trail*)
  (*East Fork Trail*)

- SPECIAL FEATURES: Ellicott Wilderness Area, historic markers

- TRAILHEAD AND DESCRIPTION: From the jct of US-64 and NC-28 in Highlands, drive SE on Main St, which becomes Horse Cove Rd (SR-1603) for 4.6 mi down the mountain to the end of the pavement and a jct with Bullpen Rd (SR-1178). Turn R and go 3 mi to the bridge over the Chattooga River and continue for 2.7 mi to a small parking area and sign for Bad Creek Trail, R. Follow the orange-blazed trail through a forest of hemlock, white pine, and laurel on an old forest road. Cross a stream at 0.2 mi and enter a rhododendron grove. Turn R at 0.6 mi at a gate, reach a ridgecrest at 0.8 mi, curve L on the ridge slope, but return to the ridge at 1.3 mi. Reach Ellicott Wilderness Area boundary at 1.4 mi where a sign indicates that the area was designated in 1975. Turn R from an old road to a foot trail in beds of galax and huckleberry. At 1.8 mi the Chattooga River is audible; jct with the *Fork Mtn Trail* at 1.9 mi, L. Continue ahead and descend on ten switchbacks to a grove of large hemlock by the Chattooga River at 3 mi. (Here is a jct with the E terminus of *Ellicott Rock Trail* requiring a river fording.) Proceed downstream for 0.1 mi to Ellicott Rock where a simple "NC" has been chiseled. Ten ft downstream is Commissioner Rock, the true intersection of North Carolina, Georgia, and South Carolina. Carved on this rock is "LAT 35 AD 1813 NC + SC." Both rocks are named for surveyors who first surveyed the state lines. Backtrack, or continue downstream on the *Chattooga Trail* for 1.8 mi to jct with *East Fork Trail,* which ends at the Walhalla Fish Hatchery after 2.4 mi. (See Chapter 1, Section 1 in *South Carolina Hiking Trails.*)

The *Fork Mtn Trail* leaves the *Bad Creek Trail* in North Carolina but after 265 yd enters South Carolina and follows a well-graded trail that weaves in and out of more than 20 coves and as many spur ridges. Blazed a rust color, it follows a S-side slope in hardwoods and laurel. Cross a small stream at 0.5 mi and at approx 0.8 mi reenter North Carolina. Pass a rock formation at 1 mi, and at 1.2 mi and 1.4 mi cross the dual forks of Bad Creek where the rocks are moss covered, the hemlocks tall, and the fetterbush thick. Pass a hugh yellow poplar at 1.5 mi (near the reentry to South Carolina) and another large poplar at 2 mi. Indian pipe and pink lady slippers are along the trail. Cross an old woods road at 2.5 mi and a ridgecrest at 3 mi. Enter an arbor of laurel at 3.3 mi for 0.3 mi. Pass through a fern glen in an open forest and enter a grove of exceptionally large hemlocks and poplars to cross Indian Camp Branch at 3.9 mi. At 5.2 mi cross a ridge into a beautiful open forest of hardwoods. Cross Slatten Branch at 5.7 mi near good campsites. Walk through an unforgettable virgin grove of rhododendron and laurel and cross more small streams. Arrive at SC-107 at 6.4 mi. It is 0.1 mi, R, across the East Fork of the Chattooga River bridge to the Sloan Bridge Picnic Area. (At the E corner of the picnic area is the *Foothills Trail* described below.) For a vehicle shuttle to the *Bad Creek Trail* entrance, drive N on SC-107 for 1.7 mi and turn L on Bull Pen Rd (SR-1100) for 2.6 mi. (It is 6.3 mi on SC/NC-107 N to Cashiers.) (*USGS-FS Map:* Cashiers)

### Slick Rock Trail (USFS #15)     64

• LENGTH AND DIFFICULTY: 0.2 mi round-trip, easy

• TRAILHEAD AND DESCRIPTION: Follow the directions given above from Highlands, turn R on Bullpen Rd (SR-1178), go 0.7 mi, and park on a narrow road shoulder, R. An unmarked trail ascends for 0.1 mi to a large rock formation with scenic views W into the Chattooga River basin. A wide variety of mosses and lichens grow in the apertures. This scenic spot was the site for the filming of *The Mating Game*. (*USGS-FS Map:* Highlands)

### Ellicott Rock Trail (USFS #820)     65

• LENGTH AND DIFFICULTY: 7 mi round-trip, moderate

• SPECIAL FEATURES: Ellicott Wilderness Area

• TRAILHEAD AND DESCRIPTION: From Highlands follow the directions given above, turn R on SR-1178, and go 1.7 mi. (Pass primitive Ammons campsite on the R at 1.1 mi.) Turn R onto a parking spur with a trail sign. Hike an old road with an even grade for a gradual descent to Ellicott Rock Wilderness Area boundary at 2 mi. The forest is mainly hardwoods with mixed sections of hemlock. At 3 mi bear L off the old road, descend steeply, and reach the Chattooga River at 3.5 mi. To locate Ellicott Rock, a survey marker for the North Carolina-South Carolina-Georgia state boundaries, ford the river (wading is usually necessary, and impossible during high water), and go downstream for approximately 0.1 mi. Exploratory trails in the area can be confusing, and another rock, Commissioner Rock (10 ft downstream from Ellicott Rock), is the true boundary jct of the three states. Commissioner Rock bears the inscription "LAT 35 AD 1813 NC + SC." Both of these rocks were named for early surveyors of the state lines. The vegetation in this area is mixed hardwoods with scattered pine, hemlock, and thick rhododendron. Backtrack, or hike out on the 3.1-mi *Bad Creek Trail* described above. *(USGS-FS Maps: Highlands, Cashiers)*

### *Chattooga River Trail (USFS #825)* 66

- LENGTH AND DIFFICULTY: 2.2 mi, easy

- TRAILHEAD AND DESCRIPTION: This trail is not the same as the *Chattooga Trail* in South Carolina and Georgia. Follow the directions given above from Highlands, turn R on SR-1178, and go 3 mi to park at the Chattooga River bridge. (If hiking the loop section of the trail the old road L of the parking area could be used for parking, because the trail will exit there.) Follow a well-graded gray- and green-blazed trail through the forest of large oak, maple, white pine, beech, and thick understory of large holly and two species of rhododendron. The Chattooga River cascades nearby on the R through huge boulders, large potholes, sandbars, and pools. At 0.8 mi turn L on the *Loop Trail*, ascend on switchbacks to an old road, and return to the parking area. (The *Chattooga River Trail* becomes a fisherman's trail upstream through stands of hemlock and white pine near large rock formations.) *(USGS-FS Map: Highlands)*

## ▶ WHITEWATER RIVER AREA
### (Transylvania County)

### *Whitewater Falls Trail (USFS #7)* 67

- LENGTH AND DIFFICULTY: 2 mi round-trip, easy

- SPECIAL FEATURES: Whitewater Falls, geology

• TRAILHEAD AND DESCRIPTION: From the jct of US-64 and NC-281 in Sapphire, take NC-281 (formerly SR-1171) for 8.6 mi S to the Whitewater Falls Scenic Area. Turn L for 0.3 mi to a parking area with views of Lake Jocassee. Hike for 0.2 mi on a paved trail to an overlook of the spectacular 411-ft Upper Whitewater River Falls. (The *Foothills Trail* crosses here; see below.) Turn L at the overlook to Tongue Rock L at 100 yd. Follow an old road to the river at 0.6 mi, ford it (unless the water is too high for safety), and go upstream for another 0.4 mi. Backtrack. Picnicking and primitive camping are allowed in the area. (Use extreme care in exploring downstream because lives have been lost at the falls.) Vegetation in the area includes white pine, hemlock, oak, maple, thimbleberry, rhododendron, and woodland sunflowers. (*USGS-FS Map:* Cashiers)

## *Foothills Trail* (USFS #20)                        68

• LENGTH AND DIFFICULTY: 4 mi, moderate to strenuous (elev change 1,240 ft)

• SPECIAL FEATURES: Whitewater River Falls, hemlock forest

• TRAILHEAD AND DESCRIPTION: The 74.8-mi *Foothills Trail* passes through the Highlands District for 4 mi from its trailheads in Oconee State Park and Table Rock State Park in South Carolina. From the W, entrance is necessary at the Sloan Bridge Picnic Area on SC-107, 8 mi S of Cashiers. Begin on the E side of the highway and ascend gently the W slope of the Chattooga Ridge. After 1 mi leave Sumter National Forest and enter North Carolina. After 0.3 mi begin a switchback, reach a ridgecrest for partial views of Lake Jocassee, and start a decline. At 0.7 mi descend steeply. Reach the gap between Grassy Knob and Round Mtn at 1.1 mi in a setting of ferns, rhododendron, and wildflowers. Turn R at 1.3 mi on an old woods road, cross a small stream, and parallel a tributary of Whitewater River. At 2.3 mi turn sharply R, off the old woods road, and on a footpath ascend to NC-281 at 2.5 mi. (It is 7.8 mi L on NC-281 to the town of Sapphire, and 0.8 mi R to the Whitewater Falls Scenic Area.) Cross the road and guardrail for a descent to the bank of the Whitewater River. Follow an old road jointly with the *Whitewater Falls Trail* to the main overlook of Upper Whitewater Falls at 3 mi. (To the R is a paved 0.2-mi trail to the parking area.) Follow the white-blazed *Foothills Trail* down the steps; after the first 100 steps (in a series of 400 to the base of the gorge) is another superb view of the 411-ft falls and cascades. Descend steeply and cross the river on a hemlock log footbridge. Rock-hop Corbin Creek and enter a damp evergreen understory of tall hemlock. Leave North Carolina at 4 mi. Backtrack, or continue downstream to a campsite at 5.1 mi (6.1 mi if including the first 1 mi in South Carolina). The *Foothills Trail* turns sharply L, but a spur trail leads downstream to a gravel road for 0.5 mi to the Lower Falls—a dangerous area anytime and extremely so when wet or slippery (*USGS-FS Map* for this description: Cashiers). The *Foothills Trail* returns to North Carolina on its route E through properties of the Duke Power Company. (For a detailed description of the *Foothills Trail* see *South Carolina Hiking Trails* by Allen de Hart, Globe Pequot Press, tel: 1–800-243-0495, and *Guide to the Foothills Trail* by the Foothills Trail Conference, Box 3041, Greenville, SC 29602, tel: 803-232-2681.)

▶**WEST BLUE VALLEY AREA**
**(Macon County)**

***West Fork Trail*** *(0.9 mi; USFS #14);* ***Hurrah Ridge Trail*** *(0.6 mi; USFS #808)*                                    **69–70**

• LENGTH AND DIFFICULTY: 1.9 mi round-trip and combined, moderate

• TRAILHEAD AND DESCRIPTION: These two spur trails form a loop with the *Bartram Trail*. From US-64 and NC-28 jct in Highlands, take NC-28 S for 6 mi to Blue Valley Rd (SR-1618), which becomes FR-79. Turn R on SR-1618 and go 6 mi to West Fork of Overflow Creek to park. Begin on the R before crossing Overflow Creek; ascend on a rocky and frequently wet trail for 0.9 mi to the *Bartram Trail*. (On the *Bartram Trail*, R, it is 0.7 mi to Osage Mtn Overlook at NC-106). Turn L on the *Bartram Trail* and go 0.4 mi. Turn L again on *Hurrah Ridge Trail.* (The *Bartram Trail* continues on for 2.9 mi to Hale Ridge Rd, FR-7.) Descend on the *Hurrah Ridge Trail* through a dry area with mixed hardwoods and hemlock to the parking area. Other vegetation on the trail is rhododendron, laurel, white pine, ferns, and wildflowers. (*USGS-FS Maps:* Highlands, Scaly Mtn)

## ▶ YELLOW MOUNTAIN AREA
### (Macon and Jackson Counties)

### *Yellow Mountain Trail (USFS #31)*      71

* LENGTH AND DIFFICULTY: 9.4 mi round-trip, strenuous (elev change 1,047 ft)

* SPECIAL FEATURES: vistas from Yellow Mtn summit

* TRAILHEAD AND DESCRIPTION: From the jct of US-64 and NC-28 in Highlands, proceed E on US-64 for 2.6 mi to Cole Mtn Rd (SR-1538, also called Buck Creek Rd), and turn L at the Shortoff Baptist Church sign. (From Cashiers W on US-64 it is 7.4 mi to Cole Mtn Rd.) Go 2.2 mi to Cole Gap (4,200 ft) and park on the L side of the road; trail sign is R. The gray-blazed trail ascends gradually on old woods road through hardwoods and abundant wildflowers. Orchids, trillium, false foxglove, Solomon's seal, hellebore, starry campion, and a number of rare species such as wolfsbane (*Aconitum reclinatum*) and grass-of-Parnassus (*Parnassia asarifolia*) line the trail. After 0.4 mi, narrow spur trails, L, extend a few yd to the Western Cliffs for scenic vistas of Round Mtn and Panther Mtn. There is a small spring at 0.6 mi, R. Reach Cole Mtn (4,600 ft) at 0.9 mi, descend gradually, and begin a steep climb on switchbacks to Shortoff Mtn at 1.4 mi. Skirt S of the summit for scenic views; descend and ascend along Shortoff Mtn range (5,000 ft). At 2 mi bear L (N) along the Jackson-Macon county line. Descend to a gap at 2.5 mi, and ascend to Goat Knob (4,640 ft) at 2.7 mi. Descend steeply, join an old road, turn R, and reach Yellow Mtn Gap at

3.2 mi. Continue on the graded trail up switchbacks bordered by laurel, rhododendron, berries, and hardwoods to the summit of Yellow Mtn (5,127 ft) at 4.7 mi. Spectacular views from Yellow Mtn are of Standing Indian, Whiterock Mtn, and Albert Mtn. The old fire tower, no longer used, has been vandalized but part of it is locked and used for two-way radio transmissions. The rock formations are composed mainly of gneiss. Backtrack, or arrange for a shuttle 1 mi from the summit by driving 6.8 mi E on US-64 from Highlands to Norton Rd (SR-1143) and turning L. Go 2.1 mi to Norton and turn L on Joddy Town Rd (SR-1150, also called Norton Creek Rd and Yellow Mtn Rd) for 1.8 mi, and park at jct L with jeep trail to the summit. (*USGS-FS Maps:* Highlands, Glenville)

### *Silver Run Trail (USFS #435)* 72

• LENGTH AND DIFFICULTY: 0.2 mi round-trip, easy

• TRAILHEAD AND DESCRIPTION: From Cashiers at the jct of US-64 and NC-107, take NC-107 S for 4 mi and park on the L side of the highway. Descend on a graded trail into a damp forest of rhododendron, hemlock, and poplar. Cross a stream on a footbridge to beautiful 30-ft Silver Run Falls, wading pool, and small beach. It is part of the headwaters of the famous Upper Falls of the Whitewater River described above. Backtrack. (*USGS-FS Map*: Cashiers)

## ▶ HORSEPASTURE RIVER AREA
### (Transylvania County)

### *Horsepasture River Trail* 73

• LENGTH AND DIFFICULTY: 2.8 mi round-trip, moderate to strenuous

• SPECIAL FEATURES: outstanding series of waterfalls

• TRAILHEAD AND DESCRIPTION: On October 27, 1986, this 435-acre tract officially became part of the National Wild and Scenic

River System. Earlier the area was threatened by an out-of-state power company that planned to destroy the water flow of the magnificent falls. Local conservationists immediately began a grassroots campaign, and legislators and state and federal organizations and agencies saved the Horsepasture River falls.

From the jct of US-64 and NC-281 in Sapphire (10.1 mi E of Cashiers), turn S on NC-281 and go 1.8 mi to a parking area on the L side of the highway by the Horsepasture River. Climb down any of a number of steep rocky spurs to the main trail downstream and pass Drift Falls at 0.1 mi. The ungraded trail requires considerable back and neck bending as it passes through a rugged concourse of rhododendron and rocks. Each trail spur provides outstanding views of waterfalls. Cross a small stream at 0.3 mi and reach Turtleback (also called Umbrella) Falls at 0.4 mi. At 0.6 mi Rainbow Falls thunders 150 ft into a deep pool, spraying a mist against the canyon walls to form a rainbow when the sun is right. On the high side of the trail wildflowers grow in profusion. A creek crosses the trail at 1 mi. Ascend for 240 yd and bear sharply R to descend again to the riverside at Stairway Falls at 1.4 mi. Backtrack. (Beyond this point extreme care should be used in the 0.8-mi treacherous descent to Windy Falls, an extraordinary group of falls and cascades.) (*USGS-FS Map:* Reid)

▶ **EAST FORK AREA**
  **(Jackson County)**

*Whiteside Mountain Trail*                                    **74**

• LENGTH AND DIFFICULTY: 2 mi, moderate

• TRAILHEAD AND DESCRIPTION: A national recreation trail, it was completed in 1974. From Cashiers go W on US-64 to the Jackson and Macon county line, and turn L on Wildcat Ridge Rd (SR-1600). Go 1 mi to the Whiteside Mtn sign L, into a parking area. (From Highlands jct of US-64/NC-28, go E on US-64 5.4 mi and turn R on SR-1600.) From the parking area begin the hike up steps. Ascend on a gray-blazed trail to the ridge at 0.2 mi and turn L. At 0.7 mi reach Devils Point, the summit (4,930 ft), for magnificent views of the Chattooga River Valley, Timber Ridge, Blackrock Mtn, Yellow Mtn, and Terrapin Mtn. Follow the precipitous edge of sheer cliffs, 400 to 600 ft high, to an overlook at 1.1 mi. Begin the descent on an old road to the parking area to complete the loop. The granite landmark is composed of feldspar, quartz, and mica. Vegetation consists of oak, birch, maple, rhododendron, laurel, flame azalea, sweet pepperbush, abundant wildflowers, and scattered conifers. (*USGS-FS Map:* Highlands)

## ▶ BONAS DEFEAT AREA
### (Jackson County)

There are a few unofficial trails in the Bonas Defeat area of the Tuckasegee River Gorge, Wolf Creek Gorge, and the Tanasee Creek basin. The area is scenic, rugged, and remote. Because there are pockets of private property (particularly along NC-281), Lake Toxaway, Sam Knob, and Big Ridge *USGS* (modified for FS use) *maps* are recommended to determine boundary lines. (Also, contact the ranger's office at 704-526-3765 if you have questions.) Two exciting routes are described below.

Access to the Tuckasegee River Gorge from the W is to take NC-281 from its jct with NC-107 in Tuckasegee (SE of Cullowhee) E 14.2 mi to the old Phillips Store (which may be closed), L, and park. (From the E take NC-281 from US-64 [8 mi W of Rosman], and drive 11.2 mi to the old Phillips Store.) If walking to Tuckasegee River Gorge from the store, request permission from the store owner (or if closed, the nearest neighbor) to walk over private property. (Or you may enter the gorge from a private driveway 0.2 mi W of the store on NC-281. Permission there should be requested from the landowner, whose house is off the curve, S. This road route is 2 mi W to the powerhouse for access to the gorge, L.) If going across the fence in front of the old store, cross the pasture to the SW corner at 0.2 mi. Cross a barbed-wire fence and descend to a road. Pass a water gauging sta, follow a pathway through the forest by Tanasee Lake, and reach another road. Follow the road, but take a sharp L to the lake at 0.5 mi. Climb down to the spillway and descend on rock layers below the dam. Descend with care by twisting around boulders, rock-hopping, and avoiding a fall into hundreds of water-carved potholes. (The area can be extremely dangerous. Non-slip shoe soles are a necessity. Avoid sections with red markings.) After passing Slickens Creek and Doe Branch mouths, L, the Bonas Defeat Cliffs loom upward, L. (The legend of "Bonas Defeat" is that a hunting dog named Boney chased a deer to the cliff edge; the deer jumped sideways, missing the cliff, but Boney dived over it, meeting his defeat.) Continue the descent to the powerhouse. Backtrack, or follow the gravel road (described above). At the first fork, take a R and return to the next fork near the dam. Bear L and return on the entrance route for a strenuous round-trip of 4 mi.

Less known than the Tuckasegee, the Wolf Creek Gorge also has soft spots in the rocks where the rapids have shaped the design. Access is to follow the directions as given above for the Tuckasegee River Gorge, except the *Wolf Creek Gorge Trail* is W, 1.5 mi from the old Phillips Store, and 0.5 mi W of the Wolf Creek Dam. Park at the Wolf Creek Baptist Church. Descend on a clear footpath behind the church and bear slightly L and down (across an old road) at 0.2 mi. At 0.4 mi reach Wolf Creek, whose fury has sculpted potholes, pools, waterfalls, and water slides. Huge hemlock, birch, white pine, and oak tower over rhododendron, laurel, ferns, and wildflowers. Return on the same route for a round-trip of 1 mi. (Wolf Creek flows SW for 1.4 mi to a confluence with the Tuckasegee River at the powerhouse. A descent to the river can also be made on Pioneer Lodge Rd [SR-1139] by going 0.3 mi W on NC-281 from the church.) (Part of the *Wolf Creek Gorge Trail* is on USFS property.)                                                              **75**

---

▶ **SECTION 3: TUSQUITEE RANGER DISTRICT**

---

The Tusquitee (the Cherokee word for "where the water dogs laughed," based on a legend of thirsty, talking water dogs)

Ranger District is the state's most western district and the largest—158,348 acres—in the Nantahala National Forest. Mainly in Cherokee County its NW corner adjoins the Unicoi Mtns and the Cherokee National Forest in Tennessee. Its N border is with the Cheoah Ranger District along the ridgeline of the Snowbird Mtns. On the E boundary is the Wayah District and a small connection with the Georgia state line in the SE. Three major TVA lakes, the Hiwassee and Appalachia in Cherokee County and Chatuge in Clay County, provide large areas for fishing and other water sports. The largest of the lakes, Hiwassee, is 22 mi W of Murphy. It was completed in 1940 at the cost of $23 million. In addition to the Unicoi Mtn range, the Chunky Gal Mtn range in the SE, and the Tusquitee Mtn range in the center, there are outstanding areas for wildlife and natural beauty. The Fires Creek Wildlife Management Area with Fires Creek running through its basin and the *Rim Trail* circling its rim to Tusquitee Bald (5,240 ft) is the most distinctive and eminent area. Its 14,000 acres are a bear sanctuary, but other game-hunting and trout fishing are allowed. The district's other major trail is the *Chunky Gal Trail,* a NW-SE route from Tusquitee Bald to the *AT* in the Wayah District.

The district has two USFS developed campgrounds: Jack Rabbit at Lake Chatuge and Hanging Dog at Lake Hiwassee. Both places have camping, picnicking, and fishing with boat launching facilities. Other recreation areas are Cherokee Lake Picnic Area off NC-294, SW of Murphy, and Bob Allison, a primitive camping and picnic area N of the community of Tusquitee.

• ADDRESS AND ACCESS: District Ranger, Tusquitee Ranger District, USFS, 201 Woodland Drive, Murphy, NC 28906, tel: 704-837-5152. The office is across the Hiwassee River at the first traffic light L from the jct of US-19/219 and US-64.

▶ **FIRES CREEK AREA**
**(Clay County)**

The 16,000-acre Fires Creek Wildlife Management Area has three recreational sites, one of which is a picnic area at Leatherwood Falls. The primitive campgrounds are at Huskins Branch Hunter Camp near the Fires Creek entrance and Bristol Camp, 4 mi up Fires Creek Rd from the Leatherwood Falls parking area. Other sites for camping are along the creeks and roads. No camping is allowed in designated wildlife openings. Fishing for rainbow, brook, and brown trout is allowed according to North Carolina Game Lands regulations. Bear hunting and use of ORVs are prohibited. Hunting for wild turkey, deer, and grouse is permitted in season. Both the copperhead and the timber rattler are in the sanctuary. Among the bird species are woodpeckers, warblers, owls, hawks, towhees, and doves. Vegetation includes all the Southern Appalachian hardwood species and six species of pine. Rhododendron and laurel slicks are commonplace, and wildflower species number in the hundreds. The area is considered ideal for backpacking. The longest trail, the *Rim Trail,* traverses the boundary on a high, elongated rim for 25 mi with spur trails down to the basin. Some old trails, such as the *Bald Springs Trail,* USFS #78, are overgrown and may not be passable.                                    **76**

• ACCESS: At the jct of US-64/NC-69 in Hayesville go W on US-64 for 4.9 mi, and turn R on Lower Sweetwater Rd (SR-1302). (From Murphy go E 9.2 mi on US-64 from US-129/19.) Follow SR-1302 for 3.7 mi and turn L on a gravel road, Fires Creek Rd (SR-1344). After 1.7 mi enter the gate and reach Leatherwood Falls parking area and picnic ground after 0.3 mi.

• SUPPORT FACILITIES: The nearest store with groceries and gasoline is at the jct of US-64/SR-1302 described above. Hayesville has other supply and service stores, and the commercial campground with the longest season is Ho Hum Campground, 8 mi E of Hayesville on NC-175. It is open March 15–November 15, full svc, rec fac, tel: 704-389-6740. Also see Chatuge Lake Area below. Murphy has shopping centers, restaurants, and motels.

### *Rim Trail* (USFS #70)                                    **77–84**

• LENGTH AND DIFFICULTY: (25 mi, easy to strenuous, elev change 3,390 ft)

- CONNECTING TRAILS:
  *Leatherwood Falls Loop Trail* (0.7 mi, easy)
  *Trail Ridge Trail* (2.7 mi; USFS #382, strenuous, elev change 1,425 ft)
  *Shinbone Ridge Trail* (1.5 mi; USFS #80, strenuous, elev change 1,349 ft)
  *(Chunky Gal Trail)*
  *Bristol Cabin Trail* (1.2 mi; USFS #76, moderate)
  *Omphus Ridge Trail* (1.3 mi; USFS #75, strenuous, elev change 1,000 ft)

- SPECIAL FEATURES: Leatherwood Falls, heath balds, remote

- TRAILHEAD AND DESCRIPTION: Water is infrequent on the *Rim Trail*, but four springs are usually dependable and are described below. Signs and blazes are sparse. Begin R of the parking area, and follow a blue blaze across the arched bridge into a white pine stand. Turn L of the comfort station at 0.1 mi, curve L to Leatherwood Falls over an elevated bridge, and jct with the *Leatherwood Falls Loop Trail* at 0.3 mi. (The *Leatherwood Falls Loop Trail* turns L and skirts the mountainside through rhododendron and hardwoods with occasional views of the falls. The trail descends to the FR at 0.6 mi for a L turn to cross the bridge, and a return to the parking area at 0.7 mi.) Turn R on the *Rim Trail*, reach a FR at 0.4 mi, take a sharp turn R up the bank at 0.6 mi, and follow switchbacks. Join and rejoin old logging roads. At 1.6 mi there is a jct with the old trail on the ridge; bear R. Pass through an experimental forest section of hardwoods, and begin a steep rocky ascent at 1.8 mi. Reach a plateau at 2 mi, and an intermittent spring at 2.2 mi. Ascend on switchbacks constructed by the YACC in 1980 to another ridgecrest on the Cherokee/Clay county line at 3.2 mi. Follow the old road W of Shortoff Knob to a spring on the L at 3.3 mi, and cross Big Peachtree Bald (4,186 ft) with Peachtree Valley to the L at 4.4 mi. Follow the rim with Valley River on the SE and a precipitous edge on the NW to Will King Gap at 5.4 mi. At 5.7 mi are occasional N views of the Chestnut Flats drainage. Follow a contour grade until an ascent to Big Stamp Lookout (4,437 ft) is reached at 7.9 mi. The trail skirts the summit, but an access route of 0.2 mi to the top is on the S side. Views are limited because the fire tower has been dismantled. (The access route, FR-427, R, descends 4 mi to Long Branch Rd. From there, R, it is 1 mi to Fires Creek Rd, and R 6.1 mi to Leatherwood Falls parking area. After a 0.3-mi descent on the access road from the *Rim Trail,* the *Trail Ridge Trail* begins, R. It is a 2.7-mi blue-blazed trail that descends steeply on rough Trail Ridge. At 2.2 mi are unique weathered or carved bowls in the rocks and surveyor's benchmarks. The trail reaches Fires Creek Rd a few yd N of Bristol Camp. From here it is 4 mi W on Fires Creek Rd to the Leatherwood Falls parking area.)

Continue along the rim, with exceptionally steep drops on the N side; pass at 9.1 mi a faint trail descending N, the *McClellan Creek Trail.* Ascend and descend over knobs—Whiteoak Knob, Defeat Knob, Beal Knob—and reach Sassafras Knob at 12.3 mi. Skirt S of Weatherman Bald (4,960 ft) at 12.9 mi and reach the boundary of Cherokee, Macon, and Clay counties at County Corner at 13.6 mi (5,149 ft). A sign indicates the boundary, but the bears may have chewed all or parts of the sign. Here is a good open grassy spot for a campsite. (To the L [N] is the unmaintained *Old Road Gap Trail* that descends 1.6 mi to a FR, and L 1.1 mi to Junaluska Gap Rd [SR-1505]. Left on SR-1505 it is 3.5 mi to Andrews.) A spring is on the *Shinbone Ridge Trail,* 65 ft SE from the campsite on the *Rim Trail* and 140 ft R in a rhododendron grove. The spring is small but is usually dependable. It had water during the summer of 1986, a major drought period.

(From the spring the blue-blazed *Shinbone Ridge Trail* gradually descends on Shinbone Ridge in and out of grassy paths for 0.5 mi. In a scenic forest of white pine, hemlock, hardwoods, ferns, and flame azalea, there are views through the trees of Sassafras Ridge N and the Fires Creek watershed S. Descend steeply; a clearcut is L at 1.2 mi. At 1.5 mi descend on steps to a timber road. There is space for three vehicles on a level area in the ridge curve. From here, L, it is 10.2 mi down the mountain on Fires Creek Rd to Leatherwood Falls parking area.)

Continue ahead on the *Rim Trail* to a spur trail, L, at 14.7 mi. (The spur leads 0.1 mi to views from Signal Bald, named for the Cherokee usage of smoke signals. From Signal Bald the spur extends another 0.1 mi to Tusquitee Bald [5,240 ft] and makes a jct with the *Chunky Gal Trail* along the way. The *Chunky Gal Trail* is described below.) Descend from Tusquitee Bald and rejoin the *Rim Trail.* After 0.2 mi there is a small saddle and a water source. Reach Potrock Bald (5,215 ft) at 16.1 mi. Here is a good campsite with vistas of Chatuge Lake and beyond into Georgia. Potrock received its name from small and large "bowls" appearing to have been carved by the Indians or the weather. A good spring is on the R at 17.1 mi.

On a gentle grade reach Matlock Bald (4,949 ft) at 17.2 mi. The rim edge on the S becomes steep down to Snake Branch as the trail continues SW on the rim to Chestnut Stomp Knob (4,400 ft) at 18.4 mi. From here continue the descent to Shearer Gap, Cold Spring Gap, and finally to Carver Gap (2,996 ft) at 22.3 mi. (*Bristol Cabin Trail* jct is here; it descends R for 1.2 mi to Bristol Camp on Fires Creek Rd.) After 0.4 mi farther on *Rim Trail, Omphus Ridge Trail* jct R. (Both of these trails leave Fires Creek Rd 2 mi apart and connect with the *Rim Trail* 0.4 mi apart. They provide an excellent 4.9-mi loop trail combination from Bristol Camp. From the *Omphus Ridge Trail* jct on Fires Creek Rd, it is 2 mi on the road SW to Leatherwood Falls parking area.)

From the *Omphus Ridge Trail* jct, continue on the ridge and enter a rhododendron arbor before crossing Graveyard High Knob at 23.6 mi. Descend and level off slightly at 23.9 mi, take an old road R, and follow the N side of the main ridge at 24.7 mi. Continue to descend to a small cove and leave the forest at a new timber road at 24.8 mi. Follow the road L to Fires Creek Rd for 0.1 mi, turn L, and go another 0.1 mi to the Leatherwood Falls parking area at 25 mi. (*USGS-FS Maps:* Andrews, Hayesville, Topton)

# ▶ CHUNKY GAL MOUNTAIN AREA
## (Clay County)

Chunky Gal Mountain is a high, remote, 8-mi ridge that averages 4,500 ft in elev from the Tennessee Valley Divide of the Blue Ridge Mtns NW to Shooting Creek Bald. It has three major gaps, the lowest of which is Glade Gap (3,679 ft). Through it passes the celebrated US-64 from Manteo to Murphy, the state's longest highway (569 mi). The legend of Chunky Gal Mtn is that a plump Indian maiden fell in love with an Indian youth of another tribe in another valley. To break up the romance her parents banished the young brave, but she deserted her family and followed him over the mtn that bears her sobriquet. Access to the mtn is described below under the *Chunky Gal Trail.*

• SUPPORT FACILITIES: The nearest towns for supplies are E 17.4 mi on US-64 to Franklin and W 16 mi to Hayesville. The nearest campgrounds are the Chatuge Lake Area (described below), or the Standing Indian Area, 7.5 mi E, and described in detail in Section 4 of this chapter.

### *Chunky Gal Trail (USFS #77)*                                  85–86

• LENGTH AND DIFFICULTY: 21.7 mi, moderate to strenuous (elev change 2,160 ft)

• SPECIAL FEATURES: gem stones, isolated wild herbs

• TRAILHEAD AND DESCRIPTION: This trail has exceptional potential for an extended backpacking trip. It is a connector trail between the *AT* at the Southern Nantahala Wilderness Area and the *Rim Trail* on the E rim of the Fires Creek Basin. Access to either end is by foot: 2.9 mi using the *AT,* or 2.8 mi using the *Shinbone Ridge Trail* and the *Rim Trail.* Whichever route you choose, the minimum hiking distance is 27.3 mi. To extend the excursion, more than 10 mi of the *Rim Trail* can be used, or long distances on the *AT.*

On US-64, 2 mi W of Rainbow Springs, or 0.3 mi W of the Macon/Clay county line, turn L on unmarked gravel FR-71. Follow the narrow, winding road for 5.4 mi to Park Gap and 1.4 mi farther to its jct with the *AT* in Deep Gap. Here is a parking and picnic area. From here begin the hike S on the graded *AT* section; ascend steeply, cross outcrops, and cross a footbridge at a water source at 1.2 mi. Circle the Yellow Mtn ridgecrest at 1.6 mi and descend to Wateroak Gap at 2.1 mi. Ascend to the ridge, skirt NW of Big Laurel Mtn (5,100 ft), descend, and reach a jct with the blue-blazed *Chunky Gal Trail* R at 2.9 mi (4,700 ft).

Follow the trail along Chunky Gal Mtn ridge for 0.7 mi to a scenic escarpment L (W) with views of Ravenrock Ridge and the Muskrat Branch basin. Shooting Creek Knob can be seen NW beyond the valley. Follow a ridge spine in a forest of oak, birch, hemlock, rhododendron, laurel, and wildflowers. The escarpment contains quartz, garnet, and olivine. Descend steeply to Bear Gap at 1.5 mi. Ascend steeply to a high unnamed knob and descend to Grassy Gap at 2.3 mi. Deer are frequently seen here. For the next 1.3 mi ascend and descend across four knobs and saddles and jct R with an old trail, *Riley Cove Trail*, at 3.6 mi. Continue ahead to climb Riley Knob (4,480 ft) at 4.4 mi. Descend and begin switchbacks at 5 mi. Cross a woods road and at 5.2 mi exit to US-64 in Glade Gap. (It is 6.8 mi W to Shooting Creek and 16 mi to Hayesville. To Franklin, E, it is 17.4 mi.)

Cross US-64, turn L on old US-64, and turn R on an old jeep road at 5.4 mi. Pass under the powerline, cross Glade Branch on a footbridge, and on switchbacks pass under the powerline again. (Avoid the shortcuts that have been made under the powerline.) Jct with an old road at 5.6 mi. Turn R and ascend on Chunky Gal Mtn with a combination of old roads and footpaths for 12 switchbacks before a more gradual contour at 6.4 mi. Enter a rhododendron tunnel at 7.1 mi, pass large boulders, and at 7.9 mi jct with a faint trail ahead. (The faint trail leads to Shooting Creek Bald [5,010 ft], also called Boteler Peak.) The R turn makes a radical change in direction, but descend N on the ridge and pass through a natural garden of laurel, flame azalea, and ferns. At 8.7 mi pass R of a clearcut, re-enter the forest, and exit at another clearcut at 9.1 mi. Columbine (*Aquilegia canadensis*), sun drops (*Oenothers fruiticose*), spiderwort (*Tradescantia virginiana*), and flame azalea grow in profusion here, and in the forest are a variety of herbs collected by the mountain residents under contract with the USFS. After another section in the forest and another clearcut, turn L on an old woods road at 9.3 mi. Skirt around the ridge and descend to a jct with a FR in Perry Gap at 10.3 mi. (It is 4 mi R [E] down the mtn to Buck Creek and US-64.) Continue ahead, N, on a gated FR through a clearcut to Tate Gap at 11.4 mi. Leave the road, follow on an old jeep road on the ridge with knobs for 1.9 mi where a sharp L (W) is made for a steep descent to Woods Rd (SR-1307), also called Tusquitee Rd, in Tusquitee Gap at 13.9 mi. (SR-1307 is an access S for 3.7 mi to a paved road and jct with the Tuni Gap Rd described below.) Cross the road, ascend NW to a spur ridge of Little Niggerhead peak at 14.3 mi. Curve around another spur and descend steeply to a gap at 15 mi. Pass old roads, ascend to the ridgecrest, and skirt W of an unnamed knob. Leave the main ridge and descend to follow rippling spur ridges and coves with banks of galax, fire pink, and trailing arbutus to a trail jct at 17.3 mi. Here is a relocation: the *Chunky Gal Trail* turns sharply L. (Ahead the trail goes to Tuni Gap and ends.) Descend on a poorly designed and constructed trail to the Bob Allison Camp. At 17.5 mi reach an old road; turn L, and leave, R, at 17.6 mi into a partial clearing. Reach an old RR grade at 17.7 mi, cross two streams on a rough RR grade, and rock-hop the Big Tuni Creek at 18 mi. Enter the edge of the campground and go upstream through a stand of hemlock and poplar for a jct with FR-400 at 18.2 mi. The Bob Allison Camp has a vault toilet, drinking water, picnic tables, and a grassy area for camping. (The camp can be reached from Hayesville Town Square by following the Tusquitee Rd [SR-1307] NE for 8.7 mi to the end of the pavement. Continue L [N] for 4.3 mi on Mosteller Rd [SR-1311], which becomes FR-400, to the camp, 0.8 mi S of Tuni Gap.)

On FR-400, turn R and cross the cement bridge over Big Tuni Creek to enter L a scenic area with cascades. Follow the blue blazes on a relocated trail that is rough, steep, and rocky. Part of the trail is not well-graded and follows a wet treadway. Timber cuts affect its direction. After 1.2 mi turn L and ascend steeply on switchbacks to Dead Line Ridge. Curve around a knoll to follow a narrow ridge that ends in a gentle saddle between Signal Bald R and Tusquitee Bald (5,240 ft) L, an elev gain of 2,160 ft at 21.5 mi. Both peaks have outstanding scenery and Tusquitee provides views of Shooting Creek Bald SE, Wine Spring Bald E, Chatuge Lake S, and Nantahala Lake NE. Exit to the *Rim Trail* at 21.7 mi. Backtrack to Allison Camp or use the

*Rim Trail* for egress. *USGS-FS Maps*: Rainbow Springs, Shooting Creek, Topton)

## ► CHATUGE LAKE AREA
### (Clay County)

The Jackrabbit Mountain Recreation Area has 103 camping sites, picnic facilities, boating, swimming, skiing, lake fishing, nature study, and hiking. Comfort stations and cold-water showers are available. The area is open usually from the middle of May to the end of October. (The nearest commercial campground is Ho Hum Campground on NC-175 near the entrance to Jackrabbit Mtn Campground. It is open from March 15 to November 15. Full svc, rec fac, tel: 704-386-6740.)

• ACCESS: Entry to Jackrabbit is from US-64 jct with NC-175 (4.7 mi E of NC-67 jct in Hayesville). Go S on NC-175 for 3.4 mi, turn R at Jackrabbit on Philadelphia Rd (SR-1155), and proceed 1.2 mi to the campground.

### *Jackrabbit Mountain Scenic Trail*                    87

• LENGTH AND DIFFICULTY: 2.4 mi, easy

• TRAILHEAD AND DESCRIPTION: Follow the trail sign R of entry to a blue-blazed trail through generally open forest of white oak, sourwood, and pine. Cleared spots provide views of Chatuge Lake. Reach the crest of a ridge at 0.6 mi, cross wooden bridge near a spring at 1.3 mi, pass the edge of Chatuge Lake at 1.6 mi, and reach the boat ramp parking area at 2.1 mi. Return to the camping area and parking lot at 2.4 mi. (*USGS-FS Map:* Shooting Creek)

## ► HIWASSEE LAKE AREA
### (Cherokee County)

Located on Lake Hiwassee, Hanging Dog Recreation Area has 69 campsites, a picnic area with tables and grills, and boat-launching facilities for fishing, boating, and skiing. Flush toilets are available, but there are not any showers. The area is usually open from April 1 to the end of October. (One of the nearest commercial campgrounds is Pied Piper Camp Resorts, Rte 6, Box 100, Murphy NC 28906, tel: 704-644-5771. Full svc, excellent rec fac. Open all year.)

• ACCESS: From downtown Murphy, at the jct of Tennessee St and Valley River Ave (Business US-19), take Tennessee St W (it becomes Brown Rd, SR-1326) and drive 4.4 mi to the campground sign, L, and go 1.1 mi to the entrance.

### *Ramsey Bluff Trail* (USFS #81)                                      88

• LENGTH AND DIFFICULTY: 2.1 mi round-trip, easy

• TRAILHEAD AND DESCRIPTION: The trail connects from Section B, spaces 25–26, to Lake Kiwassee, and from Section B to Section C, spaces 42–43, on an even-grade hike through oak, pine, sourwood, dogwood, maple, and birch. (This trail has also been called the *Shore Trail*.) (*USGS-FS Map*: Murphy)

---

## ▶ SECTION 4: WAYAH RANGER DISTRICT

---

The Wayah Ranger District has 133,894 acres of which 12,076 are in the Southern Nantahala Wilderness Area. The W side of the district is within the Macon County line where it borders the Tusquitee and Cheoah districts. Its NW boundary extends into Swain County to Fontana Lake and includes an isolated section of the Cowee Mtns at the jct of Swain, Macon, and Jackson counties. The Highland District is E and the Georgia state line and the Chattahoochee National Forest is the S boundary. The *AT* goes NW for 59.8 mi on the Nantahala Mtn range from Bly Gap at the state line to Wesser at the Nantahala River. Some of the magnificent peaks on the *AT* are Standing Indian Mtn (5,490 ft), Albert Mtn (5,280 ft), Siler Bald (5,216 ft), Cooper Bald (5,249 ft), Rocky Bald (5,180 ft), and Wayah Bald (5,336 ft). In addition to the *AT*, another long trail, the

*Bartram Trail*, passes through the district. The wilderness boundary surrounds the *AT* in the Standing Indian area and at the headwaters of the Nantahala River. Adjoining the wilderness boundary in the NE is Coweeta Experimental Forest.

The district has nine recreational areas: Standing Indian with a campground, picnic and fishing areas; Wayah Crest campground; Nantahala Gorge with fishing and water sports facilities; the Apple Tree Group Camp (requires reservation); Wayah Bald and Arrowwood Glade picnic areas; and Almond Point, Mark Dowell, and Greasy Branch serving as boating sites at Fontana Lake.

• ADDRESS AND ACCESS: District Ranger, Wayah Ranger District, USFS, Rte 10, Box 210, Franklin, NC 28734, tel: 704-524-4410. From the jct of US-441/23 and US-64 in Franklin, go W on US-64 for 1 mi and turn R on SR-1153 at the sign and go 0.3 mi.

## ▶ NANTAHALA LAKE AREA
### (Macon County)

Access to all the trails in this area can begin at the Apple Tree Group Camp. The camp received its name from the fruit trees that once grew near Apple Tree Branch, the route of the Cherokee Indians between areas that are now Franklin and Robbinsville. At least two distinguished travelers passed this way. It is likely that Atakullakulla, "Little Carpenter," a Cherokee peace chief known to British royalty, met the famous botanist William Bartram in this location. (See the *Bartram Trail* description in the beginning of this chapter.) The camp is designed for group tent camping at four campsites, each of which can serve up to 40; they are signed A through D. Water, sanitary facilities, and cold showers are provided. Reservations are necessary from the ranger's office. (*USGS-FS Map:* Topton)

• ACCESS: From Wesser on US-19 go SW to Beechertown Power Station. Turn L on SR-1310, follow up the river for 4.4 mi to FR-308, R, at a horseshoe curve. Go 3.1 mi on FR-308 to a jct with Dicks Creek Rd (SR-1401). Turn R, cross the bridge, and turn R to the camp entrance. From Franklin on US-64, go W 3.8 mi to Wayah Gap sign R and follow SR-1310 W 18.6 mi to Andrews Rd (SR-1400), which becomes SR-1401, L. Go 2.4 mi to the camp entrance, R. From Andrews take the Junaluska Rd (SR-1505) and go 12.5 mi E to the camp entrance, L.

### *Apple Tree Trail* (USFS #19B)      **89–92**

- LENGTH AND DIFFICULTY: 2.2 mi, strenuous (elev change 1,640 ft)

- CONNECTING TRAILS:
  *Junaluska Trail* (4.3 mi; USFS #19, moderate)
  *Diamond Valley Trail* (0.9 mi; USFS #19D, easy)
  *Laurel Creek Trail* (1.5 mi; USFS #19F, easy)
  *(London Bald Trail)*

- TRAILHEAD AND DESCRIPTION: Park across the road from Apple Tree Branch and follow the yellow blazes R of the branch on an old road. Cross the branch and pass a jct with the blue-blazed *Junaluska Trail* L at 0.3 mi.

(On the *Junaluska Trail* skirt E of the mtn, curve SW with SR-1401 on the L to jct with the white-blazed *Diamond Valley Trail* at 1.6 mi. Continue on an even grade through mixed hardwoods, hemlock, and rhododendron, occasionally going in and out of small coves to jct with *Hickory Branch Trail* at 3 mi. [*Hickory Branch Trail* is a 1.3-mi connector trail between this point and the *London Bald Trail.*] Cross Matherson Branch at 3.5 mi, and jct with the *London Bald Trail* at 4.2 mi. Turn L to the highway, SR-1401, in Junaluska Gap at 4.3 mi. Backtrack, or make a loop with the London Bald Trail, or use a vehicle shuttle.)

Continue on the *Apple Tree Trail*, cross the stream again at 0.7 mi, and then pass a faint road jct. Proceed on a gradual grade through a forest of oak, elm, white pine, beech, sassafras, silver bell (*Halesia carolina*), laurel, rhododendron, and numerous wildflowers. At 1.1 mi pass a jct with the green-blazed *Laurel Creek Trail*, R.

(*Laurel Creek Trail* is similar to *Diamond Valley Trail* in that access and exit are dependent on other trails. On the *Laurel*

*Creek Trail* descend, first on a slight ridge in hardwoods, and then into a deep dense grove of rhododendron along Piercy Creek and to the mouth of a tributary, L, at 1.5 mi. A loop trail at the jct with the *Bartram Trail* [formerly the *Nantahala Trail*], R, requires another 5.5 mi of hiking to the campground. A turn L for 1.5 mi connects with the *London Bald Trail* to form a loop back to the camp for 5.9 mi.)

Continue ahead on the *Apple Tree Trail* to the white-blazed *Diamond Valley Trail* jct at 1.4 mi, L.

(Descend on the *Diamond Valley Trail* for 0.9 mi, following Diamond Valley Creek to a jct with the *Junaluska Trail* in a clearing at SR-1401 and Dicks Creek. Backtrack, or return L on the *Junaluska Trail* for a loop total of 4.2 mi.)

On the *Apple Tree Trail* reach the summit of a knob at 1.7 mi. Climb steeply on a second knob, reach the summit of a third peak SE of London Bald, and reach a jct with the blue-blazed *London Bald Trail* at 2.2 mi. Backtrack, or turn L to follow the *London Bald Trail* for 6.5 mi out to Junaluska Gap and SR-1401, or turn R and follow the *London Bald Trail* for 2.2 mi to its NE terminus at Sutherland Gap and jct with the *Nantahala Trail*. A return loop can be made from here for a total of 11.5 mi. (See *Nantahala Trail* below.)

## *Nantahala Trail* (USFS #19G)                    **93**

* LENGTH AND DIFFICULTY: 6.5 mi, moderate

* CONNECTING TRAILS:
  *(London Bald Trail)*
  *(Laurel Creek Trail)*
  *(Bartram Trail)*

* TRAILHEAD AND DESCRIPTION: Except for the last 0.5 mi W on this trail, it is now the *Bartram Trail*. It requires either backtracking for a total of 13 mi, or connecting with other trails such as the N trailhead of *London Bald* in Sutherland Gap, or *Laurel Creek* (1.5 mi E from Sutherland Gap) on the *Bartram Trail* as described above. (See the beginning of Chapter 2 for details of the Nantahala/Bartram Trail from Apple Tree Group Camp.)

*London Bald Trail (6.6 mi; USFS #19C); Hickory Branch Trail (1.3 mi; USFS #19A)*                    **94–95**

- LENGTH AND DIFFICULTY: 7.9 mi combined, strenuous (elev change, 820 ft)

- CONNECTING TRAILS:
  *(Junaluska Trail)*
  *(Apple Tree Trail)*
  *(Nantahala Trail)*

- TRAILHEAD AND DESCRIPTION: This trail requires either back-tracking for a total hike of 13.2 mi, connecting with other trails for longer loops, or using longer trail connections with vehicle shuttles. Begin at Junaluska Gap on SR-1401/1505 at the Macon/Cherokee county line on the N side of the road, and follow a blue-blazed trail L from a jct with the *Junaluska Trail*. Ascend and cross a ridge before bearing L to go upstream at Pine Branch. After crossing Pine Branch continue to ascend and skirt the E boundary of the Cherokee/Macon county line. Near Hickory Knob reach the jct with the *Hickory Branch Trail* at 3.5 mi R. (The *Hickory Branch Trail* descends for 1.3 mi, first on a ridge, and then near the stream to jct with the *Junaluska Trail*.) Reach a jct with the *Apple Tree Trail* at 4.4 mi. (The *Apple Tree Trail* descends R for 2.2 mi to the campground.) Continue on the blue-blazed trail, descending and skirting E on ridges to Sutherland Gap at 6.6 mi. Backtrack, or take the *Nantahala Trail* R and the *Bartram Trail* for another 6.5 mi to the campground. (*USGS-FS Map*: Topton)

▶ **STANDING INDIAN AREA**
  **(Macon County)**

The Standing Indian Campground, a FS facility, has camping and picnic sites that are open all year. Reservations are not required except at the adjoining Kimsey Creek Group Camp. Water and sanitary facilities are provided, but there are not any electrical or sewage hook-ups. A special parking area for hikers and backpackers has been constructed at the Backcountry Information Center on FR-67/2 (0.2 mi L of the campground and picnic entance gate). The Nantahala River, which flows through the campground, is a popular trout stream. The campground is exceptionally well landscaped in an area where the Ritter Lumber Company had its main logging camp for the Upper Nantahala basin. Downstream, at Rainbow Springs, the company had a double-head rig bandsaw mill to process huge trees. Although timber harvesting has continued in the area since it was first purchased in the 1920s, the upper headwaters are now protected by the 12,076-acre Southern Nantahala Wilderness Area. The *AT* wraps around the S and E ridge of the basin and provides a master connecting route for the ascending trails. Forest vegetation in the area includes all the Southern Appalachian hardwoods with groves of pine and hemlock. Bear, deer, turkey, grouse, fox, squirrel, raccoon, hawks, and owls are part of the wildlife.

The Cherokee Indian legend of Standing Indian Mountain is that a Cherokee warrior was posted on the mountaintop to warn the tribe of impending danger from an evil winged monster that had carried off a village child. Beseeching the Great Spirit to destroy the monster, the tribe was rewarded with a thunderstorn of awesome fury that destroyed the beast, shattered the mountaintop to bald rubble, and turned the warrior into a stone effigy, the "standing Indian," in the process.

• ACCESS: From the jct of US-64 and Old US-64 (0.4 mi E of the Nantahala River bridge in Rainbow Springs and 12 mi W from Franklin) take old US-64 for 1.8 mi to Wallace Gap and turn R on FR-67/1.

• SUPPORT FACILITIES: A commercial campground, The Pines RV Park, is 5 mi W from Franklin on US-64. Full svc, open all year, address: 490 Hayesville Hwy, Franklin, NC 28734, tel: 704-524-4490.

## *Pickens Nose Trail (USFS #13)*     **96**

• LENGTH AND DIFFICULTY: 1.4 mi round-trip, easy

• SPECIAL FEATURES: rock climbing area, nature study

• TRAILHEAD AND DESCRIPTION: From the Backcountry Information Center drive 8.7 mi on FR-67/2 up the mtn to a parking area, L (0.7 mi beyond the *AT* crossing in Mooney Gap). Hike across the road and ascend before leveling on a rocky ridge. The first vistas, E-S, are at 0.3 mi, but the vistas W-S at 0.7 mi at Pickens Nose (5,000 ft) are exceptionally scenic. The Chattahoochee National Forest is S and the Betty Creek Basin is down 2,000 ft from the top sheer cliffs. A beautiful area any season with all the evergreens, June is particularly colorful with laurel, rhododendron, azalea, black locust, and Bowman's root (*Gillenia trifoliata*). (*USGS-FS Map*: Prentiss)

### Bearpen Gap Trail (USFS #22)                          97

• LENGTH AND DIFFICULTY: 4.8 mi round-trip, strenuous (elev change 1,200 ft)

• TRAILHEAD AND DESCRIPTION: From the Backcountry Information Center drive 3.2 mi on FR-67/2 to the trail sign and parking area. (Parts of this trail have been relocated because of a timber sale.) Enter the forest L of a locked gate, hike 0.2 mi to a logging road, and take the R fork. Follow the road, and at 1 mi take the R fork to curve around a ridge. At 1.9 mi cross the last stream near a large quartz rock in a hemlock grove. Galax, blue beads, and wood betony are along the trail. Ascend steeply in a mixed forest; at 2.4 mi reach the *AT* on gated FR-83 (Ball Creek Rd) in Bearpen Gap. (Across the road it is 0.3 mi up a steep and rocky path to Albert Mtn [5,280 ft] fire tower for the most panoramic views in the Standing Indian area. Backtrack to the *Bearpen Gap Trail* or take the *AT* N 3.1 mi to *Long Branch Trail* and 1.9 mi down to the Information Center, or S on the *AT* for 6.3 mi to *Timber Ridge Trail*, R, which descends 2.5 mi to FR-67/2, and another 1.6 mi on the road to the W trailhead of *Bearpen Gap Trail* and parking area for a loop of 12.8 mi.) (*USGS-FS Maps*: Prentiss, Rainbow Springs)

### Kimsey Creek Trail (USFS #23)                          98

• LENGTH AND DIFFICULTY: 7.4 mi round-trip, moderate

• TRAILHEAD AND DESCRIPTION: From the Backcountry Information Center follow the blue-blazed trail to the picnic area, cross the Nantahala River bridge, follow *Park Creek Trail* N for 0.1 mi, and turn L at *Kimsey Creek Trail* sign. Skirt E of the mtn and follow a gradually ascending grade up Kimsey Creek. Three wildlife grazing fields are on this route. At 2.6 mi pass the confluence with Little Kimsey Creek; reach Deep Gap and the *AT* at 3.7 mi. Backtrack, or go L on the *AT* for 2.5 mi to Standing Indian (5,499 ft) and return L on the *Lower Ridge Trail* to the campground and picnic area for a total circuit of 9.7 mi. (*USGS-FS Map*: Rainbow Springs)

### *Lower Ridge Trail* (USFS #28)                    99

• LENGTH AND DIFFICULTY: 7.8 mi round-trip, strenuous (elev change 2,105 ft)

• SPECIAL FEATURES: views from Standing Indian

• TRAILHEAD AND DESCRIPTION: This is a frequently used and exceptionally steep trail to the top of Standing Indian. There are views of the Nantahala Basin on its ascent. Begin at the Backcountry Information Center parking area, follow the blue-blazed trail to the campground road, cross the bridge over the Nantahala River, and turn L to begin the trail. Go up the riverside and cross a road and footbridge over Kimsey Creek at 0.2 mi. Cross another stream at 0.5 mi. At 1 mi begin a series of switchbacks in a forest of hardwoods, hemlock, and colorful patches of trillium and hepatica. At 1.5 mi reach the ridgecrest and follow the ridge L to arrive on top of a knob at 1.8 mi. Descend to John Gap at 2.1 mi. Skirt W of a knob, reach another gap, skirt W of Frog Mtn, and reach Frank Gap at 3.1 mi. Continue a steep ascent and jct with the *AT* at 3.9 mi for a spur climb of 0.2 mi to Standing Indian (5,499 ft). Here from rock outcroppings are magnificent views of the Blue Ridge Mtns and the Tallulah River Gorge running into Georgia. Backtrack, or loop back to camp on the *Kimsey Creek Trail*, going R on the *AT* for 2.5 mi at Deep Gap for a return at 10.3 mi; or go L on the *AT* for 3.5 mi to *Beech Gap Trail*, turn L and descend for 2.8 mi to

FR-67/2 at a parking area (4 mi from the Backcountry Information Center parking area, the point of origin). (*USGS-FS Map:* Rainbow Springs)

### Big Laurel Falls Trail *(0.6 mi; USFS #29);* Timber Ridge Trail *(2.5 mi; USFS #30)* 100–102

- LENGTH AND DIFFICULTY: 6.2 mi round-trip combined, easy to moderate

- SPECIAL FEATURES: scenic area at Big Laurel Falls

- TRAILHEAD AND DESCRIPTION: From the Backcountry Information Center parking area drive 4.7 mi on FR-67/2 to joint trailheads of *Big Laurel Falls Trail* and *Timber Ridge Trail.* The blue-blazed *Big Laurel Falls Trail* goes R and crosses a footbridge over Mooney Creek in a forest of hemlock, yellow birch, and rhododendron. Follow an old RR grade arbored with rhododendron, curve L around Scream Ridge, and follow to the base of Big Laurel Falls at the confluence of Kilby Creek, Gulf Fork, and Big Laurel Branch at 0.6 mi. Backtrack. For the *Timber Ridge Trail* follow the blue blazes L from FR-67/2, ascend steeply on switchbacks, and skirt L of Scream Ridge in an area of rhododendron, birch, ferns, and cohosh. Cross an old forest road on the ridge at 0.7 mi and begin a descent through large beds of galax. Rock-hop Big Laurel Branch at 1 mi. Ascend to Timber Ridge and go through fern beds with a canopy of oaks. Reach the *AT* at 2.5 mi, 0.5 mi W of the *AT* Carter Gap Shelter. Backtrack, or make a loop by turning R on the *AT* for 2.5 mi and descending R on the *Beech Gap Trail* for 2.8 mi to FR-67/2. From here proceed up the road for 0.5 mi to the parking area, a total of 7.7 mi. Another route would be to turn L on the *AT* and hike 4.3 mi to Betty's Creek Gap, turn L on *Betty's Creek Trail* (USFS #367) for 0.2 mi to FR-67/2, and descend L on the road for 1.7 mi to the beginning of *Timber Ridge Trail.* It is a loop of 8.7 mi. (*USGS-FS Maps:* Prentiss, Rainbow Springs)

### Mooney Falls Trail *(USFS #31)* 103

- LENGTH AND DIFFICULTY: 0.2 mi round-trip, easy

• TRAILHEAD AND DESCRIPTION: From the Backcountry Information Center go up FR-67/2 for 5.5 mi to roadside parking for Mooney Falls. Hike 0.1 mi through a tunnel of rhododendron and laurel to a cascading fall on Mooney Creek. Remains of a fallen American chestnut tree are at the falls and on the ground are prominent wildflowers. Backtrack. (*USGS-FS Map: Prentiss*)

**Park Ridge Trail** *(3.2 mi; USFS #32);* **Park Creek Trail** *(4.8 mi; USFS #33)* **104–105**

• LENGTH AND DIFFICULTY: 8 mi round-trip combined, moderate to strenuous (elev change 880 ft)

• CONNECTING TRAILS:
*(Lower Ridge Trail)*
*(Kimsey Creek Trail)*

• TRAILHEAD AND DESCRIPTION: These trails connect at both the N and S trailheads to form a loop. From the Backcountry Information Center parking area follow signs and blue blazes through rhododendron and hemlock to cross a footbridge over Wyant Branch at 0.1 mi. On the paved campground road, turn L, cross the Nantahala River bridge, and jct L with the *Lower Ridge Trail*. (The 3.9-mi *Lower Ridge Trail* is a scenic route to the *AT* and Standing Indian Mtn.) Turn R and follow an old RR grade. At 0.3 mi jct with the *Kimsey Creek Trail*, L. (The 3.7-mi *Kimsey Creek Trail* goes upstream to Deep Gap and a jct with the *AT*.) At 0.4 mi jct with the *Park Ridge Trail*, L. Ahead on the old RR grade is the *Park Creek Trail*. If choosing the *Park Ridge Trail*, ascend, cross a small stream, and skirt E of Bee Tree Knob from a cove. At 1 mi arrive at a gap and ascend Middle Ridge in a hardwood forest. Leave the ridge at Penland Gap at 2.9 mi and reach FR-71/1 at Park Gap picnic and parking area at 3.2 mi. To the R is a jct with *Park Creek Trail*. (FR-71/1 goes L for 1.4 mi to Deep Gap and the *AT*, and R for 5.4 mi to US-64, 2.4 mi W of US-64/Old US-64 jct at Rainbow Springs.)

To follow the *Park Creek Trail* from N to S continue downstream of the Nantahala River after leaving the *Park Ridge Trail*.

After 0.2 mi a narrow footpath leaves the old RR grade, L, and parallels the old RR grade for 0.9 mi. Either route can be hiked, but the footpath appears to be in need of more use by hikers; it is also a high-water route. The small dam on the river at 1.2 mi is constructed to permit upstream migration for spawning trout. Reach Park Creek at 1.6 mi and cross on a footbridge. Follow up the cascading Park Creek where the trail is flanked by mixed hardwoods, hemlock, rhododendron, ferns, mossy rocks, and profuse wildflowers. At 2.6 mi cross a small stream and ascend gradually on the E side of the slope to cross two more streams before beginning switchbacks at 4.5 mi. Reach FR-71/1 and the Park Gap picnic and parking area at 4.8 mi. Backtrack or return on the *Park Ridge Trail*. (*USGS-FS Map:* Rainbow Springs)

**Big Indian Trail** *(1.6 mi; USFS #34);* **Beech Gap Trail** *(2.8 mi; USFS #34A)* **106—107**

• LENGTH AND DIFFICULTY: 4.4 mi combined, moderate to strenuous (elev change 910 ft)

• TRAILHEAD AND DESCRIPTION: From the Backcountry Information Center drive 2.8 mi on FR-67/2 to the parking area and signs for *Big Indian Trail* and Big Indian Rd (FR-67/A). The trail is designated a horse trail, but it is used by hikers, fishermen, and hunters. The road is used by ORVs and not recommended for hikers. Begin at the footbridge crossing the Nantahala River. Ascend and follow the W slope by cascading Big Indian Creek through rhododendron slicks and hardwoods. At 1.4 mi cross the creek and ascend to Indian Ridge to jct with the *Beech Gap Trail* at 1.6 mi in an open forest. The blue-blazed *Beech Gap Trail* descends L 0.6 mi to FR-76/2 and crosses a footbridge over the Nantahala River in the process. (On FR-76/2 L, it is 1.9 mi downstream to the point of origin for a loop of 4.1 mi.) At the trails jct on Indian Ridge, the *Beech Gap Trail* continues up the ridge on the horse trail. Reach Kilby Gap at 1.4 mi from FR-76/2. At 1.8 mi the horse trail turns sharply R, but the *Beech Gap*

*Trail* ascends through a forest of hardwoods, laurel, and flame azalea. Cross a small stream in a deep cove and reach Beech Gap at a jct with the *AT* at 2.8 mi. Backtrack, or hike 2.5 mi L on the *AT* to the *Timber Ridge Trail*, turn L, and descend 2.5 mi to the parking area at Mooney Creek and FR-67/2. It is 0.5 mi L to the trailhead of *Beech Gap Trail* for a loop of 7.7 mi. (*USGS-FS Map*: Rainbow Springs)

### Long Branch Trail (USFS #86)                    108

- LENGTH AND DIFFICULTY: 3.8 mi round-trip, moderate

- TRAILHEAD AND DESCRIPTION: From the parking area at the Backcountry Information Center go E across the road and climb gradually to a partial lookout of the Nantahala Basin at 0.6 mi. Pass through a forest of hemlock, yellow birch, maple, and wildflowers, and cross a horse trail and grazing field with strawberries at 1.5 mi. At 1.7 mi cross Long Branch, which has remnants of an old RR grade. Cross a seeded road, begin a steep climb at 1.8 mi, and at 1.9 mi reach the *AT* on the main ridge line. Backtrack, or make a loop by hiking R on the *AT* for 3.4 mi to Albert Mtn, described above, and jct with the *Bearpen Gap Trail* for a descent to FR-67/2 for 2.4 mi. Hike downstream on FR-67/2 for 3.2 mi to the point of origin for a total of 10.9 mi. (*USGS-FS Map:* Rainbow Springs)

### John Wasilik Memorial Poplar Trail            109

- LENGTH AND DIFFICULTY: 1.4 mi round-trip, easy

- TRAILHEAD AND DESCRIPTION: From Wallace Gap on Old US-64 go 0.4 mi on the Standing Indian Campground road, FR-67/1, to Rock Gap. Follow the trail sign to a graded trail through an impressive and significant stand of yellow poplar and cherry to the second largest yellow poplar in the U.S. (25.5 ft in circumference and 8.5 ft in diameter). An early Wayah District ranger, John Wasilik, has been remembered by naming the poplar in his honor. (*USGS-FS Map:* Rainbow Springs)

## ▶ WESSER AREA
### (Swain and Macon Counties)

### *Wesser Creek Trail* (USFS #26)                    110

• LENGTH AND DIFFICULTY: 3.5 mi, strenuous (elev change 2,227 ft)

• TRAILHEAD AND DESCRIPTION: This blue-blazed trail is part of the former white-blazed *AT,* which was relocated in 1980 to avoid highway traffic and a residential district. At the jct of US-19 and Wesser Creek Rd (SR-1107), drive up SR-1107 for 1.7 mi and turn L to a parking area. Hike 0.4 mi to cross Wesser Creek in a grassy meadow near the old shelter. Ascend on switchbacks and join the roadway in sections to cross a small stream at 1.5 mi. At 1.7 mi cross another small stream and leave the road to a graded trail with switchbacks. In a forest of hardwoods ascend steeply in sections and at 3.5 mi jct with the new route of the *AT.* A spring is to the L. Backtrack, or take the *AT* for an extended hike. To the L it is 0.7 mi to Wesser Bald (4,627 ft) for panoramic vistas of the Nantahala mtn range. Beyond the peak it is 1.4 mi to Tellico Gap and Tellico Rd (SR-1365). If taking the *AT* N, it is 4.8 mi of undulating trail to the A. Rufus Morgan Shelter and another 0.8 mi to US-19 and the Nantahala Outdoors Center by the Nantahala River. (*USGS-FS Map:* Wesser)

## ▶ WAYAH GAP AREA
### (Macon County)

### *A. Rufus Morgan Trail* (USFS #27)                    111

• LENGTH AND DIFFICULTY: 1 mi round-trip, moderate

• TRAILHEAD AND DESCRIPTION: From US-64 and US-441/23 jct S of Franklin, go W on US-64 for 3.8 mi. Turn R at sign for Wayah Bald, and go 0.2 mi to sign for Lyndon B. Johnson Conservation center at jct of Old US-64 and SR-1310. Turn L and go 4.1 mi to Broadlee Rd (FR-388) and turn L. Proceed for 2 mi on a gravel road and park at the trail sign, R. Ascend on switchbacks through open woods of tall poplar, cucumber tree, maple, oak, and birch, with ferns and wildflowers banking the trail. Deer may be seen on the trail. Cross a stream at 0.2 mi and reach the lower cascades of Left Prong of Rough Fork at 0.4 mi. Continue on the trail to the base of the upper falls at 0.5 mi. Backtrack.

(The trail is named in honor of the Rev. Albert Rufus Morgan, 97 years old when he died in Asheville, February 14, 1983. Affectionately called the "Modern Moses" and "Uncle Rufus," no one has ever loved the mountains, and the *AT* in particular, more than he. One of his favorite peaks was Mt LeConte in the Smokies; he climbed it 172 times, the last on his 92nd birthday. "He was a poet, a priest, and a great friend of the *Appalachian Trail*," wrote Judy Jenner in a tribute to him in the *Appalachian Trailway News*, May/June, 1983. She also wrote a feature story on him in the Nov/Dec edition of *ATN*, 1979.) (*USGS-FS Map:* Wayah Bald)

### *Shot Pouch Trail* (USFS #17)                                112

This trail is unique in that it runs only 75 yd from the parking area to the *AT* and another 25 yd to a grazing field for wildlife. An excellent connector point for the *AT*, the parking area is 0.9 mi from Wayah Gap on the Wayah Bald Rd. Access from Franklin is the same as for the *A. Rufus Morgan Trail* described above, except at FR-388 continue up the mtn on SR-1310 to Wayah Gap and turn R. (*USGS-FS Map:* Wayah Bald)

## ▶ SAVANNAH RIDGE AREA
### (Jackson County)

### *Cullowhee Trail* (USFS #370)                                113

• LENGTH AND DIFFICULTY: 5.1 mi, strenuous (elev change 2,160 ft)

• TRAILHEAD AND DESCRIPTION: The N access to *Cullowhee Trail* is from the jct of NC-107 and Speedwell Rd (SR-1001), 1.3 mi SE on NC-107 from the main entrance of Western Carolina University. Turn R on SR-1001 and go 6.4 mi to Cullowhee Gap (3,700 ft). Park in a small area on the L of the highway. (S access to the trail is from the jct of US-64/NC-28 and SR-1001, 3.3 mi E on US-64/NC-28 from Franklin. Turn L on SR-1001 and go 9.7 mi to Cullowhee Gap and park on the R of the highway.) Hike across the highway and climb steps through a white pine stand. Follow the graded trail with gradual incline to the SE side of Kirby Knob for 0.7 mi to steep switchbacks and a vista of Cowee Mtns. Reach the ridgecrest of Savannah Ridge at 0.9 mi bearing N through hardwoods on an even grade except for knobs. Reach Kirby Knob at 1.5 mi, and Sheep Knob at 2.8 mi. Descend through hardwoods to a white pine stand near Tatham Creek at 3.9 mi. Bear R and follow seeded FS road downstream; reach the FS gate at 5 mi. Continue on a woods road past the Buchanan house, L, to the trail terminus and end of Tatham Creek Rd (SR-1309) at 5.1 mi. Backtrack or use vehicle shuttle. If a vehicle shuttle, the entrance is at the jct with Tatham Creek Rd (SR-1555), which becomes (SR-1309) and US-441/23 at Tatham Campground. (It is 5.2 mi S from the jct of US-441/23 and business 23 Bypass in Sylva, and 11.4 mi N from the jct of US-441 and US-64/NC-23 in Franklin.) Go 0.9 mi on SR-1309 to the end of the road and the trailhead. Do not park at the private gated road R; instead, request permission to park on the edge of his property from the landowner to the L, Harvey Buchanan. (*USGS-FS Maps*: Corbin Knob, Greens Creek, Glensville, Sylva South)

• SUPPORT FACILITIES: Fort Tatham Campground at the road entrance on US-441/23. Full svc, excellent rec fac. Open year-round but full svc is April 15 to November 1. Address: Rte 2, Box 206, Sylva, NC 28779, tel: 704-586-6662.

# 3.

## Pisgah National Forest

*I enjoy hiking for the wholesome exercise, the thrill of accomplishment, and for the beauty of nature.*                    —Arch Nichols

Pisgah National Forest, with 495,979 acres, is the oldest of the state's four national forests. Its scattered boundaries encircle four districts—Pisgah in Buncombe, Haywood, Henderson, and Transylvania counties; Grandfather in Avery, Burke, Caldwell, McDowell, and Watauga counties; Toecane in Avery, Buncombe, Madison, Mitchell, and Yancey counties; and the French Broad in Haywood and Madison Counties.

The Pisgah is a natural world unto itself with the Blue Ridge Parkway dividing it, the *AT* on its border with Tennessee, and such extraordinary natural attractions as Looking Glass Rock and Falls, Mt Pisgah, Bald Mountain, Roan Mountain Gardens, Table Rock, Hawksbill Mtn, Harper Creek Falls, Sliding Rock, Shortoff Mtn, Upper Creek Falls, Black Mtns, and Big Lost Cove Cliffs. It is also the site of a number of historic firsts. Gifford Pinchot, hired by George Vanderbilt to manage his vast Biltmore Estate, initiated the first forest management program here in 1892, and six years later Carl A. Schenck opened here the first school of forestry in America, the Biltmore Forest School. (Reconstructed and named the Cradle of Forestry, it is located in the Pisgah Ranger District on US-276.) After Vanderbilt's death in 1914, the area was sold to the U.S. government and in the process became one of the first tracts of the Pisgah National Forest. The first property purchased under the Federal Weeks Act of 1911 was 8,100 acres on Curtis Creek in the Grandfather Ranger District.

There are three wilderness areas: Middle Prong (7,900 acres) and Shining Rock (18,500 acres) in the Pisgah Ranger District and Linville Gorge (10,975 acres) in the Grandfather Ranger District. Two others in the Grandfather District, Lost Cove and Harper Creek, have been proposed and are in the process of being approved. The wilderness areas, watershed, and streams provide protection for the many species of wildlife common to the Appalachian region. More than 200 species of plants have been found in the Roan Mtn area alone, and 39 of 55 species of wild orchids in the state are found in the Pisgah. Dominant trees are oak, birch, maple, and poplar. Conifers range from short-leaf pines to red spruce and fragrant fir. Primary among the fish is the brook trout, often stocked in the cascading tributaries. Deer among the big game and squirrel among the small game are the most plentiful.

Pisgah has 40 recreational areas for fishing, picnicking, nature study, hiking, and camping. Some of the areas are designed for primitive camping and have limited facilities to protect the ecology. A directory of these facilities may be requested from one of the addresses below. The new *Mountains-to-Sea Trail (MST)* now being planned and under construction from Clingmans Dome to Nags Head will incorporate numerous trails (already on the NF inventory) through the Pisgah National Forest from the Rough Butt Bald area to the Beacon Heights area (see Chapter 16).

The four districts of the Pisgah National Forest are as follow:

*French Broad Ranger District,* USFS, PO Box 128, Hot Springs, NC 28743, tel: 704-622-3202. (On Main Street, US-25/70, in Hot Springs.)

*Grandfather Ranger District,* USFS, PO Box 519, Marion, NC 28752, tel: 704-652-2144. (Downtown in the Library Bldg, corner of West Court and Logan streets.)

*Pisgah Ranger District,* USFS, 1001 Pisgah Highway, Pisgah Forest, NC 28768, tel: 704-877-3350. (From jct of US-276/64 and NC-280, N of Brevard, 2 mi W on US-276.)

*Toecane Ranger District,* USFS, PO Box 128, Burnsville, NC 28714, tel: 704-682-6146. (On US-19 Bypass in Burnsville.)

## ▶ SECTION 1: FRENCH BROAD RANGER DISTRICT

The French Broad Ranger District has 78,683 acres, some of which are the most rugged and isolated terrain in the Appalachians. Its boundaries are almost exclusively in Madison County with the NE corner of Haywood County adjoining. Its W boundary is flanked by the Cherokee National Forest in Tennessee. Along most of this border is 74 mi of the *AT* on high, scenic, and remote ridges and peaks such as Big Butt (4,838 ft); Camp Creek Bald (4,844 ft), the district's highest; Rich Mtn (3,643 ft); Bluff Mtn (4,686 ft); Walnut Mtn (4,280 ft); Max Patch Mtn (4,629 ft); and Snowbird Mtn (4,263 ft). Sparse population and few industries in Madison County allow this beautiful area to remain a tranquil and natural place to live and visit. Hunting, fishing, and running the white water of the French Broad River are popular sports in the district. The varied flora is an enticement to any botanist. An example is described below in the *Big Laurel Creek Trail* section.

The district has four recreation areas: Rocky Bluff picnic and campground (3.3 mi S from Hot Springs on NC-209), a primitive camp in Harmon Den, and picnic areas at Murray Branch and Big Creek. Of the 25 trails in the district's inventory, three are horse trails, a few are combination hiking/ORV, and nine have trailheads on private property. The latter are identified below; hikers are requested to honor private property boundaries and to show trail courtesy. The trails of three of these areas are described. All trails N of NC-208 are under the Camp Creek Bald Area, trails S of NC-208 are under the Hot Springs Area, and trails in Haywood County are under the Harmon Den Area. In addition to obtaining information from the RS, Roger Shelton, who is a private citizen, has offered to assist hikers with information on the mountain terrain and the little known backcountry trails and roads. His address is 261 Big Creek Rd, Marshall, NC 28753, tel: 704-656-8176. For horseback riders a local outfitter in Waynesville can be contacted at tel: 704-452-4341/1096, and for river sports maps the Land of Sky Regional Council, PO Box 2175, Asheville, NC 28802, tel: 704-254-8131. Among the river outfitters is Nantahala Outdoor Center, US-19 W, Box 41, Bryson City, NC 28713, tel: 704-488-2175.

• ADDRESS AND ACCESS: District Ranger, French Broad Ranger District, USFS, PO Box 128, Hot Springs, NC 28743, tel: 704-622-3202. The office is on US-25/70 in the center of Hot Springs.

• SUPPORT FACILITIES: Because Rocky Bluff Campground does not have hook-ups or showers, a nearby commercial facility is Stone Mtn Recreation Area, Del Rio, TN 37727, tel: 615-623-3509. It has full svc, excellent rec fac, and is located 14 mi W of Hot Springs and 11 mi E of Newport on US-25/70. For *AT* hikers the Hiker Hostel (maintained by the Jesuits of the Catholic Church) is located in Hot Springs. Address: Hiker Hostel, PO Box 7, Hot Springs, NC 28743, tel: 704-622-3248. In Hot Springs are a motel, restaurant, grocery store, and service stations.

## ▶ CAMP CREEK BALD AREA
### (Madison County)

*Fork Ridge Trail (USFS #285)*         **114**

• LENGTH AND DIFFICULTY: 4 mi round-trip, strenuous (elev change, 1,610 ft)

• TRAILHEAD AND DESCRIPTION: This trail is also known as *Big Creek Trail.* From the jct of US-25/70 and NC-208, follow NC-208 up Big Laurel Creek for 3.5 mi to jct with NC-212 at Belva. Turn R on NC-212 and proceed for 10.7 mi to Big Creek Rd (SR-1312), which forks L at Carmen Church of God. Follow SR-1312 for 0.7 mi where the pavement ends at a fire warden station. Continue for another 0.6 mi on a gravel road and enter Pisgah National Forest where the road becomes FR-111. After 1 mi farther reach parking space, L, at Wildcat Hollow Creek's confluence with Big Creek.

From the R side of the parking area ascend gradually on a well-graded slope that runs E of Fork Ridge. Reach the ridge-crest at 0.7 mi. Forest flora consists of hardwoods with the lower elev having rhododendron and buckeye, and the higher elev having laurel, flame azalea, and copious patches of large, sweet, high bush blueberries. Spots of wintergreen, dwarf iris, and galax furnish a groundcover. The wildlife includes bear, deer, turkey, grouse, and chipmunk. After reaching a ridge sag at 0.9 mi, ascend steadily, sometimes steeply, on switchbacks to jct with the *AT* at 2 mi. (It is 0.2 mi R on the *AT* to the Jerry Cabin Shelter.) Backtrack, or make an 8.4-mi loop on the *AT* for 3 mi L to the 4.4-mi *Whiteoak Flats Trail* and return on FR-111. (See *Whiteoak Flats Trail* below.) Another loop, 9.2 mi, is possible with a R (E) on the *AT* for 4.3 mi to a jct with the 3.9-mi *Green Ridge Trail* and a return on FR-111, but the *Green Ridge Trail* is not signed or marked (see below). (*USGS-FS Maps:* Greystone, Flagpond)

### *Whiteoak Flats Trail (4.4 mi; USFS #286); Hickorylog Branch Trail (2.6 mi; USFS #289); Rock Branch Trail (1.1 mi)*
**115–117**

- LENGTH AND DIFFICULTY: 8.1 mi combined, moderate to strenuous (elev change 2,240 ft)

- SPECIAL FEATURES: Whiteoak Flats cascades, Whiteoak Flats

- TRAILHEAD AND DESCRIPTION: (The E/SE trailheads of these trails are on private property. However, there is an access for most of the trail distance by driving into the NF on Hickey Fork Rd [SR-1310] from NC-212 as described below.) From the jct of US-25/70 and NC-208, take NC-208 N for 3.5 mi to jct with NC-212 at Belva. Turn R on NC-212 and go 10.7 mi to Big Creek Rd (SR-1312), which forks L at Carmen Church of God. Follow SR-1312 for 1.2 mi to a private drive, L (and bridge across Big Creek). Park on the R side of SR-1312, but avoid blocking any private driveways or entrance to Shelton's Sawmill. Cross the bridge to the Jimmy Hensley residence and request permission to cross private property to the forest boundary. (If he is not there, make your request at the Paul Shelton residence across the road.) From the bridge go R of Whiteoak Flats Branch but L of the Hensley house into a damp area of apple trees and white pines, upstream on the unmarked Whiteoak Flats Trail. At 0.2

mi reach the USFS boundary and cross the branch near cascades. Ascend steeply at 0.7 mi to view a 100-ft cascade plunging into the gorge. Cross the branch at 1 mi and a tributary 100 yd beyond. Signs of the old RR grade are near the branch in a forest of hemlock, hardwoods, and dense rhododendron. At 1.5 mi enter the open field of Whiteoak Flats. To the L on a woods road is the N trailhead of *Hickorylog Branch Trail* (described below). Continue ahead through the meadows and reach a multiple road jct at 1.8 mi. (The road L is Hickey Fork Rd, of which the first 3.1 mi from here is in the NF and the other 1 mi is SR-1310 out to NC-212 [6.8 mi N of NC-208 jct, or 0.3 mi N of Cutshalls Grocery]. The last 0.5 mi to this point is steep, rough, and may require a 4WD.) Ascend on the *Whiteoak Flats Trail* (avoid level roads R) on a jeep road up the mtn to Huckleberry Gap at 3.8 mi. (Baxter Cliff is 0.1 mi SE.) Beyond the gap, leave the road at the first foot trail L and ascend a S slope to Bearwallow Gap and jct with the *AT* at 4.4 mi. Backtrack, or go R for 3 mi to a jct with *Fork Ridge Trail*, R (Jerry Cabin Shelter is 0.2 mi ahead). Descend on the *Fork Ridge Trail* (also called *Big Creek Trail*) for 2 mi to FR-111, and go downstream on the road to your vehicle at Whiteoak Flats Branch for 10.5 mi. Also, at Bearwallow Gap it is 0.4 mi L on the *AT* to White Rock Cliffs for superb vistas.

The *Hickorylog Branch Trail* that connected with the 1.8 milepost of the *Whiteoak Flats Trail* has its S trailhead as follows. On NC-212, 3 mi N from Cutshalls store (1.4 mi S from Carmen Church of God) turn L on a private road (sometimes called Shelton Cemetery Rd). Park near here or drive up the road for 0.5 mi and use care not to block any driveways. Hike past two cabins, a barn, and a Christmas tree farm to where the trail follows an old logging route. Ascend near cascades at 0.8 mi, cross Hickorylog Branch six times, and jct with *Rock Branch Trail*, L, in a flat at 1.5 mi. (*Rock Branch Trail* is a 1.1-mi trail that begins at the end of Rock Branch Rd [SR-1311]. Access to Rock Branch Rd is 1.3 mi N of NC-212 from Cutshalls store and goes 0.6 mi to a dead end. Permission should be requested of the Blake Shelton family or the Franklin family who live at the end of the road. Avoid parking in the turnaround because the mailman and the school-bus driver must turn here. The trail follows a farm road past hillside farms, barns, and some of the best blackberries in the world for 0.5 mi before entering the forest and the NF boundary. Well-graded, the *Rock Branch Trail* ascends to a saddle and dips into a glen of tall trees to cross Hickorylog Branch and jct with *Hickorylog Branch Trail* at 1.1 mi.) Continue steeply upstream on the *Hickorylog Branch Trail* in a scenic gorge of cascading water and dense rhododendron to cross the branch at 1.9 mi. Bear R and away from the branch to climb 0.3 mi to a saddle. Forest roads go R and L and ahead. Take the one ahead, descend, and reach the Whiteoak Flats grazing fields and *Whiteoak Flats Trail* R and L at 2.6 mi. (A loop could be made by descending R on the *Whiteoak Flats Trail* to SR-1312, R to NC-212 at Carmen, and R again on NC-212 to point of origin at 6.7 mi.) (*USGS-FS Maps:* Greystone, White Rock)

### Green Ridge Trail *(USFS #287)* 118

• LENGTH AND DIFFICULTY: 3.9 mi, strenuous (elev change 2,420 ft)

• SPECIAL FEATURES: underground creek, remote, wildflowers

• TRAILHEAD AND DESCRIPTION: From the jct of NC-208 and NC-212 at Belva, turn on NC-212 and proceed 10.7 mi to the Carmen Church of God. Turn L at the fork on Big Creek Rd (SR-1312) and go 1.3 mi to the Shelton Sawmill, R. Cross Dry Creek at the FR-111 sign and park in a small area. Otherwise, park near the sawmill without blocking any entrances. Hike upstream, preferably on the L side, to the wood's edge. Follow an old road, cross the creek repeatedly, and at 0.5 mi bear R at a fork in the road. Forest vegetation is ironwood, poplar, white pine, hemlock, oak, and birch. Both spring and summer wildflowers are exceptionally profuse; they include starry campion, bee balm, trillium, orchids, twisted-stalk, hellebore, meadow rue, Indian-physic, and phlox. Among the forest animals are bear, bobcat, turkey, grouse, owls, chipmunk, and the timber rattlesnake. The creek goes underground in places, appearing dry, thus its name. (Some of the mountain residents have a number of ghost stories about this hollow.) At 1.4 mi the old road ends and the trail begins across the creek. Cross small cove streams in switchbacks at 1.7 and 1.8 mi. Waterfalls are R at 1.9 mi. Curve L and continue to ascend on a well-graded trail that is often overgrown with nettles and may need clearing. After ascending the slope of Green Ridge, reach the top in a flat area and jct with the *AT* at 3.9 mi. Backtrack. The jct is likely to be unsigned, but it is 4.4 mi R to Devil Fork Gap on the *AT* to NC-212, and L on the *AT* for 4.3 mi to the jct with *Fork Ridge Trail* (see *Fork Ridge Trail* above). (*USGS-FS Maps:* Greystone, Flagpond)

### *Pounding Mill Trail* (USFS #297)    119–120

• LENGTH AND DIFFICULTY: 4.7 mi, strenuous (elev change 2,764 ft)

• TRAILHEAD AND DESCRIPTION: From the jct of US-25/70 and NC-208, take NC-208 for 7.2 mi to a bridge over Little Laurel Creek. Sixty yd beyond is a USFS gated and seeded road, R. (The space for parking is small. If space is passed, turn around at the Gulf sta on the R around the highway curve.) The forest road, which is becoming overgrown, is used by hikers more than the trail to Pounding Mill Gap. If using the trail, hike back across the bridge to a numbered electricity pole (3/41), descend from the highway bank, cross the creek at 0.1 mi, and cross Pounding Mill Branch at 0.2 mi. The area is filled with trees and rhododendron, hiding the stream confluence. Wildflowers such as buttercups, blood root, trillium, and water leaf are prominent. Follow the infrequently used trail upstream for 2.5 mi to Pounding Mill Gap and jct with the forest road described above. (To the R is an old FR, Angelico Knob Rd, that leads 0.7 mi to Angelico Knob [3,429 ft] and that descends to connect with Duckmill Rd [SR-1308].) Continue ahead on the FR to Seng Gap at 3.3 mi, where the faint *Hickey Fork Trail* (USFS #292) leads R. (It is 1.7 mi to FR-465, which leads to Hickey Fork Rd [SR-1310].) Ascend and descend on two knobs and reach a faint trail, R, at 4.1 mi. (It is the old *White Oak Trail*

[USFS #293] that descended 2.3 mi to FR-465 on the East Prong of Hickey Fork.) Continue straight on the Seng Ridge and at 4.7 mi reach the jct with the *AT,* SW of the Camp Creek Bald Lookout Tower (4,844 ft). The spur to the R leads 0.2 mi to the fire tower for impressive views of the Smokies. Backtrack, or use the *AT* for shuttle routes. (On the *AT* it is 6.2 mi S to Allen Gap at NC-208, and 13.9 mi N to Devil Fork Gap at NC-212.) (*USGS-FS Maps:* Greystone, Hot Springs, White Rock)

## ▶ HOT SPRINGS AREA
### (Madison County)

### *Shut-in Creek Trail (USFS #296)*      121

• LENGTH AND DIFFICULTY: 4 mi round-trip; easy

• TRAILHEAD AND DESCRIPTION: From Hot Springs drive W on US-25/70 for 2.7 mi to Upper Shut-in Creek Rd (SR-1183) and turn L at a store. Go 2.3 mi to a small parking area on the N side of the Shut-in Creek bridge. Follow an old jeep road, SE and upstream of the East Fork of Shut-in Creek, in a hollow. Frequently rock-hop the stream and its small tributaries. Other sections of the trail are wet from mountain seepage. Liverwort covers some of the rocks. At 1 mi pass through a beautiful meadow of clovers, asters, daisies, and other wildflowers. Deer have been seen here. Enter a white pine stand and at 1.7 mi a hemlock stand. Ascend to ruins of a pioneer homestead at 1.8 mi. Jct with the *AT* and FR-3543 at 2 mi in Garenflo Gap. Backtrack. (L it is 6.6 mi on the *AT* to Hot Springs, and R it is 3.5 mi to Bluff Mtn [4,686 ft].) (*USGS-FS Maps:* Lemon Gap, Paint Rock)

### *Brigman Hollow Trail (USFS #298)*      122

• LENGTH AND DIFFICULTY: 1.2 mi, strenuous (elev change 1,040 ft)

• TRAILHEAD AND DESCRIPTION: From US-25/70 and NC-208, go 5 mi on NC-208 to Brigman Hollow Rd (SR-1306). Turn L on a cement bridge over Little Laurel Creek, with Brigman Chapel on the R after the crossing. Go 0.7 mi to the end of the road at the Gosnell residence. Request permission to park. Hike up the road by the barn and grain and hay fields to the NW corner of the pasture. Enter the NF at 0.4 mi on a faint road, cross a fence, and begin a difficult climb on a primitive, unmarked, and unmaintained roadbed of hummocks, loose rocks, and nettles. At 0.7 mi climb up an enbankment, R, near Deep Creek. For the next 0.3 mi the old roadbed has been washed out under dense rhododendron. Considerable gymnastic ability is required to rock-hop through. Stay with the main stream all the way up the ravine. At 1 mi, and out of the rhododendron thicket, begin to climb the L slope up the ridge away from the creek bed, which may be dry in places. Reach Deep Gap, also called Little Paint Gap, at 1.2 mi; here is the jct with the *AT* and *Little Paint Creek Trail* that descends into Tennessee. Backtrack, or use the *AT* to extend the hike. (To the R it is 2 mi to Allen Gap and jct with NC-208. To the L it is 0.2 mi to a spring, R, and another 1.5 mi to Spring Mtn Shelter.) (*USGS-FS Map:* Hot Springs)

### *Jack Branch Trail* (USFS #299)        **123**

• LENGTH AND DIFFICULTY: 2.5 mi, strenuous (elev change 1,400 ft)

• TRAILHEAD AND DESCRIPTION: From US-25/70 at the N end of the French Broad River bridge in Hot Springs, turn on Paint Rock Rd (SR-1304). Follow downriver for 4.1 mi to end of pavement, and continue another 0.3 on a gravel road. Park L by the river, across from Bartley Island. Enter the trail near a sign and follow an unmarked trail on an old road in a deep ravine up the E slope, away from Jack Branch, for 0.1 mi. The forest flora includes mixed hardwoods with hemlock, rhododendron, fetterbush, and buffalo nut (*Pyrularia pubera*) in the lower elev, and chestnut oak, laurel, and pines in the upper elev. At 0.4 mi leave the damp area and reach a ridgecrest at 0.5 mi. Follow the ridge in a generally xeric environment with patches of wintergreen, trailing arbutus, blueberries, and azalea. At 0.9 mi turn

NW, follow an upgrade in and out of coves to 1.9 mi, and begin a NE ascent. Reach the Tennessee state line in a gentle gap at 2.5 mi. Backtrack. (Primitive trails lead L for 1.9 mi to Bearpen Gap and *Ricker Branch Trail* into Tennessee, and R for 3.5 mi to Rich Mtn Lookout Tower and the *AT*.) (*USGS-FS Map:* Hot Springs)

### *Pump Gap Trail* (USFS #309)      **124**

- LENGTH AND DIFFICULTY: 1.5 mi, moderate

- SPECIAL FEATURES: FS explosive storage bunkers, access to Lover's Leap Rock

- TRAILHEAD AND DESCRIPTION: From the N side of the French Broad River bridge on US-25/70 in Hot Springs, curl under the bridge on Lover's Leap Rd for 0.3 mi to the FS boundary gate and parking area at Silver Mine Creek. Begin the hike on an old road, cross Silver Mine Creek a number of times, pass two FS explosive storage bunkers, and enter a narrow blue-blazed trail at 0.4 mi. Flora includes poplar, maple, hemlock, ironwood, and locust. The stream has moss-covered rocks, cascades, and pools. At 1.1 mi take the R fork, cross a stream, and begin a steep ascent in a vale. Reach the *AT* in Pump Gap at 1.5 mi. Backtrack, or make a loop R on the *AT* for 2.5 mi to the point of origin at the FS gate. (This section of the *AT* has spectacular views of the French Broad River from craggy overlooks 500 to 1,000 ft high. Lover's Leap Rock is 0.6 mi from the trailhead.)

(*Pump Gap Trail* can be extended beyond the *AT* jct in Pump Gap. Descend by faint blue blazes for 0.6 mi to a fork. The L fork curls for another 0.6 mi to a peak and a FS road. The R fork is an unmarked and overgrown trail that follows an old roadbed to the confluence of the Big Laurel River and the French Broad River at 1.3 mi from Pump Gap. Options here are to return on the same route, follow the RR down the river for 3 mi to Hot Springs, or go up the French Broad River on the RR for 0.5 mi to the *Big Laurel Creek Trail*. The latter route runs 3 mi up a gentle grade to Hurricane at US-25/70. Vehicle shuttle is necessary.) (*USGS-FS Map:* Hot Springs)

### *Big Laurel Creek Trail* (USFS #310)                     **125**

• LENGTH AND DIFFICULTY: 6 mi round-trip, easy

• SPECIAL FEATURES: RR history, exceptional diversity of plant life

• TRAILHEAD AND DESCRIPTION: Park at the jct of US-25/70 and NC-208 in the parking area on the E side of Big Laurel Creek (1,600 ft). Enter on a private gravel road, descend slightly, and bear R to a fork at 0.1 mi. Arrive at a private dwelling and a gate at 0.2 mi. Follow an old RR grade with vertical cliffs L and whitewater rapids R. Pass a spring at 0.4 mi L and a burley tobacco barn L at 0.7 mi. Cross the Pisgah National Forest boundary at 0.9 mi. On a trail unsurpassed for riverside beauty, pass a series of rapids at 1.2 mi. Turn L at 2.9 mi to Runion, logging and mining settlement of the past. Reach the Southern RR tracks and the French Broad River at 3 mi. Backtrack.

In the spring and summer of 1977 and 1978, the North Carolina Natural Heritage Program of the Department of Natural Resources and Community Development made a botanical study of this 3-mi trail. The discovery of over 250 species of vascular plants was an overwhelming surprise. Five species listed as threatened or endangered were found. Among them are alumroot (*Heuchera longiflora*), wild rye grass (*Elymus riparius*), saxifrage (*Saxifraga caroliniana*), and a species each of phacelia and corydalis. Bluebells, Dutchman's pipe, orchids, and soapwort (*Saponaria officinalis*) were among the common wildflowers. (*USGS-FS Map*: Hot Springs)

### ► ROCKY BLUFF RECREATION AREA
#### (Madison County)

The Rocky Bluff Recreation Area provides camping, picnicking, hiking, nature study, and fishing in Spring Creek. The area is open usually from mid-April to mid-December. It has flush toilets, lavatories, and water fountains but no showers. The campground is on a high ridge under tall white pines and oaks and has cement tables, grills, and graveled tent sites.

- ACCESS: From Hot Springs go S on NC-209 for 3.3 mi.

### Spring Creek Nature Trail (1.6 mi; USFS #312); Van Cliff Trail (2.7 mi; USFS #313)                                        126–127

- LENGTH AND DIFFICULTY: 4.3 mi combined, easy to moderate

- TRAILHEAD AND DESCRIPTION: From the S edge of the center of the Rocky Bluff Recreation Area (3.3 mi S of Hot Springs on NC-209), follow the trail sign and descend gradually on the *Spring Creek Nature Trail*. At 0.5 mi arrive at a vista of Spring Creek near a large rock formation. Turn L for 65 yd and then turn R to follow a well-graded and scenic trail around the mtn on the L side of the cascading stream. At 1.2 mi turn L and begin an ascent on an old road to the campground and picnic area. Flora includes white pine, hemlock, fetterbush, basswood, oak, liverwort, and abundant wildflowers.

For the more strenuous *Van Cliff Trail*, follow the blue blazes SW from the S edge of the center of the picnic area on a grassy road. At 0.1 mi turn R over a rocky treadway (with poison ivy) and climb to NC-209 at 0.3 mi. Turn L on the highway for 50 yd and go R on an old road. Ascend, sometimes steeply, R of cascading Long Mtn Branch. At 0.7 mi turn sharply L over the branch and follow another old road; hike the N side of the ridge. Forest trees consist of white pine, hemlock, basswood, oak, and hickory. Parts of the trail have running cedar, cancer root (*Conopholis americana*), and Indian pipe (*Monotropa uniflora*). Make a sharp L over a stream in a cove at 0.9 mi. Reach the top of a ridge at 1.3 mi, and begin a descent into a rocky ravine at 1.6 mi. Follow an old road and switchbacks to NC-209 at 2.2 mi. Cross the highway and descend steeply, turn sharply R among boulders at 2.4 mi, cross Long Mtn Branch at 2.5 mi, and return to the campground at 2.7 mi. (This trail is also known as the *Long Mtn Branch Trail*.) (*USGS-FS Map*: Spring Creek)

## ▶ HARMON DEN AREA
**(Haywood County)**

*Cherry Creek Trail (USFS #300)*                    **128**

• LENGTH AND DIFFICULTY: 2.5 mi, moderate to strenuous (elev change 1,350 ft)

• TRAILHEAD AND DESCRIPTION: From the jct of I-40 and FR-148, Harmon Den exit, and 7 mi E of the Tennessee state line, drive up the mtn on FR-148 for 4.4 mi to the S trailhead in a curve at Cherry Creek. (Beause the trail has a 1,350 ft elev gain, the N trailhead may be preferred with a vehicle switch.) Continue up the mtn on FR-148 for 1.8 mi to take a L on Max Patch Rd (SR-1182) and go 1.6 mi to jct with the *AT* at the state line. (To the R the *AT* leads 0.8 mi to the grassy bald of Max Patch Mtn [4,629 ft]. If you have not hiked this priceless natural wonder, do not leave until you experience its awesome panoramic beauty. It is the "crown jewel of the Appalachian Mountains," wrote Bob Proudman. Dedicated July 9, 1983, as part of a 5-mi relocation of the *AT*, it is the result of 14 years of work and negotiations by Arch Nichols and the Carolina Mountain Club, USFS, and others.) Begin the *Cherry Creek Trail* on the *AT* (S), but after 0.2 mi leave the *AT*, L, at a blue blaze. In a forest of oak, hemlock, flame azalea, galax, and blue bead, reach a logging road at 0.7 mi. Turn L and then R after 75 yd. Descend into a pristine forest of large hemlocks and rock formations with leafy lichen at 1.1 mi. Cross a stream at 1.5 mi and pass cascades at 2 mi. At 2.3 mi reach a timber road, turn R for 50 ft and then L. On the W side of Cherry Creek descend to FR-148 at 2.5 mi. (*USGS-FS Map:* Lemon Gap)

*Groundhog Creek Trail (2.3 mi; USFS #315); Rube Rock Trail (4 mi; USFS #314)*                    **129–130**

• LENGTH AND DIFFICULTY: 6.3 mi combined, moderate to strenuous (elev change 1,880 ft)

• TRAILHEAD AND DESCRIPTION: On I-40, 5.9 mi W from the Welcome Center and Rest Area (0.5 mi before I-40 tunnel and 4.7 mi from the TN-NC state line), park at a parking space by a locked gate, FR-3522. Hike 0.2 mi on the loop road and look for the blue-blazed *Groundhog Creek Trail*, R. Follow through poplar, hemlock, maple, and birch in a ravine. Reach a ridgecrest at 0.4 mi and jct with the *Rube Rock Trail*, R, at 0.5 mi. (The *Rube Rock Trail* runs 4 mi to the *AT* on Harmon Den Mtn. Skirt Hickory Ridge and cross Rube Rock Branch at 0.7 mi. Skirt another ridge near I-40. Turn NE and cross Tom Hall Branch at 1.9 mi, the first of a number of crossings. Ascend to a clearcut at 3 mi. If trail blazes are missing, stay on the main crest, N, to jct with the *AT* at 4 mi. Backtrack or use as a loop, L, for 2.3 mi on the *AT* to join the *Groundhog Creek Trail*. It is 3.3 mi R on the *AT* to Max Patch Rd.) To continue on the *Groundhog Creek Trail*, turn L on an old RR grade up Groundhog Creek. At 1.3 mi cross Chestnut Orchard Branch, followed by Ephraim Branch. At 2.1 mi reach Groundhog Creek Shelter, a stone shelter with five bunks. A spring is nearby. Continue ahead for 0.2 mi to reach the *AT* at Deep Gap (also called Groundhog Creek Gap). A loop can be made R to join the *Rube Rock Trail* after 2.3 mi on the *AT* for a return loop of 8.6 mi. (On the *AT* at Deep Gap it is 5.6 mi NE to Max Patch Rd [SR-1182], and 7.8 mi SW to Pigeon River and I-40.) (*USGS-FS Map*: Waterville)

▶ **SECTION 2: GRANDFATHER RANGER DISTRICT**

The Grandfather Ranger District with 186,735 acres is partially in McDowell, Burke, Caldwell, and Avery counties. The Linville Gorge Wilderness Area, in the center of the district, is in Burke County and has 10,975 acres that protect the natural environment of the Linville River and its divides. Two other wilderness areas, Lost Cove and Harper Creek, are proposed in the Harper Creek Area of Caldwell and Avery counties. The district's W boundary is the Blue Ridge Parkway, and a section of the Toecane Ranger District adjoins in the SW near Mt Mitchell. Among the outstanding localities for scenic beauty are Table Rock, Hawksbill Mtn, Shortoff Mtn, the three cliffs of Lost Cove, the major waterfalls of Harper and North Harper creeks, and Wiseman's View. There are four picnic areas; Barkhouse on NC-181, Mulberry NW of Lenoir, Old Fort W of Old Fort, and Table Rock NW of Morganton. Two picnic and camping areas (without hook-ups) are at Curtis Creek, N of Old Fort, and Mortimer, SE of Edgemont. Chestnut and Kawana primitive campgrounds are in the Wilson Creek Area.

The district has 69 hiking trails on inventory. The shortest path (0.2 mi) is *Wiseman's View Trail* (USFS #224). The longest (14.7 mi) is *Wilson Ridge Trail* (USFS #269), used primarily by motorcyclists and ATVs. There is one fitness trail, the 14-station, 0.5-mi-loop *Woodlawn Trail* (USFS #220), at the Woodlawn Picnic Area. It is 6.5 mi N of Marion on US-221. Limited maintenance has made a large percentage of the trails difficult for backpackers. The impassable trails are not described in this book. Trails are not blazed in this district (with the exception of the *MST*). The *MST* runs through the district for 46.5 mi, 8 mi of which are new routes, from the *Overmountain Victory Trail* (USFS #308) W of the Linville Gorge rim to Beacon Heights near Grandfather Mtn. (See *MST* in Chapter 16.)   **131–133**

• ADDRESS AND ACCESS: District Ranger, Grandfather Ranger District, USFS, PO Box 519, Marion, NC 28752, tel: 704-652-2144, downtown in the ground floor of the Library Bldg, corner of West Court and Logan streets.

## ▶ OLD FORT PICNIC AREA
### (McDowell County)

*Young's Ridge Trail* (USFS #206)                    **134**

• LENGTH AND DIFFICULTY: 4.2 mi, moderate to strenuous (elev change 1,565 ft)

• TRAILHEAD AND DESCRIPTION: (This trail includes the former *Kitsuma Peak Trail* and the *Young's Ridge Trail*.) In Old Fork on US-70 at the jct with Catawba Ave, go W 0.3 mi on US-70 and turn R on Mill Creek Rd (SR-1407). Drive N 3 mi and turn L on Old US-70 (SR-1400) to the Old Fort Picnic Area, L. Park and follow the trail upstream on the L through a ravine dark with heavy hemlock shade. (On the R there is a 0.5-mi loop trail near Swannanoa Creek.) Goats beard (*Aruncus dioicus*) grows on the damp banks. Follow the switchbacks to the ridgetop at 0.9 mi. Turn R and continue W up and down knobs to Kitsuma Peak (3,195 ft) at 3.6 mi. Views of Greybeard Mtn and Mt Mitchell Wildlife Management Area are impressive. Descend on switchbacks to an open path by a fence at I-40, the FS boundary line, at 4 mi. Turn R and at 4.2 mi reach a parking overlook at Ridgecrest. (Overlook gate usually closed at 8 pm. Check with the Blue Ridge Baptist Conference Center across the street from the gate for information on parking.) (*USGS-FS Maps*: Black Mtn, Old Fort)

## ▶ CURTIS CREEK RECREATION AREA (McDowell County)

Recreation activities here are camping (with vault toilets and hand water pump), picnicking, fishing, and hiking. A natural spring is at the Snooks Nose trailhead. The area is historic because it is part of the first 8,100-acre tract purchased under the 1911 Weeks Act. The tract is dedicated to Chase Ambler of Asheville for his efforts to establish the national forests.

• ACCESS: From I-40 exit at Old Fort, go 0.2 mi into town, turn R on US-70, and go 1 mi to jct, L, on Curtis Creek Rd (SR-1227), which becomes FR-482. After 5.1 mi from US-70, reach the campground.

• SUPPORT FACILITIES: A year-round commercial campground in the area is Triple C Campground, 6 mi N on NC-80 from its jct with US-70, NW of Marion. Full svc, rec fac. Address: 1666 Buck Creek Rd, Marion, NC 28752, tel: 704-724-4099. Service stores in Old Fort; motels and shopping centers are in Marion.

### *Snooks Nose Trail (USFS #211)*                    **135**

• LENGTH AND DIFFICULTY: 4 mi, strenuous (elev gain 2,800 ft)

• SPECIAL FEATURES: Views of Iron Mtn range and Newberry Creek watershed

• TRAILHEAD AND DESCRIPTION: At the S entrance to the campground (near old rock post of former CCC camp) enter on the old road (a natural spring is R in the hemlocks), curve in a cove, rock hop a stream at 0.3 mi in a forest of hemlock, poplar, birch, and beech, and ascend steeply. At 0.7 mi reach a spur ridge, level off, then ascend steeply again, R, off the old road (trail direction is vague here). Reach a ridgecrest, turn L at 1.2 mi. Pass R of a large cliff at 1.3 mi and reach an outcropping with vistas at 2 mi, after a number of switchbacks. A religious testimony about the mountains is lettered on the rocks. Continue along the ridgecrest, ascend to Laurel Knob (4,325 ft) without views at 3 mi. In a forest of galax, laurel, and rhododendron reach a gap at 3.4 mi. Ascend steeply to the Green Knob Overlook and a sign about the USFS on the Blue Ridge Parkway (mp 350.4) at 4 mi. Backtrack or use vehicle shuttle up to the BRP from the campground on FR-482. (*USGS-FS Map:* Old Fort)

## *Hickory Branch Trail* (USFS #213)                    136–137

• LENGTH AND DIFFICULTY: 4 mi round-trip, moderate to strenuous (elev change 1,100 ft)

• SPECIAL FEATURES: primitive, waterfalls, wildlife

• TRAILHEAD AND DESCRIPTION: There are two campground trailheads. One ascends the hillside by the hand water pump, the other from the lower end of the campground on a FR. They join 0.6 mi up Hickory Branch. From the pump ascend to the ridge, descend, and follow an old woods road upstream to a ravine wash and jct with the other route. If using the FR route, rock-hop Curtis Creek on the FR but leave the road at the end of the meadow at a holly tree and a beech tree. Go upstream, cross the branch, and join the other route near cascades and pools in the ravine. Hemlocks and rhododendron are prominent. At 0.8 mi reach the confluence of streams, cross the L fork, and ascend L of scenic cascades. After 11 switchbacks through laurel, blueberry, and turkey grass reach the ridgetop in a saddle at 2 mi. Backtrack. (The *Leadmine Gap Trail* [USFS #212] goes L but is obstructed with forest growth. The old open trail R leads down to Mackey Creek.) (*USGS-FS Map:* Old Fort)

### *Mackey Mountain Trail (USFS #216)*        **138–139**

- LENGTH AND DIFFICULTY: 8 mi, moderate to strenuous (elev gain 2,115 ft)

- SPECIAL FEATURES: bear sanctuary, remote

- TRAILHEAD AND DESCRIPTION: The NW access to this trail is at the jct of Curtis Creek Rd (FR-482) and Sugar Cove Rd (FR-1188), 4.4 mi up from the Curtis Creek Campground on FR-482 and 1.8 mi down the mtn on FR-482 from BRP mp 333. The trail is not blazed, but the orange bear sanctuary markers make good directions for the first 5 mi. Water is infrequent or nonexistent on the ridge line. Begin at the road jct and ascend an embankment or follow the old road R through rhododendron and oak to the W slope of the ridge. In addition to the bear, grouse, and turkey habitat, yellow-jacket nests are commonplace on the trail banks. At 1 mi switch to the E side of the ridge, but soon return to follow across a long knob and to a narrow ridge before ascending Narrow Knob (3,440 ft) at 2.8 mi. Follow a narrow rim, then a level area to skirt W of Mackey Mtn (4,035 ft) at 4 mi and jct with an old trail, R. Continue ahead along the ridge, ascend to a knob (3,960 ft), and descend to a trail jct at 6.2 mi, R. *Greenlee Mtn Trail* (USFS #222) descends 2 mi to Maple Hill Rd (SR-1414). It is used extensively by ATVs. Turn L on the *Mackey Mtn Trail* and descend, partially on steep woods roads among virgin poplar. Follow switchbacks (difficult to follow in places) and cross a dry streambed at 6.7 mi. Bear R at an old road jct at 7.5 mi. Leave the forest boundary at 7.6 mi, cross Deep Cove Creek, go 160 yd, turn a sharp L, cross the creek again, go 35 yd, and turn R on an old road at 7.8 mi. Exit from the trees in the center of two private driveways. Go across the bridge over Clear Creek to a small parking area on public Clear Creek Rd. (If parking here, use caution not to block the gated road upstream or to drive across the private bridge to park.) Vehicle shuttle necessary. It is 2.6 mi downstream on Clear Creek Rd (SR-1422) to US-70, and R 5.4 mi on US-70 to Curtis Creek Rd, R. (*USGS-FS Maps:* Old Fort, Marion W)

## ►WOODS MOUNTAIN AREA
### (McDowell County)

*Woods Mountain Trail (USFS #218)*                    **140–142**

- LENGTH AND DIFFICULTY: 10.6 mi round-trip, moderate

- CONNECTING TRAILS:
  *Armstrong Creek Trail* (2.5 mi; USFS #223, strenuous, elev
    change 1,420 ft)
  *Bad Fork Trail* (2.5 mi; USFS #227, strenuous, elev change
    1,060 ft)

- SPECIAL FEATURES: chinquapin patches, remote

- TRAILHEAD AND DESCRIPTION: Park at the Buck Creek Gap jct
of NC-80 and BRP mp 344.1, on the E side. Follow a sign up the
BRP svc road that parallels the BRP for 0.7 mi to Hazelwood
Gap, the beginning of the *Woods Mountain Trail.* Turn R on the
trail, opposite a large oak, and skirt S of the knob. After 0.2 mi
jct with *Armstrong Creek Trail,* L in a small gap.
  (The *Armstrong Creek Trail* is primitive but passable in its steep
descent on switchbacks to the headwaters of Armstrong Creek
at 0.7 mi. In a forest of oak, birch, poplar, hemlock, and rhododendron, it parallels the creek generally, but crosses it eight
times and crosses some small drains. Reach a cul-de-sac in the
road at the Armstrong Fish Hatchery at 3 mi. Ingress here is up
Armstrong Creek Rd [SR-1443] for 4.5 mi from NC-226A, 7.4
mi SE of Little Switzerland.)
  On the *Woods Mtn Trail* at 0.9 mi the ridge becomes a narrow
spine covered with blueberries, turkey grass, laurel, and chinquapin. Dominant trees on the trail at this point are oak and
pitch pine. Scenic views of Table Rock, Hawksbill, Mt Mitchell,
Green Knob, and Armstrong Valley are found at 1.3 mi and 3.6
mi. Other views along the ridge include Mackey Mtn and Lake
Tahoma. A number of unmarked spur trails, most of which
dead end, exist along the ridge. At 2.4 mi reach a jct with old
*Bad Fork Trail,* L, but go 0.9 mi farther to a gap for the current
route of the *Bad Fork Trail.* (The *Bad Fork Trail* descends steeply
to headwaters of Bad Fork at 0.7 mi. Cross and follow the W

bank of the stream into a rough but exceptionally scenic route on rock formations with flumes, oblique cascades, and pools. Hardwoods and conifers rise tall above the ferns, shrubs, and profuse wildflowers. At 2 mi join an old logging road, but leave it after 0.3 mi to descend for a rock-hopping of Armstrong Creek at 2.5 mi and exit to Armstrong Creek Rd. Upstream it is 1.1 mi to Armstrong Fish Hatchery; and 0.4 mi beyond is the *Armstrong Creek Trail* trailhead [a loop option of 9.2 mi].)

Continue on the *Woods Mtn Trail* and at 3.3 pass another old *Bad Fork Trail,* L. District Ranger Pat Cook calls this and other similar foot trails "bear trails" after routes made by bear hunters. From here the trail continues to undulate. At 5 mi jct with an old trail, R. Ahead it is 0.3 mi to Woods Mtn (3,646 ft), the site of a dismantled lookout tower. Backtrack. (Hikers exploring old trails from the mtn should have a topo map and compass.) (*USGS-FS Maps:* Celo, Little Switzerland)

• SUPPORT FACILITIES: (See Curtis Creek Rec Area.)

## ▶ LINVILLE GORGE WILDERNESS AREA
### (Burke and McDowell Counties)

The Linville Gorge Wilderness Area has 10,975 acres of wild, rugged, and scenic terrain. It is a distinct challenge to the climber, hiker, camper, and naturalist. Its boundaries are on the canyon rims. Its west side is near the Kistler Memorial Highway (SR-1238), a gravel road on Linville Mtn. The E boundary extends from Jonas Ridge to the S base of Shortoff Mtn. The wilderness does not include the famous Linville Falls, 0.3 mi upstream from the N boundary. (The Falls are part of the NPS described in Chapter 6.) For 14 mi through the wilderness, the Linville River's white water cascades in a descent of 2,000 ft. Major escarpments rise on the river's walls. The wilderness is rich in both plant and animal life. There are five species of rare plants, four species of rhododendron, and virgin forests in the deep coves. Among the flowering plants are sand myrtle (*Leiophyllum prostratum*), red chokeberry (*Sorbus arbutifolia*), azalea, turkey beard, bristly locust, yellow root, silverbell, orchids, ninebark, and wild indigo (*Baptisia tinctoria*). The major species of animals are deer, bear, squirrel, raccoon, grouse, turkey vulture, hawks, owls, and brown and rainbow trout. The poisonous snakes are the timber rattler and the copperhead. Hunting and fishing are allowed but state licenses are necessary. Free permits from the USFS are required for camping in the gorge only on weekends and holidays from May 1 through October 31. Time limit in the gorge is three consecutive days and two nights, one weekend permit per month per visitor, and group size not to exceed ten. No-trace camping is the rule. Permits may be obtained at the ranger's office in Marion M-F, 8–4:30, or by mail (see address in the introduction). Also, permits are available in person at the Linville Falls Visitor Center, open April 15 to November 1, 9–5. Access to the Center is 0.5 mi S on Kistler Memorial Highway from NC-183, 0.7 mi E from its jct with US-221 in Linville Falls.

The *Linville Gorge Trail* is the major trail; its traverse is in the gorge, paralleling the river on the W side. Seven short but steep access trails descend from SR-1238 along the W rim. (Another trail, the 0.2 mi *Wiseman's View Trail*, is only an overlook into the gorge. It is 3.8 mi from NC-183 on SR-1238.) The E rim has two short access trails from FR-210, but other trails on the E rim connect with each other. There are some trail signs at access points to the gorge, but inside the wilderness the trails are not blazed or signed. The use of a recent topo map or the Linville Gorge Wilderness Map is recommended. (*USGS-FS Maps:* Linville Falls, Ashford)

• SUPPORT FACILITIES: Campgrounds, motels, restaurants, svc sta, and small grocery stores are at Linville Falls on US-221.

### *Linville Gorge Trail* (USFS #231)        143–151

• LENGTH AND DIFFICULTY: 11.5 mi, strenuous (elev change 2,025 ft)

• CONNECTING TRAILS, WEST RIM:
*Pine Gap Trail* (0.7 mi, easy)
*Bynum Bluff Trail* (1 mi; USFS #241, moderate)

*Cabin Trail* (0.8 mi; USFS #246, strenuous, elev change 900 ft)

*Babel Tower Trail* (1.2 mi; USFS #240, strenuous, elev change 920 ft)

*Sandy Flats Trail* (1 mi; USFS #230, strenuous, elev change 900 ft)

*Conley Cove Trail* (1.4 mi; USFS #229, strenuous, elev change 930 ft)

*Pitch-In Trail* (1.4 mi; USFS #228, strenuous, elev change 1,760 ft)

- CONNECTING TRAILS, EAST RIM:
  *(Devil's Hole Trail)*
  *(Spence Ridge Trail)*

- SPECIAL FEATURES: rugged, geology

- TRAILHEAD AND DESCRIPTION: All the trails on the W rim can be used as loops with SR-1238 as a connector. A vehicle shuttle is another option. The nearest and easiest access to the Linville Gorge is on the *Pine Gap Trail* on SR-1238, 0.9 mi from the jct of NC-183 and SR-1238 (0.7 mi from the US-221/NC-183 jct in Linville Falls). From the parking area descend easily into the gorge and at 0.7 mi jct with the *Bynum Bluff Trail,* R. To the L is a short spur to views of the canyon, and the *Linville Gorge Trail* begins ahead. (The *Bynum Bluff Trail* ascends 1 mi, steeply at first, to a parking area on SR-1238, 1.5 mi from NC-183). Descend in a forest of hardwoods, hemlock, and dense rhododendron. At 1.2 mi jct with the *Cabin Trail,* R. (The 0.8-mi *Cabin Trail* is a primitive spur that is extremely steep and rough to SR-1238, 1.9 mi from NC-183.) At 2 mi on the *Linville Gorge Trail* jct R with the *Babel Tower Trail* at a cliffside for overlooks of a horseshoe bend and river rapids. (The *Babel Tower Trail* ascends 1.2 mi to a parking area on SR-1238, 2.7 mi R to NC-183. It is a popular route with switchbacks, but generally a scenic ridge route. It is 1.1 mi S on SR-1238 to Wiseman's View.)

Continue the descent on a slope near the river for excellent views of the gorge at 2.5 mi. At 3.4 mi pass the jct L with the *Devil's Hole Trail.* (The 1.5-mi *Devil's Hole Trail* may be difficult to locate, but it crosses the river at a less steep area than usual and follows up Devil's Hole Branch to a ridge between Sitting Bear Mtn and Hawksbill Mtn to exit at FR-210.) At 3.7 mi are scenic views of Hawksbill Mtn. At 3.8 mi is a spring, and a campground, and a jct R with *Sandy Flats Trail.* (The *Sandy Flats Trail,* primitive and steep, ascends 1 mi to SR-1238, 3.7 mi S of NC-183.) Reach *Spence Ridge Trail,* L, at 4.6 mi. (*Spence Ridge Trail* fords the river and ascends for 1.7 mi on switchbacks to a level area and then the rim's parking area on FR-210, described below.) Continue downriver and at 5.5 mi jct with *Conley Cove Trail,* R. (The *Conley Cove Trail* ascends on a well-graded route through a forest of oak, pine, cucumber tree, silverbell, and wildflowers. At 1 mi is a water source and a few yd farther is a primitive trail jct, L. [The unmaintained route is *Rock Jock Trail,* USFS #247, which follows above the escarpment for 2.8 mi.] Pass a cave and on switchbacks reach SR-1238 at 1.4 mi, 5.3 mi from NC-183.) The *Linville Gorge Trail* continues 100 yd downriver to a swimming hole and a large open outcropping with views of the Chimneys and Table Rock on the E rim. Other views follow. Cross a small branch at 6.8 mi. The next 2 mi of the trail and the river have a mild decline. Jct with the *Pitch-In Trail,* R, at 9.1 mi. (The *Pitch-In Trail* ascends 1.4 mi with excellent views of the gorge, particularly of Shortoff Mtn, to SR-1238, 7.3 mi R to *Pine Gap Trail.* To the L on SR-1238 it is 2.3 mi to the *MST* and the Pinnacle 0.2 mi off the road E, and 0.8 mi farther to the trailhead and parking area R (W) of the *Overmountain Victory Trail.* Down the mtn on SR-1238 it is 4.1 mi to NC-106, from where it is 16 mi E to Morganton and 10.2 mi W to I-40 at the Mt Nebo exit.)

The *Linville Gorge Trail* follows an old jeep road and passes through grassy glades under tall poplar and elm. At 10.9 mi is a good swimming hole. In a few yd wade the river in a flat area and reach the wilderness boundary at private property at 11.5 mi. Backtrack.

*Devil's Hole Trail* (1.5 mi; USFS #244); **Jonas Ridge Trail** (4.4 mi round-trip; USFS #245); **Hawksbill Mountain Trail** (1.4 mi round-trip; USFS #217); **Spence Ridge Trail** (1.7 mi; USFS #233); **Table Rock Gap Trail** (1.6 mi; USFS #243);

*Little Table Rock Trail (1.2 mi; USFS #236); Table Rock Summit Trail (1.4 mi round-trip; USFS #242)* **152–158**

- LENGTH AND DIFFICULTY: 13.2 mi combined and round-trip, moderate to strenuous (elev change from 520 ft to 1,340 ft)

- SPECIAL FEATURES: exceptional vistas

- TRAILHEAD AND DESCRIPTION: These short trails are grouped because they have an access from FR-210 on the E rim; two of them descend to connect with the *Linville Gorge Trail*. A longer trail that follows the rim, *Shortoff Mtn Trail*, is described below separately. From the jct of NC-183/181 at Jonas Ridge go S on NC-181 for 3 mi to the Old Gingercake Rd (SR-1264) and turn R. At 0.3 mi turn L, at the first fork, on Gingercake Acres Rd (SR-1265), which becomes FR-210. At 2.6 mi reach the *Devil's Hole Trail* parking area, R. Ascend the slope 0.1 mi to the ridgecrest (L it is 0.6 mi on a primitive ridge trail to Hawksbill Mtn and jct with *Hawksbill Mtn Trail*). Turn R, ascend the ridge to the primitive *Devil's Hole Trail*, L at 0.1 mi. (Ahead is the primitive dead-end *Jonas Ridge Trail* to Gingercake Mtn.) Descend on one major switchback into a cove with large hemlocks and dense rhododendron to follow the Devil's Hole Branch. At 1.5 mi ford the Linville River and jct with the *Linville Gorge Trail*. The descent is an elev change of 1,160 ft.

Drive down FR-210 another 1.3 mi and park L for the *Hawksbill Mtn Trail*, R (W). Ascend steeply on Lettered Rock Ridge through laurel and rhododendron arbors to a trail jct at 0.5 mi. Turn L. (The R trail follows the ridge for an access L to rock climbing and N for 0.7 mi to SR-210 at Devil's Hole access.) Reach the rocky summit (4,020 ft) of Hawksbill Mtn at 0.7 mi at the E boundary of the wilderness. Vistas are superior. Mountain ash and blueberry bushes are colorful in autumn. Backtrack.

The rim access to *Spence Ridge Trail* is another 1 mi on FR-210 to the parking area, R and L. A frequently used route, the first 0.2 mi is level and arbored with rhododendron. At 0.4 mi curve R in a jct and descend. (Ahead on the old road is a primitive trail, *Little Table Rock Trail*, which descends to a curve L and crosses a small stream at 0.3 mi. It ascends on a spur ridge, descends to a small drain, and ascends a very steep grade through white pine and hemlock. At 1.1 mi it reaches the top of Little Table Rock. A campsite and vistas are R. To the L is another primitive route, *Little Table Rock Trail,* to a water source at 160 yd. Ahead is a jct with *Table Rock Summit Trail* at 1.2 mi and an access to *Table Rock Gap Trail,* L.) Continue on the *Spence Ridge Trail.* Descend on switchbacks to a jct across the river with the *Linville Gorge Trail* at 1.7 mi.

At the parking area for the *Spence Ridge Trail,* the *Table Rock Gap Trail* follows an old road (used by vehicles) S for 0.4 mi to a cul-de-sac and jct with the *MST.* Turn R, ascend steeply, and after two switchbacks in a rhododendron slick reach a jct with the *Table Rock Summit Trail.* Backtrack, or use the *Table Rock Summit Trail,* L, for a 0.4-mi ascent to the top, or take a R 100 yd for an option to descend on the *Little Table Rock Trail* described above, or continue on the *Table Rock Summit Trail* for 0.3 mi to the Table Rock Picnic Area and parking lot.

For vehicle access to the Table Rock Picnic Area, drive ahead on FR-210 for 1.1 mi to FR-210B. Turn R and go 2.9 mi to the picnic area (passing an entrance to the Outward Bound School and climbing steeply the last mile). The picnic area has a vault toilet but no water source. Camping is not allowed here. Follow the *Table Rock Summit Trail* N on white-blazed *MST.* Jct with the *Little Table Rock Trail,* L, at 0.3 mi. Pass the *Table Rock Gap Trail* 100 yd ahead, and ascend on six rocky switchbacks to the summit (3,909 ft) at 0.7 mi with magnificent views and a 360 panorama.

### *Shortoff Mountain Trail* (USFS #235)     159–160

• LENGTH AND DIFFICULTY: 11.2 mi round-trip, strenuous (elev change 1,048 ft)

• SPECIAL FEATURES: The Chimneys, vistas of Linville Gorge

• TRAILHEAD AND DESCRIPTION: This trail is also the *MST,* and it skirts the E rim of the wilderness except at the Shortoff Mtn area, which is in the wilderness. From the S edge of the Table Rock Picnic Area (described above), follow the trail on a gentle path to an open ridge of chinquapin, blueberry, and bracken at 0.4 mi. Pass W of The Chimneys (3,557 ft), an area of fissures, irregular spires, and overhangs, to the ridge return at 0.8 mi. Descend steeply to a cliff with a view of Table Rock and a deep watershed at 1.3 mi. Descend to Chimney Gap (2,509 ft) at 1.8 mi. At 2.1 mi in a saddle, R, is the obscure and primitive 1.3-mi *Cambric Ridge Trail,* which dead ends at the river). At 2.3 mi is an intermittent spring, L (60 yd from the trail) in a grove of galax and rhododendron. Ascend and descend, reach a knob at 2.7 mi, turn R at 3 mi at an old trail jct, and soon follow an old jeep road. At 5 mi pass a natural wildlife water hole. Turn R at an old road jct at 5.4 mi to reach the precipitous edge of Shortoff Mtn (3,000 ft) at 5.6 mi. Here are exceptionally scenic views of the gorge and both rims. Vegetation includes hemlock, spruce, blueberry, oak, and bristly locust. South 0.1 mi on the trail is a usually dependable spring in a gulch. Backtrack or continue ahead on the *MST.* (The *MST* descends to an old road R and crosses the Linville River for a climb to the Pinnacle and jct with SR-1238. See Chapter 16.) A private road access from NC-126 on the Old Wolf Pit Rd should not be used. The parking sign on the 1986 wilderness map is in error, according to George Cook, former district ranger.

▶ **NORTH CATAWBA AREA**
**(McDowell County)**

*Overmountain Victory Trail (USFS #308)*          **161**

• LENGTH AND DIFFICULTY: 3.5 mi, moderate

• TRAILHEAD AND DESCRIPTION: In celebration of the bicentennial (1780-1980) of the "Overmountain Men," this yellow-blazed trail was planned, constructed, and designated a National Historic Trail in 1980. During the American Revolution, when Col. Patrick Ferguson of the Loyalist Army sent word to the frontier mountain men that he would destroy them, the men responded by mustering a troop of 1,000 from Virginia, Tennessee, and North Carolina to seek out Col. Ferguson, who was killed at the Kings Mountain battle in South Carolina.

Marching for 12 days from Sycamore Shoals in Tennessee, the men passed along this route on September 30, 1780. (See introduction to Section 4 of this chapter.) East access is on the Kistler Memorial Highway (SR-1238), 0.8 mi S from the Pinnacle and 4.1 mi N from NC-106. From the parking lot follow an old wagon road through a forest of white pine, laurel, and hardwoods. Cross a small stream at 0.3 mi and the Yellow Fork at 1 mi in thick rhododendron. At 1.5 mi cross a FR (accessible by vehicle 1.9 mi N from the trailhead on SR-1238). Descend gradually on a grassy road through hardwoods. Pass two grazing fields, L, and reach a flat ridge at 3.1 mi. A water source is R. Reach the W terminus at a FS gate, trail sign, and paved Old Linville Rd (SR-1560), L and R, at 3.5 mi. Bridge Branch is R in a residential area. It is 2.5 mi, R (N), on SR-1560 to a jct with US-221 in Ashford. (*USGS-FS Map:* Ashford)

▶ **WILSON CREEK AREA**
  **(Avery, Burke, and Caldwell Counties)**

This large area has a network of more than 25 trails. They are concentrated in the deep valleys and gorges from the foldings of metamorphic rock that runs NW to SE from the Blue Ridge Mtn crest to the hill country W of Lenoir. From S to N the drains that flow E are Steels Creek, Upper Creek, Harper Creek, North Harper Creek, Lost Cove Creek, and the major basin, Wilson Creek. In the center of the area is Mortimer Recreation Area, the only family campground (no hook-ups), but commercial full-svc campgrounds are near the NF boundary. Mortimer has facilities for picnicking, camping, fishing, and hiking. The 4.5-mi *Thorpe Branch Trail* (USFS #279) at the edge of the campground is not maintained as a double-loop trail because of forest-fire damage. It is the location of a former CCC camp. The area also has two other picnic sites, Barkhouse on NC-181 and Mulberry N of Lenoir. Mortimer is now a ghost area; once nearly 1,000 residents worked here at the Riddle Lumber Company or other plants. Major forest fires devastated the mountains in 1916 and 1925, and floods washed away the town in 1916 and 1940. The rough but scenic state road that provides access to the community was constructed on an old RR grade in 1950. Streams are stocked with trout; the forests have bear, turkey, deer, grouse, raccoon, skunk, and squirrel. Rattlesnakes and copperheads are also in the area. The forests are chiefly birch, oak, hickory, poplar, hemlock, white pine, laurel, and rhododendron. The area is well-known for its Brown Mtn Lights, a mysterious flickering light that according to legend is the spirit of a Civil War slave with a lantern looking for his master.                                                    **162**

• ACCESS: To reach Mortimer Recreation Area from Morganton go 10.5 mi N on NC-181 to jct R on Brown Mtn Beach Rd (SR-1405, also called Collettsville Rd) at Smyrna Baptist Church. Go 5 mi on SR-1405 to SR-1328, L at the Mortimer sign. Go 4.5 mi to jct across the Wilson Creek bridge and turn R. After another 4.5 mi reach the campground. From Collettsville go SW on Adako Rd (SR-1337) for 2.2 mi and turn R at the Mortimer sign to follow the directions above.

• SUPPORT FACILITIES: Two commercial campgrounds in the area are Steels Creek Park, tel: 704-433-5660, 1.2 mi N on NC-181 from Smyrna Baptist Church, and Daniel Boone Family Campground, tel: 704-433-1200, 1.7 mi N on NC-181 from Smyrna Baptist Church, approx 13.5 mi N of Morganton. Full svc, rec fac; open April 1 to late fall. A small general store is at the corner of NC-90 and Wilson Creek Rd (SR-1328) at Mortimer Rec Area, and another store is about 2.6 mi S on SR-1328. A community store is on NC-181, near Jonas Ridge, 2.7 mi S from the jct of NC-181/183. Motels and restaurants are at Linville Falls. Morganton and Lenoir have shopping centers, restaurants, motels, and hospitals.

*Lower Steels Creek Trail (2.9 mi; USFS #238);* **Upper Steels Creek Trail** *(2.9 mi; USFS #237)*                        **163–164**

• LENGTH AND DIFFICULTY: 5.8 mi combined, moderate

• SPECIAL FEATURES: waterfalls, fishing, wildlife

• TRAILHEAD AND DESCRIPTION: These trails can be connected with 1.8 mi on FR-288 for a total of 7.6 mi. To reach the trailheads of the *Lower Steels Creek Trail,* turn off NC-181 on FR-228 (9.6 mi S of NC-181/183 jct in Jonas Ridge and 4.4 mi up the mtn from SR-1405 at Smyrna Baptist Church), and drive 2.1 mi to jct with FR, L. Park and walk on the road for 0.2 mi to a gate and descend to Steels Creek at 0.5 mi. Rock-hop, pass a fish barrier, L, and at 0.8 mi leave the road L into a grazing field. Reenter the forest at 0.9 mi and rock-hop the creek. Immediately rock-hop again and follow a path through white pine, birch, and ironwood. At 1.2 mi rock-hop the creek, L (watch for a N.C. Wildlife Commission trout sign on a white pine facing the stream, otherwise you may miss the crossing). Rock-hop again at 1.4 mi and pass through a clearcut. Cross the stream at 1.6 mi (either on a log bridge or by wading). Enter a rhododendron canal with orange-fringed orchids (*Habenaria ciliaris*) in sunny spots. At 2 mi turn L at remnants of an old log cabin and ascend gently on an old road to NC-181 at 2.9 mi. Descend the embankment. (There are not any trailhead signs here, but one landmark to watch for is the end of a guardrail across the road from the trailhead, 0.3 mi up the mtn from the National Forest sign and 0.2 mi down the mtn from FR-4095.) Backtrack or use a shuttle 1.7 mi up the mtn to FR-228, L.

For the *Upper Steels Creek Trail* follow the same route to FR-288, but pass the parking area for the *Lower Steels Creek Trail* and drive 1.8 mi farther to a parking area at the road terminus. Hike upstream on a jeep road to creek cascades at 0.2 mi. Rock-hop the creek and jct with the white-blazed *MST* after 75 yd. Turn R, ascend through a rhododendron thicket with rapids and pools, R. Pass a waterfall at 0.6 mi. At 0.9 mi turn sharply L, ascend steeply to an old RR grade, and at 1.3 mi pass through an ideal camping area of tall trees and grassy grounds. Enter a grazing field and reach a FR, R. Cross Gingercake Creek and Steels Creek to follow under tall poplar and white pine. At 1.9 mi rock-hop the creek and again at 2 mi. Follow a well-graded FR to a ridgetop at 2.8 mi and at 2.9 mi leave the *MST* (which goes R). Continue ahead for 120 yd to a locked FR gate and jct with FR-496. Backtrack or take FR-496, R, for 1.3 mi to NC-181, then R to FR-228. (*USGS-FS Map:* Chestnut Mtn)

**Woodruff Branch Trail** *(2.4 mi; USFS #256);* **Bill Camp Trail** *(1.2 mi; USFS #251)*                                **165–166**

- LENGTH AND DIFFICULTY: 4.8 mi round-trip, easy

- TRAILHEAD AND DESCRIPTION: These trails do not connect, but both have trailheads on FR-45 within 1.6 mi of each other and are old roads closed to vehicular use. For access go N from Edgemont on SR NC-90, which becomes FR-45 for 4.7 mi (pass *Wilson Creek Trail* access at 2 mi) to *Woodruff Branch Trail,* R. Cross hummock (also called "tank trap") and follow pleasant seeded road across Barn Ridge, and descend to a parking area near the mouth of Woodruff Branch at Anthony Creek to Anthony Creek Rd (SR-1362) at 2.4 mi. Backtrack, or use a vehicle shuttle 2.1 mi NW to Gragg on FR-45, R, for 4.5 mi (SE) on Globe Rd (SR-1516), which becomes SR-1362. The *Bill Camp Trail* is 1.6 mi up FR-45 from the *Woodruff Branch Trail.* A rarely used trail, it descends S and crosses Cary Flat Branch in a young forest of laurel, hemlock, and oak. It drops to the nose of a hill and dead ends at a private road. Backtrack. (*USGS-FS Maps:* Grandfather Mtn, Globe)

**Wilson Creek Trail** *(6.6 mi; USFS #258);* **Wilson Creek Access Trail** *(1.4 mi; USFS #268A);* **White Rocks Trail** *(0.8 mi; USFS #264)*                                **167–169**

- LENGTH AND DIFFICULTY: 8.8 mi combined, moderate to strenuous

- SPECIAL FEATURES: remote, fishing, wildlife, rugged

- TRAILHEAD AND DESCRIPTION: These primitive trails combine to provide two accesses NW and two SE. Signs and blazes are absent except unofficial markings by hikers or fishermen. Wading is necessary at some of the fordings, particularly downstream. For the SE trailheads, from Mortimer Rec Area, drive N on NC-90 through Edgemont, cross *Wilson Creek Trail* trailhead, L, at 4.0 mi. Parking area is small. Another 1.5 mi up the mtn on FR-45 is the *White Rocks Trail* trailhead, L (it is an 0.8 mi shortcut down Bark Camp Ridge to jct with the *Wilson Creek*

*Trail* at the mouth of Laurel Mtn Branch). Begin the *Wilson Creek Trail* by ascending Bark Camp Ridge in a forest of oak, white pine, and laurel. Curve L of a knob, descend, and in a cove cross Crusher Branch at 0.8 mi. Ford the creek twice and jct with *White Rocks Trail* at 1.8 mi. Cross Laurel Mtn Branch and ford the creek frequently in the next 3 mi. Campsites are good at Turkey Branch and Flat Land Branch. At 4.8 mi reach the confluence of Andrews and Wilson creeks. Between them, in a fork, *Wilson Creek Trail* turns R at red paint marks and the *Wilson Creek Access Trail* proceeds ahead. (If following the *Wilson Creek Access Trail*, rock-hop Andrews Creek a number of times and reach the convergence with Slack Creek, R, at 0.8 mi. In a rhododendron thicket are scenic cascades and pools. Arrive at a grazing field at 1.2 mi, turn R, and follow a gated old road to FR-192 at 1.4 mi [6.2 mi from FR-45]. It is 1 mi L to Old House Gap and 2.6 mi R to Edgemont Rd [SR-1514].) The main *Wilson Creek Trail* is overgrown, but you may follow the red markers up Wilson Creek to its jct with an alternate route. Cross Wilson Creek immediately after forking R from *Wilson Creek Access Trail,* pass two huge rock overhangs, cross the creek twice more, and at 0.5 mi reach a frequently used campsite. Two signs are on trees in memory of Mike Borders and J.C. Bryant, both killed in a vehicular accident. There are two routes out from here. The roughest is to go 390 ft upstream in a manway to a rocky island and a paint marker. Cross the creek at a cucumber tree and the mouth of Bee Branch. Turn sharply R and follow red "B.B." initials on a poplar to an old RR grade. Follow the "B.B." and white markers to the convergence of Wilson Creek and Little Wilson Creek, R. Ascend an old RR grade between the creeks but leave the grade at 0.4 mi. Pass through a rhodo-dendron grove and exit by a campsite at FR-192 at 0.6 mi (5.9 mi from FR-45 entrance). The other option is to follow the jeep road at the memorial campsite. After 0.8 mi jct with an old logging road. Turn L and follow to FR-192 at 1.3 mi. From here it is 0.3 mi L to the Little Wilson Creek Access, and 1.9 mi farther to *Wilson Creek Access Trail.* To the R it is 0.6 mi to the Edgemont Rd (SR-1514). From this jct it is 4.1 mi L to US-221 (0.5 mi E of the BRP); R on SR-1514 it is 5.8 mi down the mtn to

FR-45 and the SE trailhead of *Wilson Creek Trail*. Along FR-45 are two other isolated trails described above.

### *Harper Creek Trail* (USFS #260)                          **170–176**

* LENGTH AND DIFFICULTY: 6.3 mi, strenuous (elev change 1,000 ft)

* CONNECTING TRAILS:
  *Yellow Buck Trail* (2.1 mi; USFS #265, moderate)
  *Raider Camp Trail* (2.8 mi; USFS #277, moderate)
  *(MST)*
  *(Simmons Ridge Trail)*
  *North Harper Creek Trail* (4.5 mi; USFS #266, strenuous, elev change 1,320 ft)
  *Persimmon Ridge Trail* (2.7 mi; USFS #270, moderate)
  *North Harper Creek Access Trail* (1 mi; USFS #266A, easy)
  *North Harper Creek Falls Trail* (1.3 mi; USFS #239, moderate)

* SPECIAL FEATURES: waterfalls, fishing

* TRAILHEAD AND DESCRIPTION: If using the E trailhead at Wilson Creek, the combination of Harper Creek and North Harper Creek trails is shaped like a crooked Y with North Harper forking R. An advantage for using one or both of these trails is to create options for eight loop routes from modest to more challenging lengths. All but *Simmons Ridge Trail* are in the proposed Harper Creek Wilderness Area. The clear rushing streams have sculpted the metamorphic rocks in falls, flumes, and pools. Trout are stocked and the USFS requires artificial lures. The two main trails follow the stream banks and cross the creeks frequently. Under normal weather conditions all fording can be rock-hopping. Water snakes and copperheads are seen sunning in the summer, and brilliant cardinal flowers (*Lobelia cardinalis*) bloom on wet grassy islands in late summer. Trail access routes connect from SR-1328 (E), FR-464 (N), and FR-85 (W).

Begin the *Harper Creek Trail* at a narrow parking area on Wilson Creek Rd (SR-1328), 1.4 mi S of the Mortimer Rec Area. Ascend gradually on a well-graded trail to a ridgecrest and jct,

R, with *Yellow Buck Trail* at 0.4 mi. (The *Yellow Buck Trail* ascends steeply on an old skid road for 0.7 mi to slope W of Yellow Buck Mtn [2,470 ft] and continues on a gentle route with white pine and bristly locust [*Robina hispida*] to jct with the *Persimmon Trail*, L, at 1.8 mi. Ahead it is 0.3 mi to FR-464, the trail's end, and 4 mi E on FR-464 to Mortimer.) Continue on the *Harper Creek Trail* on a wide clear woods road to a jct, L, with *Raider Camp Trail* at 1.3 mi. The *Harper Creek Trail* turns R.

(The *Raider Camp Trail*, also the white-blazed *MST,* goes 135 yd to cross Harper Creek, turn L, and jct with *Phillips Creek Trail*, L, at 0.3 mi. The trail follows up Raider Creek through good campsite areas 0.7 mi before ascending on an eroded old road to a ridgecrest and crossroads at 2 mi. It goes straight to follow a level and scenic woods road in an open forest to jct with *Greentown Trail*, L, at 2.6 mi. Turn R at the jct and descend to a cliff for views of the spectacular 200-ft waterfall and cascades known as South Harper Creek Falls. Continue on switchbacks to cross Harper Creek and intersect with *Harper Creek Trail* at the top of the falls at 2.8 mi. Harper Creek Trail goes L for 1.1 mi to its terminus on FR-58 and R downstream for 3.9 mi to its first encounter with *Raider Camp Trail* and back to SR-1328 for a loop of 9.3 mi.)

To continue on *Harper Creek Trail* from the first encounter, turn R, ascend gently for 0.1 mi to a spur route, and go another 0.2 mi to views of the scenic Harper Creek Falls and pool. Continue on the main trail, also the white-blazed *MST,* and pass the falls on a precipitous slope. Rock-hop the creek three times before a jct at the mouth of North Harper Creek, R, at 3.4 mi. *North Harper Creek Trail* ascends 4.5 mi to FR-58 and is described in more detail below. Continue on the Harper Creek Trail where the treadway becomes rough in some sections. At 4.1 mi cross a tributary in a forest of hemlock, hardwoods, and rhododendron. At 5.2 mi arrive at the spectacular 200-ft falls and cascades known as South Harper Creek Falls. A few yd beyond the top of the falls jct L with *Raider Camp Trail,* described above, for a reverse loop. Curve R at the nose of a ridge and ascend for 0.1 mi to an easy grade through oak, maple, and laurel and reach FR-58 at 6.3 mi, the W trailhead. Across the road is the S trailhead of *Simmons Ridge Trail*, described below. On FR-58, L, it is 0.5 mi to private property (the early settlement of Kawana), and R on FR-58 it is 0.5 mi to the W trailhead of *Persimmon Ridge Trail*. Here is another potential loop route, using *North Harper Creek Trail*, for a return total of 12.8 mi to SR-1328.

At the confluence of Harper and North Harper creeks the *North Harper Creek Trail* starts upstream, R, and at 0.5 mi it intersects with *Persimmon Ridge Trail*, L and R.

(*Persimmon Ridge Trail*, L, is a steep ascent W for 0.1 mi to a ridge line. Ascend gradually to a knob [2,785 ft] at 1.7 mi and drop to FR-58 on a woods road at 2.1 mi. It is 0.5 mi L on FR-58 to the W trailhead of *Harper Creek Trail* and 3 mi R on FR-58 to the N trailhead of *Simmons Ridge Trail*. The E section of *Persimmon Ridge Trail* leaves North Harper Creek and ascends 0.6 mi to a jct with *Yellow Buck Trail*. A turn L is 0.3 mi to FR-464; a turn R on *Yellow Buck Trail* would provide a loop of 8.1 mi back to SR-1328.)

Continue on the *North Harper Creek Trail*, rock-hop the creek three times while passing through a flat area for campsites at 0.6 mi and by a deep pool, flumes, and ferns at 1.4 mi. At 1.8 mi jct with *North Harper Creek Access Trail* (also called *Clearcut Trail*), R. (*Clearcut Trail* is a well-graded, scenic, open-woods access route of 1 mi from FR-464, 5.4 mi from Mortimer.) Cross the creek a number of times and reach another campsite at 3.1 mi. At 3.3 mi, L, is Chestnut Cove Branch Falls, and at 3.4 mi is jct, R, with a dubious trailhead of *North Harper Creek Falls Trail*. An ax mark on a tulip poplar, L, is a simple sign.

(The *North Harper Creek Falls Trail* ascends 0.3 mi on an erratic manway to a logging road. Follow the road through dense blackberry patches and saplings, and bear L at another old road to reach FR-464 at 1.3 mi. It is 1.3 mi R to *North Harper Creek Access Trail* and L on FR-464 1.9 mi to FR-58.)

Continue up *North Harper Creek Trail*, ascend steeply through rhododendron to a large, high rock formation, L. Cross the creek and arrive at the base of an exceptionally beautiful North

Harper Creek Falls at 3.6 mi. Ascend on switchbacks to the top of the falls for another scenic area of cascades and pools. Cross the creek to campsites, turn L, ascend, cross the creek three more times, the last at 4.4 mi. Reach the W terminus of the trail at 4.5 mi. Left on FR-58, it is 0.4 mi to *Simmons Ridge Trail,* and R on FR-58 it is 0.2 mi to FR-464. Here is a primitive campsite and picnic area. It is 8.6 mi R on FR-464 and NC-90 to Mortimer Rec Area, and L it is 4.5 mi to jct of NC-181/183 in Jonas Ridge. For the NC-181 access route, go 2.5 mi L on FR-464 to Long Ridge Baptist Church, turn L on SR-1518, and go 0.5 mi. Turn R on SR-1471, go 0.8 mi to jct with NC-181 and BRP, and turn L on NC-181 for 0.7 mi to jct of NC-181/183. (*USGS-FS Maps:* Chestnut Mtn, Grandfather Mtn)

### *Simmons Ridge Trail (USFS #267)* 177

- LENGTH AND DIFFICULTY: 5.2 mi, moderate

- SPECIAL FEATURES: RR grade, wildlife

- TRAILHEAD AND DESCRIPTION: Access is described above from NC-181 to the W trailhead of *North Harper Creek Trail.* From that trailhead on FR-58 go 0.4 mi to a small parking space, L, but the trailhead is R at a large cucumber tree (or an ATV route at a large poplar). Ascend 90 yd to a ridge and follow an old logging road in a hardwood forest to the top of Headquarters Mtn (3,970 ft) at 1.4 mi. Descend to a gated dirt FR (R, 0.4 mi to old Jonas Ridge Rd [SR-1518, also called Mortimer Rd]. Left, SR-1581 becomes SR-1401 in Burke County and leads 2.1 mi to NC-181 in Jonas Ridge. Right, SR-1501 is 0.7 mi to Long Branch Baptist Church and R to FR-464.) Cross the dirt road and descend to join an old RR grade at 2.8 mi. Follow it for the remainder of the trail through a forest of oak, locust, maple, laurel, and rhododendron. Exit at FR-58 at 5.2 mi. Ahead is the W trailhead of *Harper Creek Trail* described above. On the R it is 0.5 mi to private property and the South Fork of Harper Creek. It is 3.5 mi L to the N trailhead of *Simmons Ridge Trail.* (*USGS-FS Maps:* Chestnut Mtn, Grandfather Mtn)

*Timber Ridge Trail* (1.5 mi; USFS #261); *Lost Cove Trail* (7.5 mi; USFS #262); *Hunt-Fish Falls Trail* (0.8 mi; USFS #263)      **178–180**

- LENGTH AND DIFFICULTY: 9.8 mi combined, moderate to strenuous

- SPECIAL FEATURES: wildlife, waterfalls, vistas

- TRAILHEAD AND DESCRIPTION: These trails connect as a group and are within the proposed Lost Cove Wilderness Area. The N access (described first) is on FR-981 and the S access is on FR-464. From the Mortimer Rec Area go 2 mi W on NC-90 to the S edge of Edgemont and turn L on FR-981. Drive 4 mi to a parking space, L, before crossing the bridge of Gragg Prong, opposite FR-192. (Ahead on FR-981 it is 0.4 mi to Roseborough and Roseborough Rd, SR-1511.) It goes 4.5 mi up the mtn to the BRP and Linville.) Hike across the bridge, turn L on a short jeep road, and begin the *Lost Cove Trail* (also the white-blazed *MST* route) at the downstream corner of a small meadow. Rock-hop Gragg Prong four times in the first 2 mi. At 1 mi jct with a spur trail, R, that ascends gradually to *Timber Ridge Trail* for 0.4 mi. At 1.2 mi are falls, sunbathing rocks, pools, and campsites in a forest of white pine, oak, laurel, hemlock, and rhododendron. Pass a high falls at 1.5 mi, jct with *Timber Ridge Trail*, R, at 2.3 mi near convergence with Lost Cove Creek. Rock-hop Lost Cove Creek and reach the high cascades L and three-tiered Hunt-Fish Falls, R at 3 mi, an excellent fishing and sunning area. (The *Hunt-Fish Falls Trail* ascends L steeply, 0.8 mi on switchbacks to FR-464 for a S access. This access is 1.7 mi W from Mortimer Rec Area on NC-90 to FR-464, L, and 3.1 mi farther up the mtn to the trailhead parking area, R.) Cross the creek and turn upstream. (At this point, to the R is a 0.6-mi spur trail that ascends steeply to *Timber Ridge Trail*.) For the next 1.7 mi are dense rhododendron groves but also good campsites. At 4.3 mi, L, is Little Lost Cove Creek and falls, and at 4.7 mi, L, arrive at FR-464A, a rough 4WD access from FR-464. Turn R, cross the creek, and ascend on switchbacks to jct with the old trail, L, at

5.4 mi. Turn R, curve around Bee Mtn to follow the ridgecrest. Views of the Grandfather Mtn range and Hughes Ridge are seen from here and *Timber Ridge Trail* ahead. Jct L with *Timber Ridge Trail* at 5.4 mi. (*Timber Ridge Trail* goes ahead 1 mi to jct with the spur trail, L, and descends another 0.5 mi to jct with the *Lost Cove Trail*.) At 6.5 mi descend into a huge natural amphitheater landscaped by nature with ferns, rocks, wildflowers, and a spring. At 7.5 mi return to the parking area. (*USGS-FS Map:* Grandfather Mtn)

### *Greentown Trail* (5.7 mi; USFS #258); *Greentown Short-cut Trail* (1.2 mi; USFS #268A)          181–182

* LENGTH AND DIFFICULTY: 6.9 mi combined, strenuous (elev change 1,268 ft)

* CONNECTING TRAILS:
  *(MST)*
  *(Raider Camp Trail)*

* TRAILHEAD AND DESCRIPTION: The trailhead is on the E side of NC-181 (across the road from FR-496), 0.4 mi S of Barkhouse Picnic Area. Follow an old logging road (white-blazed *MST*) and descend into a cove. At 1 mi reach Upper Creek, but go upstream to cross at 1.2 mi; turn R. At 2.3 mi jct with *Greentown Short-cut Trail*, R near the mouth of Burnthouse Branch. (*Greentown Short-cut Trail* descends in a gorge on the E side of Upper Creek to the scenic Lower Upper Creek Falls at 0.7 mi. Exit at a parking area to FR-197 at 1.2 mi. FR-197 descends to FR-982, R to NC-181, 4 mi S from the *Greentown Trail* entrance.) Continue on an old eroded road; reach an old parking and primitive campsite at a jct, R, with FR-198 at 3.8 mi. Bear L, make a long curve to a saddle with forks at 4.5 mi. Avoid the forks, go straight (from Burke County to Avery County), and descend. At 4.9 mi take the L fork; reach *Raider Camp Trail* at 5.7 mi. (*Raider Camp Trail*, described above, goes L for 0.2 mi to South Harper Creek Falls and *Harper Creek Trail*, and R for 2.6 mi to jct with the E trailhead of *Harper Creek Trail*. (*USGS-FS Map:* Chestnut Mtn)

### *Upper Creek Falls Trail* (USFS #268B)                    **183**

• LENGTH AND DIFFICULTY: 1.6 mi round-trip, moderate

• TRAILHEAD AND DESCRIPTION: From the Barkhouse Picnic Area on NC-181, drive N 0.8 mi to the parking lot, R. (From the jct of NC-181/183, drive S, down the mtn, 4.1 mi to the parking lot, L.) Descend on switchbacks through hardwoods and rhododendron groves to the rocky creek. Cross the creek and ascend steeply to the base of the falls in a scenic area. The rocks can be slippery. Backtrack. (*USGS-FS Map*: Chestnut Mtn)

### *Big Lost Cove Cliffs Trail* (1.2 mi; USFS #271); *Little Lost Cove Cliffs Trail* (1.3 mi; USFS #271A); *Darkside Cliffs Trail* (0.5 mi; USFS #272)                    **184–186**

• LENGTH AND DIFFICULTY: 5.7 mi, round-trip combined, moderate

• SPECIAL FEATURES: geology, spectacular vistas

• TRAILHEAD AND DESCRIPTION: These three trails do not connect but are grouped because of proximity and similarity. The easiest access is from NC-181, 0.7 mi N of jct with NC-183. Turn R on SR-1471 and go 0.8 mi, turn L on SR-1518 and go 0.5 mi, and turn R at Long Branch Baptist Church on FR-464. Descend 2 mi to a narrow parking edge in a sharp L curve. The trail ascends 0.4 mi in laurel and rhododendron with ground cover of wintergreen (*Gaultheria procumbens*) to an old jeep road. Descend to the cliffs at 1.2 mi for a grand 180 view of Lost Cove, Grandfather and Grandmother mtns, and the BRP. Drive down FR-464 for 1.1 mi to W trailhead of *Little Lost Cove Cliffs Trail*. Park R, and ascend on an old jeep road. At 0.6 mi is first of a number of spurs for a 360 view of Grandfather Mtn, Timber Ridge, Wilson Creek basin, Harper Creek basin, Hawksbill Mtn, and Blowing Rock area. Descend to FR-464 on a gated jeep road at 1.3 mi. Drive down FR-464 another 0.6 mi to *Darkside Cliffs Trail*, L, but park R of road. Walk this easy 0.5-mi route first through hardwoods and then rhododendron and pitch pine for superb views of the Wilson Creek basin, Blowing

Rock area, and Grandfather Mtn range. Backtrack. On FR-464 it is 6.1 mi down the mtn to NC-90 and to Mortimer Rec Area. (*USGS-FS Map*: Grandfather Mtn)

### *Phillips Creek Trail* (USFS #278)                    187

* LENGTH AND DIFFICULTY: 1.9 mi, moderate

* SPECIAL FEATURES: waterfalls, scenic gulch

* TRAILHEAD AND DESCRIPTION: Park in a cove on Wilson Creek Rd (SR-1328), 2.2 mi S of Mortimer Rec Area. On an unsigned trail ascend steeply for 60 yd to an old RR grade, turn L, and at 0.4 mi climb steeply to the top of Phillips Creek Falls. Cross the creek, continue ascent in a gorge with tall hemlock and white pine. Curve R from stream confluence, ascend to old logging road, and turn L. Reach a saddle at 1.4 mi, cross old roads, and descend rapidly into a scenic gulch with dense fetterbush and rhododendron. Cross Raider Creek to good campsites and jct R and L with *Raider Camp Trail* at 1.9 mi (between two large poplars with initials "R.J."). Backtrack, or make a loop by turning R. Go 0.3 mi to jct with *Harper Creek Trail,* turn R and follow it to SR-1328. Turn R on SR-1328 and follow it downstream to the point of origin at 4.3 mi. (*USGS-FS Map:* Chestnut Mtn)

---

## ▶ SECTION 3: PISGAH RANGER DISTRICT

---

This district of 156,103 acres and historic distinction is the flagship of the state's NF districts. It is the most popular, attracting approximately five million visitors annually. "What we do is for the public and for future generations," said Art Rowe, the district ranger, reflecting the philosophy of the area's first forest manager, Gifford Pinchot. The district is a hiker's mecca with over 275 mi of trails, most of which are blazed in white, orange, blue, or yellow (except in the two wilderness areas). Hikers have an exceptionally wide choice of trails—for ecological study and forest history; on steep rocky balds, dry ridges, and in remote forested canyons and coves; into the backcountry for solitude; and by creeksides and waterfalls. The longest and most challenging trails are the 30-mi *Art Loeb Trail* and the 31.7-mi *MST* that runs through the district but mainly follows other trails.

Two loop trails begin at the RS parking area. The *Pisgah Environmental Trail* (USFS #288), a national recreation trail constructed by the YCC, is a 0.6-mi loop that has 21 interpretive stations, some on an elevated walkway. Connecting with it is the 1.4-mi *Exercise Trail* that parallels and crosses US-276 and the Davidson River at the English Chapel, NW, and the campground entrance, SE. A frequently used route to the campground, it was constructed by volunteers as part of a Boy Scouts of America Eagle Service Project.                    **188–189**

In the preceding districts the order of trail descriptions has followed the order of USFS trail inventory numbers, as seen on USFS maps, from lowest to highest. Because the Pisgah district has assigned area trail numbers indiscriminately (except the trails in the Lake Powhatan area), the trails are described according to contiguity (and numerically where possible) in areas that are listed alphabetically.

Recreational facilities provide four family campgrounds: Davidson River, the largest, across the Davidson River from the RS; Lake Powhatan in the Bent Creek Experimental Forest near the French Broad River, off NC-191 near the BRP; North Mills River, W of North Mills; and Sunburst on NC-215, N of the BRP at Sunburst. There are three group camps that require reservations: Cove Creek, near the U.S. Fish Hatchery; White Pines, near the RS; and Kuykendall, off US-64 between Rosman and Brevard. Picnic areas are Coontree, Pink Beds, Sliding Rock, and Sycamore Flats, all on US-276 between the BRP and Brevard, and Stony Fork on NC-151, S of Chandler. Among the major natural attractions are Looking Glass Falls, Looking Glass Rock, and Sliding Rock, all on US-276 W of the RS, Courthouse Creek Falls off NC-215 NW of Rosman, and Shining Rock N of the BRP. Other attractions are the U.S. Fish Hatchery off US-276 NW of the RS and the Pink Beds Visitor Center N of Sliding Rock on US-276. The district has five special areas: two wilderness areas—Middle Prong (7,900 acres) and Shining Rock (18,500 acres), both NW in the district; Bent Creek Experimental Forest (where a number of state champion trees may be observed) at the N edge of the district; the Cradle of Forestry on US-276 E of the BRP and at the Pink Beds; and Rosman Research Station, NW of Rosman. The district has numerous streams for fishing, game animals for hunting, old roads and trails for ORVs and equestrians, routes for cross-country skiing, and domes for rock climbers. (Inquire at the RS for information on native trout fishing.)

The district boundaries are N at the French Broad River near and S of Asheville, W with the Highlands District of the Nantahala National Forest, S by the Toxaway River area, and E by US-64 and NC-280. Sections are in Buncombe, Henderson, Transylvania, and Haywood counties, and through the district runs the BRP. The district is named after Pisgah Mtn (5,721 ft), now managed by the NPS. According to legend the peak was named after the Biblical mtn where Moses saw the "promised land" by the Rev. James Hall, an Indian-fighting Presbyterian chaplain who was in the area in 1776 with Gen. Griffith Rutherford's expedition against the Cherokee. Another legend is that George Newton, a Presbyterian teacher-minister gave it the name. The district originated when George W. Vanderbilt acquired more than 125,000 acres upon which was constructed Biltmore Estate, a reproduction of a sixteenth-century French chateau. His vast forests, which included Mt Pisgah (earlier owned by Thomas Clingman, for whom Clingmans Dome is named), were first managed by conservationist Gifford Pinchot and later by Carl A. Schenck, the famous German forester. It was Schenck who established the Biltmore Forest School in 1898, the birthplace of scientific forestry in America (see *Cradle of Forestry Trail* in this section). After Vanderbilt's death in 1914, his heirs sold tracts of the forest in 1917 to the U.S. government for forest preservation.

• ADDRESS AND ACCESS: District Ranger, Pisgah Ranger District, USFS, 1001 Pisgah Highway, Pisgah Forest, NC 28768, tel: 704-877-3350. Access is 1.6 mi W on US-276 from the jct of US-276/64 and NC-280, N of Brevard.

## ▶ COURTHOUSE CREEK AREA
### (Transylvania County)

*Courthouse Creek Trail (USFS #128)*    **190**

- LENGTH AND DIFFICULTY: 1.8 mi, strenuous (elev change 1,382 ft)

- TRAILHEAD AND DESCRIPTION: There are three accesses to FR-140: (1) From the jct of the BRP in Beech Gap and NC-215 descend E 6.6 mi on NC-215 to Courthouse Creek Rd (FR-140); turn L. (2) From US-64 and NC-215 jct in Rosman drive N 10.2 mi on NC-215; turn R. (3) From US-276 (3.5 mi NW of RS) turn L on Davidson Creek Rd (FR-475), which becomes McColl Rd (SR-1327), for 8 mi to NC-215. Turn R and drive 2.6 mi to FR-140; turn R. Follow gravel FR-140 for 0.9 mi, veer L, and continue 3 mi to a parking area at the road's end. The trail is unsigned and unblazed. Ascend steeply upstream, L, by cascades and flumes. Cross the scenic stream twice. There are remnants of an old RR grade at 0.5 mi. At 0.6 mi bear R at creek's fork, and at 0.8 mi ascend steeply L of a large cascade. Through a rocky and rough gorge, climb to the jct of an unmarked trail at 1.7 mi (used by mtn climbers to the Devil's Courthouse wall), turn L, and ascend to the Devil's Courthouse parking overlook at BRP mp 422.4. Vegetation on the trail includes dense fetterbush and rhododendron, black cohosh, birch, buckeye, white snakeroot, oak, and red spruce. (*USGS-FS Map:* Sam Knob)

*Summey Cove Trail (USFS #129)*    **191**

- LENGTH AND DIFFICULTY: 2.1 mi, moderate

- SPECIAL FEATURES: Courthouse Falls, wildflowers

- TRAILHEAD AND DESCRIPTION: Follow the same directions described above for access to *Courthouse Creek Trail,* except follow FR-140 for 3.1 mi (0.8 mi before road's end) and park on the R. The trail is unsigned and unblazed. Hike downstream, at the bridge, on an old road. At 0.2 mi, L, is a narrow path (with sections of steps) that descends 0.1 mi to a pool at the scenic

Courthouse Falls. Continue on the old road to campsites at Mill Station Creek at 0.5 mi; turn L, cross the creek. Ascend in a forest of poplar, basswood, hemlock, and buffalo nut. Curve R at the ridgeline at 1 mi and descend gently to good campsites in Summey Cove at 1.3 mi. Cross the stream and ascend Big Fork Ridge; descend in a hardwood cove with numerous wildflowers, including orange fringe orchids that bloom in mid-August. Arrive at NC-215, the S trailhead, at 2.1 mi. (It is 5.4 mi R to Beech Gap at the BRP, and 1.2 mi L to FR-140.)

## ▶ DAVIDSON RIVER AREA
### (Transylvania County)

The Davidson River Area includes the drainage of the Davidson River and Looking Glass and Avery creeks, which flow into the river from the N. A popular area, it has three campgrounds (two are group camps) and two picnic areas. The RS, Schenck Job Corps Camp, Sliding Rock, and the U.S. Fish Hatchery on the Davidson River are here. Also here is the Davidson River Rec Area, the district's largest family campground with 161 sites (56 of which are shaded by forest) for tents, RVs, and motorhomes. There are grills, tables, group water sources, flush toilets, and hot showers (but no hook-ups). Activities are mainly hiking and fishing. A fee campground, it is open usually from the last week in March to the middle of December. It serves as an excellent base camp for day hikes. For example, the *North Slope Loop Trail* (USFS #359) is an access to the *Art Loeb Trail* (which ascends to the Shining Rock Wilderness Area) and to the *Exercise Trail*, which connects with the *Black Mtn Trail* for connections to the Pink Beds and South Mills River areas.

The *North Slope Loop Trail* begins at a parking area 0.1 mi L, after the main campground entrance. Orange-blazed, the 3.3-mi easy treadway passes the amphitheater to an old timber road. It weaves in and out of coves on the N side of the North Slope Ridge. Hardwoods and wildflowers are dominant. At 1.5 mi cross a small stream and jct with a 0.5-mi spur, L, that ascends steeply to connect with the *Art Loeb Trail* in Neil Gap.

Turn R, downstream, and at 1.9 mi turn R on an old RR grade. Jct with the *Exercise Trail* at the English Chapel at 2.8 mi and parallel the Davidson River in a forest of hemlock and rhododendron and mixed hardwoods. Return to the point of origin at 3.3 mi.                                                              **192**

• ACCESS: From the jct of US-276/64 and NC-280 (N of Brevard) drive 1.2 mi NW on US-276 and turn L at the campground sign.

• SUPPORT FACILITIES: At the access jct listed above there is a motel, restaurant, camping and fishing supplies, laundromat, svc sta, and grocery. Shopping centers and other services are in Brevard.

**Farlow Gap Trail** *(5.2 mi; USFS #106);* **Lanning Ridge Trail** *(2.3 mi; USFS #330)*                                        **193–194**

• LENGTH AND DIFFICULTY: 7.5 mi combined, moderate to strenuous (elev change 1,924 ft)

• SPECIAL FEATURES: cascades for sliding, Shuck Ridge Creek waterfalls

• TRAILHEAD AND DESCRIPTION: From the RS go 3.5 mi W on US-276, turn L on Davidson River Rd (FR-475), and go 4.1 mi to FR-137, R, and park. Cross the cement bridge at the pool and sunbathing rocks. At 0.1 mi turn L off the main road. Follow upstream to the site of a former fish hatchery and fork in the trail. The L route is near the river with campsites, pools, and sliding rocks. The R route follows an old RR grade and rejoins the other trail at 1.2 mi at a pool and campsite. Turn R to another RR grade; jct with the *Lanning Ridge Trail,* R, at 1.8 mi. (The *Lanning Ridge Trail* slopes S of Lanning Ridge on an old logging road to cross a creek at 1.2 mi. It descends to jct with *Cove Creek/Caney Bottom Trail* at 2.3 mi. Because of timbering the trail may have relocations.) Continue 250 ft upstream on the blue-blazed trail and rock-hop the Right Fork of the Davidson River. Ascend gradually on an old road and cross the Fork River Ridge Creek at 3.3 mi. Curve around Daniel Ridge and ascend to the top of scenic Shuck Ridge Creek waterfall at 4.1 mi. Ascend steeply to pass an old mica mine at 4.6 mi and reach Farlow Gap and jct with the *Art Loeb Trail* at 5.2 mi. The lower elev of the trail has hemlock, poplar, rhododendron, locust, and fetterbush, and the higher elev has maple, oak, and birch. Backtrack, or take the road L. Follow FR-229 for 1.6 mi to a parking area and continue another 2.3 mi to Gloucester Gap and jct with FR-475. Turn L and arrive at point of origin at 6.2 mi (loop of 11.2 mi). (*USGS-FS Map:* Shining Rock)

### *Looking Glass Rock Trail (USFS #114)*      195

• LENGTH AND DIFFICULTY: 6.2 mi round-trip, strenuous (elev change 1,369 ft)

• SPECIAL FEATURES: scenic granite dome, rock climbing

• TRAILHEAD AND DESCRIPTION: From the jct of US-276 and FR-475, go 0.4 mi on FR-475 to a parking area, R. Ascend steadily on the yellow-blazed trail that has numerous switchbacks for the first 1.8 mi. A frequently used trail, it is eroded in sections on the steep E slope. Pass through a mixed hardwood forest with scattered Carolina hemlock (*Tsuga caroliniana*) and an understory of laurel. At 2.7 mi arrive at the edge of the N face; ascend to the highest point and trail terminus (3,969 ft) at 3.1 mi. Here is the NW face with magnificent views of the Pisgah National Forest and the BRP areas. The dome is not protected with guard rails and is dangerous when wet or icy. Backtrack. (*USGS-FS Map:* Shining Rock)

### *Case Camp Ridge Trail (USFS #119)*      196

• LENGTH AND DIFFICULTY: 3.4 mi round-trip, strenuous (elev change 1,100 ft)

• TRAILHEAD AND DESCRIPTION: From the RS go W on US-276 8.6 mi, turn L on Headwaters Rd (FR-475B), and proceed 0.8 mi to Case Ridge Gap for parking. Ascend R on the blue-blazed *Case Camp Ridge Trail* through a forest of oak, laurel, hemlock, locust, buckberry, and blueberry to a gap at 0.2 mi (avoid the old road, L). At 0.5 mi reach the ridgeline where there are excellent views of Looking Glass Rock when the leaves are off the trees. Ascend on switchbacks, pass ruins of an old house at 1.3 mi, and arrive at BRP mp 415.9. Backtrack. (*USGS-FS Map:* Shining Rock)

**Cat Gap Trail** (*4.7 mi; USFS #120*); **Butter Gap Trail** (*2.7 mi; USFS #123*)                    **197–198**

- LENGTH AND DIFFICULTY: 7.4 mi combined, moderate

- TRAILHEAD AND DESCRIPTION: At jct of US-276 and FR-475, go 2 mi on FR-475 to the U.S. Fish Hatchery, L, and to the parking area. (Visitors are welcome at the hatchery where 60,000 trout are raised annually.) At the restroom begin the orange-blazed *Cat Gap Trail* across Cedar Rock Creek on a gated road bridge. Bear R on this frequently used trail in a forest of hardwoods, hemlock, and running cedar. Cross a footbridge at 0.3 mi. Ascend, pass R of cascades and pools. Jct with the blue-blazed *Butter Gap Trail,* R, at 0.8 mi in Picklesimer Fields.

(The *Butter Gap Trail* follows an old RR grade, crosses Grogan Creek at 0.4 mi, and follows upstream on the W side through a forest of mixed hardwoods, hemlock, and rhododendron. It passes cascades, and at 1.1 mi a waterfall. At 2.1 mi the trail becomes steep at the headwaters of the creek, and at 2.7 mi it reaches the trail terminus and jct with the *Art Loeb Trail* at Butter Gap. Here are multiple trails and roads. The spur trail, L, ascends 0.5 mi to Cedar Rock Mtn with outstanding views. Ahead the *Art Loeb Trail* descends 0.2 mi to an A-frame shelter, and 2.3 mi farther to *Cat Gap Trail* at Cat Gap for a loop of 8.5 mi to the fish hatchery.)

Continue on the *Cat Gap Trail* among blueberries, yellow root, spice bush, white pine, and oak. At 1.9 mi jct, L, with a blue-blazed spur to Horse Cove Gap. Ascend to Cat Gap (3,350 ft) at 2.5 mi and jct with the *Art Loeb Trail.* (See description above for loop option on the *Butter Gap Trail.*) Turn L and descend on the former *Horse Cove Trail.* After 0.3 mi jct, L, with the blue-blazed spur mentioned above. Ahead is an unblazed

0.6-mi spur to scenic views from John Rock, a monolith that is part of a 435-acre "special interest area." (It is proposed for the National Register of Landmarks.) Turn R, descend in a forest of poplar, hickory, and wildflowers. Cross a small stream, reach an old RR grade at 3.8 mi, and pass through a fern glen by campsites. Exit in a field E of the parking area at 4.6 mi. (*USGS-FS Map:* Shining Rock)

### *Black Mountain Trail* (USFS #127)  199–204

- LENGTH AND DIFFICULTY: 8.7 mi, strenuous (elev change 2,086 ft)

- CONNECTING TRAILS:
  *(Starnes Branch Trail)*
  *(MST)*
  *Pressley Cove Trail* (1.4 mi, strenuous, elev change 1,035 ft)
  *(Turkey Pen Trail)*
  *Buckhorn Gap Trail* (4.1 mi; USFS #103, moderate)
  *Clawhammer Cove Trail* (4.5 mi; easy to moderate)
  *Avery Creek Trail* (3.2 mi; USFS #327, strenuous, elev change 1,340 ft)
  *Buckwheat Knob Trail* (1.5 mi; USFS #122, moderate)

- SPECIAL FEATURE: views from Clawhammer Mtn

- TRAILHEAD AND DESCRIPTION: Using the *Black Mtn Trail,* connecting trails, and short sections of Avery Creek Rd (FR-477), there are at least six loop options. Examples are the *Buckwheat Knob Trail* and FR-477 (4.6 mi); *Avery Creek Trail* and *Buckhorn Gap Trail* (6.7 mi); and *Pressley Cove Trail, Clawhammer Cove Trail,* and FR-477 (8.4 mi). Because of the White Pine Group Camp Area, gates are locked May to September from dusk to 7 am on FR-477 between US-276 (0.5 mi W of RS) and the last bridge crossing of Avery Creek (1.9 mi). Affected are S trailheads of *Clawhammer Cove* and *Pressley Cove* and E trailhead of *Bennett Gap.*

On US-276, 0.2 mi E of the RS, park outside the fence at the work center. Follow the trail sign upstream on an old timber road. At 0.2 mi jct, R, with the *Starnes Branch Trail* at another timber road. (The *Starnes Branch Trail* makes a 2-mi loop and returns to the work center. It is described below with the *Sycamore Cove Trail*.) At 0.3 mi jct, R, with the *MST* near Thrift Creek. (The *MST* goes R on a separate trail to join the *Art Loeb Trail* at Davidson River, but from here it runs jointly on the *Black Mtn Trail* for 7.8 mi before leaving it on the N side of Rich Mtn ridge. See Chapter 16.) Continue ascent in Thrift Cove on the old timber road, cross Thrift Creek four times, and at 1.4 mi pass an old road, R (the former *Thrift Cove Loop Trail* that connected with *Starnes Branch Trail*). At 1.8 mi the road becomes more of a path. Reach Hickory Knob at 2.4 mi, and descend to Pressley Gap at 2.9 mi. Here are two old timber roads, R, and L is N trailhead of *Pressley Cove Trail*.

(The orange-blazed *Pressley Cove Trail* descends in a tunnel of laurel. Cross a small stream at 0.4 mi, descend steeply on a S slope with scenic views of the cove, L. Pass through hemlock and beech. Reach a grazing field at Avery Creek Rd [FR-477] at 1.4 mi. It is 126 yd, L, to the bridge over Avery Creek, 1.4 mi to US-276, and 0.5 mi, L, on US-276 to the RS. Right on FR-477 it is 0.3 mi to a parking area at Clawhammer Rd [FR-5058], R. It can be used for a loop to the *Black Mtn Trail* at Buckhorn Gap.)

From Pressley Gap follow the ridge on sections of old logging roads, and at 3.9 mi jct with *Turkey Pen Gap Trail*, R. Here is a small spring in a forest of large oak and hickory with beds of hayscented and cinnamon ferns. (The *Turkey Pen Gap Trail* follows a ridgeline E for 5.5 mi to Turkey Pen Gap and FR-297 off NC-280.) Ascend to skirt W of Black Mtn peak in arbors of rhododendron and laurel to rejoin the ridge at 4.2 mi. Descend steeply and follow a narrow ridge to reach a rock overhang at 4.4 mi. Ascend to Clawhammer Mtn (4,140 ft) at 4.6 mi. From rock outcroppings are superb views of Pilot Mtn, Looking Glass Rock, and NW to Pisgah Ridge. Blueberries, rhododendron, and galax are prominent. Descend steeply to Buckhorn Gap (3,520 ft) to cross the orange-blazed *Buckhorn Gap Trail* in an old RR grade cut at 5.7 mi.

(The R [E] section of the *Buckhorn Gap Trail* follows the old road 1.7 mi to a horseshoe curve in South Mills River Rd [FR-476] that leads in either direction to *South Mills River Trail*, 0.8

mi L, 2.6 mi R. But the *Buckhorn Gap Trail* can also follow the road L for 110 yd where it abruptly leaves the road, R, into a laurel thicket, and follows Grassy Ridge for 0.9 mi down to jct with the *South Mills River Trail* at Clawhammer Creek [see *South Mills River Trail* described below]. The L [W] section of the *Buckhorn Gap Trail* descends on a footpath to cross a gravel logging road at 0.1 mi and into a sapling grove by a stream to jct with Clawhammer Cove Rd [FR-5058] at 0.3 mi. Turn L and follow the road for 0.5 mi to a sharp R at a sign. Descend to Henry Branch, curve L, and parallel the stream to the trail's end at Avery Creek and jct with the blue-blazed *Avery Creek Trail* at 2.4 mi. On the *Avery Creek Trail* it is 2 mi, R, to Club Gap and the *Black Mtn Trail;* L, it is 1.2 mi to Avery Creek Rd [FR-477]. Also out of Buckhorn Gap is the *Clawhammer Cove Trail* used mainly by equestrians. It follows L on the old RR grade in a gentle descent for 0.4 mi to join a more recent logging road, the Clawhammer Cove Rd [FR-5058]. Turn L. At 0.7 mi, near a huge hemlock, the *Buckhorn Gap Trail* joins the road for 0.5 mi and leaves, R, at a sign. Continue on the road through sections of timber harvesting for 3.3 mi more. Exit at a gate and parking area in a field near Avery Creek Rd [FR-477]. It is 0.3 mi L to *Pressley Cove Trail,* L, and 126 yd ahead to the road bridge over Avery Creek.)

Continue on the *Black Mtn Trail* up log steps from Buckhorn Gap. After 0.3 mi, R, is the Buckhorn Gap Shelter with bunk beds. A spring is nearby. Ascend on the ridge. Pass coves with cinnamon ferns and ascend on switchbacks to SW slope of Soapstone Ridge. At 6.6 mi reach the crest of Rich Mtn in an oak-hickory forest. At 6.8 mi, L, are a rock outcropping and views of the Avery Creek drainage. The *MST* leaves the trail at 7 mi, R, near a large oak, and descends to the Pink Beds (see Chapter 16). Continue on an old woods road where woodland sunflowers, mountain mint, and wood betony are commonplace. Descend to Club Gap at 7.8 mi, and multiple trail jcts: *Black Mtn Trail,* R (formerly the *Club Gap Trail*); *Buckwheat Knob Trail* ahead; and *Avery Creek Trail,* L.

(The blue-blazed *Avery Creek Trail* descends steeply on a W slope in a hardwood forest. It passes under a powerline at 0.4 mi and 0.9 mi, and follows switchbacks to an old RR grade near Avery Creek at 1.1 mi. In a forest of mixed hemlock, poplar, and rhododendron, it passes excellent campsites by the creek-side. At 2.2 mi jct with the *Buckhorn Gap Trail,* L. [The *Buckhorn Gap Trail,* described above, crosses the creek to a grassy meadow with sparse poplar and locust.] The *Avery Creek Trail* continues downstream, first as a footpath and then as an old graded road for 1 mi to its end at a parking lot on Avery Creek Rd [FR-477]. The road L is 0.8 mi to a jct L with Clawhammer Cove Rd [FR-5058]; the road R ascends 2.3 mi to Bennett Gap and jct R with *Buckwheat Knob Trail.* Another 2.3 mi on the road leads to US-276 near the Cradle of Forestry.)

(The yellow-blazed *Buckwheat Knob Trail* ascends from Club Gap, passes under a powerline, and reaches Buckwheat Knob at 0.5 mi. Descend to a shallow gap, cross another knob, and descend partially on a jeep road to the trail's end in Bennett Gap and Avery Creek Rd [FR-477]. Across the road begins the white-blazed *Bennett Gap Trail,* described below. To the R on FR-477 it is 2.3 mi to US-276 near the Cradle of Forestry, and L it is 2.3 mi to the *Avery Creek Trail* parking area.)

The *Black Mtn Trail* descends R on an old woods road to a fork at 8.6 mi for trail-end options: a reverse L for 0.2 mi on an old road to a parking area at FR-477 (0.3 mi from US-276), or ahead for 0.1 mi on a svc road with tall white pine by the work center to the gated and fee entrance of the Cradle of Forestry. Vehicles cannot be parked overnight at the Cradle of Forestry parking area. (*USGS-FS Maps:* Pisgah Forest, Shining Rock)

### *Bennett Gap Trail* (2.9 mi; USFS #138); *Coontree Loop Trail* (3.7 mi; USFS #144)                                    **205–206**

• LENGTH AND DIFFICULTY: 6.6 mi combined, strenuous (elev change 1,000 ft)

• TRAILHEAD AND DESCRIPTION: From the RS go W on US-276 for 3 mi to park at the Coontree Picnic Area parking lot, L. Cross the road to the *Coontree Loop Trail* entrance. Follow up-stream through ironwood and other hardwoods. At 0.2 mi is the loop fork. If taking the R prong, follow an old road by a stream through ferns, wildflowers, and rhododendron. Ascend to Coontree Gap (2,960 ft) at 1.2 mi and jct with the white-blazed *Bennett Gap Trail,* R and L. The *Bennett Gap Trail* goes 0.9 mi R through a forest of hardwoods and hemlock on a N slope to Avery Creek Rd (FR-477) at a road bridge. (It is 1.4 mi downstream on FR-477 to US-276, 0.5 mi W of the RS. It is 140 yd L on FR-477 to the *Pressley Gap Trail* trailhead, R, and described above.) The *Bennett Gap Trail* runs L jointly with the *Coontree Loop Trail* for 0.5 mi, where the *Coontree Loop Trail* goes L. It descends steeply on switchbacks and follows Coontree Creek downstream to rejoin the loop at 3.5 mi. The *Bennett Gap Trail* continues on the ridgeline, ascends the E slope of Coontree Mtn, dips gently to Saddle Gap, and arrives at its W terminus in Bennett Gap (3,516 ft) on FR-477. (Across the road is the S terminus of the *Buckwheat Knob Trail,* which connects with the *Black Mtn Trail.*) (It is 3.5 mi R on FR-477 to the SE end of *Bennett Gap Trail,* and 2.3 mi L on FR-477 to US-276 near the Cradle of Forestry.) (*USGS-FS Maps:* Pisgah Forest, Shining Rock)

**Sycamore Cove Trail** *(1.9 mi);* **Starnes Branch Loop Trail** *(2.3 mi; USFS #143)*                                             **207–208**

• LENGTH AND DIFFICULTY: 3.9 mi combined, moderate

• TRAILHEAD AND DESCRIPTION: Access to the *Sycamore Cove Trail* is on US-276, 0.3 mi W from the Sycamore Flats Picnic Area and 150 ft E from the roadside parking by the Davidson River. Ascend gradually on a blue-blazed trail in a forest of hemlock, beech, and poplar. Cross the stream six times and turn L at 0.4 mi on an old timber road. Enter groves of laurel and rhododendron beginning at 1.2 mi. At 1.9 mi the trail ends at a jct with the blue-blazed *Starnes Branch Loop Trail.*

The *Starnes Branch Loop Trail* begins at a parking area near a dumpster on US-276, 124 ft W of the Davidson River Campground sign. Follow a driveway E 0.1 mi to a work-center residence. Enter the forest at a large black walnut tree. Cross the *MST* in a hemlock grove after 0.2 mi. (It is 0.6 mi R on the *MST* to the roadside parking on US-276 described above.) Cross

Starnes Branch at 0.7 mi and at 0.9 mi jct R with the *Sycamore Cove Trail*. Follow the *Starnes Branch Loop Trail* L on an old unmarked seeded road. Curve L to a ridge and follow a wildlife road L on the return through wildlife grazing fields. Cross the *MST* at 2 mi. Descend to jct with the *Black Mtn Trail*, R and L, at 2.3 mi. Turn L and follow the *Black Mtn Trail* past the work center to the parking area at the dumpster for another 0.3 mi. *USGS-FS Map:* Pisgah Forest; 1981 map incorrect)

## *Art Loeb Trail* (30 mi; USFS #146)          **209–213**

- LENGTH AND DIFFICULTY: Section I, 12.2 mi, strenuous; Section II, 7 mi, strenuous; Section III, 7 mi, moderate; Section IV, 3.8 mi, moderate to strenuous (elev change 4,084 ft)

- CONNECTING TRAILS:
  *(North Slope Loop Trail)*
  *(Cat Gap Trail)*
  *(Butter Gap Trail)*
  *(Farlow Gap Trail)*
  *(MST)*
  *Black Balsam Ridge Trail* (0.6 mi, easy)
  *Ivestor Gap Trail* (4.3 mi; USFS #101, easy)
  *(Graveyard Ridge Trail)*
  *(Shining Creek Trail)*
  *(Old Butt Knob Trail)*
  *Cold Mtn Trail* (1.4 mi; USFS #141, strenuous, elev change 1,025 ft)

- SPECIAL FEATURES: Pilot Mtn, Black Balsam Knob, Shining Rock Wilderness Area, geology, vistas

- TRAILHEAD AND DESCRIPTION: The *Art Loeb Trail*, designated a national recreation trail in 1979, is named in honor of the late Arthur J. Loeb, a hiking enthusiast and dedicated leader of the Carolina Mountain Club. The trail is the district's longest and most challenging. Its elev gain from the Davidson River to Black Balsam Knob is 4,084 ft, or 2,926 ft if ascended from the Daniel Boone Boy Scouts Camp. It undulates between cols and peaks with rapturous vistas. Although the full trail can require much exertion if backpacked S to N, it is divided into four sections with connecting or loop trails to allow for modest excursions and easier vehicle shuttle. For the first 18 mi the white-blazed *MST* jointly follows the trail that continues to be blazed either with yellow vertical bars or the distinctive yellow blaze of a hiker silhouette. It is rarely marked in its passage through the Shining Rock Wilderness Area. The trail passes through an exceptional variety of hardwoods and conifers, heath gardens, wildflowers, and shrubs. Mammals common to the area are bear, deer, gray fox, red and gray squirrels, rabbit, chipmunk, and woodchuck. Among the songbirds are Carolina junco, winter wren, nuthatch, scarlet tanager, warblers, and vireos. Snow buntings are seen in the winter. Other birds in the area are hawks, owls, turkey, grouse, raven, and woodpeckers.

**Section I:** From the Pisgah Ranger Station go E 0.3 mi to the Davidson River Campground sign (1.3 mi W from US-276/64, NC-280 jct). Turn, and before the bridge turn L. Proceed 0.2 mi to the parking area near the swinging bridge. Cross the swinging bridge over the Davidson River, turn L, and follow white and yellow blazes on a river plain through bee balm, cone flowers, and virgin oak and poplar. Cross a footbridge at 0.5 mi, turn R and then L to begin an ascent W on the Shut-In Ridge. Ascend through rosebay rhododendron and reach the crest at 2.9 mi. Descend to Neil Gap at 3.3 mi and jct R with a 0.5-mi spur trail to the *North Slope Loop Trail* (which, including the spur, descends for 2 mi to the Davidson River Campground parking lot; it is described above in the Davidson Rec Area). Climb to Chestnut Knob (3,840 ft), and descend to Cat Gap and a double trail jct at 6.3 mi. (The *Cat Gap Trail* goes R [NE] for 2.2 mi to the Fish Hatchery on FR-475 [a section formerly called *Horse Cove Trail*], and the *Cat Gap Trail* goes L [NW] for 2.5 mi for a loop to the same exit.) At 6.9 mi in Sand Gap, pass the *Cedar Rock Spur Trail,* R, that ascends 0.3 mi to Cedar Rock Mtn (4,056 ft). (Cedar Rock Mtn is a partially exposed massif with exceptional views, but it can be dangerous for climbing in wet or icy weather, or on slick pine needles.) Cross a stream at 7 mi, circle S of Cedar Rock, and reach an A-frame shelter at 8.6 mi. Two streams are nearby. Ascend to Butter Gap at 8.8 mi, a jct of seven roads and trails. (*Butter Gap Trail* descends R [N] for 2.7 mi to join *Cat Gap Trail* for 0.8 mi for an exit to the Fish Hatchery on FR-475. The *Cedar Rock Spur Trail* goes R [E] for 0.5 mi to the summit.) Continue ahead, L, on the ridge through open woods of hickory, oak, maple, locust, and sourwood with an understory of buckberry. Reach the summit of Chestnut Mtn, cross FR-471 at 11.6 mi, reach the summit of Rich Mtn at 11.8 mi, and descend to Gloucester Gap (3,250 ft) and Glouces- ter Rd (FR-475) at 12.2 mi. (To the R, FR-475 descends 6.7 mi to jct with US-276, and L for 2.7 mi to jct with NC-215 via SR- 1321. Also at Gloucester Gap is FR-471, which goes SE for 8.2 mi on Cathey Creek Rd to US-64 at Selica. Another road here is FR-229, which ascends NW from Gloucester Gap for 2.5 mi to a parking area near Deep Gap.) (*USGS-FS Maps:* Pisgah Forest, Shining Rock)

**Section II:** Cross FR-475, ascend, cross FR-229 at 12.8 mi and again at 13.8 mi. Begin strenuous multiple switchbacks on Pilot Mtn and reach the summit (5,040 ft) at 14.4 mi. Vegeta- tion is chinquapin, bush honeysuckle (*Diervilla sessilifolia*), lau- rel, blueberry, and chestnut oak. Hundreds of ladybird beetles have been seen here. Views are outstanding. Descend on switchbacks through yellow birch and other hardwoods to Deep Gap, follow FR-229 for 0.1 mi, and reach an A-frame shelter at 15.2 mi. A spring is 75 yd NW of the shelter. Climb Sassafras Knob with a groundcover of galax and wood betony and an understory of laurel, mountain ash, and azalea. Descend to Farlow Gap at 16.1 mi and jct with *Farlow Gap Trail.* (The blue- blazed *Farlow Gap Trail,* described above, goes 5.2 mi down the mtn to Davidson River Rd [FR-475].) Ascend to Shuck Ridge through oak, beech, and spruce. Reach BRP mp 421.2 at 17.6 mi. Turn L on the road and go 90 yd to trail steps up an embankment. Ascend on an exceptionally steep treadway with steps to the crest and jct with the *MST*, L, at 18 mi. (The *MST* leaves the *Art Loeb Trail* here and goes 3.2 mi to NC-215 and beyond. See Chapter 16.)

On a narrow trail through fir and spruce pass Silvermine Bald and reach FR-816, the end of Section II, at 19.2 mi. To the R it is 0.8 mi to the BRP. To the L it is 0.3 mi to a water source and at 0.5 mi the Black Balsam Parking Area, a popular base for hikes deep into the Shining Rock Wilderness Area and W into the Laurel Creek drainage. From here the 0.6-mi *Black Balsam Ridge Trail* ascends to Black Balsam to jct with the *Art Loeb Trail.* The *Ivestor Trail* goes W on a broad old RR grade for 4.3 mi to jct with the *Art Loeb Trail* at Ivestor Gap and again at Shining Rock Gap. It is used more than any other access trail by hikers and backpackers to the Shining Rock Wilderness. It is also used by blueberry pickers, birders, equestrians, and hunters who are allowed use of ORVs to the wilderness boundary at Ivestor Gap from September 1 to December 31. Springs are at 0.9 mi and 1.6 mi.) (*USGS-FS Maps:* Shining Rock, Sam Knob)

**Section III:** Cross FR-816 and ascend through a heath bald area to jct L at 19.5 mi with the *Black Balsam Ridge Trail.* Reach the grassy scenic summit of Black Balsam Knob (6,214 ft), the highest peak in the district, at 19.6 mi. Continue N on the ridge to Tennent Mtn (6,046 ft) at 20.8 mi. (The mtn is named in honor of Dr. G.S. Tennent, an early leader in the Carolina Mountain Club.) Descend and follow an old road entry to Ivestor Gap and the E boundary of the Shining Rock Wilderness at 21.5 mi. (R is *Graveyard Ridge Trail,* which connects after 0.2 mi with *Greasy Cove Trail* before it goes 3.2 mi farther E to the BRP, mp 418.8.) Contact here is with the *Ivestor Trail,* which continues to parallel the W side of the ridge toward Shining Rock Gap. At 22.7 mi reach Flower Gap and skirt E of Flower Knob on an old RR bed through an arbor of beech with bush honeysuckle, purple *Habenaria* orchids, and sundrops in sunny places. A spring is R at 23.1 mi. Proceed to Shining Rock Gap at 23.3 mi, an overused camping area and trail terminal. (The *Ivestor Trail* ends here after collecting the traffic from *Fork Mtn Trail* and *Little East Fork Trail* from the W. This is the W terminus for the *Shining Creek Trail* and the *Old Butt Knob Trail,* both separately but steeply ascending from Big East Fork at US-276.) Ahead are the white quartz outcrops (less pretentious than some visitors expect, but geologically venerable) that have given the area its name. It is easily reached in 0.2 mi partially by the *Old Butt Knob Trail.* (Overuse camping has damaged the thick stands of laurel, bristly locust, fetterbush, blueberry, and fly poison). Continue the *Art Loeb Trail* on an old RR bed N of Shining Rock Gap to a spur trail R at 23.8 mi (which leads 0.5 mi to *Old Butt Knob Trail*). Reach Crawford Creek Gap at 23.9 mi, leave the old RR grade, and ascend to Stairs Mtn (5,869 ft) at 24.1 mi. Enter a red spruce grove at 24.9 mi, and pass through the scenic Narrows where painted trillium and a number of rhododendron species create color and fragrance at 25.2 mi. At 25.6 mi and 25.7 mi are two magnificent views of the W Fork of the Pigeon River Valley, Lickstone Ridge, and Great Balsam Mtn. Descend to Deep Gap, an open grassy area with scattered locust at 26.2 mi. (Ahead is the 1.4 mi *Cold Mtn Trail,* infrequently used, which ascends to a dead end on the summit of Cold Mtn [6,030 ft]. Backtracking is required.) (*USGS-FS Maps:* Cruso, Shining Rock, Sam Knob)

**Section IV:** The *Art Loeb Trail* makes a 90 turn L for its descent into the lush headwaters of Sorrell Creek. The first seepage is at 26.9 mi, and at 28 mi are cascades, campsites, and part of a copious display in a mixed hardwood forest of such wildflowers as saxifrage, umbrella leaf, lady's slipper, golden Alexander, and trillium. At 28.9 mi leave the ridgecrest of laurel and descend on switchbacks to the trail's N terminus and parking area at the S edge of the Daniel Boone Boy Scouts Camp at 30 mi. Access here is on Little East Fork Rd (SR-1129), which goes 3.8 mi downstream to NC-215 (13 mi L [S] to the BRP and 5.3 mi R [N] to US-276). (*USGS-FS Maps:* Cruso, Waynesville)

### *Moore Cove Trail* (USFS #318)        214

• LENGTH AND DIFFICULTY: 1.2 mi round-trip, easy

• TRAILHEAD AND DESCRIPTION: Go 1 mi W of Looking Glass Falls on US-276 and park near a bridge (between the highway and the creek). Hike across the stone bridge, turn R on steps, and ascend 150 ft to an old RR grade. Cross Moore Branch three times on footlogs in a rhododendron area. There are abundant wildflowers. Reach 45-ft Moore Branch cascades at 0.6 mi. Walk behind the falls. Backtrack. (*USGS-FS Map:* Shining Rock)

## *Caney Bottom Loop Trail* (USFS #361)    **215**

- LENGTH AND DIFFICULTY: 4.6 mi, easy to moderate

- TRAILHEAD AND DESCRIPTION: At the jct of US-276 and David-son River Rd (FR-475), follow FR-475 upstream (past the U.S. Fish Hatchery) for 3.5 mi to a parking area, L. Cross the road to the gated entrance road of Cove Creek Group Camp. Cross a footbridge over Cove Creek at 0.1 mi. Reach an open area at 0.4 mi and jct L with the blue-blazed *Lanning Creek Trail*. (The *Lanning Creek Trail* goes up Lanning Ridge before a turn W to jct with the *Farlow Gap Trail* at 2.3 mi. A timber cut may have altered the route.) Continue ahead on a frequently used trail, cross Cove Creek on a footbridge and enter a field at 0.6 mi. Past the field, enter a forest of hemlock, laurel, oak, and poplar and follow up Caney Bottom Creek on a blue-blazed trail. Pass waterfalls, R, at 0.9 mi. Cross a number of tributaries on foot-bridges, follow old RR grades and old roads, and reach an intersection of trails at 1.8 mi; turn L and leave Caney Bottom. At 2 mi are good campsites. At 2.4 mi cross Cove Creek on a footbridge and follow sections of old RR grades and roads to a descent at 4.1 mi at the group camp restroom. Return on the road to FR-475 at 4.6 mi. (*USGS-FS Map:* Shining Rock)

## ▶ LAKE POWHATAN RECREATION AREA
### (Buncombe County)

The Lake Powhatan Rec Area is in the Bent Creek Experi-mental Forest with a system of connecting trails. The fee camp-ground has 96 sites (no hook-ups), flush toilets, sewage dispos-al, picnic tables with grills, and central water. Lake Powhatan, fed by Bent Creek, provides swimming and fishing. The camp-ground is open from the last weekend in April to mid-Decem-ber. (Also in the area are ten state-champion big trees [white walnut, northern white and Port Orford cedar, sweet cherry, ponderosa, red and Scotch pine, spicebush, and white and Nor-way spruce], the Southeastern Forest Experiment Station, and the Western N.C. Arboretum. Information: Project Leader,

Southeastern Forest Experiment Station, Rte 3, Box 1249, Asheville, NC 28806, tel: 704-259-0331.)

• ACCESS: From the jct of I-40/26 in SW Asheville, take I-26 1.5 mi to jct with NC-191, turn L, and follow NC-191 2.1 mi to the Lake Powhatan sign, R. Go 0.3 mi on SR-3480, turn L on Wesley Branch Rd (SR-3484, which becomes FR-806), and go 3 mi. (From BRP mp 393.6, turn at the French Broad River bridge and drive 0.3 mi to NC-191; turn L and go 0.3 mi to entrance road, L.) The Experimental Station entrance is on NC-191 between the BRP and the Lake Powhatan sign.

**Homestead Trail** (1.1 mi; USFS #333); **Small Creek Trail** (0.4 mi; USFS #334); **Deerfield Loop Trail** (0.6 mi; USFS #335); **Pine Tree Loop Trail** (1.8 mi; USFS #336); **Explorer Loop Trail** (3 mi; USFS #337); **Grassy Knob Trail** (0.5; USFS #338); **Sleepy Gap Trail** (1 mi; USFS #339)          **216–222**

• LENGTH AND DIFFICULTY: 8.4 mi combined, easy to moderate

• TRAILHEAD AND DESCRIPTION: The trails are not marked or color-coded; therefore a map from the campground office may clarify the original trails and the spur trails made by hikers and campers. From the beach parking area at Lake Powhatan follow E on the *Homestead Trail* at a hiking sign, and go around the lake through a hardwood and white pine forest. Pass an area where Carl A. Schenck (see *Cradle of Forestry Trail* in this section) had a lodge from where he managed the Biltmore Forest. Cross Bent Creek at FR-480 and return around the lake at 1.1 mi. The *Small Creek Trail* is a 0.4-mi connector from the *Deerfield Loop Trail* and the *Homestead Trail*.

For the *Deerfield Loop Trail,* leave the beach parking area, follow E (but S of the *Homestead Trail*), and meander through a mixed forest and a wildlife field to a jct with *Pine Tree Loop Trail* at 0.6 mi. Turn L and at 0.9 mi jct L with the *Grassy Knob Trail.* (The *Grassy Knob Trail* crosses South Ridge Rd [FR-479M] and ascends on a ridge 0.5 mi to jct with the *Shut-In Trail/MST.*) After another 0.6 mi jct with the *Explorer Loop Trail,* but follow a new trail, R, on the S side of Bent Creek in a return to the campground beach area at 2.4 mi.

From the trail sign on Bent Creek Gap Rd (FR-479) parking area, follow the *Explorer Loop Trail* sign across Bent Creek, and at the fork, turn L. Cross Beaten Branch, jct L with the *Pine Tree Loop Trail,* cross Beaten Branch again, and jct L with *Sleepy Gap Trail* at 0.5 mi. (The *Sleepy Gap Trail* ascends an E slope, crosses South Ridge Rd [FR-479M] and ascends in a forest of hardwoods and rhododendron for 1 mi to Sleepy Gap at BRP mp 397.3 and jct with the *Shut-In Trail/MST*.) Continue on the *Explorer Loop Trail* to a jct with Cold Knob Rd (FR-479H) at 1.7 mi. Turn R on FR-479H, and after 0.4 mi (before the gate) leave the road and parallel Bent Creek to the point of origin after a loop of 3 mi. (*USGS-FS Map:* Dunsmore Mtn, Skyland)

## ▶ MIDDLE PRONG WILDERNESS AREA
### (Haywood County)

In 1984, a wild, remote, and rugged 7,900-acre section of the district officially became the Middle Prong Wilderness Area. Its boundary is NC-215 (E), the BRP (S and W), and near the toe of Big Beartrail Ridge (N). In the center of the wilderness is long Fork Ridge, whose waters drain E into the W Fork of the Pigeon River and W into the Middle Prong of the W Fork at Sunburst. Sunburst was a lumber town for the Champion Paper Company in the early 1900s. It had more than ten camps harvesting the huge hemlock, chestnut, and poplar. Although the forest is recovering, parts of old RR and skid grades and logging equipment remain scattered in the Middle Prong area. Wildlife includes bear, deer, red and gray squirrel, turkey, and grouse, and Middle Prong has native brook trout. Rich lush coves are full of wildflowers, and large sweet blueberries are prominent on the grassy meadows of Fork Ridge and its E escarpment. Old roads and old trails provide numerous manway options, but none of them are blazed, marked, or signed. Two of the longer and better known trails are described below. Access to them is easy, but once in the wilderness it is advisable to have a topo map and compass or hike with experienced companions familiar with the similar ridges and coves. A developed base camp can be Sunburst Rec Area. It has campsites with water and toilets and a picnic area.

• ACCESS: Sunburst Rec Area is on NC-215, 8.6 mi W from the BRP, and 9.6 mi S from US-276 near Woodrow. Access on the BRP is described below.

• SUPPORT FACILITIES: The nearest groceries and services are in Woodrow, with full provisions and services 5 mi W from Woodrow to Waynesville.

### Haywood Gap Trail (5.8 mi; USFS #142); Buckeye Gap Trail (4 mi; USFS #126)                                                    223–225

• LENGTH AND DIFFICULTY: 13.8 mi, combined and round-trip, strenuous (elev change 2,468 ft)

• TRAILHEAD AND DESCRIPTION: From the S end of Sunburst Campground hike 1.6 mi upstream W of Middle Prong on FR-97 and ascend two switchbacks. On the third major curve leave FR-97, L, and follow a primitive route across Little Beartrap Branch. Enter the wilderness boundary to campsites near the mouth of Big Beartrap Branch, R, at 2.7 mi. Rock-hop the Middle Prong at an area once called the "cattle crossing." Cross Camp Two Branch and at 3.4 mi jct with the *Buckeye Gap Trail.* At this point either trail can be ascended to jct with the *MST,* which can be used for a connector to return here after 8 mi. If taking *Haywood Gap Trail,* cross the Grassy Ridge Branch and follow the main stream for 2.2 mi to Sweetwater Spring (W side of trail). From here it is 0.2 mi to Haywood Gap (5,225 ft) and BRP mp 426.5. Turn L on the white-blazed *MST,* go 1.8 mi on a graded footpath to jct with the *Buckeye Gap Trail* on an old RR grade. (The *Buckeye Gap Trail* access here is out 0.2 mi across a small stream to Rough Butt Bald Overlook [mp 425.4], elev 5,300 ft. If vehicle is left on the BRP overnight, the BRP ranger should be informed at tel: 704-456-9530, weekdays, 9–4:30.) Turn L on the *Buckeye Gap Trail* and follow jointly with the *MST* for 1 mi where Buckeye Creek is crossed in a rhododendron grove. The forest also has birch, beech, cherry, maple, and scattered fir and spruce. After 75 yd ahead, the *MST* turns sharply R up the slope, but the *Buckeye Gap Trail* continues on the old RR grade with numerous seeps. Descend gradually and after 1.5 mi from the *MST* turn abruptly L off the old RR grade. (For exploratory hikers who wish to follow part of the old and obscure 7-mi *Green Mtn Trail* [USFS #113] bushwhack R [E] approx 0.4 mi up to scenic Fork Ridge anywhere along the 1.5-mi stretch after leaving the *MST*.) Descend steeply to cross Grassy Ridge Branch and rejoin the *Haywood Gap Trail* at 4 mi. Turn R downstream and return to the Sunburst Rec Area. (*USGS-FS Map:* Sam Knob)

## ▶ NORTH MILLS RIVER AREA
### (Henderson County)

*Big Creek Trail (4.9 mi; USFS #102); Spencer Branch Trail (2.5 mi; USFS #140); Fletcher Creek Trail (2.4 mi; USFS #350); Middle Fork Trail (1.8 mi; USFS #352); Trace Ridge Trail (3.1 mi; USFS #354)*  **226–230**

• TOTAL LENGTH AND DIFFICULTY: 17.5 combined or round-trip, easy to strenuous (elev change 2,400 ft)

• TRAILHEAD AND DESCRIPTION: From the jct of NC-191/280 in the community of Mills River, drive N for 0.9 mi to North Mills River Rd (SR-1345), L (W) at the North Mills River Rec Area sign. Drive 5 mi on SR-1345 to the edge of the North Mills River Rec area campground and turn R on Wash Creek Rd (FR-5000). Drive 2 mi, turn L on Hendersonville Reservoir Rd (FR-142), and after 0.5 mi reach gated roads and parking area. From here the five trails spread out NW to the North Mills River watershed.

The unsigned, unblazed *Trace Ridge Trail* begins N (R of the gated FR-5097) on an old forest road used as a horse and hiking trail. Follow a dry ridgeline through oak, maple, white pine, dogwood, locust, laurel, and azalea. Descend to a gap at 2.7 mi and jct with the *Spencer Branch Trail,* L. Ascend steeply and at 3.1 mi reach BRP mp 401.8 (0.1 mi W of Beaverdam Gap Overlook). Backtrack. (At *Spencer Branch Trail* is a return option that follows downstream for 2.5 mi to the Hendersonville Reservoir and another 1.5 mi on FR-142 to the parking area.)

Access to the *Fletcher Creek Trail* is on gated FR-142 (L of the gated FR-5097). Descend to the N edge of the North Fork of Mills River and at 1 mi pass cascades of Long Branch, R. At 1.2 mi is the *Fletcher Creek Trail* trailhead, R. (Ahead on FR-142 it is 0.3 mi to the jct of *Spencer Branch Trail* and *Big Creek Trail* at the Hendersonville Reservoir.) Turn R off FR-142 on the un-marked *Fletcher Creek Trail* (an old road) and ascend. Achieve a minor crest on the slopes of Coffee Pot Mtn after 0.6 mi. Begin slight descent and reach the confluence of Middle Fork and Fletcher Creek at 1.1 mi at good campsites. Cross Fletcher Creek and bear L a few yd on *Spencer Branch Trail* before turning R up Middle Fork on an old RR grade. After 0.5 mi cross Middle Fork, enter wildlife clearings at 0.6 mi and 1 mi. Cross a new logging road and rock-hop Middle Fork at 1.5 mi and 1.7 mi. At 1.9 mi the trail fades out in upper flats. Backtrack to *Spencer Branch Trail*.

*Spencer Branch Trail* goes downstream for 0.9 mi to FR-142 and it goes upstream conjointly with the *Fletcher Creek Trail* for 0.2 mi. (If going downstream, after 0.6 mi rock-hop Fletcher Creek, pass a large rock overhang, L, at 0.7 mi, and jct with *Big Creek Trail* at the reservoir at 0.9 mi.) Go upstream and after 0.2 mi the trails fork. *Fletcher Creek Trail* goes L, across Fletcher Creek, and follows an old RR grade (now a 4WD track) in a forest of hardwoods, hemlock, and rhododendron. Pass two wildlife clearings and end near a logging area where the trail fades out at FR-5097 after 1.1 mi from the *Spencer Branch Trail*. Backtrack. *Spencer Branch Trail* continues upstream, E of Fletcher Creek, but crosses the stream a number of times before crossing FR-5097 at 0.6 mi. After another 0.5 mi upstream veer R and ascend for 0.3 mi to jct with the *Trace Ridge Trail* described above.

To reach *Big Creek Trail,* follow FR-142 1.5 mi from the parking area, go around the N side of the Hendersonville Reservoir, and jct with *Spencer Branch Trail* described above. Follow around the back side of the reservoir and go upstream (SW and W) on an old RR grade. Numerous good campsites are along the route in a forest of birch, poplar, oak, and rhododendron. At 2.5 mi cross Bee Branch and begin an ascent on an old timber road on a S slope with switchbacks. At 3.5 mi follow a footpath, steep in sections, among oak, maple, laurel, and locust along Little Pisgah Ridge. Reach the trail's W terminus at BRP mp 403.1 at the S end of Little Pisgah Ridge Tunnel. Backtrack, or arrange a vehicle shuttle. (The unmarked trail may be difficult to locate from the BRP, but cues are to cross a landfill E for 0.1 mi to steps and a more obvious trail route.) (*USGS-FS Map:* Dunsmore Mtn)

• SUPPORT FACILITIES: The North Mills River Rec Area has a campground with tent/trailer sites (no hook-ups), flush toilets, picnic tables, and sewage disposal. Facilities are usually open from the last of April to the middle of December. Groceries, restaurant, svc sta, and other supplies are at Mills River, 6 mi E from the campground.

## ▶ PINK BEDS AREA
### (Transylvania County)

The Pink Beds is an unusual forested upland bog with an average altitude of 3,250 ft. It extends more than 5 mi between the E slopes of the Pisgah Ridge and the W slopes of Soapstone Ridge and Dividing Ridge. The headwaters of the South Fork of Mills River converge here. Its name most likely has come from the dense pink rosebay rhododendron and laurel common throughout the area. Other sources may be the pink rock formerly quarried in the region or the masses of wild pink phlox among the fern meadows. A gravel forest road and trails give access into its floral displays and near its numerous serpentine streams. On US-276 is the Cradle of Forestry Interpretive and Education Center and nearby is Pink Beds Picnic Area. Yellow Gap Road (FR-1206) from US-276 to North Mills River Rec Area goes through the Pink Beds. Trails that connect with FR-1206 for 8.7 mi between US-276 and Yellow Gap are described in this section.

Two loop trails originate at the Education Center's main building. The *Biltmore Forest Campus Trail* (USFS #006) is a 0.9-mi easy, paved, national-recreation loop trail that provides an historic tour of the buildings of the Biltmore Forest School. It was founded by Carl A. Schenck, a German forester employed by George Vanderbilt to manage his vast forest empire. Schenck became the father of American forestry management because of his work here from 1897 to 1909. The school opened in 1898, and had 367 alumni before closing in 1914. In 1968, Congress passed the Cradle of Forestry in America Act, which established 6,400 acres for commemorating a natural national historic site. The *Forest Festival Trail* (USFS #319) is also a paved, easy, 1-mi interpretive loop trail that features exhibits of forestry management and logging equipment, based on Dr. Schenck's Biltmore Forest Fair of 1908. From the parking area there is an access to the N trailhead of the former *Club Gap Trail,* now the *Black Mtn Trail,* described in the Davidson River Area. The Education Center is open from the first of May to the end of October, daily, 10 am to 6 pm. A small fee is charged for entrance.                    **231–232**

• ACCESS: From BRP mp 412, descend E on US-276 for 3.8 mi, or from Brevard jct of US-64/276 follow US-276 W for 12 mi.

### Buck Spring Trail *(USFS #104)*                    233

• LENGTH AND DIFFICULTY: 6.2 mi, moderate (elev change 1,200 ft)

• TRAILHEAD AND DESCRIPTION: On US-276 (2.3 mi E from the BRP and 1.3 mi W from the Pink Beds Picnic Area) park on the N side of the highway. Follow the trail sign on a gently graded footpath. Cross Bearwallow Branch at 0.3 mi, the first of 13 streams on this scenic trail that winds in and out of coves and around ten ridges on a gradual ascent to the Pisgah Inn. At 1.1 mi jct with the white-blazed *MST*, R, which jointly runs with the trail for the remainder of the route. At 4.3 mi begin a steeper ascent to where two long switchbacks reach an old RR grade at 5.9 mi. On a level area with superb vistas of the Pink Beds and Black Mtn, arrive at the Pisgah Inn at 6.2 mi. The *MST* continues (see Chapter 6 and 16). (*USGS Maps:* Shining Rock, Cruso)

### Pink Beds Loop Trail *(USFS #118)* 234

- LENGTH AND DIFFICULTY: 5 mi, easy

- CONNECTING TRAILS:
  *(MST)*
  *(South Mills River Trail)*

- TRAILHEAD AND DESCRIPTION: On US-276 (0.2 mi W of the Cradle of Forestry entrance) enter the Pink Beds Picnic Area and parking lot. At the NE end follow the trail sign, descend to cross Pigeon Branch and to a meadow where the trail begins its loop at 0.1 mi. Turn R, follow the orange blaze into a hemlock grove with soft duff, and cross a number of tributaries of the South Fork of the Mills River on footbridges. Most of the tread-way is on an old RR grade and can easily accumulate standing water in rainy seasons. At 1.6 mi jct with the white-blazed *MST* (L on the *MST* it is 0.3 mi to the N side of the *Pink Beds Loop Trail*). After 75 yd the *MST* veers R on its route to join the *Black Mtn Trail*. Continue ahead downstream in a natural garden of tall ferns, white azaleas, fox grapes, and pink wild roses at 1.9 mi. Turn sharply L at 2.7 mi at a jct with the *South Mills River Trail*, R. (It is 0.9 mi downstream to the gauging sta and FR-476 described in the South Mills River Area.) Follow an old RR grade in sections of open forest of oak, poplar, birch, and pine, and cross Barnett Branch on a footbridge 120 yd before a jct with the *MST* at 3.8 mi. (R it is 0.5 mi to FR-1026, and L it is 0.3 mi to the S side of the trail loop.) Continue ahead and return to the meadow and point of origin at 5 mi. (*USGS-FS Maps:* Pisgah Forest, Shining Rock)

### Laurel Mountain Trail *(USFS #121)* 235

- LENGTH AND DIFFICULTY: 7.4 mi, strenuous (elev change 1,658 ft)

- TRAILHEAD AND DESCRIPTION: From the jct of US-276 and Yellow Gap Rd (FR-1206) (0.4 mi W of the Pink Beds Picnic Area), drive 8.5 mi to the trailhead L, but park on the R side of the road. (It is 0.2 mi ahead to Yellow Gap, and a descent of 3 mi to North Mills Rec Area. Beyond on North Mills River Rd [SR-1345] it is 5.2 mi to NC-191, 0.9 mi W of the community of Mills River.) This trail is an infrequently used trail with undependable water sources. It has occasional views of the Pink Beds Valley, Dividing Ridge, and Funneltop Mtn. Ascend over hummocks on an old roadbed and follow the blue-blazed trail through a clearcut of young oak, poplar, locust, and hemlock. Ascend gradually through sections of overgrowth on Laurel Mtn, S and NW slopes, for 2.6 mi to Rich Gap. Continue the slope W, pass another gap, and reach Johnson Gap at 4.4 mi, Sassafras Gap at 5.2 mi, and Good Enough Gap at 5.6 mi. Follow the ridgecrest to Turkey Spring Gap at 6.4 mi, and jct L with a side trail that goes 0.2 mi to *Pilot Rock Trail.* Continue ahead on the E slope of Little Bald Mtn in oak, birch, laurel, and rhododendron on switchbacks into the BRP boundary. Jct with the *Buck Spring Trail,* R and L, at 7.4 mi (see Chapter 6). It is 0.3 mi R to the BRP Buck Spring Overlook parking area, mp 407.7, or L 0.8 mi to Pisgah Inn. Backtrack or use vehicle shuttle. (*USGS-FS Map:* Dunsmore Mtn)

### *Pilot Cove/Slate Rock Creek Trail* (USFS #320)    236

• LENGTH AND DIFFICULTY: 4.3 mi, moderate

• TRAILHEAD AND DESCRIPTION: From the jct of US-276 and Yellow Gap Rd (FR-1206) (0.4 mi W of the Pink Beds Picnic Area), take FR-1206 5.2 mi to a parking area and primitive camping area at Pilot Cove. Backtrack 275 yd to the trail entry, R. Ascend on the white-blazed trail for 0.9 mi and jct with FR-5014 in a forest of rhododendron, poplar, alder, and maple. Turn R, and at 1 mi cross a small stream in Pilot Cove. Ascend steeply to a gap (3,840 ft) on Slate Rock Ridge at 1.5 mi. Descend to a tributary confluence and follow an old RR grade along the NE side of Slate Rock Creek through a forest of poplar, birch, hemlock, and rhododendron. There are good campsites along the way. Reach Yellow Gap Rd at 4.3 mi, and return R on the road 1.6 mi to complete the loop at the point of origin. (*USGS-FS Map:* Dunsmore Mtn)

*Pilot Rock Trail (USFS #321)*                                  **237**

- LENGTH AND DIFFICULTY: 3.6 mi, strenuous (elev change 1,690 ft)

- SPECIAL FEATURES: Pilot Rock monolith, laurel groves

- TRAILHEAD AND DESCRIPTION: From the jct of US-276 and Yellow Gap Rd (FR-1206) (0.4 mi W of the Pink Beds Picnic Area), take FR-1206 4 mi to a parking area at Grassy Lot Gap. Ascend the orange-blazed trail on the N side of the road into a forest of poplar, beech, locust, and oak. Cross small Bradley Creek after 100 yd, pass through a clearcut, and begin switchbacks on a well-graded trail at 0.4 mi. At 0.9 mi are scenic views of the Pink Beds, South Mills River Valley, and Funneltop Mtn (4,266 ft). Ascend a ridge on switchbacks among beds of galax and trailing arbutus and groves of laurel and chestnut oak. At 2.3 mi jct with a 0.3-mi side trail, R, that connects with *Laurel Mtn Trail.* Continue ahead and descend from the ridge to the watershed of Thompson Creek at 3.1 mi. Ahead jct with the old (closed) *Thompson Ridge Trail* (USFS #132), turn R, ascend and jct with the *Buck Spring Trail* at 3.6 mi behind the Pisgah Inn, BRP mp 408.6. Backtrack or use vehicle shuttle. (*USGS-FS Map:* Dunsmore Mtn)

▶ **SHINING ROCK AREA**
  **(Haywood County)**

   To emphasize connecting trail options from the East Fork (parallels US-276) and West Fork (parallels NC-215) of the Pigeon River and from the BRP (S) into the Shining Rock Wilderness Area (N), the following 18 trails are grouped under the title of Shining Rock Area. Because the longest section of the *Art Loeb Trail* is in the Davidson River Area, it and three other connecting trails have been described earlier in this chapter. Also, the *MST* is described in Chapter 16. All the trails connect directly with or have trail access to the *Art Loeb Trail,* the area trail most impacted by visitors. Four trails are hiker/horse trails:

*Little East Fork, Ivestor Gap* (another highly impacted route), *Flat Laurel,* and the road section of *Sam Knob.* Among the least used trails are *Little East Fork, Fork Mtn, Fire Scald Ridge, Old Butt Knob, Cold Mtn,* and *Little Sam.* The highest concentration of people is at the Black Balsam Parking Area at the end of FR-816 (1.2 mi from BRP mp 420.2). Four official trails (and one created by hikers) fan out from the parking area. Camping permits are not required in the Shining Rock Wilderness Area, and in 1982 the FS established a "volunteer ranger program" to educate and monitor the public on "wilderness ethics." Nevertheless, high-impact camping remains a problem. (See "Wilderness Experience" in the Introduction to Part I.) Five trails are found exclusively in the Shining Rock Wilderness Area: *Big East Fork, Cold Mtn, Greasy Cove, Old Butt Knob,* and *Shining Creek.*

## *Little East Fork Trail* (USFS #107)                    **238**

* LENGTH AND DIFFICULTY: 5 mi, strenuous (elev change 2,312 ft)

* TRAILHEAD AND DESCRIPTION: From the jct of NC-215 and the BRP go N 13 mi on NC-215 to Little East Fork Rd (SR-1129) and turn R (5.3 mi S from US-276 and turn L). Proceed 3.8 mi to the parking area past the Daniel Boone Boy Scouts Camp, R. Hike up the road a few yd, cross the Little East Fork of the Pigeon River bridge, and turn L through Boy Scout camps named for a variety of Indian tribes. Follow an old RR grade, rough in sections, for the entire distance. The river has numerous cascades and pools. The forest is mainly hardwood with groves of hemlock and rhododendron in the lower elevations and spruce with birch near the top. Enter the NF at 0.3 mi, and cross Cathey Cove Creek. At 1 mi enter the Shining Rock Wilderness Area. Cross Hemlock Branch at 1.3 mi and at 2.8 mi cross the Little East Fork. The gradient increases, but follow switchbacks for the remainder of the route to jct at 5 mi with *Ivestor Gap Trail.* Left it is 0.4 mi to Shining Rock Gap and connection with the *Art Loeb Trail,* and R it is 3.9 mi to the Black Balsam Parking Area. (Using the *Art Loeb Trail,* N, a loop of

12.1 mi can be made for a return to Camp Daniel Boone.)
(*USGS-FS Maps:* Sam Knob, Shining Rock, Waynesville)

### *Fork Mountain Trail (6.2 mi; USFS #109); Fire Scald Ridge Trail (1.1 mi; USFS #111)*     239–240

• LENGTH AND DIFFICULTY: 7.3 mi combined, strenuous (elev change 2,620 ft)

• TRAILHEAD AND DESCRIPTION: From the BRP/NC-215 jct in Beech Gap, descend N on NC-215 8.4 mi to parking space, R, beside the river (0.2 mi before the Sunburst Rec Area). Because the footbridge has been washed away, rock-hop or wade (river may be impassable with high water) the West Fork of the Pigeon River. After crossing, immediately turn R, go upstream for 0.4 mi, cross and turn L at the mouth of Turnpike Creek, and turn sharply R to leave the stream at 0.8 mi. Ascend on switchbacks to a narrow gap on the Fork Mtn ridgeline at 2 mi. (The old timber road L is 0.4 mi to High Top [5,263 ft].) Turn R and follow an old road (except in a few relocations), undulate on knobs but leave the ridge to skirt E of Birdstand Mtn at 3.2 mi. The forest is chiefly hardwoods with laurel, rhododendron, blueberries, and ferns. Except for Birdstand Mtn, the trail remains W of the Shining Rock Wilderness Area boundary edge. At 4.7 mi, in a shallow gap, jct with the primitive *Fire Scald Ridge Trail,* R.

(The *Fire Scald Ridge Trail* W access is from NC-215. From the BRP described above, descend 5.3 mi to a narrow space for parking against a rock wall, L, on a curve. Cross the road, and climb over the guard rail, and descend steeply through wildflowers, tall basswood, poplar, and locust to the rapids of the West Fork of the Pigeon River at 0.1 mi. If the river is high, crossing can be made on double steel cables. Across the river climb an exceptionally steep trail, faint in most places, to a fork on the old skid road at 0.3 mi. Bear R or L for climb to *Fork Mtn Trail.* If L, follow up the stream for a short distance and climb the slope 0.8 mi for a rapid, rugged, 1,240-ft elev gain. If R, ascend gradually on spur ridges for 0.8 mi and make a curve up Fire Scald Ridge for another 0.6 mi to rejoin the trail at *Fork Mtn*

*Trail,* a total loop of 2.8 mi. Some of the vegetation is sweet pepperbush, arrow-wood, rhododendron, and liverwort.)

Continue ahead on the *Fork Mtn Trail* and skirt E of the ridge for the final mile to reach *Ivestor Gap Trail* at 6.2 mi. (It is 1.7 mi R to the Black Balsam Parking Area, and 0.5 mi L to Ivestor Gap and connections with the *Art Loeb Trail.*) (*USGS-FS Maps:* Sam Knob, Shining Rock, Waynesville)

### **Sam Knob Trail** *(3.2 mi; USFS #344);* **Flat Laurel Trail** *(1.4 mi; USFS #346);* **Little Sam Knob Trail** *(1.8 mi; USFS #347)* **241–243**

- LENGTH AND DIFFICULTY: 6.4 mi combined, easy

- CONNECTING TRAILS:
  *(MST)*
  *(Ivestor Trail)*
  *(Black Balsam Ridge Trail)*

- SPECIAL FEATURES: scenic views of Sam Knob and Fork Ridge

- TRAILHEAD AND DESCRIPTION: At the BRP/NC-215 jct in Beech Gap, descend N on NC-215 0.8 mi to parking area, R, to begin the *Sam Knob Trail,* which can be used for hiking, horse travel, or cross-country skiing. Rock-hop Bubbling Spring Branch and follow an old RR grade with borders of bush honeysuckle, rhododendron, cherry, maple, blackberry, blueberry, and gentian. Cross a cement bridge at 0.7 mi where a 125-ft cascade is R. At 1.6 mi are scenic views of Mt Hardy, Fork Ridge, and the gorge of the West Fork of the Pigeon Valley. Spectacular views of Sam Knob (6,130 ft) begin at 1.8 mi, and at 2 mi, L, near a landslide are scenic views of Flat Laurel Creek cascades and pools. Campsites are 0.3 mi farther in a flat area near Flat Laurel Creek, as are three routes to the Black Balsam Parking Area. Two routes are across the creek and the other route follows the old RR grade. To continue on the *Sam Knob Trail,* rock-hop the creek in a rhododendron grove and reach a trail fork in a flat area. Turn L and cross a streamlet, follow any of a number of camp trails up to a large wildlife field with scenic views, L, of Sam Knob. Bear R, and ascend easily in the field to an old logging road at 2.7 mi. Follow the road to a gate and pass the restrooms to the Black Balsam Parking Area.

The second route is from the fork, mentioned above. Veer R on an open field path that ascends casually 0.8 mi to the SW corner of the Black Balsam Parking Area. (Some hikers call the path the *Goldenrod Trail* for the magnificent exhibition of *Solidago* species that bloom in late September. It is a time when the fall colors come early to these gentle hillsides, mile-high meadows, and heath balds, all covered with the xanthous and ochre of goldenrod, purples of asters, and crimson of the blueberry bushes.)

The third route is the *Flat Laurel Trail,* which begins on the old RR grade where the *Sam Knob Trail* turned L. Follow the wide trail 180 yd to rock-hop a stream and jct, R, with the *Little Sam Knob Trail* at 0.4 mi. At 0.8 mi rock-hop Flat Laurel Creek in an area of scattered spruce, mountain ash, and blackberries. Cross culverts for other small streams in an easy scenic approach to Black Balsam Parking Area at 1.4 mi. (The *Ivestor Trail* begins here, N, on an old RR grade, and the *Black Balsam Ridge Trail* ascends E to jct with the *Art Loeb Trail.* On FR-816, S, it is 1.3 mi to BRP mp 420.2.)

The *Little Sam Knob Trail,* mentioned above, follows an old RR grade through a forest of spruce, birch, and rhododendron SE of Little Sam Knob (5,862 ft). Rock-hop a stream at 0.8 mi, ascend to a jct with an unnamed trail, L, turn sharply R, and follow an old RR grade on the W slope of Chestnut Bald Ridge. At 1.2 mi is a scenic view of Mt Hardy; jct with the *MST* at 1.8 mi. (It is 1 mi L to jct with the *Art Loeb Trail* and 2.2 mi R to NC-215. The latter could form a 7-mi loop to the beginning of the *Sam Knob Trail* on NC-215.) (*USGS-FS Map:* Sam Knob)

### *Yellowstone Falls Trail* (3.2 mi; USFS #358); *Graveyard Ridge Trail* (3.4 mi; USFS #356) 244–245

- LENGTH AND DIFFICULTY: 6.6 mi combined, easy to moderate

- SPECIAL FEATURES: Yellowstone Prong waterfalls

- TRAILHEAD AND DESCRIPTION: (The *Yellowstone Falls Trail* is listed as the *Graveyard Fields Loop Trail* by the NPS.) On the BRP at the Graveyard Fields overlook mp 418.8 (5,120 ft), begin on a paved trail through dense rhododendron. Descend to a rocky area and bridge over the Yellowstone Prong of the East Fork of the Pigeon River at 0.2 mi. Cross and turn R for a trail to the Second Falls at 0.3 mi. Backtrack to the bridge, but stay on the N side of the stream for an immediate jct, R, with the *Graveyard Ridge Trail.*

(The *Graveyard Ridge Trail* follows an old logging road that ascends gently 0.4 mi to Graveyard Ridge, but quickly curves to follow the S slope. At 1.5 mi, hiking N, cross a low gap [E of Black Balsam Knob]. Cross the headwaters of Dark Prong, curve E at the base of Tennent Mtn in a forest of birch, rhododendron, and spruce, and jct with *Greasy Cove Trail,* R, at 3.2 mi. Turn sharply L and reach Ivestor Gap at 3.4 mi to jct with the *Art Loeb Trail.*)

Continuing on the *Yellowstone Falls Trail,* after another 0.6 mi jct L with a return loop but continue ahead for 0.5 mi to the scenic Upper Falls. Return for a complete loop at 3.2 mi. (Yellowstone is named from the yellow mosses, lichens, and minerals on the rocks. The area received its name from moss-covered fallen spruce trunks and stumps that resembled a graveyard. The trunks were destroyed by a fire in November 1925 that burned 25,000 acres of prime timber.) (*USGS-FS Map:* Shining Rock)

### Big East Fork Trail *(3.6 mi; USFS #357);* Greasy Cove Trail *(3 mi; USFS #362)*      246–247

• LENGTH AND DIFFICULTY: 6.6 mi combined, moderate to strenuous (elev change 2,256 ft)

• SPECIAL FEATURES: scenic river, fishing

• TRAILHEAD AND DESCRIPTION: At the BRP/US-276 jct in Wagon Rd Gap, descend W on US-276 2.9 mi to the Shining Rock Parking Area, L. Hike up US-276 (across the Big East Fork bridge) 0.1 mi and turn R at the *Big East Fork Trail* access. Follow an old road that becomes an old RR grade. At 0.4 mi jct R with a 0.2-mi spur connector to *Shining Creek Trail* (on the other side of the river.) Ahead the trail forks L at 0.5 mi. (The R fork is a dead-end side trail to a waterfall and pool.) At 1.1 mi pass a rocky area with rapids, white azalea, and cinnamon ferns. At 1.3 mi leave the river and ascend on the slope, rock-hop Bennett Branch, and return to the riverside at 1.8 mi. For the next 1.8 mi follow the scenic riverside where the loud rattle of kingfishers can be heard over the roar of the rapids. Excellent camping and fishing locations are along the way, and scenic flumes and clear pools are frequent. The forest is mostly birch, hemlock, rhododendron, maple, poplar, buckeye, and wildflowers. At 3.6 mi reach the end of the *Big East Fork Trail* at Bridges Camp, a frequently used campsite. Rock-hop or wade the East Fork of the Pigeon River to begin the *Greasy Cove Trail*. (The continuing trail on the S side of the river is a fisherman's trail. There are not any signs or blazes for the *Greasy Cove Trail*, but look for double cuts in a maple tree and a locust tree before crossing the river.)

Across the river, follow *Greasy Cove Trail* steeply upstream on the N side of Greasy Cove Prong, a splashing stream with moss-covered rocks. At 0.9 mi leave the stream and veer R up a steep hollow of birch, hemlock, and poplar to a level area on Grassy Cove Ridge at 1.7 mi. Continue the ascent and end the trail at the jct with the *Graveyard Ridge Trail* at 3 mi. (The *Graveyard Ridge Trail* goes L 3.2 mi to its S end and jct with the *Yellowstone Falls Trail* at the BRP. Ahead the trail gently ascends 0.2 mi to its N end at a jct with the *Art Loeb Trail* and *Ivestor Gap Trail* in Ivestor Gap. It is 1.7 mi N on the *Art Loeb Trail* for a return loop on either the *Shining Creek Trail* or the *Old Butt Knob Trail* described below.) (*USGS-FS Map:* Shining Rock)

### *Shining Creek Trail (4.1 mi; USFS #363); Old Butt Knob Trail (3.6 mi; USFS #332)* 248–249

- LENGTH AND DIFFICULTY: 7.7 mi combined, strenuous (elev change 2,556 ft)

- CONNECTING TRAILS:
  (Art Loeb Trail)
  (Ivestor Gap Trail)

- SPECIAL FEATURES: vistas from outcroppings

• TRAILHEAD AND DESCRIPTION: At the BRP/US-276 jct in Wagon Rd Gap, descend W on US-276 2.9 mi to the Shining Rock parking area, L. At the end of the parking area follow the *Shining Creek Trail* through a clearing, and at 0.3 mi turn R at a fork. (The L fork is a spur trail that goes to the East Fork of the Pigeon River, where wading or rock-hopping is necessary to jct with the *Big East Fork Trail*. The best approach to this trail is to follow the directions described above under *Big East Fork Trail*.) Ascend on switchbacks to a small saddle, Shining Creek Gap, at 0.7 mi, and jct R with *Old Butt Knob Trail* in a rhododendron thicket.

(The *Old Butt Knob Trail* ascends on the extremely steep Chestnut Ridge in sections of dense rhododendron, laurel, oak, and chestnut saplings to a knob at 1.5 mi. Follow an easier grade for the next 0.5 mi to Old Butt Knob and pass outcroppings along the way for scenic views of Shining Rock Wilderness Area. Descend to Spanish Oak Gap in a forest of oak, birch, and maple. Ascend to Dog Loser Knob and more off-trail vista points at 2.8 mi. Descend gradually to Beech Spring Gap and a spring, L, at 3 mi. Ascend on switchbacks to Shining Rock [5,940 ft], the highest point of the trail, and curve L [S] to Shining Rock Gap at 3.6 mi. Here is a jct with the *Art Loeb Trail, Ivestor Gap Trail,* and *Shining Creek Trail*.)

To continue on the *Shining Creek Trail,* descend from Shining Creek Gap to the bank of Shining Creek in a forest of hemlock and mixed hardwoods at 1 mi. Follow large boulders upstream on the steep R and flumes, cascades, and pools, L, in the creek. Among abundant wildflowers cross Daniels Cove Creek at 2 mi, and at the confluence of the N and S prongs of Shining Creek, stay R. Follow the streamside in a forest of tall hickory, oak, and birch, and at 3.1 mi cross at a stream fork to begin a steep climb on a ridge slope. On switchbacks enter sections of rhododendron, beech, spruce, and moss beds to reach Shining Rock Gap at 4.1 mi. Jct here with *Art Loeb Trail, Ivestor Gap Trail,* and *Old Butt Knob Trail*. A return loop on the *Old Butt Knob Trail* totals 8.4 mi to the parking area. (*USGS-FS Map: Shining Rock*)

# ▶SOUTH MILLS RIVER AREA
## (Henderson and Transylvania Counties)

### *South Mills River Trail* (USFS #133)                250–254

- LENGTH AND DIFFICULTY: 12 mi, easy to moderate

- CONNECTING TRAILS:
  *(Turkey Pen Gap Trail)*
  *(Vineyard Gap Trail)*
  *(Bradley Creek Trail)*
  *Mullinax Trail* (1.2 mi; USFS #326, easy)
  *Poundingmill Trail* (1.5 mi; USFS #349, easy)
  *Wagon Road Gap Trail* (0.7 mi; USFS #134; moderate)
  *Cantrell Creek Trail* (1.9 mi; USFS #148, moderate)
  *(Squirrel Gap Trail)*
  *(Buckhorn Gap Trail)*
  *(Pink Beds Loop Trail)*

- SPECIAL FEATURES: fishing, forestry history, wildlife

- TRAILHEAD AND DESCRIPTION: From the jct of US-276/64 and NC-280 near Brevard, proceed NE on NC-280 5 mi to Henderson/Transylvania county line. Turn L between private homes on Turkey Pen Rd (FR-297) and drive 1.2 mi on a narrow gravel road to a parking area in Turkey Pen Gap, a source of multiple trailheads for both hikers and equestrians. To the L begins the *Turkey Pen Gap Trail;* to the R begins *Vineyard Gap Trail.* Ahead (on a continuation of the FR) is the *Bradley Creek Trail* beginning at a gate, and on a footpath (L of the gate) is the E trailhead of the *South Mills River Trail.* This remarkable trail stays almost exclusively in sight and sound of the fast-moving South Fork of Mills River, whose headwaters are in the Pink Beds and the E slope of the BRP Pisgah Range. Although high peaks, such as Black Mtn (4,286 ft) on the S and Funneltop Mtn (4,266 ft) on the N, rise from the gorge, they are never seen from the trail's forested route. The trail crosses the river 13 times, nine of which must be forded. Because crossing the river can be difficult or impossible after heavy rains, alternate routes or plans are advised. The route basically follows an old RR grade that entices historic fantasies of the way it was a century ago. A hiker has written "visitation is only by ghosts" on a sign at the chimney of the former Cantrell Creek Lodge. It is a multiple-use trail for horses and hikers and trophy trout anglers, and short sections are used by ATV riders. In addition to some of the less used connecting trails, there are numerous old logging roads that offer hikers solitude.

Begin the *South Mills River Trail* by descending on a heavily used footpath to the river at 0.4 mi, cross the swinging footbridge, and ascend to an old road (R and L) at 0.6 mi. Turn L and follow a S slope of maple, poplar, birch, and rhododendron. At 0.7 mi jct with *Mullinax Trail*, R. (The *Mullinax Trail* follows an old seeded road that is rough in places and is used both by hikers and equestrians to the jct with *Squirrel Gap Trail* at 1.2 mi. A 5-mi loop can be made from this point by going L on the *Squirrel Gap Trail* 0.7 mi to turn R on the 1.8-mi *Laurel Creek Trail*, another R on the *Bradley Creek Trail*, and a final R at the E-end jct with the *Squirrel Gap Trail*.)

At 2 mi jct R with the *Poundingmill Trail*. (The *Poundingmill Trail* follows the Poundingmill Branch upstream and follows sections of old logging roads. At 1.5 mi jct with the *Squirrel Gap Trail* on Poundingstone Mtn after a steep ascent from the branch. It is 0.8 mi R on *Squirrel Gap Trail* to jct R with *Mullinax Trail*.)

Continue on the *South Mills River Trail,* pass a grazing field, R, at 2.7 mi, and cross the South Mills River on a swinging footbridge at 2.2 mi. At 3.1 mi jct with the *Wagon Road Gap Trail*. (The *Wagon Road Gap Trail* is a white-blazed foot trail that ascends 0.7 mi on a steep and sometimes rocky treadway in Big Cove to jct with the *Turkey Pen Gap Trail* in Wagon Road Gap. It is 2.5 mi L on the *Turkey Pen Gap Trail* to Turkey Pen Gap parking area.)

At 3.7 mi cross the South Mills River on a swinging footbridge. Enter a large grassy meadow with tall poplar and oak. Rock-hop Cantrell Creek at 3.9 mi and arrive at the remnants of Cantrell Creek Lodge in a meadow at 4 mi. Only a chimney with a double fireplace remains; the lodge was moved in 1978 to the Cradle of Forestry on US-276. A few yd N, at the edge of the forest, is the S terminus of the *Cantrell Creek Trail.* (This is the trail route to follow for avoiding the eight fordings of the South Mills River in the next 4.7 mi. It ascends gradually upstream 1.9 mi to a jct with *Squirrel Gap Trail,* but along the way at 1 mi, L, is the *Horse Cove Gap Trail,* a 0.8-mi connector that shortens the route from 5.4 mi to 3.8 mi to the *South Mills River Trail* at Wolf Ford.)

To continue on the *South Mills River Trail,* cross the meadow of wildflowers at Cantrell Creek Lodge site, ascend a low hill, and return to the riverside. Follow the old RR grade and wade the river eight times before a jct with the blue-blazed *Squirrel Gap Trail,* R, at 8.7 mi at a swinging footbridge. Cross the bridge to the E end of South Mills River Rd (FR-476), a gated road used mainly by riders of horses, ATVs, and ORVs. At 8.8 mi leave the road, R, in the first curve and follow a footpath across Clawhammer Creek. (After 80 yd, jct L with a faint 0.9-mi extension route of *Buckhorn Gap Trail* that ascends Grassy Ridge to FR-476. See *Buckhorn Gap Trail* in this section.) Pass scenic High Falls with cascades and pools in a forest of hemlock, rhododendron, and fetterbush. Rock-hop or wade the river at 9.4 mi. Cross West Ridge Branch at 9.7 mi and jct with an unmarked obscure trail, L. (It fords the river and ascends steeply 0.3 mi to a curve in FR-476, where it turns L and meets the *Buckhorn Gap Trail* in the road's horseshoe curve at 0.4 mi.) Continue up the gorge to cross a few tributaries and arrive at FR-476 at 10.2 mi. Follow the road upstream, arrive at the gate and to the parking area at the water-level gauging station (built in 1935) at 11.1 mi. (It is 1.3 mi N on FR-476 to Yellow Gap Rd [FR-1206] and another 3.3 mi L to US-276 near the Pink Beds Picnic Area.) The trail continues upstream on a beautiful footpath among laurel, ferns, fetterbush, and white azalea. Cross the river on a log bridge at 11.8 mi and a small log bridge into a flat area of ferns in the approach to a jct with the orange-blazed *Pink Beds Loop Trail* at 12 mi. (*USGS-FS Map:* Pisgah Forest)

***Squirrel Gap Trail*** *(7.5 mi; USFS #147);* ***Bradley Creek Trail***
*(3.7 mi; USFS #351)*                                    **255–256**

- LENGTH AND DIFFICULTY: 11.2 mi combined, moderate

- CONNECTING TRAILS:
  *(Mullinax Trail)*
  *(Laurel Creek Trail)*
  *(Poundingmill Trail)*
  *(Cantrell Creek Trail)*
  *(Horse Cove Gap Trail)*
  *(South Mills River Trail)*
  *(Vineyard Gap Trail)*

- TRAILHEAD AND DESCRIPTION: To reach *Squirrel Gap Trail,* the
hiker must hike part of another trail for access. For example,
from the W terminus follow the description under the *South
Mills River Trail,* or from the Turkey Pen Gap parking area take
the *Vineyard Gap Trail* 3.3 mi. Another access is also from Turkey Pen Gap parking area on the *Bradley Creek Trail,* 1.7 mi to
the E terminus of *Squirrel Gap Trail* in Pea Gap. The latter route
of entry is described below. At the gate descend on the logging
road to South Mills River at 0.4 mi and turn downstream. Ford
the river at 0.8 mi (the county line), continue downstream to
where the road forks (one fork goes L, the other fords the river).
Turn L and ascend gradually to Pea Gap; descend to and cross
Pea Branch for a jct L with the E terminus of *Squirrel Gap Trail*
at 1.7 mi.

(The *Bradley Creek Trail* follows Pea Branch downstream to
Bradley Creek where it crosses Case Branch at 2.2 mi and jct R
with *Vineyard Gap Trail.* Continue upstream, cross Bradley
Creek a number of times [twice on bridges], and encounter
frequent seepage in wet weather. At 3.4 mi jct L with the 1.8-mi
*Laurel Creek Trail* that is moderately difficult and lightly used on
its ascent to the *Squirrel Gap Trail.* Continue up Bradley Creek
for another 0.3 mi to the Bradley Creek Reservoir and the trail's
N terminus. Backtrack.)

Begin the blue-blazed *Squirrel Gap Trail* up Pea Branch, reach
jct, L, with *Mullinax Trail* at 0.7 mi, and ascend through Mul-

linax Gap for a jct, R, with the *Laurel Creek Trail* at 1.4 mi on the N side of Poundingstone Mtn. After 260 yd, jct L with the *Poundingmill Trail.* Continue ahead, first on the ridge of Laurel Mtn and then on the N slope through a forest of hardwood, laurel, and rhododendron. Pass through Laurel Gap (3,480 ft, the trail's highest point) and follow the S slope of Rich Mtn in and out of coves. Jct L with *Cantrell Creek Trail* and Cantrell Creek crossing at 4 mi. In a forest of oak, maple, hemlock, and hickory, reach the jct L with the *Horse Cove Gap Trail* (an 0.8-mi connector to the *Cantrell Creek Trail*) at 5.4 mi. Cross the headwaters of Laurel Brook and pass through Squirrel Gap (3,320 ft) at 6.7 mi. Descend gradually to Glady Branch waterfalls, L, at 7.3 mi, and reach the trail terminus at 7.5 mi at a jct with the *South Mills River Trail.* Backtrack, or exit upstream on the *South Mills River Trail* 2.4 mi to parking area of FR-476 for a vehicle shuttle. (*USGS-FS Map:* Pisgah Forest)

### *Turkey Pen Gap Trail* (USFS #322)      257

• LENGTH AND DIFFICULTY: 5.5 mi, moderate

• CONNECTING TRAILS:
(*Wagon Road Gap Trail*)
(*Black Mountain Trail*)

• TRAILHEAD AND DESCRIPTION: From Turkey Pen Gap parking area at the end of FR-297, ascend L (W) on a dry ridge to Simpson Gap at 0.7 mi. At 1.1 mi begin a 0.4-mi climb on switchbacks to Sharpy Mtn. Descend moderately in an oak forest with an understory of laurel, rhododendron, blueberry, and ground patches of galax. Arrive at Wagon Road Gap and *Wagon Road Gap Trail,* R, at 2.5 mi. (The white-blazed *Wagon Road Gap Trail* descends rapidly 0.7 mi to jct with the *South Mills River Trail.*) Ascend to McColl Mtn. Descend to Deep Gap at 4 mi. Continue on the ridge and enter Muleshoe Gap at 4.7 mi (N of Horse Knob). Begin a 0.8-mile ascent to a jct with the *Black Mtn Trail* (S of Black Mtn peak, 4,286 ft) at 5.5 mi. (It is 1.8 mi N on the *Black Mtn Trail* to *Buckhorn Gap Trail,* where a R turn offers a potential 18.8-mi loop by using the *South Mills River Trail.* It is

3.9 mi L on the *Black Mtn Trail* to the RS on US-276.) (*USGS-FS Map:* Pisgah Forest)

### *Vineyard Gap Trail (USFS #324)* 258

- LENGTH AND DIFFICULTY: 3.3 mi, moderate

- TRAILHEAD AND DESCRIPTION: From Turkey Pen Gap parking area at the end of FR-297, ascend R (E) on a dry ridge, and at 0.2 mi bear R on the ridge. Follow the ridgeline, but descend to a damp hollow before ascending to another ridge. Descend to Vineyard Gap and turn L. (The trail ahead follows Forge Mtn ridge to private property.) Descend on a spur ridge and ford South Fork of Mills River at 2.3 mi. Pass the mouth of Bradley Creek and follow Bradley Creek upstream. Twice wade or rock-hop the stream in a forest of hardwoods, hemlock, and rhododendron. Arrive at campsites and a crossing of Bradley Creek to *Bradley Creek Trail* at 3.3 mi. Backtrack or follow *Bradley Creek Trail* L for 2.2 mi to Turkey Pen Gap parking area. (*USGS-FS Map:* Pisgah Forest)

---

## ▶ SECTION 4: TOECANE RANGER DISTRICT

The Toecane Ranger District received its name from the Toe and Cane rivers. According to legend the white settlers shortened the name of an Indian princess, Estatoe, who wished to marry a brave from another tribe, whom her tribe rejected and killed. In her grief she drowned herself in the South Fork of the Toe River.

The district's 74,458 acres are in four major segments: two in the N that border the Tennessee state line and the Cherokee NF, and two in the S that border the BRP and a portion of the Grandfather Ranger District. The most SW section covers the Craggy Mtn Scenic Area in the NE corner of Buncombe County. The most E section is the Black Mtn range, an area with 18 peaks over 6,300 ft in elev, and the South Toe River drainage area in Yancey County. A new 1,500-acre tract is between Grassy Knob Ridge and Winter Star Ridge, SW of Celo Knob.

Mt Mitchell State Park, the state's oldest and highest, adjoins the W side of this section. The largest NW segment in Yancey and Mitchell counties is a remote area through which flows the Nolichucky River in a canyon inaccessible except by white water and the Clinchfield RR. The N section of the district is the majestic Roan Mtn Area and its famous gardens in Mitchell County.

The district's first 25,000 acres were purchased in 1913 to protect the South Fork of the Toe River's watershed and for its great supply of timber. Because the major timbering and railroad building were abandoned in 1915, large groves (some of the largest in the U.S.) of red spruce and Fraser fir have remained.

The *AT* route of 55.7 mi follows the ridgeline in and out of North Carolina and Tennessee except in an area near Erwin where it crosses a highway bridge over the Nolichucky River. Another famous trail, the *Overmountain Victory Trail (OVT)* (USFS #308), a national historic trail, enters this district from Tennessee at the Yellow Mtn Gap intersection with the *AT*. It descends for nearly 1 mi on the historic footpath, Creek Rd (FR-1132). It was near the state line that the frontier patriots camped September 27, 1780, on their march S. The route of the *OVT* is approximately 315 mi, beginning in Craig's Meadow in Abingdon, Virginia, and ending at Kings Mtn National Park battlefield in South Carolina. Except for about 12 mi on federal lands, the *OVT* is a motor route. The trail commemorates the route used by the mountainmen in their march to find and fight Col. Patrick Ferguson who had pledged to "lay their country waste with fire and sword" if they did not support the British forces. Col. Ferguson's death in the October 7, 1780, battle at Kings Mtn was a turning point of the Revolutionary War. In 1980 thousands of hikers, equestrians, and motorists celebrated the bicentennial on a march from Abingdon to Kings Mtn. (For more information on the *OVT* route contact the Regional Office, NPS, 75 Spring St SW, Atlanta, GA 30303, tel: 404-221-5185. The battle trails on Kings Mtn are described in *South Carolina Hiking Trails* by Allen de Hart.)

Recreational facilities include two family campgrounds, one at Black Mtn on FR-472 and Carolina Hemlock on NC-80, both along the South Fork of the Toe River. One group campground is at Briar Bottom, adjoining Black Mtn. Picnic areas are Corner Rock on FR-74 E of Barnardsville, Lost Cove on FR-472 near Black Mtn, Roan Mtn off NC-261, Spivey Gap (also called Bald Mtn) on US-19W near the Tennessee border, and Carolina Hemlock Pavilion on NC-80 at the Carolina Hemlock Campground. Some of the special-interest areas are Douglas Falls in the Craggy Mtn Scenic Area, Roan High Knob and Gardens, Elk Falls, Nolichucky River, Yellow Mtn, and Hump Mtn. A forest-associated, but not USFS-sponsored, annual event in mid-October is Lumberjack Day in Burnsville. National and local contestants compete in log chopping and sawing, pole felling, log stacking, and other allied skills. For information contact the Yancey County Chamber of Commerce, 2 Town Square, Burnsville, NC 28714, tel: 704-682-7413.

• ADDRESS AND ACCESS: District Ranger, Toecane Ranger District, USFS, PO Box 128, Burnsville, NC 28714, tel: 704-682-6146. Access is on the US-19 E bypass between NC-197 and Hickory Lane (SR-1139) in Burnsville.

▶ **BIG IVY AREA**
**(Buncombe County)**

*Big Butt Trail (USFS #161)*                                    **259**

• LENGTH AND DIFFICULTY: 6.2 mi, moderate to strenuous

• SPECIAL FEATURES: remote, ramp beds

• TRAILHEAD AND DESCRIPTION: From Burnsville on NC-197, go SW 16 mi to the top of Cane River Gap, or, from Barnardsville on NC-197 go NE 10 mi. Begin at a parking area and ascend on a white-blazed trail along the Yancey/Buncombe county line. Reach Mahogany Knob, after 22 switchbacks, at 1.7 mi, Flat Spring Knob at 2.4 mi, and Flat Spring Gap at 2.6 mi.

Primitive campsite and water are available here. Ramps, a long-lasting, garlicky wild onion, is massed in sections throughout the trail area. Bypass Big Butt (5,900 ft) on the E slope but climb Little Butt Knob at 3.8 mi. Reach Point Misery at 4.7 mi, and at 6.2 mi the BRP parking area in Balsam Gap, mp 359.8 (5,320 ft). Some of the vegetation on the trail consists of birch, beech, spruce, hemlock, hickory, maple, trillium, and grassy groundcovers. (*USGS-FS Maps:* Mt Mitchell, Montreat)

*Halfway Trail (3.1 mi; USFS #162); Bullhead Ridge Trail (1 mi; USFS #1005)*                                         **260–261**

• LENGTH AND DIFFICULTY: 4.1 mi combined, moderate to strenuous (elev change 1,114 ft)

• SPECIAL FEATURES: Douglas Falls, wildflowers

• TRAILHEAD AND DESCRIPTION: Begin at the N end of the parking lot at Craggy Gardens Visitor Center, which is at mp 364.1 on the BRP. Skirt Craggy Knob on the white-blazed trail, and turn L at 0.5 mi. Descend, cross a stream at 0.9 mi, and pass through a canopy of moosewood under yellow birches and by wildflowers such as twistedstalk and merrybells (*Uvularia grandifloria*). Cross a stream at 1.4 mi, and reach the scenic Cascade Falls at 1.8 mi. (Hold on to the cable for safety.) Descend steeply to 2.3 mi and cross a stream at 2.4 mi. Turn sharply L at 2.7 mi and descend on switchbacks. (The trail to the R is *Bullhead Ridge Trail;* it leads 1 mi through a splendid stand of maple, birch, and hemlock to the parking lot at FR-74. The trail has primitive campsites.) Turn R by large boulders at 2.9 mi and reach the 70-ft Douglas Falls at 3.1 mi. Return by the same route, or hike 0.5 mi on a wide, well-graded access trail to FR-74 and the parking lot. Here also is the W trailhead of *Bullhead Ridge Trail,* which can be used for a 1.9-mi loop to Douglas Falls and back to the parking lot. FR-74 winds down the mtn for 8.7 mi to Dillingham Rd (SR-2173), which goes 5 mi more to Barnardsville and NC-197. (*USGS-FS Maps:* Craggy Pinnacle, Montreat)

## ►CAROLINA HEMLOCKS RECREATION AREA
### (Yancey County)

The Carolina Hemlocks Rec Area has facilities for tent and RV camping (no hook-ups, but water and comfort sta), picnicking (a shelter pavilion can be rented for groups), fishing, swimming, and hiking. The *Hemlock Nature Trail* (USFS #1003) makes a 1-mi loop and begins at the swimming beach, follows the South Toe River, crosses NC-80, and enters an interpretive loop around the campground. Two other trails, *Colbert Ridge Trail* and the *Buncombe Horse Range Trail*, have trailheads nearby. Season of operation is usually from the middle of April to the end of October.                                                    **262**

• ACCESS: From Micaville, jct of NC-80 and US-19E, drive 8.6 mi S on NC-80 to the Carolina Hemlocks Rec Area. From BRP mp 351.9 in Buck Creek Gap, drive 5.3 mi N on NC-80.

• SUPPORT FACILITIES: A nearby commercial campground is Clear Creek Camping Park with full svc, open May 1 to October 31. Address is Rte 5, Box 189, Burnsville, NC 28714, tel: 704-675-4510. Access from the Carolina Hemlocks Rec Area is 1 mi S on NC-80 to Clear Creek Campground Rd (SR-1199) for 0.5 mi. From BRP mp 351.9 it is 4.3 mi N on NC-80. Groceries are available on NC-80 to Micaville, and 4 mi farther W on US-19E to Burnsville are motels, restaurants, and supplies.

### *Colbert Ridge Trail* (USFS #178)                    **263–264**

• LENGTH AND DIFFICULTY: 3.6 mi, strenuous (elev change 2,950 ft)

• TRAILHEAD AND DESCRIPTION: From the Carolina Hemlocks Rec Area go N 0.4 mi on NC-80, turn L on Colbert Creek Rd (SR-1158), and after 0.5 mi park at the trailhead, R. Follow the white-blazed trail, ascending gently at first. Rock outcroppings provide scenic views of South Toe River Valley, Black Mtn range, Roan Mtn, and Grandfather Mtn. At 2.7 mi ascend switchbacks on the E side of Winter Star Mtn. Reach a spring, L, at 3.3 mi, and jct with the *Black Mtn Crest Trail* at 3.6 mi. (A turn L extends 0.1 mi to Deep Gap [5,700 ft] and the Deep Gap shelter. Space for tent camping is nearby. A return loop can be made from here by going S on the *Black Mtn Crest Trail* for 2.3 mi, turn L for 0.5 mi on the *Big Tom Gap Trail,* turn L on the *Buncombe Horse Range Trail* for 6 mi, and go another 0.5 mi to the point of origin on Colbert Creek Rd for a loop of 13 mi.) (*USGS-FS Maps:* Mt Mitchell, Celo)

### *Buncombe Horse Range Trail* (USFS #191)    265

* LENGTH AND DIFFICULTY: 16.5 mi, moderate to strenuous (elev change 2,860 ft)

* CONNECTING TRAILS:
  (*Big Tom Gap Trail*)
  (*Mt Mitchell Trail*)

* SPECIAL FEATURES: RR history, Camp Alice, spruce/fir groves

* TRAILHEAD AND DESCRIPTION: This trail is rugged and is used both by horseback riders and hikers. Access is described from the NE trailhead. From the Carolina Hemlocks Rec Area go N 0.4 mi on NC-80, turn L on Colbert Creek Rd (SR-1158), and proceed 0.8 mi to jct with Aunt Julie Rd (SR-1159). Turn R, go 0.2 mi, and park L near a private home. Follow the white blazes on an old jeep road. Take the L fork at 0.6 mi. Cross rocky Middle Fork at 1.3 mi. At 1.8 mi bear R at the jct to begin steep switchbacks up Maple Camp Ridge in a hardwood forest. Cross Maple Camp Creek at 3.4 mi, and reach a heath bald with good views at 4.8 mi. Arrive at Maple Camp Bald (5,613 ft), R, at 5.3 mi. At 6 mi cross Thee Creek and jct with primitive *Big Tom Gap Trail,* R, which leads 0.5 mi to jct with the *Black Mtn Crest Trail.* Jct with the blue-blazed *Mt Mitchell Trail,* R and L, at 7.8 mi near a spring. Reach the Camp Alice Shelter on Community Hill (5,782 ft) at 8 mi. (The shelter has ten wire bunks, a picnic shed, a horse corral, and a spring nearby.) Continue ahead on the old RR grade to the site of Camp Alice at 8.5 mi, R. (Camp Alice was a thriving logging camp in the 1920s. It later served as a lodge

for Mt Mitchell visitors. Only remnants of the stone foundations remain.) Cross Lower Creek at 8.7 mi and a number of
small streams that drain into Middle Fork and South Fork before approaching the base of Potato Knob at 11.7 mi. (Here is
an access route, R, to NC-128, the road from the BRP to the top
of Mt Mitchell.) Turn L and pass through a beautiful spruce/fir
grove at 12.6 mi. At 14 mi enter a large wildlife habitat clearing
with fine views and soon begin to follow an old logging road on
long, level switchbacks that descend to the Right Prong of the
South Toe River. At 16.5 mi reach FR-472 (3,560 ft), the SW
trailhead. (To the R it is 2 mi to the BRP on FR-472, and L it is
2.9 mi to Black Mtn Rec Area on FR-472.) (*USGS-FS Maps:* Mt
Mitchell, Celo, Montreat, Old Fort)

## ▶ BLACK MOUNTAIN RECREATION AREA
### (Yancey County)

The Black Mtn Rec Area has facilities for tent and RV camping (no hook-ups, but water and comfort sta), fishing, picnicking, and hiking. The Briar Bottom Group Campground (reservation required) adjoins upstream on the South Toe River. The
1-mi loop *Briar Bottom Trail* (USFS #1006) serves both as a
route for bicycling and hiking. The trail begins at the gate to the
group campground, parallels the river to loop the campground, and crosses two locust footbridges in the process. An
unnamed short trail goes up (W) Setrock Creek to a scenic
cascading waterfall. Two other trails are accessible from the rec
area, *Mt Mitchell* and *Lost Cove Ridge*.                    **266**

• ACCESS: From the BRP mp 347.6 at Big Laurel Gap descend
2.5 mi on FR-2074 to jct with FR-472. Turn L, go 0.7 mi, and
cross South Toe River, R. Or, from BRP mp 351.9, descend 4.9
mi on FR-472 and turn L at the campground entrance. The N
access is from the jct of NC-80 and FR-472 near the Mt Mitchell
Golf Course, followed by a 3-mi drive upstream. Support facilities are the same as for the Carolina Hemlocks Rec Area (see
above).

### *Lost Cove Ridge Trail (USFS #182)* 267

• LENGTH AND DIFFICULTY: 3.3 mi, moderate to strenuous (elev change 2,070 ft)

• TRAILHEAD AND DESCRIPTION: This trail is also called the *Green Knob Trail.* From BRP mp 350.4 at Flinty Gap (4,782 ft), stop at the parking lot and cross the road to climb switchbacks to Green Knob Lookout Tower (5,070 ft). The 360 views are outstanding, particularly of the Black Mtn Range. Turn R a few yd before reaching the tower and descend on a white-blazed trail between FR-472 and Big Lost Cove Creek. Trees are hardwoods and scattered conifers. At 2.7 mi the trail descends steeply to FR-472. Cross the road, the South Toe River, and enter the Black Mtn Rec Area at 3.3 mi. (*USGS-FS Maps:* Old Fort, Celo)

### *Bald Knob Ridge Trail (USFS #186)* 268

• LENGTH AND DIFFICULTY: 2.8 mi, easy to moderate (elev change 1,300 ft)

• SPECIAL FEATURES: virgin spruce and fir groves

• TRAILHEAD AND DESCRIPTION: From the parking area at BRP mp 355 (5,200 ft), descend 0.1 mi on the white-blazed trail to the FS boundary, and follow Bald Knob Ridge N of the Left Prong of South Toe River. At 1 mi begin switchbacks. The trail passes through magnificent stands of virgin red spruce and Fraser fir. Reach FR-472 at 2.8 mi. Return by the same route or have a vehicle at FR-472, 1 mi down the mtn from BRP mp 351.9 in Deep Gap.

### *Mt Mitchell Trail (USFS #190)* 269–270

• LENGTH AND DIFFICULTY: 5.6 mi, strenuous (elev change 3,684 ft)

• CONNECTING TRAILS:
  *(Briar Bottom Trail)*
  *(Higgins Bald Trail)*
  *(Buncombe Horse Range Trail)*

- SPECIAL FEATURES: rugged, highest point E of the Mississippi River

- TRAILHEAD AND DESCRIPTION: (Also see *Mt Mitchell Trail* description in Mt Mitchell State Park, Chapter 10.) Begin the hike near the bridge in the Black Mtn Rec Area. Walk across a meadow and pass the amphitheater at the upper level near the campground host's residence. Follow a blue-blazed, well-graded trail past Devil's Den Forest walk at 0.1 mi. Ascend on switchbacks in a virgin hardwood forest. Large banks of meadow rue are passed at 0.9 mi. Jct with *Higgins Bald Trail* at 1.5 mi, L. (The *Higgins Bald Trail* [USFS #190A] is a 1.5-mi alternate route from Long Arm Ridge to Flynn Ridge where it rejoins the *Mt Mitchell Trail.* At its crossing of Setrock Creek is an outstanding cascade and waterfall.) A forest of conifers predominates for the next 0.4 mi. Jct with the old *Old Ridge Trail*, R, at 1.7 mi. Cross Setrock Creek at 2.6 mi, and jct with the *Higgins Bald Trail*, L, at 2.7 mi. Jct with the *Buncombe Horse Range Trail* (described above), formerly the *Maple Camp Trail*, at 3.9 mi. Turn L and at 4 mi turn R into the forest. (Camp Alice Shelter is 200 ft L; it has wire bunks for ten hikers. A spring is nearby.) Ascend steeply over a rough and eroded treadway for 1.6 mi to the summit of Mt Mitchell and the picnic area at the parking lot. Backtrack or use a vehicle shuttle. (*USGS-FS Maps:* Celo, Mt Mitchell)

## ▶ BLACK MOUNTAINS
### (Yancey County)

### *Black Mountain Crest Trail* (USFS #179)                   271

- LENGTH AND DIFFICULTY: 12 mi, strenuous (elev change 3,550 ft)

- CONNECTING TRAILS:
  *(Big Tom Gap Trail)*
  *(Colbert Ridge Trail)*

- SPECIAL FEATURES: rugged, high altitude, solitude

• TRAILHEAD AND DESCRIPTION: (Sections of this trail were formerly called *Deep Gap Trail* and *Celo Knob Trail*. A former 3.5-mi access route, *Woody Ridge Trail* [USFS #177] from the community of Celo is no longer in use.) The S trailhead is in Mt Mitchell State Park, and vehicles must be registered with the park ranger if left overnight. The N trailhead is on FR-5578 off Bowlens Creek Rd (SR-1109), 3 mi S of Burnsville.

Leave the Mt Mitchell picnic area and parking lot to hike N on what is considered to be the most rugged trail in the district. It is also the highest with a traverse of a dozen peaks over 6,000 ft within 6 mi. Follow the orange-blazed trail over rocky terrain and through dense vegetation. Sections of spruce/fir groves are dying from acid rain and woolly aphids. At 1 mi ascend to Mt Craige (6,645 ft), the park's second highest peak. It was named in honor of Governor Locke Craige (see Mt Mitchell State Park in Chapter 10). Reach Big Tom Mtn after another 1 mi (6,593 ft); it was named in honor of Thomas Wilson. There is a jct at 1.6 mi with the primitive *Big Tom Gap Trail,* R. (The *Big Tom Gap Trail* is a 0.5-mi steep connector to the *Buncombe Horse Range Trail* described above.) Continue on the crest among ferns, thornless blackberry, Clinton's lily, moosewood, spruce, and fir to the summit of Balsam Cone (6,611 ft) at 1.9 mi. Ascend to Cattail Peak (6,583 ft) at 2.5 mi. Leave the state-park boundary and enter the NF boundary to ascend Potato Hill at 3 mi. Reach Deep Gap shelter at 3.9 mi. (The shelter has four large wood bunks, tent camping sites are nearby, and water is 300 yd down the mtn in front of the shelter.) Jct with the *Colbert Ridge Trail,* R, at 4 mi. (The *Colbert Ridge Trail* is a 3.6-mi access route from Carolina Hemlocks Rec Area.) Reach the summit of Deer Mtn (6,200 ft) at 4.5 mi. Jct with an old road L at 6.2 mi. Continue ahead on an old road, skirting W of Gibbs Mtn and Horse Rock. Leave the old road at 7.2 mi, and reach the summit of Celo Knob (6,427 ft) at 7.4 mi. Turn L and begin the descent into Bowlens Creek watershed on an old logging road at 7.6 mi. Pass a spring on the R. Cross a small stream at 8.8 mi, pass a dangerous open mine shaft L at 9.5 mi, and go past a gate at 10.3 mi. (Note the unique four-trunked tree at 10.4 mi.) From

11 mi, follow the cascading Bowlens Creek to gated FR-5578, the N trailhead, and a small parking space. Follow the road through an area of private property and reach Bowlens Creek Rd (SR-1109, also called Low Gap Rd) at 12 mi. (It is 2.4 mi N to NC-197 and 0.7 mi to jct of US-19E in Burnsville.) (*USGS-FS Maps:* Mt Mitchell, Celo, Burnsville)

▶ **ROAN MOUNTAIN AREA**
**(Mitchell County)**

*Cloudland Trail (3 mi round-trip; USFS #1000); Roan Mtn Gardens Trail (1 mi; USFS #1002)*                     **272–273**

• LENGTH AND DIFFICULTY: 4 mi round-trip combined, easy

• TRAILHEAD AND DESCRIPTION: Take the Roan Mtn Rd (SR-1348) for 1.8 mi at jct with NC-261 in Carvers Gap on the Tennessee-North Carolina state line (13 mi N of Bakersville). For the *Cloudland Trail* turn R to parking lot #1. Follow the trail sign W on the crest of Roan Mtn through spruce, fir, mountain avens (*Geum radiatum*), rhododendron, and sections of heavy moss on the trees and the ground. Pass parking lots #2 and #3 and climb to Roan High Bluff (6,267 ft) at 1.5 mi for superb views of Bald and Unaka mtns. Backtrack. For the *Roan Mtn Gardens Trail* follow a triple-loop paved trail from parking lot #2 through an extraordinary display of purple rhododendron (*catawbiense*) and flame azalea. One of the trails has 16 interpretive signs, and another loop passes through a large grassy bald with rhododendron—usually at their flowering peak the last two weeks in June. The trail has easy access for the handicapped. (Contact the RS for information on the date and events of the Rhododendron Festival.) (*USGS-FS Map:* Bakersville)

• SUPPORT FACILITIES: Roan Mtn State Resort Park. From jct of US-19E and TN-143 go 5 mi S from the town of Roan Mtn on TN-143 (which becomes NC-261 in N.C. at Carvers Gap). Tel: 615-772-4178. Full svc, rec fac, open all year.

▶ **ELK FALLS AREA**
**(Avery County)**

*Big Falls Trail* *(USF #1007)*                                  **274**

• LENGTH AND DIFFICULTY: 0.5 mi round-trip, easy

• TRAILHEAD AND DESCRIPTION: From Main St in Elk Park proceed N on Elk River Rd (SR-1305), which becomes FR-190, for 5 mi to Elk Falls parking area. Begin the hike on a timber access road to Elk River, and descend to the bottom of the 50-ft amphitheater-like falls. Camping is not permitted. Backtrack. (*USGS-FS Map:* Elk Park)

# 4.

## Uwharrie National Forest

*Red Clay and laurel and rocky streams, Uwharries, my home in the evergreens.*
                                                        —James H. Price, III

In the center of the state, the 46,888-acre Uwharrie National Forest spreads into a patchwork of private and public tracts in three counties, mainly Montgomery but more than 8,000 acres in Randolph and another 1,000 acres in Davidson. Nearly 300 miles of county, state, and private roads form part of that patchwork, and another 185 miles of forest roads give easy access to its streams, recreational areas, and trails. With its mountainous ranges rarely over 900 ft in elevation, it disguises its 400-million-year history. Archeologists have reported that the composite geography has been eroded by the Yankin, Pee Dee, and Uwharrie rivers to expose parts of the hard basalt and rhyolite deposits in the oldest known mountain range in North America. Its rocky and worn ridges have been mined for gold, silver, copper, and lead, and the early settlers impoverished an already poor soil with inadequate timber and farm management. In 1931 much of the acreage was identified as the Uwharrie Purchase Unit, and in 1935 it was transferred to the USFS for administration. Finally, in 1961 it became a national forest, the state's youngest. During the 1930s the CCC and subsequently the USFS reforested hundreds of acres with pines and allowed groves of hardwoods to mature in the coves and by the streambanks. Slopes with mountain laurel, dogwood, and sourwood

187

became natural understory gardens with 700 species of plants and abundant wildflowers and ferns. A further preservation was made in 1984 when Congressional Public Law 98-324 created the 4,790-acre Birkhead Wilderness Area. The Final Environmental Impact Statement of the 1986 Land and Resource Management Plan reported 225 historic sites as "recommended for further testing or preservation." The origin of Uwharrie's name is unclear; perhaps it came from the Suala Indians. As early as 1701 it was spelled Heighwaree, an early map of 1733 lists it as Uharie, and it is listed as Voharee on a 1770 map.

Recreational facilities include two family campgrounds (no hook-ups but with sanitary facilities), one at Badin Lake near Uwharrie and the other at Uwharrie Hunt Camp between Uwharrie and Badin Lake. Badin Lake Group Camp requires reservations. There are two primitive camps (with pit toilets only), West Morris Mtn Camp on the Ophir Rd (SR-1303) near the Uwharrie community and Yates Place Camp on Mountain Rd (SR-1146). In-season hunting and fishing are allowed in the NF according to state laws and licenses. Badin Lake has largemouth bass, white bass, bream, yellow perch, and sunfish. Forest game animals are deer, turkey, raccoon, squirrel, fox, rabbit, quail, and duck. Numerous species of songbirds, owls, and hawks are here, too. Among the species of reptiles are the box turtle, lizards, skunks, and snakes (including the infrequently seen rattlesnake and the copperhead). There are horse trails, ORV trails, and ten foot trails, the longest of which is the 20.5-mi *Uwharrie Trail,* formerly routed for 33 mi but reduced because of its traverse on private property and the *Birkhead Trail* becoming independent. An interpretive trail, *Densons Creek Trail* (USFS #97) is at the RS. It is an easy double loop with options for 0.9 mi and 2.2 mi. Numbered posts describe flora, fauna, farm history, and geology. The trail area has copious milky quartz. The district trails are blazed and signed, and in contrast to other NF wilderness areas in the state the Birkhead Wilderness Area is well-maintained, blazed, and signed. Volunteer assistance for trail maintenance is provided by the Central

Piedmont Group of the Sierra Club from Charlotte and the Uwharrie Trail Club from Asheboro. **275**

• ADDRESS AND ACCESS: District Ranger, Uwharrie National Forest, USFS, Rte 3, Box 470, Troy, NC 27371, tel: 919-576-6391. Access is on NC-24/27, 1.8 mi E of Troy.

• SUPPORT FACILITIES: In addition to the campgrounds described below, a commercial campground is Holly Bluff Family Campground, Rte 3, Box 247, Asheboro, NC 27203, tel: 919-857-2761, open April 1 to November 1, full svc, rec fac. Approach is 8 mi S of Asheboro on NC-49. Motels, restaurants, and shopping centers are in Troy, Asheboro, and Albemarle, and hospitals are in the latter two. A store for groceries and outdoor-sports equipment is at Uwharrie, jct of NC-109 and SR-1303/1150.

## ▶ BADIN LAKE, BADIN LAKE GROUP CAMP, AND COVE BOAT RAMP RECREATION AREAS
### (Montgomery County)

These three recreational areas are near each other on the E shore of Badin Lake. Facilities for boating, fishing, hiking, and picnicking are available at all three sites. Water skiing is available only at Badin Lake and Cove Boat Ramp Rec Area. Camping facilities with drinking water and toilets (but no hook-ups) are provided at Badin Lake and the Group Camp, but the latter requires reservations for both camping and picnicking. All the areas are open year-round. A number of trails in the area have been abandoned, grown over with dense vegetation, or designated ORV routes. Examples are USFS #85, #88, and #93 on the 1985 Uwharrie National Forest USFS Map. (*USGS-FS Map:* Badin)

• ACCESS: From the jct of NC-109 and Checking Station Rd (SR-1153) (1.5 mi N from the community of Uwharrie) go 0.4 mi on SR-1153 to FR-576, turn R, and go 2.9 mi to FR-597. Turn R.

The first L off FR-597 goes to Cove Boat Ramp and the second L off FR-597 is Badin Lake.

### *Dutch John Trail* (3.6 mi; USFS #90); *Badin Lake Trail* (5.6 mi; USFS #94) 276–277

• LENGTH AND DIFFICULTY: 9.2 mi combined, easy

• TRAILHEAD AND DESCRIPTION: For the *Dutch John Trail* follow the access route described above, but go only 1.5 mi on FR-576 and turn L on FR-533. Drive 2 mi and park at Dutch John Creek for the S trailhead. From the bridge follow the trail upstream adjacent to Dutch John Creek for 1.3 mi in a forest of hardwoods, laurel, and scattered pine. Veer R from the creek and gradually ascend to FR-576 at 2.7 mi. Cross the road and reach FR-597 at 3.4 mi. To reach Cove Boat Ramp, cross the road, hike 280 yd to jct with *Badin Lake Trail*. Backtrack, or turn L and reach Cove Boat Ramp parking lot at 4.2 mi. Return by the same route or use a vehicle shuttle.

For the *Badin Lake Trail* follow the access description above to Cove Boat Ramp and parking lot. From the parking lot hike N, taking either the lakeside L or the switchbacks R on the yellow-blazed loop trail. If ascending R, reach a jct with the *Dutch John Trail* at 0.6 mi. Turn L, continue through a forest of hardwoods, and cross forest roads at 0.9 mi and 1.4 mi. Pass a stream and skirt the rocky side of a hill at 1.6 mi. A shorter loop is L at 1.9 mi. Reach a lake cove at 2 mi and a scenic peninsula at 2.8 mi. Turn L and reach a large rock slope by the lake at 3.7 mi. The area has abundant cedars, mosses, and wildflowers. Continue by the lakeside, cross a road at 4.3 mi, and reach the jct with the short trail loop at 5.1 mi. Return to the parking lot at 5.6 mi. (*USGS-FS Map:* Badin)

## ▶ BIRKHEAD MOUNTAIN WILDERNESS AREA (Randolph County)

• ACCESS: From the Asheboro jct of US-220 and NC-49, go W on NC-49 for 5.7 mi, turn L (S) on Lassiter Mill Rd (SR-1107),

*old,*

*from 49 turn L (1170 Maclanie) turn Rt at forks*

2nd entrance)

and go 2.6 mi to a fork. Continue L for 1.8 mi to FR-6532, L, and drive 0.5 mi to the parking area at the end of the road. If from the S, Uwharrie for example, take SR-1303 for 5.3 mi N to Ophir, SR-1134 and SR-1105 for 2.7 mi N to Eleazer, and SR-1107 5.1 mi N to FR-6532, R.

### *Robbins Branch Trail* (3.2 mi); *Birkhead Trail* (5.6 mi; USFS #100); *Hannahs Creek Trail* (1.4 mi)                    278–280

- LENGTH AND DIFFICULTY: 10.2 mi combined, easy to moderate

- SPECIAL FEATURES: pioneer history

- TRAILHEAD AND DESCRIPTION: Follow the trail sign and at 0.4 mi reach a fork where the *Robbins Branch Trail* goes L and the *Hannahs Creek Trail* goes R. If following the *Robbins Branch Trail* proceed through a young forest; ascend gently. At 1.2 mi pass through an open area of sumac and wildflowers with a vista of the Uwharrie Mtns. Descend gradually, enter an older forest at 1.5 mi, and at 1.7 mi pass R of rock erosion barriers left by pioneer farmers. Turn sharply L on a footpath at 1.9 mi. After 92 yd cross Robbins Branch, bordered with Christmas ferns, and continue upstream to cross the branch three times and a tributary once. (In late August cardinal flowers are brilliant near the branch.) Leave the branch headwaters and jct with the *Birkhead Trail* at 3.2 mi.

To the L, the *Birkhead Trail* goes 2.6 mi to Tot Hill Farm Rd (SR-1142), its N terminus. To the R it runs 2 mi to a jct with *Hannahs Creek Trail* and another 1 mi to its S terminus at the forest boundary. If taking the N route, curve R at 0.2 mi to a shallow saddle for a traverse on the Coolers Knob Mtn crest. Pass Camp #1-B, L, with water at 0.7 mi. Reach Coolers Knob with a scenic view E on a 50-yd spur at 1.4 mi. Cedar Rock Mtn and peaks from 900 to 1,050 ft are visible from here. Descend, and at 1.5 mi leave the Birkhead Mtn Wilderness Area and cross private land for 0.2 mi before reentering the NF. Cross Talbotts Creek at 2.4 mi and reach SR-1142 at 7.2 mi. (It is 2 mi L to NC-49 and 5.1 mi R on NC-49 to Asheboro.) If taking the *Birkhead Trail* R (S), pass patches of wild quinine (*Parthenium integrifo-*

*lium*) and Camp #5 with a grill at 0.4 mi. Descend gradually in a hardwood forest. Reach the remnants of the Birkhead Plantation at 1.0 mi. (Boy Scout Troop 570 has erected a sign about John W. Birkhead [1858–1933] and his wife Lois Kerns [1868–1943] and their ten children. The family later moved to Asheboro where Mr. Birkhead was clerk of court and county sheriff.) At 1.7 mi pass Camp #4, R, with a yellow-blazed spur. At 2.0 mi is the site of the Christopher Bingham Plantation (ca 1780) and jct, R, with the *Hannahs Creek Trail*. Ahead the *Birkhead Trail* goes another 0.4 mi to cross the North Prong of Hannahs Creek and to a campsite at 0.9 mi with water. At 1 mile arrive at the S boundary of the Birkhead Mtn Wilderness Area, and the trail's S terminus. (Ahead it is 1 mi on a private jeep road to a crossing of the South Prong of Hannahs Creek and entry to SR-1109 at Strieby Church. From here it is 0.6 mi on the road to jct with SR-1143. To the R [W] it is 2.1 mi to Lassiter Mill crossroads with SR-1107, and L [E] 10.8 mi to Ulah and US-200.)

On the *Hannahs Branch Trail* follow the old woods road, cross a streamlet, and pass a chimney and foundation L at 0.2 mi. Cross another streamlet at 0.5 mi, pass a man-made rock wall, and cross Robbins Branch at 0.9 mi. Ascend to the jct with the *Robbins Branch Trail* at 1.4 mi. Veer L and return to the parking area. (*USGS-FS Maps:* Eleazer, Farmer)

## ▶ UWHARRIE TRAIL AREA
### (Montgomery County)

### *Uwharrie Trail* (USFS #276)                 281–283

- LENGTH AND DIFFICULTY: 20.5 mi, moderate

- CONNECTING TRAILS:
  *West Morris Mtn Trail* (2.2 mi; USFS #95, moderate)
  (*Dutchmans Creek Trail*)

- SPECIAL FEATURES: Dennis Mtn, Island Creek

- TRAILHEAD AND DESCRIPTION: The *Uwharrie Trail* (a national recreation trail since 1980) is a N-S route, which at the S end forms a reversed "S", crosses the middle of *Dutchmans Creek Trail,* and forms an irregular figure eight. Access to the S trailhead is at a parking lot on NC-24/27, 2 mi E of the Pee Dee River bridge and 10 mi W from the center of Troy. From the NW corner of the parking space, enter a footpath through small oaks and descend on the white-blazed trail into a more mature forest of hardwoods, pine, and laurel. Pass under a powerline at 0.3 mi. At 1 mi cross Wood Run Creek in a laurel grove, and at 2 mi jct with a 0.3-mi spur, R, to Wood Run primitive campsite. At 2.4 mi pass a spur a few yd R to FR-517. Follow the trail downstream, cross it six times, observe crested dwarf iris, and pass the remnants of an old automobile at 2.5 mi. Cross a timber road at 3.5 mi, ascend steeply to the top of Dennis Mtn (732 ft) at 3.7 mi for views W of Morrow Mtn State Park and Lake Tillery. Descend, join an old woods road R, rock-hop Island Creek at 4.6 mi, turn R on a footpath, and go upstream in a scenic forest with galax and royal ferns. After crossing the creek four times, ascend to and cross the terminus of FR-517 at 5.6 mi. At 5.7 mi arrive at a cross-trail with the yellow-blazed *Dutchmans Creek Trail.* (*Dutchmans Creek Trail* goes 5.3 mi L to rejoin the *Uwharrie Trail* N, and 5.9 mi R [S] to the NC-24/27 parking area. A loop can be formed here for either trail.) Continue on the *Uwharrie Trail* and jct at 6 mi with a 0.3-mi spur, R, the *Pond Camp Trail,* which goes to a small pond at the headwaters of Clarks Creek. For the next 2.2 mi the trail ascends and descends three hilltops, crosses three old forest roads and four streamlets, and reaches Dutchmans Creek at 7 mi. Deer and turkey may be seen in this area. The forest is open in a number of places, but laurel is dense near some of the stream areas. At 8.2 mi ascend from a young forest to jct with the *Dutchmans Creek Trail,* L at 8.4 mi. At 8.9 mi jct R with a spur trail of 0.5 mi to primitive Yates Place Camp. At 9 mi arrive at Mtn Road (SR-1146) where the trail crosses. (Left it is 2.1 mi to SR-1150; R it is 0.5 mi to Yates Place Camp and beyond for 5 mi on Carrol Rd [SR-1147] and NC-109 to Troy.)

Continue ahead on the *Uwharrie Trail,* and cross a tributary of Cedar Creek at 9.3 mi and Watery Branch at 10 mi. Follow downstream, R, for 0.5 mi. Begin a steep rocky climb and reach the hill summit at 10.8 mi. At 11.3 mi make a sharp turn off a logging road and reach NC-109 at 11.9 mi. Cross the road to a parking space. (It is 1.8 mi L on NC-109 to jct with SR-1150 and Uwharrie for groceries, telephone, gasoline, and supplies; R it is 5 mi to Troy.)

At 12.4 mi is a spring, L. Cross Cattail Creek at 12.8 mi and cross Spencer Creek hiking bridge at 14 mi. Ascend and pass a bed of running cedar at 14.1 mi and intersect with the yellow-blazed *West Morris Mtn Trail*, L at 14.3 mi. (The *West Morris Mtn Trail* descends 1 mi to the West Morris campground, a primitive camp without water or tables on Ophir Rd [SR-1303], 1.2 mi N of Uwharrie. The loop trail leaves the campground, S, descends to Spencer Creek, and ascends to complete a loop of 2.2 mi.) On the *Uwharrie Trail* ascend and reach the mtn summit at 14.6 mi. Cross an old forest road at 15 mi and at 17 mi cross two streams on bridges a few feet apart at Panther Branch. Cross Robinson Rd (SR-1134) at 18.1 mi. Reach a high ridge at 19.2 mi and continue to a rocky peak of Dark Mtn (953 ft) at 19.4 mi. Here is an excellent W view. After a rocky descent, reach a parking area on Flint Hill Rd (SR-1306) at 20.5 mi. Ophir is 1.8 mi L, Flint Hill is 2.8 mi R, and it is 7 mi to NC-134. (A former 5.4-mi *Uwharrie Trail Extension* [USFS #99] from here to SR-1143 has been discontinued because of its traverse on private property.) (*USGS-FS Maps:* Lovejoy, Morrow Mtn, Troy)

### *Dutchmans Creek Trail* (USFS #98)                    284

- LENGTH AND DIFFICULTY: 11.1 mi, moderate to strenuous

- CONNECTING TRAILS:
  (*Uwharrie Trail*)

- SPECIAL FEATURES: reforestation, old mines, remote, Dutchmans Creek

- TRAILHEAD AND DESCRIPTION: The S-shaped *Dutchmans Creek Trail* begins, ends, and crosses the middle of the S-section of the *Uwharrie Trail* to jointly form the shape of an erratic figure eight. The trailheads are at a parking lot on NC-24/27, 2 mi E of the Pee Dee River bridge and 10 mi W from the center of Troy.

The yellow-blazed trail begins at the NE corner of the parking lot, across FR-517. Cross a natural-gas line at 0.3 mi, then enter a clearcut at 0.4 mi and leave it at 1 mi. Cross a small branch at 1.1 mi and Dumas Creek at 2.2 mi. Ascend steeply to an open area for S views, and at 2.5 mi turn sharply L (N) at a 1978 reforestation project. Leave the clearcut, dip into a ravine, and at 3 mi cross a road in use to the private Piedmont Sportsmen Club. Pass under a powerline at 3.1 mi. Ascend gently to the top of a long flat ridge at 4.4 mi and descend to cross FR-517 at 4.9 mi. Cross Island Creek twice, ascend. Cross FR-517 again at 5.5 mi to ascend a rocky ridge. Reach a level area and a crosstrail jct with the *Uwharrie Trail* at 5.9 mi. (On the *Uwharrie Trail* it is 5.7 mi L to NC-24/27 and 3.3 mi R to NC-1146; see description below.) Follow the *Dutchmans Creek Trail* R of a clearcut, and reach a rocky hill at 6.3 mi. Descend into a grove of laurel and follow Little Island Creek for four crossings before ascending steeply on a rocky scenic mtn of hardwoods, Virginia pine, and wildflowers at 7.3 mi. (In the winter you can see Badin Dam [W] through the trees.) Reach the mtn summit at 7.6 mi. Descend for the next 0.4 mi and notice disturbed earth from old mines. Cross a streamlet three times before climbing another steep mtn to reach the top at 8.6 mi. (Badin Lake area can be seen through the trees in the winter, and Lick Mtn can be seen to the E.) At 9.1 mi descend to a garden-like area of laurel, galax, trailing arbutus, and wild ginger (*Hexastylis shuttleworthii*). At 9.5 mi rock-hop Dutchman's Creek and go upstream in a scenic area of gentle cascades and clear pools. Pass through a mature forest of tall oak, beech, and poplar with scattered holly. Rock-hop the creek three times before reaching a jeep road at 10.4 mi. Turn L and follow the jeep road to a private road at 10.8 mi. Turn L, go 50 yd, turn R on an old road, and leave it after 0.1 mi on a footpath to reach a jct with the *Uwharrie Trail* at 11.1 mi. It is 0.6 mi L on the *Uwharrie Trail* to SR-1146, and 2.7 mi R to rejoin the *Dutchmans Creek Trail*. (*USGS-FS Map:* Morrow Mtn)

# PART II

# Trails in the National Park System

# 5.

## Appalachian National Scenic Trail

*With my pack for days I've sought the high trail,*
*I have found primeval nature there.*
*Where the balsam bends before the fierce gale,*
*There in peace I find congenial air.*

—A. Rufus Morgan

Albert Rufus Morgan (1885-1983) loved the 2,100-mi *Appalachian National Scenic Trail (AT)* (USFS #1). He loved it so much that for many years he alone maintained 55 mi of it from Georgia to the Nantahala River Gorge. "For years I tried to keep the trail marked. I painted blazes until I began to lose my eyesight," he said in 1979. In 1950 he founded the Nantahala Hiking Club and served for 18 years as its president. Called a "modern Moses," this conservationist, poet, and Episcopal priest has been an inspiration to all hikers, and because of him and others like him the *AT* through 14 eastern states will always be there for others to enjoy. **285**

A continuous scenic corridor from Maine to Georgia, the *AT* is a living, changing masterpiece of incredible dreams, design, and dedication. To hike from end to end, the average number of footsteps is 5,240,000 and the average time is between four and five months. More than 1,550 known hikers have officially completed the world's most famous trail, and millions of other hikers have been lured by its mystique and natural beauty to walk parts of its trailway.

The first to hike the *AT* in one trip was Earl Shaffer, a WW II veteran from Pennsylvania, who was 29 years old when he began his solitary attempt. At the time (1948), trail leaders thought such a feat impossible, but he started at Mt. Oglethorpe, Georgia, April 4, and completed the journey August 5 at Katahdin, Maine. His remarkable adventure is documented in his journal *Walking with Spring,* which was first privately printed in 1981 and later published by the Appalachian Trail Conference (ATC) in 1984. Shaffer hiked the *AT* in the opposite direction in 1965, the first hiker to complete the *AT* in both directions. He started at Katahdin on July 19 and finished at Springer Mtn, Georgia, on October 25. The second hiker straight through was Gene Espy of Cordele, Georgia, in 1951. The first person to hike the *AT* in sections was Myron H. Avery, from the 1920s to 1936. A notable trio that completed the *AT* in 1964 was Chuck Ebersole, his teenage son Johnny, and their beagle Snuffy. The first woman to hike the complete distance in one continuous trip was the late Mrs. Emma Gatewood ("Grandma Gatewood") of Ohio. She started at Mt. Oglethorpe on May 3, 1955, and finished at Katahdin on September 25. She followed the same route again in 1957, and by 1964 at the age of 77 completed the third trip she had earlier taken in sections. She was dearly loved by the trail world for many reasons. Among them were her stamina, her love for people, and her great sense of humor. For example, on one occasion she was lost and was reminded of it when found by a forest official in Maine. "Not lost" she said, "just misplaced." The first woman to complete the *AT* in sections was Mary Kilpatrick of Philadelphia. She finished in 1939. Another solitary female hiker is Dorothy Laker of Tampa, Florida, who completed the *AT* in 1957 when a teenager, and again in 1964 and 1972.

The name and the concept of this supertrail belong solely to Benton MacKaye, a forester and author from Shirley Center, Massachusetts. He has said that he thought of it in the early 1900s, before the *Long Trail* was begun in Vermont in 1910. It was that year that James P. Taylor, a Vermont schoolmaster, established the Green Mountain Club and the concept of the Long Trail from Canada to Massachusetts. Others who had long trail and connecting-trail concepts were Philip W. Ayers, a New Hampshire forester, and Allen Chamberlain, a Boston newspaper columnist and early president of the Appalachian Mountain Club (founded in 1876). They formed the New England Trail Conference in 1916. One of the conference's goals was to connect the New England trails, a linkage that remarkably resembles the later path of the *AT*.

Two other founding fathers were U.S. forester William Hall, who envisioned a link with the southern Appalachians, and Will S. Monroe, professor and seer of the Green Mountain Club. Monroe's concept was to connect the New England trails to trails in New York and New Jersey. In December, 1921, Monroe's friend, J. Ashton Allis, proposed connecting the trails as far as the Pennsylvania state line. Two months before Allis' proposal the *Journal of the American Institute of Architects* carried MacKaye's article, "An Appalachian Trail: A Project in Regional Planning." The response to a singular name for the trails was immediate and within a year the Palisades Trail Conference (which later became part of the New York-New Jersey Trail Conference) began construction of a 6-mi section between Lake Tiorati Circle and Arden to connect with another trail in Palisades Interstate Park. The trail opened on Sunday, October 7, 1923, the first and original section of the *AT*. (The entire *AT* design was initially completed on August 15, 1937, but considerable relocation was to follow.)

In 1926 the leadership of Arthur Perkins of Hartford, Connecticut, began to translate MacKaye's dream and proposal into reality, but it was Myron H. Avery of Lubec, Maine, who probably more than any other leader was instrumental in implementing MacKaye's proposals. He worked and coordinated agreements with government agencies, including the important CCC and thousands of volunteers to complete the *AT*. He was the first president of the Potomac Appalachian Trail Club, formed in November 1927 in Washington, D.C., and served as chairman of the Appalachian Trail Conference from 1930 to 1952. In his final conference report he gave what has since become a classic definition of the *AT*: "Remote for detachment, narrow for chosen company, winding for leisure, lonely for contemplation, it beckons not merely north and south but upward to the body, mind, and soul of man."

Congress created the National Trails System Act in 1968 and gave further protection to the *AT* with the Appalachian Trail Act in 1978. In 1988 less than 175 mi of the *AT* remain unprotected, the longest sections of which are in Maine and Pennsylvania. Congressional appropriations to the NPS for this purpose will determine additional protective purchases.

*AT* mileage in North Carolina is 301.9 mi, most of which (205.9 mi) frequently weaves back and forth on the Tennessee border between Doe Knob in the Smokies and Elk Park NE of Roan Mtn. The *AT* is jointly maintained by private clubs of the ATC, USFS, and NPS. The Nantahala Hiking Club maintains 59.8 mi from the Georgia–North Carolina state line to the Nantahala River at Wesser on US-19. From there the Smoky Mountains Hiking Club maintains 97.4 mi to Davenport Gap at NC-284/TN-32. For the next 89.7 mi, the Carolina Mountain Club maintains the *AT* to Spivey Gap, US-19W. At that point the Tennessee Eastman Hiking Club maintains 55 mi to Elk Park (and 67.3 mi exclusively in Tennessee, which takes the *AT* to the Virginia state line 3.3 mi S of Damascus). (See club information in the Appendix.)

Hikers on the *AT* should acquire the latest edition of the *AT Guide to Tennessee-North Carolina* and *AT Guide to North Carolina-Georgia*. If not available in the local bookstore, the guidebooks can be ordered from the ATC, PO Box 807, Harpers Ferry, WV 25425, tel: 304-535-6331.

• ACCESS: To reach the *AT* at the Georgia-North Carolina state line at Bly Gap (3,840 ft), begin in Georgia at US-76, Dicks Creek Gap (2,675 ft), 11 mi E from Hiawassee and 18 mi W from Clayton. After 4.4 mi arrive at Plumorchard Gap Shelter, and at 8.7 mi arrive at the state line at a cleared crest. If beginning at the N end of the *AT* in the state, follow US-19E 1.6 mi W from Elk Park, N.C., or 16 mi E from Hampton, Tennessee.

The following information is a condensed listing of the major locations and prominent features of the *AT* through North Carolina. Milepoints are listed north to south and south to north. Features include shelters, post offices, highway crossings, support services, and other trail connections. Bold type numbers (the first is 286 for *Russell Field Trail*) are for the purpose of matching trails in the book to the pocket maps. They run W into Tennessee and are not described in this book. The other connecting trails (that are not numbered here) run E into North Carolina. They are described and numbered under GSMNP, Chapter 7.

### Appalachian National Scenic Trail

| Milepoints | | Location and Prominent Features |
|---|---|---|
| N to S | S to N | |
| | | The first 77.5 mi of the *AT* are in Georgia, beginning at Springer Mtn. |
| 301.9 | 0.0 | Bly Gap, NC-GA state line (3,840 ft). Nearest all-weather road is 8.7 mi S on US-76 in Georgia. |
| 300.4 | 1.5 | Court House Bald (4,650 ft). |
| 298.7 | 3.2 | Muskrat Creek Shelter. |
| 298.1 | 3.8 | Whiteoak Stamp, spring E. |
| 297.9 | 4.0 | Jct W with *Chunky Gal Trail* (5.2 mi to US-64). |
| 294.8 | 7.1 | Deep Gap (4,330 ft). FR-71 leads 6 mi W to US 64. |
| 294.0 | 7.9 | Standing Indian Shelter. |
| 292.0 | 9.9 | Standing Indian Mountain (5,490 ft). A rocky heath bald with excellent views of Georgia and the Tullulah River gorge. |
| 289.0 | 12.9 | Beech Gap (4,508 ft). |
| 285.8 | 16.1 | Carter-Gap Shelter (4,550 ft). |
| 281.1 | 20.8 | Mooney Gap, FR-67–2 (8 mi W to Standing Indian Campground). |
| 279.5 | 22.4 | Albert Mtn (5,280 ft) (named for the grandfather of A. Rufus Morgan). Fire tower and outstanding views of Coweeta Experimental Forest. |
| 279.0 | 22.9 | Big Spring Gap Shelter. |
| 273.8 | 28.1 | Rock Gap Shelter (3,750 ft). |

| | | |
|---|---|---|
| 273.0 | 28.9 | Wallace Gap (3,738 ft). US 64. Town of Franklin is 15 mi E. |
| 268.8 | 33.1 | Campsites. |
| 266.1 | 35.8 | Siler Bald Shelter and Siler Bald Mtn (5,216 ft) (named in honor of William Siler, great grandfather of Rufus Morgan). |
| 263.9 | 38.0 | Wayah Gap (4,180 ft). Cross SR-1310. |
| 261.7 | 40.2 | Jct W with yellow-blazed *Bartram Trail* and Wine Spring. |
| 259.8 | 42.1 | Wayah Bald Observation Tower and John B. Byrne Memorial. |
| 259.2 | 42.7 | E jct with *Bartram Trail* and *Big Locust Trail.* |
| 257.4 | 44.5 | Licklog Gap (4,408 ft). |
| 255.0 | 46.9 | Burningtown Gap, SR-1397. |
| 253.7 | 48.2 | Cold Springs Shelter. |
| 253.3 | 48.6 | Copper Bald (5,249 ft), scenic view of Nantahala River Valley. |
| 252.9 | 49.0 | Tellico Bald (5,130 ft), laurel. |
| 252.4 | 49.5 | Black Bald (5,000 ft), rhododendron. |
| 252.0 | 49.9 | Rocky Bald (5,180 ft), heath bald of rhododendrons and azaleas. |
| 249.8 | 52.1 | Tellico Gap (3,850 ft), FR-Otter Creek, leads E to SR-1310. |
| 248.4 | 53.5 | Wesser Bald Firetower (4,627 ft). |
| 247.7 | 54.2 | Wesser Creek Trail, E. |
| 242.9 | 59.0 | A. Rufus Morgan Shelter. |
| 242.1 | 59.8 | US-19, Wesser, N.C. (1,650 ft), lodging, groceries, and restaurant. |
| 242.0 | 59.9 | Cross Nantahala River bridge. |
| 239.9 | 62.0 | Tyre Top (3,760 ft). |
| 239.2 | 62.7 | Grassy Gap (3,050 ft). |
| 238.4 | 63.5 | The Jump-Up, near an extraordinary view of Nantahala River Valley. |
| 235.3 | 66.6 | Sassafras Gap Lean-to. |
| 234.3 | 67.6 | Cheoah Bald (5,062 ft), magnificent panoramas. |
| 229.9 | 72.0 | Stekoah Gap (3,165 ft). |

| 225.5 | 76.4 | Jct W with *Wauchecha Bald Trail,* 1.2 mi to Wauchecha Bald (4,385 ft). |
| 222.3 | 79.6 | Yellow Creek Gap. Tuskeegee Rd (SR-1242) E to NC-28. |
| 220.5 | 81.4 | Cable Gap Shelter. |
| 219.5 | 82.4 | High Top (3,786 ft), highest in Yellow Creek range, no vistas. |
| 217.7 | 84.2 | Walker Gap (3,450 ft). Jct with *Yellow Creek Mtn Trail,* W. |
| 215.0 | 86.9 | NC-28, Fontana Dam, N.C., lodging, groceries, restaurant, recreational facilities, post office. (Permit required for camping in the Smokies.) |
| 213.7 | 88.2 | Visitor Center, Fontana Dam Shelter. |
| 213.3 | 88.6 | Cross Fontana Dam. |
| 209.3 | 92.6 | Shuckstack Mtn (4,020 ft). Shuckstack Tower for scenic views. |
| 208.1 | 93.8 | Birch Spring Shelter (3,830 ft). |
| 203.6 | 98.3 | Mollies Ridge Shelter (4,600 ft). 0.1 mi ahead to Devils Tater Patch. |
| 201.3 | 100.6 | Russell Field Shelter (4,400 ft). *Russell Field Trail* descends W 3.5 mi toward Cades Cove Campground, Tenn. **286** |
| 198.9 | 103.0 | Spence Field Shelter (4,890 ft). *Eagle Creek Trail* descends E leading to Fontana Lake. Bote Mtn Rd leads W 6.6 mi to Cades Cove Rd in Tenn. |
| 198.5 | 103.4 | Side Trail E, *Jenkins Ridge Trail* leading S in N.C. |
| 197.8 | 104.1 | Rocky Top (5,440 ft). |
| 197.1 | 104.8 | East Peak of Thunderhead (5,530 ft). |
| 196.6 | 105.3 | Beechnut Gap (4,840 ft). |
| 194.7 | 107.2 | Starky Gap (4,530 ft). |
| 192.9 | 109.0 | Derrick Knob Shelter (4,880 ft). |
| 192.6 | 109.3 | Sams Gap (4,840 ft). *AT* goes E, *Greenbrier Ridge Trail* descends W 5.1 mi to Tremont Rd, Tenn. **287** |

| | | |
|---|---|---|
| 190.6 | 111.3 | Cold Spring Knob (5,240 ft). |
| 190.3 | 111.6 | *Miry Ridge Trail* exits W to Elkmont Campground, Tenn. **288** |
| 189.8 | 112.1 | Buckeye Gap (4,820 ft). |
| 187.5 | 114.4 | Silers Bald Shelter (5,440 ft) (named after Jesse Siler, great-great uncle of A. Rufus Morgan). Two shelters. Scenic view of Mt LeConte NE. |
| 187.1 | 114.8 | *Welch Ridge Trail* descends E to High Rocks and connects with Hazel Creek trails in N.C. |
| 185.8 | 116.1 | Double Springs Gap Shelter (5,590 ft). *Goshen Prong Trail* exits W to Little River Rd in Tenn. **289** |
| 183.5 | 118.4 | Mt Buckley (6,580 ft). |
| 183.0 | 118.9 | Clingmans Dome (6,643 ft), highest elevation on the entire *AT*. Tower provides panoramic views, 0.5 mi to parking area and Clingmans Dome Rd (named for Thomas L. Clingman, U.S. Senator, explorer). |
| 179.9 | 122.0 | Mt Collins (6,190 ft) and Mt Collins Shelter. *Sugarloaf Mtn Trail* exits W in Tenn. *Fork Ridge Trail* exits E in N.C. **290** |
| 177.2 | 124.7 | Indian Gap. *Road Prong Trail* exits W 3.3 mi to Chimney Tops parking area in Tenn. **291** |
| 175.5 | 126.4 | Newfound Gap (5,040 ft) and highway (formerly US-441). GSMNP headquarters W and Gatlinburg; Cherokee E. |
| 173.8 | 128.1 | *Sweat Heifer Trail* exits E 3.6 mi to Kephart Prong Shelter (5,830 ft). |
| 172.8 | 129.1 | *Boulevard Trail* (6,030 ft) exits W to Mt LeConte and the Jumpoff, outstanding vistas. **292** |
| 172.6 | 129.3 | Ice Water Spring Shelter (5,900 ft). |
| 171.4 | 130.5 | Charlies Bunion (5,400 ft). Outstanding view of the Smokies and Mt LeConte. Crowded by visitors; dangerous in icy weather. |
| 171.1 | 130.8 | Dry Sluice Gap (5,380 ft). *Richland Mtn Trail* exits E to connect with *Bradley Fork* and *Kephart Prong* trails in N.C. |

| | | |
|---|---|---|
| 166.5 | 135.4 | Bradleys View (5,800 ft) provides excellent vistas into Bradley Fork gorge. |
| 165.2 | 136.7 | Pecks Corner Shelter (5,850 ft), 0.4 mi E. *Hughes Ridge Trail* exits E, 11.8 mi to Smokemont Campground in N.C. |
| 162.5 | 139.4 | Mt Sequoyah (5,980 ft). |
| 161.2 | 140.7 | Mt Chapman (6,220 ft), forests of balsam and spruce. |
| 160.3 | 141.6 | Tri-Corner Knob Shelter (5,920 ft). *Balsam Mtn Trail* exits E 5.8 mi to Laurel Gap Shelter in N.C. |
| 158.2 | 143.7 | Mt Guyot Spur (6,180 ft) leads to summit of Mt Guyot (6,621 ft). |
| 156.4 | 145.5 | *Maddron Bald Trail* exits W to *Snake Den Mtn* and *Indian Camp Creek* trails in Tenn. |

**293–295**

| | | |
|---|---|---|
| 155.0 | 146.9 | Camel Gap (4,700 ft). *Yellow Creek Trail* goes E 5.2 mi to Walnut Bottoms in N.C. |
| 153.6 | 148.3 | Cosby Knob Shelter (4,800 ft). |
| 152.0 | 149.9 | Low Gap (4,240 ft). *Low Gap Trail* exits E 2.3 mi to Walnut Bottoms in N.C. *Cosby Creek Trail* exits W 2.5 mi to Cosby Campground in Tenn. **296** |
| 149.7 | 152.2 | Mt Cammerer side trail goes W 0.6 mi to summit (5,025 ft), spectacular 360 panorama. |
| 145.6 | 156.3 | Davenport Gap Shelter (2,200 ft). |
| 144.7 | 157.2 | Davenport Gap, TN-32, NC-284 (1,975 ft), groceries E 2 mi, camping another 0.5 mi. |
| 142.8 | 159.1 | Big Pigeon River bridge (1,400 ft) and I-40, 15 mi W to Newport, Tenn. |
| 139.9 | 162.0 | Painter Branch, camping. |
| 137.5 | 164.4 | Snowbird Mtn (4,263 ft), excellent scenic views. |
| 135.0 | 166.9 | Deep Gap, 0.2 mi E to Groundhog Creek Shelter. *Ground Hog Creek Trail* leads E 2.3 mi to I-40. |
| 132.7 | 169.2 | Harmon Den Mtn (3,840 ft), *Rube Rock Trail* E, 4 mi to I-40. |

| | | |
|---|---|---|
| 132.1 | 169.8 | Brown Gap, campsites. |
| 129.6 | 172.3 | Jct *Cherry Creek Trail*, E, 2.5 mi to FR-148. |
| 129.4 | 172.5 | Max Patch Rd (SR-1182) 1.6 mi E to FR-148. |
| 128.6 | 173.3 | Max Patch Mtn (4,629 ft). Panoramic views of the Smokies, Tenn. Valley, Mt Mitchell. |
| 123.2 | 178.7 | Lemon Gap, SR-1182 and TN-107 (3,550 ft). |
| 121.9 | 180.0 | Walnut Mtn Shelter. |
| 119.5 | 182.4 | Bluff Mtn (4,686 ft). |
| 116.0 | 185.9 | Garenflo Gap (2,500 ft), FR, E; *Shut-In Trail*, NW, 2 mi to SR-1183. |
| 112.6 | 189.3 | Deer Park Mtn Shelter. |
| 109.7 | 192.2 | Jesuit Hostel for *AT* hikers, Hot Springs, N.C. |
| 109.4 | 192.5 | Hot Springs, N.C. (1,326 ft). Lodging, groceries, PO, restaurant, laundromat. Roads US-25/70 and NC-209. |
| 108.1 | 193.8 | Lovers Leap Rock. Scenic view of the French Broad River. |
| 106.2 | 195.7 | Pump Gap. *Pump Gap Trail* leads W as alternate *AT* route to French Broad River. |
| 103.6 | 198.3 | Tanyard Gap (2,278 ft). Cross US-25/70. |
| 101.3 | 200.6 | Rich Mtn Firetower (3,643 ft). Panoramic views of Black Mtn range and the Smokies. |
| 98.7 | 203.2 | Spring Mtn Shelter (3,300 ft). |
| 95.0 | 206.9 | Allen Gap (2,234 ft). Roads NC-208 and TN-70, groceries. |
| 90.1 | 211.8 | Little Laurel Shelter. |
| 88.8 | 213.1 | Camp Creek Bald (4,844 ft). Jct with *Pounding Mill Trail*, S 4.8 mi to NC-208. |
| 86.8 | 215.1 | Blackstack Cliffs, superb views of N and W Tenn. |
| 86.6 | 215.3 | Bearwallow Gap. Jct E with *Whiteoak Flats Trail*, 4.4 mi to SR-1312. |
| 83.6 | 218.3 | Jct *Fork Ridge Trail*, S, 2 mi to FR-111. |
| 83.4 | 218.5 | Jerry Cabin Shelter. |
| 80.4 | 221.5 | Big Butt (4,838 ft) campsites. |
| 78.9 | 223.0 | Shelton gravestones. Great-great nephew and other relatives live S of here in Big Creek and Laurel Creek valleys. |

| 74.9 | 227.0 | Devil's Fork Gap (3,107 ft), NC-212, N to US-23. |
| 69.3 | 232.6 | Hogback Ridge Shelter. |
| 68.7 | 233.2 | High Rock (4,460 ft). |
| 67.2 | 234.7 | Sams Gap (3,800 ft). Road US-23, groceries, restaurant 3 mi E. |
| 61.2 | 240.7 | Big Bald (5,516 ft). Grassy bald with spectacular views. |
| 60.1 | 241.8 | Bald Mtn Shelter. |
| 58.7 | 243.2 | Little Bald (5,185 ft). |
| 55.5 | 246.4 | Campsites. |
| 55.0 | 246.9 | Spivey Gap (3,200 ft). Road US-19W. |
| 50.5 | 251.4 | No Business Knob Shelter. |
| 48.1 | 253.8 | Temple Hill Gap (2,850 ft). |
| 44.8 | 257.1 | Nolichucky River (1,700 ft). Erwin, Tenn. Lodging, groceries, restaurant, PO, 1.8 mi W. |
| 43.4 | 258.5 | Nolichucky Whitewater Exp., groceries, accommodations. |
| 40.5 | 261.4 | Curley Maple Gap Shelter (3,080 ft). |
| 36.4 | 265.5 | Indian Grave Gap (3,360 ft). 3 mi W to USFS Rock Creek Rec Area. |
| 35.3 | 266.6 | FR-230, N. 50 yd to spring. |
| 34.1 | 267.8 | Beauty Spot (4,337 ft), grassy scenic bald. |
| 32.0 | 269.9 | FR-230, W. |
| 31.0 | 270.9 | Unaka Mtn (5,180 ft), summit of conifers. |
| 28.3 | 273.6 | Cherry Gap Shelter. |
| 25.6 | 276.3 | Iron Mtn Gap. TN-107/NC-226 roads (3,723 ft), groceries 0.5 mi E. |
| 21.5 | 280.4 | Greasy Creek Gap, campsites. |
| 19.6 | 282.3 | Clyde Smith Shelter. |
| 17.5 | 284.4 | Hughes Gap (4,040 ft). Accommodations 2 mi E; town of Buladean E on NC-26, 5.3 mi. Town of Burbank W, 3.2 mi. |
| 14.8 | 287.1 | Roan High Knob (6,285 ft). Cloudland Rhododendron Gardens. Summit forested with evergreens. |
| 14.2 | 287.7 | Roan High Knob Shelter. |

| | | |
|---|---|---|
| 12.9 | 289.0 | Carvers Gap (5,512 ft). TN-143/NC-261 roads. |
| 10.0 | 291.9 | Roan Highlands Shelter in Low Gap (5,050 ft). |
| 8.3 | 293.6 | Yellow Mtn Gap (4,682 ft). Site of John Sevier's "Overmountain Men," historic Bright's Trace, and *Overmountain Victory Trail*. Overmountain Shelter 0.3 mi E. |
| 6.6 | 295.3 | Big Yellow Mtn (5,459 ft). Grassy balds with extraordinary views. |
| 5.0 | 296.9 | Hump Mtn (5,587 ft). Superb panorama of Doe River Valley NW, Whitetop and Mt Rogers in Virginia, Beech Mtn to NE, and Grandfather Mtn to E. |
| 0.5 | 301.4 | Apple House Shelter. |
| 0.0 | 301.9 | US-19E, Elk Park, N.C. Lodging, groceries, restaurant, PO, 2.3 mi E. *(AT* continues 70.6 mi NW through Tenn. to Damascus, Va.) |

# 6.

## Blue Ridge Parkway

*No fairer land surely than this, where the hills*
*Are feathered with forests, and braided with rills.*
                                                  —A.M. Huger

The Blue Ridge Parkway (BRP), a 469-mi highway described as the most scenic in America, averages 3,000 ft in elev and runs along the majestic crest of the Blue Ridge Mountains. In the beginning it was a trail made by surveyors, landscape architects, and naturalists. "They stamped out a trail with their hobnailed boots/ Cutting blazes on trees as they went/ Over ridges and hollows they marked the way/ For the men and machines that would follow," wrote Albert Clarke Haygard, Jr., in his 1959 *The Skyline Saga.* It is a link between Shenandoah National Park at Rockfish Gap in Virginia and Cherokee at the edge of Great Smoky Mountains National Park in North Carolina. It is a "road of unlimited horizons, a grand balcony," wrote Harley E. Jolley in 1969 in *The Blue Ridge Parkway.* It is also a classic piece of engineering that has preserved the physical and cultural aspects of the Blue Ridge.

Although the NPS archives have not identified a single originator of the BRP idea, a number of historians give the credit to Harry F. Byrd, a U.S. senator from Virginia. (Another claim for the credit is from Theodore E. Straus of Maryland, a member of the Public Works Administration [PWA], who said in 1962, "I am the originator of the mountain road connecting the Skyline

Drive to the Smokies." Fred L. Weede, from Asheville and one of the leaders in the routing of the BRP through Asheville, said in 1954 that he recognized Straus as "the father of the idea.") Senator Byrd accompanied President Franklin D. Roosevelt on an inspection tour of the CCC camps in the Shenandoah National Park in August 1933. When the President expressed his enjoyment of such natural beauty, Byrd suggested an extension of the mountaintop route to the Smokies. President Roosevelt liked the suggestion, even stated that it should begin in New England. Senator Byrd later stated that the President said, "You and Ickes (Harold L. Ickes, Roosevelt's Secretary of the Interior, who was with them on the CCC tour) get together for the right of way." It was not that simple. Not only did a political controversy arise over the routing through North Carolina and Tennessee, but a final right of way was not deeded until October 22, 1968. (The original construction route was long opposed by the owners of Grandfather Mountain.) Initially the plan called for the BRP to be a toll road, something North Carolina Governor J.C.B. Ehringhaus opposed. After considerable political debate, Secretary Ickes decided in 1934 to eliminate any Tennessee routing, probably due to the strong influence of Ambassador Josephus Daniels, a North Carolinian and close friend of President Roosevelt and Secretary Ickes.

On September 11, 1935, the first rocks were blasted on the BRP near the Cumberland Knob area, and 52 years later the missing link (6.5 mi that included the engineering wonder of the Linn Cove viaduct on the E slope of Grandfather Mountain) was completed and dedicated September 11, 1987. The day of dedication was one of great pride for those who had spent a lifetime as part of this innovative dream. Many had not been aware of the political perils in its construction. Once begun, Virginia and North Carolina were determined to complete it with or without federal assistance. Congress debated the management of the parkway as much or more than its financing. In July 1934, Secretary Ickes notified the NPS that he desired that agency to maintain and administer the parkway. But Congress had to approve this idea, and on April 24, 1936, N.C. congressman Robert Lee Doughton introduced the bill. "I think that this is the most ridiculous undertaking that has ever been presented to Congress . . . a colossal steal," argued Jesse P. Wolcott, a congressman from Michigan. The bill barely passed on June 20, 1936 (145 for, 131 against, and 147 abstaining). It was approved quickly by the Senate, and President Roosevelt signed the bill into public law (#848) on June 22, 1936.

The BRP is a popular tourist attraction (more than 21.5 million visitors in 1986 for example) with a wide range of cultural and recreational facilities. Its 241 mi through N.C. begin at milepost 217 in Cumberland Knob Park. Along the way are facilities for camping, fishing, bicycling, picnicking, horseback riding, hiking, and cross-country skiing. In addition there are lodges, historic exhibits, museums, parks, and mountain-culture preserves. Campgrounds are at Doughton Park, Price Park, Linville Falls, Crabtree Meadows, and Mt Pisgah. There are more than 50 trails; some are graded and manicured, some are simple pathways, others are rugged and natural. Long segments of the *MST* will follow its narrow corridor, and its newest and most expensive trail, the *Tanawha Trail,* is a crown jewel of design and natural beauty on the E slopes of Grandfather Mtn. A number of BRP trails join a network of trails in the adjoining national forests.

Because of the density of visitors and user damage to the natural environment, the NPS has a number of regulations for the benefit of all. Some of them are listed here to assist hikers in their planning. Camping is not allowed on any BRP trail—only in the campgrounds or in primitive camps with a permit. No alcohol or open containers of alcohol are allowed in passenger compartments of vehicles. Pets must be kept on leashes. Quiet hours in the campgrounds are 10 pm to 6 am. Weapons are unlawful (including bows, airguns, and slingshots). Fires are allowed only at designated campgrounds. All plants and animals are protected—berries, nuts, and edible fruits may be gathered for personal consumption. Maximum speed is 45 mph. No swimming in lakes or ponds and no rock climbing unless permission is obtained from a ranger of the NPS. Emergency dispatch telephone numbers are 704-259-0701 and 704-298-9612.

• INFORMATION: The following BRP offices are open from 9 am to 4:30 pm weekdays: Doughton Park (mp 217–261), 919-372-8568; Cone Park (mp 261–305), 704-295-7591; Gillespie Gap (mp 305–355), 704-765-2761; Swannanoa (mp 355–407), 704-259-0701; Balsam Gap (mp 407–469), 704-456-9530. Headquarters office: 700 Northwestern Bank Bldg, Asheville, NC 28801, tel: 704-259-0779. (Trails: 704-259-0809)

## ▶ CUMBERLAND KNOB RECREATION AREA (mp 217.5)

The Cumberland Knob Recreation Area is a 1,000-acre forest and park, 1 mi from the Virginia state line. It is the first recreation area constructed as part of the first 12.7 mi of the BRP in 1935-1936. It is probably named for William Augustus, Scottish Duke of Cumberland (1721-1765). Picnic areas and a visitor information center are open May 1 to October 31. Camping is not available. Elev 2,740 ft. Galax, Va., is 8 mi N on NC/VA-89. (*USGS Map:* Cumberland Knob)

### *Cumberland Knob Trail* (1.7 mi); *Gully Creek Trail* (2.7 mi) 297–298

• LENGTH AND DIFFICULTY: 4.4 mi combined, easy

• TRAILHEAD AND DESCRIPTION: Follow the signs to the information center, turn R, and reach the summit (2,855 ft) at 0.3 mi. Circle the Knob and return through picnic areas, or descend on the *Gully Creek Trail*. Follow the *Gully Creek Trail* L of the visitor center, descending on a well-graded trail with switchbacks to Gully Creek at 0.8 mi. Trail crisscrosses the stream and begins ascent on switchbacks at 1.3 mi. A scenic knob is at 1.9 mi. Return by the Cumberland Knob, or take a shorter trail, R, to the parking lot.

### ▶ FOX HUNTERS PARADISE TRAIL (mp 218.6)    299

The trail is an easy 0.2-mi path that provides a scenic view of forests in western Surry County where fox hunters listen to their hounds from High Piney Knoll.


### ▶ LITTLE GLADE POND TRAIL (mp 230)    300

The trail is an easy 0.3-mi loop around the site of a turbine-type mill operated about 1895 to 1915.


### ▶ DOUGHTON PARK (mp 238.5–244.7)

Doughton Park is named in honor of Robert Lee "Muley Bob" Doughton, an enduring congressman (1911-1953) from N.C.'s 9th district, and a leader and advocate for establishing and developing the BRP. The 6,000-acre park has a lodge (open May through October), svc sta, camp store, campground, backcountry camping, picnic area, nature studies, special exhibits, fishing, and more than 30 mi of trails. Its most frequently used trail is the scenic *Fodder Stack Trail*. It goes 0.7 mi NE from the parking lot at the lodge to Wildcat Rock and to Fodder Stack outcropping. From here are impressive views of the Basin Creek watershed and the pioneer cabin of Martin and Janie Caudill seen deep in the valley. Along the trail are Fraser magnolia, hemlock, rhododendron, minnie-bush, white moss, and, for this far S, a rare grove of large-toothed aspen. All other trails are interconnecting; they form loops that converge as a funnel into Basin Cove. Backpack camping is allowed near the confluence of Basin and Cove creeks, but a permit is required from the ranger's office. There is a trail system signboard at Alligator Back Overlook, mp 242.2. (*USGS Map:* Whitehead)
**301**

• ADDRESS: District Ranger, Rte 1, Box 263, Laurel Spring, NC 28644, tel: 919-372-8568.

### *Bluff Mountain Trail*            302–307

* LENGTH AND DIFFICULTY: 7.2 mi, easy to moderate

* CONNECTING TRAILS:
  *Cedar Ridge Trail* (4.3 mi, strenuous, elev change 2,265 ft)
  *Bluff Ridge Trail* (2.8 mi, strenuous, elev change 2,229 ft)
  *Basin Cove Trail* (3.3 mi, moderate)
  *Grassy Gap Trail* (6.7 mi, strenuous, elev change 1,805 ft)
  *Flat Rock Ridge Trail* (5 mi, strenuous, elev change 1,880 ft)

* SPECIAL FEATURES: Brinegar and Caudill cabins, Bluff Mtn

* TRAILHEAD AND DESCRIPTION: Park at the Brinegar Cabin parking lot, mp 238.5 (3,508 ft). The Brinegar Cabin has a handicraft exhibit. The cabin was the home (begun in 1885) of Martin Brinegar (1856-1925), his wife, the former Caroline Jones (1863-1943), and their children. From the parking lot follow the trail sign 0.2 mi to the trailheads of *Bluff Mtn Trail,* R, and the *Cedar Ridge Trail,* L. A long loop of 16.5 mi can be made by going in either direction to include the *Flat Rock Ridge Trail,* or a shorter loop of 12.9 mi if using the primitive *Bluff Ridge Trail.* The description below follows these trails in a counter-clockwise route. (The *MST* follows the *Bluff Mtn Trail* S to Alligator Back, but it goes 1.5 mi N on a separate route also to Air Bellow Gap, mp 237.1, where it leaves the BRP on its E route. See Chapter 16.)

Begin the yellow-blazed *Bluff Mtn Trail* on an easy grade of grassy fields, wildflowers, and groves of white pine, and after 1 mi enter the campground for long RVs. Cross the BRP and briefly parallel the tent and small RV section of the campground. Cross the BRP at Low Notch (mp 239.9) at 1.6 mi and ascend slightly to open and more level areas. Cross the BRP again to arrive at the svc sta at 2.6 mi. From here go past the souvenir shop into the forest, come out to the BRP and cross. Immediately cross the picnic road and follow the trail through the heath and grassy meadows of Bluff Mtn to the picnic parking area at 3.9 mi. Continue ahead to the jct of primitive *Bluff Ridge Trail,* L at 4.1 mi.

(The primitive *Bluff Ridge Trail* passes a picnic shelter after 240 ft and follows the ridge of the Alligator Back escarpment.

There are views of the Cove Creek drainage and Flat Rock Ridge. Descend on the red-blazed trail to a gap after 0.5 mi, ascend to Brooks Knob at 0.7 mi, and consistently descend for 1.2 mi to the trail terminus and jct with the *Grassy Gap Trail* (fire road) R and ahead, and the *Basin Creek Trail,* L. The *Grassy Gap Trail* goes 5 mi up Cove Creek to the *Bluff Mtn Trail* and the BRP; it goes ahead, downstream, 1.7 mi to jct with the *Cedar Ridge Trail,* the *Flat Rock Ridge Trail,* and a parking area at Long Bottom Rd. If hiking the *Basin Creek Trail,* follow the dark blue-blazed old wagon road 3.3 mi up Basin Creek. Rock-hop the creek frequently in a lush valley of poplar, oak, maple, and rhododendron. Pass L of the mouth of Caudill Branch at 1.5 mi. Reach Wildcat Branch, which flows from the L at 3.2 mi. Turn R from here and ascend 0.1 mi to an open area and the one-room cabin of Martin and Janie Caudill. Although the Caudill family had 16 children, only a few were born here. In 1916 a flood washed away most of the houses downstream and drowned some of the residents. The Caudill cabin was not damaged. Backtrack.)

Continuing on the *Bluff Mtn Trail,* descend from the jct with the *Bluff Ridge Trail,* in the picnic area, on switchbacks to Alligator Back overlook (mp 242.2) at 4.6 mi. Bear L and parallel the BRP to reach Bluff Mtn overlook (mp 243.4) at 5.7 mi. Here are views of the rock wall and cliffs of Bluff Mtn. Join the *Grassy Gap Trail* (fire road) and follow it 0.1 mi before leaving it R, at 6.1 mi.

(The *Grassy Gap Trail* descends on a green-blazed winding road to jct with *Bluff Ridge Trail* and *Basin Creek Trail* at 5 mi. Thirty yd L of the jct is the gravesite of Alice Caudill, a child bride, who was drowned in the 1916 flood. Downstream after 0.1 mi is the primitive campsite, and beyond the trail crosses Basin Creek to end at Long Bottom Rd at 6.7 mi.)

Proceed on the *Bluff Mtn Trail* and reach the Basin Cove overlook (mp 244.7) at 7.2 mi. Here the *Bluff Mtn Trail* ends and the light-blue-blazed *Flat Rock Ridge Trail* begins. It is 100 yd R to the Basin Cove overlook. The *Flat Rock Ridge Trail* descends on a scenic ridge in a hardwood forest with scattered pines, two species of rhododendron, and a number of open rocky outcroppings. At 1.6 mi and 1.7 mi are some of the best views of Bluff

Mtn and the Cove Creek drainage area. At 5 mi reach the end of the trail at Long Bottom Rd and jct with the *Cedar Ridge Trail* and the *Grassy Gap Trail*. Vehicle access to this point is from the jct of the BRP and NC-18, 7 mi SW on the BRP from Doughton Park. Turn S on NC-18, go 5.9 mi to McGrady, turn L on Long Bottom Rd (SR-1728), and drive 7.1 mi to the parking area and gated road L. (Long Bottom Rd becomes SR-1730 enroute.) (Absher is 2.5 mi ahead on Long Bottom Rd, and 3 mi farther is the W entrance to Stone Mtn State Park.)

To complete the loop begin the orange-blazed *Cedar Ridge Trail* (90 yd inside the gated *Grassy Gap Trail* gate) on a series of switchbacks for 0.6 mi. Ascend gradually along the ridgeline and park boundary in a forest of hardwoods, conifers, and laurel. At 3.5 mi begin another series of switchbacks, and at 4.3 mi return to the *Bluff Mtn Trail* jct and Brinegar Cabin parking lot.

▶ **JUMPINOFF ROCKS TRAIL (mp 260.3)**          308

Follow the trail 0.5 mi through a forest with beds of galax and tufts of arbutus to rocky cliffs (3,165 ft) for scenic views. Backtrack.

▶ **THE LUMP TRAIL (mp 264.4)**          309

The trail leads 0.3 mi to a grassy bald with 360 scenic views, particularly of the Yadkin Valley.

▶ **E.B. JEFFRESS PARK (mp 271.9)**          310

The park has restrooms, drinking water, and picnic tables. It is named in honor of the 1934 State Highway Commission chairman who crusaded for the BRP. The *Cascades Nature Trail* loops through a forest of hardwoods, laurel, and hemlock to cascades on Falls Creek. Complete the loop after 1.2 mi.

## ▶ TOMPKINS KNOB TRAIL (mp 272.5)     311

The trail is a 0.6-mi loop from the parking lot around the historic (log) Cool Spring Baptist Church and the Jesse Brown Cabin.

## ▶ MOSES H. CONE MEMORIAL PARK (mp 292.7–295)

The 3,517-acre mountain estate of Moses H. Cone (1857-1908), textile "denim king," was donated to the NPS in 1950 as a "pleasuring ground" for the public. The Southern Highlands Handicraft Guild occupies part of Cone Manor. A stable is nearby and down the mtn in front of the mansion is the 22-acre Bass Lake. To the L (W) of the manor is the *Craftsman's Trail,* a 0.7-mi figure-eight self-guiding trail with medicinal herbs. There are more than 25 mi of old carriage trails that provide one-way trips, loops, and crosstrail connections for hikers, equestrians, and cross-country skiers. High pastureland, deep and damp coves, and a forest with plenty of wildlife make this area ideal for an all-day hike. Access to the network of trails (carriage roads) is from the parking area to the paved road in front of the manor and E to the gravel road at the stable. Three of the trails are N of the BRP; all others are S. The *MST* follows two of the trails—*Rich Mtn Trail* and *Watkins Trail*—(see Chapter 16). The shorter trails that connect S of the manor are the 2.7-mi *Duncan Trail,* the 0.6-mi *Black Bottom Trail,* the 1.8-mi *Bass Lake Trail,* the 2.3-mi *Maze Trail,* and the 1-mi *Rock Creek Bridge Trail.* The three longest trails are described below (*USGS Map:* Boone)     **312–317**

### Rich Mountain Trail *(4.3 mi);* Flat Top Mountain Trail *(3 mi);* Watkins Trail *(4 mi)*     318–320

- LENGTH AND DIFFICULTY: 11.3 mi combined, moderate

- SPECIAL FEATURES: Cone Manor and cemetery

- TRAILHEAD AND DESCRIPTION: From the parking area, walk E to the gravel road behind the stable. To the L follow the road and enter the BRP underpass to a fork at 0.1 mi. To the L is the *Rich Mtn Trail,* to the R is the *Flat Top Mtn Trail.* If hiking L, descend to a crossing of Flannery Fork Rd (SR-1541, also called Payne Branch Rd) at 0.7 mi. Follow E of Trout Lake (permanently drained) to the dam, turn L, and follow switchbacks up a stream under tall hemlocks. Pass a gate at 2.2 mi. After ascending to a scenic open pasture, turn R at the curve at 2.6 mi. Reenter the forest. At 3.2 mi the *MST* turns sharply L off the road. (The *MST* descends W on its route to Price Park. See Chapter 16.) Continuing on the road reach a scenic circle and advance to the top of Rich Mtn (4,370 ft) at 4.3 mi. Backtrack to the BRP underpass.

On the *Flat Top Mtn Trail* ascend in a pasture. At 0.8 mi take a spur trail L and enter an avenue of Fraser fir to the Cone family cemetery. Continue on the ascent with switchbacks and reach the scenic summit of Flat Top Mtn (4,558 ft) at 3 mi. Backtrack to the stable. From the stable go S, but turn sharply L in front of the manor (at 0.2 mi from the BRP). Descend into a forest of hemlock and white pine; go straight at a curve at 0.7 mi. Follow the well-graded switchbacks through large rhododendron slicks and groves of hemlock. At 2.8 mi keep L in a curve. (The road R is *Black Bottom Trail,* which leads to the *Maze Trail* and the *Bass Lake Trail.*) Pass L of a lake and spillway, and at 3.8 mi cross Penley Branch in a forest of exceptionally tall maple, oak, and hemlock. Turn R at a road used by residents and arrive at US-221 at 4 mi. Across the highway is the New River Inn. (It is 1 mi R on US-221 to Blowing Rock, 0.2 mi L to the BRP, and 2.3 mi L on the BRP to Cone Manor.)

## ▶ JULIAN PRICE MEMORIAL PARK (mp 295.5–300)

Julian Price purchased this land in the early 1940s to develop it into a resort for the employees of Jefferson Standard Life Insurance Company. Because of his unexpected death in 1946, the company gave the property to the NPS with an agreement that a lake and park would bear his name. Although the area had been logged in the early part of the century, few settlers ever lived here. One early settler, probably between 1810 and 1817, was Jesse Boone, nephew of Daniel. Boone Fork, which flows N from the lake, bears his name. The 4,344-acre plateau has a developed campground with 134 tent sites (some open all year) and 60 sites for trailers (no hook-ups). There is also a large scenic picnic area, trout fishing, boat rentals, and hiking. The *MST* follows part of the *Boone Fork Trail*. (*USGS Maps:* Boone, Valle Crucis, Grandfather Mtn)

### Green Knob Trail                                            321

• LENGTH AND DIFFICULTY: 2.3 mi, moderate

• TRAILHEAD AND DESCRIPTION: From the Sims Lake parking lot (E of the picnic area on the BRP) descend to the lake, cross the bridge, and circle L. Follow up the side of Sims Creek and cross under the BRP bridge at 0.7 mi. Cross the stream in a forest of hemlock, poplar, birch, and oak to ascend Green Knob. Reach the top (3,930 ft) at 1.5 mi, and descend to the BRP parking lot.

### Price Lake Loop Trail                                       322

• LENGTH AND DIFFICULTY: 2.4 mi, easy

• TRAILHEAD AND DESCRIPTION: Follow the signs counterclockwise around the lake from any beginning point in the lakeside camping area. Cross Cold Prong stream at 0.7 mi, Boone Fork stream at 0.9 mi, and Laurel Creek at 1.6 mi. The trail is well-graded and wet only in a few spots near the upstream marshes. Parts of the trail are arbored with rhododendron. Return at the dam and the parking lot to reenter the campground at 2.4 mi.

### Boone Fork Trail                                            323

• LENGTH AND DIFFICULTY: 4.9 mi, moderate

• TRAILHEAD AND DESCRIPTION: From the picnic area parking lot, cross Boone Fork on a bridge to the trail system sign and enter the woods ahead for a clockwise loop. Ascend gently to the campground and pass through Section B (between campsites) at 0.6 mi to enter a low area. Ascend through a rhododendron grove and jct, R and L, with the *Tanawha Trail* (described below) at 0.7 mi. Turn R and jointly follow the *Tanawha Trail* to a stile and pasture at 1.1 mi. After 35 yd the *Tanawha Trail* turns L, but the *Boone Fork Trail* picks up the *MST* that has come up from the S on the *Tanawha Trail.* Continue on the *Boone Fork Trail,* jointly with the *MST,* on an old farm road through the pasture. Keep straight at a road fork at 1.3 mi, ascend slightly in a patch of woods, and at 1.4 mi turn abruptly R at a signpost. Descend 40 yd to a stile and enter a dense forest to the headwaters of Bee Tree Creek. Cross it 16 times, sometimes on a footbridge. At 2.6 mi turn sharply R off the old RR grade, cross Bee Tree Creek for the final time, and reach Boone Fork at 2.7 mi. Stay on the high N side of the mtn in dense rhododendron, birch, and hemlock. Ascend in a large rocky area at 3.2 mi, elevated from the cascades. Reach an old dam site, L, at 3.6 mi. Pass a large scenic rock slope to immediately leave the *MST* at 3.8 mi. (The *MST* requires rock-hopping Boone Fork on its journey upward to Rich Mtn. See Chapter 16.) Continue upstream on an old RR grade and exit into a partial field that has copious patches of blackberries and wild pink roses at 4.6 mi. (This is a good area for birders.) Pass a fence and return to the picnic area at 4.9 mi.

### *Tanawha Trail*                                        324–327

- LENGTH AND DIFFICULTY: 13.3 mi, moderate

- CONNECTING TRAILS:
  *(Boone Fork Trail)*
  *(MST)*
  *(Cold Prong Pond Trail)*
  *(Upper Boone Fork Trail)*
  *(Grandfather Trail)*
  *(Grandfather Mtn Access Trail)*
  *(Daniel Boone Scout Trail)*
  *(Beacon Heights Trail)*

- SPECIAL FEATURES: trail design, Rough Ridge boardwalk, Linn Cove

• TRAILHEAD AND DESCRIPTION: This exceptional trail has been designed, constructed, and supervised at the cost of $700,000. There is not a similar trail elsewhere in the state. The Cherokee Indian name means "fabulous hawk," the name they gave the mtn now called Grandfather. Markers with a feather logo are placed at strategic points on the trail. The trail parallels the BRP from the Price Lake parking area (mp 297.3) to the Beacon Heights parking area (mp 305.3). In the process it passes through pastureland, deep forest coves, ascends to rocky outlooks, crosses cascading streams, and goes under the engineering marvel of the Linn Cove Viaduct. It is a trail for day hikes; no camping is allowed. Camping options are either in Price Park or outside the BRP boundary with fee permits for designated campsites from Grandfather Mtn, Inc. (see Chapter 14). The trail is described N to S, beginning at the Price Lake parking area. Except for the first 0.7 mi, the trail is also the *MST* route (see Chapter 16). (*USGS Maps:* Grandfather Mtn, Valle Crucis, Boone)

Follow the trail sign and cross the BRP to Section B of the park's campground. Bear L of the campsites and enter a rhododendron grove. At 0.3 mi jct R with the *Boone Fork Trail* (described above). Arrive at a pasture and stile at 0.7 mi. Go 35 yd and turn sharply L into the woods. (The *Boone Fork Trail* continues ahead.) Cross two small footbridges and exit from the woods into the pasture at 0.9 mi. Ascend gently to enter the woods again, and pass through 3 more stiles before crossing Holloway Mtn Rd (SR-1559) at 1.7 mi. (It is 1 mi L on the road to BRP mp 298.6.) Enter another stile across the road to ascend a scenic pasture. Views of the Grandfather Mtn range can be seen ahead. Enter another forest and another pasture before passing the last stile at 2.8 mi. Descend gently into a low area of poplar, ash, and white snakeroot at 3 mi. Pass through a forest of tall hardwoods and groves of rhododendron to reach at 3.7 mi a jct with *Cold Prong Pond Trail,* L. (It goes 0.2 mi to the Cold Prong parking area and Cold Prong Pond at mp 299.2. Backtrack.) For the next 1 mi cross small streams and pass through a mature forest deep into Price Park. Upon coming out around a ridge, leave the Price Park boundary (but the trail continues unchanged within the BRP corridor). Pass a rich display of rosebay rhododendron, witch hazel, and at 5.5 mi a patch of flame azalea. Follow an old RR grade a short distance before arriving at an access to Boone Fork parking at 5.6 mi. (A sharp L goes 135 yd to Boone Fork parking, mp 299.9. Along the way, the 0.5-mi *Upper Boone Fork Trail* forks R and follows the Boone Fork under the BRP to scenic Calloway Peak overlook at mp 299.7.) Immediately after the jct cross a high footbridge over cascades and pools of Boone Fork. Within 100 yd, L, is the 0.4-mi *Grandfather Mtn Access Trail,* which is also the *Daniel Boone Scout Trail* access. (It descends on an old road under the BRP bridge to a parking area on US-221. This route is recommended for hikers with required fee permits to the trails of Grandfather Mtn, Inc.) At 5.9 mi jct R with the *Grandfather Trail Ext*, and at 6 mi the *Daniel Boone Scout Trail,* R. (Both trails require fee permits and are described in Chapter 14.) Descend to a stream crossing at 6.2 mi, curve around a ridge, and descend to a footbridge over Dixon Creek at 7.1 mi. Pass through a lush cove of tall hardwoods, jewel weed, and black cohosh at 7.4 mi. At 8.6 mi jct L with the 0.1-mi access route to Raven Rocks overlook, mp 302.3 on the BRP. Cross a footbridge over a fork of cascading Little Wilson Creek at 9 mi. A 60-yd access trail to Rough Ridge parking on the BRP, mp 302.9, is at 9.3 mi. Immediately cross a footbridge over a fork of Little Wilson Creek. Curve around and up the ridge to the spectacular views from the Rough Ridge boardwalk at 9.5 mi. In late September and early October the rocky mountainside turns multiple hues of red from the blueberry bushes. Other plants here are turkey grass, Allegheny sand-myrtle, red spruce, and mountain ash. Descend into a scenic area of rocky overhangs at 10.4 mi, and after 0.2 mi cross a footbridge over the cascading Wilson Creek. To the L is a 70-yd access trail under the BRP to the Wilson Creek overlook at mp 303.7. Reach a pedestrian overlook at 11.4 mi, descend to cross Linn Cove Branch and pass under the Linn Cove Viaduct to an observation deck at 11.6 mi. After 200 yd arrive at the Linn Cove parking area, mp 304.4. Reenter the forest to a section of huge boulders, descend to cross a footbridge over cascading Stack Rock Creek, and reach Stack Rock, L, at 13.2

mi. Reach the BRP Stack Rock parking area, R, mp 304.8, at 12.5 mi. Cross a footbridge over Andrews Creek, follow a boardwalk alongside the BRP, and cross US-221 at 13 mi. (US-221 is a serpentine route of asphalt between Blowing Rock and Linville. It follows the route the Cherokee called the *Yonahlossee Trail.* There is an overlook on the BRP, mp 303.9, which gives a view of part of the route.) At 13.3 mi jct R and L with the *Beacon Heights Trail* and the end of the *Tanawha Trail.* (A turn L goes 0.2 mi to Beacon Heights [described below], and the *MST* goes with it nearly to the top before forking R to descend to Old House Gap in the Pisgah National Forest. See Chapter 16.) Turn R and after 130 yd arrive at the Beacon Heights parking area, mp 305.3.

## ▶ GWYN MEMORIAL TRAIL (mp 298.6)      328

This 91-yd garden trail honors Rufus Lenoir Gwyn (1877-1963), whose efforts were influential in the location of the BRP through the Blue Ridge. The trail is at a jct with Holloway Mtn Rd 1 mi from US-221.

## ▶ BEACON HEIGHTS TRAIL (mp 305.3)      329

An easy 0.3-mi graded trail ascends to a bare quartzite summit (4,205 ft) for spectacular views of the Pisgah National Forest, Hawksbill and Table Rock mtns, and Grandfather and Grandmother mtns. Along the way the trail jct with the *Tanawha Trail,* L, and the *MST* running jointly L and R. The summit was named by A.M. Huger, poet and trailblazer at the turn of the century.

## ▶ GRANDMOTHER MOUNTAIN TRAIL (mp 307.4)    330

From the Grandmother Mtn parking lot ascend 0.2 mi on a moderate trail arbored with rhododendron to the NP boundary.

▶ **FLAT ROCK TRAIL (mp 308.2)** 331

The easy 0.7-mi trail is a well-graded, self-guiding loop. Signs provide geological and biological information. The summit supplies outstanding views of Grandfather Mtn, Linville Valley, Black Mtn, and Roan Mtn. The quartzite outcropping is weather-sculptured.

▶ **LINVILLE FALLS RECREATION AREA (mp 315.5–316.5)**

The 440-acre Linville Falls Rec Area was acquired by the NPS from the philanthropy of John D. Rockefeller, Jr., in 1952. It is named for William Linville and his son, who were killed by Indians in 1766 while they slept near the river's headwaters. Sixteen-year-old John Williams, left for dead, survived. At the major falls the Linville River cuts through quartzite to plunge dramatically into a hidden drop before it thunders from a lower open level. The area has 100 picnic sites, a camp store, two campgrounds (190 sites), trout fishing, and an information shelter. There are four nature trails, but other trails, such as the long *Linville Gorge Trail,* are in the Linville Gorge Wilderness Area under the jurisdiction of the Pisgah National Forest (see Chapter 3, Section 2). (*USGS-FS Map:* Linville Falls)

**Linville Falls Trail** *(1 mi);* **Plunge Basin Overlook Trail** *(0.8 mi);* **Linville Gorge Trail** *(0.9 mi);* **Duggers Creek Trail** *(0.3 mi)* **332–335**

• LENGTH AND DIFFICULTY: 4.9 mi combined round-trip, easy to moderate

• TRAILHEAD AND DESCRIPTION: To hike the *Linville Falls Trail,* begin at the parking lot and cross the Linville River bridge to follow a wide and heavily used trail to Upper Falls. Ascend from the Upper Falls through hemlock and rhododendron to a choice of three lookouts for outstanding views of the 90-ft (total) Linville Falls. (This trail is also known as *Erwins Trail* and goes to Erwins Lookout at 1 mi.) Backtrack. For the *Plunge Basin Overlook Trail* and the *Linville Gorge Trail,* leave the parking lot, L. Ascend through rhododendron to jct with *Plunge Basin Overlook Trail,* R. Turn R and descend to the overlook for a superb view of the Lower Falls. Carolina, catawba, and rosebay rhododendron bloom on the weather-sculptured walls of the gorge. Return to the jct with the *Linville Gorge Trail* and turn at the sign to descend steeply on a rocky slope to the basin of the Lower Falls at 0.9 mi. Backtrack. For the *Duggers Creek Trail,* follow the signs E of the parking lot for an interpretive loop trail over a rocky area with thick mosses and fern patches. Return to the parking lot.

## ▶ CHESTOA VIEW TRAIL (mp 320.8)                336

This scenic, short, and easy 0.8-mi route to Chestoa View was named by A.M. Huger. (Chestoa is the Cherokee Indian word for rabbit.) From the parking lot enter a paved trail and follow the loop through mature hardwoods and numerous wildflowers, including large clusters of Bowman's root. Take the gravel trail to return and pass scenic views of the Linville Gorge Wilderness Area and Grandfather Mtn.

## ▶ CRABTREE MEADOWS RECREATION AREA (mp 339.5–340.3)

The 253-acre Crabtree Meadows has a restaurant that is open from May through October and a gift shop, camp store, and svc sta. Adjoining are an amphitheater and campground with tent and trailer sites (no hook-ups). The picnic area is on the S edge of the park on the BRP. Crabtree Falls is the central feature of the campground, but the more than 40 species of wildflowers and 35 species of songbirds are significant also. (*USGS Map:* Celo)

### *Crabtree Falls Trail* 337

• LENGTH AND DIFFICULTY: 2.5 mi, moderate

• TRAILHEAD AND DESCRIPTION: From the campground parking lot follow the posted directions N to 0.4 mi and begin at the steps. Reach the waterfalls at 0.8 mi and cross the bridge to begin a return climb. At 1.4 mi cross the stream and walk through spreads of trillium and wild orchids at 1.7 mi. Follow L at all trail jcts until the jct with the original trail.

## ▶ WOODS MOUNTAIN ACCESS TRAIL (mp 344.1) 338

This is a moderate 0.7-mi access route to the *Woods Mtn Trail* (USF #218) in the Pisgah NF (see Chapter 3, Section 2). From the Buck Creek Gap jct with NC-80, follow N an old svc road that parallels the BRP to Hazelnut Gap and jct with the W trailhead of *Woods Mtn Trail* (opposite a large oak).

## ▶ GREEN KNOB TRAIL (mp 350.4) 339

From the Green Knob Overlook (4,761 ft) follow the trail N and across the parkway and up switchbacks to reach the fire-tower at 0.6 mi for outstanding views of the Black Mtn range. (The trail R at the ridgeline is *Lost Cove Ridge Trail,* USFS #182; it descends 3.3 mi to Black Mtn Recreation Area. See Chapter 3, Section 4.)

## ▶ BALD KNOB RIDGE TRAIL (mp 355) 340

This is a terminus point (0.1 mi) of the *Bald Knob Ridge Trail* (USFS #186), which descends 2.8 mi toward Black Mtn Rec Area on a white-blazed trail to FR-472.

## ▶ BIG BUTT TRAIL (mp 359.8)                                341

The terminus point (0.2 mi) of the *Big Butt Trail* (USFS #161) follows a ridgeline of wildflowers and ramps before descending on numerous switchbacks 6 mi to NC-197W. This trailhead is near the highest point (5,676 ft) on the BRP N of Asheville.

## ▶ CRAGGY GARDENS RECREATION AREA (mp 364–367)

The 700-acre Craggy Gardens (5,220 ft) has a grassy picnic ground in Bear Pen Gap with tables, grills, water, and comfort sta. The visitor center has exhibits and BRP information. Although this area is colorful during all seasons with wildflowers, mountain ash, and wild crabapple, the highlight of color is in mid-June when the Craggy summits turn purple with catawba rhododendron. In addition to the trails listed below, the E terminus of the *Halfway Trail* (USFS #162) is in the NW corner of the visitor center parking lot.

To hike the *Pinnacle Trail* (0.8 mi round-trip), follow the signs from the parking lot at Craggy Garden's Overlook up switchbacks to the summit (5,840 ft) with 360 scenic views. For the *Craggy Gardens Self-Guiding Trail,* follow signs from the visitor center to the picnic area, a one-way distance of 0.8 mi. The *Bear Pen Gap Trail* is 0.2 mi long and runs through the picnic area. (*USGS Map:* Craggy Pinnacle)                        342–344

## ▶ RATTLESNAKE LODGE TRAIL (mp 374.4)          345

The strenuous 0.4-mi *Rattlesnake Lodge Trail* is accessed from a parking area at the S end of the Tanbark Tunnel. Ascend steeply on an orange-blazed trail to connect with the *MST* and the ruins of the summer home of Dr. Chase P. Ambler, an Asheville physician who built the lodge in 1900. To the R of the jct is a spring and the N route of the *MST*. To the L it is 10 mi on the *MST* to the Folk Art Center (mp 382). (See Chapter 16.)

▶ **SHUT-IN TRAIL (mp 393.6–407.7)**          **346**

• LENGTH AND DIFFICULTY: 16.4 mi, strenuous (elev change 3,611 ft)

• TRAILHEAD AND DESCRIPTION: A national rec trail and the *MST* route, it follows mainly a horse trail named and constructed in the 1890s by George Vanderbilt as an access route from Biltmore to his Buck Spring Hunting Lodge. It was originally 20 mi long and included a fording of the French Broad River. With the creation of the BRP, parts of the trail were obliterated and the remainder became overgrown. But in the 1970s Pop Hollandsworth of the Asheville School, Jack Davis and Arch Nichols of the CMC, and others cleared sections of the old trail and relocated others. It is listed on the inventories of both the BRP and the Pisgah NF because it weaves in and out of the boundaries. Water is infrequent.

For the NE access, turn off the BRP ramp at the NC-191 jct (sign for I-26), and immediately turn L on FR-479. Go 0.3 mi, take the first gravel road L, and go 0.1 mi to Bent Creek and the parking area. Follow the hiking sign and after 125 ft jct with the *MST*. (The *MST* goes L 0.5 mi to its crossing of the French Broad River bridge. It goes R, jointly, with the *Shut-in Trail*. See Chapter 16.) Ascend on switchbacks through rhododendron thickets and reach an old road at 0.4 mi. Jct with a gravel road at 1.7 mi; turn L. Leave the road and begin an ascent at 1.8 mi. Reach a crest at 2.4 mi and BRP at 3.1 mi; this is Walnut Cove Overlook (2,915 ft). Ascend and skirt NW of Grassy Knob (3,318 ft) at 5.5 mi. From Chestnut Cove Gap follow signs, descending into Chestnut Cove and skirting N of Cold Knob to reach mp 400.3 at Bent Creek Gap (3,270 ft) at 8.3 mi.

From Bent Creek Gap enter an old road by a gate and ascend. Excellent views of the city of Asheville and Craggy Mtns at 8.5 mi. Reach the summit of Ferrin Knob (4,064 ft) at 9.5 mi, then descend on a ridge through oak and locust. Turn R at 9.7 mi and reach Beaver Dam Gap Overlook (3,570 ft) at 10.2 mi. Reach Stoney Bald (3,750 ft) and continue to Big Ridge Overlook (3,820 ft) at 12.3 mi. Reach Mills River Valley Overlook (4,085 ft) at 13.4 mi and then Elk Pasture Gap (4,235 ft) to jct with NC-151 at 14.6 mi. Cross the BRP and climb to a plateau through large oaks and dense understory; reach the crest of Little Pisgah Mtn at 15.1 mi. (A side trail is R for 1.2 mi to Mt Pisgah.) Ahead descend slightly to Buck Spring Gap parking area at 16.4 mi (4,980 ft). Across the parking space the *MST* continues and joins the *Buck Spring Trail* for 1.1 mi to arrive at the Pisgah Inn. (*USGS-FS Maps:* Asheville, Dunsmore Mtn)

## ▶ MT PISGAH (mp 407–409)

The mile-high Mt Pisgah complex has a modern motel and dining hall at the 52-room Pisgah Inn. It is open by May 1 through October. There are sweeping views over the Pisgah NF that melt away toward South Carolina. Writer William G. Lord has said that "sleep is quiet as a moth's wing" at the inn. The area is part of the original 100,000-acre estate owned by the late George W. Vanderbilt. (George Weston, who was Vanderbilt's farm superintendent, built and opened the first inn in 1920. In the 1940s it fell into disrepair but was reopened in 1952 by Leslie and Leda Kirschner of New York. The new current inn was opened in 1967 and operates under a concession contract with the NPS.) There is a svc sta, a picnic area, and a large (140 sites) campground for trailers and tents (no hook-ups), with water and flush toilets. Information: Pisgah Inn, PO Box 749, Waynesville, NC 28786, tel: 704-235-8228. (USGS-FS Maps: Cruso, Asheville, Skyland, Dunsmore Mtn)

*Buck Spring Trail (1.1 mi); Mt Pisgah Trail (1.2 mi); Mt Pisgah Campground Trail (1 mi); Frying Pan Mtn Trail (2 mi)* **347–350**

- LENGTH AND DIFFICULTY: 6.5 mi round-trip, combined, easy to strenuous

- SPECIAL FEATURES: Mt Pisgah and Frying Pan Mtn vistas

- TRAILHEAD AND DESCRIPTION: To hike the *Buck Spring Trail,* a national recreation trail, begin at a signboard at the NE corner of the Pisgah Inn parking lot. (There is a connection here for the *Buck Spring Trail* in the Pisgah NF [6.2 mi, USFS #104] and *Pilot Rock Trail* [3.6 mi, USFS #321]. Follow the easy trail through a natural garden of laurel banks and bluets [*Houstonia caerules*] and weather-formed chestnut oaks. At 0.7 mi jct R with the *Laurel Mtn Trail* [7.4 mi, USFS #121], which descends into the Pisgah NF.) At 1 mi visit the historic site of Vanderbilt's Buck Spring Hunting Lodge. Reach the Buck Spring Gap parking overlook at 1.1 mi. (The *Shut-In Trail* begins on the N side of the parking area, and the *MST* follows both of these trails.)

To hike the *Mt Pisgah Trail* follow the paved access road N 0.2 mi to the Mt Pisgah parking area. Enter at the trail sign and into the Pisgah NF to begin a strenuous climb at 0.4 mi. After a rocky route to the summit (5,721 ft) reach an observation deck for panoramic views of the Pigeon River and the Blue Ridge range. Backtrack. An easy return to the Pisgah Inn is on the *Mt Pisgah Campground Trail* from the Mt Pisgah parking area. Descend, parallel W of the BRP, pass through the picnic area, and reach the campground at 1 mi. From the campground entrance gate there is a sign for the *Frying Pan Mtn Trail*. Ascend to Big Bald where azaleas, filbert, mountain ash, and leatherflowers (*Clematis viorna*) thrive. Reach Frying Pan Gap (4,931 ft, mp 409.6) at 1.3 mi. (The gap was named by pioneer livestock herders.) Follow FR-450 to the fire tower at 2 mi for panoramic views. Backtrack.

## ▶ GRAVEYARD FIELDS LOOP TRAIL (mp 418.8)     351

• LENGTH AND DIFFICULTY: 3.2 mi, easy

• TRAILHEAD AND DESCRIPTION: From the parking overlook examine the trail design board. Enter a paved trail through a dense section of rhododendron to the Yellowstone Prong of the East Fork of the Pigeon River at 0.2 mi. Cross a bridge, turn R to view Second Falls, and return to the bridge, but keep R. Immediately jct R with the *Graveyard Ridge Trail* (USFS #356) that ascends 3.4 mi to Ivestor Gap (see Chapter 3, Section 3). Continue upstream, jct at 0.6 mi with a return loop, but continue ahead another 0.5 mi to the scenic Upper Falls. Backtrack for a loop of 3.2 mi. (This same loop trail is listed as *Yellowstone Falls Trail,* USFS #358 in the Pisgah NF.) (The area received its name from moss-covered fallen spruce trunks and stumps that resembled a graveyard. The trunks were destroyed by a fire in November 1925 that burned 25,000 acres of prime timber.) (*USGS-FS Map:* Shining Rock)

## ▶ DEVIL'S COURTHOUSE TRAIL (mp 422.4)     352

From the parking lot and signs (5,462 ft) follow the paved trail 0.1 mi toward the BRP tunnel and ascend on a steep but moderately difficult trail. At 0.3 mi jct L with a 0.1-mi spur to the *MST.* Turn R and reach the summit (5,720 ft) at a stone observation deck and disk directors at 0.4 mi. (According to the Cherokee Indian legend, Judaculla, a slant-eyed giant devil, had his legal chambers inside this mtn.) Views from this point are spectacular; on clear days you can see North and South Carolina, Georgia, and Tennessee. The SE side of the rock face is used by rock climbers. Backtrack. (*USGS-FS Map:* Sam Knob)

## ▶ TANASEE BALD/HERRIN KNOB TRAIL (mp 423.5) 353

From the jct of the BRP and NC-215 go S on the BRP for 0.3 mi to the Courthouse Valley parking overlook (5,362 ft), L, and park at the second parking area. The trail begins at the SW corner behind a picnic table. Follow an unmarked, narrow (perhaps overgrown) trail under beech, fir, hawthorne, arrow wood, and birch. The ground cover is ferns, galax, and wood sorrel. Pass R of Tanasee Bald at 0.4 mi and turn R at a fork at 0.5 mi. After a few yd enter a natural summertime garden of fragrant wildflowers, birds, butterflies, and blueberries. At 0.7 mi climb steeply to the SW slope of Herrin Knob (5,720 ft), named for James P. Herren (correct spelling), a prominent timberman. This rocky bluff is naturally landscaped with laurel, orchids, and multiple moss species. Descend to BRP, mp 424.2, at 1.2 mi. Backtrack, or hike the BRP for 0.8 mi as a loop. (*USGS-FS Map:* Sam Knob)

▶ **GRASSY RIDGE TRAIL (mp 424.2)**                    **354**

The *Grassy Ridge Trail* (across the BRP from the *Tanasee Bald/Herrin Knob Trail* begins on the R (N) side of the BRP at Mt Hardy Gap. (There is no designated parking place here.) Enter the forest in a dense stand of beech and yellow birch to climb rocky switchbacks on the N side of Mt Hardy. At 0.6 mi reach a faint trail, R, on open Fork Ridge. (Fork Ridge is in the Middle Prong Wilderness Area of the Pisgah NF with a number of bald areas.) Turn L up the ridge to a partially bald summit of Mt Hardy (6,110 ft) at 0.8 mi. (Formerly called Black Mtn, it was named in honor of Dr. James F. E. Hardy, Asheville Civil War physician, by the United Daughters of the Confederacy [UDC] in 1942.) Backtrack. (An old unmarked trail follows the ridgeline W through a fir/spruce forest with plush carpets of moss and wood sorrel for 1.1 mi to jct with an access trail to the *MST*. A left turn leads a few yd to Rough Butt Bald Overlook, mp 425.4. A turn R on the access trail leads 100 yd to the *Buckeye Gap Trail* (USFS #126). (*USGS-FS Map:* Sam Knob)

▶ **BEAR PEN GAP TRAIL (mp 427.6)**                **355–356**

The trailhead is at the SE corner of the parking lot (5,560 ft). It is only 0.1 mi within the BRP boundary, but it is an excellent access route to the *MST* and to the *Gage Bald/Charley Bald Trail* at 1.3 mi in the Wet Camp Gap of the Nantahala NF (see Chapter 16).

▶ **RICHLAND BALSAM TRAIL (mp 431.4)**              **357**

At the Richland Balsam Overlook the BRP attains its highest point (6,053 ft). To hike the 1.4-mi round-trip trail, begin at the NW corner of the parking area and follow an interpretive sign. The trail runs through a damp Canadian-zone type of forest, chiefly of fir and spruce. (The Fraser fir has been devastated by the balsam woolly aphid in this area.) Other vegetation includes mountain ash, Rowan tree, birch, pin cherry, witherod, wood sorrel, golden moss, and blueberry. Reach the summit (6,292 ft) at 0.6 mi and return on the loop. (An old trail, *Lickstone Ridge Trail*, is heavily overgrown from the summit.) (*USGS-FS Map:* Sam Knob)

### ▶ WATERROCK KNOB TRAIL (mp 451.2) 358

A plaque here honors H. Getty Browning (1881-1966), a leader in the location of the North Carolina BRP route. From the parking area's E side, enter the paved trail (which becomes a rocky path) for a moderate climb to the summit (6,400 ft) at 0.6 mi. Here are superb views of the Smokies and Pisgah and Nantahala NFs. (A faint trail L of the summit follows the ridge for 2.5 mi to Mt Lyn Lowery, and NE on the high Plott Balsams to Oldfield Top after another mi.) Some of the vegetation is fir, birch, gooseberry, bush honeysuckle, turtlehead (*Chelone lyonii*), meadow parsnip, and mountain lettuce (*Saxifraga micranthidifolia*). Views from the summit are panoramic. Backtrack. (*USGS-FS Map:* Sylva North)

### ▶ BLACK CAMP GAP TRAIL (mp 258.2) 359

On the Heintooga Rd (a spur from Wolf Laurel Gap) drive 3.6 mi to the 66-yd trail R. It approaches a Masonic plaque, but its name is from the black ashes of a long-ago forest fire.

# 7.

## Great Smoky Mountains
## National Park

*To conserve the scenery and the natural and historic objects and the wildlife therein . . .*
—from an Act of Congress, April 25, 1916, establishing the National Park Service

One of the oldest uplands on earth, the magnificent Smokies cover 520,004 acres, of which 275,895 are in North Carolina, the rest in Tennessee. Authorized by Congress in 1926 and dedicated in 1940 by President Franklin D. Roosevelt, the Great Smoky Mountains National Park receives over ten million visitors annually and is the nation's most heavily used national park. The property was not acquired easily. Initially, Congress did not appropriate federal funds for land purchase, and 85 percent of the proposed land was owned by timber industries, most of which were initially unwilling to sell. Although state legislatures appropriated funds and local fund-raising campaigns were widespread, it was not enough. The turning point came in 1928 when John D. Rockefeller, Jr., donated $5 million. By the early 1930s Congress had appropriated another $3.5 million. Finally, after 14 years of negotiations (and some litigation) with 18 timber companies and the purchase of more than 6,000 separate tracts, the park became a reality, a former domain of the Eastern Cherokee would be preserved forever.

More than 60 percent of the luxuriant virgin forest had been cut by the timber companies prior to the land sales. Today the second-growth forests are maturing and blending in natural succession. Since 1966, the beginning of wilderness hearings about the Smokies, there has been public demand to protect the wilderness character. With this trend it is likely that the 50-mi North Shore road between Fontana Dam and Bryson City, promised by the NPS in 1943, will never be completed. (The road is also called Lake View Rd, Lakeshore Drive, and the Road to Nowhere.) Six mi have been constructed from Bryson City to Forney Ridge (also called Tunnel Ridge because the road dead ends after passing through a tunnel). An editorial in the *Raleigh News and Observer,* March 12, 1987, stated that a U.S. Senate bill to designate 90 percent of the park as wilderness (and compensate Swain County with $11 million for a broken promise) would be a "reasonable compromise between competing goals of public use and environmental preservation."

For the naturalist, the park is a paradise with more than 1,400 varieties of flowering plants, 150 species of trees, 300 mosses, and 2,000 fungi. There are more than 200 species of birds, 50 species of fur-bearing animals, 26 species of reptiles, and 80 different kinds of fish. Because the park is a wildlife sanctuary, it is forbidden to disturb any of the plants or animals. The park has ten developed campgrounds, five of which are in North Carolina. In addition to camping as a recreational activity, the park has 600 mi of streams for fishing. The park is famous for its hundreds of miles of trails for hiking, horseback riding, and cross-country skiing.

The highest mountain in the park is Clingmans Dome (6,643 ft), accessible within 0.5 mi by auto road or by hiking the *AT.* There are 16 other peaks that tower over 6,000 ft. Geologists estimate that the original peaks in the Smokies were over 15,000 ft in elev when formed 250 million years ago. It is to these high peaks and ridges and into the lower coves that more than 920 mi of hiking and horse trails (of which 510 mi are in North Carolina) form a vast network of highly visible back-country routes. At least 54 trails are classified by the park as "quiet walkways," "nature trails," or "sidewalk trails," and another ten are cemetery trails. The longest trail is the 69-mi *AT* from Fontana Dam to Davenport Gap, and the second longest is the 43-mi *Lakeshore Trail* on the N shore of Fontana Dam.

During the 1930s the CCC operated 16 camps in the Smokies. As a result numerous trails were regraded from old RR grades or roads, and others were rerouted. Trail usage declined during the WW-II years, but hiker and horse traffic has continuously increased since the 1960s. The increase has made permits and reservations necessary for those who stay overnight in the backcountry. Only the trails on the North Carolina side of the park are described in this book.

There are a number of rules and regulations for hiking the backcountry; they are designed to protect both the quality of the natural environment and the quality of the backpacking experience. "It is our attempt to enable you and others to love this wild place without loving it to death," say park officials. Overnight trips require a free permit. Self-registration permits are allowed at any ranger station by following the posted instructions, but some campsites are rationed due to heavy use and require reservations. On the North Carolina side they are Upper and Lower Walnut Bottoms (#36 and #37); Mt Sterling (#38); Lower Chasteen Creek (#50); Pole Road (#55); Bryson Place (#57); and Bone Valley (#83). Hikers must telephone the Backcountry Reservation Office (615-436-1231, seven days a week, 24 hours a day) to obtain permission. Also, all shelters are rationed with the exception of the following: Davenport Gap and Mollies Ridge on the *AT* and Laurel Gap on the *Balsam Mtn Trail*. Reservations are recommended up to a month in advance.

The following rules are listed by the park: Maximum size of party is eight; only one consecutive night at a shelter and three at a campsite; campers must stay in designated sites of the itinerary; do not reserve more space than you intend to occupy; do not damage animal or plant life; carry out all food and trash; use toilet at least 100 ft from campsite (bury all solid waste); do not wash dishes or bathe with soap in a stream; use only wood that is dead and on the ground; no pets, motorized vehicles, or bicycles; no firearms or hunting of animals; notify the ranger of a change in plans.

Bears are more prominent in the park than anywhere else in the state. Remain watchful for them and report all bear incidents to the ranger. The most dangerous bears in the park are the solitary males, but that does not mean a female (with or without her cubs) will not be aggressive. Because the bears are generally shy and secretive and have a keen sense of detecting people, the average hiker will probably not see them. The best way to avoid any bear problems is to avoid attracting them with food. Proper food storage is a necessity, so do not keep food in tents or sleeping bags and do store it in an odor-proof bag tied with a rope at least four ft from the nearest limb and ten ft above the ground. Also, refrain from throwing any food to a bear or leaving food for the bear to eat. Bears are more likely to visit campsites and shelters from June to October.

• ADDRESS AND ACCESS: The park has three visitor centers: Oconaluftee, 4 mi N of Cherokee on the Newfound Gap Rd (designated US-441 outside the Park), tel: 704-497-9146; Sugarlands, 2 mi SW of Gatlinburg, tel: 615-436-1255; and Cades Cove, tel: 615-448-6222, 12 mi SW of Townsend, Tennessee. (The centers are open daily except December 25.) Headquarters address: GSMNP, Gatlinburg, TN 37738, tel: 615-436-5615; District Ranger Office, Box 4, Park Circle, Cherokee, NC 28719, tel: 704-497-9147. Other addresses for the RS are listed at the end of each park area introduction.

## ▶ BIG CREEK AREA
### (Haywood County)

The Big Creek Area is the most northern corner of the park. The area comprises the Big Creek drainage from Balsam Mtn (SW), Mt Sterling (SE), Mt Cammerer Ridge (N), and Mt Guyot (W) along the state line. The area was logged in the early 1900s, and a logging town was established at Crestmont, the site of a CCC camp in the 1930s. The site is now Big Creek Campground, a developed fee camp of 12 campsites for tents only. It has flush toilets, grills, and tables. A pay telephone is nearby at the RS. Big Creek, which flows on the E side of the camp, is a good rainbow trout stream. Bear, rattlesnake, deer, raccoon, grouse, and squirrel are in the area. Spring wildflowers are prominent.

• ADDRESS AND ACCESS: From I-40 at the state line at Waterville, take exit #451, cross the Pigeon River bridge, turn L on Waterville Rd (SR-1332), pass the Waterville Power Plant, and at 2 mi intersect with Old NC-284 Rd (SR-1397, also called Mt Sterling Rd). (It is 2.5 mi R to Davenport Gap and the *AT* at the state line; L the road passes through the Mt Sterling village and ascends to Mt Sterling Gap for a descent to the Cataloochee area after 16 mi.) Cross the road to the RS. Address: Big Creek RS, GSMNP, Star Route, Newport, TN 37821, tel: 704-486-5910.

• SUPPORT FACILITIES: There is a general store at the crossroads near the RS. Shopping centers, motels, and restaurants are in Newport, Tenn., 15 mi W on I-40. Camper's Paradise, a commercial campground in Cosby, Tenn., is 13.5 mi W on TN-32, tel: 615-487-2502.

## Big Creek Trail                                    360–364

• LENGTH AND DIFFICULTY: 5.8 mi, moderate (elev change 1,375 ft)

• CONNECTING TRAILS:
   *Swallow Fork Trail* (3.8 mi, strenuous, elev change 2,180 ft)
   *Low Gap Trail* (2.3 mi, strenuous, elev change 1,240 ft)
   *Gunter Fork Trail* (4.5 mi, strenuous, elev change 2,430 ft)
   *Yellow Creek Trail* (5.2 mi, moderate, elev change 1,611 ft)

• TRAILHEAD AND DESCRIPTION: From the RS follow the gated road 0.5 mi to the camping/parking area. *Big Creek Trail* goes to Walnut Bottoms where the other four trail connections begin. Go R of the campground to a jeep road and go upstream of Big Creek. Pass Mouse Creek Falls (on the far L of the river) at 2 mi, and at 2.9 mi pass Brakeshoe Spring. Forest vegetation includes maple, oak, hemlock, butternut, rhododendron, phacelia, and ramps. Cross Flint Rock Cove Branch at 4.5 mi and jct with Swallow Fork Trail, L, at 5.2 mi, at the lower edge of Walnut Bottoms. It is a former logging camp and now backcountry campsite #37. (*Big Creek Trail* ends at 5.8 mi upstream at Upper

Walnut Bottoms campsite #36, but the *Yellow Creek Trail* and the *Gunter Fork Trail* begin here.)

The *Swallow Creek Trail* leaves Walnut Bottoms and ascends dramatically to Pretty Hollow Gap. At 0.4 mi pass a spring, R. Ascend and follow an old RR grade for a short distance. At 0.9 mi cross Swallow Fork. Cross a number of small tributaries, the last of which is at 2.5 mi on the ascent. After another 0.5 mi make a switchback and ascend to Pretty Hollow Gap at 3.8 mi to jct with the *Mt Sterling Ridge Trail* and the *Pretty Hollow Gap Trail*. (The *Mt Sterling Ridge Trail*, L, goes 1.3 mi to jct with the *Baxter Creek Trail* and the Mt Sterling fire tower. To the R it goes 4 mi to Laurel Gap to jct with the *Balsam Mtn Trail*.)

The *Yellow Creek Trail* and the *Gunter Fork Trail* run jointly the first 0.5 mi from their origin at the end of the *Big Creek Trail* in Walnut Bottoms (near Upper Walnut Bottoms campsite #36). At the separation follow the *Yellow Creek Trail* straight ahead on an old RR grade along the N side of Big Creek. Turn sharply R from the creek at 3.2 mi (near the confluence with Yellow Creek). Ascend steeply and at 4.3 mi begin scenic views of the valley. Reach Camel Gap at the state line to jct with the *AT* at 5.2 mi. A loop can be made here, R, on the *AT* for 2.3 mi to *Low Gap Trail* described below.

The *Gunter Fork Trail* forks L from the *Yellow Creek Trail*, crosses Big Creek, and ascends by cascades of Gunter Fork. At 2.3 mi cross the base of a major cascade that drops nearly 200 ft. At 2.5 mi leave the stream and ascend steeply on a ridge with laurel, rhododendron, oak, and hemlock where there are scenic views of the Big Creek Valley. Continue ascent in an evergreen forest and thick mossy duff. Arrive at the crest of the Balsam Mtn range and jct R and L with the *Balsam Mtn Trail*. (From here, R, it is 4.5 mi to the *AT* and Tricorner Knob. To the L it is 1 mi to Laurel Gap and jct with the *Mt Sterling Ridge Trail*.)

The *Low Gap Trail* leaves Big Creek at the lower end of the Walnut Bottoms campsite (0.4 mi before the upstream end of *Big Creek Trail*). On the W side of Big Creek turn R and parallel downstream with Big Creek. Pass R of an old cemetery at 0.4 mi, and at 0.8 mi leave the Big Creek area at the mouth of Low

Gap Branch. Turn L upstream and cross the branch at 1.8 mi, the last water on the ascent to Low Gap and the *AT*. To the R it is 7.1 mi on the *AT* to Davenport Gap. Left it is 0.8 mi to the Cosby Shelter and another 1.5 mi to *Yellow Creek Trail* in Camel Gap. (A loop of 12 mi back to Walnut Bottoms is possible using *Yellow Creek Trail*.) (*USGS Maps:* Cove Creek Gap, Luftee Knob, Waterville)

### Baxter Creek Trail                                                365

- LENGTH AND DIFFICULTY: 6 mi, strenuous (elev gain 4,142 ft)

- CONNECTING TRAIL:
  (*Mt Sterling Ridge Trail*)

- SPECIAL FEATURE: Mt Sterling (5,842 ft)

- TRAILHEAD AND DESCRIPTION: From the Big Creek Campground, cross the swinging bridge at the lower end of the campground, turn R upstream, and pass through old fields and homesites. At 0.7 mi ascend beside Baxter Creek and soon begin the climb on switchbacks in a hardwood forest with laurel. At 4 mi reach Mt Sterling Ridge and veer R up the ridge. After 4.5 mi spruce and fir become dominant. Reach the top at 6 mi to Mt Sterling backcountry campsite #38. Climb the fire tower for a spectacular view of the Smokies (W), Snowbird Mtn and Max Patch (N), and the Pisgah NF (E and S). (The *Mt Sterling Ridge Trail* jct is 0.3 mi E, from where it is 2.3 mi L to Old NC-284 Rd. See description below.) A loop can be made by taking the *Mt Sterling Ridge Trail* R at the jct and following it to Pretty Holly Gap after 3.6 mi for a R on *Swallow Fork Trail* and descent to *Big Creek Trail*. A return to the point of origin is a loop of 17.2 mi. (*USGS Maps:* Cove Creek Gap, Waterville)

▶ CATALOOCHEE AREA
(Haywood County)

In Cherokee, Cataloochee means "waves of mountains or ridges." This area has ridges, a picturesque valley, and a history of the model pioneering spirit of endurance and resilience. Descendants of the early settlers lived in the basin into the 1960s and return each summer to special homecomings and dinner-on-the-grounds at the chapel. A number of the original buildings are preserved by the NPS. An example is the Palmer Chapel, built in 1898. The drainage, like the Big Creek drainage, flows N into the Pigeon River, and except for the Cataloochee Creek that flows into Waterville Lake the basin is surrounded by mtn ridges. The Balsam Mtn range is on the W edge, Mt Sterling Ridge on the N, and the Cataloochee Divide on the S and E. Only two roads, one over Cove Creek Gap (SR-1395) and the other over Mt Sterling Gap (SR-1397) connect with the outside world. Plans by the NPS in the 1960s to construct a fast route from I-40 to the heart of the basin were only partially completed. Fortunately, conservationists were successful in stopping a major recreational development that would have destroyed the character of the peaceful valley. The valley has a developed campground with flush toilets for tenting, and a RS is nearby. All trails in the area are horse/hiker trails except the *Asbury Trail* for hikers only. Fishing is popular in Cataloochee Creek. Flora and fauna are similar to the Big Creek area described above.

• ADDRESS AND ACCESS: On US-276 (on the W side of the bridge) before its jct with I-40 (Exit 20) in Cove Creek, turn N on Little Cove Rd (SR-1331). (There may be a Cataloochee sign here.) Drive 1.3 mi and turn R on Old NC-284 Rd (SR-1395, also called the Cataloochee Rd). After 4.5 mi reach Cove Creek Gap, the park boundary. Descend 1.8 mi to a paved road, turn L, and after 2.7 mi bear L across the Cataloochee Creek bridge and jct with the Cataloochee Rd, R. (It is 7 mi to Mt Sterling Gap and another 7 mi to the Deep Creek RS described above.) From the jct it is 0.7 mi on the paved road to the Cataloochee RS, R. Address: Cataloochee RS, GSMNP, Route 2, Box 555, Waynesville, NC 28786.

• SUPPORT FACILITIES: Shopping centers, motels, restaurants, and commercial campgrounds (some open all year) are in Maggie Valley, 6.5 mi S from Cove Creek on US-276 and W on US-19.

### Caldwell Fork Trail                                366–371

- LENGTH AND DIFFICULTY: 5.8 mi, moderate

- CONNECTING TRAILS:
  *Booger Man Trail* (3.8 mi, moderate)
  *Big Fork Ridge Trail* (2.8 mi, moderate)
  *McKee Branch Trail* (2.5 mi, strenuous, elev change 1,710 ft)
  *Double Gap Trail* (2.2 mi, strenuous, elev change 1,800 ft)
  *Rough Fork Trail* (6.5 mi, strenuous, elev change 2,380 ft)

- TRAILHEAD AND DESCRIPTION: The *Caldwell Fork Trail,* named after the valley's Caldwell families, begins 0.1 mi SW of the Cataloochee campground, a good base camp. Cross a footbridge and go upstream in a forest of hemlock, beech, birch, and rhododendron. At 0.8 mi jct L, with the *Booger Man Trail* near Den Branch. (The *Booger Man Trail* follows an old rough road built by Robert Palmer who built his cottage on the mountainside, a clearing at 2 mi on the trail. Huge oak and poplar seen on this trail are there because Palmer never allowed logging. At 2.9 mi descend near Smoke Branch to return to the *Caldwell Fork Trail* at 3.8 mi.)

    Continue on the *Caldwell Fork Trail;* cross the creek a number of times. At 2.5 mi jct with the returning *Booger Man Trail,* L, and after another 0.5 mi jct R with the *Big Fork Ridge Trail.* (The *Big Fork Ridge Trail* descends to the Caldwell Fork to cross on a footbridge and ascend on an old jeep road to the site of a former Caldwell Fork schoolhouse at 0.3 mi. It reaches the crest of the Big Fork Ridge at 1.2 mi and descends gradually to cross Rough Fork on a footbridge to jct with the *Rough Fork Trail* at 2.8 mi. Here is the gated Cataloochee Rd and parking area for the *Rough Fork Trail* N trailhead. (It is 2.4 mi R on the road to the N trailhead of the *Caldwell Fork Trail* for a loop of 8.2 mi.)

    On the *Caldwell Fork Trail* it is 0.1 mi from *Big Fork Ridge Trail* to jct with the *McKee Branch Trail,* L. (The *McKee Branch Trail* ascends 2.5 mi, steeply, to Purchase Gap on the Cataloochee Divide to the *Cataloochee Divide Trail* and the park boundary. This grassy horse-trail route was used by the early settlers to get over the mtn to Maggie Valley.)

At 4.4 mi on the *Caldwell Fork Trail* jct with the *Double Gap Trail,* L. (The *Double Gap Trail* ascends for 0.4 mi before crossing a stream. At 1.9 mi, R, is a huge black cherry tree. Continue to ascend steeply to reach the *Cataloochee Divide Trail* at 2.2 mi.)

Ahead on the *Caldwell Fork Trail* cross Double Creek to Caldwell Fork backcountry campsite #41. Enter a forest of tall poplar and ascend gradually to the trail terminus at 5.8 mi and jct with *Rough Fork Trail,* L and R. (If turning R on the *Rough Fork Trail,* descend 1.4 mi to Big Hemlock backcountry campsite #40. Pass through a grove of large trees and at 1.9 mi arrive at a well-preserved log house (now a larger frame building), which was the original home of Jonathan Woody and his family in the 1860s. From here follow the NPS road downstream in a forest of rhododendron, birch, and white pine to the road gate and parking area. Another 2.4 mi on the road to the N trailhead of *Caldwell Fork Trail* is a loop of 11.1 mi. If taking the *Rough Fork Trail* L from the jct with the *Caldwell Fork Trail,* ascend steeply for the first 0.7 mi before joining an old RR grade that leads another 2.8 mi to a jct with the *Cataloochee Divide Trail* in Paul's (also called Polls) Gap. Here is a connection with the BRP Balsam Mtn spur road (2.4 mi S of the Balsam Mtn Campground and 6.2 mi N of the BRP.) (*USGS Maps:* Bunches Bald, Cove Creek Gap, Dellwood)

### *Cataloochee Divide Trail*                                        372–373

- LENGTH AND DIFFICULTY: 11.5 mi, moderate

- CONNECTING TRAILS:
  *(Spruce Mtn Trail)*
  *(Rough Fork Trail)*
  *(Double Gap Trail)*
  *(McKee Branch Trail)*
  *Asbury Trail* (7 mi, strenuous, elev change 1,810 ft)

- TRAILHEAD AND DESCRIPTION: The *Cataloochee Divide Trail* follows the Cataloochee Divide and is a ridge trail with a road access at either end. If beginning in the N, park at Cove Creek Gap on the Old NC-284 Rd (SR-1395) at the park boundary (see access direction in the introduction). Follow the sign and reach Panther Spring Gap and a spring at 2 mi. Jct R with the *McKee Branch Trail* at 4.9 mi. (To the L, on private property, is a short trail to Purchase Knob, 5,086 ft.) At 6.2 mi jct R with *Double Gap Trail* where a water source is a few yd downhill. Ascend along the ridge and at 7 mi reach scenic Hemphill Bald (5,540 ft) with vistas of the Plott Balsam range, the highest point of the trail. Descend the Pine Tree Gap at 7.5 mi, ascend to the N side of Sheepback Knob and reach Maggot Spring Gap at 9 mi. At Garrett Gap follow an old RR grade to reach Paul's Gap at 11.5 mi and jct with the *Rough Fork Trail* and *Spruce Mtn Trail,* R. Here also is a connection with the BRP Balsam Mtn spur road (2.4 mi S of the Balsam Mtn Campground).

The *Asbury Trail* begins R (N) at Cove Creek Gap. A foot trail, it is usually not maintained except by Boy Scout troops. Follow the trail 1 mi through a forest of white pine and hardwoods to Hogan Gap (where the incomplete new highway to I-40 ends), and after another 1.2 mi on the ridgeline of Whiteoak Mtn turn L on a spur ridge. Descend and ford Cataloochee Creek (2,474 ft), or go upstream 0.2 mi to cross the Cataloochee Rd bridge at 3.6 mi. Go R 0.2 mi, leave the road, R, after a horseshoe curve, and ascend to Scottish Mtn (4,287 ft) at 5.4 mi. Follow the park boundary to Mt Sterling Gap at 7 mi. From here the trail follows SR-1395 to Davenport Gap. The trail is named after Bishop Francis Asbury, the Methodist-circuit preacher who rode this route on horseback in 1810. (*USGS Maps:* Bunches Bald, Cove Creek Gap, Dellwood)

### *Mount Sterling Ridge Trail*      374

• LENGTH AND DIFFICULTY: 7.7 mi, strenuous (elev change 1,950 ft)

• CONNECTING TRAILS:
  *(Asbury Trail)*
  *(Baxter Trail)*
  *(Pig Pen Trail)*
  *(Swallow Fork Trail)*

*(Pretty Hollow Gap Trail)*
*(Balsam Mtn Trail)*

- SPECIAL FEATURES: Mt Sterling

- TRAILHEAD AND DESCRIPTION: The trail can be assessed from two directions. In the Cataloochee basin at the jct of the paved road and the graveled Cataloochee Rd (0.7 mi N of the RS), drive 7 mi N on the Cataloochee Rd to Mt Sterling Gap. The other access is 7 mi S on the same road (usually called Old NC-284 Rd) from the Big Creek RS to Mt Sterling Gap. In the gap, the trailhead of the *Asbury Trail* is SE and the *Mt Sterling Ridge Trail* goes W. On an old jeep road ascend on the *Mt Sterling Ridge Trail* 0.4 mi to jct L with the rarely used *Pig Pen Trail*. At 0.7 mi begin switchbacks. Enter a spruce/fir forest, and reach the ridgetop at 2.3 mi. (To the R is a 0.3-mi spur to connect with *Baxter Creek Trail,* backcountry campsite #38, and panoramic views from the Mt Sterling fire tower.) Continue along the ridge. Reach Pretty Hollow Gap and cross trails at 3.6 mi. *Pretty Hollow Gap Trail* goes 5.5 mi L, down the mtn to Cataloochee Rd, and the *Swallow Fork Trail* goes R 3.8 mi to join the *Big Creek Trail.* Continue on the ridge and pass Big Cataloochee Mtn (6,122 ft) on the S slope. Cross streamlets at 6 mi and 7 mi. At 7.7 mi the trail ends at a jct with the *Balsam Mtn Trail,* R and L. (Left it is 0.1 mi to the Laurel Gap Shelter and R it is 5.5 mi to the *AT.*) Backtrack, or make a 21.2-mi loop by using the *Balsam Mtn Trail,* R, to the *AT,* followed by *Gunter Fork Trail* and the *Swallow Fork Trail.* If turning L, a 23.9-mi loop can be made by using the *Balsam Mtn Trail,* the *Palmer Creek Trail,* and the *Pretty Hollow Gap Trail.* (*USGS Maps:* Cove Creek Gap, Luftee Knob)

### Palmer Trail                                     375–378

- LENGTH AND DIFFICULTY: 4.6 mi, strenuous (elev change 1,775 ft)

- CONNECTING TRAILS:
  *Little Cataloochee Trail* (5 mi, moderate)
  *Pretty Hollow Gap Trail* (4 mi, strenuous, elev change 2,190 ft)
  *(Pig Pen Trail)*

*(Mt Sterling Ridge Trail)*
*(Swallow Fork Trail)*

• SPECIAL FEATURE: pioneer history

• TRAILHEAD AND DESCRIPTION: On the Cataloochee Rd, 1.1 mi
upstream from the RS, park near the trail sign at Palmer Creek.
Hike up the road that parallels the scenic stream. At 0.7 mi jct R
with the *Little Cataloochee Trail.*

   (The *Little Cataloochee Trail* follows an old road alongside a
creek 1.2 mi and reaches Davidson Gap at 1.8 mi. Pass through
Noland Gap at 2.2 mi, cross Coggin Branch, and pass the foundations of what was once the Daniel Cook house (1856). Cross
Coggin Branch again and at 3 mi pass L of the Little Cataloochee Baptist Church (1889) with its tall belfry. Cross Little Cataloochee Creek and a bridge at 3.5 mi. At 3.9 mi pass R of the
John Hannah cabin (1862) built of logs hewn on location. Ascend and jct with the rarely used *Pig Pen Trail,* L, at 4 mi. (The
*Pig Pen Trail* ascends 3.6 mi as a connector to the *Mt Sterling
Ridge Trail.*) Continue on the dirt road and cross Dude Branch
to terminate at Cataloochee Rd at 5 mi. It is 4.5 mi L on Cataloochee Rd to the RS.)

   To continue on the *Palmer Creek Trail,* enter a clearing at 1.5
mi and jct with the *Pretty Hollow Gap Trail* that goes ahead, but
the *Palmer Creek Trail* turns L. (The *Pretty Hollow Gap Trail*
follows Pretty Hollow Creek and passes Turkey George Horse
Camp at 0.2 mi. Cross the stream three times and at 3 mi cross
Onion Creek. Arrive at the N terminus at 4 mi to a crosstrail jct
with the *Mt Sterling Ridge Trail,* R and L, and *Swallow Fork Trail*
down the other side of Mt Sterling Ridge.)

   The *Palmer Creek Trail* crosses the Pretty Hollow Creek on a
footbridge and begins an ascent. Cross Lost Bottom Creek at
2.5 mi and Beech Creek at 3 mi. At 4.6 mi arrive at the end of
the trail at the one-way (S to N) Heintooga/Round Bottom Rd.
(To the L on the road it is 1.8 mi to the N terminus of *Spruce Mtn
Trail* and 0.7 mi R on the road to the S trailhead of the *Balsam
Mtn Trail.* Either trail can be used for connections with other
trails to form long loops in rejoining the *Palmer Creek Trail.*)
(*USGS Maps:* Cove Creek Gap, Luftee Knob)

## ▶ BALSAM MOUNTAIN AREA
### (Swain County)

The Balsam Mtn Ridge is the only ridge that connects the Smokies with the Blue Ridge Mtns. Much of the Balsam Mtn area with its dark green forest of fir (balsam) and spruce can be seen from the BRP, but a special paved spur road, Balsam Mtn Rd, takes the visitor 9 mi into a section of the ridge. Wildlife is frequently seen, and wildflower species are numerous. The Balsam Mtn developed campground has 46 campsites, usually open from late May to late September. There are flush toilets and water but no hook-ups. The 0.5-mi *Balsam Mtn Nature Trail* begins R, soon after entrance. It descends into a forest of fir, birch, white snakeroot, and rhododendron. The Heintooga Picnic Area, 0.6 mi beyond the campground, has 41 picnic sites and a loop parking area. From here the easy *Flat Creek Trail* begins at a gated access. Follow a sign to the Heintooga overlook (5,335 ft) for exceptional vistas of the ridges and the Raven Fork drainage. Follow the trail through spruce, birch, and rhododendron for 2.6 mi to the Balsam Mtn Rd. Along the way (at 1.8 mi) is a side trail, R, 0.2 mi to Flat Creek Falls. At the road it is 3.7 mi back (L) to the picnic area. **379–380**

• ACCESS: From BRP mp 458.2, turn onto Balsam Mtn Rd (closed in winter) and go 8.4 mi to the Balsam Mtn campground. From there it is 0.6 mi to the Heintooga Picnic Area. (A one-way, 14-mi gravel road continues N to Round Bottom where the road becomes open for two-way traffic as Big Cove Rd. No trucks, buses, or trailers; gates are closed at dark.)

• SUPPORT FACILITIES: All provisions and other camping needs are 20 mi in either direction of the BRP to Cherokee or Maggie Valley.

*Spruce Mountain Trail* (4.8 mi); *Balsam Mtn Trail* (10 mi) **381–383**

• LENGTH AND DIFFICULTY: 14.8 mi, moderate to strenuous (elev change 1,650 ft)

- CONNECTING TRAILS:
  *(Rough Fork Trail)*
  *(Cataloochee Divide Trail)*
  *(Palmer Creek Trail)*
  *(Beech Gap Trail)*
  *(Mt Sterling Ridge Trail)*
  *(Gunter Fork Trail)*
  *(AT)*

- SPECIAL FEATURE: spruce/fir forest groves

- TRAILHEAD AND DESCRIPTION: Although separated by 2.5 mi of road, the descriptions of these two trails are combined because they cover the same major ridgeline and have similar terrain and vegetation. Begin the *Spruce Mtn Trail* at Paul's Gap, 2.4 mi S of the Balsam Mtn campground. (At the parking area, *Rough Fork* and *Cataloochee Divide* trailheads are R.) Ascend in a mixed hardwood and spruce/fir forest to the highest point of the trail, the top of Cataloochee Balsam Mtn (5,970 ft) at 1.8 mi. Descend and ascend to Chiltoes Mtn at 3 mi. Reach Balsam Mtn Rd at 4.8 mi and Spruce Mtn backcountry campsite (#42), which has a spring. (A jeep road goes NW for 1 mi to the site of the dismantled Spruce Mtn fire tower.)

To reach the *Balsam Mtn Trail* follow Balsam Mtn Rd N for 2.5 mi to Pin Oak Gap (8.3 mi from Heintooga picnic area). Jct with *Palmer Creek Trail* along the way at 1.8 mi. Ascend to Ledge Bald (5,184 ft), descend to Beech Gap at 2.3 mi, and jct L with the *Beech Gap Trail*, a 3-mi steep and rough access trail from Balsam Mtn Rd in Round Bottom. Ascend in a spruce/fir forest to Balsam High Top (5,640 ft) at 3.6 mi; descend to Laurel Gap at 4.1 mi. A shelter (space for 14) and a spring are here. At 4.3 mi jct R with the *Mt Sterling Ridge Trail*. At 5.2 mi jct R with the *Gunter Fork Trail*. Continue on a generally level trail in a mixed forest with ferns, mosses, and white flowering moosewood. Pass L of Luftee Knob (6,200 ft) and reach Mt Yonaguska at 9.5 mi. Turn R and reach the *AT* and Tricorner Knob Shelter at 10 mi. (See Chapter 5 for other trails connecting with the *AT*.) (*USGS Maps:* Luftee Knob, Mt Guyot)

## ▶SMOKEMONT AREA
### (Swain County)

The developed Smokemont Campground is on the NE side of the Oconaluftee River and at the confluence of the Bradley Fork in the Oconaluftee Valley. Oconaluftee in Cherokee means "by the riverside." The watershed for this area begins from the high elev near Newfound Gap (N), Mt Kephart (N), Hughes Ridge (NE), Richland Mtn (N), and Thomas Divide (NW). The campground has 150 sites (no hook-ups) and three group camps. Fully operational from mid-April to the first of November, 35 sites are open all year. There are flush toilets, water, and sewage disposal. Its crowded condition during the summer and fall months is not suitable for a hiker who loves solitude and remoteness, but it is a good base camp for hikers with such multiple interests as hiking, fishing, and horseback riding. Reservations for the campground are made through Ticketron (May 1 to October 31). Call 615-436-5615 for information. Hitchhiking is forbidden on Newfound Gap Rd.

• ACCESS: From Cherokee drive N 5.7 mi on US-411 (becomes Newfound Gap Rd at the park boundary) to entrance, R.

• SUPPORT FACILITIES: Cherokee has shopping and service centers, motels, commercial campgrounds, restaurants, and a hospital.

### Hughes Ridge Trail                                       384

• LENGTH AND DIFFICULTY: 11.8 mi, strenuous (elev change 3,340 ft)

• CONNECTING TRAILS:
  (Chasteen Creek Trail)
  (Enloe Creek Trail)
  (Taywa Creek Trail)
  (AT)

• TRAILHEAD AND DESCRIPTION: Enter the Smokemont Campground, turn R, and park. Ascend to the chapel and go straight.

After 0.1 mi bear L from a horse trail. Turn L again at 0.6 mi with another horse-trail jct. At the third horse-trail jct at 1 mi, bear R. After the switchbacks begin, the route is more certain. Ascend in a forest of white pine, dense rhododendron, laurel, and oak on a climb of Hughes Ridge. Cross a small stream at 4.4 mi, the last source of water on the ridge. At 6.5 mi jct L with the *Chasteen Creek Trail* (which descends 4 mi to the *Bradley Fork Trail*). After another 0.5 mi jct R with the *Enloe Creek Trail*. (The 3.6-mi *Enloe Creek Trail* is the only trail route from the Smokemont area to the Raven Fork drainage. It is described below.) Continue to ascend on a wide treadway, mainly on the W side of the ridge in an oak/hickory forest with sections of galax and wintergreen groundcover. At 9.6 mi jct L with the *Taywa Creek Trail* (which descends 3.6 mi to the *Bradley Fork Trail*). Ascend and descend into a number of low gaps and reach Hughes Ridge Shelter (also called Pecks Corner Shelter) and spring at 11.3 mi. Ascend another 0.5 mi to the *AT* and the state line. (*USGS Maps:* Mt Guyot, Smokemont)

### Hyatt Ridge Trail                                    385–387

- LENGTH AND DIFFICULTY: 4.5 mi, strenuous (elev change 2,065 ft)

- CONNECTING TRAILS:
  *Enloe Creek Trail* (3.6 mi, moderate)
  *Hyatt Bald Trail* (2.9 mi, strenuous, elev change 1,860 ft)

- TRAILHEAD AND DESCRIPTION: From the Smokemont Campground drive 3 mi S on Newfound Gap Rd and turn L on a 0.6-mi connector road (across the Oconaluftee River) to Big Cove Rd. Turn L and follow Big Cove Rd (which becomes Straight Fork Rd) 11 mi to the trailhead, L. (A hiking route to this point is 12.6 mi from the campground on *Hughes Ridge Trail, Enloe Creek Trail,* and *Hyatt Ridge Trail.*) Follow an old jeep road beside Hyatt Creek and begin a steep ascent at 1 mi. Reach Low Gap at 1.9 mi and jct L with the *Enloe Creek Trail.*

(The *Enloe Creek Trail* descends on an old jeep road into a beautiful forest of tall hardwood and hemlock. At 1 mi reach

Raven Fork, a stream of rapids that would be impossible to cross after heavy rains. Enloe Creek backcountry campsite #47 is near the creek. Continue ahead and after 0.4 mi the treadway is rocky and sometimes muddy from horse traffic. Pass a number of small waterfalls and arrive at Enloe Creek at 2 mi. Ford the creek [difficult after heavy rains] and at 2.7 mi ascend on switchbacks to jct with *Hughes Ridge Trail* at 3.6 mi. [To the R it is 4.7 mi to the *AT,* and L it is 7.1 mi to the campground.])

Continue on the *Hyatt Ridge Trail,* ascend steeply on the ridge, and jct at 3.8 mi with the *Hyatt Bald Trail,* R. (The *Hyatt Bald Trail* descends, steeply in sections, on an E slope of a hardwood forest. After 2.7 mi it emerges to an old road and jct, R and L, with the *Beech Gap Trail* that follows the old road L for 2.8 mi in a steep 2,000 ft climb to connect with the *Balsam Mtn Trail.* Turn R on the old road, pass a spring, R, and reach the gated road entrance at Round Bottom at 2.9 mi. Here in a horseshoe curve Balsam Mtn Rd—5.9 mi from the Heintooga Picnic Area—becomes Straight Fork Rd. Down the mtn it is 1.2 mi to *Hyatt Ridge Trail,* R.)

The *Hyatt Ridge Trail* continues to ascend and ends at the McGhee Spring backcountry campsite #44 at 4.5 mi. Back-track. (The continuation of *Hyatt Ridge Trail* and the adjoining *Raven Fork Trail* at McGhee Spring have been deleted from the park's trail inventory.) (*USGS Maps:* Bunches Bald, Luftee Knob, Smokemont)

### Bradley Fork Trail                                        388–392

- LENGTH AND DIFFICULTY: 5.3 mi, easy to moderate

- CONNECTING TRAILS:
  *Smokemont Loop Trail* (5.9 mi, moderate)
  *Chasteen Creek Trail* (4 mi, strenuous, elev change 2,300 ft)
  *Taywa Creek Trail* (3.6 mi, strenuous, elev change 2,130 ft)
  *Richland Mtn Trail* (4.3 mi, strenuous, elev change 2,540 ft)

- TRAILHEAD AND DESCRIPTION: On entry to the campground, turn L and go to a gate at the end of the campground (this trail may also be signed *Richland Mtn Trail*). The *Smokemont Loop*

*Trail* begins here also. Hike on the service road that parallels Bradley Fork. Pass a hemlock grove at 1 mi; at 1.2 mi jct with *Chasteen Creek Trail,* R.

(The *Chasteen Creek Trail* begins as a gated jeep and horse trail. After 0.1 mi reach Lower Chasteen Creek backcountry campsite #50, and at 0.8 mi is a waterfall in a forest of poplar, oak, and maple. Cross a stream at 2.4 mi and leave the jeep road at 2.7 mi. Ascend on switchbacks to jct with *Hughes Ridge Trail* at 4 mi. (A loop of another 6.6 mi can be made by taking the *Hughes Ridge Trail,* R, to the campground.)

Continue upstream. At 1.7 mi the *Smokemont Loop Trail* leaves the *Bradley Fork Trail.* (The *Smokemont Loop Trail* forks L from the main trail and crosses Bradley Fork on a footbridge. Ascend on the lower slopes of Richland Mtn in a forest of poplar, hickory, hemlock, birch, and laurel. Reach the ridgecrest at 2.7 mi and begin a descent. Return to Bradley Creek at 4.3 mi, pass L of the Bradley cemetery at 5 mi, and through a white-pine grove to join the service road at 5.2 mi. Go L, cross Bradley Fork on a road bridge, and return to the origin at 5.9 mi.)

On the *Bradley Fork Trail* pass a waterfall at 2.5 mi, and cross the creek twice on road bridges before a jct with the *Taywa Creek Trail* at 4 mi. (The *Taywa Creek Trail* ascends on Long Ridge to a number of outcroppings with scenic views. Cross Taywa Creek twice, at 1 mi and again at 1.6 mi. Ascend steeply on switchbacks and reach *Hughes Ridge Trail* at 3.6 mi. It is 2 mi L to the *AT* and 9.6 mi R to the Smokemont Campground.)

The *Bradley Fork Trail* continues upstream, crosses Bradley Fork and Tennessee Branch before bearing R at a jct with the *Richland Mtn Trail* at 4.3 mi. One mi farther the trail ends at Cabin Flats backcountry campsite #49. (The *Richland Mtn Trail* ascends and crosses a bridge over Tennessee Branch at 0.1 mi. It crosses the branch three more times and a number of drains to 0.9 mi. Ascend steeply and jct L with *Grassy Branch Trail* at 2.9 mi. Begin an easier gradient and pass views of Thomas Divide L [W]. At 4.3 mi jct with the *AT* near Dry Sluice Gap. (It is 0.3 mi L to the spectacular views of the *AT's* Charlies Bunion and 4.1 mi farther to Newfound Gap Rd.) (*USGS Maps:* Mt Guyot, Smokemont)

### Kephart Prong Trail                                393–395

- LENGTH AND DIFFICULTY: 2.1 mi, easy

- CONNECTING TRAILS:
  Grassy Branch Trail (2.3 mi, strenuous, elev change 1,740 ft)
  Sweat Heifer Trail (3.5 mi, strenuous, elev change 2,270 ft)

- TRAILHEAD AND DESCRIPTION: From the Smokemont Campground drive up Newfound Gap Rd for 3.7 mi to the parking
  area, R. Cross the Oconaluftee River on a road bridge and pass
  the remains of an old CCC camp. Cross Kephart Prong on a
  footbridge and pass the site of an old fish hatchery. Cross Kephart Prong three more times and reach an overused Kephart
  Prong Shelter (accommodates 14) at 2.1 mi. (The shelter is
  named for Horace Kephart [1862-1931], authority on mtn lore
  and author of Our Southern Highlanders. Mt Kephart, NW of the
  shelter, was named in his honor, October 3, 1928.) Go R from
  the shelter to follow the Grassy Branch Trail, which parallels
  Kephart Prong. At 0.8 mi it crosses Lower Grassy Branch near a
  cascade and crosses the stream again at 2.1 mi. Here are views
  of the valley and Thomas Divide beyond. Jct with the Richland
  Mtn Trail at 2.3 mi. (On the Richland Mtn Trail it is 1.4 mi L to
  the AT; R it descends 2.9 mi to the Bradley Fork Trail.)
  
  Left of the shelter is the infrequently used Sweat Heifer Trail.
  Cross a small stream, ascend, and reach an old RR grade at 0.7
  mi. Ascend and cross a cascading stream at 1.8 mi and leave the
  old RR grade at 2.1 mi. Wildflowers are prominent in a hardwood forest. Reach the AT at 3.5 mi. It is 1.7 mi L to Newfound
  Gap Rd. (The trail's name may derive from the practice of
  driving livestock over the mtn on the Oconaluftee Turnpike, a
  wagon road constructed in 1931.) (USGS Maps: Clingmans
  Dome, Mt Guyot, Smokemont)

### Kanati Fork Trail                                        396

- LENGTH AND DIFFICULTY: 3 mi, strenuous (elev change 2,110
  ft)

- CONNECTING TRAIL:
  (Thomas Divide Trail)

• TRAILHEAD AND DESCRIPTION: From Smokemont, drive 3.9 mi NW to the trailhead parking area, L (0.2 mi beyond the *Kephart Prong Trail* described above). Follow the graded trail, parallel to Kanati Fork, in a cove of oak, poplar, maple, and birch. At 1 mi leave the cove and ascend on switchbacks in a section of hemlock. Cross a small branch at 1.6 mi and ascend in a forest with rhododendron and laurel to jct with the *Thomas Divide Trail* at 3 mi. (To the R it is 1.8 mi to the Newfound Gap Rd, and L it is 12.3 mi to the *Thomas Divide Trail* access in Deep Gap. See the Deep Gap Area descriptions below.) (*USGS Maps:* Clingmans Dome, Smokemont)

### *Newton Bald Trail* 397

• LENGTH AND DIFFICULTY: 5.3 mi, strenuous (elev change 2,900 ft)

• CONNECTING TRAILS:
  *(Mingus Trail)*
  *(Thomas Divide Trail)*

• TRAILHEAD AND DESCRIPTION: Park across the road from the Smokemont Campground entrance. Hike up the Newfound Gap Rd (NW) for 0.1 mi, and turn L on an old woods road. At 0.3 mi join a horse trail, turn R, but leave it, R, at 0.5 mi on a well-graded trail. Ascend steadily on a N slope. Cross a small stream in an area of hemlock and rhododendron at 2.7 mi and another water source at 3 mi. Jct L with the former *Mingus Creek Trail* at 4.4 mi on the ridgecrest of Newton Bald (5,142 ft). Descend slightly and jct with the *Thomas Divide Trail* at 5.3 mi. (The *Thomas Divide Trail* goes R 5.2 mi to Newfound Gap Rd, and L for 9.8 mi to Deep Creek Campground.) (*USGS Map:* Smokemont)

## ▶ DEEP CREEK AREA
### (Swain County)

Some of the longest and most scenic trails on the E side of the Smokies are on the ridges and valleys that run N-S in or near the Deep Creek basin. The *Thomas Divide Trail* is on a high E border, the central *Deep Creek Trail* weaves through a lush valley to its watershed near Newfound Gap, and the *Noland Divide Trail* is a lofty W-side route to Clingmans Dome. The famous conservationist Horace Kephart had a permanent camp, Bryson Place, on Deep Creek, and the stream remains a popular route (eight separate backcountry campsites) for hikers, equestrians, and fishermen. With the exception of the *Noland Divide Trail,* all access routes to the trails begin at the *Deep Creek Trail* parking area N of the Deep Creek Campground. The developed campground has 128 sites for tents or RVs (no hook-ups), flush toilets, water, and a large picnic area. It is open all year. The RS is R after the entrance gate. Waterfalls, cascading streams, outcroppings, and virgin forests provide an area of natural beauty. Unfortunately, the wild swine wallow in the springs and destroy plant life and the food chain for the native animals. The proposed *MST* is routed through this area from Clingmans Dome to include all of the *Fork Ridge Trail,* parts of *Deep Creek Trail, Sunkota Ridge Trail,* and *Thomas Divide Trail,* and all of *Newton Bald Trail* for 26.4 mi to Smokemont. The E trailhead and 25 mi of the 42.7-mi *Lakeshore Trail* are also in the Deep Creek jurisdiction.

• ADDRESS AND ACCESS: From downtown Bryson City on US-19, turn N at the Swain County Courthouse, turn R after crossing the bridge, and follow the signs for 3 mi. Address: Deep Creek RS, GSMNP, 970 Park Rd, Bryson City, NC 28713, tel: 704-488-3184. All inquiries about the trails in the areas of Noland Creek, Forney Creek, and Chambers Creek should also be directed to the Deep Creek ranger.

• SUPPORT FACILITIES: Bryson City has motels, restaurants, shopping centers, commercial campgrounds, and a hospital.

### *Deep Creek Trail* 398–401

• LENGTH AND DIFFICULTY: 12 mi, strenuous (elev change 2,820 ft)

- CONNECTING TRAILS:
  *Indian Creek Trail* (6.7 mi, moderate to strenuous, elev change 1,555 ft)
  *Pole Road Creek Trail* (3.2 mi, strenuous, elev change 1,800 ft)
  *Fork Ridge Trail* (5.1 mi, strenuous, elev change 2,880 ft)

- SPECIAL FEATURES: Bryson Place, virgin hemlock, fishing

- TRAILHEAD AND DESCRIPTION: From the parking area N of the campground, hike upstream on the gated Deep Creek Rd. Pass Tom's Branch Falls, R, at 0.4 mi, and pass at 0.9 mi the jct R with the S trailhead of *Indian Creek Trail* and *Thomas Divide Trail.* At 1.9 mi pass Jenkins Place, a former homesite, and jct R with the 1.1-mi *Indian Creek Loop Trail* (which connects with the *Sunkota Ridge Trail* described below). At 2.2 mi reach the end of the road and begin the *Deep Creek Trail* upstream. Follow the sign to an old jeep road that will follow the E side of the creek up and down spur ridges of Sunkota Ridge for 3.9 mi. Pass the first backcountry campsite, Bumgardner Branch #60, at 0.5 mi. At 1 mi is a view of the valley from the highest spur on the route. A spring is 0.2 mi ahead. At 3 mi pass McCracken Branch backcountry campsite #59, and Nicks Nest Branch backcountry campsite #58 at 3.5 mi. Emerge at Bryson Place backcountry campsite #57 at 3.9 mi. It is a large grassy area with tables, a horse hitching rack, and a clear stream at the campsite entrance. Before crossing the stream, L, at 200 ft, is a memorial plaque on a millstone honoring Horace Hephart, the "Dean of American Campers." On the R (E) of the campsite is a jct with the *Indian Creek Trail.*

(The well-graded *Indian Creek Trail* ascends through a beautiful forest of hardwood, white pine, rhododendron, and fern beds for 1.5 mi to Martin's Gap [3,430 ft] on the Sunkota Ridge and a crosstrail jct with the *Sunkota Ridge Trail.* [To the L the *Sunkota Ridge Trail* goes 4.8 mi to jct with the *Thomas Divide Trail,* and 5 mi R to jct with the *Deep Creek Trail.*] Descend rapidly on the E side of the ridge on switchbacks to cross Indian Creek for a sharp R turn downstream at 2.4 mi. Arrive at the end of a road at 3 mi and follow it to its entrance gate at Deep Creek Rd at 6.7 mi. Along the way at 5.9 mi pass a 1-mi spur trail [*Indian Creek Loop Trail*] R that leads to *Sunkota Ridge Trail* and to the *Deep Creek Trail* at Jenkins Place. At 6.2 mi pass R of the *Thomas Divide Trail* S terminus, and at 6.6 mi pass the 50-ft Indian Creek Falls. Jct at Deep Creek Rd at 6.7 mi for a loop distance of 13.7 mi back to the parking area.)

From Bryson Place slightly descend to the riverbank and proceed upstream to pass Burnt Spruce backcountry campsite #56 at 4.4 mi. Jct with *Pole Road Creek Trail,* L, at 4.6 mi. (The *Pole Road Creek Trail* crosses a high scenic footbridge over Deep Creek and serves chiefly as a wide connecting trail between Deep Creek and Noland Divide. It crosses Pole Road Creek a number of times, but after 2 mi ascends steeply in a forest of tall hardwood and hemlock to reach Upper Sassafras Gap. Here it jct with the *Noland Divide Trail* at 3.2 mi. It is 3.6 mi N to Clingmans Dome Rd and 7.9 mi S to the Deep Gap campground.)

Continuing upstream, the *Deep Creek Trail* passes Pole Road backcountry campsite #55 at 4.7 mi, and Nettle Creek backcountry campsite #54 at 5.5 mi. Pass banks of Fraser sedge (*Carex fraseri*) at 5.9 mi, and ascend R of a precipice at 7.1 mi. At 8.1 mi jct L with *Fork Ridge Trail.* Poke Patch backcountry campsite #53 is here.

(The *Fork Ridge Trail* crosses the footbridge over Deep Creek and ascends steeply but soon more gradually. At 0.9 mi is a scenic view of Clingmans Dome Rd area and Bearpen Ridge. Enter a dense laurel grove at 1.5 mi, one of a number of groves on the route through a forest of maple, birch, cucumber tree, and flame azalea. At 2.6 mi are huge hemlocks. After the final switchback on the ridge at 3.8 mi, the trail turns R on a more moderate grade, passes seeps and springs [the last one at 5 mi], and exits at a small parking area on Clingmans Dome Rd at 5.1 mi. [To the L it is 3.5 mi to Clingmans Dome parking area, and R it is 3.5 mi to Newfound Gap Rd.] Across the road it is 125 ft to the *AT.*)

On the *Deep Creek Trail* ascend upstream on a bank and parallel the creek until veering R at 10.5 mi. Ascend steeply in a forest dominated by hemlock before a final ascent on switchbacks that leads to the N terminus at the Newfound Gap Rd and parking area at 12 mi. (From here, on the road, it is 1.6 mi L [N] to Newfound Gap and 1.6 mi R [S] to the *Thomas Divide Trail.*) (*USGS Maps:* Bryson City, Clingmans Dome)

### Thomas Divide Trail                                      402–406

- LENGTH AND DIFFICULTY: 14.1 mi, strenuous (elev change 3,310 ft)

- CONNECTING TRAILS:
  *Deeplow Gap Trail* (3.8 mi, moderate)
  *Sunkota Ridge Trail* (9.8 mi, strenuous, elev change 2,640 ft)
  (*Indian Creek Trail*)
  (*Newton Bald Trail*)
  (*Kanati Fork Trail*)

- TRAILHEAD AND DESCRIPTION: From the N side of the Deep Creek campground go past the gated road and after 0.9 mi turn R at the *Indian Creek Trail,* cross Indian Creek on a bridge, and at 0.5 mi turn R at the S trailhead. Cross Indian Creek again and begin ascending on a gradual grade to Stone Pile Gap at 1.4 mi. Follow an unused road (had been planned as part of the Indian Creek Motor Trail) and at 3.4 mi turn sharply R. In a forest of hardwood, laurel, and flame azalea reach a knob at 5 mi. Descend to a spring at 5.2 mi and to a jct with the *Deeplow Gap Trail,* R and L, in Deeplow Gap at 5.8 mi.

(The *Deeplow Gap Trail* descends R [E] on the S slope of Thomas Divide and enters a cove to cross Little Creek at 0.5 mi. At 0.8 mi it reaches the base of 75-ft Little Creek Falls. It crosses the creek, follows a series of switchbacks down to a jeep road, and jct with the *Cooper Creek Trail* at 1.5 mi. Because the park has closed the *Mingus Creek Trail,* a route to the Newfound Gap Rd at Mingus Mill and the Oconaluftee Visitor Center, the 2.3-mi *Cooper Creek Trail* does not serve its former purpose as a connector route. Instead, use the *Thomas Divide Trail* to the *Newton Bald Trail* for an alternate route. The *Deeplow Gap Trail* goes L [W] from the *Thomas Divide Trail* and descends on switchbacks to a hemlock grove where it joins a jeep road at 1.8 mi. It crosses Georges Branch at 2.1 mi and Indian Creek on a bridge to jct with *Indian Creek Trail*, R and L. A 12-mi loop could be made L on the *Indian Creek Trail* to the parking area at the Deep Creek campground.)

Continue ahead on the *Thomas Divide Trail* to jct R with the W end of the *Newton Bald Trail* at 8.9 mi. (The *Newton Bald Trail* goes E 5.3 mi to Newfound Gap Rd at Smokemont.) At 9.4 mi jct with the N terminus of the *Sunkota Ridge Trail*, L.

(The *Sunkota Ridge Trail* descends moderately and in some places gently for 4.8 mi to Martin's Gap where it intersects with *Indian Creek Trail*. Along the way it is on the E slope for almost the entire distance. It has trail banks of trailing arbutus, gentian, ferns, and wood betony. Sassafras, flame azalea, and striped green maple make up part of the understory. Intermittent springs are at 3.5 mi and 4.3 mi. [In Martin's Gap the *Indian Creek Trail* goes R 1.5 mi to jct with the *Deep Creek Trail*, and L 5.2 mi to jct with Deep Creek Rd.] From Martin's Gap the trail begins on the E slope among rhododendron and laurel and follows the slope and the ridgeline for another 3.8 mi before beginning a steep descent of 1.2 mi to reach its S terminus and jct with a connector trail, the *Indian Creek Loop Trail* at 9.8 mi. Left it is 0.4 mi to the *Indian Creek Trail*; R it is 0.6 mi to the *Deep Creek Trail* at Jenkins Place. From here it is 1.9 mi back to the parking area at the Deep Creek campground, a total loop of 22.8 mi using part of the *Thomas Divide Trail* and all of the *Sunkota Ridge Trail*.)

Continue on the *Thomas Divide Trail*. (Although not known just where on this historic ridge, the Cherokee, Tsali, hid his family from the infamous "Trail of Tears" in 1838 somewhere "on the far side of this ridge." It was William Thomas (1805-1893) who located him and requested he turn himself in to the U.S. Army for accidentally killing a soldier. Thomas had been adopted by the Cherokee chief Yonaguska as his son, Little Will, near the age of 12. At the death of Yonaguska in 1839, Thomas became the Cherokee chief. Because Thomas was a white citizen he was able to represent the Cherokee in their land claims. His strong leadership before Congress had a permanent influence on the U.S. government establishment of the Qualla Reservation that adjoins part of the park. Thomas Divide is named in his honor. See introduction and *Tsali Trail* in Chapter 2.) Descend to Tuskee Gap and ascend to Nettle Creek Bald at 11.8 mi. At 12.2 mi jct R with the *Kanati Fork Trail* (which descends 3 mi to Newport Gap Rd). At 13 mi arrive at Turkey Flyway (5,160 ft) for general views of Mt Kephart and Richland Mtn. Follow a narrow ridge to Beetree Ridge before descending to a gap at 13.8 mi. Ascend to Newfound Gap Rd and trail terminus at 14 mi. (On the highway it is 0.3 mi R to an overlook and parking area, and 1.7 mi N to jct L with the N trailhead of the *Deep Creek Trail*.) (*USGS Maps:* Bryson City, Clingmans Dome, Smokemont)

## Noland Divide Trail                                    407

• LENGTH AND DIFFICULTY: 11.5 mi, strenuous (elev change 4,155 ft)

• CONNECTING TRAILS:
  (*Noland Creek Trail*)
  (*Pole Road Creek Trail*)

• SPECIAL FEATURES: vistas and botanical variation

• TRAILHEAD AND DESCRIPTION: This hiker/horse trail has the highest elev change of any trail on the E side of the Smokies. (Other high elev changes are *Baxter Creek Trail* and *Forney Creek Trail*.) An outstanding display of flora is on the trail, ranging from the poplar of the valley to the pine, laurel, and blueberries of the dry ridges and spruce/fir near the trail's highest point. Trillium, galax, asters, ferns, orchids, berries, and lichens are present in great variation. Begin at the sign to the L (W) of the campground entrance. Follow an easy route for 0.4 mi. Ascend to a ridge, but leave it at 1.2 mi to follow an exceptionally steep slope to the headwaters of Juney Whank Branch at a long switchback. Reach Beaugard Ridge at 3.5 mi with vistas of Bryson City and the Alarka Mtns, S, in the Nantahala National Forest. Curve R and ascend steeply on the crest to springs at 4.9 mi, the last water source up the trail. Slope R of Coburn Knob and arrive at the ridgeline of Noland Divide. Reach Lower

Sassafras Gap at 7.2 mi and Upper Sassafras Gap at 8 mi at crosstrails. (The N end of *Noland Creek Trail* is L; it leads S 9.5 mi to North Shore Rd. On the R the W end of *Pole Road Creek Trail* descends E 3.2 mi to jct with the *Deep Creek Trail*.) Continue the ascent on Noland Divide and at 11 mi turn R on a road that emerges at Clingmans Dome Rd at 11.5 mi. (To the L on the paved road it is 1.5 mi to Clingmans Dome parking; to the R it is 2 mi to *Fork Ridge Trail*, described above.) (*USGS Maps:* Bryson City, Clingmans Dome)

## ▶ NORTH SHORE AREA
### (Swain County)

This large area covers the rugged drainage pattern of Noland, Forney, Hazel, and Eagle creeks, which flow S and SW into Fontana Lake from the crest of the Smokies. Hiking trails ring its borders and provide an interconnecting web within the loop. The spectacular outer loop of 80.6 mi includes 29.6 mi of the *AT* from Clingmans Dome to the *Lakeshore Trail* near Fontana Dam, 38.6 mi of the *Lakeshore Trail* to 11.4-mi *Forney Creek Trail,* and a final mi of *Forney Ridge Trail* to the Forney Ridge parking area at Clingmans Dome. The route is one of the most scenic, adventuresome, and unforgettable in the Smokies backcountry. Many of the trails in this area were built by the CCC in the 1930s, and others are old roads used by generations past. An historic area, its lush coves were once populated, predominately by employees of mining and lumber companies. There are many memories about this vast and beautiful forest and its people. The famous writer on mountain lore, Horace Kephart, lived in a mining cabin in the remote hollow of Little Fork for three years in the early part of the century. Uninhabited since 1943, when the Little Tennessee River was impounded by the Fontana Dam TVA project, there remain more than 20 cemeteries. They have such family names as Proctor, Bradshaw, Mitchell, Posey, and Welch, and such locations as Fairview and Bone Valley. Descendants are provided regular, free boat access (the easiest route) by the NPS. But the bitter controversy of a North Shore road and a designated wilderness area continues. "The public value of that park for wilderness preservation is more important than a road for those cemetery people," said Ronald J. Tipton of the Wilderness Society in Atlanta. "We won't give up," said Fred Chandler of the North Shore Cemetery Association. "We got children and grandchildren, they won't give up." (See the introduction to this chapter.)

• ACCESS: From downtown Bryson City at the Swain County Courthouse, drive N on Everette St, cross the bridge, and go straight on what becomes Fontana Rd (SR-1364) to the park gate after 3 mi. Continue ahead on what is also called Lakeview Rd, 5 mi to *Noland Creek Trail* access, L, and another 0.7 mi to an access parking area at the tunnel for all North Shore trails. The W access is at the Fontana Dam parking area where a hike of 1.1 mi on the *AT* (across the dam) connects with the *Lakeshore Trail* for an access to all other trails. Another vehicle access is at Forney Ridge parking area at Clingmans Dome. (Clingmans Dome Rd is closed in winter.) (See Chapter 5 for *AT* access points.) Address for the ranger who supervises the trails for Noland, Forney, and Chamber creeks area is the same as for Deep Creek.

• SUPPORT FACILITIES: Bryson City has motels, restaurants, shopping centers, commercial campgrounds, and a hospital. Fontana Village has limited seasonal services; call 704-498-2211 for information. A TVA campground with hot showers is at the base of Fontana Dam, open April 15 to October 1. Boat access, rentals, and shuttle service are available at Fontana Marina off NC-28, 1.6 mi E of Fontana Village.

## *Noland Creek Trail* 408–409

• LENGTH AND DIFFICULTY: 9.5 mi, strenuous (elev change 2,440 ft)

• CONNECTING TRAILS:
  *Springhouse Branch Trail* (2.8 mi, moderate)

*(Noland Divide Trail)*
*(Poles Road Creek Trail)*

• TRAILHEAD AND DESCRIPTION: Follow the access description above, from Bryson City. At the trail sign ascend a few ft to the gate and then descend 0.2 mi to where the trail divides. Left it is 1 mi to the edge of Fontana Lake and Lower Noland Creek backcountry campsite #66. Backtrack, and pass under the highway bridge. Cross Noland Creek on a bridge, and follow upstream in a forest of hardwood, hemlock, and rhododendron. At 1.7 mi reach the mouth of Bearpen Branch and the Bearpen Branch backcountry campsite #65, L. Cross Noland Creek on a bridge at 3 mi and follow the R bank. Arrive in Solola Valley, an area once inhabited, at 4 mi. At 4.5 mi reach the mouth of Springhouse Branch and the Mill Creek backcountry campsite #64.

(The *Springhouse Branch Trail* begins L and ascends gradually up Mill Creek. Evidence of old farms [rock piles] is noticeable at 0.5 mi. Cross Mill Creek at 0.6 mi. Pass a spring at 2.4 mi and reach the crest of Forney Ridge in Board Camp Gap at 2.8 mi, the trail's terminus. Jct here with the *Forney Ridge Trail*, R and L. (It is 1.3 mi L on *Forney Ridge Trail* to *Bee Gum Branch Trail,* and 5.5 mi R to Clingmans Dome Rd.)

After leaving Solola Valley pass a waterfall and cross Noland Creek at 5 mi. Ford the stream twice more and ascend. At 5.4 mi is Jerry Flat backcountry campsite #63, and at 6.5 mi is Upper Ripshin backcountry campsite #62. Cross Upper Ripshin Branch at 7.2 mi and immediately cross Noland Creek again. Ascend to and cross Sassafras Branch at 8.6 mi and turn R at the trail fork. To the L is Bald Creek backcountry campsite #61. Ascend steeply by Sassafras Branch for 0.4 mi and turn R to approach Sassafras Gap, the trail's terminus at 9.5 mi and crosstrail jct. (It is 3.6 mi L on the *Noland Divide Trail* to Clingmans Dome Rd and 1.5 mi L on the road to *Forney Ridge Trail*. At Sassafras Gap the *Pole Road Creek Trail* descends 3.2 mi to the *Deep Creek Trail*.) (*USGS Maps:* Bryson City, Clingmans Dome, Noland Creek, Silers Bald)

### *Lakeshore Trail*         **410**

- LENGTH AND DIFFICULTY: 42.7 mi, moderate

- CONNECTING TRAILS:
  *(Forney Creek Trail)*
  *(Hazel Creek Trail)*
  *(Sugar Fork Trail)*
  *(Jenkins Ridge Trail)*
  *(Pinnacle Creek Trail)*
  *(Eagle Creek Trail)*
  *(Lost Cove Trail)*
  *(AT)*

- SPECIAL FEATURE: settlements of former inhabitants

- TRAILHEAD AND DESCRIPTION: Access is described above in the North Shore Area. (Boat access is possible at Chambers Creek, Pilkey Creek, Hazel Creek, and Eagle Creek at normal lake level. The trail follows a contour generally between 1,800 and 2,000 ft. An infrequent orange blaze and trail signs help guide the hiker in and out of scores of ridge spines, coves, and cross-trails. The forest is predominantly hardwood with a mixture of pine, hemlock, rhododendron, laurel, and azalea. Leucothoe and ferns are commonplace near the many streams. Wild-flowers are profuse and include orchids, cohosh, arbutus, cardinal flower, turtlehead, and dwarf iris. In some of the former settlements are vines, shrubs, and domestic flowers. Bear, wild boar, deer, fox, beaver, grouse, and wild turkey are among the wild animals. Songbirds are prominent. (The park staff have set boar traps to assist in transferring the animals out of the park.)

At the tunnel parking area, the "Portals to the Wilderness," there is a choice of trail directions. The short route is through the tunnel to the other trail jct, L, at 0.5 mi. To follow a longer route, the "tunnel bypass," cross the road from the parking area to a trail sign. At 0.4 mi jct L with an old trail route. (It descends to the Goldmine Branch and follows the branch upstream to rejoin the *Lakeshore Trail*.) Continue ahead, cross two small streams, and rejoin the tunnel route at 1.6 mi. Follow a graded treadway to a ridgecrest at 2.4 mi. At 2.9 mi turn L, downhill to an unnamed trail jct. Reach another jct, bear R on an old road, and cross a bridge at 3.1 mi. At 4 mi jct with *Forney Creek Trail* (which follows an old RR grade for most of its 11.4 mi to *Forney Ridge Trail,* 1 mi from Clingmans Dome Rd). Cross an old bridge over Forney Creek to Lower Forney backcountry campsite #74 at 4.1 mi. Follow a gradual and graded ascent to curve the multiple ridge spines of Pilot Knob. At 6.2 mi is a minor gap and jct with old trails; go straight. Descend slightly, cross small Jenny Branch at 7.1 mi and Gunter Branch at 7.7 mi. At 8.2 mi cross a small branch in a small glade by old walls. For the next 2 mi pass through a former settlement with evidence of homesites. (The McClure cemetery is on a gentle knoll, R [0.1-mi side trail], at 9.9 mi.) Cross Chambers Creek on a park footbridge at 10.6 mi. Here is Chambers Creek backcountry campsite #98. From here Fontana Lake is visible for the next 5 mi, the section most visible for the entire route. Arrive at Hicks Branch backcountry campsite #75 at 12.3 mi. At 12.7 mi pass an old homesite chimney and arrive at Kirkland Creek backcountry campsite #76 at a bridge over *Kirkland Creek* at 12.9 mi. Pass an old rusty antique car at 14.1 mi. Where side trails jct at 16 mi, go straight on an old road. Cross a park bridge over Pilky Creek at 17 mi (the vicinity of the old *Deep Gap Trail,* R, now an overgrown manway). Reach a gap on Welch Ridge at 23.6 mi; descend to Hazel Creek valley and jct with the *Hazel Creek Trail,* L, at a service road, before crossing the Hazel Creek bridge at 25.2 mi. (The *Hazel Creek Trail* descends 0.3 mi to the lake entrance and Proctor backcountry campsite #86.) Cross the bridge and turn R. (To the L it is 0.2 mi to the Lower Bunkhouse, a cottage from which the park staff monitor the area.) Go upstream jointly with the *Hazel Creek Trail* to follow a long curve called the Horseshoe around the stream. At 28.1 mi, R, pass Sawdust Pile backcountry campsite #85. Arrive at a jct, L, with *Sugar Fork Trail* and stream confluence at 29.7 mi. Sugar Fork backcountry campsite #89 is R. (The *Hazel Creek Trail* continues R on the service road for 10.1 mi and ends at a jct with the *Welch Ridge Trail,* 0.5 mi from the *AT.*) Here at Sugar Fork is the former pioneer settlement of Medlin. A preeminent mountaineer, Granville Calhoun (and devoted friend of Horace Kephart) lived here. Turn L and follow the *Sugar Fork Trail* parallel with Sugar Fork. At 30.2 mi, the Higdon Cemetery is L. At 31.4 mi, R, is the mouth of Little Fork. (Kephart lived three years in a simple cabin up this remote hollow.) Arrive at Pickens Gap at 32 mi. Here is a jct R with *Jenkins Ridge Trail* (which ascends 5.9 mi to the *AT*). *Sugar Fork Trail* ends here and *Pinnacle Creek Trail* begins. Descend and at 34.3 mi pass Pinnacle Creek back-country campsite #88, R. Ahead the treadway may be wet and wading necessary at the stream crossings. At 36 mi cross the first of three log bridge crossings. Here is the end of *Pinnacle Creek Trail* and the jct with *Eagle Creek Trail,* L and R. (To the R the *Eagle Creek Trail* ascends 8 mi to the *AT;* L it ends at the jct of the *Lost Cove Trail* after 1 mi. Continue L on the *Eagle Creek Trail* to Lost Cove at 37 mi. To the L is Lost Cove backcountry campsite #90 and continuance of the *Lakeshore Trail.* To the R the *Lost Cove Trail* ascends 3.1 mi to the *AT*.) From here pass through a lush cove and begin a steep ascent on a footpath before a level contour in and out of ridge spines of Snaken Ridge and Shuck-stack Ridge. At 42.4 mi the footpath ends and an abandoned road begins. Jct with the *AT,* R and L, at 42.7 mi (41.6 mi if the tunnel route is used). Follow the *AT* on the paved road 1.1 mi to cross the Fontana Dam and reach the parking area. (*USGS Maps:* Noland Creek, Tuskeegee, Fontana Dam, Thunderhead Mtn, Cades Cove)

### Forney Creek Trail                                   411–415

- LENGTH AND DIFFICULTY: 11.4 mi, strenuous (elev change 4,030 ft)

- CONNECTING TRAILS:
  (*Lakeshore Trail*)
  *Jumpup Ridge Trail* (5.8 mi, strenuous, elev change 3,100 ft)
  *Bee Gum Branch Trail* (2.9 mi, strenuous, elev change 1,640 ft)
  *Jonas Creek Trail* (3.5 mi, strenuous, elev change 3,200 ft)
  *Forney Ridge Trail* (6.8 mi, strenuous, elev change 2,500 ft)

- TRAILHEAD AND DESCRIPTION: Follow the Lakeshore Drive and the *Lakeshore Trail* descriptions above. (Another access is 1 mi on the *Forney Ridge Trail* from Clingmans Dome Rd.) After 4 mi (2.9 mi if using the tunnel route) on the *Lakeshore Trail* jct with *Forney Creek Trail*, R. (To the L the *Forney Creek Trail* crosses a bridge to Lower Forney backcountry campsite #74 and the lake after 0.2 mi. The *Lakeshore Trail* continues from the campsite W to Fontana Dam.) Go upstream on the *Forney Creek Trail* on an old RR grade for the first 9 mi. It crosses the creek at least 15 times; wading or rock-hopping is necessary. At 0.6 mi jct L with the *Jumpup Ridge Trail* and Bear Creek backcountry campsite #73.

(The *Jumpup Ridge Trail* follows an old RR grade near Bear Creek. At 2.8 mi it leaves the creek area at Poplar Flats on an old jeep road. Ascent becomes steeper on curves and switchbacks to terminate on the ridgeline of Welch Ridge at 5.8 mi. (To the R it is 6.2 mi on the *Welch Ridge Trail* to Silers Bald and the *AT*. To the L it runs 0.6 mi to jct with *Cold Spring Branch Trail* and scenic High Rocks.)

Reach the site of an old CCC camp with scattered old farm artifacts at 2.8 mi. Here is CCC backcountry campsite #71. After crossing the creek, jct with the *Bee Gum Branch Trail*, R. (The *Bee Gum Branch Trail* ascends by Bee Gum Branch to leave it at 2.3 mi in a cove. Reach the S end of *Forney Ridge Trail* at 2.9 mi. From here the *Forney Ridge Trail* is 6.8 mi to Clingmans Dome Rd, described below.)

Continue on the *Forney Creek Trail* through cove hardwood and a mixture of rhododendron, hemlock, and white pine. At 4 mi arrive at the *Jonas Creek Trail*, L, and Jonas Creek backcountry campsite #70. (The *Jonas Creek Trail* fords Forney Creek and follows an old RR grade up Jonas Creek for 1.5 mi where it becomes a path. After crossing Jonas Creek and Yanu Branch begin switchbacks that end at 2.6 mi. Jct with the *Welch Ridge Trail* on Welch Ridge at 3.5 mi. To the L it is 4.4 mi on the *Welch Ridge Trail* to its S terminus at High Rocks. To the R it is 2.4 mi to Silers Bald and the *AT*.)

Continue on the *Forney Creek Trail*, crossing Forney Creek frequently, and reach the mouth of Huggins Creek and Huggins backcountry campsite #69, L, at 5.3 mi. From here the old RR grade gradually ascends on switchbacks to cross other streams such as Buckhorn Branch and Little Steeltrap Creek. After the old RR grade ends at 9 mi, follow an old timber road for 0.5 mi to cross Forney Creek for the last time. Ascend on a footpath with a number of seeps in a damp forest of hemlock, fir, and beech. Terminate the trail at 11.4 mi to jct with the *Forney Ridge Trail,* R and L.

(To the L the *Forney Ridge Trail* ascends 1 mi on a rough and rocky footpath in a spruce/fir forest to the parking area on Clingmans Dome Rd. A 0.4-mi spur trail to the *AT* goes L 0.1 mi before reaching the parking area. To the R the *Forney Ridge Trail* descends 5.8 mi to jct with the *Bee Gum Branch Trail* described above. At 0.8 mi it reaches Andres Bald, which received its name from mountain-born Andres (not Andrews) Thompson, who built a hand-hewn cabin here in the 1850s. Owning 1,280 acres here and elsewhere in the vicinity, he became a prosperous cattle raiser, and four of his nine children were born here. A scenic area with views of the Little Tennessee River Valley and beyond, the bald's grassy beauty is enhanced in late June when a concentration of flame azalea and purple rhododendron is in bloom. Ferns, wildflowers, spruce, and fir assist in the display. Descend to gaps and lower knobs to reach *Springhouse Branch Trail* at 4.3 mi. (The *Springhouse Branch Trail* runs 2.8 mi to the *Noland Creek Trail,* described above.) Reach a scenic area at 6.5 mi and slope R of the knob to jct with *Bee Gum Branch Trail,* also described above. From here it is 2.9 mi to the *Forney Creek Trail,* a potential loop of 17.3 mi. (*USGS Maps:* Clingmans Dome, Noland Creek, Silers Bald)

### *Hazel Creek Trail* 416–420

* LENGTH AND DIFFICULTY: 15 mi, strenuous (elev change 3,580 ft)

* CONNECTING TRAILS:
  *(Lakeshore Trail)*
  *Sugar Fork Trail* (2.4 mi, moderate)
  *Bone Valley Trail* (1.7 mi, easy)
  *Cold Spring Branch Trail* (3.9 mi, strenuous, elev change 2,450 ft)
  *Welch Ridge Trail* (6.8 mi, moderate)

• SPECIAL FEATURES: trout fishing, sites of former communities, High Rocks, Hall Cabin

• TRAILHEAD AND DESCRIPTION: The *Hazel Creek Trail*, widely known for its trout fishing, is in the heart of the North Shore Area. Access to it is by other trails or by boat on Fontana Lake. The latter provides the quickest (approx 6 mi) route from the Fontana Boat Dock; the *AT* route from Clingmans Dome Rd is the shortest (4.6 mi) trail route. From the lake trailhead, follow the park jeep road and reach Proctor backcountry campsite #86 at 0.3 mi and jct R with the *Lakeshore Trail*, described above. (It is 25.2 mi on the *Lakeshore Trail* to its E terminus.) The two trails are adjoined for 4.6 mi to the mouth of Sugar Fork and *Sugar Fork Trail*, L. Along the way on the old RR grade, after about 1 mi, is the vanished timber community of Proctor. During its thriving history it is estimated that its population was more than 1,000. At 3.3 mi is Sawdust Pile backcountry campsite #85. Another backcountry campsite at 4.9 mi, Sugar Fork #84, is where the *Hazel Creek Trail* bears R and the *Lakeshore Trail* runs jointly with the *Sugar Fork Trail*.

(The *Sugar Fork Trail* passes the confluence of Little Fork at 1.7 mi. Horace Kephart lived up Little Fork while doing his research on mountain culture. Ascend to Pickens Gap at 2.4 mi and end of *Sugar Fork Trail*. Ahead begins *Pinnacle Creek Trail*, which descends to jct with *Eagle Creek Trail*. To the R begins *Jenkins Ridge Trail*, which ascends 5.9 mi to the *AT* at Spence Field.)

Continue up the old road, close to Hazel Creek, and reach Bone Valley backcountry campsite #83 at 5.6 mi. Here is the jct, L, with *Bone Valley Trail*. (The *Bone Valley Trail* begins across the bridge and gently ascends by the Bone Valley Creek. Cross the stream four times enroute to the Crate Hall Cabin, a national historic site, at 1.7 mi. The Hall cemetery is N of the cabin. Ruins of other buildings are nearby. Backtrack.

Continue following Hazel Creek upstream and jct R with the *Cold Spring Branch Trail* at 6.8 mi. (The *Cold Spring Branch Trail* ascends by the stream mainly on an old RR grade and passes evidence of former homesites, particularly at 0.5 mi and 1 mi. The old RR grade ends at 3 mi and trail steepness increases. It reaches Cold Spring Gap at 3.4 mi, turns L, and after 0.5 mi the trail ends at Welch Ridge. Here the *Welch Ridge Trail* goes sharply L to the scenic High Rocks, and R 6.5 mi to jct with the *AT* at Silers Bald.)

On the *Hazel Creek Trail* at 8.5 mi reach Calhoun Place backcountry campsite #82 (named in honor of Josh Calhoun, former homesteader). At 10.3 mi the jeep trail ends and a footpath begins. Also here is the confluence of Proctor and Hazel creeks. Begin a grade increase and wade or rock-hop the creek a number of times. Pass the old Cascades campsite at 13.2 mi. At 14 mi begin a steep incline to reach Welch Ridge at 15 mi. The trail ends at a jct with the *Welch Ridge Trail*, R and L.

(The *Welch Ridge Trail* runs 0.5 mi L to the meadows of Silers Bald at a jct with the *AT*. On the *AT*, R, it is 4.1 mi to the Clingmans Dome Rd parking area. The *Welch Ridge Trail* runs R through meadows, rhododendron groves, and mixes of hardwoods and conifers. At 1 mi from the *AT* it descends on switchbacks to Mule Gap. At 2.4 mi it meets *Jonas Creek Trail*, L. The *Jonas Creek Trail* descends 3.5 mi to *Forney Creek Trail*. At 3.8 mi it passes a rock outcrop and descends to a gap at 4.4 mi. It ascends steeply to Mt Glory at 4.7 mi. It passes R of Hawk Knob at 5 mi, a spring at 5.2 mi and a beautiful open area at Bearwallow Bald before a jct L with *Jumpup Ridge Trail* at 6.2 mi. The *Jumpup Ridge Trail* descends 5.8 mi to *Forney Creek Trail*. At 6.5 mi jct with the *Cold Spring Branch Trail*, described above. Turn R and ascend 0.3 mi to High Rocks [5,190 ft] for superb views from the rocks or the fire tower of the surrounding North Shore, the Little Tennessee River Valley, and the Steoah Mtn range.) (*USGS Maps:* Fontana Dam, Noland Creek, Thunderhead Mtn, Tuskeegee, Silers Bald)

## *Eagle Creek Trail*                                   421–424

• LENGTH AND DIFFICULTY: 9.1 mi, strenuous (elev change 3,170 ft)

- CONNECTING TRAILS:
  *(Lakeshore Trail)*
  *(AT)*
  *Lost Cove Trail* (3.1 mi, strenuous, elev change 1,930 ft)
  *Pinnacle Creek Trail* (3.5 mi, moderate)
  *Jenkins Ridge Trail* (5.9 mi, strenuous, elev change 2,076 ft)

- TRAILHEAD AND DESCRIPTION: The easiest and shortest trail access to the *Eagle Creek Trail* is on *Lakeshore Trail* for 6.6 mi from the Fontana Dam parking area. The trail begins at a jct of *Lost Cove Trail, Lakeshore Trail*, and Lost Cove backcountry campsite #90.

  (The *Lost Cove Trail* is the only trail connecting directly from the North Shore Area to the Twentymile Creek Area. It gradually ascends by Lost Cove Creek, a stream crossed a number of times on its route. At 1.4 mi is Upper Lost Cove backcountry campsite #91. The trail ascends on switchbacks after leaving the stream and ends at Sassafras Gap on the *AT* at 3.1 mi. Ahead begins the *Twentymile Creek Trail.* Left on the *AT* it is 0.4 mi to the Shuckstack fire tower and 4.5 mi farther to the Fontana Dam parking area. On the *AT*, R, it is 1 mi to Birch Spring Gap Shelter.)

  Follow the *Eagle Creek Trail* up Eagle Creek and make two long curves, the latter around Horseshoe Bend, and jct with *Pinnacle Creek Trail* at 1 mi. (The *Pinnacle Creek Trail* is the lateral connection to the trails in the Hazel Creek Area, and the *Lakeshore Trail* runs with it. It is unique because most of the distance is an old graded roadway built by the Corps of Engineers in the 1940s. It follows up Pinnacle Creek and passes Pinnacle Creek backcountry campsite #88 at 1.6 mi. The forest is a mixture of oak, maple, locust, sourwood, white pine, hemlock, and rhododendron. At 3.5 mi jct L with *Jenkins Ridge Trail.* An isolated trail, the *Jenkins Ridge Trail* ascends 5.9 mi to Spence Field on the *AT*, 0.3 mi E of the *Hazel Creek Trail* terminus on the *AT*.)

  Continuing on the *Eagle Creek Trail*, cross Ekaneetlee Creek at 2 mi to Ekaneetlee Creek backcountry campsite #89. Both this creek and Hazel Creek are good trout fishing streams. At

3.4 mi reach another backcountry campsite, Eagle Creek Island #96. Arrive at the site of an old logging camp at Tub Mill Branch at 5.3 mi. Here is Big Walnut backcountry campsite #97. Begin a steep ascent after passing Fodderstack Rock at 6.5 mi. Follow up Spence Cabin Branch and reach the trail's N terminus on the *AT* at 9.1 mi. A turn R to return on the *Jenkins Ridge Trail,* described above, is a loop of 19.8 mi to the S terminus of *Eagle Creek Trail.* (*USGS Maps:* Cades Cove, Fontana Dam, Thunderhead Mtn)

## ▶ TWENTYMILE CREEK AREA
### (Swain County)

In the W corner of the park, in North Carolina, the Twenty-mile Creek Area is bordered by the state line N and W, the Twentymile Ridge E, and NC-28 and Cheoah Lake (Little Tennessee River) S. The area received its name from being 20 mi downstream from the confluence of the Little Tennessee River and the Tuckasegee River. (Farther W, into Tennessee, the park extends to Chilhowee.) The *AT* formerly followed the state line from Doe Knob over Gregory Bald, Parson Bald, Sheep Wallow Knob, and down to Deals Gap. Here it crossed US-219 and descended to Cheoah Dam where it crossed the bridge to ascend Yellow Creek Mtn; see *Yellow Creek Mtn Trail,* Chapter 2, Section 1.) High on the mountain balds were the grazing fields for cattle and sheep before the 1930s. It is on these balds that spectacular displays of flame azalea are seen in mid-June. The ranger at Twentymile Area also supervises the Eagle Creek and Hazel Creek areas.

• ADDRESS AND ACCESS: From Fontana Village drive W on NC-28 for 6 mi to Twentymile RS, R. Access to the trails is here. Address: Twentymile RS, GSMNP, Fontana, NC 28733, tel: 704-498-2327.

• SUPPORT FACILITIES: The nearest developed campground is Fontana Dam Campground at the base of Fontana Dam, 5 mi E from the RS. It has hot showers (no hook-ups) and is usually open from April 15 to early October. Groceries, gas, telephone, motel, and restaurant are W on NC-28, 2.8 mi from the RS.

### Twentymile Creek Trail                                    425–429

- LENGTH AND DIFFICULTY: 4.6 mi, strenuous (elev change 2,355 ft)

- CONNECTING TRAILS:
  *Wolf Ridge Trail* (5.9 mi, strenuous, elev change 3,345 ft)
  *Twentymile Loop Trail* (2.9 mi, moderate)
  *Gregory Bald Trail* (6.9 mi, strenuous, elev change 1,740 ft)
  *Long Hungry Ridge Trail* (4.4 mi, strenuous, elev change 2,240 ft)
  *(AT)*
  *(Lost Cove Trail)*

- SPECIAL FEATURES: heath balds, flame azalea groves

- TRAILHEAD AND DESCRIPTION: From the RS parking lot, take a svc road past the RS and cross a bridge over Moore Springs Branch at 0.5 mi. The *Wolf Ridge Trail* turns L, and the *Twentymile Creek Trail* turns R. (The *Wolf Ridge Trail* goes 1.1 mi up Moore Springs Branch and crosses three bridges and two wading crossings. At the confluence with Dalton Branch, L, is Long Hungry Ridge backcountry campsite #74. To the R is *Twentymile Loop Trail*.) (The *Twentymile Loop Trail* goes E, climbs over Long Hungry Ridge, crosses Twentymile Creek, and ends at *Twentymile Creek Trail* near Proctor Field Gap after 2.9 mi.)

(On the *Wolf Ridge Trail* go upstream on Dalton Branch 0.7 mi before making a sharp R, away from the stream, to begin a climb up Wolf Ridge. Reach Wolf Ridge backcountry campsite #95 at 3.2 mi, near a stream. Ascend to the crest of scenic Parson Bald at 5.5 mi; follow up the crest and reach the trail's end at a jct with the *Gregory Bald Trail*, L and R, at 5.9 mi. Here is Sheep Pen Gap backcountry campsite #13.) (Half of the *Gregory Bald Trail* descends L, 3.5 mi, to Sams Gap, its beginning on Parson's Branch Rd. The road, closed in winter, is a one-way vehicle route, S only, 5.6 mi from Cades Cove. The other half of the trail, R, follows the main ridge to end at the *AT* in Doe Gap after 3.4 mi. Along the way it is 0.8 mi to Gregory Bald [4,948 ft], a grassy field with incredible views and beauty from the flame azaleas that bloom usually from mid- to late June. It is another 0.7 mi to jct L with the 5-mi *Gregory Ridge Trail* that descends to Forge Creek Rd, 2.3 mi S of Cades Cove. To the R of the jct is *Long Hungry Ridge Trail,* described below. A loop of 14.9 mi can be made by returning to the RS on the *Long Hungry Ridge Trail* and *Twentymile Creek Trail.*)

On the *Twentymile Creek Trail* follow the svc road upstream in a forest of poplar, maple, oak, rhododendron, and hemlock. Ferns and wildflowers are prominent on the roadside. Cross two bridges and at 1.7 mi pass Twentymile Creek backcountry campsite #93, near another bridge. Cross Turkey Cove Branch at 2.1 mi. Soon cross a bridge and move away from Twentymile Creek, but follow the N side of Proctor Branch to Proctor Field Gap at 2.6 mi. Jct here with *Long Hungry Ridge Trail,* L, but the *Twentymile Creek Trail* continues ahead.

(The *Long Hungry Ridge Trail* crosses Proctor Branch at 0.1 mi, and goes to a ridge nose to parallel Twentymile Creek upstream. At 1.2 mi pass Upper Flats backcountry campsite #92, R. Cross Twentymile Creek and another stream on the E-slope climb of Long Hungry Ridge to the crest at scenic Rye Patch [4,400 ft] at 3.5 mi. Reach *Gregory Bald Trail* L and R at 4.4 mi. To the R it is 1.9 mi to the *AT* at Doe Knob. To the L it is 0.7 mi to scenic Gregory Bald described above.)

To complete the *Twentymile Creek Trail,* ascend, cross Proctor Branch at 3.1 mi, and follow switchbacks, steeply near the end, to Sassafras Gap (3,653 ft) at the *AT,* R and L, at 4.6 mi. To the L it is 1 mi to Birch Spring Gap Shelter, and to the R it is 0.4 mi to the Shuckstack fire tower for magnificent views of Fontana Lake. Ahead begins the *Lost Cove Trail* described above. (*USGS Maps:* Fontana Dam, Cades Cove, Calderwood, Tapoco)

# 8.

## Other Trails in the National Park System

*I must go down to the seas again,*
*for the call of the running tide . . .*

—John Masefield

## ▶ CAPE HATTERAS NATIONAL SEASHORE
### (Dare and Hyde Counties)

Cape Hatteras, a chain of barrier islands E of Pamlico Sound, has 30,318 acres of sandy Atlantic beaches, dunes, and marshlands. It is the nation's first national seashore. Authorized as a park by Congress on August 17, 1937, the islands are havens for more than 300 species of migratory and permanent shorebirds. Major shore fish are flounder, bluefish, and spot, and offshore are marlin, dolphin, mackerel, and tuna. Often referred to as the Outer Banks and the "Graveyard of the Atlantic," the offshore area has two ocean currents near Diamond Shoals that are used as shipping lanes and which are hazardous for those navigating the seas. More than 600 ships have fallen victim to the shallow shoals, winds, and storms over the past 400 years.

For hikers and campers on the string of islands, the NPS permits camping at designated campgrounds only. Facilities are limited to cold showers, drinking water, tables, grills, and modern restrooms. Oregon Inlet, Cape Point, and Ocracoke fee campgrounds are usually open from mid-April to mid-October. Salvo and Frisco fee campgrounds have a mid-June to late August schedule. Campsites may be reserved through Ticketron (tel: 919-473-2111) or taken as available. Hikers using tents are requested to use stronger tents and longer stakes than usual for protection against the sand and wind. Protection against sunburn and insects is essential. Also be aware of strong littoral currents, rip currents, and shifting sand when swimming. Tidal currents near inlets are hazardous, and the NPS recommends swimming only where lifeguards are on duty.

Short nature trails are located at the visitor centers at Cape Hatteras, Bodie Island Lighthouse, and near the campground on Ocracoke Island. The *Cape Hatteras Beach Trail* (the E terminal route of the *MST*) follows the park's entire chain of islands. It is described below. In addition to the Cape Hatteras park, the same office administers two other area parks. The Wright Brothers National Memorial (9 mi N of the US-64/NC-12 jct at Whalebone Junction) is a 431-acre memorial museum to Wilbur and Orville Wright, who on December 17, 1903, were the first to successfully achieve air flight with machine power. The other park is the Fort Raleigh National Historic Site (8 mi W of Whalebone Junction on US-64). Designated an historic site on April 5, 1941, it covers 144 acres and includes parts of the former 1585 and 1587 settlements. The Lindsay Warren Visitor Center displays excavated artifacts, and exhibits tell the story of Sir Walter Raleigh's "lost colony." In addition, the park includes a reconstruction of Fort Raleigh, the Waterside Theatre (which presents Paul Green's symphonic drama of the "Lost Colony" in the summer), an Elizabethan garden maintained by the Garden Club of North Carolina, Inc., and the *Thomas Hariot Trail.* The trail is a 0.3-mi interpretive loop with signs about the plant life that Hariot found in the area in 1585. It begins at the visitor center. **430**

• ADDRESS AND ACCESS: Superintendent, Cape Hatteras National Seashore, Rte 1, Box 675, Manteo, NC 27954, tel: 919-473-2111. To reach the park headquarters turn off US-64/264, 3 mi W of Manteo at the park sign.

• SUPPORT FACILITIES: In addition to the park campgrounds there are commercial campgrounds to choose from, some open all year. For this and other information contact the Dare County

Tourist Bureau, PO Box 399, Manteo, NC 27954, tel: 919-473-2138. Open M–F, 9–5; Sat 10–3.

## Cape Hatteras Beach Trail                    431–434

- LENGTH AND DIFFICULTY: 75.8 mi, easy
- SPECIAL FEATURES: lighthouses, wildlife refuge, seashore
- TRAILHEAD AND DESCRIPTION: This unique trail generally follows the beach line, but in shorter sections it climbs dunes with sea oats and beach holly; winds through forests of water oak, pine, and sweet bay; passes salt marshes of sedge and cord grass; and clings to road shoulders. In a given season the hiker will see scores of bird species—swans, geese, ducks, gulls, egrets, terns, herons, songbirds, and shorebirds—migratory and permanent. The trail crosses the Oregon Inlet bridge, passes historic coast-guard sites, and requires a ferry ride to pass the wild ponies on Ocracoke Island. (Through-backpackers should plan camping arrangements and shuttle service well in advance; see introduction above.) The trail is not blazed.

Begin the hike at the jct of US-64/264/158/NC-12 at Whalebone Junction in Nags Head and proceed S on NC-12 for 0.1 mi to the Cape Hatteras National Seashore Information Center, R. (Hatteras and Ocracoke ferries sign is nearby.) Hike the L shoulder of NC-12 by a border of myrtle, beach holly, bayberry, sedge, and cattails. Pass parking areas on the R at 1.5 mi, 3.2 mi, and observation decks at 3.8 mi and 4.4 mi. At 4.7 mi pass a park maintenance area, L, a park svc road on the R at 4.9 mi, and reach the Coquina Beach road entrance, L, at 5.3 mi. The Sand Castle interpretive center for children is at 5.5 mi. (The area has facilities for picnicking and, during the summer season, showers and comfort stations.) At 5.7 mi, L, are remnants of the *Laura A. Barnes,* a 629-gross-ton, four-masted schooner wrecked in 1921. Continue ahead on paved access road for a return to NC-12 at 5.9 mi. Cross the highway and enter a paved road to Bodie Island Lighthouse Station and Visitor Center. Reach the visitor center and lighthouse (built in 1871) at 6.9 mi. (The 0.4-mi *Bodie Island Nature Trail* with an observation tower starts L of the lighthouse.)

From the visitor center follow the paved loop road S for 0.1 mi to the NPS gate. Enter on a sandy road and follow red-topped markers for 0.2 mi over a small bridge and freshwater lake overflow. Turn sharply L. Follow the markers, using care not to follow the Environmental Study Area signs into the black nettle rush and salt meadow cord grass, a route sure to get your feet wet. Instead, follow the dike line of the lake on an old road through cedar, myrtle, and greenbriar to NC-12. Turn R and follow the road shoulder to Oregon Inlet Campground on the L at 8.6 mi. Begin to cross the Herbert C. Bonner bridge on the L, facing traffic at 9 mi. Observe traffic carefully because pedestrian walk space on the 2.4-mi bridge is only 45 inches wide. Views from the bridge are spectacular. Reach the end of the bridge at the Coast Guard Station at 11.4 mi and enter the Pea Island Wildlife Refuge. Pass a ferry schedule sign, R, at 12.2 mi, and a parking area for beach access at 13.8 mi (125 yd to the Atlantic Ocean). At 14.1 mi turn R off NC-12 to follow a hiking sign on the N dike of North Pond in the Pea Island National Wildlife Refuge. (The 5,915-acre refuge has 265 species of birds, 24 species of reptiles, and 23 species of mammals. The waterfowl numbers are greater in January, but a greater variety of species can be observed during the fall migration of October-November. For information contact the Refuge Manager, Pea Island National Wildlife Refuge, PO Box 150, Rodanthe, NC 27968, tel: 919-987-2394.) Reach an observation deck of the impoundment at 14.3 mi. Continue on the trail around the W side of North Pond for 1.7 mi. Turn L at 16.2 mi, pass an observation deck at 16.7 mi, and reach NC-12 parking area and comfort station (open all year) at 16.8 mi. (If the South Pond area is hiked, permission must be granted from the refuge office.) Cross NC-12, follow a cement trail to dunes and then to the beach at 16.9 mi. Hike S on the beach 2.3 mi to exit over the dunes at Pea Island National Wildlife Refuge office on NC-12. Pass an interpretive exhibit area where signs indicate the Pea Island Life-Saving Station was authorized by Congress in 1873. The station's crews rescued more than 600 people by 1915. After a visit to the refuge headquarters return across NC-12 and to the beach at 19.4 mi. For the next 30 mi you will be hiking on the beach.

At 24.8 mi, pass an exit over dunes to a parking area at NC-12, near the end of the Pea Island Refuge. At 25.6 mi pass dune exit to old Chicamacomico Coast Guard Station, a historic site, on NC-12, 0.5 mi from the beach. A general store, laundry, and private campground are over the dunes at 25.8 mi, 0.5 mi from the beach. The Rodanthe post office is at 26.1 mi, and a restaurant and fishing pier are at 26.3 mi. The original KOA is at 27.7 mi (125 yd from the beach to the KOA bathhouse and another 0.3 mi to the KOA office near NC-12). Holiday KOA is at 28.1 mi, 125 yd from the beach. Waves post office is at 28.3 mi, 0.4 mi from the beach, and Salvo post office is at 30.5 mi, 0.5 mi from the beach. Salvo NPS campground is at 31 mi, 0.5 mi from the beach. Beach exit and parking area are at 35.4 mi on off-road vehicle ramp #27. Another beach exit and parking area are at 37.6 mi, another at 41.9 mi. Avon post office and shopping center are at 43.7 mi, followed by a fishing pier. Another ORV ramp exit, #38, is at 45.9 mi. A parking area and beach exit are also here. At 46.8 mi cross over the dunes for 100 yd to the parking area at the old beach road; NC-12 is 100 yd ahead. Follow S on NC-12 for 0.2 mi and take an old jeep trail R. Hike this road for 2.6 mi to near Buxton. Cross over NC-12 to the beach at 49.6 mi, turn R, and after 1.4 mi arrive at historic Cape Hatteras Lighthouse.

From the lighthouse go W to the Hatteras Island Visitor Center (tel: 919-995-4474) at 51.4 mi. Continue straight on the road to Buxton Woods parking area and picnic area at 51.5 mi. Here is the *Buxton Woods Nature Trail,* R, a self-guided, interpretive, 0.6-mi scenic loop. Ahead pass a maintenance area, L, and at 51.9 mi, R, enter the Open Pond Rd where exists the largest forest on Cape Hatteras. (Camp trailers disposal system is L at this point and the paved road continues L 0.9 mi to ORV ramp #44. Nearby is the NPS Cape Point Campground.

Follow the sandy road and cross a stream at 53.2 mi; reach a Y in the road at 53.3 mi. Take the R fork where a sign restricts ORVs, and follow the S side of the lake at 53.4 mi. Enter an open area of dunes at 53.5 mi and follow the sandy road to NPS Frisco Campground at 55.8 mi. After the campground go to the gate at 56.1 mi, turn L, and follow the ramp to the beach at 56.3 mi. Turn R on the beach, pass a fishing pier, and after 6 mi on the beach turn R at ramp #55 to a parking lot and NC-12. Turn L and after 0.1 mi reach the Hatteras Ferry at 62.6 mi. (From the NPS Frisco Campground it is 1.1 mi on a paved road to NC-12 and the Frisco post office.)

Take the Hatteras Ferry to Ocracoke Island (the time is usually 40 minutes), and after arrival hike 0.7 mi on NC-12 to a parking area L. Go over the dunes to the beach at 63.3 mi. A parking area for the beach is also at 66.5 mi. At 68.1 mi cross the dunes from the ocean for 100 yd to a parking area. A short hike on NC-12 leads to the observation deck for the Pony Pen to view the wild ponies. Return to the beach. At ORV ramp #68 reach NPS Ocracoke Campground at 72.4 mi. The *Ocracoke Boardwalk Trail* is a 0.1-mi walk (with handicapped access) to observe the ocean. Follow either the beach or the road to ORV ramp #70 at the Ocracoke airstrip, which is 0.2 mi from the beach, at 75.3 mi. From here follow NC-12 to the town boundary at 75.8 mi, the trail's terminus. Another 1.3 mi goes to the Ocracoke Island Visitor Center (tel: 919-928-1461) and Ocracoke Ferry. Toll ferries leave the port to Swanquarter to US-264, or to Cedar Island to US-70 (tel: 919-928-3841). The town has motels, restaurants, a marina, and supply stores. (*USGS Maps:* Roanoke Island, Oregon Inlet, Pea Island, Rodanthe, Little Kinnakeet, Buxton, Cape Hatteras, Hatteras, Green Island, Howard Reef, Ocracoke)

▶ CAPE LOOKOUT NATIONAL SEASHORE
(Carteret County)

Across Ocracoke Inlet from the Cape Hatteras National Seashore begins the Cape Lookout National Seashore. These barrier islands are narrow with low dunes, bare beaches at the Atlantic Ocean, and flat grasslands and salt marshes on the sound side. It includes Portsmouth Village (part of the N Core Banks), S Core Banks from Drum Inlet to Cape Lookout, and Shackleford Banks, W of the cape and ending S of Beaufort. Authorized by Congress in 1966 and established in 1976, the 58 mi of islands remain uncommercialized and present a fragile natural resource. Although the islands are best known as a fisherman's haven, hikers, campers, and beachcombers use the beach as a trail. There are not any signs or distance markers or campsites or lifeguard-protected beaches (there are sharks and jellyfish in the Atlantic Ocean).

Choose comfortable packs and shoes. Wear a hat, shirt, and plenty of sunscreen lotion. Take plenty of potent insect repellent (insects are worst May through October). Use a strong tent with fine insect netting and, because of the wind, use ft-long tent stakes. Carry in plenty of food and water. Pets must be kept on leashes. Only driftwood campfires are allowed. All trash must be carried out.

At Portsmouth Village, the 1-mi, easy *Portsmouth Village Trail* goes from the dock to the old schoolhouse, homes, cemeteries, Methodist church, and former U.S. Life-Saving Station. From here it is another 1 mi to the beach. Now a ghost town, parts of the village are preserved by the NPS. Portsmouth began in 1753 as a trans-shipment point for goods entering Ocracoke Inlet. Its population reached nearly 600 by 1860, but most of the inhabitants went ashore upon Federal occupation during the Civil War. (*USGS Maps:* Portsmouth, Wainwright Island, Styron Bay, Davis, Horsepen Point, Harkers Island, Cape Lookout, Beaufort) **435**

• ADDRESS AND ACCESS: Superintendent, Cape Lookout National Seashore, PO Box 690 (415 Front St), Beaufort, NC 28576, tel: 919-728-2121. Access is by private concession ferries that operate from Harkers Island to Cape Lookout and the lighthouse (tel: 919-728-3907); from Davis to Shingle Point (tel: 919-729-2791); from Atlantic to North New Drum Inlet (tel: 919-225-4261); and Ocracoke to Portsmouth Village (tel: 919-928-4361 or 919-928-1951). Call for rates and schedules.

• SUPPORT FACILITIES: Shopping centers, restaurants, and motels are in Beaufort and Moorehead City. There are at least a dozen commercial campgrounds in the area. Contact the Cape Lookout National Seashore office for a list of the local campgrounds, beach driving permits, fishing information, tide table, and map. Waters forecast can be heard by calling the Coast

Guard Base at Fort Macon (tel: 919-726-7550) or a five-day forecast from the National Weather Service in Wilmington (tel: 919-762-3240) or Cape Hatteras (tel: 919-995-5610).

## ▶ GUILFORD COURTHOUSE NATIONAL MILITARY PARK
### (Guilford County)

The park was established March 2, 1917, in honor of the 4,300 officers and soldiers of Commanding General Nathanael Greene's Continental Army in the battle against British Field Commander Charles E. Cornwallis, March 15, 1781. Although the battle was not a total victory for either side, it was significant in that Cornwallis retreated to Wilmington, practically abandoning the Carolinas. The end of the Revolutionary War came seven months later at Yorktown, Virginia, October 19, 1781. The 220.4-acre park has a museum in the visitor center; there are seven tour stops of historical interest. Camping is not allowed. Open daily except Christmas Day.

• ADDRESS AND ACCESS: Superintendent, Guilford Courthouse National Military Park, PO Box 9806, Greensboro, NC 27429 (tel: 919-288-1776). Access is 0.5 mi on New Garden Rd from US-220 N 6 mi from downtown Greensboro.

### *Guilford Courthouse Battlefield Trail*                    436

• LENGTH AND DIFFICULTY: 2.5 mi, easy

• TRAILHEAD AND DESCRIPTION: From the visitor center follow the paved trail SW of the parking area through a mature forest of oak, hickory, walnut, and poplar with an understory of dogwood, redbud, and sourwood. The first tour stop, the American first line, is at 0.4 mi. Cross Old Battleground Rd and reach a spur trail, L, to the General Greene monument at 0.6 mi. Continue on trails through open fields of large scattered oak and poplar with senna, milkweed, evening primrose, lobelia, and bur marigold among the wildflowers. At 1.3 mi reach stop five at the site of Guilford Courthouse. Return by stop six, American third line, at 1.9 mi for a return to the visitor center at 2.5 mi.

▶ **MOORES CREEK NATIONAL BATTLEFIELD**
**(Pender County)**

The battlefield was established June 2, 1926, by the NPS. It has 87 acres and is significant because it is where the North Carolina patriots won a victory February 27, 1776, that notably advanced the American cause against the British loyalists. On April 12, 1776, North Carolina became the first colony whose delegation at the Continental Congress in Philadelphia voted for independence. The 1-mi *Moores Creek Trail* begins on the *Pathway to History Trail*, W of the visitor center, and follows interpretive signs through pine and hardwoods with Spanish moss to a bridge at 0.4 mi. The nature trail part begins at 0.7 mi in the loop. There are facilities for the handicapped. Open daily except Christmas Day. **437–438**

• ADDRESS AND ACCESS: Superintendent, Moores Creek National Battlefield, PO Box 69, Currie, NC 28435 (tel: 919-283-5591). Access from the jct of US-421/NC-210 is 3 mi to Currie on NC-210; follow the signs another 3 mi.

▶ **CARL SANDBURG HOME NATIONAL HISTORIC SITE**
**(Henderson County)**

Carl Sandburg (1878–1967), poet, author, lecturer, and social philosopher, won the Pulitzer Prize for history in 1940 with his *Abraham Lincoln: The War Years* and the Pulitzer Prize for poetry in 1951 with *Complete Poems*. He lived his last 22 years at "Connemara," a 240-acre farm at Flat Rock. A constant hiker, he refreshed himself by walking the trails designed by the first owner of the property (attorney Christopher G. Memminger of Charleston, South Carolina). On October 17, 1968, Congress authorized the farm as a historic site; it acquired the property from the Sandburg family in 1969 for commemorative purposes, and opened to the public in May 1974. It is open daily, 9 to 5.

• ADDRESS AND ACCESS: Superintendent, Carl Sandburg Home National Historic Site, PO Box 395, Flat Rock, NC 28731 (tel: 704-693-4178). Entrance is by Little River Rd (SR-1123) off US-25 (near the Flat Rock Playhouse), 3 mi S of jct with US-64 in Hendersonville.

*Memminger Trail* (0.7 mi); *Little Glassy Trail* (0.2 mi); *Big Glassy Trail* (1 mi); *Spring Trail* (0.3 mi); *Jerusalem Trail* (0.3 mi); *Loose Cow Trail* (0.1 mi); *Front Lake Trail* (0.5 mi)
**439–445**

• LENGTH AND DIFFICULTY: 3.1 mi combined round-trip, easy

• TRAILHEAD AND DESCRIPTION: From the main building parking lot ascend on a trail to the main house and follow the signs (or use a brochure map) to begin on the *Memminger Trail.* It connects with, but circles, the *Little Glassy Trail,* which leads to an outcrop in the circle. From the trail gap and jct with the *Big Glassy Trail,* go 1 mi through oak, hickory, hemlock, and white pine to Big Glassy Mtn, a large rock face with scenic views. Backtrack to the woodshed for the *Spring Trail.* The *Jerusalem Trail, Loose Cow Trail,* and *Front Lake Trail* are all near the main house and are interconnected. (*USGS Map:* Hendersonville)

# PART III

# Trails in Other U.S. Government Properties

# 9.

## National Wildlife Refuges and the Army Corps of Engineers

*The quality of the environment is the centerpiece of the quality of life.* —Jay D. Hair

The origins of the National Wildlife Refuge System began in September 1937 with passage of the Federal Aid in Wildlife Restoration Act. Its conservationist sponsors were Senator Key Pittman of Nevada and then Representative Willis Robertson of Virginia. It did not come too soon, because the impact of plundered forests and uncontrolled slaughter of wildlife in the early twentieth century had wiped out some species and threatened and endangered others. Some earlier efforts had been made. For example, President Theodore Roosevelt in 1903 signed an executive order protecting wildfowl on Florida's Pelican Island. Later, migratory bird bills were passed in the 1930s, the Fish and Wildlife Act in 1956, and the National Wildlife Refuge System Administration Act of 1966. Other acts have followed, each one a building block of a process to save and protect the nation's native wildlife.

There are over 400 refuges in the United States and its trust territories that encompass nearly 90 mil acres. They range in size from the smallest (less than an acre), Mille Lacs in Minnesota, to the Yukon Delta (nearly 20 mil acres) in Alaska. All these refuges are under the jurisdiction of the U.S. Fish and Wildlife Service of the Department of the Interior. The regional headquarters for North Carolina is at 75 Spring St, SW, Atlanta, GA

30303, tel: 404-221-3588. There are also numerous citizen clubs and organizations in the nation whose mission is to conserve natural resources and protect wildlife. One is the National Wildlife Federation, which has 13 regions (Region 3 for North Carolina). Its national headquarters is at 1412 16th St, NW, Washington, DC 20036, tel: 202-797-6800. Other names and addresses of government and citizen groups are listed in the Appendix. It is estimated that 28 mil people annually visit the refuges for hunting, fishing, boating, and nature study. In North Carolina there are seven refuges, two of which (Great Dismal Swamp and Mackay Island) extend into Virginia. Only the refuges with designated trails are described below. The *Cape Hatteras Beach Trail* passes through the Pea Island National Wildlife Refuge and is described in Chapter 8.

## ▶ MACKAY ISLAND NATIONAL WILDLIFE REFUGE (Currituck County)

The refuge is in the extreme NE corner of the state, with 842 of its 7,055 acres in Virginia. Established in 1960 as a wintering ground for migratory waterfowl, it is at its peak from December to February when flocks of ducks, geese, and swans travel through their Atlantic flyways. The refuge lists 174 species of birds, including many songbirds. Some of the most rare fly-ins are the white ibis, peregrine falcon, red-necked grebe, and cinnamon teal (*Anas cyanoptera*). There are two designated trails. The 0.3-mi *Great Marsh Trail,* used heavily by fishermen, leads to a pond where there are excellent views of the marsh and waterfowl. It is on the S side of the Causeway of the Great Marsh, N 4.8 mi on NC-615 from the ferry dock at Knotts Landing. The other trail is described below. No camping is allowed in the refuge.                                    **446**

• ADDRESS AND ACCESS: Refuge Manager, Mackay Island NWR, PO Box 31, Knotts Island, NC 27950, tel: 919-429-3100. At the jct of NC-168/615 in Currituck, take the free auto ferry to the island. Drive 2.4 mi on NC-615 and turn L on Mackay Island Rd (opposite the United Methodist Church). Go 0.3 mi to the manager's office, R.

### *Mackay Island Trail* 447

• LENGTH AND DIFFICULTY: 3.8 mi, easy

• TRAILHEAD AND DESCRIPTION: From the manager's office drive 0.7 mi to a small parking area and gated entrance. Begin the hike on an open service road about 3 ft above sea level. At 0.5 mi arrive at a road fork, where either direction completes the loop. If continuing ahead, go through a forest of loblolly pine, yaupon, bays, and cedar, with cord grass and cattails at the clearings. At the next road jct, turn L and follow the open route through a marsh. Turn L again at 1.9 mi at another road jct. There is evidence of beavers in the refuge, and waterfowl are prominent, particularly egrets, ducks, grackle, and grebe. Complete the loop at 3.3 mi and turn R for a return to the parking area. (*USGS Maps:* Knotts Island, Barco)

## ▶ PEE DEE NATIONAL WILDLIFE REFUGE
### (Anson and Richmond Counties)

Containing 8,443 acres, this refuge was established in 1965 to protect the habitat of resident wildlife and wintering geese and ducks. It is the state's most inland refuge where the rolling hills of the piedmont level out to flood plains (mostly on the S side) of the Pee Dee River. More than 175 species of birds have been classified, including Canada geese, mallards, wood ducks, herons, owls, hawks, and songbirds. There are 28 species of mammals and 48 species of amphibians and reptiles. There is a 2.5-mi wildlife drive with interpretive management panels that is open April 1 through October 15. The 0.5-mi *Pee Dee Nature Trail* has interpretive history signs about flora and fauna. It passes a photo-blind on Sullivan Pond and is open all year. Both routes are located directly behind the refuge headquarters. No camping is allowed. **448**

• ADDRESS AND ACCESS: Refuge Manager, Pee Dee NWR, PO Box 780, Wadesboro, NC 28170, tel: 704-694-4424. Access is on US-52, 6 mi N of Wadesboro and 3 mi S of Ansonville.

## U.S. ARMY CORPS OF ENGINEERS

Formed during the early years of the nation as part of the Continental Army, the U.S. Army Corps of Engineers had its beginning at West Point, a garrison on the Hudson River. In 1798 the Corps was enlarged, and in 1802 Congress made West Point a military academy for the United States. Since then, Congress has authorized a wide range of Corps projects. Among them have been blazing and building roads, clearing waterways and harbors, building dams for flood control and hydropower, protecting and restoring shorelines, providing natural disaster relief, fish and wildlife development, and multiple recreation opportunities. While emphasizing diversity in recreational usage year-round, the Corps enforces zoning regulations to protect the ecology.

There are four major Corps projects in North Carolina: Falls Lake (Neuse River); Jordan Lake (Haw and New Hope rivers); Kerr Dam and Reservoir (Staunton/Roanoke and Dan rivers); and Scott Dam and Reservoir (Yadkin River). All were constructed for the major purpose of preventing downstream flood damage. With the exception of the Scott project, acreage is leased by the state's Department of Natural Resources and Community Development (DNRCD) for recreational purposes and managed by the Division of Parks and Recreation. These properties are described by the DNRCD as State Recreation Areas (SRA). The Corps also leases acreage to the state's Wildlife Resources Commission for wildlife management and motorboat registration on all four projects. Examples of other types of leases are Wilkes County Park at the Scott Reservoir project and commercial leases (such as marinas) on all the projects (usually subleased by the DNRCD). All the projects have trails except Jordan Lake (nature trails are planned). (Jordan Lake, named for U.S. Senator B. Everett Jordan [1896–1974] has 24 proposed or existing public-use sites. Primary access points are on US-64 between Apex and Pittsboro, and US-1 between Apex and Moncure. Address: Manager, Jordan Lake, PO 144, Moncure, NC 27559, tel: 919-542-4501.)

► **FALLS LAKE**
**(Durham, Granville, Wake Counties)**

The 38,886-acre (11,620 water and 27,266 land) Falls Lake project has seven public-use sites, three of which are state recreational areas managed by the Division of Parks and Recreation. Boating, water skiing, sailing, fishing, and picnicking are the major activities. A 42-mi hiking trail (to be part of the *MST*) is being constructed on the S boundary of the lake as a joint project of the Division of Parks and Recreation, Triangle Greenways Council, and the Corps. A section of it is described below. Falls Lake received its name from the Falls of Neuse, a short section of rapids below the dam.

*Falls Lake Trail*                                          **449**

• LENGTH AND DIFFICULTY: 13.2 mi, easy

• TRAILHEAD AND DESCRIPTION: This well-designed and well-maintained trail was designated a state trail as part of the *MST* on April 11, 1987. Through a hardwood forest, it weaves in and out of coves and crosses numerous small drainages. It ascends to a number of gentle ridges and offers occasional scenic views of the lake. The mature forest has a few old-growth trees and some specific evidence of succession. For example, a few places have young growth among former tobacco rows. Holly, laurel, loblolly pine, Christmas fern, wild ginger, and running cedar comprise the winter greenery. Among the ferns are royal, cinnamon, sensitive, resurrection, ebony, southern lady, and bracken. Wildflowers include three species of wild orchids, coral bell, squirrel cups (*Hepatica americana*), mandrake, yellow root, and spring beauty (*Claytonia virginica*). Some of the more evident mammals are deer, beaver, fox, squirrel, and raccoon.

Access to the E trailhead is at a parking lot below the dam on

Falls of Neuse Rd (SR-2000) in N Raleigh, and 2.4 mi S from Old NC-98, 0.7 mi W of US-1 at Wake Forest. (Other access points will be described along the trail route.) Follow the white blaze from the parking lot (S end of the bridge) into the forest on an old service road. Pass through loblolly pine, sweet gum, tulip poplar, and oaks with an understory of holly and dogwood. At 0.1 mi turn L on a foot trail and after 110 yd the trail forks near a unique double tulip poplar. Take either route. (The blue-blazed trail, L, goes 0.6 mi to rejoin the main trail.) On the main trail, turn R, cross the paved dam road, and arrive at the parking lot of the Corps' Operational Management Center at 0.3 mi. Follow the Lakeside road and after 0.2 mi re-enter the forest that has scattered jessamine and redbuds. Cross a Corps service road and jct with the blue-blazed alternate route at 0.9 mi. Turn R. At 1.5 mi cross a pipeline right-of-way and a scenic stream area at 2 mi. Cross footbridges over streams at 2.3 mi and 2.6 mi. Pass some fine views of the lake between the streams and the arrival at Raven Ridge Rd (SR-2002) at 3.4 mi. (It is 3.9 mi L on Raven Ridge Rd and Falls of Neuse Rd to the E trailhead.) Turn R and cross the Honeycutt Creek causeway to re-enter the woods R at 3.5 mi. Enter a clearcut area at 4.4 mi, followed by a series of small stream crossings and an old powerline clearing at the edge of a residential area. At 5 mi pass an old farm pond and old farm area, followed by a cove and large beech trees. Arrive at a residential area and exit to Possum Track Rd (SR-2002) at 6.1 mi. (The road R is barricaded, but the road L is a vehicle access back to the trail's origin for 6.2 mi; 1.4 mi to Raven Ridge Rd, L; 2.9 mi to Falls of Neuse Rd, L; and 1.9 mi to the parking lot, L.)

Continuing on *Falls Lake Trail,* cross the road into a grove of loblolly pine. Cross a paved road at 6.4 mi, and enter another pine forest grove at 6.6 mi. Pass lake views at 7.7 mi. Cross a couple of ravines before crossing a footbridge at 8.5 mi. At 8.8 mi reach an old woods road, turn R and arrive at Possum Track Rd at 9 mi. (It is 0.2 mi L to Raven Ridge Rd jct.) Turn R and cross the Cedar Creek causeway. At 9.2 mi turn R into a pine forest with cedar and honeysuckle. Pass remnants of an old homestead, R, at 10.1 mi. Enter a scenic area of large beech trees and cross a footbridge at 10.2 mi. After views of the lake at 10.7 mi, enter a section of laurel for the next 0.6 mi. At 12 mi arrive at Bayleaf Church Rd (SR-2003). (To the R is the Yorkshire Center of Falls Lake Rec Area, and to the L, on the gated road, it is 1 mi to Bayleaf Baptist Church and jct with Possum Track Rd.) Cross the road at the exit sign of the Yorkshire Center and re-enter the forest. Cross a number of small streams in rocky areas and arrive at the end of the guard rail on Six Forks Rd (SR-1005), at the Lower Barton Creek causeway, at 13.2 mi. (To the R it is 2.2 mi to NC-98. To the L it is 7.9 mi back to the parking lot below the dam. The vehicle route is 0.7 mi on Six Forks Rd where a L turn follows Possum Track Rd and Raven Ridge Rd as described above.) (*USGS Maps:* Bayleaf, Wake Forest)

## ▶ JOHN H. KERR DAM AND RESERVOIR
### (Granville, Vance, Warren Counties in N.C.; Charlotte, Halifax, Mecklenburg Counties in Virginia)

The reservoir of 48,900 acres was completed in 1952 and named for the N.C. congressman whose leadership made the project possible. Over three-fourths of the area project is in Virginia. There are 29 rec areas, of which 9 are in N.C., including 6,200 land acres leased to the state by the Corps. Chief activities are boating, sailing, skiing, fishing, swimming, picnicking, and camping. There are over 850 numbered campsites among the following parks: Bullocksville, County Line, Hibernia, Henderson Point, Kimball Point, Nutbush Bridge, and Satterwhite Point. All campgrounds open April 1 or Easter (whichever comes first) and close as late as November 1. After that date all water sources are cut off. Three campgrounds (Cooper Point at Satterwhite, Nutbush Bridge, and Hibernia) have portions open all year. All campgrounds have portions with electrical and water hook-ups. Three commercial marinas offer full svc for fishermen, boaters, and campers. Among the special events in the parks is the Governor's Cup Invitational Regatta in June. Only the rec areas with nature trails are covered below. (See

*Hiking the Old Dominion* by Allen de Hart, published by Sierra Club Books, for trails on the Virginia side of the Reservoir.) (*USGS Maps:* Middleburg, Townsville, John H. Kerr Dam, Tungsten)

• ADDRESS AND ACCESS: Superintendent, Kerr Reservoir State Rec Area, Rte 3, Box 800, Henderson, NC 27536, tel: 919-438-7791. At the I-85 jct in North Henderson take Satterwhite Rd (SR-1319) N 6 mi.

The 0.4-mi *Big Poplar Trail* and the 0.6-mi *Henderson Nature Trail* are at Satterwhite Point; the access is described above. Access to the *Big Poplar Trail* is in the J.C. Cooper Campground. It is a linear trail between the washhouse (L of the fork) at campsite section 105–123 and the entrance loop, R, of campsite section 1–15. The wide trail in a mature forest could also be called big beech (tree-carving dates are in the late 1800s) or big white oak. A large tulip poplar grows halfway on the trail at a streamlet. On Satterwhite Rd, across the road from the J.C. Cooper Campground entrance, is the entrance to *Henderson Nature Trail*. It loops from the Henderson kiosk at the Outdoor Lab of the Vance Salt and Water Conservation District sign. The graded interpretive trail is bordered with pieces of old RR crossties. If following the trail clockwise, reach a cleared area at 0.2 mi, pass the lakeshore, and at 0.5 mi pass the Richard Henderson (1735–1785) gravesite.                    **450–451**

At the Nutbush Bridge campground is the 0.3-mi *Sycamore Springs Trail*. Access from Henderson, at the I-85 and NC-39 jct, is 4.5 mi N on NC-39 to Harris Crossroads. Turn R on Harris Rd (SR-1308) and after 1.8 mi turn L at the campground entrance. Park in a pine grove at the first fork. The linear path through mature hardwoods, young pine, and honeysuckle exits on the R fork road 0.1 mi from its origin. The trail gets its name from a spring that feeds a drain into Kerr Lake. (The area has hazelnut bushes, which the Saponi Indians called a "nutbush.")
                                                    **452**

At Bullocksville Rec Area is the 0.5-mi *Old Still Trail*, a loop trail whose entrance is opposite the baseball field at the RS. At 0.3 mi it turns sharply L to ruins of an old illegal liquor still. Access is 3.3 mi W from Drewry on Bullocksville Rd (SR-1366), and Drewry is accessible 2.3 mi W on Manson Rd (SR-1237) from I-85, Exit 223, or 2.4 mi W on Ridgeway Rd (SR-1224) from I-85, Exit 226. Both I-85 exits are N of Henderson. To reach County Line Rec Area, use either of the accesses to Drewry and drive N on Drewry Rd (SR-1200) for 3 mi. Turn L on Buchanan Rd (SR-1202) and go 2.1 mi to the entrance. Park L of the fork at the RS for *Hollow Poplar Trail*. The 0.4-mi loop trail goes through a mature forest of oak, loblolly pine, sweet gum, and red maple. A large, partially hollow tulip poplar gives the trail its name.                                    **453–454**

## ▶ W. KERR SCOTT DAM AND RESERVOIR
### (Wilkes County)

The project was constructed by the Corps from 1960–1962 and named in honor of former U.S. Senator and N.C. Governor W. Kerr Scott (1896–1958). There are 16 recreational areas, one of which has been leased to Wilkes County and another to a commercial establishment. The lake contains 1,470 acres and is surrounded by 2,284 land acres. Popular aquatic sports are boating, skiing, swimming, and fishing. Small-game hunting is allowed at selected areas. Land activities are camping (Bandits Roost Park and Warrior Creek Park have electrical and water hook-ups and hot showers), picnicking, and hiking. At the manager's office is a 0.3-mi self-guiding loop, *Scott Dam Nature Trail*. It has 27 interpretive points for the local trees, flowering shrubs, and ferns. Access is described below. Another short trail is the 0.8-mi *Bandits Roost Trail*. It goes from the boat-ramp parking lot of Bandits Roost Campground in Area B along the shoreline to a terminus between campsites #25 and #26 in Area A. Access is 1.9 mi W on NC-268 from the dam entrance. A longer trail is described below.                         **455–456**

• ADDRESS AND ACCESS: Resource Manager, W. Kerr Scott Dam and Reservoir, PO Box 182, Wilkesboro, NC 28697, tel: 919-921-3390. The entrance road to the manager's office is on NC-268, 3 mi SW from the jct of US-421 in Wilkesboro.

## *Overmountain Victory Trail* 457

• LENGTH AND DIFFICULTY: 2.7 mi, easy

• TRAILHEAD AND DESCRIPTION: Now a national historic trail, this trail was formerly called the *Warrior Creek Trail*. Warrior Creek is historically significant because the mouth of the creek at the Yadkin River (now underwater) was where the Overmountain Men of the Wilkes County militia crossed the Yadkin, September 28, 1780. The army of 350 men continued to Lenoir where it joined the main patriot army (from the mtns of N.C., Tenn., and Va.) at Quaker Meadows. Their march to the historic Battle of Kings Mountain in S.C., where Col. Pat Ferguson was killed and his Tory army defeated on October 7, 1780, was a turning point in the Revolutionary War. To commemorate this route, the Corps and local citizen groups have established this trail.

From the NC-268 entrance to the dam, continue SW 4.3 mi on NC-268 to Section F, Warrior Creek Park, and turn R. Go 0.6 mi and turn L at the campground sign. (If the campground is open, usually May 1 to September 30, ask for a campground and trail map and drive the 1 mi to the trailhead, following the signs.) If the campground is closed, park outside the gate and walk to the trailhead. From the trailhead parking lot descend the steps on a well-graded and well-maintained trail. Pass through a forest of white pine, holly, and tall hardwoods. Galax, yellow root, ferns, and fetterbush decorate the trail and stream banks. Cross two footbridges and arrive at Area C camping road at 0.5 mi. Cross the road; pass through Area E camping at 0.6 mi, and pass a natural spring at 1.1 mi. Pass a picnic area at 1.3 mi. Descend into a lush cove on the lake, and arrive at an abandoned picnic area at 2 mi. Ahead, follow an old woods road and ascend to an abandoned parking area at 2.5 mi. Turn L and follow the road to a Corps gate at 2.7 mi. To the L is a parking overlook and picnic shelter with scenic views of the lake. To the R it is 1.3 mi on the paved campground road to the E trailhead and point of origin. (*USGS Map:* Boomer)

# PART IV

# Trails in the State Parks and Recreation System, Forests, Natural Areas, Historic Sites, and Other State Properties

# 10.

## The State Parks and Recreation System

*We can take pride in the state's beauty, only if we actively protect it.*
—Ann Taylor

The Department of Natural Resources and Community Development (DNRCD) has 12 divisions, three of which are Parks and Recreation, Forest Resources, and the N.C. Zoological Park. The current administrative form was completed in 1977 after a reorganization began in 1971. A number of reorganizations preceded this most recent one; for example, in 1955 the state legislature transferred all the historic sites from Parks and Recreation to a new Department of Archives and History. The park system is divided into three categories: parks (with regular recreational facilities); state recreation areas (SRAs, designed and managed to tolerate intense usage); and natural areas (NAs, without recreational facilities). All the trails in the parks are covered in this chapter, the NAs in Chapter 11, and the SRAs (which are leased property from the Corps of Engineers) in Chapter 9.

Interest and concern about the state's natural resources began in the late nineteenth century. A specific example was the establishment of a state Geological Survey in 1891 to determine the state's mineral and forest resources. State geologist Joseph A. Holmes was appointed to direct and present biennial reports. In 1905, the state legislature reorganized the Survey to create the N.C. Geological and Economic Survey. Its duty was expanded to "all other material resources." When the legislature and Governor Locke Craige learned in 1914 that timber harvesting and forest fires were destroying such valuable areas as Mt Mitchell, the Governor (a strong conservationist) went to the area for a personal inspection. The result was a bill passed in 1915 to create the state's first park (cost not to exceed $20,000). The management of Mt Mitchell State Park became the responsibility of the Geological and Economic Survey. The state's second state park came in 1924 after director Holmes and the legislature were successful in acquiring the 410-acre Fort Macon Military Reservation from the Federal government for one dollar.

In 1925 the legislature expanded responsibility to fire prevention, reforestation, and maintenance of the state parks and forests when the Geological and Economic Survey was phased into the new Department of Conservation and Development. Acquisition was slow; only three of the Baden Lake areas were added to the list in the 1920s, and unfortunately did not include any land acreage at White Lake. But in the 1930s there was a change when federal assistance programs became available, particularly the CCC. Between 1935 and 1943 the state acquired six new parks: Morrow Mtn, Hanging Rock, Pettigrew, Singletary Lake, Jones Lake, and Crabtree (now Umstead). The Congressional Recreation Area Study Act of 1936 became the blueprint for state park systems, but the N.C. state legislature appropriated only sporadic capital funds. From 1945 to 1961 only Mt Jefferson was acquired. Five state parks and a natural area were added in the 1960s, and there was a notable increase in the 1970s with 11 new parks, eight new natural areas, and the first SRA at Kerr Lake (the facilities had been parks since 1951). This decade of growth was under the administrative leadership of governors Bob Scott and James E. Holshouser. Within a three-year period the park lands nearly doubled (50,000 acres more). Other advances during this period were the beginning of the state zoo, a heritage trust fund (for the natural areas), and in 1973 the State Trails System Act, which created a master plan with procedures for implementing a statewide network of multi-use trails for hikers, bicyclists, equestrians, canoeists, and

ORV users. It also created a seven-member citizens' Trail Committee to advise the Director of Parks and Recreation.

During the 1980s three SRAs were opened—Jordan Lake, Falls Lake, and Fort Fisher—and one state park—Waynesborough. Legislative appropriations were increased but continued to be inadequate for park maintenance and land acquisition. The *Winston-Salem Journal* editorialized in May 1987 that "North Carolina has a large financial investment and a priceless natural heritage in its parks . . . it needs a master plan to overcome a starvation diet." The same month the legislature passed the State Parks Act, led by Senator Henson P. Barnes. The act would establish a master plan that "firmly defines the purpose of state parks and requires sound strategy in managing the system."

Among the park system's 27 regular parks, 23 have trails for a total of 107 trails and 183 miles. All the parks are open all year. An exception is Mt Mitchell, which has to close when snow closes the Blue Ridge Parkway. Other western parks may close temporarily if there are unusually heavy snowstorms. Parks open daily at 8 am and close at 6 pm November through February; 7 pm in March and October; 8 pm in April, May, and September; and 9 pm June through August (except Carolina Beach at 11 pm). There are exceptions: Boone's Cave closes mid-November to mid-March; Hammocks Beach 8 am to 6 pm year-round; Lake Waccamaw, 9 am to 6 pm; and Singletary Lake, open to groups 8 am to 5 pm.

Park rules are posted conspicuously in the parks. Alcohol, illegal drugs, and firearms are prohibited. Fishing is allowed but a state license is necessary. Camping facilities for individual parks are described in this chapter. Some of the parks without a campground have the nearest commercial campground listed under support facilities. Descriptions are also made about primitive and youth-group camping. When visiting a park, first go to the park office and request brochures and maps available to make your stay a pleasurable and educational experience.

The state's physiographic regions are divided into mountains (17 western counties in the Appalachian Mtns chain); piedmont

(42 counties from the Appalachian foothills through the central part of the state to the fall line); and the coastal plains (41 eastern counties from the fall line 150 mi E on flatlands to the Atlantic Ocean. (The fall line designates the area that separates the hard, resistant rocks of the Piedmont Plateau from the softer rocks and sediments of the coastal plains. This common term also designates where the rivers cease to have falls or rapids.) Geographically, the coastal plains include a series of seven sloping terraces that range in descent from about 275 ft in elev to sea level at the barrier islands. Because Mt Mitchell is the only state park in the mountain physiographic region, parks in the adjoining counties (with elev ranging from 2,305 ft to 4,900 ft) are included in the mountain region in this guidebook.

• INFORMATION: Division of Parks and Recreation, PO Box 27687 (512 North Salisbury St), Raleigh, NC 27611, tel: 919-733-7275.

▶ SECTION 1: COASTAL REGION

▶ CAROLINA BEACH STATE PARK
(New Hanover County)

The 1,773-acre Carolina Beach State Park is considered a naturalist's delight with more than 50 species of flora (including the rare Venus' fly trap and five other insectivorous plants native to the coastal environment). Its trail system enables the hiker to study salt marshes, sandhills, rainwater ponds, and swamp lands. One historic sandhill, Sugarloaf, was the settlement area of the Coree Indians in the 1500s and a navigational landmark as early as 1738. Park facilities include a tent/trailer campground, picnic area, marina to the Cape Fear River for fishing and boating, and hiking. (*USGS Map:* Carolina Beach)

• ADDRESS AND ACCESS: Superintendent, Carolina Beach State Park, PO 274, Carolina Beach, NC 28428, tel: 919-458-8206 (office), 919-458-8207 (marina). From Greenfield Park in Wilmington, go S 12 mi on US-421 to entrance R, at jct with Dow Rd (SR-1573).

***Sugarloaf Trail*** *(2.8 mi);* ***Fly Trap Trail*** *(0.4 mi);* ***Campground
Trail*** *(1 mi);* ***Swamp Trail*** *(0.8 mi)*                **458–461**

- LENGTH AND DIFFICULTY: 5 mi round-trip combined, easy

- TRAILHEAD AND DESCRIPTION: Trailheads are at Fly Trap
parking area, the campground, and the marina parking area.
(If Fly Trap parking is chosen, take the first paved road L after
the park entrance. The campground trailhead is the second
paved road, R.) Follow the road signs to the marina parking
area. From here enter the yellow-blazed *Sugarloaf Trail* at the
trail sign and follow it through a forest of pines, oak, and
yaupon. At 0.2 mi the red-blazed *Swamp Trail* is L. Continue
ahead along the river bank to 0.6 mi and turn L in a forest of live
oaks, pines, mosses, and pink spiderwort (*Tradescantia rosea*).
On white sandhills reach an old road's jct at 1 mi; turn sharply
L, pass two cypress ponds with white water lilies, and make
another sharp L at a lily pond at 1.7 mi. At 2.3 mi jct with the
red-blazed *Swamp Trail,* L. Continue ahead, cross paved road,
pass a jct R with the blue-blazed *Campground Trail,* and reach
the terminus of the *Sugarloaf Trail* at the Fly Trap parking area.
The *Fly Trap Trail* begins here near a kiosk that describes the
Venus' fly trap (*Dionaea muscipula*). Charles Darwin described it
as the "most wonderful plant in the world." Protected by law, it
is found only in SE N.C. and NE S.C. After the 0.4-mi loop on
the *Fly Trap Trail,* return on the *Sugarloaf Trail* to the *Campground Trail,* turn L, and follow the trail across Marina Rd to the
campground. Turn R, go to area #2, and turn R at the sign at
3.5 mi. Blue lupine grows here (*Lupinus perrennis*). Cross Marina Rd again, jct with *Sugarloaf Trail* at 4 mi, turn R, and go 75 yd
to jct with the *Swamp Trail.* Turn L and after 0.8 mi reach the
*Sugarloaf Trail* again. Turn R and return to the marina parking
area.

▶ **CLIFFS-OF-THE-NEUSE STATE PARK**
**(Wayne County)**

Cliffs-of-the-Neuse State Park covers 608 acres, chiefly of
forests, on the W bank of the Neuse River. The park's most

extraordinary attraction is the 90 ft cliff carved over thousands of years to show countless fossil shells, the remains of other marine species, and sedimentation at what was once the Atlantic shoreline. Spanish moss drapes the oaks and pines. Galax, a more mountainous plant, grows on the N bank of Mill Creek. Picnicking, swimming, and boating (in the lake), fishing, and hiking are the activities. Year-round family camping is provided at tent/RV sites that have water, flush toilets, tables and grills, and hot showers (no hook-ups). Tent camps for youth groups are available. (*USGS Map:* Seven Springs)

• ADDRESS AND ACCESS: Superintendent, Cliffs-of-the-Neuse State Park, Rte 2, Box 50, Seven Springs, NC 28578, tel: 919-788-6234. Entrance to the park is on SR-1743, E 0.5 mi from NC-111, 13 mi SE of Goldsboro.

### *Spanish Moss Trail* (0.5 mi); *Galax Trail* (0.5 mi); *Bird Trail* (0.8 mi)                    462–464

• LENGTH AND DIFFICULTY: 1.8 mi combined, easy

• TRAILHEAD AND DESCRIPTION: From the parking area follow the trail signs R and descend to a scenic area by the river bank and Mill Creek. Turn L on red-blazed *Bird Trail* to loop across Still Creek and reach the jct with a yellow-blazed loop, the *Galax Trail,* at 0.8 mi. Follow the *Galax Trail* 0.5 mi and return to the parking lot. The *Spanish Moss Trail* is L of the parking lot but R of the Interpretive Center. Descend and circle back to the parking lot after 0.5 mi. (Campers have made numerous connecting trails in this area.)

## ▶ FORT MACON STATE HISTORIC PARK
### (Carteret County)

The Fort Macon State Historic Park is best known for its restored fort at Beaufort Inlet. Emphasis is on its Civil War history. Facilities and services in the 389-acre park include ocean swimming (June 1 through Labor Day), fishing, picnicking, and hiking. A short nature trail and beach hiking provide

over 2 mi of walking. The 0.4-mi *Fort Macon Nature Trail* begins
R between the parking area and the fort's covertway. Follow the
signs on a loop trail through a shrub thicket to Beaufort Inlet
and back. Some trees and shrubs are live oak, black locust,
Hercules' club (*Zanthoxylum clava-herculis*), and yaupon. Camping is not allowed in the park. (*USGS Map:* Beaufort)    **465**

• ADDRESS AND ACCESS: Superintendent, Fort Macon State Park,
PO Box 127, Atlantic Beach, NC 28512, tel: 919-726-3775. To
reach the park (which is on the E tip of Bogue Banks), turn S off
US-70 in Moorehead City to cross the bridge to Atlantic Beach.
At the jct with NC-58 turn L on Fort Macon Rd (SR-1190), and
go 2.2 mi.

▶ **GOOSE CREEK STATE PARK**
   **(Beaufort County)**

Goose Creek State Park is a coastal park that covers 1,327
acres on the N side of the Pamlico River. Special features are the
tall loblolly pines and live oaks draped with ghostly gray Spanish moss and both freshwater and saltwater fishing. Primitive
camping, picnicking, swimming (June 1 to Labor Day), fishing,
boating, and hiking are provided in this sandy wilderness. Bogs,
sandy natural beaches, excellent freshwater fishing for bass,
bluegill, and perch, and saltwater fishing for bluefish and
flounder are features of a distinctive recreational area. Native
mosquitoes and ticks welcome visitors; a maximum-strength
repellent is advisable. (*USGS Map:* Blounts Bay)

• ADDRESS AND ACCESS: Superintendent, Goose Creek State
Park, Rte 2, Box 372, Washington, NC 27889, tel: 919-923-
2191. Access from Washington at jct of US-264/17 is 9 mi on
US-264 and a R turn on Hawkins Beach Rd (SR-1334) for 2.4
mi to park entrance.

• SUPPORT FACILITIES: Shopping centers, motels, and restaurants are in Washington. A nearby private campground is Whi-
chard's Beach Campground, Rte 2, Box 656, Chocowinity, NC
27817, tel: 919-946-1748. From the jct of US-265/17, go 1.7 mi

S on US-17 and turn SE on SR-1166 for 3 mi. Full svc, rec fac. Open all year.

> ***Live Oak Trail** (1.1 mi);* ***Goose Creek Trail** (2.9 mi);* ***Ragged Point Trail** (0.5 mi);* ***Flatty Creek Trail** (0.4 mi);* ***Ivey Gut Trail** (1.9 mi)*                                      **466–470**

- LENGTH AND DIFFICULTY: 6.8 mi, combined, easy

- SPECIAL FEATURES: Spanish moss displays, estuarine wildlife

- TRAILHEAD AND DESCRIPTION: A combination trip on the trails, beginning with the *Live Oak Trail,* could be as follows: Begin from the parking lot on the E side of the park and follow the signs for a loop around the river bank. Pass the swimming area at 1.2 mi. The *Goose Creek Trail* connects near the swimming area but goes W. After 0.2 mi jct, L, with the *Ragged Point Trail.* (This is a boardwalk trail that can be used by the handicapped. It goes to an observation tower for viewing the Pamlico River and nearby wetlands. Backtrack.) Continue on the *Goose Creek Trail* and at 0.9 mi cross boardwalks over low areas. At 1.5 mi reach a jct with the W parking lot, and at 1.8 mi reach jct with *Flatty Creek Trail.* (This is another boardwalk trail and observation tower. Backtrack.) Continue around the peninsula and return to the W parking lot at 2.9 mi. The *Ivey Gut Trail* leaves from the W parking area and campground and meanders near Goose Creek to an exit on the park road and parking area at 1.9 mi. (There is a legend that the ghost of a Goose Creek pirate walks through these woods after dark looking for a cache of gold.) Some of the plants seen along the trails are prickly pear, blue flag iris, bays, lizard's tail, blueberry, and marsh pennywort.

## ▶ HAMMOCKS BEACH STATE PARK
### (Onslow County)

Hammocks Beach State Park with 892 acres occupies all of Bear Island SE of Swansboro. The island is reputed to be one of the most unspoiled and beautiful beach areas on the Atlantic coast. For the hiker there is 3.8 mi of a wide beach trail from Bear Inlet to Bogue Inlet. It is an unmarked trail that shifts its sandy treadway with each change of the tide. There are high dunes; one in the SW section of the island is 60 ft. In addition to hiking, other activities are fishing, swimming, and birding. Vegetation is sparse, but there are sea oats, croton, elder, yaupon, cord grass, and near the marsh side some water oaks and cedars. A few deer, rabbits, and raccoons live on the island. It is also the nesting ground of the loggerhead sea turtle. The park has a bathhouse, refreshment stand, and picnic tables. A free passenger ferry operates daily (10 to 6) from Memorial Day to Labor Day. The distance to the park is 2.5 mi through a web of marshy islands. Visitors using private boat service for day use or overnight camping must contact the park office to register for a permit. (*USGS Maps:* Hubert, Brown's Inlet)

• ADDRESS AND ACCESS: Superintendent, Hammocks Beach State Park, Rte. 2, Box 295, Swansboro, NC 28584, tel: 919-326-4881 or 919-326-2205. From the W edge of Swansboro on NC-24, take Hammock Beach Rd (SR-1511) S to the ferry landing.

## ▶ JOCKEY'S RIDGE STATE PARK
### (Dare County)

Jockey's Ridge State Park, better known as a center for hang gliding than for hiking, covers 385 acres of "marching" sand dunes adjacent to Nags Head Woods, a maritime forest of 1,980 acres. Jockey's Ridge is named, according to one among a number of local stories, for its use as a natural grandstand for races of Banker ponies. It has a 140-ft-high dune, the largest and highest on the Atlantic coast. A hike to the top of the ridge presents an outstanding view of both the Atlantic Ocean and Roanoke Sound, particularly at sunset. Activities include hiking, nature study and photography, hang gliding, and kite flying. Hikers on the 1.1-mi *Jockey's Ridge Trail* are advised to stay on the designated routes to the ridge. Contact the park ranger for information concerning hang glider take-off and landing zones. Facilities include a park office, restrooms, and picnic shelters with tables and grills. Camping is not available at the park. (*USGS Maps:* Manteo, Roanoke Island NE)    **471**

• ADDRESS AND ACCESS: Superintendent, Jockey's Ridge State Park, PO Box 592, Nags Head, NC 27959, tel: 919-441-7132. Access is from US-158 W of Nags Head on West Hollowell St.

## ▶JONES LAKE STATE PARK
### (Bladen County)

Jones Lake is an example of the Bay Lakes area, where shallow depressions (none deeper than 10 ft) are filled with cool, clear water. Geologically, it is thought that the oval depressions were caused by a meteorite shower. Other theories are the ancient ocean springs theory and the ancient ocean lagoons theory. These formations are also found in coastal S.C. and NE Ga. The Bay Lakes area is also known for a wide variety of bay trees and shrubs. The park covers 2,208 acres with facilities for camping, picnicking, swimming, boating, fishing (mainly for yellow perch and blue-spotted sunfish), hiking, and guided nature study (in the summer). The campground has tent/RV sites with drinking water, flush toilets, tables and grills, and hot showers (no hook-ups). Open April 1 through November. (Bladen Lakes State Forest is across the road from the park. See Chapter 11.) (*USGS Map:* Elizabethtown)

• ADDRESS AND ACCESS: Superintendent, Jones Lake State Park, Rte 1, Box 945, Elizabethtown, NC 28337, tel: 919-588-4550. Access is from the jct of NC-53/242 and US-701 on NC-242 N for 4 mi.

### *Jonas Lake Trail*                                          **472**

• LENGTH AND DIFFICULTY: 3.8 mi, easy

• SPECIAL FEATURES: species of bay trees

• TRAILHEAD AND DESCRIPTION: Enter from either the campground or the picnic area to make the loop around the lake.

Follow the signs from the parking lot by the water fountain (70 yd from the entrance). Enter the forest of juniper, pine, gum, and cypress with Spanish moss. Pass sweet bay (a shrub bog plant with large showy leaves and fragrant flowers related to the magnolia); red bay (a small evergreen with a scent of bay rum); the loblolly bay (a member of the tea family with evergreen leaves and white fragrant blossoms); and the bull bay tree (*Magnolia grandiflora*, with large creamy-white petals and scarlet seeds). In hiking counterclockwise, pass a total of six lake-view stations. The trail is sometimes narrow and wet. There are a number of side trails. At 2.5 mi a side trail leads to the parking area. Return to the point of origin at 2.8 mi. Animal life in the park includes deer, raccoons, snakes, bears, and a variety of waterfowl. Yellow perch and blue-spotted sunfish are in the lake, but high acidity makes fishing only fair.

## ▶ LAKE WACCAMAW STATE PARK
### (Columbus County)

Lake Waccamaw State Park, with 9,219 acres, is the second largest state park in the coastal district. The lake, one of the clear lakes of the Carolina Bays, received its name from the Waccamaw Indians. On a remote, gated wilderness road, the undeveloped park offers picnicking, primitive group camping, fishing, and hiking. A pier built into the lake allows for sunbathing and wading. Overnight campers must register with the park ranger. The park comprises three vegetative communities— white sand ridges, pocosin, and cypress-gum swamps. Among the flora are running oak, Carolina ipecac, queen's delight, and pond pine. Wildlife is abundant; there are bear, swamp rabbit, fox, deer, mink, alligator, snakes (including three species of rattlesnakes), and 36 species of fish. (*USGS Maps:* Whiteville, Bolton, Juniper Creek)

• ADDRESS AND ACCESS: Superintendent, Lake Waccamaw State Park, Rte 1, Box 63, Kelly, NC 28448, tel: 919-669-2928 or 919-646-3852. From US-74/76 (W 3 mi from Bolton) on NC-214, turn L on the first paved road, Bella Coola Rd (SR-1947).

## ▶MERCHANT'S MILLPOND STATE PARK
**(Gates County)**

Merchant's Millpond State Park is home for more than 180 species of birds in its 2,592 acres. Warblers stop over in their fall and spring migrations and a large number of waterfowl make this their winter home. Wildlife includes deer, raccoon, turtle, beaver, mink, river otter, and snakes. The major fish are large-mouth bass, bluegill, chain pickerel, and black crappie. The park is a rare ecological community with huge bald cypress and tupelo gum trees in the 760-acre millpond and Lassiter Swamp. (The state champion water tupelo [*Nyssa aquatica*] is here.) The trees are draped with Spanish moss and resurrection fern. Large beech groves, oaks, pines, and holly are in the forest surrounding the wetlands. Activities include fishing, hiking, nature study (with a summer naturalist), canoeing (with rentals), and camping (family tent/RV, group and primitive). The family campsites contain drinking water, a picnic table and grill, flush toilets, and hot showers (no hook-ups). (*USGS Map:* Beckford)

• ADDRESS AND ACCESS: Superintendent, Merchant's Millpond State Park, Rte 1, Box 141-A, Gatesville, NC 27938, tel: 919-357-1191. Park entrance is on US-158, 6 mi NE of Gatesville, immediately NE of Merchant's Millpond Rd (SR-1403).

### *Merchant's Millpond Trail*                                    473

• LENGTH AND DIFFICULTY: 6.8 mi, easy

• SPECIAL FEATURES: ecological study of plantlife

• TRAILHEAD AND DESCRIPTION: Begin the loop trail NW from the parking lot on Merchant's Millpond Rd (SR-1403). After hiking 0.3 mi across the bridge, turn R at the trailhead and enter a forest of cypress, maple, oak, and pine. At 0.6 mi jct L, with a 0.5-mi access route to the family campground. Cross a boardwalk at 0.8 mi and ascend to a division of the loop at 0.9 mi. Turn R, skirt the millpond, and pass a family canoe camp at

1.2 mi. Cross a park fire road at 2.4 mi and reach the backpack primitive camp near Lassiter Swamp at 3.8 mi. Turn L on the return trail and pass through a carpet of running cedar. Cross the park fire road at 4.6 mi. Complete the loop at 6 mi, jct R with the family campground at 6.2 mi, and return to the road at 6.8 mi. (A loop trail, 0.3 mi, extends to a peninsula with picnic tables below the canoe rental building and parking area on SR-1403.)

▶ **PETTIGREW STATE PARK**
**(Washington and Tyrrell Counties)**

Pettigrew State Park covers 17,376 acres, the state's largest. Of this acreage, Lake Phelps has 16,600 acres; it is the second largest natural lake in the state. The lake is unique because it is not fed by any known surface streams, thus it may be the cleanest lake in the state. Its origin may date to 135 million years ago, and in 1775 it was called the "haunt of the beasts" by hunters. Recently archeologists have discovered such artifacts of American Indians as a 31-ft dugout canoe. The lake has bass, catfish, bluegill, and shellcracker. Ducks, swans, and other waterfowl winter here. Exceptionally large cypress, poplar, sweet gum, and sycamore are in the 776 land acres of the park. Another part of history in the park is Somerset Place, a plantation home of the Josiah Collins family (named for Somersetshire, Collins' home county in England), and Bonarva, home of Confederate General James Johnston Pettigrew (for whom the park is named). The Pettigrew family cemetery is here. Activities at the park are picnicking, fishing, boating, hiking, and camping. The campsites are tent/RV with table and grill, water, flush toilets, and hot showers (no hook-ups). (*USGS Map:* Creswell)

*Carriage Drive Trail*                                    **474**

- LENGTH AND DIFFICULTY: 8.2 mi round-trip, easy

- SPECIAL FEATURES: Somerset Place, scenic carriage route

• TRAILHEAD AND DESCRIPTION: From the parking lot near the park office follow the old carriage road W on a level, wide, grassy trail through virgin stands of cypress, sycamore, and poplar bordered with willows, papaw, and honeysuckle. Views of the lake, through patches of wildflowers such as wood sorrel, are found on the L at 0.4 mi, 0.6 mi, and 1.2 mi. Reach the Western Canal at 2.2 mi, and the trail terminus near Moccasin Canal at 2.7 mi. Return by the same route. For the E section, hike past the historic Collins House, an outstanding nineteenth-century coastal plantation estate, at 0.4 mi. Pass the Bonarva Canal at 0.7 mi and at 1.1 mi jct L, with a short side trail to the Pettigrew cemetery. Continue ahead, R, to the Bee Tree Canal and overlook at 1.4 mi. Return by the same route.

▶ **SINGLETARY LAKE STATE PARK**
**(Bladen County)**

Singletary Park is headquarters for the Carolina lakes area—White, Waccamaw, Jones, Salter's, Bay Tree, and Singletary lakes. The major activity of the 1,221-acre park is organized group camping. Of the two camps, one is open all year. Facilities provide a mess hall and kitchen, campers' cabins, and washhouses. Swimming, fishing, and boating are activities open to the group campers. The easy 1-mi *Singletary Lake Trail* makes a loop around the lake. It goes 290 yd from the main road to the lake and follows into a forest, R, with cypress, bayberry, gum, poplar, and juniper. Spanish moss is prominent. At 0.4 mi it crosses a svc road, follows green blazes through groves of scrub oak and long leaf pine, and returns to the point of origin. (*USGS Map:* White Lake)                    **475**

• ADDRESS AND ACCESS: Superintendent, Singletary Lake State Park, Rte 1, Box 63, Kelly, NC 28448, tel: 919-669-2928. Access is 12 mi SE of Elizabethtown on NC-53.

► SECTION 2: MOUNTAIN REGION

► HANGING ROCK STATE PARK
(Stokes County)

Hanging Rock State Park, with 6,000 acres in the Sauratown Mtns, has more than 18 mi of named and side trails. They go to scenic heights, waterfall areas, rocky ridges, and caves, and in the process provide the hiker with views of as many as 300 species of flora, including the mountain camelia (*Stewartia ovata*). Canadian and Carolina hemlock grow together here, a rarity, and a species of *lespedeza* is found only in this area. Animal life includes deer, fox, skunk, woodchuck, squirrel, raccoon, owls, and hawks. The park has camping (also cabins), picnicking, swimming, fishing, and mtn climbing. All trails connect except the *Lower Cascades Trail.* It can be reached by going W from the park entrance on Moores Springs Rd 0.3 mi. Turn L on Hall Rd (SR-2012) and go 0.4 mi to the parking area, R. The 0.6-mi round-trip *Lower Cascades Trail* descends to the scenic falls and pool under a huge overhang. The park is open all year. (*USGS Map:* Hanging Rock)                                **476**

• ADDRESS AND ACCESS: Superintendent, Hanging Rock State Park, PO Box 186, Danbury, NC 27016, tel: 919-593-8480. To reach the park, turn off NC-8, 1.5 mi N of Danbury onto Moores Springs Rd (SR-1001), across the road from Stokes County Community Hospital. The W entrance route is off NC-66, 0.5 mi N of Gap, on Moores Springs Rd.

• SUPPORT FACILITIES: The park has a campground with 74 tent/trailer campsites (no hook-ups) and family vacation cabins. The campground is open all year (water off mid-November to mid-March); the cabins are available (with reservations) from April 1 to October 31. Groceries, restaurant, gasoline, and PO are in Danbury.

### Hanging Rock Trail                                                477

• LENGTH AND DIFFICULTY: 1.4 mi round-trip, moderate

• TRAILHEAD AND DESCRIPTION: From parking lot #1 follow the trail sign E across Indian Creek and begin the ascent. (Heavy visitor traffic has caused serious erosion.) After 0.3 mi a side trail R leads to Wolf Rock. A red blaze leads to the steep 200-ft climb to the summit for excellent views. The metamorphic rock is composed of quartzite. Backtrack. (The *MST* is planned to pass through this area.)

### Hidden Falls Trail *(0.4 mi)*; Window Falls Trail *(0.6 mi)*; Upper Cascades Trail *(0.2 mi)*                                    478–480

• LENGTH AND DIFFICULTY: 1.6 mi round-trip combined, easy

• TRAILHEAD AND DESCRIPTION: From parking lot #1 follow the trail signs from the picnic area at the N end of the parking lot. Descend 0.4 mi to a shady area and Hidden Falls on Indian Creek. Continue to Window Falls at 0.6 mi. Return to the parking lot at 1.2 mi. Go W from the parking lot to Upper Cascades Falls at 0.2 mi and return by the same route. (A new trail is planned along Indian Creek to the Dan River.)

### Chestnut Oak Trail *(0.7 mi)*; Wolf Rock Trail *(1.9 mi)*; Magnolia Spring Trail *(0.4 mi)*; Moores Wall Trail *(2.3 mi)*; Moores Knob Trail *(1.5 mi)*                                              481–485

• LENGTH AND DIFFICULTY: 6.8 mi, combined round-trip, moderate

• SPECIAL FEATURES: Devils Chimney and Moores Knob vistas

• TRAILHEAD AND DESCRIPTION: This combination of trails required ascending and descending on some rocky terrain. From parking lot #2, follow the trail signs around the fence at the bathhouse. Follow S on *Chestnut Oak Trail* but leave it L at 0.4 mi. Reach Wolf Rock at 0.8 mi. (The trail L leads to *Hanging Rock Trail*). Turn R and follow the ridge to jct at 1.3 mi, R, with *Magnolia Spring Trail*. Continue ahead to House Rock at 1.5 mi.

Here are excellent views of Hanging Rock, NE, and the vicinity of Winston-Salem, S. At 1.9 mi reach Devils Chimney over rocky Cooks Wall for a view of Pilot Mtn. Backtrack, but turn L at 2.5 mi on *Magnolia Spring Trail.* Descend to a bridge and go through a rhododendron tunnel. At 2.9 mi jct with the red-blazed *Moores Wall Trail,* R and L. (The R leads 1 mi back to the parking lot.) Turn L and at 3.5 mi jct with the blue-blazed connector to the *Sauratown Trail* and the *Torys Den Trail* (described below). Turn R and ascend to a rocky area with hemlock and turkey grass at 4.1 mi. An observation tower (2,579 ft) with spectacular views is reached at 4.8 mi. Descend on white-blazed *Moores Knob Trail;* pass Balanced Rock and Indian Face on an old road. Cross Cascade Creek at 5.9 mi. Pass through the camping area and rejoin the red-blazed trail at 6.1 mi. Turn L and return to the parking lot at 6.8 mi. This combination of trails could also include the *Torys Den Trail* for a total of 12 mi.

### *Torys Den Trail*                                                486

• LENGTH AND DIFFICULTY: 4.2 mi, easy

• CONNECTING TRAILS:
  *(Chestnut Oak Trail)*
  *(Moores Knob Trail)*
  *(Moores Wall Trail)*
  *(Magnolia Spring Trail)*
  *(Sauratown Trail)*

• TRAILHEAD AND DESCRIPTION: From parking lot #2, follow the trail signs on the E side of the bathhouse and lakeshore. Follow the *Chestnut Oak Trail,* but leave it, R, at 0.3 mi and follow the red-blazed trail. At 0.4 mi pass jct R with *Moores Knob Trail.* Cross a stream and boardwalk and jct L at 1 mi with *Magnolia Spring Trail* (which ascends 0.4 mi to jct with *Wolf Ridge Trail).* Continue ahead, ascend slightly to a saddle at 1.5 mi, and jct with a blue-blazed trail, L. (The trail R is *Moores Wall Trail.)* Follow the blue-blazed trail, and after 0.5 mi reach the crest of Huckleberry Ridge near a large rock formation. Descend, and jct with the *Sauratown Trail* at 2.4 mi R and L. (*Sauratown Trail* is also a horse trail.) Turn R, descend and cross a small stream at 3.5 mi. Ascend to Charlie Young Rd (SR-2028) at 3.6 mi and turn R. Follow the road 0.4 mi to a Torys Den sign L (across the road from a stone house). (*Sauratown Trail* continues ahead on its route to the horse parking center on Hall Rd, SR-2012.) Follow the trail 0.1 mi to an outcrop, but turn R on the approach. Descend 90 yd near a small cave L and turn R. (Ahead it is a few yd to a view of Torys Den Falls.) Descend 100 yd on the path to the 30-ft Torys Den. Backtrack, or use a vehicle shuttle. Vehicle access is to drive W from the park entrance on Moores Springs Rd to Mickey Rd (SR-2011); turn L, and turn L again on Charlie Young Rd, a total of 4.3 mi.

## ▶ MOUNT JEFFERSON/NEW RIVER STATE PARK
### (Ashe and Alleghany Counties)

Mount Jefferson State Park covers 541 acres and includes the summit (4,900 ft) of Mt Jefferson; it is halfway between the towns of Jefferson and West Jefferson. Panoramic views from the fire tower reveal other mtn ranges in a three-state area—Whitetop Mtn in Virginia, Grandfather and Pilot mtns in N.C., and Cherokee National Forest mtns in Tennessee. The park has a wide variety of trees, shrubs, and flowers. Its chestnut-oak forest is considered to be one of the finest in the southeast. In addition, there are maple, ash, white and red oaks, black locust, and poplar. Rhododendron, laurel, and flame azalea are also prominent as are banks of galax and scattered wood lilies and dutchman's breeches. Animal life includes the fox, ground hog, and red and gray squirrels. Picnicking and hiking are the major activities; camping is not allowed. (*USGS Map:* Jefferson)

• ADDRESS AND ACCESS: Superintendent, Mt Jefferson State Park, PO Box 48, Jefferson, NC 28640, tel: 919-982-2587 or 919-246-9653. Access is from US-221 between Jefferson and West Jefferson; turn on Mt Jefferson Rd (SR-1152) for 3 mi to the summit.

• SUPPORT FACILITIES: The nearest campground is Greenfield Campground at the base of the park, 0.7 mi SW on Mt Jefferson

Rd (SR-1149 from the park road). Address is West Jefferson, NC 28694, tel: 919-246-9106. Open year-round. Full svc, rec fac. Other information can be obtained from the Jefferson Chamber of Commerce, tel: 919-246-9550. Shopping centers, restaurants, and motels are in nearby Jefferson/West Jefferson.

### *Rhododendron Trail* 487

- LENGTH AND DIFFICULTY: 1.4 mi round-trip, easy

- TRAILHEAD AND DESCRIPTION: From the parking lot climb 0.2 mi to the N.C. Forest Service lookout tower, and continue to a loop that provides information on the natural history of the area. Reach Luther's Rock overlook for views of the New River and beyond. Complete the loop and return.

(New River State Park is a 26-mi stretch of the South Fork from Dog Creek to the Virginia state line. It has been designated a national scenic river, and its chief recreational activities are canoeing and fishing. Three access points provide picnicking and canoe-in camping. Because a continuous strip of publicly owned land has not been achieved, river users are advised to remain on park property. There are no admission fees or permit requirements to canoe the river, but a permit is required for canoe-in camping. There are a number of area outfitters for canoe rental and livery. Contact the park office listed above for a list of outfitters and river guidelines. A major access is the Wagoner Rd Access. To reach it, go 4.7 mi SE on NC-88 from its jct with US-221 in Jefferson, to the community of Wagoner. Turn L on New River State Park Rd [SR-1590] and go 0.8 mi to the picnic and parking area.)

## ▶ MOUNT MITCHELL STATE PARK
### (Yancey County)

Mount Mitchell State Park, extending over 1,469 acres of the Black Mountains ridge, is the state's highest park (6,684 ft), and Mt Mitchell itself is the highest peak east of the Mississippi. This is also the state's oldest park, having been designated in 1915 thanks to the influence of early environmentalists such as Governor Locke Craige and U.S. President Theodore Roosevelt. The park is listed in the National Registry of Natural Landmarks. Mt Mitchell is named in honor of Elisha Mitchell, a clergyman and University of North Carolina geology professor, who fell to his death in a gorge N of Little Piney Ridge (about 2 mi from Mt Mitchell summit) while on one of his scientific explorations. A creek and waterfall also bear his name. Geologically, the Black Mtn range is estimated to be over 1 billion years old, erosion having worn down the summits about 200 million years ago. Fraser fir (damaged by the woolly aphid and acid rain) and red spruce give the crest an alpine look reminiscent of Canada or Maine. Some of the flowering plants are white hellebore, blue-beaded Clinton's lily, and bearberry. Among the forest animals are bear, deer, bobcat, and squirrel. There are 18 mi of hiking trails, including Commissary Road but not including the many connecting trails into the Pisgah National Forest. The restaurant and observation lounge are open May 15 to October 15. (*USGS-FS Maps:* Montreat, Mt Mitchell)

• ADDRESS AND ACCESS: Superintendent, Mt Mitchell State Park, Rte 5, Box 700, Burnsville, NC 28714, tel: 704-675-4611. Entrance is from NC-218 off the BRP near mp 355, 30 mi NE of Asheville and 11.2 mi S from Buck Creek Gap and jct with NC-80.

• SUPPORT FACILITIES: Primitive camping is restricted in the park; inquiry should be made at the park office. The nearest campground is Black Mountain Recreation Area in Pisgah NF. Access is from the BRP, mp 351.9, at Deep Gap. Descend 4.9 mi on FR-472 and turn L at the campground entrance. (There are no hook-ups.)

*Mt Mitchell Summit Trail (0.2 mi); Old Mt Mitchell Trail (2 mi); Camp Alice Trail (1.1 mi); Balsam Trail (0.7 mi); Mt Mitchell Trail (1.6 mi)*                                              **488–492**

• LENGTH AND DIFFICULTY: 5.6 mi combined, easy to strenuous

• SPECIAL FEATURES: Mt Mitchell summit, spruce/fir forest

• TRAILHEAD AND DESCRIPTION: From the summit parking area, ascend the wide *Mt Mitchell Summit Trail* in a damp forest of conifers and mosses for 0.2 mi to an observation tower and the tomb of the Rev. Elisha Mitchell, who "39 years a professor at the University of North Carolina lost his life in the scientific exploration of this mountain in his 64th year, June 27, 1857." Vistas from the observation tower are magnificent. Along the ascent, other trails branch off. After 140 yd the *Old Mt Mitchell Trail* goes R and the *Camp Alice Trail* branches from it. The *Balsam Trail* and the *Mt Mitchell Trail* branch off L after 0.1 mi. They are described below in that order.

From the *Mt Mitchell Summit Trail,* branch off R on *Old Mt Mitchell Trail.* At 0.3 mi jct L with *Camp Alice Trail.* (It descends steeply on a blue-blazed trail to Camp Alice, an old logging and railroad camp of the 1920s at 1.1 mi. Regardless of the name, no camping is allowed. Return on the switchbacks to *Old Mt Mitchell Trail.*) Continue ahead, descending easily to a tent camping area at 0.8 mi, the park restaurant at 1.5 mi, and the trail's S terminus at the park office parking lot at 2 mi. This yellow-blazed trail is the oldest route to the summit, probably used by explorers in the early 1840s.

For the *Balsam Trail,* branch off *Mt Mitchell Summit Trail* at 0.1 mi, L. Follow the self-guided loop nature trail back to the parking lot, turning L at each jct. The highest spring in eastern America, with an average temperature of 36, is on this trail.

The *Mt Mitchell Trail* also follows jointly with the *Balsam Trail* for the first 0.1 mi, but continues ahead. At 0.3 mi the blue-blazed trail begins a steep descent over rough terrain. Switchbacks begin at 0.7 mi. Reach Commissary Road and jct with *Buncombe Horse Range Trail* (see Toecane Ranger District, Chapter 3), at 1.6 mi. (The Camp Alice Shelter is here with space for ten campers. A spring is nearby.) Backtrack, or continue for another 4.4 mi on switchbacks to the Black Mtn campground in the Pisgah National Forest.

### Deep Gap Trail                                                   493

• LENGTH AND DIFFICULTY: 5.4 mi round-trip, strenuous

• TRAILHEAD AND DESCRIPTION: This trail is also part of the *Black Mountain Crest Trail* described in the Toecane Ranger

District, Chapter 3. From the summit parking and picnic area, follow an orange blaze N over rough terrain to Mt Craige (6,645 ft) at 1.1 mi; at 1.5 mi reach Big Tom (6,593 ft), named in honor of Thomas Wilson (1825–1900), who found the body of Dr. Mitchell. Continue over strenuous treadway to Balsam Cone (6,611 ft) at 2.1 mi, and reach Cattail Peak (6,583 ft) at 2.4 mi. Leave the state park boundary and go another 1.5 mi to Deep Gap Shelter. (The shelter has four large wood bunks, tent camping space, and a spring.) (Ahead the *Black Mountain Crest Trail* goes to Bowlens Creek Rd [SR-1109] for a total of 12 mi.)

## ▶ PILOT MOUNTAIN STATE PARK
### (Surry and Yadkin Counties)

Pilot Mountain State Park covers 3,748 acres in two sections—Pilot Mountain and the S and N side of the Yadkin River—and is connected by a 6.5-mi 300-ft-wide forest corridor for hikers and equestrians. In the park is the Big Pinnacle, rising 200 ft from its base, 1,400 ft above the valley floor and 2,420 ft above sea level. Dedicated as a national nature landmark in 1976, it is geologically a quartzite monadnock. Park activities are canoe camping, picnicking, horseback riding, hiking, and camping. A family-type tent/trailer campground is near the base of the N side of the mtn. It has hot showers but no hook-ups (water off mid-November to mid-March). Trails connect easily with the exception of *Yadkin River Trail* that is on the S side of the Yadkin River. *Sauratown Trail* has its W terminus at the park, and the *MST* will pass through the *Corridor Trail*. (*USGS Maps:* Pinnacle, Siloam)

• ADDRESS AND ACCESS: Superintendent, Pilot Mountain State Park, Rte 1, Box 21, Pinnacle, NC 27043, tel: 919-325-2355. Entrance to the park is at the jct of US-52 and Pilot Knob Rd (SR-2053), 14 mi S of Mt Airy and 24 mi N of Winston-Salem.

*Sassafras Trail (0.5 mi); Jomeokee Trail (0.8 mi); Ledge Springs Trail (1.6 mi); Mountain Trail (2.5 mi); Grindstone Trail (1.6 mi)* **494–498**

- LENGTH AND DIFFICULTY: 7 mi combined, easy to strenuous

- SPECIAL FEATURES: Big Pinnacle, scenic ledges

- TRAILHEAD AND DESCRIPTION: All of these trails connect and can be reached from the parking lot at the top of the mtn. From the parking lot go past and behind the comfort station to a rocky area and a sign for the *Jomeokee Trail*. To the L, 30 yd, is the *Sassafras Trail*. (Follow the *Sassafras Trail* N on a self-guiding loop. It is an interpretive trail among pitch pine, chestnut oak, laurel, and groundcover patches of galax.) At the *Jomeokee Trail* sign descend among rocks and follow a much used access to the Big Pinnacle. (Jomeokee is an Indian word for "Great Guide" or "Pilot.") At 0.2 mi pass the base of Little Pinnacle and jct R with the yellow-blazed *Ledge Springs Trail*. Ahead, after another 0.1 mi, turn R to follow a rocky loop around the Big Pinnacle. The trail walls have caves, eroded rock formations, ferns, wildflowers, lichens, and mosses. Park officials say that ravens nest on the summit. (Climbing or rappelling is prohibited.) On the return from the loop take the *Ledge Springs Trail*, L. Descend on a rocky, rough, and sometimes strenuous base of the ledges. At 1 mi reach Ledge Springs, R, 30 yd from the jct with the *Mountain Trail*. (Formerly the *Mountain Bridle Trail*, the *Mountain Trail* is a rough connector trail to the *Corridor Trail* described below. Blazed red, it descends through a hardwood forest with scattered patches of laurel and pine in the beginning. At 1.8 mi it reaches large boulders pushed up in a row from a former clearing. After another 0.4 mi it leaves the row and follows a footpath to an exit at the Surry Line Rd [SR-2061] to jct L with *Grassy Ridge Trail* and R with the *Corridor Trail* at 2.5 mi.) To continue on the *Ledge Springs Trail* turn R and begin a steep ascent over the ledges to jct with *Grindstone Trail*, L, at 1.3 mi. (*Grindstone Trail* follows first on an easy contour, but soon descends in a rocky area with hardwoods and laurel. It crosses a footbridge and small stream at 1.3 mi, an old road at 1.5 mi, and exits at 1.6 mi between campsites #16 and #17). Continue the ascent ahead on *Ledge Springs Trail,* pass R of the picnic area, and return to the SW corner of the parking lot at 1.5 mi.

### *Grassy Ridge Trail (1.7 mi); Corridor Trail (6.5 mi); Horne Creek Trail (1.3 mi); Canal Trail (1 mi round-trip)* 499–502

• LENGTH AND DIFFICULTY: 10.5 mi combined, easy

• TRAILHEAD AND DESCRIPTION: (With the exception of *Canal Trail,* these trails are horse/hiker trails.) The N terminus of the white-blazed *Grassy Ridge Trail* is on Pilot Knob Rd (SR-2053 in Surry County and SR-1151 in Stokes County) under the US-52 bridge, 0.2 mi E of the park entrance. At this trailhead is the W terminus of *Sauratown Trail* (see Chapter 14). (Vehicular access to the S end of *Grassy Ridge Trail* and the N end of *Corridor Trail* from here is E on Pilot Knob Rd, 1.1 mi to jct with VFW Rd [SR-1152]. Turn R, go 0.4 mi, and turn R on Old US-52 [SR-1236]. After another 0.4 mi turn R across the RR on Surry Line Rd [SR-1148] and drive 1.6 mi.)

Enter *Grassy Ridge Trail* at a poplar tree and into a hardwood forest. Cross a streamlet at 0.1 mi and reach a jct, R, at 0.2 mi. (To the R it is 0.3 mi on a footpath to the park office.) Continue L, pass an old tobacco barn at 0.4 mi. Cross small streams at 0.5 mi and 1.3 mi. Arrive at Surry Line Rd (SR-2061 in Surry County) at 1.7 mi. (To the R, on the road, it is 75 yd to the S terminus of the red-blazed *Mountain Trail.*) Cross the road to a road jct with SR-2063 and a parking area in the corner of Pilot Mtn State Park Corridor. Here is the N terminus of the *Corridor Trail.* (Vehicular access to the S terminus of the *Corridor Trail* is W on SR-2061 for 2.6 mi to jct with Shoals Rd [SR-2048]. Turn L, and go S 4 mi [turning neither R nor L] but partly on SR-2069, also called Shoals Rd, to a fork. Ahead is a dead-end sign. Turn L on gravel Hauser Rd [SR-2072] and go 1 mi to the S terminus, L. Ahead it is 0.2 mi, R, to the park's Yadkin River section.)

Begin the yellow-blazed *Corridor Trail* on an old farm road in a grove of Virginia pine and pass under a powerline at 0.1 mi. At 0.3 mi is a view (looking back) of the Pinnacles. Cross two footbridges with a meadow of wildflowers and elderberry in between. At 0.7 mi leave the forest and enter a field with another good view of the Pinnacles (looking backward). After 0.1 mi enter a forest of pine and cedar. Pass remnants of an old tobacco barn, L, at 1.2 mi. Cross a small stream bordered with pinxter at 1.4 mi, and another stream at 1.5 mi. At 1.6 mi cross paved Mt Zion Rd (SR-2064). Follow the trail through areas of old farm land and young-growth forests. Descend to rock-hop a tributary of Grassy Creek at 2.6 mi. Pass patches of yellow root and wood betony among the river birch. Exit from the woods into an open area of honeysuckle, blackberry, and poison ivy, and cross paved Shoals Rd (SR-2048) at 3 mi. Follow the woods' edge into the forest, cross a stream, cross a number of old woods roads, and descend gently to another stream with beds of sensitive fern at 4.7 mi. Cross a footbridge constructed by the YACC. Cross paved Stoney Ridge Church Rd (SR-2070) at 5 mi. Follow the trail through beautiful routes of alternating pine groves and open hardwoods. At 6 mi cross a rocky tributary of Horne Creek. (Upstream are two large mill stones.) Pass under a powerline at 6.3 mi and reach the trail's S terminus at 6.5 mi at Hauser Rd (SR-2072). Across the road begins the *Horne Creek Trail*. (To the L on the road it is 0.2 mi to the entrance, R, of the Yadkin River section of the park at a log shed.) (A vehicular access to US-52 from here is on SR-2072, E, 2.8 mi to Perch Rd [SR-2065]. Turn L, and go 3.5 mi to US-52 in Pinnacle.)

(Vehicular access to the S end of the *Horne Creek Trail* is on the park road. Drive in at the park gate by the log shed, ford the small Horne Creek three times, pass through a picnic area, and reach a cul-de-sac on a bluff by the Yadkin River. The *Canal Trail* begins here, on the W side of the cul-de-sac at a wide trail opening, and connects with *Horne Creek Trail,* after 80 yd, at the Southern Railway track.)

At the N end of *Horne Creek Trail* enter a partial field with walnut trees. After 0.3 mi arrive at the park road, turn R, rock-hop Horne Creek, and at 0.5 mi re-enter the woods. Ascend and rejoin the park road in a grove of pines at 0.8 mi. Turn R, follow the road, but leave it after 0.2 mi. Descend to the Southern Railway track and jct, L, with the *Canal Trail* (which begins

80 yd up the bank to the cul-de-sac). Cross the RR tracks and after 60 yd reach the Yadkin River, the trail's end. (To the R the *Canal Trail* crosses a footbridge. It goes upstream 0.5 mi between the river and the RR tracks among sycamore, poplar, and river birch. At 0.2 mi pass a long rock wall, R. Backtrack.) Although *Horne Creek Trail* ends at the river, horses can ford the river to two islands and to *Yadkin River Trail* described below.

### *Yadkin River Trail*                                   503

• LENGTH AND DIFFICULTY: 0.7 mi, easy

• TRAILHEAD AND DESCRIPTION: To reach this trail take NC-67 to East Bend and follow Old NC-67 (SR-1545) into town. Turn NW on Fairground Rd (SR-1541), go 0.5 mi, turn R on Shady Grove Church Rd (SR-1538) for 0.4 mi, and turn R on Old Shoals Rd (SR-1546) for 2.5 mi to the picnic and parking area. Follow the yellow-blazed trail to the river and return on a loop through a pine forest W of the RS. (This is also an area for a bridle trail that crosses the Yadkin River N to *Horne Creek Trail* and *Corridor Trail* described above.) There are two renovated campsites for individual canoeists on the 45-acre islands in the Yadkin River. Group camping is not permitted.

### ▶ SOUTH MOUNTAINS STATE PARK
### (Burke and Cleveland Counties)

South Mountains State Park is an undeveloped, remote park covering 5,783 acres of upper piedmont ecology. Composed of numerous mountain knobs, all under 3,000 ft elev, the area is underlain by a mixture of mica schist and gneiss with quartzite. Mature forests of oak, poplar, hemlock, and pine grow here; they support an understory of three species of rhododendron, mulberry, holly, and laurel. Wildflowers are abundant along the streams. The major attraction in the park is the 70-ft High Shoals Falls. The area is the site of a former CCC camp. It provides 12 mi of fishable trout streams, backpack camping, picnicking, and 13 mi of old CCC roads for horseback riding and hiking. The four pack-in campsites are High Shoals (sites 1–4); Shinny Creek (sites 5–8); Murray's Branch (sites 9–11); and Little River (sites 12–14). All campers must register at the park office. (*USGS Maps:* Casar, Benn Knob)

• ADDRESS AND ACCESS: Superintendent, South Mountains State Park, Rte 1, Box 206, Connelly Springs, NC 28612, tel: 704-433-4772. Access from Morganton is S on NC-18 from its jct with I-40. Go 10.8 mi to Sugar Loaf Rd (SR-1913), take a sharp R at the Pine Mtn sign, and go 4.2 mi to Old NC-18 (SR-1924) and make a L. After 2.7 mi turn R on Sliding Rock Rd (SR-1901), go 1.3 mi, cross Jacob's Fork Creek bridge, and turn R on South Mtn Park Rd (SR-1904). Proceed for 3.6 mi to the park office.

• SUPPORT FACILITIES: Shopping centers, motels, restaurants, and hospitals are in Morganton.

**High Shoals Falls Trail** *(1 mi);* **Upper Falls Trail** *(0.9 mi);* **Shinny Creek Trail** *(2.1 mi);* **Jacob's Fork Trail** *(0.8 mi);* **Fox Trail** *(1.1 mi)* **504–508**

• LENGTH AND DIFFICULTY: 12.2 mi round-trip combined, moderate to strenuous

• SPECIAL FEATURES: High Shoals Falls, remote areas

• TRAILHEAD AND DESCRIPTION: (Although none of the trails are loops, a combination of trails and old roads can form loops of 2.4 mi to 9.5 mi.) From the parking and picnic area opposite the park office, follow the trail signs upstream past the restrooms on Hq Rd. At 0.5 mi the main trail forks where *High Shoals Falls Trail* is L and *Upper Falls Trail* is R. On *High Shoals Falls Trail* the treadway is rocky, has roots, and can be slippery through a dense area of rosebay rhododendron. Follow the yellow dots over the stream crossing to massive boulders and a deep pool at the base of the waterfall. Backtrack. To follow *Upper Falls Trail* begin at the fork, ascend steeply on an old road with three switchbacks in a forest of black gum, hemlock, poplar, and rhododendron. Pass a spring at 0.4 mi and a stile at 0.5

mi. Ahead it is 0.2 mi to the entrance of High Shoals pack-in campground, R, and to the L another 0.2 mi to scenic Upper Falls and pools. No picnicking or camping is allowed near Upper Falls. Backtrack to the stile, turn L on the old road, ascend 0.2 mi, and leave the road, R. Follow an unnamed yellow-blazed trail around a ridge and descend into a deep rocky gorge with dense hemlock and rhododendron. Rock-hop Shinny Creek to Shinny Creek pack-in campground, in a meadow, after 0.8 mi. Here the Hq Rd leads R for 1.1 mi to the park office and L for 3.1 mi to Lower CCC Rd.

Across the road (near the bridge) is the E terminus of the white-blazed *Shinny Creek Trail*. Go upstream, rock-hop the creek of cascades and pools at 0.2 mi. Cross two footbridges over Shinny Creek and another over Dark Creek in a forest of hemlock and rhododendron (bridge construction here and other work on this trail were made possible by the Adopt-a-Park program of the Z. Smith Reynolds Foundation and the South Mountains Sierra Group). Follow an old RR grade and turn sharply L at 0.8 mi. Ascend on a ridge, rocky and steep in sections, in areas of hardwoods, yellow pine, and turkey beard. Reach the ridgecrest at 1.4 mi, follow an old woods road, and arrive at the trail's end and jct with Hq Rd, R and L, at 2.1 mi, the end of the trail. (It is 0.8 mi R to Lower CCC Rd.) Turn L on Hq Rd, and after 0.5 mi jct R with the white-blazed *Jacob's Fork Trail*. (*Jacob's Fork Trail* descends and crosses Jacob's Fork at 0.2 mi. Ascend to the trail's end at 0.8 mi with the jct of the *Fox Trail* [a forest road]. Turn R, pass the gravesite of William Crotts, CSA [Confederate States of America], and unmarked graves, R, at 0.6 mi. At 0.7 mi is the first access to the pack-in campsites #9–11 in a former wildlife field. The second access is 100 yd ahead. Arrive at the end of *Fox Trail* at 1.1 mi and jct with Lower CCC Rd, R and L. Turn R, go 0.4 mi, turn R on gated Hq Rd, and go 1.3 mi to the beginning of *Jacob's Fork Trail* for a loop of 3.6 mi.)

To return to the park office, continue E on Hq Rd, pass a wildlife field, R, at 0.9 mi, and old road jct, R, at 1 mi. (The old road goes 0.8 mi to jct with *Upper Falls Trail.*) Continue L, descend, cross the Shinny Creek bridge, pass the Shinny Creek trailhead at 2.3 mi (a trail and road loop of 4.4 mi), cross another road bridge at 2.6 mi, pass large cascades and a flume at 2.7 mi, reach *High Shoals Falls* and *Upper Falls* trails jct, R, at 2.9 mi, and return to the parking area at 3.4 mi.

## ▶ STONE MOUNTAIN STATE PARK
### (Alleghany and Wilkes Counties)

Stone Mountain State Park, with 11,500 acres of forests, trout streams, waterfalls, and rugged medium-grained biotite granite domes, borders the eastern edge of the Blue Ridge Mountains. The largest granite area is Stone Mountain, rising in grandeur 600 ft above its base and 2,305 ft above sea level. The granite is estimated to be 300 mil years old. The park's protected environment provides a habitat for deer, beaver, mink, otter, bobcat, squirrel, bear, and a number of smaller mammals. Spring wildflowers are prominent. The major activities are picnicking, fishing, hiking, climbing, and camping. There is a 37-unit tent/trailer campground (0.8 mi N of the park office on SR-1100) with grills and tables, flush toilets, and hot showers (water off mid-November to mid-March). Walk-in campsites are also available in the backcountry at designated areas. Group walk-in campers must have advance reservations. Climbing is allowed on the south face of Stone Mountain, and climbers are requested to receive information on the regulations and routes from the ranger's office. Access is by way of *Stone Mtn Trail* (described below) to the mtn base where a panel diagrams the 12 climbing routes. The mtn is closed to climbing when the rocks are wet, and all climbers (as well as all hikers) must be out of the area before dark. (*USGS Map:* Glade Valley)

• ADDRESS AND ACCESS: Superintendent, Stone Mountain State Park, Star Rte 1, Box 15, Roaring Gap, NC 28668, tel: 919-957-8185. The main access is from US-21 in Thurmond. Follow Traphill Rd (SR-1002) W 4.3 mi to jct with John P. Frank Parkway (SR-1784), and follow SR-1784 N 2.5 mi to the park office, R.

• SUPPORT FACILITIES: McGrady Grocery Store is 0.6 mi W on SR-1002 from the park's S entrance (W of Traphill). Shopping centers, restaurants, motels, and other services are in Elkins, 15 mi SE on US-21.

**Stone Mountain Trail** *(3.3 mi);* **Wolf Rock Trail** *(1 mi);* **Cedar Rock Trail** *(0.7 mi);* **Blackjack Ridge Trail** *(1.4 mi);* **Stone Mountain Nature Trail** *(0.5 mi);* **Indian Den Rock Trail** *(0.5 mi);* **Middle and Lower Falls Trail** *(1.6 mi round-trip)* **509–515**

• LENGTH AND DIFFICULTY: 9 mi combined, easy to strenuous

• SPECIAL FEATURES: granite domes, waterfalls

• TRAILHEAD AND DESCRIPTION: Access to all these trails is at the parking lot; they all connect and provide multiple loop options. The longest trail is *Stone Mtn Trail.* It begins and ends at the parking lot. Counterclockwise, it passes in front of the S face of Stone Mtn, in a valley, on its route to ascend Stone Mtn ridge from Stone Mtn Falls. It descends from the dome to the parking lot. (If it is necessary to park at the main road parking area, walk 0.4 mi up the access road to the trailhead.) From the parking lot cross the road to a small picnic area and trail sign. After 75 yd to the top of the steps, jct R with the *Wolf Rock Trail.*

(The *Wolf Rock Trail* enters a rhododendron slick and ascends on an old wagon road to the summit of the mtn in a flat area. At 0.5 mi jct R with the group campsite connector trail that descends to the East Prong of Roaring River. Ahead pass a long stone wall, L, and a former homestead area. At 0.8 mi reach a short spur, R, to the pock-marked flat dome of Wolf Rock. Views W are of Little Stone Mtn and SW of Greenstreets Mtn. After another 0.1 mi, jct L with a narrow path that ascends 120 yd to a cement box spring. Descend, pass a seepage L and two old sheds R. At 1 mi jct L with *Cedar Rock Trail,* and end *Wolf Rock Trail* to begin *Blackjack Ridge Trail.* At this point you have a choice of two return loops to the parking lot. If taking *Cedar Rock Trail,* ascend 100 yd to a granite slope and outstanding view of Stone Mtn. Follow the yellow blaze painted on the rock. Descend to join *Stone Mtn Trail,* turn L on it, and complete the loop after 1.9 mi. If taking *Blackjack Ridge Trail,* follow the old road in a forest of oak, laurel, and pine to pass Buzzard Rock, R, at 0.2 mi. Leave the ridge, L, at 0.6 mi [at yellow blazes] and soon descend to rock-hop Cedar Rock Creek. Ascend steeply and terminate the trail at a jct of *Cedar Rock Trail* at 1.4 mi. Bear R on *Cedar Rock Trail* to *Stone Mtn Trail,* where a L for 0.2 mi will complete the loop of 2.8 mi.)

To hike *Stone Mtn Trail,* continue beyond *Wolf Rock Trail* jct and enter a grassy meadow for views of the S face of Stone Mtn. A plaque described the dome as a registered natural landmark. At 0.2 mi (at the edge of the woods), jct L with *Stone Mtn Nature Trail.* (It crosses the meadow, N, to the base of the mtn. Enter the woods to an information panel of the climbing routes, L. Turn R on a yellow-blazed trail with interpretive signs among the boulders. Cross a small stream and return to *Stone Mtn Trail* after 0.5 mi.) On *Stone Mtn Trail,* 25 yd from the edge of the woods, jct with *Cedar Rock Trail.* (A sign here may refer to *Stone Mtn Trail* as *Stone Mtn Falls Trail;* they are the same.) Cross Big Sandy Creek twice, and at 0.7 mi jct L with the *Indian Den Rock Trail.* (*Indian Den Rock Trail* ascends steeply 0.2 mi to a spur, R, that goes 150 yd to a granite outcrop before connecting with the *Stone Mtn Trail* after another 0.3 mi.) Continue downstream on the *Stone Mtn Trail,* and jct R with the *Middle Falls Trail* and *Lower Falls Trail* at 0.9 mi. (Both of the falls trails dead-end. Rock-hop Big Sandy Creek, follow an old road, and after 0.2 mi jct with the *Middle Falls Trail,* R. Follow it for 0.1 mi to a view of the cascades. For the Lower Falls continue on the old road and rock-hop or wade Big Sandy Creek twice to see the cascades after 0.5 mi. Backtrack.)

Proceed on the *Stone Mtn Trail,* which becomes a footpath through a rhododendron grove. Arrive at the beautiful 200-ft tumbling Stone Mtn Falls (also called "Beauty Falls") at 1.2 mi. Climb carefully the steep trail to the fall's summit, pass an old stone chimney at 1.5 mi, turn L at the next fork, and jct L with the *Indian Den Rock Trail* at 1.9 mi. Follow the ridge and pass Hitching Rock with its magnificent views of Wolf Rock and Cedar Rock, W at 2.1 mi. Begin a steep incline and reach the summit of Stone Mtn (2,305 ft) at 2.7 mi. Views N are of the Blue Ridge Mtns and SW of Cedar Rock. Large patches of lichens, mosses, and pines cling to the rocks. Follow the yellow blaze painted on the barren granite and begin the descent at 2.8 mi. Return to the parking lot at 3.3 mi.

---

## ▶ SECTION 3: PIEDMONT REGION

---

## ▶ BOONE'S CAVE STATE PARK
### (Davidson County)

The park consists of 110 acres of hardwoods—beech, oak, poplar, elm, and hornbeam; laurel, rhododendron, wild hydrangea, and wild pink are among the flowering plants. On the E side of the Yadkin River and generally undeveloped, the park provides picnicking, fishing, hiking, and a canoe rest-stop on the 165-mi *Yadkin River Trail.* (For information on the *Yadkin River Trail,* contact the Yadkin River Trail Assoc Inc, 280 South Liberty St, Winston-Salem, NC 27101, tel: 919-722-9346.) *Daniel Boone's Cave Trail* is an easy 0.5-mi route. From the parking lot descend on a gravel trail with steps 100 yd to Boone's Cave, R. (Legends are that Daniel Boone hid from the Indians here, or that he discovered and explored the 80-ft cave, thus the park's name. Cave explorers should be prepared to crawl and have dependable flashlights.) Follow the elevated boardwalks to the river bank access before following a footpath, L, toward the cabin of Squire Boone (who, according to legend, moved here in 1750 when Daniel was 16). Return to the parking lot on the service road to complete the loop. (*USGS Map:* Churchland)

**516**

• ADDRESS AND ACCESS: West District Office, Rte 2, Box 224M, Troutman, NC 28166, tel: 704-528-6514. From I-85 jct with NC-150, halfway between Lexington and Salisbury, go 5 mi N on NC-150 to Churchland. Turn L on Boone's Cave Rd (SR-1162) and go 3.8 mi to the parking area.

## ►CROWDER'S MOUNTAIN STATE PARK
### (Gaston County)

Crowder's Mountain (1,625 ft), named in honor of Ulrick Crowder, a German merchant who settled in the area in the 1780s, is part of 1,966 acres of Crowder's Mountain State Park. In 1987 Kings Pinnacle (1,705 ft) was acquired. Family and group backpack camping is available in separate camping areas. Registration at the park office is necessary. The park has been designated a Natural Heritage Area; some infrequent plants— ground juniper (*Juniperus communis*) and Bradley's spleenwort (*Asplenium bradleyi*) found in acidic rocks—and a wide variety of flora and fauna make it ideal for natural preservation in the future. Recreational opportunities are picnicking, fishing, camping, rock climbing, and hiking. (*USGS Maps:* Kings Mtn, Gastonia)

• ADDRESS AND ACCESS: Superintendent, Crowder's Mtn State Park, Rte 1, Box 159, Kings Mountain, NC 28086, tel: 704-867-1181. One access from I-85 jct is US-74/29 (E toward Gastonia). Turn R on Freedom Mill Rd (at sign) and after 2.5 mi turn R on Sparrow Spring Rd. Reach the park entrance on R after another 0.6 mi.

*Crowder's Trail (3 mi); Backside Trail (0.9 mi); Tower Trail (2 mi); Rocktop Trail (2.1 mi)* **517–520**

• LENGTH AND DIFFICULTY: 5.2 mi, round-trip, moderate to strenuous

• SPECIAL FEATURES: views from Crowder's Mtn

• TRAILHEAD AND DESCRIPTION: From the park office follow the signs on a well-graded and well-maintained trail N to jct with *Pinnacle Trail* at 0.1 mi. Turn R, follow yellow dot markers through mature hardwood to Freedom Mill Rd (SR-1125) at 0.8 mi. Cross the road, turn L, and skirt the ridge to jct with *Backside Trail* at 2.6 mi. Turn R. (The *Backside Trail* is a 0.9-mi connector trail with *Tower Trail*, which runs from Camp Rotary Rd [SR-1131] to Crowder's Mtn. It is 1.8 mi round-trip. The *Tower Trail* is 4 mi round-trip.) At 2.9 mi climb steps and at 3 mi reach the summit for impressive views from 150-ft cliffs. Return SW on *Rocktop Trail,* whose jct with *Tower Trail* loop is at 3.4 mi; continue on rocky quartzite ridge, descend, and reach SR-1125 at 4.4 mi. Return to the park office parking lot at 5.2 mi.

*Pinnacle Trail (1.7 mi); Turnback Trail (1.2 mi); Fern Nature Trail (0.7 mi); Lake Trail (1 mi)*           **521–524**

- LENGTH AND DIFFICULTY: 4.5 mi combined, easy to strenuous

- SPECIAL FEATURES: views from Kings Pinnacle

- TRAILHEAD AND DESCRIPTION: From the parking lot at the park office go N on a gravel trail 0.1 mi to jct with the *Pinnacle Trail* and *Crowder's Trail.* Take the L (*Bridle Trail* joins the *Pinnacle Trail* for 0.1 mi), and at 0.7 mi pass an access route to walk-in campground. Continue ahead to a rocky ridge treadway and jct with *Turnback Trail,* L, at 1.1 mi. Ahead, climb steeply to ridge at 1.5 mi. (To R is outcrop with vistas.) Descend to a light saddle and climb steeply to Kings Pinnacle at 1.7 mi for scenic views of Crowder's Mtn and pastoral scenes, W. Vegetation has blueberry, scrub oak, pine, sourwood, and sassafras. Backtrack, or take the *Turnback Trail,* R, at the base of mtn, a portion of *Fern Nature Trail* and *Bridle Trail,* in a 1.4-mi return to the park office. The *Fern Nature Trail* is a loop that can be reached either from the office parking area or the picnic parking area. Among the plants are yellow root, sweet pepperbush, pine, and hardwoods. Between the office and the picnic area is a lake parking lot where a 1-mi *Lake Trail* circles the lake.

## ▶ DUKE POWER STATE PARK
### (Iredell County)

Located on the northern shore of Lake Norman, the largest man-made lake in the state, is Duke Power State Park. It has 1,501 acres (mostly donated by Duke Power Company) set aside for swimming, boating, fishing, picnicking, camping, and hiking. The park is divided into two sections, consisting of two peninsulas separated by Hicks Creek. Lake Norman covers 32,510 acres and has a 520-mi shoreline. A 33-site campground is open all year (no hook-ups) with hot showers, flush toilets, tables and grills, and a sanitary dumping station (water off mid-November to mid-March). The park harbors over 800 species of plants. The forest is mainly hardwoods with Virginia and loblolly pines. A subcanopy of sweet gum, dogwood, and sour-wood tops numerous ferns and wildflowers. Among the water-fowl are green-winged teal, blue heron, wood duck, and osprey. Black crappie, bass, and perch are the chief fish. An 0.8-mi access trail, the *Alder Trail*, begins at the parking lot of picnic area #1. It loops around the peninsula among stands of wild-flowers to picnic tables and to the swimming area. (*USGS Map:* Troutman) **525**

• ADDRESS AND ACCESS: Superintendent, Duke Power State Park, Rte 2, Box 224M, Troutman, NC 28166, tel: 704-528-6350. From the town of Troutman (6 mi S of Statesville and 3 mi N of I-77 on US-21/NC-115) go 3.6 mi W on State Park Rd (SR-1330).

• SUPPORT FACILITIES: Groceries, gasoline, and other stores are in Troutman. Statesville has shopping centers, motels, and restaurants.

### *Lakeshore Trail* 526

• LENGTH AND DIFFICULTY: 5.4 mi round-trip, easy

• TRAILHEAD AND DESCRIPTION: Begin at the parking lot of pic-nic area #2, and follow the sign R of the restrooms to white blazes. At a jct, after 0.5 mi, turn either R or L for a loop. If R, follow to Hicks Bridge Rd (SR-1402) and cross near a gate. (It is 0.7 mi S on the road to the campground.) At a red-blazed jct, follow ahead by the lakeside to the end of the peninsula. (For a shortcut, the red blazes can be followed for a 2.5-mi loop.) In the process pass the amphitheater and the campground before continuing around the lakeshore on the return trip.

## ▶ ENO RIVER STATE PARK
### (Durham and Orange Counties)

Eno River State Park is a popular hiking and fishing area along 20 mi of the river between Hillsborough and Durham. Covering 1,965 acres, the park is segmented into four sections (Cate's Ford, Cabe's Land Access, Cole Mill Rd Access, and Pump Station Access), but they are similar, with flood plains, rocky bluffs, and some low-range white water. Remnants of mill dams and rock piles illustrate the settlements of pioneer millers and farmers. Sycamore, river birch, and sweet gum are prominent on the riversides. Wildflowers are profuse; it is a park with a million trout lilies. Among the wildlife are deer, beaver, squirrel, fox, chipmunk, and wild turkey. Anglers will find Roanoke bass, largemouth bass, bream, redhorse sucker, and catfish. Other activities include picnicking, canoeing, and horseback riding. The latter is allowed only at Cate's Ford. Canoe launching points are below Pleasant Green Dam, Cole Mill Rd, and Guess Rd. There is no park campground, but organized group camping is allowed at two primitive campsites at Cate's Ford. A pack-in with supplies (including water and firewood) is necessary, and reservations are required. (*USGS Maps:* Durham NW, Hillsborough)

• ADDRESS AND ACCESS: Superintendent, Eno River State Park, Rte 2, Box 436-C, Durham, NC 27705, tel: 919-383-1686. One access to the park office is 5.3 mi from I-85 in W Durham, N on Cole Mill Rd (SR-1401 in Durham County, which becomes SR-1569 in Orange County). Westbound traffic on I-85 has a ramp to Cole Mill Rd, but eastbound traffic must take the US-70 lane, R, 0.4 mi to turn L, and go under I-85.

*Wilderness Shelter Access Trail (0.7 mi); Eno Nature Trail (0.3 mi); Cox's Mountain Trail (2.3 mi); Fanny's Ford Trail (0.9 mi)*
**527–530**

• LENGTH AND DIFFICULTY: 4.9 mi combined and round-trip, easy

- TRAILHEAD AND DESCRIPTION: All these trails connect and are red-blazed. From the park office drive to the second parking area, R. Follow a well-maintained trail 0.1 mi to a jct L with the *Eno Nature Trail*. (The self-guiding trail is also called the Eno Trace; it loops 0.3 mi through large hardwoods with 12 interpretive posts.) Continue on the *Wilderness Shelter Access Trail* to cross the swinging footbridge over the Eno River. Reach the Wilderness Shelter campsite, L at 0.3 mi. The trail ends at 0.7 mi and *Cox's Mountain Trail*, a loop trail, begins L up the mtn and R on the old road. If hiking L, ascend and pass under a powerline at 0.2 mi to Cox's Mtn. Descend to a stream at 0.5 mi and follow downstream to the Eno River at 0.9 mi. Turn R and go downriver among river birch and beech. Turn R on an old wagon road at 1.3 mi, pass under a powerline, and follow the old road in a forest with beds of running cedar. At 2.1 mi jct with *Fanny's Ford Trail*, L. (*Fanny's Ford Trail* is a 0.9-mi loop by the river bank and the pack-in primitive campsite. The trail's name comes from Fanny Breeze, a beloved black midwife and hospitable neighbor to the river community during and after the Civil War.) To complete *Cox's Mtn Trail* loop, bear R on the old road and return to the point of origin at 2.3 mi.

### *Buckquarter Creek Trail* (1.5 mi); *Holdon's Mill Trail* (2 mi)
### 531–532

- LENGTH AND DIFFICULTY: 3.5 mi combined and round-trip, easy

- TRAILHEAD AND DESCRIPTION: From the park office drive ahead to the first parking lot, R. Walk down to the Eno River, turn R, upriver to a loop fork at 0.1 mi. If hiking R follow an old road, but turn L at 0.2 mi off the road and into a forest of laurel, oak, and pine. Join an old logging road at 0.5 mi. Pass through a cedar grove and curve L to follow downstream of Buckquarter Creek. At 0.8 mi jct R with *Holdon's Mill Trail*. (*Holdon's Mill Trail* crosses Buckquarter Creek on a footbridge and after 160 yd ascends on an old farm road in a hardwood forest. Pass rock piles from early farm clearings. Pass under a powerline and descend to the Eno River at 1 mi. To the R is the site of Holdon's Mill. Return downriver on a scenic path of rocks and wild-flowers near occasional rapids. Rejoin the *Buckquarter Creek Trail* at 2 mi.) Continue downriver and complete the trail after another 0.7 mi.

### Pea Creek Trail *(1.3 mi)*; Cole Mill Trail *(1.2 mi)*; Bobbitt Hole Trail *(2.5 mi)*                                    533–535

* LENGTH AND DIFFICULTY: 5 mi combined and round-trip, easy

* TRAILHEAD AND DESCRIPTION: These trails are at Cole Mill Rd Access, Section 2. Activities are picnicking, fishing, canoeing, and hiking. Access is as described above to the park office, except from I-85 go 3.2 mi and turn L on Umstead Rd (SR-1449). The trails connect, may overlap in parts, and are red-blazed. From the lower end of the parking area follow the sign down to the Eno River at 0.3 mi to *Pea Creek Trail*, L, and *Cole Mill Trail*, R. On the *Pea Creek Trail* pass under the Cole Mill Rd bridge, and at 0.6 mi under a powerline. Rock-hop Pea Creek in an area of wildflowers and ferns. Curve L and recross Pea Creek and complete the loop at 1 mi. Hike upriver on the *Cole Mill Trail*, and at 0.6 mi jct with *Bobbitt Hole Trail* that continues upriver, but *Cole Mill Trail* turns R under a powerline. This route rejoins *Bobbitt Hole Trail*, L, after 300 yd. (From here, R, it is 0.4 mi on *Cole Mill Trail* to the upper parking lot and picnic area.) If taking the higher elev of *Bobbitt Hole Trail*, follow a beautiful wide trail through pine, oak, and holly on the ap-proach to the river. A turn R for a few yd is to a sharp curve in the river and the large scenic pool called Bobbitt Hole after 0.9 mi. Return, downriver, and after 0.6 mi jct with *Cole Mill Trail* for a return to the parking area.

### Old Pump Station Trail                                    536

* LENGTH AND DIFFICULTY: 1.5 mi, easy

* TRAILHEAD AND DESCRIPTION: This loop trail is the Pump Station Access, Section 4. Access is as above, except after I-85, go 2.3 mi and turn R on Rivermont Rd (SR-1402). Drive 0.6 mi to Nancy Rhodes Creek and park, L. Follow the trail sign to

remains of the old Durham Pump Station at 0.4 mi. Turn L upriver of the Eno and make a sharp L at 1 mi. Return under a powerline and reach Rivermont Rd at 1.3 mi. Turn L and follow the road back to the parking area.

### Cabe's Mill Trail                                                      537

*   LENGTH AND DIFFICULTY: 0.9 mi, easy

*   TRAILHEAD AND DESCRIPTION: This loop trail is at Cabe's Land Access, Section 3. Access is as above, except after I-85, go 2.3 mi and turn L on Sprager Rd (SR-1400). Go 1.3 mi, turn R on Howe St (Howell Rd on county maps), and after 0.5 mi reach parking space on R. Follow an old service road to the Eno River, passing carpets of periwinkle, ivy, and running cedar. Reach the river at 0.4 mi, turn L, pass beaver cuts and old mill foundations at 0.4 mi. Cross a small stream and ascend to the point of origin.

## ▶ MEDOC MOUNTAIN STATE PARK
### (Halifax County)

The 2,286-acre park is on the granite fall line of the piedmont where the coastal plain zone begins. The area was named Medoc, for a grape-producing region in France, when a large vineyard was operated here in the nineteenth century. Although locally called a mtn because of its higher than usual elev in the area, it is more a low ridge with the summit at 325 ft above sea level. Winding through the park is Little Fishing Creek with bluegill, largemouth and Roanoke bass, redbreast sunfish, and chain pickerel. Plant life is diverse; it is unusual for laurel to be this far E. Activities include fishing, picnicking, hiking, and tent camping. Camping facilities include tables, grills, tent pads, a central water source, and hot showers (water off mid-November to mid-March). (*USGS Maps:* Hollister, Aurelian Springs, Essex)

*   ADDRESS AND ACCESS: Superintendent, Medoc Mtn State Park, Rte 3, Box 219-G, Enfield, NC 27823, tel: 919-445-2280. Park

office is on Ringwood Rd (SR-1002), 4.6 mi E of NC-561 intersection at Hollister, and 2 mi W of NC-48.

• SUPPORT FACILITIES: Groceries and gasoline are in Hollister.

### Summit Trail (2.9 mi); Dam Site Loop Trail (0.9 mi)    538–539

• LENGTH AND DIFFICULTY: 3.8 mi combined and round-trip, easy

• TRAILHEAD AND DESCRIPTION: From the park office parking lot follow the trail sign, and after 125 yd turn L to begin the loop of *Summit Trail*. At 0.5 mi cross Rocky Spring Branch, and reach the E bank of Little Fishing Creek at 0.7 mi. Turn R and go upstream. Pass a large granite outcropping, the core of the summit, at 1.4 mi. After a few yd the trail ascends R 0.1 mi to the peak, but to include the *Dam Site Loop Trail* continue ahead, N, and pass an artesian well. Pass the ruins of a dam built by the Boy Scouts in the early 1920s, and the ruins of another dam upstream. Circle back to the *Summit Trail* through groves of laurel at 2.5 mi. Follow a gravel road, but turn from it at 3.1 mi. Pass an old cemetery, L, and return to the parking lot.

### Stream Trail (2.2 mi); Discovery Trail (0.1 mi); Bluffs Trail (2.8 mi)    540–542

• LENGTH AND DIFFICULTY: 5.1 mi combined, easy

• TRAILHEAD AND DESCRIPTION: Access to these connecting trails is 2.2 mi W from the park office on SR-1002 to Wood Rd (SR-1322). Turn R and follow the park signs 1 mi to the picnic parking area. From the parking area go 60 yd R of the picnic shelter to the trail sign. *Stream Trail* is L. (The *Bluffs Trail* is R.) *Stream Trail* is a beautiful, well-designed, and carefully maintained trail. It passes through a forest of loblolly pine, oak, and beech with laurel, holly, and aromatic bayberry part of the understory. Rattlesnake orchid, partridge berry, and running cedar are part of the groundcover. At 0.2 mi arrive at Little Fishing Creek and go upstream. At 0.4 mi jct L with a 0.1-mi shortcut named Discovery Trail. At 1.2 mi is a confluence with

Bear Swamp Creek. Enter an open area with kudzu and trumpet vine at 1.6 mi. Exit the forest at 2 mi and cross the picnic grounds to the parking area at 2.2 mi. On *Bluffs Trail,* pass through an old field on a wide manicured trail into a forest. At 0.4 mi turn R downstream by Little Fishing Creek. Pass through large loblolly pine, beech, river birch, and oak. Climb to a steep bluff at 1 mi. Reach the highest bluff (over 60 ft) at 1.4 mi. Descend, bear R on a return ridge, cross a stream at 2.6 mi, and return to the parking lot at 2.8 mi.

## ▶ MORROW MOUNTAIN STATE PARK
### (Stanly County)

This 4,641-acre park is in the heart of the lower piedmont region and in the ancient Uwharrie range. Over 500 million years ago it was covered by a shallow sea in which volcanic islands developed; they later became the hard basalt and rhyolite deposits of this area. Established in 1935, the park is on the Pee Dee River and Lake Tillery. Named after J.M. Morrow, a former landowner, the park is scenic and historic. It offers a nature museum, picnicking, boating, fishing, nature programs, swimming, hiking, equestrian trails, and camping. Family camping, with 106 tent/RV campsites, is open all year with water, showers, and restrooms (no hook-ups, water off mid-November to mid-March). Backpack camping and youth-group tent camping are also provided, but advance registration is necessary. Rental cabins, available from April 1 through October, also require advance registration. Historic in its own right (the state's fourth oldest and a former CCC camp), the restored homestead of Dr. Francis Kron is another example of the park's effort to maintain cultural resources with its natural resources. (*USGS Maps:* Badin, Morrow Mountain)

• ADDRESS AND ACCESS: Superintendent, Morrow Mountain State Park, Rte 5, Box 430, Albemarle, NC 28001, tel: 704-982-4402. An access route from Albemarle is 1.8 mi NE on NC-740 (from jct with NC-24/27/73) to Morrow Mtn Rd (SR-1798) and 2.5 mi to the park entrance.

***Laurel Trail** (0.6 mi); **Morrow Mountain Trail** (3 mi); **Quarry Trail** (0.6 mi); **Hattaway Mountain Trail** (2 mi)*     **543–546**

- LENGTH AND DIFFICULTY: 6.2 mi combined, easy to moderate

- TRAILHEAD AND DESCRIPTION: Park at the Natural History Museum and begin the *Laurel Trail* behind the museum. If going clockwise, stay on the main trail through a mature forest of hardwoods, pine, laurel, and pink azalea for a loop of 0.6 mi. (After 0.2 mi jct L with *Morrow Mountain Trail*, which goes to the top of Morrow Mountain. Ascend W of Sugarloaf Creek and jct with *Sugarloaf Mtn Trail* at 0.7 mi. Follow the *Sugarloaf Mtn Trail* for 0.6 mi and turn L. Cross a small stream and arrive at the E side of Morrow Mtn at 2.5 mi. Ascend steeply on switchback to jct with the *Mtn Loop Trail*. Exit at either the overlook or the picnic area to the Morrow Mtn parking area.)

For the *Quarry Trail,* hike NW from the museum, past the swimming pool, to the picnic area (or drive to the picnic parking area). The loop of 0.6 mi reveals a man-made gorge where volcanic slate of the Slate Belt can be studied. On the *Hattaway Trail,* begin at the pool bathhouse and follow the 2-mi loop trail up and over dry, rocky Hattaway Mtn, the park's third highest. The mature forest has oak, sourwood, maple, and laurel.

***Three Rivers Trail** (0.6 mi); **Fall Mountain Trail** (3.7 mi)*     **547–548**

- LENGTH AND DIFFICULTY: 4.3 mi combined, easy to moderate

- SPECIAL FEATURES: Kron House, river views, rhyolite

- TRAILHEAD AND DESCRIPTION: Park at the boathouse near the boat launch. The *Fall Mountain Trail* begins at the S end of the parking lot. If taking the W route, jct L with *Three Rivers Trail.* (*Three Rivers Trail* is a 0.6-mi self-guiding interpretive trail that crosses the boat-launch road and loops by an open marsh of swamp rose and arrowwood. It passes through a damp forest area and to the riverside for views of the Yadkin, Pee Dee, and Uwharrie rivers.) Continuing on *Fall Mtn Trail,* twice cross an access path to the youth-group tent campsites. At 1.2 mi pass the historic Kron House, L. (Dr. Kron, physician, lived here from 1829 until his death in 1883. His 6,000-acre farm was used for numerous horticultural experiments.) Ascend N to cross the Fall Mtn ridge in a forest of oak, laurel, and scattered pine at 1.7 mi. Descend on a rough area of rhyolite and volcanic outcroppings. There are excellent views of the Falls Dam and the Yadkin River. Silverbell, coneflower, and lip fern are among the flowering plants and ferns. Pass through a crack in a boulder the size of a house, and follow the shore back to the boathouse. Deer and squirrel may be seen in these areas.

### Rocks Trail                                                              549

- LENGTH AND DIFFICULTY: 2.6 mi round-trip, easy

- TRAILHEAD AND DESCRIPTION: Park at the administrative building and begin at the rear of the building, hiking E. Arrive at the family campground and follow the yellow blazes on *Rocks Trail* (which is also a bridle trail). At 0.2 mi from the campground turn L. (Because of numerous campground trails and extra lead-in trails to *Mountain Creek Bridle Trail,* the hiker may need to watch carefully for the yellow blazes.) Pass R of a jct with the bridle trail at 0.6 mi. Continue ahead to an excellent view of the Pee Dee River. Descend over a rocky area to trail's end at 1.3 mi. Return by the same route.

### Sugarloaf Mountain Trail *(2.8 mi)*; Mountain Loop Trail *(0.8 mi)*                                                          550–551

- LENGTH AND DIFFICULTY: 3.6 mi combined, moderate

- TRAILHEAD AND DESCRIPTION: (These trails connect with the *Morrow Mtn Trail,* bridle trails, and Morrow Mtn Rd.) Park at the parking lot R and E of the staff residences. Follow the trail sign for hikers, bearing L from the bridle trail. Cross two small streams and Morrow Mtn Rd. Ascend and follow the NW ridgeside of Sugarloaf Mtn (858 ft). Jct L with *Morrow Mtn Trail* at 1.4 mi. Turn R (jointly with *Morrow Mtn Trail*) and after 2 mi continue R (*Morrow Mtn Trail* goes L in its ascent to the top of Morrow Mtn), cross Morrow Mtn Rd at 2.2 mi, cross a stream at 2.7 mi, and enter a field near the parking lot to complete the loop. For the *Mountain Loop Trail,* drive to the top of Morrow Mtn. The trailhead can be found at the picnic shelter or the overlook. It leads to a loop around the peak (938 ft). The trail is graded, with bridges over the ravines. It also connects on the E side with *Morrow Mtn Trail,* described above. From Morrow Mtn are views E to Lake Tillery and Dennis Mtn (the route of the *Uwharrie Trail*) in the Uwharrie National Forest (see Chapter 4).

## ▶ RAVEN ROCK STATE PARK
### (Harnett County)

Established in 1970, Raven Rock State Park is a large 5,500-acre wilderness-type forest. The Cape Fear River runs through its center. A major geological feature of the area is the 152-ft-high crystalline rock jutting out toward the river. Ravens once nested here, thus the park's name. It is unusual for rhododendron and laurel to grow this far E with a diverse and long list of piedmont and coastal-plain plants. The area has the largest salamander population E of the Appalachians. Some of the wild animals and birds are osprey, eagle, owls, squirrel, raccoon, and deer. Prominent fish are largemouth bass, catfish, and sunfish. Activities are picnicking, hiking, fishing, and primitive backpack camping. (All gear, including water, must be carried to the camps. Registration is required at the park office.) There are bridle trails on the N side of the river; directions and regulations are available from the park office. (*USGS Map:* Mamers)

• ADDRESS AND ACCESS: Superintendent, Raven Rock State Park, Rte 3, Box 1005, Lillington, NC 27546, tel: 919-893-4888. Access to the park is 3 mi off US-421 on Raven Rock Park Rd (SR-1314), 6 mi W of Lillington.

### Raven Rock Loop Trail                      552–556

• LENGTH AND DIFFICULTY: 2.1 mi, easy

• CONNECTING TRAILS:
*American Beech Nature Trail* (0.5 mi, easy)

*Little Creek Loop Trail* (1.4 mi, easy)
*Fish Traps Trail* (1.2 mi round-trip, easy)
*Northington's Ferry Trail* (2.2 mi round-trip, easy)

• SPECIAL FEATURE: Raven Rock overhang

• TRAILHEAD AND DESCRIPTION: From the parking lot follow the Raven Rock sign on the E side of the lot. Jct R with the *American Beech Nature Trail.* (The nature trail descends and crosses a small stream through poplar, sweet gum, red maple, beech, sweet bay, laurel, and oak. It returns on the E side of the picnic area.) At 0.8 mi the *Raven Rock Loop Trail* jct R with *Little Creek Loop Trail.* (It descends downstream by Little Creek for 0.7 mi to a canoe camp. Downriver it is another 0.5 mi to a backpack group campsite. Reach scenic Raven Rock at 0.9 mi. Descend on stairways to the riverbank and rock overhangs. Return on the steps, but take a turn R at the top. Arrive at a scenic overlook of the Cape Fear River at 1.1 mi. Jct sharply R with *Fish Traps Trail* and *Northington's Ferry Trail* at 1.7 mi. (*Fish Traps Trail* leads to a rock outcropping at 1.1 mi beside the river. [Indians placed trap baskets at the rapids to catch fish. Backtrack.] *Northington's Ferry Trail* follows a wide, easy route to the mouth of Campbells Creek [also called Camels Creek], site of the Cape Fear River crossing. The ferry served as a crossing between Raleigh and Fayetteville as early as 1770. Backtrack.) Continue on the *Raven Rock Loop Trail* on an old woods road to the parking area.

### *Campbell Creek Loop Trail* (5.1 mi); *Lanier Falls Trail* (0.4 mi) 557–558

• LENGTH AND DIFFICULTY: 5.4 mi, combined round-trip, easy to moderate

• TRAILHEAD AND DESCRIPTION: At the parking lot follow the old service road N 45 yd and turn L into young growth that enters an older forest. Descend gradually in an oak-hickory forest to a footbridge over Campbell Creek at 0.7 mi. Here the trail loops R or L. If taking the L route ascend and descend on low ridges through sections of laurel to jct with the *Buckhorn*

*Trail* at 2.1 mi. (See *Buckhorn Trail* in Chapter 14.) A park service road comes in from the L and joins *Campbell Creek Loop Trail* R. Descend to the primitive campsites at 2.3 mi, L, and *Lanier Falls Trail,* L, at 2.5 mi. (The 0.2-mi *Lanier Falls Trail* leads to a scenic rock outcropping at the Cape Fear River. Backtrack.) Continue the trail to the mouth of Campbell Creek and follow upstream to rejoin the access route at the bridge at 4.4 mi.

## ► UMSTEAD STATE PARK
### (Wake County)

William B. Umstead State Park covers 5,334 acres—3,979 in the Crabtree Creek section and 1,355 in the Reedy Creek section. Among the six largest state parks, it is a valuable oasis in the center of a fast developing metropolitan area. Adjoining on the W is the Raleigh-Durham Airport, on the N is US-70, and on the S is I-40. A former CCC camp, the park's original 5,088 acres were deeded to the state by the U.S. Government in fee simple of one dollar in 1943. It was designated Crabtree Creek State Park, but in 1955 it was named in honor of the former governor. The park lies in the Crabtree Creek watershed; Sycamore Creek (N) and Reedy Creek (S) flow into the drainage. Large stands of mature oak, poplar, and loblolly pine provide a canopy for dogwood, redbud, laurel, and sourwood. Beaver, deer, squirrel, and raccoon are among the mammals. Recreational activities are fishing, camping, hiking, nature studies, and horseback riding. There are four organized group camps; swimming is provided for group campers only. (*USGS Maps:* Cary, Raleigh West, Durham SE, Bayleaf)

• ADDRESS AND ACCESS: Superintendent, Umstead State Park, Rte 8, Box 130, Raleigh, NC 27612, tel: 919-787-3033. Access to the Crabtree Creek section entrance is on US-70, 6 mi W of the jct with US-1/64 on the Benson Beltline. The Reedy Creek section entrance is on I-40, 4 mi W of the jct with US-1/64 on the Benson Beltline.

### Sal's Branch Trail (2.4 mi); Umstead Nature Trail North (1.1 mi) 559–560

- LENGTH AND DIFFICULTY: 3.6 mi combined, easy

- TRAILHEAD AND DESCRIPTION: In the Crabtree Creek section, park at the large picnic area parking lot (nearest the lake). At the lower corner follow R a wide trail with steps 190 yd to *Sal's Branch Trail*, R. (Ahead, at the end of the steps, R, is the access to the boathouse, and L is the *Nature Trail* [Crabtree Creek Section]). Proceed on the orange-blazed trail through loblolly pine, running cedar, and Christmas ferns to a service road at 0.5 mi. Cross the road, pass Sal's Branch beech grove at 0.8 mi, and turn sharply uphill at 1.9 mi. Complete the loop at 2.4 mi. The *Nature Trail*, white-blazed, follows the lake edge briefly to the dam, descends, and goes upstream, L, on Pots Branch to a jct L to the picnic area. Ahead it goes jointly a short distance with *Sycamore Creek Trail*. It passes an old dam and stone foundations built by the CCC. Turn L from *Sycamore Creek Trail* and arrive at the small picnic area and another parking lot at 1 mi. (The self-guiding nature trail has numbered posts. A booklet from the ranger provides descriptions.) Keep L and return to the original parking lot.

### Sycamore Trail (6.5 mi); Company Mill Trail (3.5 mi) 561–562

- LENGTH AND DIFFICULTY: 10 mi combined, easy

- TRAILHEAD AND DESCRIPTION: From the parking area, described above, enter the large picnic area in a pine grove. Begin the yellow-blazed *Sycamore Trail* (and access to the self-guiding nature trail) at the L corner of the large picnic shelter. Cross a stream; cross park roads at 0.5 mi and among large oaks at 1.6 mi. At 1.9 mi arrive at the trail's fork that begins a loop. If hiking R, cross a park road (also a bridle trail) at 2.3 mi. Cross Sycamore Creek on a footbridge and jct with the blue-blazed *Company Mill Trail*, R and L, at 3 mi. (A loop can be made of 3.5 mi). Turn L and jointly follow *Company Mill Trail* along a narrow path on the stream bluff for 0.2 mi to a fork. (*Company Mill*

*Trail* goes R.) Cross Sycamore Creek on a footbridge. Pass through a scenic area (blazes may be green) of rocks, laurel, tall hardwoods, and wildflowers (such as wild orchids and crested dwarf iris) for 1.4 mi to complete the loop. Return to the point of origin at 6.5 mi. If taking the *Company Mill Trail* at the first upstream connection, ascend gradually to cross a bridle trail at 0.8 mi. Descend and reach the bank of Crabtree Creek at 1.6 mi. Follow the creek bank downstream to jct with *Beech Trail,* R, at 2.2 mi. Here is the George Linn Mill site. (At this jct the creek can be forded under normal water flow. A footbridge is planned. *Beech Trail* is an 0.8-mi exit route to the Reedy Creek Section of the park.) Continue ahead on the trail's loop to rejoin the *Sycamore Trail* at 3.3 mi. Return to the point of origin at the parking lot at 9.6 mi.

### Beech Trail *(1.6 mi round-trip);* Umstead Nature Trail South *(1.2 mi)* 563–564

• LENGTH AND DIFFICULTY: 2.8 mi combined, easy

• TRAILHEAD AND DESCRIPTION: From the Reedy Creek Section parking area, descend to the picnic area and jct with the yellow-blazed *Beech Trail,* R, and the *Nature Trail* (Reedy Creek Section), L. (The *Nature Trail* has 25 descriptive plaques about the flora and fauna.) Descend to Crabtree Creek at the George Linn Mill site at 0.8 mi. (Unless a footbridge has been constructed, wading across the rocky stream is necessary for a connection with *Company Mill Trail,* described above.) Backtrack. (The W terminus of *Loblolly Trail* is at the Reedy Creek Section parking area, described under Raleigh, Chapter 13.)

# 11.

## State Forests, Natural Areas, Historic Sites, and Other State Properties

*If no one knows the importance of preserving a beautiful place, that place is not likely to be preserved. . . .* —Ansel Adams

In addition to the state parks, the Division of Parks and Recreation in the Department of Natural Resources and Community Development (DNRCD) administers 11 natural areas, two of which have visitor centers and designated trails. They are Theodore Roosevelt Natural Area and Weymouth Woods-Sandhills Nature Preserve. (The other natural areas, in order of acquisition, are Baytree Lake and White Lake, 1929; Chowan Swamp and a tract of Dismal Swamp, 1974; Hemlock Bluffs, Masonboro Island, and Mitchell's Mill, 1976; Bushy Lake, 1978; and a tract of marshland on Baldhead Island, 1979.) An increase in public pressure to preserve the natural areas prompted the state in 1963 to adopt principles for the Natural Area System. Among the principles are to preserve, protect, extend, and develop the natural areas of scientific, aesthetic, and geological value.

The Division of Forest Resources (another division of the DNRCD) administers five educational state forests. They are Bladen Lakes, Clemmons, Holmes, Rendezvous Mountain, and Tuttle. The locations are diverse, but their purpose and facilities are generally the same. For example, they all have interpretive displays and trails, primitive walk-in campsites, and picnic areas. They serve as outdoor-living and environmental centers that teachers and other group leaders use as classrooms. Arrangements can be made with each RS for ranger-conducted programs. Campsites are free but require permits. Open seasons are March 15 to November 30 with the exception of Bladen Lakes, which is open March 1. All are closed on Mondays and Tuesdays. Also within the DNRCD (as a separate unit and no longer under the Division of Parks and Recreation) is the N.C. Zoological Park.

There are 24 state historic sites, administered by the Historic Sites Section, Division of Archives and History, Department of Cultural Resources. The sites provide visitor centers with artifacts, exhibits, and multimedia programs about such historic places as the Duke Homestead, Tryon Palace, and the Thomas Wolfe Memorial. The majority of the sites do not have admission charges. Some of the sites have trails and are described in this chapter. For more information, contact the Department of Cultural Resources, Raleigh, NC 27611, tel: 919-733-7862. Other state properties, such as the state aquariums at Pine Knoll Shores and Fort Fisher, are operated by the Office of Marine Affairs, Department of Administration. Trails at these sites are also described in this chapter. For more information contact the Office of Marine Affairs, 417 N Blount St, Raleigh, NC 27601, tel: 919-733-2290. Although the majority of trails in this chapter are short, they are ostensibly important walks for educational and cultural purposes.

## ▶ THEODORE ROOSEVELT NATURAL AREA
### (Carteret County)

This natural area of 265 acres on the island of Bogue Banks is set aside to preserve a maritime forest of laurel oak and live oak, red bay, red cedar, swamp red maple, and red ash, especially in the swales. Other plant life includes eight species of ferns, wild olive, and the toothache tree (*Zanthoxylum americana*). There are marshes (freshwater, brackish, and saltwater) and bird sanctuaries, particularly for warblers. The *Hoffman Trail,* a 0.4-mi loop, provides a visit over the dunes by the swales and the East Pond. The trail entrance is at the SE corner of the Marine

Resources Center. The property was established in 1971 from a gift by the grandchildren of President Theodore Roosevelt. Also here is the N.C. Aquarium at Pine Knoll Shores. It houses exhibits, aquariums, a public library, and meeting facilities. Field trips, boat trips, workshops, multimedia programs, and more are presented. Admission is free; it is open year-round. (*USGS Map:* Mansfield) **565**

• ADDRESSES AND ACCESS: Theodore Roosevelt Natural Area, c/o Fort Macon State Park, PO Box 127, Atlantic Beach, NC 28512, tel: 919-726-3775. N.C. Aquarium at Pine Knolls Shores, Atlantic Beach, NC 28512, tel: 919-247-4003. Access is on NC-58, 5 mi W of Atlantic Beach.

## ▶ WEYMOUTH WOODS–SANDHILLS NATURE PRESERVE
### (Moore County)

The 425-acre woodland preserve is E of the city limits of Southern Pines. Most of the acreage was donated by Mrs. James Boyd in 1963. There are more than 500 species of plants (including 135 species of wildflowers), including French mulberry, longleaf pine, turkey oak, and bays. Among the wildlife are deer, squirrel, raccoon, beaver, owls, and numerous songbirds. Butterflies are prominent, for example, black and palamedes swallowtails, painted lady, and hairstreaks. The sandy ridges, popularly known as the Sandhills Region, were formed from sediments of clay, sand, and gravel deposited by streams in the region millions of years ago when the area was part of an inland sea. The preserve has a Natural History Museum, and naturalists provide illustrated lectures and tours. Open daily Monday to Saturday. (*USGS Maps:* Southern Pines, Niagara)

• ADDRESS AND ACCESS: Superintendent, Weymouth Woods-Sandhills Nature Preserve, 400 N Fort Bragg Rd, Southern Pines, NC 28387, tel: 919-692-2167. In S Southern Pines turn off US-1 at Magnolia Drive (SR-2053) and go 1.2 mi to jct with Fort Bragg Rd (SR-2074). Turn L and go 1.7 mi to entrance, L.

***Bowers Bog Trail*** *(0.5 mi);* ***Pine Barrens Trail*** *(1 mi);* ***Gum Swamp Trail*** *(0.4 mi);* ***Holly Road Trail*** *(1.9 mi);* ***Pine Island Trail*** *(0.5 mi)*                                                                                                566–570

- LENGTH AND DIFFICULTY: 4.3 mi combined, easy

- TRAILHEAD AND DESCRIPTION: *Bowers Bog Trail* is a loop nature trail E of the museum and parking area. Begin the *Pine Barrens Trail* W of the museum and follow the white blazes through prominent displays of longleaf pine, turkey oak, bracken, and blueberry. The *Gum Swamp Trail* loop adjoins it at the N side, but it contains chiefly hardwoods. From the *Gum Swamp Trail* begin the 1.9-mi *Holly Road Trail.* After crossing James Creek at 40 yd, turn L or R at 0.1 mi on the yellow-blazed trail. If you turn R, reach a jct with the *Pine Island Trail* loop at 0.2 mi, R. (This area is lush with plant life in a swampy area of James Creek. The trail crosses James Creek twice and some tributaries.) Continue on *Holly Road Trail,* cross a stream and soon a fire road. At 1.4 mi pass L of a spring. Complete the loop at 1.9 mi, and return on the E or W sides of the *Gum Swamp Trail* loop and the *Pine Barrens Trail* loop.

▶ **BLADEN LAKES EDUCATIONAL STATE FOREST**
  **(Bladen County)**

The 32,237-acre coastal forest is spread between South River and the Cape Fear River in the bay lakes area. Within the general boundaries are Salters Lake, Singletary Lake, and Jones Lake, but the forest office, exhibits, trails, and picnic areas are concentrated near the jct of NC-242 and Smith Rd (SR-1511), across the road from Jones Lake State Park. The primitive walk-in campsites are 3.7 mi SE on Smith Rd. *Smith Swamp Trail* is a slow 3.5-mi auto tour (14 mph) past exhibit stations, and the 0.4-mi *Turnbull Creek Trail* is a manicured, interpretive foot trail. An approach to them is on Smith Rd, 0.2 mi E from the forest office. If the gate to the road is locked, walk the sandy road and at 0.2 mi pass the Naval Stores Industry exhibit, L. Turn L at the fork in a pine plantation and reach the picnic area (with exhibits and kiosk), R. *Turnbull Creek Trail* is L, opposite the picnic area. The trail dips to a natural spring and circles through Spanish moss, water and turkey oaks, fetterbush, and fragrant nettle (*Cnidoscolus stimulosus*). Turnbull Creek is on the N side. Fox squirrels (which feed on the large seed cones of the longleaf pine) may be seen here. (*USGS Map:* Elizabethtown North) **571–572**

• ADDRESS AND ACCESS: Forest Supervisor, Bladen Lakes Educational State Forest, Rte 2, Box 942, Elizabethtown, NC 28337, tel: 919-588-4964. The office is on NC-242, 4 mi N of Elizabethtown (0.6 mi N of Jones Lake State Park) and 9 mi S of Ammons.

## ▶CLEMMONS EDUCATIONAL STATE FOREST (Johnston County)

A forest of 307 acres between Clayton and Garner, it has study sites for rocks, trees, wildlife, watersheds, and forest management. Opened in 1976, it represents a transitional zone between the piedmont and coastal plain. A forestry center and exhibits explain the varied facilities of the area. Picnicking and group primitive camping facilities are available, and sections of the trails can be used by the handicapped. There are 15 ranger-conducted programs for visiting groups to choose from. The 2.2-mi *Clemmons Demonstration Trail* begins at the parking lot. Follow the signs 100 yd to a forest information board and another 100 yd to the forestry center and trail signboard. Turn R, and follow the red blazes. At 0.2 mi cross a stream near the 0.1-mi *Watershed Loop Trail.* At 0.3 mi pass a shortcut trail and pass it again at 1.3 mi. The 0.8-mi yellow-blazed *Clemmons Talking Tree Trail* loops from the trail signboard. An exceptionally well-designed trail, it provides push-button devices for recorded botanical information. All trails have easy treadway. (*USGS Map:* Clayton) **573–575**

• ADDRESS AND ACCESS: Forest Supervisor, Clemmons Educational State Forest, 2411 Garner Rd, Clayton, NC 27520, tel:

919-553-5651. Access is on Old US-70 (SR-1004), 1.5 mi N of Clayton city limits and 4.2 mi N of US-70.

## ▶ HOLMES EDUCATIONAL STATE FOREST
### (Henderson County)

The forest is named in honor of Canadian-born John S. Holmes (1868–1958), who served as the state's first forester from 1915 to 1945. The forest covers 231 acres, 25 of which are rich bottomland and 206 on steep mountainsides and rounded summits. It was a CCC camp in the 1930s, and it became a state forest in 1972. More than 125 species of flowering plants have been identified. Facilities are available for picnicking, hiking, and nature study. Primitive camping is provided on the mountaintop; it has road access. Approach to the trailheads is 0.1 mi from the main parking lot to the forestry center and trail-system signboard. For the 2.8-mi *Cliffside Demonstration Trail* with study sites, follow the red-blazed loop trail through hardwoods and white pines on switchbacks to reach the campground shortcut trail at 1 mi. Keep L, pass a small pond, cross a forest road, and jct with the shortcut, R, at 1.5 mi. Pass a scenic overlook, L, and begin a descent on switchbacks for a return to the forestry center. Also starting at the forestry center is the *Holmes Talking Tree Trail,* an 0.8-mi loop. On a green-blazed route, pass a variety of trees with audio devices explaining forest history, use, growth, and values. Cross cascades at 0.4 mi. (*USGS Map: Standing Stone Mtn*)                    **576–577**

• ADDRESS AND ACCESS: Forest Supervisor, Rte 4, Box 308, Hendersonville, NC 28739, tel: 704-692-0100. Access is from Penrose on US-64. Take Featherstone Creek Rd (SR-1528) for 2.6 mi to Little River. Turn L on Crab Creek Rd, which becomes Kanuga Rd (SR-1127), and go 4.2 mi to entrance, R. Another route is from downtown Hendersonville. From jct of US-64E and US-25S go S 0.5 mi on US-25S to jct R with Caswell St, which becomes Kanuga Rd (SR-1127), and go 10 mi.

# ▶RENDEZVOUS MOUNTAIN EDUCATIONAL STATE FOREST
## (Wilkes County)

In 1926 Judge Thomas Finley donated the 142-acre Rendezvous Mtn to the state as a park, but the state never developed it. Thirty years later it became a state forest. It is a scenic hardwood forest with rugged terrain at the foothills of the Blue Ridge Mtns. There are facilities for picnicking, hiking, and nature study (primitive camping is planned). After entering the gate, park at the first parking lot, R. Cross the road (R of the picnic area), and follow the 0.2-mi *Table Mountain Pine Sawmill Trail*. The loop has historic exhibits of timber-cutting equipment, logging methods, and a sawmill from the 1950s. At the second parking lot, R, the 0.6-mi *Rendezvous Mountain Talking Tree Trail* loops through a beautiful forest of hardwood, laurel, pinxter, and flame azalea with scattered rhododendron. Descent is moderate to steep. Also, from the parking lot is the 275-yd *Firetower Trail*, which ascends N past the forest office to the old fire tower (2,445 ft) with scenic views. (*USGS Map:* Purlear)
**578–580**

• ADDRESS AND ACCESS: Forest Supervisor, Rendezvous Mtn Educational State Forest, Box 42, Purlear, NC 28665, tel: 919-667-5072. From NC-16 in Millers Creek (5.3 mi NW of Wilkesboro), turn W on Old US-421 Rd (SR-1304) and go 2.8 mi to jct with Purlear Rd (SR-1346). Turn R on Purlear Rd and go 1.8 mi, turn L on Rendezvous Mtn Rd (SR-1348), and ascend to the forest entrance after 1.3 mi.

# ▶TUTTLE EDUCATIONAL STATE FOREST
## (Caldwell County)

The forest honors Lelia Judson Tuttle (1878–1967), a teacher and missionary whose property was deeded to the state in 1973. On the 160-acre forest are facilities for picnicking, hiking, nature study, and primitive camping. As at the other state forests, ranger programs are designed for groups from kindergarten to adults. Also, workshops are provided for continuing-education credit. Trail access is from the parking and picnic area. The easy 1.9-mi *Tuttle Demonstration Trail* follows signs past the forestry center to a signboard at 0.1 mi. Turn L on the red-blazed trail through pines (white, Virginia, and shortleaf) and hardwoods. At 0.7 mi jct with a shortcut, R. Pass Sleepy Hollow School site and go through the campsites for a return to the parking area. *Tuttle Talking Tree Trail* loops 0.6 mi on a green-blazed interpretive trail from the forestry center. The audio devices play recordings about forest succession and species of trees. (*USGS Maps:* Morganton North)     **581–582**

• ADDRESS AND ACCESS: Forest Supervisor, Tuttle Educational State Forest, Rte 6, Box 417, Lenoir, NC 28645, tel: 704-758-5645. Access is on Nick Rd (SR-1331), 0.8 mi off NC-18 (near the Burke/Caldwell county line), 6 mi SW of Lenoir.

## ▶ BENTONVILLE BATTLEGROUND STATE HISTORIC SITE
### (Johnston County)

After the capture of Savannah December 20, 1864, General William T. Sherman's troops turned N to join General U.S. Grant's troops in Virginia. On the way General Sherman continued a swath of destruction, particularly in Columbia, South Carolina, the capital city and seedbed of the Secessionist movement. Every public building in the city was destroyed (whether by accident or design) on February 17, 1865, except the new and unfinished statehouse. The Battle of Bentonville is significant because it was the last major Confederate offensive and the largest ever fought in North Carolina. General Joseph E. Johnston's troops, with less than half the number of Union troops, fought bravely but lost during March 19 to 21. They withdrew toward Smithfield with plans to protect Raleigh, the state's capital city, but the Union forces did not pursue them.

• ADDRESS AND ACCESS: Bentonville Battleground State Historic Site, PO Box 27, Newton Grove, NC 28366, tel: 919-594-0789.

Entrance is 1.4 mi off US-701 on Cox Mill Rd (SR-1008), 3 mi N of Newton Grove.

### *Bentonville Battleground History Trail (0.2 mi); Bentonville Battleground Trail (13.4 mi)*     **583—584**

- LENGTH AND DIFFICULTY: 13.6 mi combined, easy

- SPECIAL FEATURES: 27 history stations

- TRAILHEAD AND DESCRIPTION: The *Bentonville Battlefield History Trail* is a self-guiding walk that begins near the field fortifications exhibit and leads to the original trenches dug by Union forces on the first day of the battle. From the historic Harper House, begin the longer route by crossing Cox Mill Rd (SR-1008) between trailmarkers #3 and #4 and follow the public road. At 0.6 mi turn L on SR-1192. Reach a jct with SR-1008, turn R, and at 2.7 mi see the United Daughters of the Confederacy monument to the Confederate soldiers. Turn L on SR-1194, which later merges with Devils Race Track Rd (SR-1009), and arrive at the Bentonville Community Building at 5.6 mi. Continue to marker #23 at 5.8 mi; here Confederate cavalry was halted by the flooded Mill Creek. Return to the Community Building and take the road L, following 0.1 mi and turning R at marker #24. At 7.1 mi turn L at marker #25, pass markers #26 and #27, and turn R on a private dirt field road near a feed bin at 7.9 mi. Continue by the field's edge for 0.7 mi to a paved road and turn L at marker #28. Reach SR-1008 at 9 mi; turn R and go 0.6 mi to Ebenezer Church to jct with SR-1009. (A country store is across the road.) Turn R and go 0.5 mi to marker #20, return to SR-1008 at 10.6 mi. Follow it to the UDC marker at SR-1194 jct at 11.6 mi. Return on SR-1008 to the starting point for a total of 13.4 mi.

### ▶ FORT DOBBS STATE HISTORIC SITE
### (Iredell County)

Named for Royal Governor Arthur Dobbs, the fort was built (ca 1750s) during the French and Indian War to protect the settlers. Excavations of the vanished fort show a moat, cellar, magazine area, and well. A pioneer cottage has exhibits of the period. The 0.5-mi *Fort Dobbs Nature Trail* goes through a hardwood forest with footbridges over small ravines. Ferns and wildflowers are prominent among the spicebushes.          **585**

• ADDRESS AND ACCESS: Fort Dobbs State Historic Site, Rte 9, Box A-415, Statesville, NC 28677, tel: 704-873-5866. From the jct of I-40 and US-21 in Statesville, go N 1.2 mi on US-21, turn L on Fort Dobbs Rd (SR-1930), and go 1.3 mi to entrance, R.

## ▶ REED GOLD MINE STATE HISTORIC SITE
### (Cabarrus County)

Gold was discovered here, accidentally, when in 1799 Conrad Reed, son of John Reed, found a 17-pound yellow rock at Little Meadow Creek, which flowed through the family farm. It was the first gold discovery in the nation. A silversmith in Concord, 10 mi away, could not identify the substance, so the Reeds used it as a doorstop. In 1802 a Fayetteville jeweler recognized it as gold. Soon the Reeds formed a partnership with workers for mining. Underground mining began in 1831 and ended in 1912. Owned now by the state, there is a large visitor center with exhibits, illustrations, and a guided tour to both the surface and a 500-ft underground mining area. The tour may also continue to an area of archeological work and to a reconstructed stamp mill. The mill crushes ore into a fine powder and is operable in the summer. (Flat shoes are recommended for the gravel mine floor and steep steps.) The self-guided *Reed Gold Mine Nature Trail* is an easy 0.4-mi loop from the Upper Hill mining area past the Lower Hill and back to the visitor center. Markers indicate sites of mining shafts and adits. Vegetation includes oak, maple, holly, cedar, ferns, and crane fly orchids. The site is open daily and on Sunday afternoons. It is closed on Monday. There is no admission charge.          **586**

• ADDRESS AND ACCESS: Reed Gold Mine State Historic Site, Rte 2, Box 101,.Stanfield, NC 28163, tel: 919-786-8337. From the jct of US-601/NC-200, 6 mi S of Concord, take NC-200 E 3.5 mi. Turn R on Pine Bluff Church Rd (SR-1100) and go 2 mi. From Locust at NC-24/27, take NC-200 W 4.5 mi and turn L.

▶ **NORTH CAROLINA AQUARIUM/FORT FISHER**
(New Hanover County)

The 25-acre aquarium houses fish tanks, exhibits, conference rooms, research laboratories, and the University of North Carolina Sea Grant offices. It is one of three similar facilities in the state. The Pine Knoll Shores Aquarium is described under the Theodore Roosevelt Natural Area in the beginning of this chapter. Open M-F from 9–5, S-S from 1–5; closed on holidays. Free admission. Trails open year-round. (*USGS Map:* Kure Beach)

• ADDRESS AND ACCESS: N.C. Aquarium, Box 130, Kure Beach, NC 28449, tel: 919-458-8257. Entrance is from US-421, 1 mi S of Fort Fisher and 5.6 mi S of Carolina Beach State Park.

*Marsh Trail (0.8 mi); Hermit Trail (2 mi)*          **587–588**

• LENGTH AND DIFFICULTY: 2.8 mi round-trip, combined, easy

• TRAILHEAD AND DESCRIPTION: From the parking lot follow the signs, cross a boardwalk among yaupon, catbrier, and wax myrtle to a marsh meadow. Reach a fork; the *Marsh Trail* is L, the *Hermit Trail* is R. If taking the *Hermit Trail,* reach a side trail, R, at 0.7 mi. (The 0.1-mi side trail goes to Hermit's Bunker, named for George Harrill, the "Fort Fisher hermit," who lived off the land in this salt marsh for many years.) For another 0.7 mi round-trip, the trail goes to the Hermit Basin. After returning to the main trail, reach a jct with *Marsh Trail* at 1.7 mi. Turn L for a return to the parking lot at 2 mi, or turn R to make a loop on the *Marsh Trail* for 0.8 mi. Pass a tidal basin and swales to the Atlantic Ocean and return by the pond to the parking area. Among the shore and marsh birds are brown pelican, willet, egret, and blackbird.

# PART V

# Trails in Counties and Municipalities

# 12.

## County Parks and Recreation Areas

*Trails are a growing resource in a limited resource.*
—Elisabeth Hair

Fifty-two percent of the state's 100 counties have parks and recreation departments. They operate as a separate public unit in each county, usually under a county board of commissioners. A few counties and cities combine their departments or resources to provide joint services or special projects. Examples are Clinton and Sampson, Lincolnton and Lincoln, Henderson and Vance, and Sanford and Lee counties. Because of population needs and available funding, each county park varies in size, facilities, and scope from a simple day-use picnic area to complex recreational centers such as Tanglewood in Forsyth County. When the President's Commission on Americans Outdoors reported its findings in 1986, it showed rapid expansion in a number of the state's cities. With an increase in the population and less space in the city for outdoor recreation, the county parks are becoming more vital for green space. The report also showed a demographic trend to a fast-growing older segment of the population and a desire for recreation closer to home. Mecklenburg and Forsyth are examples of counties preparing for this trend. Mecklenburg's diverse park and greenway system will become what Elisabeth Hair (former chair of the board of county commissioners) called "Charlotte's green necklace." In Forsyth County, greenways will connect the county's towns to a greenway network in the city of Winston-Salem. Numerous county park and rec departments have constructed physical-fitness trails. Others, such as Craven County's rec and parks department, do not own property but maintain exercise trails on public school property. For the addresses and telephone numbers of the state's counties and cities with parks, contact the Division of Parks and Rec, PO Box 27687, Raleigh, NC 27687, tel: 919–733-PARK for the *North Carolina Parks and Recreation Directory.*

## ▶ ALAMANCE COUNTY
### Cedarock Park

The 414-acre park contains the Cedarock Park Center (for conferences and workshops in the Paul Stevens homestead); horseshoe courts; frisbee golf course; basketball courts; picnic area; playgrounds; fishing; horseback-riding trails; walk-in campsites (primitive with permits); and hiking trails. The trails are color coded and create interconnecting loops. There is also a physical-fitness trail that begins at picnic shelter #3. The park is open all year (*USGS Map:* Snow Camp)

• ADDRESS AND ACCESS: Director, Rec and Parks Dept, 217 College St, Graham, NC 27253, tel: 919-228-0506 or 919-227-8298. From jct of I-85/NC-49 in Burlington (exit #145A from the W, #145 from the E), go 6 mi S on NC-49 to jct with Friendship-Patterson Mill Rd, and turn L. Go 0.3 mi to park entrance L. The RS is at the first house (Garrett homestead), R.

### *Cedarock Trail (2.2 mi); Ecology Trail (0.5 mi)*      589–590

• LENGTH AND DIFFICULTY: 2.9 mi combined, easy

• TRAILHEAD AND DESCRIPTION: From the picnic parking lot, begin at shelter #3 at the trail signboard. Follow the yellow-blazed trail through a hardwood forest with scattered cedars and pines. At 0.2 mi cross Rock Creek on a footbridge and join the brown-blazed *Ecology Trail.* At 0.5 mi the *Ecology Trail* turns L to make a loop. (To the R you have a choice on either a blue-blazed trail or a red-blazed trail to make a loop to a tent camp-site before returning to the main trail.) Continue on the *Cedarock Trail,* leave the forest, pass through a meadow, re-enter the forest, and reach an old mill dam, L. Cross Rock Creek at Elmo's Crossing and enter a meadow of wildflowers, including the Star of Bethlehem (*Ipheion uniflorum*), at 2 mi. Pass a maintenance area to the park road and return to the parking lot.

## ▶ FORSYTH COUNTY
### Horizons Park

The 492-acre park is one of ten county rec areas and historic sites that encircle the city of Winston-Salem. The county and the city have been leading the state in parks and recreation with 20 acres per 1,000 citizens. Horizons Park is an example of how well they are serving the public. The facility has a large picnic area (with shelters), a children's playground, softball field, 18-hole frisbee golf course (the state's first), and hiking trails. (*USGS Map:* Walkertown)

• ADDRESS AND ACCESS: Director, Parks and Rec, 680 West 4th St, Winston-Salem, NC 27101, tel: 919-727-2946. One access is from the jct of US-52 and NC-8 (N of the city). Follow NC-8 4.2 mi and turn R on Memorial Industrial School Dr (SR-1920) 1.1 mi to the entrance, R.

### Horizons Hiking Trail *(2.5 mi); Horizons Nature Trail (0.1 mi)*
### 591–592

• LENGTH AND DIFFICULTY: 2.6 mi combined, easy

• TRAILHEAD AND DESCRIPTION: From the parking area go to the picnic shelter and locate the trail signs. After 110 yd jct with the nature trail that forms a loop around the playground. The trail has 20 posts identifying trees. (Ask a park attendant for the nature-trail brochure.) The *Horizons Hiking Trail* goes R and L for a shorter loop (B) and a longer loop (A). If going R, cross a stream at 0.3 mi and reach a jct with loop B, L, at 0.4 mi. If going R, go through a field, cross a bridge (one of a number on the trail), and follow the white blazes. Pass a tree nursery and cross another bridge and begin ascending and descending on rolling hills in a young forest. Red bud, Virginia pine, dogwood, and red cedar co-exist with the major hardwoods. At 1.1 mi cross a boardwalk in a damp area. Arrive at the loop-B jct at 2.1 mi, L and R. If continuing R, there is a huge holly tree at 2.3 mi, R. Here also is a nineteenth-century graveyard. Return to the nature trail and complete the loops at 2.6 mi.

## Tanglewood Park

Tanglewood is the William and Kate B. Reynolds Memorial Park, an outstanding piedmont recreation and leisure resort. Facilities include the elegant manor house and lodge, rustic vacation cottages, campground (full svc), restaurant, tennis courts, swimming pool, golf (36-holes championship courses and driving range), lake for paddleboats and canoes, picnic areas, arboretum and rose garden, deer park, horse stables and steeplechase course, 0.8-mi exercise-walking trail (near campground entrance), professional summer-stock theater, and the Walden Nature Center. (*USGS Maps:* Clemmons, Advance)

• ADDRESS AND ACCESS: Tanglewood Park, PO Box 1040, Clemmons, NC 27012, tel: 919-766-0591. From I-40 jct (Clemmons), go S 0.9 mi on Middlebrook Dr (SR-1103) to US-158. Turn R, go another 1.7 mi, and turn L (park office is L at 1.3 mi).

### *Walden Nature Trail* 593

• LENGTH AND DIFFICULTY: 1.5 mi combined, easy

• TRAILHEAD AND DESCRIPTION: From the park entrance, go E on US-158 0.4 mi to the park office, R (opposite Harper Rd, SR-1101, and svc sta) for the Walden Nature Center. Approach the *Walden Nature Trail* behind the park office and acquire a pamphlet at the signboard or from the park office. The trail has three sections, each consecutively increasing in difficulty and species variety. *Little Walden* (sec 1, 195 yd) has audio stations for the visually handicapped around a small pond (service by advance reservations); *Emerson's Walk* (sec 2, 0.7 mi round-trip) is a paved old road with 18 tree-interpretive markers and is accessible for the physically handicapped; and *Thoreau's Woods* (sec 3, 0.7 mi round-trip) has 28 interpretive markers about the trees. The trail is named after Thoreau's Walden Pond and was completed in 1982 as a memorial to the N.C. Wildlife Enforcement Officers who have died in the line of duty since 1947. Little Walden was built entirely by volunteers and through donations. Major contributors were the Reader's Digest Foundation, Winston-Salem Host Lions Club, AT & T Pioneers, and Girl Scout Troop 437. (There is an exhibit of live wildlife L of the main trailhead.)

▶ **LEE COUNTY**
**San-Lee Park**

The park is composed of 125 acres of forest, lakes, old waterworks, trails, picnic areas, family (RV) and group campgrounds. There is also an amphitheater, boat launch (and rentals), volleyball court, and other rec facilities. All the trails are well-designed and maintained. The park is open all year, tel: 919-776-6221. (*USGS Map:* Sanford)

• ADDRESS AND ACCESS: Director, Parks and Rec Dept, PO Box 698, Sanford, NC 27330, tel: 919-775-2107. At jct of US-1 (Bus) and Charlotte Ave (US-421/NC-87/42), take Charlotte Ave E 1.2 mi to Grapeviney Rd (also called San-Lee Dr, SR-1509) and turn R. After 2.2 mi turn R on Pumping Station Rd (SR-1510) and go 0.6 mi to park entrance, R.

*Muir Nature Trail (1.1 mi); Gatewood Trail (0.8 mi); Hidden Glen Loop Trail (0.2 mi); Thoreau Trail (0.9 mi)*   **594–597**

• LENGTH AND DIFFICULTY: 3 mi combined, easy

• TRAILHEAD AND DESCRIPTION: From the parking lot by Miner's Creek, cross the bridge, turn R, and follow the *Muir Nature*

*Trail* signs into the woods (there is a choice of an upper or lower loop). At 0.5 mi turn L at the lake's edge at the steps. Follow through rocks, hard- and softwoods, and wildflowers on the return. Hike a few yd or park at the refreshment stand to hike the other trails. Follow the campground road to Colter amphitheater signs. Turn R on *Gatewood Trail* and at 0.3 mi jct with *Thoreau Trail,* R. Turn L and jct with *Hidden Glen Loop Trail* at 0.5 mi. Pass Aldo Leopold Wilderness group campground on the return. The *Thoreau Trail* begins at the boat launch near the bridge over Moccasin Pond. Cross the bridge and follow the shoreline L. Cross a bridge over Crawdad Creek and jct with *Gatewood Trail* at 0.6 mi. Return either L (shorter) or R.

▶ **MECKLENBURG COUNTY**

Mecklenburg County is fast becoming an urbanized county. It has faced that challenge with ten major parks and another ten under development or proposed. In 1977 a ten-year park plan was begun, in 1982 a park's bond master plan set a goal of 9,250 acres, and in 1986 a $15 million park bond was passed by local vote. Additionally, there are community centers and historic sites in towns outside Charlotte, and a greenway master plan that will connect parks, educational centers, and points of historic significance. One connector would extend 35 miles from the N boundary at Davidson to the S boundary at Pineville. Among the first purchases for the greenway system was the McAlpine Greenway Park, described below. Unique to the county is that some of the parks are inside city limits.

• ADDRESS: Director, Parks and Rec Dept, 1200 Blythe Blvd, Charlotte, NC 28203, tel: 704-336-3854.

**Latta Plantation Park**

The 760-acre nature preserve is named for James Latta, merchant and planter, who with his wife Jane Knox lived in a handsome federal-period plantation house in the early nineteenth century. The house, near the Catawba River (Mtn Island

Lake), is restored and open afternoons Wednesday-Saturday. The park also has a visitor center; equestrian center (with 2 arenas and 80 permanent stalls) and 6 mi of bridle trails; canoe access to the lake; picnic areas (with shelters); the 55-acre Carolina Raptor Center; and hiking trails. Entrance to one of the hiking trails, *Beechwood Trail,* is at the horse-trailer parking area, the first R after entering the park. The footpath circles the headwaters of a stream that flows into Beechwood Cove. Tall beech, oak, and poplar are predominant in the 1.1-mi loop. Fragrant honeysuckle and cedar are near the entrance. At the Raptor Center is the 0.3-mi *Raptor Trail* for viewing live birds of prey, such as eagles, owls, hawks, falcons, and vultures, in a pine forest. The center is open weekends 12–5 pm; it is a non-profit, tax-exempt public corporation for rehabilitation, research, and conservation of raptors. (*USGS Map:* Mountain Island Lake)

**598–599**

- ADDRESS AND ACCESS: Mgr, Latta Plantation Park, Rte 3, Box 882, Huntersville, NC 28078, tel: 704-875-1391. Carolina Raptor Center, Inc, PO Box 16443, Charlotte, NC 28297, tel: 704-875-6521. Access from the S: At exit #38 on I-85 in Charlotte, take Beatties Ford Rd (SR-2074) N 7.3 mi to Sample Rd (SR-2125) (opposite Hopewell Presbyterian Church), and go 0.7 mi to the park entrance. From the N: Turn off I-77 at Huntersville on Gilead Rd; go W 0.9 mi, turn L on McCoy Rd (SR-2138), and go 1.6 mi to jct R with Hambright Rd (SR-2117). After 1.7 mi on SR-2117, turn L on Beatties Ford Rd and go 0.8 mi to Sample Rd, R.

### Dale Arvey Trail (1 mi); Mountain Island Lake Nature Trail (1 mi) 600–601

- LENGTH AND DIFFICULTY: 2 mi, easy

- TRAILHEAD AND DESCRIPTION: From the picnic area parking lot locate the central signboard on a paved route. For the *Dale Arvey Trail* go L, and enter the woods on a trail of natural turf. At 0.2 mi is a scenic area of the lake. Curve around a peninsula (a side trail L leads to a gazebo) and reach a fork at 0.3 mi. (A turn R leads 0.3 mi on a spur trail through a dense grove of young hardwoods, papaw, and grapevine to a floating dock and boat-access parking lot. Backtrack.) The L fork is a return to the picnic area after another 0.2 mi. From the signboard follow the paved route R, pass the restrooms, and enter the forest to the Mountain Island Lake Nature Trail. After 0.1 mi turn R at a fork on a treadway of wood chips into a mixture of sweet gum, Virginia pine, and cedar. Muscadine grapes hang from some of the trees and yellow senna borders open areas. After the trail makes its final turn, L, at 0.6 mi, there is a side trail, R, to the tip of the peninsula where a large rock faces the lake. Here is a beautiful view of the lake, particularly at sunset. Complete the loop by passing a pier to the picnic area.

### McAlpine Greenway Park

The 350-acre McAlpine Greenway Park was the first purchase for the greenway system. It has mature forests, flood plains, and open meadows along McAlpine Creek. Facilities include soccer fields, picnic areas, and well-designed biking and hiking trails (*USGS Maps:* Charlotte East, Mint Hill)

• ADDRESS AND ACCESS: Mgr, McAlpine Greenway Park, 8711 Old Monroe Rd, Charlotte, NC 28212, tel: 704-568-4044. The park is in SE Charlotte, near Matthews and between Independence Blvd (US-74) and Sardis Rd. If in Matthews, take John St W (which becomes Monroe Rd) and go NW 5 mi to the Seaboard RR overpass, R. If downtown, take East 7th St (which becomes Monroe Rd) SE 7.3 mi to the above address, L.

*McAlpine Creek Trail (1.9 mi); Cottonwood Trail (1 mi round-trip); McAlpine Creek Nature Trail (1.8 mi round-trip)* 602–604

• LENGTH AND DIFFICULTY: 4.7 mi, combined and round-trip, easy

• TRAILHEAD AND DESCRIPTION: At the parking area (N of the RR bridge) follow the signs to *McAlpine Creek Trail* (a bikeway for bikers and hikers), R of the soccer field. Cross a weir at McAlpine Creek, R, and go under the RR at 0.2 mi. Pass under the Monroe Rd bridge, downstream, where the trail becomes hard soil and sand in an open meadow. At 0.9 mi a paved jct, R, is an access trail that crosses McAlpine Creek on a cement weir. (Ahead, *McAlpine Creek Trail* goes another 1 mi to Sardis Rd, and enroute passes through a marsh.) On the access trail it is 0.2 mi to Tara Drive. Along the way, R, after 125 yd is *Cottonwood Trail,* and after another 120 yd, L, is the trailhead of *McAlpine Creek Nature Trail.* The *Cottonwood Trail* is a 0.5-mi interpretive path through a flood plain dominated by large cottonwood trees. (Plans are to extend the trail to Monroe Rd.) The *McAlpine Creek Nature Trail* is a footpath through tall sycamore, cottonwood, elm, sweet gum, and oak. A 300-yd boardwalk covers a low area. Wildflowers, raccoon, squirrel, and owls are part of the preserved area. The trail ends at the McAlpine Creek bank at 0.9 mi. Backtrack.

### McDowell Park and Nature Preserve

The park is named in honor of John McDowell, a leader of the county's recreation program in the 1960s and 1970s. The initial rolling land on the E side of Lake Wylie was a 150-acre gift to the county from the Crescent Land and Timber Corp, a subsidiary of Duke Power Co, in 1976. Now with 850 acres, the park is among the county's largest; it is open all year. It has a nature center that emphasizes natural history with exhibits and hands-on nature displays. Activities include camping (full svc), fishing, picnicking, hiking, and boating (rentals also). (A hiker symbol is on the park's entrance sign, and another sign on the main road cautions vehicular traffic that hikers have the right-of-way—a distinctive characteristic of the preserve.) The park is also good for birders; more than 85 species of birds have been catalogued. All the trails can be hiked from the nature center, either directly, by access trails, or by connecting trails (*USGS Map:* Lake Wylie)

• ADDRESS AND ACCESS: Mgr, McDowell Park and Nature Preserve, Rte 1, Box 118, Pineville, NC 28134, tel: 704-588-1436. From jct of I-77 and Carowinds Blvd, go on the Blvd for 2.4 mi. Turn L on NC-49 and go 4.2 mi to the park entrance, R.

***Creekside Trail*** *(2.1 mi round-trip);* ***Sierra Trail*** *(0.2 mi);* ***Trail for the Handicapped*** *(0.3 mi);* ***Pine Hollow Trail*** *(0.5 mi);* ***Cedar Ridge Trail*** *(0.6 mi);* ***Cove Trail*** *(1 mi);* ***Shady Hollow Trail*** *(0.6 mi);* ***Kingfisher Trail*** *(0.3 mi);* ***Chestnut Trail*** *(1.6 mi round-trip)*                                                          **605–613**

• LENGTH AND DIFFICULTY: 7.2 mi, combined and round-trip, easy

• TRAILHEAD AND DESCRIPTION: Park at the nature center parking area and enter the trail network on the L side of the nature center. Immediately jct L with the *Creekside Trail* (may have a nature trail sign), and R with the *Sierra Trail*. (The *Sierra Trail* is a sensory-interpretive loop on a hillside of hardwoods. From its loop is a connector trail to the *Chestnut Trail* and the W terminus of the *Pine Hollow Trail*.) If taking the *Creekside Trail* descend gradually 0.3 mi to a parking area and jct, L, with the *Cove Trail*. Turn R on a wide paved trail, cross a bridge over Porter Branch, and go upstream to partially follow the looped *Trail for the Handicapped*. (The 0.3-mi *Trail for the Handicapped* has benches, displays, side trails [one to the water's edge of Porter Branch], wildflowers [including the cardinal flower], and a huge white oak.) Pass a footbridge R and jct with *Pine Hollow Trail*. (The *Pine Hollow Trail* crosses the bridge into mixed hardwoods and pine, crosses a marshy area and tributary to Porter Branch, and ascends to connect with the *Sierra Trail* after 0.5 mi.) At 0.5 mi on the *Creekside Trail* jct with the *Cedar Ridge Trail*, L. (The *Cedar Ridge Trail* ascends slightly to pass under a powerline at 0.1 mi. Ahead is a kudzu patch and a forest of cedar, pine, and some large oaks near former homestead sites. Running cedar and periwinkle are groundcovers. Pass a deep ravine, R, and descend to rejoin the loop end of the *Creekside Trail* at 0.6 mi.) To continue on the *Creekside Trail,* cross the footbridge, R, ascend to pass under the powerline, and descend to the creek where the trail forks for a loop at 0.8 mi. If going L, cross the branch on a footbridge and go upstream to jct L with the *Cedar Ridge Trail* at 1 mi. Continue upstream through a beautiful forest of tall hardwoods, redbuds, and spring wildflowers such as trillium and bloodroot. Curve around a steep slope to rejoin the creekside at 1.3 mi. Backtrack to the parking area at the *Cove Trail,* or return L to the nature center.

The *Cove Trail* begins downstream at the *Trail for the Handicapped* parking area and follows a slope on a well-graded trail. At 0.2 mi approach Porter Cove in an area of wild ginger, ironwood, and sugar maple. Follow the waterfront to a peninsula ridge and a paved road. Turn R on the road and descend through the L corner of the picnic area to end the *Cove Trail* at 1 mi. Continue ahead and after 75 yd jct L with the *Shady Hollow Trail.* (The *Shady Hollow Trail* is a 0.6-mi access route through a mixed forest to the nature center.) Follow ahead 0.3 mi on the *Kingfisher Trail* to the restrooms, another picnic area, gazebo on the edge of Lake Wylie, and pedalboat dock.

Begin the *Chestnut Trail* near the restrooms and follow it to cross a gravel road, pass a playground L, and at 0.3 mi jct with the trail's loop. If going R, cross a footbridge (where a R turn is an access trail to the campground), turn L, and at 0.7 mi jct with an access R. (It is a 0.1-mi spur to the campground information station.) At 0.9 mi jct R with a connector trail to the nature center. The *Chestnut Trail,* among beech, oak, dogwood, and hickory, curves L and descends to rejoin its access at the gazebo for a total of 1.6 mi. (The 0.2-mi connector trail to the nature center from the *Chestnut Trail* crosses the main road and descends to the *Sierra Trail* for a return to the nature center.)

## ▶ ONSLOW COUNTY

Among the parks in Onslow County are two with nature trails. One is Onslow County Rec Park with a 0.4-mi *Bicentennial Nature Trail.* It is a wide, smooth, carefully designed route through a forest of bays, pines, oaks, holly, and small shrubs such as inkberry (*Ilex glabra*). Completed and dedicated in 1976 (with the assistance of Raymond Busbee of East Carolina University) it has 18 interpretive sites. A major unique site is that of plant succession. The beautiful park has ballfields, tennis courts, an arena, and picnic areas with a shelter. From the jct of US-258 and US-17 in Jacksonville, drive 3 mi S on US-17 to Onslow Pines Rd (SR-1116). Turn R; go 0.7 mi and turn R.

Another park, Hubert By-Pass Rec Park is at the corner of Hubert Blvd and NC-24, 5.3 mi E on NC-24 from the main entrance to Camp Lejeune Marine Corps Base. After a turn on Hubert Blvd (SR-1745), go 0.3 mi and turn R. The park is clean and well maintained. It has picnic areas, a soccer field, a 0.7-mi jogging trail, and a nature trail. The 0.5-mi *Mitchell Swamp Trail* begins at the most E parking area. There are 27 interpretive sites with the common name, botanical species name, and descriptions on a permanent sign. After 0.2 mi reach a rain shelter at the scenic swamp, a major focus point. Eight species of oak are on the trail; other plants include wax myrtle and sweet leaf (*Symplocos tinctoria*). (*USGS Maps:* Jacksonville S, Hubert)                                                      **614–615**

• ADDRESS: Director, Parks and Rec Dept, 433 Onslow Pines Rd, Jacksonville, NC 28540, tel: 919-347-5332.

▶ **POLK COUNTY**

The Polk County Community Foundation has constructed a 0.6-mi nature trail, the *Woodland Park Trail,* in Tryon. Entry is from Chestnut St. Turn L after crossing old tracks at the RR station on US-176. The trail can also be reached from Trade St (US-176) near the A&P store. The trail is excellent in both design and maintenance. The forest is chiefly hardwoods; no camping is allowed.                                                      **616**

• ADDRESS: Director, Polk County Rec Dept, PO Box 308, Columbus, NC, 28722, tel: 704-894-8199.

▶ **ROWAN COUNTY**
**Dan Nicholas Park**

Successful business executive and philanthropist Dan Nicholas donated 330 acres to Rowan County in 1968 for recreational activities. As a result the county commissioners established a park and recreation board to develop and administer the park. Facilities include areas for fishing, picnicking (with shelters), tennis, paddleboating, camping (full svc), and hiking. There are four ball fields, a craft shop, a nature center with plant, animal, and geological exhibits. There is also a small zoo, and the outdoor T.M. Stanback Theater. The park is open all year. (*USGS Map:* Salisbury)

• ADDRESS AND ACCESS: Director, Parks and Rec Dept, Rte 10, Box 832, Salisbury, NC 28144, tel: 704-636-2089. At the jct of I-85 and E Spencer, take Choate Rd (SR-2125) 1.1 mi E. Turn L on McCandless Rd, which becomes Bringle Ferry Rd (SR-1002) after 0.5 mi. Continue E 4.8 mi to the park entrance, L.

### *Persimmon Branch Trail (2.3 mi); Lake Trail (1 mi)* 617–618

• LENGTH AND DIFFICULTY: 3.3 mi combined, easy

• TRAILHEAD AND DESCRIPTION: From the concession stand at the dam, walk to the opposite side of the lake and turn R at 0.2 mi on the *Persimmon Branch Trail.* Follow the 32 interpretive markers that identify the trees such as oaks, pines, ash, elm, hornbeam, and mosses and ferns. Cross Persimmon Branch at 0.4 mi, turn L, and begin the return loop at 1 mi. From the dam the *Lake Trail* circles the lake along its edge through a picnic area and large campground. The lake has a large variety of ducks and other waterfowl.

### ▶ UNION COUNTY
### Cane Creek Park

This is the state's largest county-owned natural environment park; it has 1,050 acres of forest that surround a 350-acre lake. It has a large family-oriented campground (full svc), a group camp, a backcountry tent camp, and a camp store. In addition to camping, there is picnicking (with shelters); fishing (a trophy large-mouth bass lake with bluegill and crappie); horseback riding; boating (also rentals for sailboats, canoes, pedalboats and rowboats); and lake swimming. On the S side of the lake at the family campground, the 1-mi *Wilderness Trail,* for backpack primitive camping, goes SW into the forest. The other trails on the N side of the lake are for day hikes. Almost at the South Carolina state line, the park was constructed as a joint project by the county and the U.S. Soil Conservation Svc for recreation, watershed protection, and flood control of Cane Creek. The park is open all year. (*USGS Map:* Unity)          **619**

• ADDRESS AND ACCESS: Supervisor, Cane Creek Park, 5213 Harkey Rd, Waxhaw, NC 28173, tel: 704-843-3919. In E Waxhaw on NC-75, take Providence Rd (SR-1117) S 6.7 mi (crossing NC-200 at 5.8 mi) to Harkey Rd (SR-1121), turn L, and go 0.8 mi to park entrance R. (Providence Rd crossing is 11 mi S of Monroe on NC-200.)

**Bluebird Trail** *(2.2 mi round-trip);* **Swamp Trail** *(0.2 mi);* **White Oak Trail** *(4.8 mi round-trip)*          **620–622**

• LENGTH AND DIFFICULTY: 7.2 mi combined round-trip, easy

• TRAILHEAD AND DESCRIPTION: From the operations center parking lot follow the *Bluebird Trail* sign through a picnic area to the beach area, and go W along the lake's edge to open fields at 0.4 mi and 0.8 mi. Reach the Cane Creek dam at 1.1 mi. (To the L across the dam is a 0.5-mi connector route to the *Wilderness Trail.* To the R it is 0.1 mi to a gate and Harkey Rd.) Backtrack or follow the bridle trail, R (which is shorter), to the parking area. The *White Oak Trail* begins across the road from the operations center. (The first 0.8 mi was formerly part of the *Possum Trot Trail.*) Cross a service road at 0.3 mi and the paved main road at 0.4 mi. After a few yd the 0.2-mi *Swamp Trail,* R, is a link to the *Bluebird Trail.* Pass the boat dock and picnic area near a parking lot, and at 0.8 mi reach the first of a number of bridle trails (of which there are 6 mi in the park) and old backroads crossings. Through a young hardwood and pine forest, cross a stream twice before reaching a fork that forms a loop at 1.9 mi. If hiking R, follow downstream and turn L at a powerline. At 2.5 mi turn L away from the powerline and rejoin the trail at 2.9 mi. Ferns and wildflowers (such as wild phlox and sundrops) are prominent. Backtrack. (Any of the R jcts on the bridle trails or old roads will take you back to the parking area if you desire a different route.)

# 13

## Municipal Parks and Recreation Areas

*I never met a human being whose humor was not the better for a walk.*
                                                          —Donald C. Peattie

Over 120 cities and towns in the state have departments of parks and recreation. Some towns whose boundaries join have formed a joint department, and other cities have teamed with the counties for financial reasons and cooperative services. A few cities are moving swiftly with long-range master plans for greenway systems that will not only serve the innercity but connect with other cities and into the counties. An example is the Raleigh/Durham/Chapel Hill greenway plan, influenced strongly by a citizens' group, the Triangle Greenways Council. Winston-Salem has a plan to connect with other towns in Forsyth County. Other cities with plans are Charlotte/Mecklenburg County and High Point/Greensboro/Guilford County. Eventually the *MST* will connect Asheville, Greensboro, Burlington, Durham, Raleigh, Goldsboro, Kinston, and New Bern. Urban trails are usually multiple-use for walking, jogging, and bicycling. They frequently follow streams, city utility routes, recreational parks, and historic areas. The urban trails provide opportunities for appreciating the city's heritage and culture at a relaxed pace, for meeting neighbors, and for physical and spiritual health. Urban walking clubs are being organized, and books and magazines on urban trails are increasing. Examples are *The Walking Magazine* (Raben Publishing Co), *City Safaris* (Random House); and *Clues to American Architecture* (Starrhill Press). "Trails for day use must be developed in and near urban areas," stated the National Park Service in 1986 when it was developing a National Trails System Plan. On the following pages are examples of diverse trails whose treadway is city soil, asphalt, brick, and cement that leads into history and reminds us that urban trails are heritage trails.

▶ **ALBEMARLE**
**(Stanly County)**

The city has two trails, one in Rock Creek Park and another in Northwoods Park. Access to Rock Creek Park is immediately R after turning S on US-52 at the jct of NC-24/27/73. Begin *Rock Creek Trail* at the far end of the parking area and pass a number of park buildings, R. Follow a wide, easy, old RR grade 1 mi to a dead end. Tall pine and hardwoods comprise a canopy over shrubs and honeysuckle. Rock Creek, R, partially parallels the trail. Backtrack.

To reach Northwoods Park, take US-52 from Rock Creek Park N to US-52 bypass at 2.2 mi. Turn R, go 1.3 mi; turn R on Centerview Church Rd and turn L immediately. Park at the swimming pool parking lot. Begin the trail at the edge of the hardwood forest and follow *Northwood Park Trail* for a loop of 1.5 mi in either direction. The trail ascends and descends in a hilly area, both on old woods roads and through a section with physical-fitness stations. (*USGS Maps:* Albemarle SW and NW)
**623–624**

• ADDRESS: Director, Parks and Rec Dept, PO Box 190, Albemarle, NC 28001, tel: 704-983-3514.

▶ **BLOWING ROCK**
**(Watauga County)**

The 1.6-mi round-trip *Glen Burney Trail* is a scenic, moderate descent into the Glen Burney Gorge. Access is on Main St (US-221); go S, 1 block past Chestnut St (St Mary's of the Hills Episcopal Parish is across the street) and turn R on narrow

Globe Rd (SR-1537). Descend 0.1 mi on a paved road and 0.1 mi on a gravel road to the trailhead, R. Begin at the roadside; descend steeply through rhododendron, hemlock, ferns, witchhazel, and wildflowers to a bridge over the New Years Creek Cascades at 0.2 mi. Keep L and at 0.4 mi reach an observation deck at Glen Burney Falls. After another 0.2 mi descend to the fall's base. A farther descent leads to the base of beautiful Glen Marie Falls. Backtrack. The 100-year-old trail is on property donated to the town in 1906 by Emily Puruden. (Trail maintenance is assisted by the Northwest Mtn Task Force.) (*USGS Map:* Globe)                **625**

• ADDRESS: Director, Rec Dept, PO Box 47, Blowing Rock, NC 28605, tel: 704-295-3700.

## ▶ BURLINGTON
### (Alamance County)

The Burlington Rec and Park Dept and the Burlington Women's Club sponsor the Town and Country Nature Park with its easy 1.5-mi *Town and Country Nature Trail.* Access to the park is from I-85/NC-49N to US-70. Turn R (toward Haw River), and turn L on Church St for 0.9 mi. Turn on McKinney St for 0.3 mi, R on Berkley Rd, and go 0.2 mi to Regent Park Lane. Park at the end of the street. Follow the trail signs W on a well-graded trail (with picnic areas at intervals) through oak, birch, Virginia pine, black willow, and wildflowers. Cross bridges at 0.3 and 0.7 mi. Pass the S side of the Haw River at 0.9 mi. Side trails go up and down the river. (*USGS Map:* Burlington) **626**

• ADDRESS: Director, Parks and Rec Dept, PO Box 1358, Burlington, NC 27215, tel: 919-226-7371.

## ▶ CARY
### (Wake County)

The Cary Greenway System has connecting trails mainly in the residential area of the city between I-40, S, and N of US-64.

A number of trails are complete or in the planning process. Others will eventually encircle the city. Two examples are listed below. Access is from jct of US-1/64. Go W on US-64 for 1.6 mi. Turn R on Lake Pine Rd and go 1.1 mi to an intersection with Cary Parkway. (A convenience store is R.) Diagonally across the road, NW, is a forest-trail access to the trails. After 0.2 mi jct R and L with the 0.7-mi *Coatbridge Circle Trail.* Left is through a hardwood forest to the Jones Park swimming pool; R follows a wide forest route to the paved and beautiful 0.2-mi *Tarbert-Gatehouse Trail.*                    **627–628**

• ADDRESS: Greenway Planner, Parks and Rec Dept, PO Box 128, Cary, NC 27511, tel: 919-469-4066.

## ▶ CHAPEL HILL
### (Orange County)

The Chapel Hill Parks and Rec Dept maintains 13 park areas, two of which have nature trails. For access to Umstead Park, turn off Airport Rd (NC-86) W at Umstead Drive (between downtown and the airport). The *Umstead Park Nature Trail* is an easy 1.1-mi route from the parking lot. Follow it across a bridge, and turn R or L. If R, connecting trails (some from private homes) come in near the athletic facilities. Pass large sycamores beside the stream. For the 0.7-mi *Tanyard Branch Trail,* locate the Umstead Rec Center from the parking lot. Follow R of the building and along the stream to wooden steps that lead to Caldwell St. Walk along Mitchell Lane for 0.2 mi to the Hargraves Community Center.

To reach Cedar Falls Park, turn off NC-86 E at Weaver Dairy Rd (SR-1733) (N of the airport) to Cedar Falls Park. The 0.7-mi red-blazed *Cedar Falls Park Trail* leaves the parking lot through hardwoods around the tennis court. At 0.5 mi pass ruins of an old homestead, and return.                    **629–631**

• ADDRESS: Director, Parks and Rec Dept, 306 N Columbia St, Chapel Hill, NC 27514, tel: 919-968-2700.

## ▶ DURHAM
### (Durham County)

The Durham Rec Dept maintains over 70 parks in the city park system. Two of the parks have trails; they are described below. The city also has a Durham Trails and Greenway Commission with masterplans for nearly 170 mi in the city and county.

• ADDRESS: Director, Parks and Rec Dept, 101 City Hall Plaza, Durham, NC 27701, tel: 919-683-4355.

### West Point on the Eno

This 400-acre city park emphasizes the history and rec potential of the West Point Mill community (1778–1942). Restored are the McCown-Mangum farmhouse, mill, blacksmith shop, and gardens. There is also a Hugh Mangum Museum of Photography. Facilities in the park allow picnicking, fishing, rafting, canoeing, and hiking (no camping or swimming). The park is supported by Friends of West Point, Inc, 5101 N Roxboro Rd, Durham, NC 27704, tel: 919-471-1623. (*USGS Map:* Durham NW)

### *Buffalo Trail (0.5 mi); South Eno River Trail (1.7 mi); North Eno River Trail (1.7 mi)*                              632–634

• LENGTH AND DIFFICULTY: 3.9 mi combined, easy to moderate

• TRAILHEAD AND DESCRIPTION: From I-85 in Durham, take US-501 Bypass N (N Duke St) 3.4 mi and turn L into the park (across the road from the Riverview Shopping Center). Follow the park road to a small parking area, R, at the trail signboard (across the road from the picnic shelter and restrooms). *Buffalo Trail* ascends a ridge and descends to jct with *South Eno River Trail* after 0.5 mi. If taking *South Eno River Trail,* walk down the park road to the mill. Cross the mill race bridge and turn L to the dam. Ascend in a forest of hardwoods and laurel. At 0.2 mi and 0.3 mi are spur trails L to *Buffalo Trail.* At 0.6 mi jct with

*Buffalo Trail* L. Turn R, rock-hop a stream, and arrive at Sennett Hole (the site of the first grist mill on the river) for scenic views at 0.7 mi. Continue upriver on rocky ledges among laurel, rhododendron, yellow root, trillium, spring beauty, wild ginger, river birch, and sycamore. At 1.7 mi reach Guess Rd. Backtrack, or cross the bridge and locate an old road R that leads to a footpath downriver, the *North Eno River Trail*. Follow the N bank to a cement high-water bridge below the dam. Cross the bridge to the mill and return to the point of origin at 1.7 mi.

### Rock Quarry Park

The park is on Stadium Dr, 0.3 mi from N Duke St (0.9 mi from I-85). It has athletic fields, tennis courts, and a physical-fitness trail. From the parking lot at the softball field, begin the *Quarry Trail* at the wood's edge on the fitness trail. Turn L at the first fork, pass the old rock quarry, and reach at 0.3 mi a 90-yd side trail L to the Edison Johnson Rec Center. Cross the Ellerbe Creek bridge on Murray St and make an immediate L on a wide paved trail. After 125 yd pass a replica of a brontosaurus, L (part of the N.C. Museum of Life and Science). At 0.7 mi pass the Jaycee softball field. Cross Lavender St and jct L with a side trail and footbridge over Ellerbe Creek to a picnic and parking area of Northgate Park. The trail ends at Club Blvd at 1.2 mi. (Plans are to join the trail with the 0.5-mi *Pearl Mill Trail* for connections downtown.)                                **635–636**

### ▶ EDENTON
### (Chowan County)

Edenton, settled in 1658, and officially created in 1712, is one of the state's oldest communities. It is often referred to as a "stroller's paradise." Three centuries of outstanding architecture (particularly Federal, Greek Revival, and Georgian) make this national recreational trail a unique educational experience.

*Edenton Historic Trail* 637

• LENGTH AND DIFFICULTY: 1.5 mi, easy

• TRAILHEAD AND DESCRIPTION: Begin the loop at the Barker House (visitor center and headquarters for Historic Edenton) at the end of S Broad St by Edenton Bay. The visitor center is open daily except major holidays, tel: 919-482-3663. (If you do not have a map, the following will guide you past the 28 designated historic sites.) From the Barker House go R (E) on Water St to the Cannons of Edenton Bay and turn L of the Courthouse Green (1767) to E King St (where the Edenton Tea Party of 1774, the first known women's colonial political activity, took place). Turn R, but backtrack after the Coffield House, to S Broad St, and turn R. Turn R on E Church St but backtrack after the Blair House (ca 1775). Pass St. Paul's Episcopal Church (1736) R, before turning L on South Granville St. Turn R on W Eden St, but L after 1 block on Blount St (which becomes W King St). At the jct with S Broad St, turn R for a return to the parking lot and waterfront park.

• ADDRESS AND ACCESS: Edenton Chamber of Commerce, 116 E King St, Edenton, NC 27932, tel: 919-482-3400. If entering Edenton on US-17, or NC-32/37, go S on S Broad St and park at Waterfront Park at the corner of S Broad St and W Water St.

▶ **ELIZABETH CITY**
   **(Pasquotank County)**

Settled in the 1660s, the town, as Edenton described above, has numerous historic buildings. Its 30-block historic district contains the state's largest number of antebellum commercial buildings. A sidewalk trail offers unforgettable views of vintage homes with marble window sills, stained glass windows, aesthetic woodwork, and spacious gardens. In contrast, a nature trail in Knobbs Creek Park shows the unchanged swamp.

### *Elizabeth City Historic Trail*      **638**

* LENGTH AND DIFFICULTY: 1.6 mi, easy

* TRAILHEAD AND DESCRIPTION: Access is from US-158 (Elizabeth St) on Water St, S (at the W end of the Pasquotank bridge). Park at the riverfront of the Pasquotank River (corner of Water and Fearing Sts). This is the former site of Elizabeth "Betsy" Tooley's Tavern (ca 1790). (If you do not have a guide map the following will direct you past the 32 historic sites.) Follow Fearing St for six blocks, passing Christ Episcopal Church (ca 1856). At the jct of Fearing and South Rd, turn L at the Grice-Fearing House (ca 1800), R (probably the oldest structure on the hike). Turn R on Church St, and after another six blocks turn R on the original brick-pavement of Selden St to Main St. Turn R and pass 19 historic buildings (including the courthouse) on your return to Water St. Turn R, 1 block to the point of origin.

* ADDRESS: Chamber of Commerce, 502 E Ehringhaus St (PO Box 426), Elizabeth City, NC 27909, tel: 919-335-4365.

### Knobbs Creek Park

From US-17 Bus (near the N Bypass jct), take E Ward to the park entrance, L. At the parking area follow the trail sign. The 0.7-mi *Knobbs Creek Nature Trail* meanders through a dark watery area of cypress, black cherry, sweet gum, and beech. A group of Alabama supplejack (*Berchemia scandens*) hangs like lengthy jungle serpents over the cypress knees. Boardwalks built by the YCC in 1976 offer observation decks. Backtrack, or make a loop on the park meadow.      **639**

* ADDRESS: Director, Park and Rec Dept, 200 E Ward St, Elizabeth City, NC 27909, tel: 919-335-1424.

## ▶ GASTONIA
### (Gaston County)

The Schiele Museum of Natural History and Planetarium is a facility of the city of Gastonia. The 28-acre park is an example of how history can be preserved. Habitat settings in the museum show more than 25,000 mounted birds, mammals, and reptiles. The wide, well-groomed, 0.7-mi *Trail for All Seasons* introduces the visitor to natural and human history through the colonial period. There is a smokehouse, molasses boiler, log cottage, sorghum cane press, mill, and barn. The exceptional trail crosses Kendrick Creek (also known as Slick Rock Branch) twice, and passes 19 markers. The markers indicate the process of forest succession, wildflowers, shrubs, wildlife, and pioneer history. **640**

• ADDRESS AND ACCESS: Schiele Museum of Natural History, 1500 E Garrison Blvd (PO Box 953), Gastonia, NC 28053, tel: 704-864-3962. If approaching from I-85, take New Hope Rd S for 1.1 mi, and turn R on Garrison Blvd for 0.7 mi to the 1500 block.

## ▶ GOLDSBORO
### (Wayne County)

A combination of city parks and greenway planning provides a route for the *Stoney Creek Trail* to begin at Quail Park and eventually extend to the Neuse River. To approach Quail Park, turn off Bypass US-70/13 at Wayne Memorial Dr, S, to the first street L, Newton Dr. Turn L again on Quail Dr to the park. Walk past the picnic shelter to Stoney Creek and turn downstream through the Kemp Greenway. Trail blazes may be yellow or white. Plant life includes tall river birch, poplar, maple, laurel oak, ironweed, cardinal flower, day flower, beauty bush, and sensitive fern. (This trail is also good for birdwatching.) Cross Royall Ave and go under the RR trestle at 0.3 mi. At 1.1 mi cross Ash St and enter Stoney Creek Park. At 1.8 mi cross Elm St (entrance gate L to Seymour Johnson Air Force Base). Go 130 yd to a dead-end street for parking space. (The Baucom Greenway is being developed downstream.) (*USGS Maps: Goldsboro NE and SE*) **641**

• ADDRESS: Director, Parks and Rec Dept, Drawer A, Goldsboro, NC 27530, tel: 919-734-9397.

## ▶ GREENSBORO
### (Guilford County)

The city of Greensboro operates 33 parks and rec areas. It also manages the Natural Science Center of Greensboro on Lawndale Drive, and a five-lake, 137-acre municipal nursery at Keeley Park for the production of trees, shrubs, and flowers for the city. The Natural Science Center has a zoo of 123 species, a planetarium, and a museum in a 30-acre complex. It is open daily. It has a 0.6-mi *Zoo Trail* (which passes by wildlife of chiefly North and South America), and three connecting botanical trails—*Wildwood, Salamander,* and *Muskrat*—for 0.3 mi. Bioluminescent mushrooms grow on a bank near the trail stream. The center is located at 4310 Lawndale Dr, 2.5 mi N from its jct with US-200 (Battleground Ave) in the NW part of the city (tel: 919-288-3769). The city has a 100-mi labyrinth of bicycle trails (some of which are used for hiking and jogging). A number of parks have unnamed paths (such as Fisher Park Circle, traditional and beautiful), and others only physical-fitness courses. Some areas, such as Hamilton Lake, may have a path nearby, but not around the lake. The 0.9-mi *Hamilton Lake Trail* begins at the corner of Starmount Dr and E Keeling Rd at Lake Hamilton. It follows R of Starmount Dr on pea gravel through an open forest of tall and magnificent hickory, oak, poplar, pine, and beech—excellent to view for autumn foliage. The trail ends at the corner of Kemp Rd and Starmount. (Other trails are under construction in the greenway system, as are new parks and a 0.5-mi trail for the visually handicapped in Greensboro Country Park.) Discussed below are the trails with names, used primarily by pedestrians, and in parks with other facilities.

**642–646**

• ADDRESS: Director, Parks and Rec Dept, Drawer W-2, Greensboro, NC 27402, tel: 919-373-2574.

### Bicentennial Garden

At the jct of Cornwallis Drive W, turn S on Hobbs Rd to the parking area, R, at Bicentennial Garden, 1105 Hobbs Rd. Developed by Greensboro Beautiful, Inc, the park is meticulously maintained with cultivated flowerbeds and special gardens. Follow the 0.5-mi *Bicentennial Garden Trail* to the bridge over a small stream and into a lightly wooded garden where more than 75 plants are found in a fragrance garden and an herb garden. (Labels are also in Braille.) The area is to become part of the Caldwell Memorial Park, in honor of David Caldwell (1725–1824), patriot, statesman, clergyman, physician, and founder of Caldwell Log College in 1767.                       **647**

## Hagan-Stone Park

The park has 409 acres of forest, fields, and developed areas. Facilities include a tent/RV campground (with full svc), hot showers, picnic tables, and public phone. Among the rec activities are swimming, boating with rentals (no motors), fishing, picnicking, nature study, and hiking. There are two unique museums: one for tobacco and the other is Oakgrove School House.

• ACCESS: From the jct of I-85 and US-421, go SE on US-421 for 3.4 mi to NC-22 jct. Turn R and go 4.1 mi on NC-22 to Winding Rd (SR-3411). Turn L and go 0.4 mi to entrance, L.

### *Dogwood Trail (0.5 mi); Indian Head Trail (1.4 mi); Hagan-Stone Hiking Trail (3.4 mi)*                       **648–650**

• LENGTH AND DIFFICULTY: 5.3 mi round-trip combined, easy

• TRAILHEAD AND DESCRIPTION: From the parking lot enter the forest (near the maintenance area) and follow the yellow arrow to the beginning of the loop trails. The *Dogwood Trail* makes a short loop, but the *Indian Head Trail* turns R at 0.6 mi to circle the campground. Continue ahead on the *Hagan-Stone Hiking Trail* to circle the perimeter of the park. Reach the Oakgrove School House at 1.2 mi, and soon enter an open field with pine and cedar borders. Pass a picnic area at 2.4 mi, R, and enter a field L at 3.4 mi. Return to the parking area near a young forest and log cottage at 3.4 mi. The trail is exceptionally well-maintained over duff in the forest and grassy avenues in the fields.

**Hester Park**

Oka T. Hester Park is a more recent facility in SW Greensboro on Groometown Rd, E of Sedgefield Country Club. The park has a large center for community activities, a lake with paddleboats, picnic area, children's playground, tennis and volleyball courts, and physical-fitness trails. Motorized vehicles, horses, or pets are not permitted on any of the walking routes. To reach the park from the jct of I-40 and US-29A/70A, go 1.8 mi W on US-29A/70A to jct with Groometown Rd and turn L. After 0.9 mi turn L to Ailanthus St and Hester Park. The 1.3-mi *Hester Park Trail* loops the beautiful lake edge. The physical-fitness trail can also be hiked with the loop.          **651**

**Lake Brandt**

Lake Brandt, between Lake Higgins and Lake Townsend, serves as a reservoir for the city. The lake has a marina on the S side that provides fishing and boating (no swimming). Cooperative efforts between the city, the county, and private citizens' groups have created and maintain the five hiking trails described below. (*USGS Maps:* Summerfield, Lake Brandt)

• ACCESS: From the NW section of the city at the jct of US-220 (Battleground Ave) and Lawndale Dr, follow Lawndale Dr (which becomes Lake Brandt Rd) 5.3 mi N to Dillard's Store, R, and park to the side of the store.

*Nat Greene Trail (3.5 mi); Owl's Roost Trail (4.4 mi); Piedmont Trail (2.8 mi); Reedy Fork Creek Trail (3.7 mi); Laurel Bluff Trail (3.3 mi)*          **652–656**

• LENGTH AND DIFFICULTY: 17.7 mi combined, easy

• TRAILHEAD AND DESCRIPTION: (Two or more of these trails will become part of the *MST*.) At Dillard's Store, hike back (S) on the road 0.1 mi to enter the forest, R, on the *Nat Greene Trail* (a state trail designated in honor of Nathaniel Greene who led the colonial army against Lord Cornwallis at Guilford Courthouse, March 15, 1781, and for whom the city is named). Pass the parking area of Lake Brandt Marina at 0.2 mi in a forest of poplar, beech, and Virginia pine. Weave in and out of coves for periodic views of the lake. Cross a small stream at 1.6 mi and jct with *Owl's Roost Trail*, R, on an old RR grade, at 2.8 mi. Cross the old RR grade and after 0.2 mi enter a marsh. Cross a wide 225-ft long boardwalk at 3.4 mi and through a flood plain to Old Battlefield Rd at 3.5 mi, the end of the trail. (It is 0.7 mi R to US-220.)

To continue on the loop, backtrack to *Owl's Roost Trail* and follow it on the old RR grade N, cross a RR bridge at 0.3 mi, and leave the RR grade, R, into a pine grove. After a few yd enter a forest of oak, hickory, ironwood, tag alder, running cedar, and scattered crane fly and rattlesnake orchids. Cross a small stream at 1 mi and at 1.6 mi reach an excellent view of the dam and marina across the lake. At 3.1 mi enter a boggy area. Rejoin the old RR grade at 3.5 mi and cross a 295-ft RR bridge at 3.8 mi, where traffic can be seen, L, on US-220. Enter a pastoral area at 4 mi and jct R with the *Piedmont Trail* at 4.2 mi. Continue ahead for 0.2 mi to jct with Strawberry Rd (SR-2321) and a small parking area. (It is 0.2 mi L to US-220 and a grocery store.)

Backtrack on the trail to the *Piedmont Trail*, L, and enter a grazing field with cedar, honeysuckle, wild plum, and blackberry. At 0.5 mi descend into a seepage area at the base of a farm pond and lake edge. Enter another open area, cross a small stream at 1 mi and at 1.2 mi. Cross a boardwalk at 1.6 mi and a fallen bridge over a stream at 2.6 mi. (A new trail bridge is planned here.) Reach Lake Brandt Rd (SR-2347) at 2.8 mi. (To the R it is 0.3 mi across the bridge to Dillard's Store.)

Across the road from the *Piedmont Trail* begin the *Reedy Fork Creek Trail*. Enter a forest of oak, river birch, sycamore, and sweet gum to follow downstream. Cross a gas pipeline at 0.5 mi and a footbridge (built by Boy Scout Troop 275) over a stream. Enter a laurel grove. At 1.3 mi turn sharply L from Reedy Creek (the backwaters of Lake Townsend). Briefly join, R, an old woods road at 2.1 mi. Pass through wildflowers such as firepink, black cohosh, blood root, wild geraniums, and button bush before arriving at Hendricks Rd (SR-2324) at 3.2 mi, near the guardrail. Turn R on the road and cross a scenic marsh causeway, frequented by waterfowl. At 3.7 mi jct with Church St

(SR-1001). (It is 6.4 mi R on Church St to US-220.) Turn R, cross the bridge over the lake, and after 0.1 mi jct, R, with the *Laurel Bluff Trail.*

*Laurel Bluff Trail* (which runs through the Roger Jones Bird Sanctuary) enters a river birch grove at 0.1 mi. Follow an old woods road for a short distance and pass the boundary of a field at 1.6 mi. Among the trees are willow oak, shagbark hickory, black gum, maple, and poplar. Shrubs and wildflowers include wood betony, beauty bush, arum, laurel, redbud, dogwood, and filbert. Cross a small brook near the edge of the lake at 2 mi, and reach a boggy area at 2.1 mi. Bear R at a fork at 2.3 mi and pass a spur trail, L, at 2.7 mi. Pass through a large beech grove at 2.8 mi, and cross a gas pipeline at 3.1 mi. Pass by an old barn and through a vegetable garden to reach Dillard's Store at 3.3 mi.

## Lake Daniel Park

There is an easy 3.5-mi asphalt bike, hiking, and exercise trail between Lake Daniel Park complex and Latham Park. Entry can be made at a number of streets between the points of origin. To walk the distance given above, begin on Lake Drive near Battleground Ave and proceed W (near an E-flowing stream) to N Elam Ave near Wesley Long Community Hospital. Meadows are open and grassy, with sections of oak, ash, poplar, pine, and sweet gum. Trail mileage is marked on the *Lake Daniel Trail*. A city map is advisable.                                         **657**

## ▶ GREENVILLE
### (Pitt County)

The city operates 19 parks, and at least two have trails. Green Spring Park on 5th St (across the street from St Peter's Catholic Church) has an excellent 20-sta 1.2-mi physical-fitness trail that is popular with joggers and walkers. The *Green Spring Park Trail* begins at a picnic area and passes under tall cypress, sweet gum, and ash, many of which are draped with Spanish moss. Another park, River Park North, has nature trails.                     **658**

- ADDRESS: Director, Parks and Rec Dept, PO Box 7207, Greenville, NC 27834, tel: 919-752-4137 (919-758-1230 at River Park North).

### River Park North

The park was designated in 1982 with 359 acres, 290 of which are in a rich bottomland forest by the Tar River. It has four fishing lakes, a natural science center, picnic shelters, rental-boat ramp, and pack-in camping for organized groups. The park is open every day except Monday and holidays.

### *River Park North Trail* (1.1 mi); *Willow Branch Trail* (0.3 mi)
**659–660**

- LENGTH AND DIFFICULTY: 2.8 mi round-trip combined, easy

- TRAILHEAD AND DESCRIPTION: Access to the park from downtown at 5th St and Green St is to go N on Green St 1.5 mi (across the Tar River bridge) and take a R on Mumford Rd for 0.8 mi to the park, R. From the parking area follow the wide service road S toward the lakes. Near the picnic shelter a L beyond the pedalboat dock is the trailhead for the 0.3 mi *Willow Branch Trail*. It follows the lake bank with 12 interpretive posts for plants such as water oak, red mulberry, and black willow. It has a forest observation deck. It rejoins the service road in an open area with swamp rose, passion flower, rose mallow, and pink-weed. The *River Park North Trail* follows the service road, passes between the lakes and under a powerline at 0.3 mi and 0.5 mi. In a scenic forest of tall river birch, ash, cypress, and sycamore reach the Tar River bank at 0.8 mi. Turn L and arrive at the mouth of a stream, the trail's end at 1.1 mi. Backtrack.

▶ **HENDERSON**
**(Vance County)**

Fox Pond Park has lighted tennis courts, picnic area with shelters, children's playground, youth baseball field, fishing (no swimming), and trails. From the parking lot near the tennis courts, begin the 1.4-mi *Fox Pond Trail* on the E side of the lake and go counterclockwise. Cross a bridge and boardwalk at the lake's headwaters at 0.5 mi. Cross a svc road near a cement bunker at 0.9 mi, cross over the stream (near the dam) on a swinging bridge at 1.3 mi and return to the parking lot. East of the parking lot is the 0.6-mi *Conoconors Trail,* which loops through sweet gum and poplar trees around the tennis courts. *Quarry Trail* and *Sutton's Island Trail* are short loops of 0.2 mi each in the rec area. Park is open all year.          **661–664**

• ADDRESS AND ACCESS: Director, Rec and Parks Dept, PO Box 1556, Henderson, NC 27536, tel: 919-492-6111. On NC-39 (0.4 mi E of Bypass US-1) turn on Huff Rd (SR-1533) and go 0.5 mi to the park, L.

▶ **HIGH POINT**
**(Guilford County)**

The city is following the trend of its triangle cities, Greensboro and Winston-Salem, in long-range plans for a greenway system. The city also contributes approximately 65 percent of the funding for the High Point Environmental Center at High Point City Lake, a 200-acre preserve for natural-science study. One of its services is an outdoor classroom program for public-school children, and it has a special wildflower garden with emphasis on plants from the piedmont. Picnicking is allowed but no camping or swimming. The center is open daily.

• ADDRESS AND ACCESS: Supervisor, High Point Environmental Center, 1228 Penny Rd, High Point, NC 27260, tel: 919-454-4214. From the jct of US-29A/70A and Penny Road (W in Jamestown), go N 1.1 mi on Penny Rd and turn R at the center's entrance. From Greensboro, at the jct of Wendover Ave and I-40, go SW on Wendover Ave 4.5 mi to the jct with Penny Rd (at the Deep River intersection). Turn L and go 2 mi to the center, L. (The Parks and Rec Dept address is 221 Nathan Hunt Dr, High Point, NC 27260, tel: 919-887-2511.)

*Dogwood Trail, Wildflower Garden Trail, Lakeshore Trail, Hillside Trail, Fiddlehead Trail, Pine Thicket Trail, Pipsissewa Trail, Chicadee Trail* 665–672

- LENGTH AND DIFFICULTY: 3.6 mi round-trip combined, easy

- TRAILHEAD AND DESCRIPTION: From the parking area at the Interpretive Building follow the signs to the picnic shelter on the *Dogwood Trail;* pass the *Chickadee Trail,* R, then a textural trail (for use of the senses), L, and come to the *Wildflower Garden Trail* at 0.1 mi. Turn L on the *Wildflower Garden Trail,* and at 0.3 mi return to the *Dogwood Trail.* Pass *Fiddlehead Trail,* R, but continue to the *Lakeshore Trail* jct at 0.5 mi and bear L. At 0.8 mi reach the High Point City Lake viewpoint with large oak, poplar, pine, and cedar trees. Reach "Kudzu Castle" at 1.2 mi, and come to the jct with the *Dogwood Trail,* R, and the *Hillside Trail,* L. Take the *Hillside Trail* for 0.5 mi to jct with the *Fiddlehead Trail.* Follow the *Fiddlehead Trail* to the *Pine Thicket Trail* at 1.8 mi and turn R. Return to the *Dogwood Trail* and turn L. Turn L again at the jct with the *Fiddlehead Trail,* but turn R at the floating bridge at 2.8 mi. Additional jcts with *Pipsissewa Trail* and *Chicadee Trail* are at 2.9 mi and 3 mi. After loops on these trails return to the parking area at 3.6 mi.

▶ **LINCOLNTON**
**(Lincoln County)**

In 1982 the Timken Foundation donated funds to construct the *South Fork Nature Trail* at South Fork Park. Eagle Scouts of Troop 81 assisted in the project. Begin the trail S of the swimming pool at a gate. The easy and wide 0.5-mi loop trail is mainly on a flood-plain bend of the South Fork. (A primitive campsite is in the loop's center; reservations are required.) Among the flora are tall water oak, green ash, sycamore, elm, and river birch. Fragrant japonica honeysuckle covers many understory shrubs. (A physical-fitness trail adjoins the trail in a grassy meadow.) **673**

• ADDRESS AND ACCESS: Director, Rec Commission, PO Box 25, Lincolnton, NC 28092, tel: 704-735-2671. In downtown Lincolnton at the courthouse, go W on W Main St (NC-27) and turn S at the first traffic light. Turn R to the park off S Madison St.

## ▶ NEW BERN
(Craven County)

New Bern, "the land of enchanting waters," is an historic riverport at the confluence of the Trent and Neuse rivers. Settled in 1710, and named for the city of Bern, Switzerland, it is one of the most elegantly restored cities in the state. The colonial assembly met here as early as 1737, and after the completion of Tryon Palace in 1770 it was the colonial capital and the state capital until 1794. After the Revolutionary War there was a dramatic development of Federal-style architecture. Examples are the Stevenson House (ca 1805); First Presbyterian Church (1819); and the New Bern Academy (1806). On the *New Bern Historic District Trail* are 67 historic buildings (business, government, homes, and churches) within a walking (or auto) route of 4.5 mi. Because the route is divided into four sections (1.2 mi in the Palace area; 1.1 mi in the Johnson St area; 1.2 mi in the East Front St area; and 1 mi in the downtown area) that may begin or end in irregular patterns (such as in the middle of a block), it is essential that you have a tour map to know which building is in which tour section. Maps are available free of charge from the Chamber of Commerce (address below). There are guided tours sold through a travel agency or on location. Additionally, there are volunteers (arranged by the Chamber of Commerce) who will walk or ride with you to describe the history and architecture. Each building on the tour has a steel shield (yellow, black, and red) with a bear logo. 674

• ADDRESS AND ACCESS: New Bern Area Chamber of Commerce, 101 Middle St (Drawer C), New Bern, NC 28560, tel: 919-637-3111. Open daily. From US-70/17, which passes through on Broad St, turn S on Middle St and go 2 blocks to the SW corner of Middle St and Tryon Palace Drive. Tours originate at the SE corner of the Palace Auditorium, George St and Pollock St, across from the Tryon Palace main gate.

# ▶ RALEIGH
## (Wake County)

The Raleigh Parks and Rec Dept has a comprehensive system of 131 parks and areas maintained by the Department. Part of its program is the Capital Area Greenway (with 175 parcels of land), a model development for municipal planning. The greenway system was begun in 1974 when the city responded to rapid urbanization that threatened its natural beauty. The master plan provides a system of wide trails in their natural state for recreational activities such as walking, jogging, hiking, fishing, picnicking, bicycling, and nature study. The trails mainly follow on flood plains or utility areas of the city's two major streams, Crabtree and Walnut creeks, and their tributaries. Because the majority of the trails are paved, they can be used by the physically handicapped. Some of the short, unconnected trails are described below in a group. The three longest trails—Lake Johnson, Loblolly, and Shelley Lake—are described separately. A Raleigh Greenway Map is essential.

• ADDRESS: Director, Parks and Rec Dept, PO Box 590, Raleigh, NC 27602, tel: 919-890-3285.

On the Crabtree Creek flood plain are the *Alleghany, Lassiter's Mill, Fallon Creek,* and *Buckeye* trails. They will eventually be connected with the Shelly Lake trails. The paved 0.4-mi *Alleghany Trail* follows Crabtree Creek downstream in a forest of tall poplar, willow oak, and loblolly pine. It passes under the Yadkin Drive bridge. (Park on the side of Alleghany Dr either near its jct with Alamance Dr or Buncombe St.)  **675**

The 0.2-mi *Lassiter's Mill Trail* is a paved trail from Lassiter Mill Rd upstream to the dam where Cornelius Jesse Lassiter operated a 1764 grist mill from 1908 to 1958. (Park on Old Lassiter Mill Rd, a few yd from the jct of Lassiter Mill Rd.)  **676**

*Fallon Creek Trail,* a 0.3-mi 21-post interpretive paved trail, goes through tall elm, ash, poplar, and hackberry. The state-champion river birch (8.5 ft in girth) is near the creekside. Understory trees are boxelder, hornbeam, holly, and dogwood. (Park at the Kiwanis Park at the end of Noble St or on Oxford Rd, 0.1 mi downstream from its jct with Anderson Dr.)  **677**

The *Buckeye Trail* is a paved 2.4-mi scenic meandering route in a deep forest of tall river birch, poplar, willow oak, and loblolly pine. If parking at the upstream parking area on Crabtree Blvd, walk 240 yd downstream (E) on the sidewalk, around the curve, to the forest entrance. Pass a picnic area at 0.2 mi, a children's playground at 1.4 mi, and a maintenance entrance from Crabtree Blvd at 1.6 mi. At 1.9 mi, L, is an observation deck (with a ramp for the handicapped) on a knoll with views of the river. Descend and reach the E trailhead parking area at 2.4 mi (with an access to Milburnie Rd).  **678**

In the Walnut Creek area are the *Lake Johnson Trail* (described below) and *Rocky Branch, Little Rock,* and *Dacian Valley* trails. (*Walnut Creek Trail* is under construction.) *Rocky Branch Trail* is a paved 1.5-mi route. Begin at the Dix Hospital entrance (Umstead Dr) at Saunders St. (Parking space is 140 yd up Umstead Drive, L, from the trailhead, R.) Descend the steps, pass through an open meadow with large pecan trees and a picnic area. Cross Boylan Ave at 0.3 mi, enter a forest, exit onto a sidewalk of Western Blvd, cross Hunt Dr at 0.6 mi, and cross Rocky Branch bridge. At 1.1 mi cross Bilyeu St and after 0.1 mi follow an old paved roadway to the corner of Bilyeu St and Cardinal Gibbons St (near the S side of Cardinal Gibbons High School).  **679–680**

*Little Rock Trail* is a 0.7-mi paved route at Chavis Park. (Park on Chavis Way.) From the corner of Lenoir and Chavis Way, cross the Garner Branch footbridge, pass two picnic areas, cross Bragg St at 0.5 mi, and end at McMackin St. Tall elm, ash, and sycamore shade the trail.  **681**

*Dacian Valley Trail* is a 0.3-mi loop beginning at a picnic area at the end of Dacian Rd. Pass through tall hardwoods near Walnut Creek. (It will connect with the *Walnut Creek Trail.*)  **682**

Two other trails (unrelated to the above) are *Gardner Street Trail* and *Marsh Creek Trail.* At the rose garden and Raleigh

Little Theatre, the *Gardner Street Trail* begins at the corner of Gardner and Everette Sts at the greenway sign. (Park on Gardner St.) Descend and pass L of a restroom and basketball court. Cross Kilgore St and follow the sidewalk briefly. After crossing Van Dyke Ave, turn L on Fairall Dr, a gravel road shaded by tall poplar, oak, and loblolly pine. At 0.6 mi enter a forest and arrive at the Jaycee Park on Wade Ave at 0.8 mi. The paved 0.4-mi *Marsh Creek Trail* is at Brentwood Park (at the end of Vinson Ct). The wide trail follows Marsh Creek from Ingram Dr to a footbridge over the stream at the end of Glenraven Dr.

**683–684**

### *Lake Johnson Trail* 685

• LENGTH AND DIFFICULTY: 3.7 mi, easy

• TRAILHEAD AND DESCRIPTION: From Western Blvd (near the WRAL-TV sta and gardens) take Avent Ferry Rd 3.2 mi and park at the parking lot on the S side of Lake Johnson. Enter a picnic area and follow the white-blazed foot trail to an A-frame shelter at 0.3 mi. Cross a stream and pass a small waterfall at 0.6 mi. Wind in and out of coves around the lake and reach the dam spillway at 1.6 mi. Reach the Lake Dam Rd and turn L to enter the Walnut Creek Greenway system. Turn L at 1.9 mi on a paved trail and return to the Avent Ferry Rd at 2.7 mi. Turn L on Avent Ferry Rd and follow the causeway back to the parking area at 3.1 mi. (A new greenway trail continues across the road from the boat dock at Avent Ferry Rd. The wide wood-chip trail passes N of Lake Johnson in a scenic area. After 0.3 mi bear R and ascend to a parking area at 0.6 mi at William Stadium behind Athens Drive High School.) (*USGS Map:* Raleigh West)

### *Loblolly Trail* 686

• LENGTH AND DIFFICULTY: 6 mi, easy

• TRAILHEAD AND DESCRIPTION: Take the Blue Ridge Rd exit from Wade Ave, and go S 0.4 mi to Old Trinity Rd; turn R. Park near Gate D at the Carter-Finley Stadium. Enter the gate and follow white blazes to a metal gate at 0.5 mi. Cross a stile at 0.6

mi, and go through a cement culvert on Richland Creek under Wade Ave (or cross over the highway if the water is too high). Follow downstream among river birch. At 1.3 mi enter the North Carolina State University (NCSU) forest management area of conifers and broadleaves, and at 2.2 mi jct with the NCSU 1.2-mi *Frances Liles Interpretive Trail* loop, R. Between the trail accesses is a NCSU weir gaging sta. Arrive at Reedy Creek Park Rd at 2.4 mi. (Wake County Flood Control Lake is L. It is 1.7 mi R to Blue Ridge Rd.) Turn R, and after 150 yd turn off the road, L, to an obscure trail entrance (between a hickory and a loblolly pine) to continue. At 3 mi turn R at a metal fence and follow it to cross Richland Creek (below the dam) at 3.2 mi (wading may be necessary). Turn R, and then L before crossing a bridle trail at 3.5 mi. Enter Umstead State Park, cross a small stream in a beech grove, and pass R of a small lake at 3.8 mi. Cross a park svc road at 4.2 mi, and after crossing two more small streams (that feed Reedy Creek Lake), cross Reedy Creek at 5.1 mi (wading may be necessary). Pass under a powerline at 5.7 mi, cross Camp Whispering Pines Rd, and arrive at the Reedy Creek parking area of William B. Umstead State Park at 6 mi. Access here is 0.3 mi from I-40 (see Chapter 10, Section 3). (*USGS Maps:* Cary, Raleigh West)

### *Shelly Lake Trail* (2.2 mi); *Snelling Branch Trail* (0.6 mi); *Ironwood Trail* (0.8 mi); *Ironwood Trail Extension* (0.4 mi)
### 687–690

• LENGTH AND DIFFICULTY: 4 mi, easy

• TRAILHEAD AND DESCRIPTION: From the jct of US-70 and NC-50 at Crabtree Valley Mall, take NC-50 N 0.8 mi to Shelley Rd. Turn R on Shelley Rd (SR-1812) and go 1 mi to Shelly-Sertoma Park, L. (Another route to the park follows Shelley Rd 1.3 mi from Six Forks Rd.) (Parking is both at the Arts Center and below the dam.) If parking below the dam, enter the trail near Leadmine Creek at the jct L of *Shelly Lake Trail* (a national recreation trail) and *Ironwood Trail*, R. Follow the paved trail to the top of the dam and a fork. To the L, the trail crosses the dam, connects with an exercise trail, passes the pedalboat dock, and forks at 0.6 mi. To the L it goes 0.1 mi to the Arts Center, and to the R 0.4 mi to end at Rushingbrook Dr.

If following the paved trail from the dam on the grassy E side of the lake, cross a boardwalk and enter a forest of sweet gum, oak, and river birch at 0.2 mi. At 0.7 mi is an alternate trail L to an observation deck near the lake. Go upstream and return to the main trail at 1 mi. Reach North Hills Dr at 1.2 mi. Cross the street to continue on *Snelling Branch Trail,* which passes a baseball field L, Sanderson High School R, and ends at the Optimist Club parking lot at 0.6 mi. Access here is off Northcliff Dr.

The *Ironwood Trail* follows Leadmine Creek downstream from the parking area below Shelly Lake Dam. Go under the Shelly Rd bridge, S. Wind through the forest, cross the stream three times, and exit at North Hills Dr in the 5200 block. (The trail will eventually connect downstream with the *Ironwood Trail Extension* to North Hills Park and the *Alleghany Trail* at the Crabtree Creek confluence.)

Entrance to the *Ironwood Trail Extension* is from Currituck Dr to the tennis courts at North Hills Park. Descend steeply on a paved trail to Crabtree Creek. Turn R in a forest of tall poplar and river birch to cross a footbridge over Leadmine Creek at 0.4 mi. (Plans are to complete the trail upstream to join the *Ironwood Trail.*) (*USGS Map:* Raleigh West)

▶ **ROCKY MOUNT**
**(Nash County)**

Battle Park is a 54-acre recreation park, a gift from the Battle family of Rocky Mount Mills. It has a picnic area with shelters, children's playground, a boat ramp to the Tar River, and a history trail. After parking, follow *Battle Park Trail* on a paved (parts are gravel) and easy 1.6-mi loop. Pass the Donaldson Tavern site, a stage coach sta from an overland route. (Near here the Marquis de Lafayette was entertained while on his southern tour in 1825.) At 0.2 mi turn R to the waterfall overlook on the Tar River. Proceed to the children's playground through a picnic area with pine, birch, oak, elm, and dogwood. Cross the driveway at 1.3 mi and pass the site of the first Rocky

Mount post office on the return. (The trail is accessible to the physically handicapped.) **691**

• ADDRESS AND ACCESS: Director, Rec and Parks Dept, PO Box 1180, Rocky Mount, NC 27801, tel: 919-972-1151. Access is from the jct of US-64 Bypass and NC 43/48. Take NC-43/48 (Falls Rd) SE 0.5 mi to the parking area near the Confederate monument.

## ▶ ROANOKE RAPIDS
### (Halifax County)

In Emry Park, the 0.5-mi *Emry Park Trail* is a wide and neatly groomed loop trail. From the parking lot follow the signs clockwise through a forest of willow and white oak and loblolly pine. Leave the forest and pass the lighted tennis courts, children's playground, and ball field. The city is jointly planning with the Roanoke Canal Commission, Inc, a 3.1-mi historic trail, the *Roanoke Canal Trail*. It is on the banks of an old navigational canal from Roanoke Rapids to Weldon. After 0.4 mi within the city limits it will follow the river to the filter plant in NW Weldon. **692–693**

• ADDRESS AND ACCESS: Director, Parks and Rec Dept, PO Box 38, Roanoke Rapids, NC 27870, tel: 919-535-2031. (Roanoke Canal Commission is the same address, but a different tel: 919-537-3297.) From the jct of US-158/NC-48, take NC-48 (Roanoke Ave) N to Ninth Ave and turn L to Emry Park.

## ▶ SALISBURY
### (Rowan County)

The city was founded in 1753 and has a 23-block historic district that is listed in the National Register of Historic Places. It is through this area and 20 other blocks that the *Historic Salisbury Trail* loop covers 3.9 mi of industrial, commercial, and residential historic sites. A national recreation trail, it is an exceptionally grand tour past tall trees and nineteenth-century architecture. It reflects the pride of the Historic Salisbury Foundation and its dedication to preserve the city's heritage. A map and individual site description can be obtained from the address below. Otherwise, a description of the route and a few buildings is as follows: Begin at the NE corner of N Bank St and S Jackson St (2 blocks W of Main St) at the Josephus Hall House, a large antebellum house (1820) with Federal, Greek Revival, and Victorian features. Proceed N on Jackson St to the Rowan Museum (1819), which is open for guided tours. After five blocks turn L on W Kerr St to Water St R, and to the Waterworks Gallery. Turn R on W Cemetery St 1 blocks to Church St, turn L one block, and turn L again on W Franklin St to the Grimes Mill (1896). After two blocks turn L on Fulton St, go six blocks, turn R on W Fisher St, go one block, and then turn L on S Ellis St to the Governor John Ellis House (1851). Go two blocks to the R on Horah St, go one block, turn R for three blocks on S Fulton St, and turn L on Thomas St. Go three blocks to Main St and turn L. To the R is Military Ave and the Salisbury National Cemetery. (Monuments honor the nearly 5,000 Union soldiers who died here in the Civil War.) Continue N on Main St on wide sidewalks for six blocks (passing such sites as the Empire Hotel and the former courthouse square.) Turn L on W Council St for one block to pass L on S Church St for three blocks (to pass Andrew Jackson's well), and R on N Bank St to the point of origin. **694**

• ADDRESS AND ACCESS: City of Salisbury, PO Box 479, Salisbury, NC 28144, tel: 704-637-2200 or 704-636-0103. From I-85 jct with US-52 in Salisbury, go NW 1 mi to Main St (US-29/70). Continue ahead on W Innes St two blocks and turn L on S Jackson St two blocks to Hall House at 226 S Jackson.

▶ **SMITHFIELD**
**(Johnston County)**

The *Neuse River Nature Trail* in the Town Common Park is maintained by the city's Parks and Rec Dept and the Year-

Around Garden Club. It is an easy 1.6-mi route on the E banks of the Neuse River, downtown. From the parking lot on N Front St hike 0.2 mi up the E bank of the river to the terminus and return. Hike downriver past the historic site of Smith's Ferry (1759–1786) and under the US-70 bridge at 0.5 mi. Continue through a pristine forest of large sweet gum, oak, and green ash. Turn L at 0.7 mi and reach the tennis courts, children's playground, and parking area on E Market and S 2nd St at 1 mi. Return by the same route or go on N Front St for a distance of 1.6 mi. Vehicular traffic is allowed on parts of the trail. **695**

• ADDRESS AND ACCESS: Director, Parks and Rec Dept, PO Box 2344, Smithfield, NC 27577, tel: 919-934-9721. Access is on N Front St, one block from E Market St (US-70) at the bridge (or the E Church St parking lot).

## ▶ STATESVILLE
### (Iredell County)

Among the city parks is 25-acre Lakewood Park, which contains the 1.6-mi *Lakewood Nature Trail*. If approaching from I-40 and NC-115 (N Center St), go S 0.4 mi on NC-115 into the city and turn L on Hartness Rd. After 0.3 mi turn L on Lakewood Drive to the parking area. From the parking area follow the trail signs onto a paved and interconnecting trail system in a mature forest of oak, pine, and poplar. The city also has a physical-fitness trail that is used by walkers in Anderson Park and an unnamed short trail in East Stateville Park. **696**

• ADDRESS: Director, Parks and Rec Dept, 432 W Bell St, Statesville, NC 28677, tel: 704-872-2481.

## ▶ TARBORO
### (Edgecombe County)

The *Tarboro Historic District Trail* is a remarkable adventure into history. It is a trail of beauty any season of the year. A national recreation trail, it is a 2.4-mi walking or driving tour within a 45-block area of beautiful downtown Tarboro. More than 100 homes, gardens, churches, and government and business structures are designated as historically or architecturally significant. The trail begins at the tour headquarters on Bridgers St at the Blount-Bridgers House (ca 1808). (A trail map is advisable and is available here. The building is open Monday-Friday, usually on Sunday afternoons, and by appointment, tel: 919-823-8121.) In case you do not have a map, brief directions follow: Within the Bridgers St block, go N (R side of the Blount-Bridgers House) and pass the Pender Museum (ca 1810). Turn R on Philips St; L on St Patrick St; L on Battle Ave; L on Main St; R on Porter St; R on Trade St; R on Baker St; R on St Patrick St (by the Town Common [1760] at 0.9 mi); L on Church St; R on St David St (by the Calvary Episcopal Church); R on St James St; R on St Andrew St; L on Wilson St, and L on Main St. At 1.8 mi jct with Granville St; turn R and backtrack on Main St to R on Park Ave; turn L on St Andrew St and return to the Blount-Bridgers House. The Main St section of the trail has received national recognition for expansive restoration.   **697**

• ADDRESS AND ACCESS: Tarboro Dept of Planning and Economic Development, 112 W Church St (PO Box 220), Tarboro, NC 27886, tel: 919-823-8121. (Chamber of Commerce tel: 919-823-7241.) Access: turn E on Bridgers St from Main St (US-64, Bus), and go one block.

▶ **WASHINGTON**
**(Beaufort County)**

The "original Washington, 1776," is the first town in the U.S. to be named for George Washington. Settlements at this jct of the Pamlico and Tar rivers began as early as the 1690s, but the origin of the present city is traced to the early 1770s. The city's earliest buildings of historic and architectural significance were mainly destroyed by fire, first in 1864 by federal forces and again in the business district in 1900 by an accidental fire. A remarkable restoration and preservation has created an historic district of at least 29 historic buildings and special sites in the downtown area. They can be seen on the 2-mi *Washington Historic District Trail* (a national recreation trail), a walking tour among homes, businesses, churches, by the old courthouse, and along streets of magnolia and crepe myrtle. Parking is available at the corner of Gladden St and Stewart Parkway. A map of the tour is available from addresses below, but without a map the following description will assist. Also, the trail sign, a colorful shield with directional arrows, serves as an excellent guide at each turn.

Begin the trail at the NW corner of Gladden and Main Sts at the renovated Seaboard Coastline RR Depot. On Main St walk W 3 blocks and turn R on Pierce St. Go one block, turn L on W 2nd St for one block, and turn L on Washington St back to W Main St at 0.5 mi. Turn R to see (halfway down the block) the stately 1820s "Elmwood." Return on Main St to pass the Havens Warehouse and Mill to the parking lot at 1 mi. Walk R along the Stewart Parkway waterfront pavilion. After passing three eighteenth-century houses on Water St, go N two blocks on Bonner St (passing the 1860s St Peter's Episcopal Church). Turn L for one block on E 2nd St, turn L one block to Main St, and turn R for the return. **698**

• ADDRESS AND ACCESS: City of Washington, PO Box 1988, Washington, NC 27889, tel: 919-946-1033. Also, Washington Chamber of Commerce, 102 Stewart Parkway (PO Box 665), Washington, NC 27889, tel: 919-946-9168. For access to the trailhead, follow US-70 N or S to Main St. Turn E two blocks to the corner of Gladden St.

▶ **WILMINGTON**
(New Hanover County)
**Greenfield Gardens Park**

Greenfield is a magnificent 200-acre city park with trails, tennis courts, picnic areas, rental boats, amphitheater, rec center, nature study area, and fragrance garden. Millions of azalea blossoms provide a profusion of color in April. Additional color and greenery come from camellias, yaupon, magnolias, bays, live oaks, crepe myrtle, water lilies, dogwood, and Spanish moss draped on cypress. (The park is popular during the city's annual N.C. Azalea Festival [first or second weekend in April]). Open daily. No camping or swimming.

• ADDRESS AND ACCESS: Director, Parks and Rec Dept, PO Box 1810, Wilmington, NC 28401, tel: 919-341-7855. The park entrance is reached from US-421, S, at South 3rd St to Willard St. Turn L on Willard St, then R to the parking area (the park office is R, across Burnett Blvd).

### Rupert Bryan Memorial Trail (4.5 mi); Greenfield Nature Trail (0.3 mi)                                    699–700

• LENGTH AND DIFFICULTY: 4.8 mi combined, easy

• TRAILHEAD AND DESCRIPTION: The trail (also called *Greenfield Gardens Trail*) is a paved loop for hiking, jogging, and bicycling around the lake and over bridges. (It parallels, with little exception, the auto route on W and E Lakeshore Dr.) If you follow the trail R from the parking area, pass the amphitheater and rec center at 0.9 mi. At 2.4 mi jct L with the *Greenfield Nature Trail* boardwalk, which has interpretive signs. Among the plants are ferns, swamp rose, and Virginia willow. Continue ahead to Jackson Point picnic area, Indian sculpture, and a return to the parking area.

## ▶ WILSON
### (Wilson County)

There are more than 20 parks in the city, and many others are proposed. Unnamed walkways are prominent; three areas have designated trails. The wide *Hominy Canal Trail* is a 0.9-mi path between Ward Blvd and jct of Kincaid Ave and Canal Dr. Tall loblolly pine, willow and live oaks, sweet gum, and river birch shade the trail. Access to parking can be had at Williams Day Camp on Mt Vernon Dr. The 1.2-mi *Toisnot Lake Trail* circles the lake; it also extends 0.6 mi into the hardwood forest downstream to the Seaboard Coast RR. Access to Toisnot Park is on Corbett Ave, N, near its jct with Ward Blvd (NC-58/42). Corbett Ave is also the 3.8-mi access route to Lake Wilson and the *Lake Wilson Trail.* Go N 3.3 mi, turn L on Lake Wilson Rd (SR-1327) at Dunn's Cross Rd, and go 0.5 mi to the lake, R.

**701–702**

*Lake Wilson Trail*                                                    **703**

• LENGTH AND DIFFICULTY: 2.3 mi, easy

• TRAILHEAD AND DESCRIPTION: From the parking lot go either R or L on the dam. If L, cross the dam/spillway and follow an old road through a forest of river birch, alder, sweet gum, and holly. At 0.8 mi bear R, off the old road, and enter a swampy area to follow the yellow blazes. (Beavers may have dammed the area and prevented crossing.) Cross a bridge on the feeder stream to an old road at 1.3 mi. Among the swamp vegetation are button bush and swamp candles (*Lysimachia terrestris*). Turn R and follow the old road (damaged by jeeps and 4WDs) to complete the loop at 2.3 mi. (This is a good birdwatching trail.)

▶ **WINSTON-SALEM**
**(Forsyth County)**

A city and county planning board has established a growth-strategy program that encourages the development of green-way networks for rec and land-use development. A pilot project was the Salem Creek Greenway and *Salem Creek Trail.* It will extend 4.2 mi from Market Place Mall to connect with the *Salem Lake Trail,* a trail used for many years and described below. In the process it will connect with Washington, Central, Happy Hill, Civitan, and Reynolds parks. Other connections will join the campuses of Winston-Salem State University, Salem College, and the N.C. School of the Arts. Another major project is

*Bethabara Trail* in the NW part of the city. Eventually connections are planned to Kernersville, Rural Hall, and Tanglewood Park.

• ADDRESS: Director, Rec and Parks Dept, PO Box 2511, Winston-Salem, NC 27102, tel: 919-727-2087.

## Salem Lake Park

The park is a 365-acre city reservoir surrounded by 1,800 acres of land. Activities are picnicking; fishing (bass, bluegill, catfish, crappie); boating (rentals also); horseback riding; birding; and hiking (no skiing or swimming). Open daily, except Thursday, tel: 919-788-0212.

• ACCESS: From I-40, go S on US-311/NC-209 at Claremont Ave (which becomes Martin Luther King St). After 0.8 mi turn L on Reynolds Park Rd (SR-2740) and go 1.9 mi to Salem Lake Rd, L.

### *Salem Lake Trail*                                           704–705

• LENGTH AND DIFFICULTY: 7.4 mi, easy

• TRAILHEAD AND DESCRIPTION: Park R on the approach to the second entrance gate. Hike NE on a wide service road through poplar, oak, beech, Virginia pine, and sweet gum. Fern, yellow root, sweet pepperbush, sensitive briar, and wild roses grow in the open coves and lakeside. At 0.9 mi cross a cement bridge and at 2.7 mi a causeway where kingfishers and wild ducks frequent the marsh, R. Arrive at Linville Rd (SR-2662) at 3.4 mi. (To the L it is 0.7 mi to I-40.) Continue on the trail by crossing the causeway L to a re-entrance in the woods. Follow the service road under a powerline at 3.9 mi and to a scenic view by the lake at 5 mi. At 6 mi jct with a pipeline that crosses the lake, L. (To the R it is 0.2 mi to Old Greensboro Rd, a paved access road from Linville Rd.) If a bridge is not complete across the lake, follow a fisherman's trail ahead and cross the lake on the Southern RR trestle at 6.2 mi. After 0.6 mi along the RR track, turn L and go 60 yd to jct with *Salem Creek Trail,* R and L.

(When complete, *Salem Creek Trail* will go R downstream to Market Place Mall.) Turn L and go 0.1 mi to cross Salem Creek at the base of the Salem Lake dam. Ascend. If the parking lot gate is locked, follow the paved road around the guard fence to the point of origin at 7.4 mi. (When the bridge and *Salem Creek Trail* are complete, the loop will be 7 mi.)

### Winston Lake Park

The 0.7-mi *Winston Lake Nature Trail* is an easy and wide route between the Winston Lake swimming pool parking lot and the picnic shelter. From the swimming pool, pass through a playground and gate to enter a mature forest of pine, oak, and poplar near the creek. At 0.2 mi begin a curve R around the lake in an ascent to the large picnic shelter. Pass an exercise station at 0.3 mi. (No camping.) **706**

• ACCESS: From the jct of I-40 and US-311, go N for 1.9 mi on US-311, and turn R on Winston Lake Rd. Go 0.2 mi to Waterworks Rd, turn R, and immediately turn L to Winston Lake swimming pool.

# PART VI

# Trails on Private and Commercial Properties

# 14.

## Private and Commercial Trails

*I never found a companion so companionable as solitude.*
—Henry David Thoreau

Of the 19 million acres of forests in the state, 14 million acres are owned by private citizens. Named trails on these properties are rare, particularly those trails open to the public. Some landowners have been reluctant to open their properties because of liability and trail abuse, but all owners are now better protected and less liable with the passage by the state legislature in 1987 of the "Act to Limit the Liability of Landowners to Persons Using Their Land in Connection With the Trails System." Nevertheless, corporate and individual landowners have a long history of cooperation with scout troops, schools, nature-oriented groups, and hunting or fishing clubs to use their properties. Examples are in this chapter. Most private trails are not publicized and the majority have never been named. If all the pathways through farm woodlands, or those favorite forest fishing and hunting routes, or those walks to points of meditation were all counted, they would number in the thousands. There are also private resorts, retreats, and special camps where only paying or invited guests may walk the trails. A popular hiking pastime in the mountain area is to ascend highly publicized mountain peaks (particularly those with a view) on both public and private properties. Some private peak owners object and have placed no-trespassing signs at appropriate places. If you see such signs, they may apply mainly to vehicles. An inquiry to the owners would show respect for their property rights. Frequently, private owners will give an individual, or a small group, permission to walk a path or roadway if the purpose is for education or aesthetics. Access to some mountain peaks requires passage over lands of multiple owners. Bushwacking or random cross-country hiking on these premises can result in trespassing on one piece of property but not on others. Examples are Blackrock Mtn near Sylva, Sandymush Bald S of Luck, Snake Mtn near Boone, and Wesner Bald near Balsam Gap. Some commercial properties require an entrance fee, for example, Chimney Rock Park and Grandfather Mtn.

▶ **BEARWALLOW MOUNTAIN TRAIL**    **707**
   **(Henderson County)**

• LENGTH AND DIFFICULTY: 2 mi round-trip, moderate

• TRAILHEAD AND DESCRIPTION: From the jct of US-74 and Bearwallow Rd (SR-1594) in Gerton (5 mi NW on US-74 from jct of NC-9 in Bat Cave), go 2.1 mi on SR-1594 (mostly on a gravel road) to Bearwallow Gap. Park away from the L gate. Ascend on a moderate-grade pasture road through oak, hickory, locust, and maple to the firetower on Bearwallow Mtn (4,232 ft) at 1 mi. Scenic views from the tower are of Sugarloaf Mtn, Bat Cave area, and Little Pisgah Mtn. Flowering plants include bellflower, turtlehead, and phlox. Backtrack. (*USGS Map:* Bat Cave)

▶ **BLUFF MOUNTAIN TRAIL**    **708**
   **(Ashe County)**

The North Carolina Nature Conservancy, a private organization, owns and maintains a controlled-access nature preserve on

Bluff Mtn. It is described as "a naturalist's dream." To hike the 2 mi loop trail, permission is necessary from the Conservancy. Address: PO Box 805, Chapel Hill, NC 27511, tel: 919-967-7007.

▶ **BREVARD NATURE TRAIL**                                   **709**
  **(Transylvania County)**

This is a botanical trail system of extraordinary educational value in a 395-acre nature preserve, privately owned and maintained by Charles F. Moore, Box 8, Brevard, NC 28712, tel: 704-884-9614. A clear mountain stream flows through a remarkable diversity of vascular flora. Hiking and nature study permitted with guided tour only.

▶ **BOB'S CREEK TRAIL**                                        **710**
  **(McDowell County)**

• LENGTH AND DIFFICULTY: 8 mi, moderate to strenuous

• TRAILHEAD AND DESCRIPTION: From I-40 (S of Marion) turn S on US-221 for 1.9 mi. At Phillips 66 svc sta turn L on Goose Creek Rd (SR-1153) and go 0.5 mi to Old US-221 (SR-1786). Turn L for 50 yd to Glenwood Sta Rd (SR-1766), R, and go 0.5 mi to Huntsville Rd (SR-1790). After 1.8 mi on SR-1790, turn sharply L and ascend a gravel road 1.4 mi to the parking area (near a gated road). Enter the national recreation trail at a sign and go through pine, oak, sourwood, maple, and laurel. The well-designed trail is particularly scenic in the fall. Wildlife includes deer, turkey, owls, songbirds, and squirrel. For the first 3.5-mi loop the trail ascends and descends to Hemlock Falls, Split Rock Falls, Hidden Falls, and Sentinel Rock. If the S fork of the next 4.5-mi loop is taken, pass Poplar Cove Spring, follow a gentle contour, and descend to Big Alley. Halfway around the loop is a backpacking campsite, stream, and rock formations. A number of hemlock groves are on the trail in this 500-acre pocket wilderness. (*USGS Map:* Glenwood)

• INFORMATION: Bowater Carolina Company, PO Box 7, Catawba, SC 29704, tel: 803-329-6600.

▶ **BUCKHORN TRAIL** (45.4 mi)                    **711**
**(Sections A, B, C, and D in Lee County, Section E in Lee and Harnett Counties)**

The *Buckhorn Trail* is the longest hiking trail on private property in the state. It was designed and constructed in the early 1980s by volunteers under the leadership of Frank Barringer of Sanford. Assisting him were Boy Scout Troops 906, 907, 941, 942, and 944 in Lee County and Troop 61 in Lillington. Girl Scout leaders were Jane Barringer and Sylvia Adcock. From W to E the trail parallels generally the Deep River and the Cape Fear River from near the House in the Horseshoe historic site to Raven Rock State Park. The trail meanders through flood plains, on steep but low ridges, into tributary coves, and through a remarkable area of natural history, timberland, and segments of remoteness. It is described in sections with emphasis on special features and major access points. To guarantee its continued use, hikers are requested to respect the property rights of the owners. In addition to numerous individual landowners, corporate owners include the Federal Paperboard Co, Inc, Har-Lee Farm, and Boise-Cascade Corp. Support and cooperation are also given by the hunting clubs of both counties. Campsites should be carefully chosen, away from developed areas, roads, or streams. No-trace camping is the rule— the same rules that apply for public wilderness areas (see introduction to national forests). With the possibility that this route may someday be an alternate *MST* route, the blazes are white circles.

• INFORMATION: Frank Barringer, PO Box 375, Sanford NC 27330, tel: 919-776-2417 or 775-5023.

### Section A: From Euphronia Church Road to US-421

• LENGTH AND DIFFICULTY: 10.7 mi, moderate

• SPECIAL FEATURES: ruins of McLeod House, Deep River ledges

• TRAILHEAD AND DESCRIPTION: From the jct of NC-42 and Bypass US-1/15/501 in Sanford, take NC-42 W 1.8 mi and turn L on Steel Bridge Rd (SR-1318). Go 7.5 mi W to a R turn on Euphronia Church Rd (SR-1393) and go 0.2 mi to the church parking lot. Begin the trail on the old forest road N, past the church cemetery. At 0.5 mi cross the first of a number of small streams. Ahead is a mixed forest of oak, gum, hickory, poplar, pine, holly, hornbeam, wildflowers, and ferns, through which cross many old pioneer wagon roads and more current logging roads. At 1.4 mi R is the remains of the McLeod House and chimneys. (Here also is an alternate [shorter] yellow-blazed trail, R, that rejoins the main trail at 2.3 mi.) At 1.5 mi cross a stream where trout lilies bloom in profusion in March. When the tree leaves are off, Deep River can be seen from a bluff at 1.9 mi. There are remnants of the Blakley House entwined with yellow jessamine at 2.1 mi. At 2.3 mi the alternate trail rejoins near the ruins of another old house. Reach a cable gate of the Poe Hunt Club and a massive clearcut, L, at 2.8 mi, but veer R from the clearcut on an old woods road. Turn off the old road, R, onto a footpath at 3.5 mi (once the Clark Place, now remembered by the escaped jonquils and baby's breath). Follow the trail through an area of hardwoods over a rocky streambed at Smith Creek at 3.9 mi, where switch cane and wild grape provide dense understory. Soon pass L of the edge of a young loblolly pine forest. Cross a Smith Creek tributary with banks of wildflowers at 4.2 mi, and after 0.1 mi pass under a powerline to an old road. Turn off the old road, R, onto a footpath at 4.4 mi in a young forest. Old tobacco rows are evident. At 4.9 mi is an abandoned house, L, 50 yd before arriving at NC-42. Turn R to an intersection at 5 mi. (On NC-42 W it is 3 mi to Carbonton, and 6.7 mi E to US-1/15/501 in Sanford. Road mileage back to

Euphronia Church is 3.7 mi on Plank Rd [SR-1007], R, to Steel Bridge Rd [SR-1318], R, for 2 mi to Euphronia Church Rd, R.)

Cross the jct diagonally and reenter the forest. Pass rock piles, indicative of pioneer farming. Cross a stream at 5.6 mi, ascend and descend through former tobacco land, now filled with pine, sweet gum, and running cedar. Descend to scenic Little Pocket Creek and follow downstream, L, at 6 mi. At 6.7 mi cross a small stream on a living holly tree. Ahead, cross a number of drains and through timber clearcuts. Follow an old logging road and cross Big Pocket Creek on a large fallen logging bridge at 7.7 mi. Continue on the main road and turn L at a road jct at 8.5 mi. Turn L again on a less used woods road at 9.1 mi. After 0.1 mi reach the end of the road, where a foot trail begins R. (Ahead, 20 yd off the road, is a large and scenic rock ledge with views of the silent and dark Deep River. Hepatica, spring beauty, and trout lilies bloom among the ferns in a natural rock garden). Turn R on the footpath and over a high bluff above the river through laurel, and return to the road at 9.6 mi. (A clearcut may have altered the trail across the road.) Turn L and follow the road (formerly Tempting Church Rd, SR-1322). Cross Patterson Creek on an old bridge at 10.5 mi and arrive at US-421 at 10.7 mi. (Gulf is L, 2 mi; Sanford is R, 4 mi, to US-1/15/501, where a R, 1.8 mi, leads to jct with NC-42. A turn, R, on NC-42 for 4.3 mi returns you to where the trail crossed NC-42.) (*USGS Maps:* Goldston, White Hills)

### Section B: From US-421 to US-15/501/NC-87

* LENGTH AND DIFFICULTY: 5.3 mi, easy to moderate

* SPECIAL FEATURES: Endor Iron Furnace

* TRAILHEAD AND DESCRIPTION: Go N on paved Cumnock Rd (SR-1400) 0.5 mi and turn R on paved Cotten Rd (SR-1403). At 1.3 mi, after a short road descent, turn L on a service road (before the Buffalo Creek bridge) and follow up a sewage line route. Cross Big Buffalo Creek, either on the pipeline or on fallen trees. (If the water is too high, hike downstream to the RR bridge and turn R.) Ascend R of a high embankment to the

Norfolk Southern RR at 1.8 mi. Turn R; follow the RR tracks 0.1 mi, and turn L into the woods. Pass R of the chain fence and turn L on the gravel road at 2.2 mi. Pass the Buffalo Creek Wastewater Treatment Plant and leave the road at 2.4 mi, R, on a footpath. Cross a woods road used by ATVs and ORVs, and also the Carolina and Northwestern RR; follow a high berm to its end at 2.7 mi. Rejoin the ATV route, R. (A path to the L side is 50 yd to the scenic upper view of the Endor Iron Furnace, now dangerous to enter and in need of preservation.) The ATV route leads R, steeply, to the base of the furnace and to the edge of Deep River. Leave the ATV route after a few yd, R. At the Carolina and NW RR bridge turn L at 3.4 mi. Descend R, immediately after crossing the bridge into the forest, whose floor can be wet. Exit and cross the RR again at 3.8 mi. Enter a young forest on a footpath but leave it to follow an old road through a semi-open grove of pine and sweet gum. Reach a paved road, Brown Rd (SR-1462), at 4.7 mi. Turn L and arrive at the dual lane US-15/501/NC-87 at 4.8 mi. (It is 12 mi L to Pittsboro; it is 0.2 mi R to the Country Cubbard store for food and gasoline. Farther S it is 2.7 mi to US-1 in N Sanford. Road mileage back to the beginning of this section is 7.3 mi; S on US-15/501/NC-87 for 2.7 mi to Beechtree Dr, R [SR-1444]. Go 0.4 mi and turn R on Cotten Rd [SR-1403] for 3.7 mi to SR-1400 and L 0.5 mi to US-421.) To reach the beginning of the next section, cross the road and hike 0.5 mi L [N] to roadside parking at a private road, R, at 5.3 mi, the end of this section. (*USGS Maps:* Colon, Goldston)

### Section C: From US-15/501/NC-87 to Farrell Rd (SR-1423)

- LENGTH AND DIFFICULTY: 7.7 mi, moderate

- SPECIAL FEATURES: scenic riverside, white pine grove

- TRAILHEAD AND DESCRIPTION: At the roadside of US-15/501/NC-87 described in Section B, park near the small private road. Ascend, but turn off the road at a powerline after 50 yd. At 0.2 mi cross the dam of a small lake (Little Buffalo Creek) and for the next 1.3 mi cross a number of small streams that drain into the creek. Also switch from old roads to footpaths. Among the flora are sycamore, river birch, hornbeam, laurel, holly, and ferns. At 1.5 mi pass R of a small dam (residential area across the creek). Ascend and descend low ridges along the bank of Deep River after 2.5 mi. At 3.1 mi cross a much used private road. Rock-hop a stream at 3.2 mi. Reach a meadow and turn R at 3.6 mi, but reenter the forest after 130 yd to take a sharp L. Pass through a scenic area of wildflowers (blood root, coral bell, hepatica), sycamore, and oak at 4 mi. At 4.3 mi is a private access from the R to Deep River, L. Continue downstream in a partially open field. Cross a muddy stream in a slick embankment at 4.6 mi. At 5 mi pass through a new-growth area that shows rock piles from former farming; pass R of large boulders at 5.3 mi and L of big holes at 5.4 mi. Encounter an ATV route soon thereafter. Cross a stream and fence to a beautiful grazing field at 5.7 mi (deer are often seen here). At 6.1 mi enter one of the most scenic spots of the trail. On the rocky riverside there is a natural garden of laurel, wild orchids, and ferns. Out in the river are rapids and across the river is the mouth of Rocky Creek. Ascend and descend in a rocky area to pass through scattered white pine (rare this far E) at 6.5 mi. Descend to a flat area near the river before ascending an old (but used) road R. At 7.4 mi pass L of an old tobacco barn and enter the edge of a field. Follow the road to the ruins of an old plantation. Two large chimneys and a farm building partially remain. Arrive at the end of the dead-end paved Farrell Rd (SR-1423) at 7.7 mi. (For a return to the point of origin of this section, take Farrell Rd 0.6 mi to Deep Creek Rd [SR-1466], turn R, go 4.8 mi to US-15/501/NC-87, and turn R for 0.6 mi.) (*USGS Map:* Colon)

### Section D: From Farrell Rd (SR-1423) end to NC-42

• LENGTH AND DIFFICULTY: 9.4 mi, easy

• TRAILHEAD AND DESCRIPTION: (This section is entirely on backcountry state roads and can be hiked or driven. Because of crop farms, unbridged streams, and marshy lowland near Deep River and the Cape Fear River, an upland route for the section is necessary and is being scouted.) From the end of Farrell Rd (SR-1423), go 0.6 mi to Deep River Rd (Old US-1, now SR-1466). (There is a grocery store 0.6 mi, R.) Cross Deep River Rd and continue on Farrell Rd through forests and a few scattered farm fields and homes. Cross over US-1 at 1.9 mi. At 2.3 mi turn L on Lees Chapel Rd (SR-1425), and pass through small farms of tobacco, corn, and soybeans. Cross the RR tracks of the Seaboard Coastline at 3 mi, enter a forest (some timbering) and arrive at the jct with Lower Moncure Rd (SR-1002) at 4.2 mi. (L on SR-1002 is 4 mi to Moncure and R is 8 mi to Sanford). Turn R on Lower Moncure Rd, go 0.4 mi, and turn L on Cletus Hall Rd (SR-1504). Follow the road under a powerline at 4.9 mi, pass Buchanan Rd (SR-1503) L, and enter a forest to cross two streams before arriving at Lower River Rd (SR-1500) at 6.7 mi. Turn R, and cross Norfolk Southern RR at 7 mi. Pass through a low flat area and cross Hughes Creek at 7.5 mi. Cross two more streams and pass a jct, R, with Gunther Rd (SR-1505) at 8.6 mi in a hilly area. Pass under a powerline before arriving at NC-42, R and L, at 9.4 mi, the end of this section. The trail continues across the road in a private driveway. (It is 4 mi L [N] to Corinth and 9 mi R [S] to Sanford. Along the way to Sanford, at 3.1 mi, is a grocery store at the corner of Buckhorn Rd and NC-42.) (*USGS Maps:* Colon and Moncure)

### Section E: From NC-42 to Raven Rock State Park

• LENGTH AND DIFFICULTY: 12.3 mi, moderate

• SPECIAL FEATURES: Buckhorn Dam, Letts Landing

• TRAILHEAD AND DESCRIPTION: Begin in the private driveway of the Yarborough farm on NC-42 (across Lower River Rd described in Section D). Follow L of the buildings toward the woods, and turn R at the edge on an old road at 0.2 mi. Descend 85 yd to a sharp L (before the irrigation pool) and follow the white blazes through a forest of oak, poplar, maple, and beds of running cedar. Cross Bush Creek at 0.6 mi and turn downstream. For the next 1.4 mi cross a number of drains into Bush Creek and climb steep but low ridges. (Timber cutting may have altered the route. If blazes are missing look for ribbons.) Cross a stream in a scenic area of quartz, wildflowers, and ferns at 1.8 mi. At 2.3 mi arrive near the Cape Fear River; turn sharply R. (The Deep River joins the Haw River 5.5 mi upstream, the beginning of the Cape Fear River.) After crossing a ridge return to the river at 2.7 mi. Enter a clearcut and ascend steeply to pass under a powerline at 2.9 mi. Descend steeply to a small stream area. Pass through a low area, partially on an old woods road to a stream at 3.8 mi. Ascend to a bluff and cul-de-sac of an access road at 3.9 mi. To the L is scenic Buckhorn Dam. (To the R is a 0.6-mi old jeep road to a private residence and the N end of Doyle Cox Rd [SR-1540]. Parking is allowed here with permission of the property owners. It is 0.8 mi on Doyle Cox Rd to Buckhorn Rd [SR-1538] and 6.7 mi farther to the beginning of this section—3.6 mi R on Buckhorn Rd to NC-42 and R for 3.1 mi.)

From the Buckhorn Dam cross the old road and continue on the trail in and out of coves and over ridges for a descent to Fall Creek at 4.6 mi. (If the water is high, go farther upstream.) Ascend and descend on rocky quartz bluffs. At 5 mi, L, arrive at a scenic area of rapids on the Cape Fear River. Between the trail and the river is an old sluiceway; a bluff harbors laurel and yellow jessamine. Leave the riverside, ascend and descend on bluffs, and pass through beds of ferns and wildflowers. Cross the narrow Letts Landing access road (a former access to river traffic, but now an access route to farm bottomland) at 5.5 mi. (To the R it is 1 mi to the paved Buckhorn Rd.) Descend through a clearcut and cross a small creek at 5.8 mi to enter Har-Lee Farm. After 50 ft turn R on a service road and go 0.2 mi to a gravel road, R and L. Turn L, ascend and arrive at the E side of TV-40 relay building and tower at 6.6 mi. Turn L at the first old woods road and follow it past a farm pond, R. At 7.2 mi cross a small creek on a cement bridge and ascend to a pasture and gate. Climb over the locked gate to Lee County Rd (SR-1277) at 7.6 mi. (The rough road may need maintenance; it is 1.3 mi R to the paved Buckhorn Rd.) Turn L and go 85 yd to parking space, R, at an old field. Turn R and descend 0.4 mi through a field and clearcut to Daniels Creek. Cross the stream on flat rocks above cascades and a pool at 8 mi. Turn L and follow downstream to the Cape Fear River at 8.7 mi. Among large poplars follow an old road downriver and at 9.3 mi arrive at a thicket of honeysuckle and blackberry in a pine grove. After 0.2 mi through the grove arrive at an old logging road. Turn R, ascend, but after a few yd turn L for a descent into a laurel patch. At 10.4 mi cross a small stream. Return to the riverside, but soon leave it for an ascent to Womack Rd at 10.7 mi. (To the L are fine views of the Cape Fear River.) Turn R and go 0.3 mi before turning L onto an old woods road. (Ahead Womack Rd becomes SR-1267 and after 1.5 mi it joins Cool Springs Rd [SR-1265] for a 3.2-mi access to US-421 at Ryes.) At 11.5 mi leave the old woods road on a footpath, R, and descend to rock-hop picturesque Cedar Creek at 11.7 mi. Go downstream among holly and ferns to an old woods road at 11.9 mi. Turn R and ascend in oak and pine among quartz rocks. Arrive at the Raven Rock State Park boundary and access road, R and L, at 12.3 mi, the E end of the *Buckhorn Trail*. Jct here with the *Campbell Creek Loop Trail*, L and ahead. Also ahead it is 2.1 mi to the park's parking lot. (To the L, *Campbell Creek Loop Trail* descends 0.2 mi to a primitive campsite. See Chapter 10, Section 3 for details on the Raven Rock State Park trails.) (The shortest highway route back to the origin of this section is 18.6 mi. From the park's parking lot go 3.1 mi to US-421; turn R, go 6.5 mi on US-421 to Seminole, and turn R at the Broadway sign. Go 2.3 mi [through Broadway on Main St] and turn R on Berke Thomas Rd [SR-1535]. Follow it 1.7 mi to NC-42, take a R, and go 5 mi.) (*USGS Maps:* Moncure, Cokesbury, Mamers)

▶ **CATAWBA FALLS TRAIL**                                     712
   **(McDowell County)**

• LENGTH AND DIFFICULTY: 2.8 mi round-trip, easy to moderate

• TRAILHEAD AND DESCRIPTION: In the center of Old Fort, turn S on Catawba St at the jct with US-70 and go under I-40 to the R exit ramp. Follow Catawba River Rd (SR-1274) and after 3 mi park near (before crossing) the Catawba River bridge. Hike the private road; at 0.3 mi ford the river, enter an old sawmill site at 0.5 mi, and approach an old dam site at 1 mi. The road ends at

1.1 mi. Cross Clover Patch Branch and take the L trail at the fork to reach the lower falls at 1.3 mi. To view the upper falls plunging into a pool, climb R of the falls on slippery banks with rhododendron and huge hemlock. Return by the same route. The property is owned by D.W. Adams. Camping and camp-fires are prohibited. If picnicking, all trash must be carried out. (A nearby commercial campground is Catawba Falls Camp-ground on Catawba Falls Rd, 0.4 mi before reaching the bridge. It has full svc and is open all year. Address: Rte 1, Box 59-A, Old Fort, NC 28762, tel: 704-668-4831.) (*USGS Map:* Marion)

▶ **CHAMBERS MOUNTAIN TRAIL**                           713
**(Buncombe County)**

• LENGTH AND DIFFICULTY: 4.7 mi round-trip, moderate

• TRAILHEAD AND DESCRIPTION: From US-19/23 in Clyde, turn onto Charles St, and cross a RR and bridge for the distance of 0.2 mi. Turn L on SR-1513 and Jenkins Valley Rd (SR-1642), and go 0.4 mi to a R turn on Chambers Mtn Rd (SR-1534). Proceed 1.4 mi on a paved road to where a gravel road turns steeply L (NW). Parking space is limited; a resident's permission may be advisable. The summit can be reached by vehicle, but the gate (200 yd up the steep road) may be locked. Follow the road to a grassy plateau, then take the switchbacks to reach the summit (4,509 ft) at 2.35 mi. Superb views from the firetower are of Lake Junaluska, Pisgah Forest, and Newfound Mtn. Backtrack. (*USGS Map:* Clyde)

▶ **CHEROKEE ARBORETUM**
**(Swain County)**

*Cherokee Arboretum Trail (0.5 mi); Mount Noble Trail (4.6 mi round-trip)*                                                              **714–715**

• LENGTH AND DIFFICULTY: 5.1 mi combined and round-trip, easy to strenuous

• TRAILHEAD AND DESCRIPTION: From the jct of US-19 and US-441 in Cherokee, turn N on US-441 and go 0.6 mi to a sign for Oconaluftee Indian Village, L. Follow the road to a parking area and locate the trail sign for the *Cherokee Arboretum Trail* near the stockade gate. On an easy loop pass through a forest of pines and hardwoods where more than 150 species of plants are labeled. On the trail are a restored Indian log cabin, a stream, small pool, and an herb garden. A national recreation trail, it is maintained by the Cherokee Historical Association. Access to the *Mt Noble Trail* is from the upper parking lot on the R (E) side. On a moderate to strenuous climb, ascend in and out of hardwood coves, first to the W and then N to headwaters of Owl Branch at 1.4 mi. After curving around a ridge ascend more steeply to the summit of Mt Noble (4,066 ft) and a fire tower at 2.3 mi (elev gain 1,666 ft). Outstanding views are of the Cherokee area (E, SE), GSMNP (NW, N), and Nantahala NF (S). (The Village is also home for the Cherokee outdoor drama "Unto These Hills.") (*USGS Map:* Whittier)

• INFORMATION: Cherokee Historical Association, Box 398, Cherokee, NC 28719, tel: 704-497-2111.

▶ **CHIMNEY ROCK PARK**
  **(Rutherford County)**

Chimney Rock Park (2,280 ft) is a 1,000-acre scenic private nature preserve with commercial comforts. The first developer was J.B. Freeman in the late 1800s, but the first extensive developers were twin brothers, Lucius and Asahel Morse, from Missouri in the early 1900s. The park continues to be operated by their descendants. One of the park's outstanding features is the giant granite monolith, Chimney Rock, which rises sharply to 315 ft. It is a remnant of 500 million-year-old igneous rock.

Another major feature is Hickory Nut Falls, which plummets 404 ft in the gorge. There are a number of special annual events, among them an Easter Sunrise Service, Sports Car Hill-climb, Photography Contest, and Rope Climbing Exhibition. Open daily mid-March through November; an entry fee is charged. There is a large picnic area with a pavilion, but camping is not allowed. (*USGS Maps:* Bat Cave, Lake Lure)

• ADDRESS AND ACCESS: Chimney Rock Park, Chimney Rock, NC 28720, tel: 704-625-9611. Entrance is on US-74/64/NC-9 in Chimney Rock.

• SUPPORT FACILITIES: There are five campgrounds in the immediate area, including two at Lake Lure and three by the Rocky Broad River. Contact the park for additional information. Motels, restaurants, and stores are here also.

*Skyline Nature Trail (0.9 mi); Cliff Trail (0.6 mi); Hickory Nut Falls Trail (1.2 mi round-trip)*                716–718

• LENGTH AND DIFFICULTY: 2.7 mi combined and round-trip, easy to moderate

• TRAILHEAD AND DESCRIPTION: After entry to the park, drive 3 mi to the parking area and either take the tunnel to the 258-ft elevator to the sky lounge or use the steps on a route past Vista Rock or Needle's Eye. Follow the signs for *Skyline Nature Trail* (and use a brochure for the 28 interpretive stops). Among the trees and shrubs are table mtn pine, wafer ash (*Ptelea trifoliata*), chestnut oak, laurel, and rhododendron. Wildflowers include windflower, wild orchids, and shooting star (*Dodecatheon meadia*). Reach spectacular Hickory Nut Falls at 0.9 mi. Backtrack, or return on the precipitous *Cliff Trail* (which was constructed by Guilford Nanney, a local resident who also designed the intricate series of stairways in the park). Pass Inspiration Point where both Hickory Nut Falls and Lake Lure can be viewed. For the *Hickory Nut Falls Trail,* leave the parking area and walk through a picturesque and densely shaded forest of hemlock, oak, laurel, and ferns for 0.6 mi to the misty base of the lower falls. Backtrack.

## ▶ CRABTREE BALD TRAIL                                  719
### (Haywood County)

- LENGTH AND DIFFICULTY: 6.7 mi round-trip, strenuous (elev change 2,355 ft)

- SPECIAL FEATURE: views of 49 mtns over 6,000 ft elev

- TRAILHEAD AND DESCRIPTION: (This route is neither blazed nor signed; the major property owner is Jack Messer, tel: 704-627-6224, who has given his permission for day hikes, though you will see no-trespassing signs. Crabtree Bald, the SW end of a ridgeline called Crab Orchard Fields, is unique in its claim that the state's 49 peaks of 6,000 ft or higher elev can be seen from here.) From the jct of I-40 and NC-209 (Exit 24) go 2.4 mi N on NC-209 to Crabtree-Ironduff School, and turn R on Upper Crabtree Rd (SR-1503). After 2 mi turn L on Bald Creek Rd (SR-1505) at a James Chapel Baptist Church sign. Drive 3.1 mi along Bald Creek and park off the side of the gravel road near a bridge over Indian Branch with cement curbs. To the L is a cattle chute and pasture gate. Climb over the gate and follow a distinct jeep road through the pasture with Indian Branch on the R. At 0.2 mi is a second gate; cross Indian Branch and at 0.5 mi reach a road jct at the edge of the woods. Straight ahead is a shorter but steeper route; R is a longer but easier route. If following the shorter route, continue up the valley beside the stream. Cross the stream again at 1 mi in an open area and follow the old road. (From this point and for the next 0.9 mi, you can follow any old track that goes in the same direction as the power line [S or SW] because you will reach a number of forks and intersections.) At 2.3 mi reach a bend near the crest of the ridge where you can spot the two antennae on the summit of Crabtree Bald. To shortcut, climb L steeply up the crest of the mountain ridge and generally through open cattle pastures for 0.1 mi to reach a jeep route on the main crest. Bear L and hike through open fields to reach the scenic summit (5,320 ft) at 2.9 mi. If returning on the longer route follow the crest's jeep road NE in open fields for 1.1 mi to a low gap. Bear R on a used jeep road and descend, first through fields and then back into the forest of oak, maple, and locust. Arrive at the road jct for a loop at 6.2 mi, and return to the gate and Bald Creek Rd at 6.7 mi. (*USGS Map:* Fines Creek)

▶ **DE FLORA NATURE TRAIL**                                    **720**
   **(Ashe County)**

• LENGTH AND DIFFICULTY: 0.7 mi, easy

• TRAILHEAD AND DESCRIPTION: At the jct of US-421 and US-221 at Deep Gap (1 mi W of the BRP and 12 mi E of Boone) go N on US-221 for 2 mi, turn R on Pine Swamp Rd (SR-1171), and go 1.1 mi to West Pine Swamp Rd (SR-1169). Turn L and go 0.7 mi to a parking area, L. The trail is by marshes, ponds, streams, and through woodland with more than 150 species of flowering plants and numerous species of ferns. Some of the plants are rare. The owner maintains and conducts tours on the trail. For permission and a tour schedule contact Dr. F. Ray Derrick, Dept of Biology, Appalachian State Univ, Boone, NC 28608, tel: 704-262-3025 or 264-8467.

▶ **GRANDFATHER MOUNTAIN**
   **(Avery, Caldwell, and Watauga Counties)**

   Grandfather Mountain is a popular commercial tourist attraction and nature preserve with its mile-high swinging bridge over an 80-ft couloir (dedicated in 1952); natural wildlife habitats (Mildred the Bear Environmental Habitat in 1973, for example); plant and mineral exhibits; hiking trails over rugged terrain; and unspoiled natural beauty (such as the world's largest gardens of pink-shell azalea, *vaseyi*). Geologically, the mtn is unique; its metamorphic sandstone is distinct from all other surrounding mtns. "We have made it inoffensively accessible," said Hugh Morton, whose family has owned the property since his MIT-graduate grandfather, Hugh MacRae, bought it in 1885. Among the annual events are the Highlands Games (over

100 Scottish clans represented in traditional sports and arts) held the second weekend in July; "Singing on the Mountain" (a modern and traditional gospel concert) the 4th Sunday in June; and the Nature Photography Weekend (with contests and lectures) in late May. (Photography is a special interest of Morton, who was a combat newsreel photographer in the Philippines in WW II, and who is internationally known for his filmed wildlife series.) Campground facilities are not available, but picnic facilities are set up at scenic overlooks. Hang gliding is featured on weekends. An entrance fee is required at the gatehouse on US-221.

There are ten trails on the mtn, each connecting to a network of other trails. Six accesses provide convenient trail-length options—two on NC-105, one from the BRP, one from US-221, one at the visitor center, and one on the entrance road. The access to the visitor center and entrance road is for day hikes only. Overnight parking or walking up or down the entrance road is prohibited. Daily permits (unless you purchase a season hiking pass) and small fees are required on all trails and for camping at designated campsites. Permits are available at the Grandfather Mtn entrance gatehouse; at Scotchman Store (open 24 hrs daily) at the jct of NC-105 and NC-184; and at Grandfather Mtn Country Store on US-221, 6.4 mi S of Blowing Rock. Contact the backcountry manager for a list of additional permit outlets and hiking and camping regulations. (Permit fees are used for trail maintenance and development and safety patrol.) (*USGS Maps:* Grandfather Mtn, Valle Crucis)

• ADDRESS AND ACCESS: Grandfather Mountain, Linville, NC 28646, main office tel: 704-733-4337 or toll-free: 800-222-7515 (NC), 800-438-7500 (eastern U.S.). For trails: Backcountry Manager, PO Box 128, Linville NC 28646, tel: 704-733-2013 (M-F 9–5), 704-733-4337 (weekends). Gatehouse entrance on US-221, 2 mi NE from Linville; 1 mi W from the BRP.

• SUPPORT FACILITIES: Groceries, lodging, restaurants, shops in Linville. For information on campgrounds and other attractions, call N.C. High Country Host, toll-free numbers above.

*Grandfather Trail* (2.2 mi); *Underwood Trail* (0.5 mi); *Arch Rock Trail* (0.6 mi); *Black Rock Cliffs Cave Trail* (1 mi)
**721–724**

• LENGTH AND DIFFICULTY: 4.3 mi combined, strenuous

• TRAILHEAD AND DESCRIPTION: From the visitor center parking area locate the trail signs, N, on a high embankment and follow the blue-blazed *Grandfather Trail* through dense rhododendron. At 0.4 mi reach a gap, and at 0.5 mi jct L with the yellow-blazed *Underwood Trail*. (The *Underwood Trail*, which rejoins the *Grandfather Trail* after 0.5 mi, passes Raven's Nest Spring on a rocky treadway. Its purpose is for a route less arduous than the rough climbs of *Grandfather Trail*.) Continuing on the *Grandfather Trail*, ascend steeply and climb ladders to scenic MacRae Peak (5,939 ft). At 1 mi jct R with the red-blazed *Arch Rock Trail*. (The *Arch Rock Trail* turns S and descends to Grandview Pinnacle at 0.4 mi. A further descent of 0.2 mi reaches the trail's end at a jct with the yellow-blazed *Black Rock Cliffs Cave Trail*. On the *Black Rock Cliffs Cave Trail* it is 0.4 mi R on a level grade to the main entrance road and Cliffs Cave parking area. To the L it is 0.4 mi to Black Rocks, and another 0.2 mi to the cave. Flashlights are necessary. Backtrack.)

Continuing on the *Grandfather Trail* reach the Attic Window Peak (5,949 ft) at 1.1 mi, and the Indian House Cave (200 ft off the trail, R) at 1.2 mi. At 1.9 mi jct with the red-blazed *Calloway Trail*, L (described below), and reach a spur trail to Watauga View at 2.2 mi. Here also is the end (temporary) of *Grandfather Mtn Trail* and the beginning, R, of the white-blazed *Daniel Boone Scout Trail* (described below).

*Profile Trail* (2.6 mi); *Shanty Spring Trail* (1.6 mi); *Calloway Trail* (0.3 mi)
**725–727**

• LENGTH AND DIFFICULTY: 4.5 mi combined, moderate to strenuous

• TRAILHEAD AND DESCRIPTION: The *Shanty Spring Trail* is across the road from the jct of NC-105 and NC-184, and access to the *Profile Trail* is 0.6 mi N on NC-105 at a parking area, R. The trails connect near Shanty Spring on the profile side of

*Grandfather Mtn.* If a loop is considered, the *Profile Trail,* though longer, is less steep. If ascending on the *Shanty Spring Trail,* follow the graded white-blazed trail through beech, yellow and black birch, rhododendron, and oak up the Eastern Continental Divide. At 0.4 mi enter a hemlock grove and pass a spur to Little Grassy Creek Falls, R. Ascend steeply and jct L with the *Profile Trail* at 1.4 mi. Ahead, climb on a rocky route to Shanty Spring at 1.6 mi. (Here is the last dependable source of water for any of the campsites on the main ridge ahead.) Begin the red-blazed *Calloway Trail,* continue the climb to the top of the ridge, and jct with the blue-blazed *Grandfather Trail,* R and L, after 0.3 mi. (To the R it is 1.9 mi to the visitor center parking area, and L it is 0.3 mi to Calloway Park, the end of the *Grandfather Trail,* and the beginning of the *Daniel Boone Scout Trail,* which descends the E side of the mtn to jct with the *Tanawha Trail,* the BRP, and US-221.)

If ascending on the *Profile Trail* from the NC-105 parking lot, cross the Watauga River on huge flat boulders and follow a skillfully designed trail on a slope through cherry, maple, birch, beech, Fraser's sedge, ferns, and Indian pipe. Pass benches of impressive stonework. At 0.8 mi cross Shanty Spring Branch in a beautiful pristine area. Pass through a large rock formation at 0.9 mi and begin an ascent on Green Ridge switchbacks to a good view of Snake Mtn, Seven Devils, and the Foscoe Valley at 1.7 mi. At 2 mi are three campsites (50 ft L) with intricate rock work for a fireplace and bench, almost under the chin of the Grandfather profile. With good views NW, pass R of Haystack Rock at 2.2 mi (where a spur trail is planned L to ascend to the profile cliff and to join the completion of the *Grandfather Trail* on the main ridge). Jct with the *Shanty Spring Trail,* R and L, at 2.6 mi, the end of the *Profile Trail.*

### **Daniel Boone Scout Trail** *(3 mi);* **Grandfather Trail Extension** *(1.2 mi);* **Cragway Trail** *(0.9 mi)*      **728–731**

- LENGTH AND DIFFICULTY: 5.1 mi, combined, strenuous (elev change 2,082 ft)

- TRAILHEAD AND DESCRIPTION: Begin the *Daniel Boone Scout Trail* at a small parking area (W side of road) on US-221 (1.6 mi

S from the Grandfather Mtn Country Store and Motel, and 7.4 mi NE from the Grandfather gatehouse entrance). Follow an old road (the NPS has planned the route under the BRP bridge at Boone Fork to connect with the BRP's *Tanawha Trail,* and the NPS has named it the *Grandfather Mtn Access Trail*). If this route is followed, jct with the *Tanawha Trail* after 0.4 mi. (To the R, across the Boone Fork bridge, are two trail accesses to the BRP. The nearest is to Boone Fork parking after 260 yd [mp 299.9], and the other access is at the BRP Calloway Peak Overlook parking [mp 299.7] on the *Upper Boone Fork Trail* for 0.5 mi.) Continue L on the *Tanawha Trail* and go 0.2 mi to a jct, R, with the *Grandfather Trail Ext.* Ahead on the *Tanawha Trail* it is 255 yd to a jct where the *Daniel Boone Scout Trail* continues R. (See Chapter 6 for details of the *Tanawha Trail.*)

If hiking the *Grandfather Trail Ext,* follow the old woods road 0.7 mi to a jct L with the *Cragway Trail.* (The 0.9-mi *Cragway Trail* ascends, steeply in sections, to upturned cliffs that offer magnificent views of a geological cirque, the Boone Fork Bowl. Other views are of the Blue Ridge Mtns and their foothills, NE. Rhododendron, red spruce, Allegheny sand myrtle, and blueberries landscape this beautiful route. It connects with the *Daniel Boone Scout Trail.*) Continue ahead, upstream on the *Grandfather Trail Ext,* and cross Boone Fork at 1 mi. Ascend to View Rock, L, at 1.2 mi for a view of the Boone Fork Bowl and the temporary end of the trail. (From here the extension is planned to ascend White Rock Ridge on a gradual climb through blueberry patches and across a rocky cone of pinnacles to White Rock summit. From there it will curve L along the main ridge into dense fir and spruce to skirt the high, scenic cliffs of Boone Fork Bowl. A *Leeway Trail* will be routed on the E side for a less strenuous route. In a gap, N of Calloway Peak, a connector trail will go R to join the *Profile Trail.* The *Grandfather Trail Ext* will continue ahead and connect with the *Grandfather Trail* and the *Daniel Boone Scout Trail.* When completed, *"Extension"* will be dropped from the title.)

If continuing on the *Daniel Boone Scout Trail* from the *Tanawha Trail,* ascend on a ridge, eroded in sections, to a campsite L, and jct R with the *Cragway Trail* at 1.7 mi. (A dependable spring is 145 yd to the L.) It is 85 yd R on the *Cragway Trail* to the first of its major scenic views—Flat Rock View.) In a forest of spruce, mtn ash, rhododendron, birch, striped maple, galax, and ferns, ascend on a narrow, rough treadway to Hi-Balsam Shelter, L, at 2.7 mi. (The shelter sleeps six; no campfires; use a fire ring near the trail.) A few yd below the shelter from here is a view of the Linn Cove viaduct on the BRP. Continue a steep ascent to Calloway Peak (5,964 ft, the highest elev of the Blue Ridge Mtn range) at 3 mi. (Calloway Peak is named for Ervin and Texie Calloway, proprietors of the Grandfather Hotel on the W side of the mtn at the turn of the century.) Panoramic scenery from large boulders provides an awesome view of Beach Mtn and Tennessee (W); Mt Rogers in Virginia (N); Mt Mitchell (SW); and Table Rock (S). (From here it is 2.2 mi on the *Grandfather Trail* to the visitor center.)

▶ **GREENCROFT GARDENS TRAIL**                                   **732**
  **(Franklin County)**

* LENGTH AND DIFFICULTY: 2.9 mi, easy

* TRAILHEAD AND DESCRIPTION: From Louisburg jct of US-401 and NC-56 W, go S on US-401, 5.5 mi to Greencroft sign, L at private driveway. (It is 4.4 mi N on US-401 from NC-98.) Park at the designated space. The trail enters the forest at the N end of the residence. Follow the signed trail that winds down to and around a lake, a waterfall, and loops back to the parking area after 0.9 mi. (A 2-mi loop that extends beyond the gardens trail requires permission and a guide.) Founded by Allen and Flora de Hart, the gardens have over 400 wild plant species labeled, the largest private wildflower garden in eastern North Carolina. A prominent species is wild pink (*Silene caroliniana*), a tufted perennial with white, sometimes pink, petals. Open all year; daytime use only. The annual public Franklin County Outdoor Garden Concert is held here the first Sunday in May, 2 to 5 pm.

* INFORMATION: DeHart Botanical Gardens, Inc, Rte 1, Box 36, Louisburg, NC 27549, tel: 919-496-4771 or 496-2521.

▶ **HIGH WINDY TRAIL**                                    **733–737**
**(Buncombe County)**

• LENGTH AND DIFFICULTY: 6.6 mi round-trip, strenuous

• TRAILHEAD AND DESCRIPTION: In Black Mountain at jct of I-40 and NC-9, take NC-9 S and after 0.5 mi turn R on Blue Ridge Rd (SR-2500). Go 0.9 mi, turn L on Blue Ridge Assembly Rd (SR-2720) and drive 0.5 mi to the YMCA Blue Ridge Assembly entrance. From the parking area, go to the administration bldg, L, to request permission to hike the trail. (In addition to the *High Windy Trail,* there are two nature trails [including the 0.4-mi *Steve Franks Memorial Trail*] and three long loop trails, all connecting with, or partially running with the *High Windy Trail.*) From the parking area go S, curve R around the columned Robert E. Lee Hall, and take the first road R to begin the *High Windy Trail.* (The *Wolfpit Circle Trail* and the *Carolina Loop Trail* run jointly until they make their L turns on the mountainside.) Pass a vehicle shed, L, and the Earle L. Whittington Amphitheater and Chapel, R, and arrive at a metal gate at 0.5 mi. Beyond the gate ascend on a jeep road through hardwoods, rhododendron, wild hydrangea, and ferns to the first major curve R, at 0.8 mi. (The *Carolina Loop Trail* and the *Wolfpit Branch Trail* go L on an old jeep road. To the R the *Carolina Loop Trail* continues with the main trail.) Ascend to a storm shelter, L, at 1 mi. (To the R is the original *High Windy Trail.* It is badly eroded and exceptionally steep for 0.6 mi until it rejoins the main trail.) Continue L on the easier route. At 1.4 mi the *Carolina Loop Trail* goes L. At 1.6 mi cross a bridge over a tributary of Wolfpit Branch. Pass a scenic lookout at 1.8 mi, and in a forest of tall oaks jct L with the *Viewpoint Trail.* (The *Viewpoint Trail* climbs to a scenic view of the Swannanoa River Valley. It also goes to a spring and headwaters of Wolfpit Branch in a lush cove before descending to join the *Wolfpit Circle Trail* and *Carolina Loop Trail.*) At 2.1 mi jct R with the old *High Windy Trail* in an area of wildflowers and ferns. Ascend steeply to the ridgecrest at 2.5 mi, turn L, and follow an old road. After 0.4 mi turn L. Arrive at High Windy (4,360 ft) at 3.3 mi (a storm shelter is nearby). Climb the old fire tower for a panoramic view of Mt

Mitchell and Craggy Dome (N), Stone Mtn (SE), and Mt Pisgah (SW). Backtrack. (*USGS Map:* Black Mountain)

• ADDRESS AND ACCESS: YMCA Blue Ridge Assembly, 84 Blue Ridge Circle, Black Mountain, NC 28711, tel: 704-669-8422. In Black Mountain turn S on NC-9 at I-40 jct, and after 0.5 mi turn R on Blue Ridge Rd (SR-2500). Go 0.9 mi, turn L on SR-2720, and drive 0.5 mi to the Assembly entrance.

▶ **OLD COLLEGE FARM TRAIL**                                   **738**
  **(Cleveland County)**

• LENGTH AND DIFFICULTY: 8.7 mi, moderate

• SPECIAL FEATURES: Jolly Mtn, Broad River

• TRAILHEAD AND DESCRIPTION: The white-blazed trail has two major accesses. The one described below is clockwise from the parking area at the N side of the Broad River bridge on NC-150 (3 mi S of Boiling Springs). It is a multiple-use trail, mainly for hikers and equestrians, from rough footpaths to secondary roads in red clay soil. It was developed by the Cleveland County Trails Association with assistance from the Broad River Group of the Sierra Club and Boy Scout Troop 100. Among the property owners are the Federal Paperboard Co and Duke Power Co.

Follow the old road up the scenic riverside among river birch, laurel, papaw, tag alder, and oak. Cross a small stream, and at 0.5 mi cross Jolly Branch. For the next 0.8 mi follow the base of Jolly Mtn, R, and begin an ascent into a pine forest at 1.6 mi. Leave the old road at 1.8 mi on a footpath, cross a ridge, and come onto another old road for a jct at 2 mi. Go straight ahead, bear L at the next road fork, and arrive at the powerline at 2.3 mi. Views E and W show the rolling hills. Turn R, undulate in patches of elderberry, horse mint, and senna, and at 2.7 mi (immediately past a powerline tower) turn L. Descend into the forest on an eroded road to a faint trail R at 2.8 mi. (The trail is a 55-yd connector to the N side of the loop.) Continue ahead, cross a small stream, and follow an old grassy road that parallels

R of Sandy Run in a forest of loblolly and Scotch pines. Arrive at Old College Farm Rd (SR-1195) at 3.4 mi. (To the L it is 30 yd to the road bridge over scenic Sandy Run.) Turn R, up the public road, and at 3.5 mi turn L on a timber road. (It is 0.7 mi up the public road to the NW trailhead.) At 3.7 mi reach a small stream with a culvert and ascend steeply to another logging road in a clearcut at 3.8 mi. Turn R, and go straight (avoid the R fork). Continue a gradual ascent among young sourwood, wild cherry, and oak to another fork at 4.1 mi. Turn L, descend and cross the dam of an old farm pond, R. Follow a footpath R of a barbed wire fence to a pine and Arizona cedar plantation, timber road, and clearcut at 4.5 mi. (Overgrowth at a timber cut makes the next mile, L, impassable.) To bypass, turn R on the timber road and rejoin the trail after 65 yd. Stay on the timber road to pass L of a large barn (once used on the Gardner-Webb College Farm). Reach the paved Old College Farm Rd at 4.7 mi, the NW trailhead. (It is 1.3 mi NE to NC-150.)

To continue the loop, turn R, follow the public road 0.2 mi before turning L off the road for a 0.1-mi parallel route. Reach a wide forest road and veer L (here is also an entrance, R, from SR-1195). Leave the old forest road at 5.2 mi, L, to a lesser used road. After 0.1 mi turn R, descend steeply 35 yd to cross a stream. Cross another stream, enter beds of running cedar, and at 5.5 mi arrive at the faint connector route (55 yd R to the S side of the loop). Ascend to the powerline and pass under at 5.6 mi (the view R shows where you passed earlier in the opposite direction). Reenter the woods and follow the blazes on a number of turns through pines before returning to the powerline swath at 5.9 mi. Follow under the powerline, R of a private home, to an old road jct at 6.5 mi. Turn R and into the forest. Pass R of a farm house to a pleasant, wide forest road and gently ascend to Jolly Mtn. Turn R at a fork at 6.7 mi. (At 7 mi is an aqua blaze, R, on a 120-yd spur trail to scenic views of the Broad River. Among the rocky ledges are laurel, jessamine, wild quinine, and blueberries.) On the main trail take the next fork L to descend steeply and to rock-hop Jolly Branch at 7.5 mi. Ascend through periwinkle and honeysuckle to pass R of private homes at 8 mi. The footpath now becomes rough and undulates on the approach to the exit and parking area at NC-150 at 8.7 mi. (*USGS Map:* Boiling Springs)

• INFORMATION: John Hunt, Box 176, Lattimore, NC 28089, and Fred Blackley, 504 S Dekalb St, Shelby, NC 28150, tel: 704-484-1731

▶ **PEARSON'S FALLS TRAIL**                                        **739**
(Polk County)

*Pearson's Falls Trail* (0.3 mi) is part of a 250-acre nature preserve maintained and financed privately by the Tryon Garden Club (organized in 1929). Open all year, there is a small fee to view the beautiful 90-ft cascades and botanical display of over 200 species (one of which is the rare broadleaf coreopsis, *Coreopsis latifolia*). (The Club purchased the property in 1931 from the Charles W. Pearson family.) Access to the property is 4 mi N of Tryon on US-176; turn L on SR-1102 (3 mi S from Saluda). Follow the signs 1 mi.

• INFORMATION: Tryon Garden Club Nature Preserve, Rte 1, Box 327, Saluda, NC 28773, tel: 704-479-3031.

▶ **PHILLIPS KNOB TRAIL**                                          **740**
(Yancey County)

• LENGTH AND DIFFICULTY: 4.3 mi round-trip, strenuous (elev change 1,520 ft)

• TRAILHEAD AND DESCRIPTION: From the town square in Burnsville, drive N on Main St (which becomes Mitchell Branch Rd, SR-1373) and after 0.8 mi park at a fork. Begin the hike, R, on Mica Springs Heights Rd. (Although the road leads to the summit spur, the road is narrow and rough.) It is 0.8 mi to the next jct; turn R on a steep and rough road. Reach the fire tower at 2.2 mi. Views to Big Bald, Table Rock, and Black Mtn ranges are impressive. Backtrack. (*USGS Map:* Burnsville)

## ▶ SAURATOWN TRAIL                                    741
### (Stokes and Surry Counties)

• LENGTH AND DIFFICULTY: 19 mi, moderate

• TRAILHEAD AND DESCRIPTION: The trail, on both public and private properties, is open all year to hikers and equestrians. It is significant because it traverses the scenic crest of Sauratown Mtn and connects Hanging Rock and Pilot Mtn state parks. Part of the route is proposed for the *MST*. For hiking purposes, the description below follows hiking trails in Hanging Rock State Park to jct with the *Sauratown Trail,* rather than the horse-trail route exclusively. (See both state parks in Chapter 10, Section 2.)

From parking lot #2 in Hanging Rock State Park, follow the trail signs SW; pass L of the bathhouse fence, cross a feeder stream at 0.3 mi, and follow red blazes. At 0.4 mi pass jct R with *Moores Knob Trail* and pass jct L with *Magnolia Spring Trail* at 1 mi. Continue ahead, ascend slightly to a saddle at 1.5 mi and jct R with *Moores Wall Trail.* Turn L on a blue-blazed trail, the *Torys Den Trail.* After 0.5 mi reach the crest of Huckleberry Ridge near a large rock formation. Descend and jct with the *Sauratown Trail,* R and L, at 2.4 mi. Turn L.

(To the R the *Sauratown Trail* and the *Torys Den Trail* run jointly 1.6 mi. From that point, on Charlie Young Rd [SR-2028], the *Sauratown Trail,* as a bridle trail, continues 0.7 mi straight ahead to descend on a ridge to Hall Rd [SR-2012]. It turns R on the road and goes to the Horse Parking Trail Center, R, after 1.7 mi (0.1 mi E of *Lower Cascades Trail,* and 0.6 mi W of the main entrance to the park on Moores Spring Rd).

Following *Sauratown Trail* W, pass a spring at 3.5 mi, leave the park boundary at 3.9 mi, and arrive at NC-66 at 4.2 mi. (Note: The mileage accumulations are based on the hiking access trails, not the bridle trail.) Turn L on NC-66, but R on Merritt Rd (SR-1188) at 4.6 mi, and L on Sauratown Mtn Rd (SR-1172) at 5.2 mi. Ascend the gravel road to reach the summit of Sauratown Mtn (2,450 ft) at 8.5 mi. Pass R of the last radio-tower buildings and begin a SW switchback descent. Follow the ridge through chestnut oak, hickory, blueberry patches, and wild-flowers (such as fire pink) to a saddle at 9.3 mi. Pass Crystal Mine (an abandoned mining area) at 9.9 mi. Begin a steep descent at 10 mi. Follow a rocky, irregular treadway for 1.7 mi to an old tobacco barn at 11.7 mi. Pass an abandoned house and go through a honeysuckle grove at 11.9 mi; reach a farm road at 12.1 mi. Turn R and follow a farm road to Volunteer Rd (SR-1136) at 12.7 mi. Turn L for 80 yd on Volunteer Rd and turn R on a private road. Reach the West Prong of the Little Yadkin River at 13.9 mi. (The swinging bridge has been washed away. A new one is being rebuilt, and large rocks have been placed in the river for rock-hopping. During normal weather the shallow river can be waded.) Ascend steeply to Bowen Rd (SR-1160) at 14.2 mi. Turn R and follow a gravel road to High Bridge Rd (SR-1157) at 14.8 mi. (The town of Pinnacle is 0.5 L.) Cross the road, and pass through a bed of running cedar in the forest and fields of honeysuckle in open areas to Bradley Rd (SR-1155) at 16.9 mi. Cross Old US-52 at 17.6 mi, and Southern RR crossing at 17.7 mi. Turn L on paved VFW Rd (SR-1152), and at 18.3 mi turn R on Pilot Knob Rd (SR-1151). Enter Surry County at 18.5 mi, and go under US-52 bridge at 19 mi, to the end of *Sauratown Trail* and the boundary of Pilot Mtn State Park. (Here is a jct with the 1.7-mi *Grassy Ridge Trail* that leads to the 6.5-mi *Corridor Trail,* both of which are equestrian/hiker routes to the Yadkin River.)

• ADDRESS AND ACCESS: Sauratown Trails Committee, 280 South Liberty St, Winston-Salem, NC 27101, tel: 919-722-9346. Hanging Rock State Park is off Moores Springs Rd (SR-1001), 0.5 mi W of NC-8, 1.5 mi N of Danbury. Pilot Mtn State Park is off US-52, NW of Pinnacle.

• SUPPORT FACILITIES: Groceries and svc stores are in both towns. Both parks have campgrounds that are closed in the winter, but the private Moores Springs Campground is open all year at Hanging Rock State Park. It is W of the park entrance on Moores Springs Rd. Address: Rte 1, Westfield, NC 27053, tel: 919-593-8242.

▶**SPIVEY MOUNTAIN TRAIL**                                    **742**
  **(Buncombe County)**

• LENGTH AND DIFFICULTY: 2.6 mi round-trip, moderate

• TRAILHEAD AND DESCRIPTION: From the jct of I-40 and US-19/23 W of Asheville, go 0.2 mi on US-19/23 N to Old Haywood Rd (SR-1404) and turn L between Exxon and Gulf svc stations. Go 0.4 mi, turn L on Starnes Cove Rd (SR-1255), and go 2.9 mi to the end of the paved road to park. Inform someone at either one of the Chambers homes (L or R of the parking area) that you are taking the hike. Follow up the gravel road, L of a pond and barn, and at 0.4 mi pass L of a residence. At 0.8 mi reach a crest of the ridge and pass through young hardwoods. Chinquapin, wild rose, spiderwort, and spotted knapweed *(Centaurea maculosa)* are in the open areas. Pass under a powerline and ascend the ridgeline to a gravel road at 1.1 mi. Turn R on the gravel road and reach the fire tower on Spivey Mtn (3,317 ft) at 1.3 mi. Here are excellent views of Asheville and the surrounding area. Backtrack. *(USGS Map:* Enka)

• INFORMATION: Jim and Karen Chambers, Rte 8, Box 404, Asheville, NC 28806, tel: 704-667-8361.

▶**SUNSET ROCK TRAIL**                                       **743–744**
  **(Macon County)**

• LENGTH AND DIFFICULTY: 1.4 mi round-trip, easy

• TRAILHEAD AND DESCRIPTION: From the jct of US-64 and NC-28 in Highlands, proceed on E Main St 0.4 mi and park opposite the Highlands Nature Center. Follow the sign and turn R at 0.2 mi over rock slabs through pine, rosebay, rhododendron, hemlock, and locust. At 0.6 mi an 1879 rock engraving indicates that the park area is a memorial to Margaretta A. and S. Prioleal Ravenel. To the R is a large rock outcropping that provides a magnificent sunset view of the Nantahala NF and the town of Highlands. From here can also be seen Satulah Mtn (4,542 ft) about 1 mi S, a property owned by the same corporation that owns Sunset Rock, Satulah Summit-Ravenel Park, Inc. Backtrack. (Satulah Summit is accessible by a short hike on the *Satulah Summit Trail* from the Satulah Mtn Rd. From the jct of US-64 and NC-28 (4th St), go S 0.2 mi on 4th St, straight ahead off NC-28 at the curve. Follow the signs and park to avoid blocking the gate.)

• INFORMATION: Highlands Chamber of Commerce, Town Hall, PO Box 404, Highlands, NC 28741, tel: 704-526-2112.

# PART VII

# Trails on College, University, and Special Properties

# 15.

## College and University Trails

*Trails are such a uniting force, so democratic, so educational; they unite all age groups.* —Doris B. Hammett

Degree programs in parks and recreation are offered in 21 colleges and universities in the state, and 11 two-year colleges offer preliminary degree programs. Some of the large senior institutions offer degrees in forestry and a variety of environmental fields. Two university medical centers, University of North Carolina at Chapel Hill and Duke University, offer departments in recreation therapy. Although few institutions of higher education have adequate properties for a trail system, all of them require courses in physical education and 40 percent have organizations or clubs that promote hiking in outdoor sports or outings.

▶ **DAVIDSON COUNTY COMMUNITY COLLEGE (Davidson County)**

Davidson County Community College's 83-acre *Natural Garden Trail* contains 0.4 mi of multiple-loop trails to emphasize ferns, trees, and wildflowers (including orchids, trillium, and blue star, *Amsonia tabernaemontana*). A stream-and-bog area offers additional botanical study. The county garden clubs have sponsored projects since 1976, and the Garden honors Anel Black of the Garden Council of Lexington. **745**

• ADDRESS AND ACCESS: Biology Dept, DCCC, Lexington, NC 27292, tel: 704-249-8186. Access is at the corner of Business I-85 and Old Greensboro Rd (SR-1798), 3.8 mi N of the US-64 jct.

## ▶ DUKE UNIVERSITY
### (Durham, Chatham, Alamance, and Orange Counties)

The 8,300-acre Duke Forest has five major tracts, two of which (Durham and Korstian) have numerous fire roads and unnamed trails for hikers, joggers, and equestrians. It began with a gift of 4,700 acres from Durham and Orange counties in the 1920s. In 1931 the University established a Forest Program and appointed Dr. Clarence F. Korstian as its first director; he developed the forest into an area of research and a laboratory for forestry students. (The forest is coveted and threatened by commercial developers.)

The large Durham tract is located on both sides of NC-571, beginning W of its jct with Bypass US-15/501 (2 mi S from I-85), and goes 3 mi NW to US-70. Gate numbers are posted along NC-571 for loop trails and picnic sites. Gates 11 and 12 lead to the tract's highest ridge, Couch Mtn (640 ft) on the *Couch Mountain Trail*. Korstian, another large tract, is between Whitfield Rd (SR-1731) and Mt Sinai Rd (SR-1718), 3 mi E of the NC-86/I-40 jct on Whitfield Rd. New Hope Creek flows through, W to E. One trail, through Gate 25 (or 23 on the N side), descends to ford New Hope Creek on a concrete flood bridge. The trail at Gate 26 descends to a cliff and a grove of rhododendron. **746**

The other tracts are less visited. The Blackwood tract is found on both sides of Hillsborough Rd (SR-1009), 5 mi N of downtown Carrboro. The Eno tract is on Stony Creek between the triangle of NC-86 (W), Ray Rd (SR-1723) (E), and Old No 10 Rd (SR-1710) (N), 1.5 mi S from I-85 on NC-86. The Hillsborough tract is on both sides of US-70, 1.5 mi W of its jct with NC-86 in N Hillsborough. The Eno River flows through this property.

The forest contains excellent examples of plant succession. A wide range of trees and flowers common to the piedmont are here, and wildlife (such as fox, deer, raccoon, squirrel, and owls) is protected. Fishing is allowed, but camping, hunting, and use of motorized vehicles on the trails are not permitted. There are no facilities for drinking water or restrooms. Over 20.7 mi of trails are on the fire lanes, and 14.3 mi are possible on all-weather roads. (For walking in a more formal setting, the Sarah P. Duke Memorial Gardens near the University entrance are also open to the public.) (*USGS Maps:* Chapel Hill, Durham NW, Efland, Hillsborough)

• INFORMATION: Duke Forest Resource Mgr, School of Forestry and Environmental Studies, 206-A Biological Sciences Bldg, Duke University, Durham, NC 27706, tel: 919-684-2421. (Request the "Discover Duke Forest" brochure. It includes details and locator maps.)

## ▶ NORTH CAROLINA STATE UNIVERSITY
### (Wake, Durham, and Moore Counties)

The Carl A. Schenck Memorial Forest is a research laboratory of conifers and broadleaves on the university property between Wade Ave and Reedy Creek Park Rd (SR-1650) in Raleigh. The 6-mi *Loblolly Trail* (see Chapter 14) goes 1.5 mi through the forest, and the 1.2-mi *Frances Liles Interpretive Trail* is in the forest interior. It has 10 stops that describe the multiple benefits derived from forest land. Redbud groves and pine grafting are prominent on the S side of the loop. Access is either from the *Loblolly Trail* or the picnic shelter. To reach the picnic shelter take Reedy Creek Park Rd off Blue Ridge Rd (1 mi N of the State Fairgrounds) and go 0.9 mi to the forest entrance sign L. Go 0.1 mi to the entrance gate and park to avoid blocking the gate. Walk on the gated road 0.1 mi to the picnic shelter, R, and the trailhead. (*USGS Map:* Raleigh West) **747**

The Hill Forest is in Durham County and has a network of single-lane access roads that provides 10.5 mi of unnamed trails. Permission for hiking in the forest is required; contact the address below. The forest is on both sides of Flat River, which has some exceptionally steep banks. Dial Creek also flows S through the Forest. To reach the forest from I-85 and US-501 in Durham, go 12.5 mi N on US-501 to Quail Roost and turn R on Moores Mill Rd (SR-1601), immediately turning R on State Forest Rd (SR-1614) after crossing the N and W RR. Go 1 mi to the forest entrance. (SR-1614 also goes through the forest to jct at 2.2 mi with Wilkins Rd [SR-1613] and Hampton Rd [SR-1603] for a route E to Hampton.) The George K. Slocum Forestry Camp is on the L of the entrance. (*USGS Maps:* Rougemont, Lake Michie)

Goodwin Forest is in Moore County. Although there are no developed trails, there are 4.1 mi of single-lane access roads open to hikers. If approaching from Carthage, go W 1.3 mi on NC-22/24/27 to jct with Bethlehem Church Rd (SR-1261), L. After 1.5 mi enter Goodwin Forest. Follow the first road L or go straight ahead. Permission for the hike is required from the office below. (*USGS Map:* Carthage)

• INFORMATION: School of Forest Resources, NCSU, Box 8002, Raleigh, NC 27695, tel: 919-737-2891.

## ▶ UNIVERSITY OF NORTH CAROLINA-ASHEVILLE (Buncombe County)

The 10-acre University Botanical Gardens were set aside by the Board of Trustees in 1960, but the gardens have been developed and maintained by a private board of directors. There are over 400 native species along an easy 0.6-mi route on grassy and gravel trails that cross meadows and into the forest. A log cabin on the trail honors Hubert H. Hayes, author and playwright. The trail returns by Reed Creek from Heath Cove through an area of sycamore, white pine, and oak to cross a stream on a curved bridge. The gardens are open daily; free, but no picnicking or camping is permitted.

• ACCESS: From the jct of I-240 and US-19/23/70 in Asheville, turn N on the latter toward Weaverville and Marshall. Go 2 mi and turn R off the expressway to Broadway and NC-251 jct.

After 0.5 mi turn L on W.T. Weaver Blvd and go 0.1 mi. Park at the entrance. (*USGS Map:* Asheville)　　　**748**

• INFORMATION: University Botanical Gardens at Asheville, Inc, 24 Hampden Rd, Asheville, NC 28805.

## ▶ UNIVERSITY OF NORTH CAROLINA-CHAPEL HILL (Orange County)

The 525-acre North Carolina Botanical Garden is a botanical preserve of southeastern trees, shrubs, plants, ferns, wild-flowers, and herbs. Its nature trails are open daily, and the administrative offices are open M to F. Guided tours of the arboretum are offered Saturdays at 10:30 am. From the parking lot follow the signs on the *North Carolina Botanical Garden Trail* (a self-guided interpretive trail). Cross a bridge at 0.2 mi and turn R. (Another trail ascends L to connect with other unnamed trails.) Follow a combination of trails under a subcanopy of flowering trees such as dogwoods and return to the parking lot after 1.5 mi. (The Totten Research Center is across the street.)　　　**749**

• ADDRESS AND ACCESS: NC Botanical Garden, UNC-CH, Totten Center 457-A, Chapel Hill, NC 27514, tel: 919-967-2246. In E Chapel Hill the location is at Laurel Hill Rd (SR-1901), 0.7 mi S of the US-15/501 and NC-54 jct.

## ▶ WESTERN CAROLINA UNIVERSITY (Jackson and Macon Counties)

The University has a 300-acre preserve in the Wolf Creek watershed, a state natural heritage area N of Brown Mtn. Access paths are also on private and Nantahala NF properties. One access, frequently used by the university's Biology Club, is 5.4 mi S from the campus. From the jct of the main campus entrance on NC-107 in Cullowhee, go S on NC-107 for 1.3 mi to jct with Speedwell Rd (SR-1001). Turn R and drive 1.1 mi to

Cullowhee Mtn Rd (SR-1157) at the bridge over Tilley Creek. Drive 3 mi (along Cullowhee Creek, R) to a horseshoe curve in the road and park on a large grassy area beyond the curve. Hike back 50 yd to the center of the curve at Wolf Creek, R. Follow a footpath on private property past a flume with cascades, pools, and falls. Oak, birch, maple, hemlock, and rhododendron shade the gorge. In addition to the common wildflowers and mosses are less common species such as walking fern and Fraser's sedge. At 0.5 mi jct R with USFS Cherry Gap Rd. Ahead upstream are the university preserve lands and an extended pathway. Backtrack, or follow Cherry Gap Rd out to SR-1157, turn R, and descend 0.6 mi to where you parked. To hike the university and private properties, request permission from the address below. (*USGS Map:* Glenville)                **750**

• INFORMATION: Dept of Biology, WCU, Cullowhee, NC 28723, tel: 704-227-7244.

In Highlands (Macon County) the university administers the Highlands Biological Station (since 1977), an interinstitutional program of the University of N.C. system. (Serving the station is the Highlands Biological Foundation Inc, a non-profit organization with 23 member institutions from the SE region who use the facilities for research. Some international studies are also offered.) Highlands (Clark Foreman) Nature Center is part of the station. It has artifacts, minerals, a botanical garden, and local flora and fauna. It is open from Memorial Day to Labor Day, but the station is open all year. The *Highlands Botanical Garden Trail* has an herb and health garden and a special garden in memory of Effie Howell Foreman. Established in 1962 and supported by state and private funds, the Garden has more than 400 labeled species, most of which are indigenous to the Highlands area and some of which are endemic. Self-guiding, multiple, and connecting, the trails show ferns, azaleas, club mosses, and a bog succession with swamp pinks, lilies, insectivorous plants, and some rare plants. After hiking this area, take the trail R, around Lake Ravenel on the private *W.C. Coker Rhododendron Trail.* Reach the road at 0.6 mi. After another 0.2 mi, turn L, cross the dam, and return to the parking area at 1 mi. (The *Sunset Rock Trail* is across the road from the Nature Center. See Chapter 14.) (*USGS Map:* Highlands)   **751–752**

• ADDRESS AND ACCESS: Highlands Biological Sta, PO Box 580, Highlands, NC 28741, tel: 704-526-2602. From the jct of US-64/NC-28 in Highlands, go 0.3 mi on E Main St to 6th St and turn L. Go 0.2 mi to sign and turn R. Pass the station and park at the garden entrance.

# 16.

## Mountains-to-Sea Trail

*I think the time has come for us to consider the feasibility of establishing a state trail from the mountains to the seashore.*
—Howard N. Lee

After the General Assembly passed the North Carolina Trails System Act of 1973, the Department of Natural Resources and Community Development (DNRCD) staff began brainstorming about the future of trails. A catalyst was *Resources for Trails in North Carolina, 1972,* written by staff member Bob Buckner. With fresh ideas and concepts about trail purposes and usage, staff planners such as Alan Eaks and Jim Hallsey inspired others to move forward in implementing the Trails System Act. One of the act's statutes explains that "in order to provide for the ever increasing outdoor recreation needs of an expanded population and in order to promote public access to, travel within, and enjoyment and appreciation of the outdoors, natural and remote areas of the state, trails should be established in natural scenic areas of the state, and in and near urban areas." It was also a period when the trend for greenways was on the horizon. Regional councils of government and county governments were proposing canoe trails and trail connections, and Arch Nichols of the Carolina Mountain Club was proposing a 60-mi hiking trail from Mt Pisgah to Mt Mitchell. Discussing these and many other exciting ideas with the DNRCD staff was the North Carolina Trails Committee (a seven-member citizen advisory board appointed by the DNRCD secretary and authorized by the Trails System Act).

The committee began functioning in January 1974 with Louise Chatfield (Greensboro) as chair, followed by John Falter (Apex) in 1976, and Doris B. Hammett, MD (Waynesville), in 1977. It was Dr. Hammett who led a planning committee for the Fourth National Trails Symposium, which was held at Lake Junaluska, September 7 to 10, 1977. Among the distinguished state and national guest speakers was Howard N. Lee, Secretary of DNRCD (and former mayor of Chapel Hill). Lee's speech was prepared by his speechwriter and director of public relations, Stephen Meehan. Near the end of the speech Lee said, "I think the time has come for us to consider the feasibility of establishing a state trail between the mountains and the seashore in North Carolina." He explained that he wanted the Trails Committee to plan such a trail that would utilize the NPS, USFS, state parks, city and county properties, and private landowners "willing to give an easement over a small portion of their land on a legacy to future generations. I don't think we should be locked into the traditional concept of a trail with woods on both sides . . . I think it would be a trail that would help—like the first primitive trails—bring us together . . . I would depend on trail enthusiasts for maintenance . . . Beyond that, how great it would be if other states would follow suit and that the state trails could be linked nationally."

Citizen task forces for segments along the corridor were established to design, negotiate easements, construct, and maintain the "dream trail," whose name became the *Mountains-to-Sea Trail (MST)*. Its western trailhead would start at Clingmans Dome as a connector with the *AT* in the GSMNP to its eastern trailhead at Nags Head on the Outer Banks. Between 1979 and 1981 the DNRCD signed cooperative planning agreements with the NPS, the USFS, and the U.S. Fish and Wildlife Service for the *MST* to pass through federal properties. Another agreement was signed in 1985 pledging a cooperative effort to share resources to complete the state's longest trail, estimated to be between 600 and 700 mi long when completed.

Plans for the *MST* would use original trails in GSMNP to reach the Cherokee Indian Reservation and the Blue Ridge Parkway. It would follow the BRP until reaching the Nantahala NF, where it would alternate between the properties. It would also oscillate between the BRP and Pisgah NF with the exception of a long eastern curve into the Davidson River drainage of the Pisgah District and the Linville River and Wilson Creek drainages in the Grandfather District. On its return to the BRP at Mt Pisgah, it would follow the BRP corridor to the Woods Mtn Range where its eastern route would approach the Pinnacle on the Linville Gorge rim. After a long route that would cross a number of ridges it would return to the BRP corridor at Beacon Heights. Again it would follow the BRP to its final eastern turn at Air Bellows Gap at the northern edge of Doughton Park.

From there it would descend SE into the Garden Creek drainage to Stone Mtn State Park, a section to be named in honor of Louise Chatfield (1920-1986), a leader in the trails movement and founder of the North Carolina Trails Association in 1978. "We are doing this because it will be something for tomorrow, for everybody," she said. From Stone Mtn the *MST* route would enter private lands to Pilot Mtn State Park, and beyond to Hanging Rock State Park. Continuing E to Lake Brandt, N of Greensboro, it would pass through Alamance and Durham counties to approach Eno River State Park in Durham. From there it would follow the S shore of Falls Lake to Raleigh. From Raleigh it would follow the flood-plains corridor of the Neuse River through Johnston and Wayne counties to Cliffs-of-the-Neuse State Park and through Lenoir County. It would leave the Neuse River to enter Croatan NF in Jones, Pamlico, and Carteret counties. At Cedar Island the hiker would take a state ferry to Ocracoke, the beginning of the final 75 mi, and follow the *Cape Hatteras Beach Trail* on the Outer Banks through Cape Hatteras National Seashore. In addition to the main *MST* corridor across the state, regional connecting trails are planned to major cities, the Uwharrie NF, and other public areas such as state, city, and county parks.

Described below are the segments of the *MST* that have been completed (some of which are "designated," meaning officially accepted as part of the state's trail system), or in the process of completion. Of the 325 mi, 74 mi are new trails, constructed entirely for the purpose of the *MST* route. The segments are supervised by citizen task forces that have the assistance and guidance of the N.C. Trails Committee and the N.C. Trails Association, Inc. Segment 1 is the Balsam Highlands Task Force; Segment 2 the South Pisgah Task Force; Segment 3 the Central Blue Ridge Task Force; and Segment 4 the Northwest Mtns Task Force. The other 11 segments are called county task forces with the exception of the Raleigh-Durham-Chapel Hill area, which is called the Triangle Greenways Council. (The *MST* blaze is a circle with a three-inch diameter.)

Not described in this chapter are the fragmented segments E of the mountains. Because they are described in detail elsewhere in the book, the following is a brief summary of their locations. There are 4.8 mi in Doughton Park (BRP) on the *Bluff Mtn Trail;* 10.5 mi in Pilot Mtn State Park following such trails as *Horne Creek, Corridor,* and *Grassy Ridge;* 19 mi on the *Sauratown Trail* (including private property and roads); 11.2 mi at Lake Brandt in Guilford County; 5.6 mi in Eno River State Park; 13.2 mi on the *Falls Lake Trail* in Raleigh; 2 mi in Cliffs-of-the-Neuse State Park; and 75.8 mi on the *Cape Hatteras Beach Trail.* Of these the *Cape Hatteras Beach Trail* was designated a state trail in June 1982; *Nat Greene Historic Trail* at Lake Brandt in September 1983; and *Falls Lake Trail* in April 1987. There are numerous trail leaders on these task forces. They have a variety of reasons for working on the *MST,* one of which is adventure. Bob Benner of the Central Blue Ridge Task Force said, "On the trail I always feel a quiet excitement in anticipation of what awaits me around the bend, over the next rise, into the next mile. . . . " Another reason is expressed by Willie Taylor of the Guilford County Task Force. "Urban trails are the trails of the future. We are bringing the trail (MST) through Greensboro." If you are interested in being active in one of the task forces, contact the following for more information: State Trails

Coordinator, Division of Parks and Rec, Yorkshire Center, 12700 Bayleaf Rd, Raleigh, NC 27614, tel: 919-846-9991.

▶ **MOUNTAINS-TO-SEA TRAIL** 753
Segment 1

*From Clingmans Dome to Smokemont, GSMNP (Swain County)*

• LENGTH AND DIFFICULTY: 24.9 mi, moderate to strenuous

• TRAILS FOLLOWED: *AT, Fork Ridge Trail, Deep Creek Trail, Indian Creek Trail, Sunkota Ridge Trail, Thomas Divide Trail, Newton Bald Trail;* described in Chapter 7

• TRAILHEAD AND DESCRIPTION: Vehicular access in GSMNP is on Clingmans Dome Rd, 7 mi from Newfound Gap Rd (Clingmans Dome Rd is closed in the winter). Park at the Forney Ridge parking area and hike 0.5 mi on a paved access tail to the *AT* and Clingmans Dome (6,643 ft), the highest point in the Smokies and on the *AT*. An observation tower here provides spectacular panoramic views of the GSMNP. (Clingmans Dome is named in honor of Thomas Lanier Clingman, Smokies explorer, U.S. Senator and Civil War general.) (Foot-trail access is 7.5 mi on the *AT* from Newfound Gap parking area.)

Begin the *MST*, N, on the *AT*. At 1 mi reach Old Buzzards Roost in forest of spruce/fir; water is R; descend. Reach Mt Collins Gap at 2 mi among moose-wood, ferns, mosses; ascend to Mt Collins summit (6,188 ft) (named for Robert Collins in 1858 or 1859) at 3 mi. At 3.2 mi jct with *Sugarland Mtn Trail*, L, on which is the Mt Collins shelter after 0.4 mi (bunks for 12; a permit is required for overnight camping from the GSMNP, tel: 615-436-1231 for information and reservations, daily/24 hrs, see introduction in Chapter 7). Jct with a spur trail, R, at 3.5 mi that leads 125 ft to Clingmans Dome Rd. (The *AT* continues ahead for 4 mi to Newfound Gap and parking area.) Turn R on the spur trail, cross Clingmans Dome Rd to the small parking area and NW trailhead of *Fork Ridge Trail*. (To the R, on the road, it is 3.5 mi to Forney Ridge parking area; to the L it is 3.5 to Newfound Gap Rd.) Follow *Fork Ridge Trail* and descend

2,800 ft in elev for the next 5.1 mi. At 3.6 mi pass a spring, golden Alexander, and white snakeroot. Enter a virgin hemlock forest at 5.6 mi and descend on switchbacks. Galax, a laurel and azalea arbor, and views of Bearpen Ridge, R, are at 7.1 mi. At 8.6 mi cross Deep Creek footbridge. End *Fork Ridge Trail* and jct with *Deep Creek Trail,* R and L, and Poke Patch backcountry campsite #53. (Other campsites downstream are Nettle Creek #54 at 11.2 mi; Pole Rd #55 at 12 mi; Burnt Spruce #56 at 12.3 mi; and Bryson Place #57 at 12.8 mi. Self-assigned permits or reservations are required from GSMNP visitor centers or vehicle campgrounds, or call 615-436-1231.) Hike downstream in forest of tall hardwoods and hemlocks. Jct at 12.1 mi with *Pole Rd Creek Trail,* R, scenic creek area, and continue downstream; there are signs of wild boar and deer.

At 12.8 mi reach Bryson Place #57 backcountry campsite, jct with *Indian Creek Trail,* L, and ascend on it. (This area is historically significant because here Horace Kephart, often referred to as a principal founder of GSMNP and "Dean of American Campers," had his last long-term campground. Kephart was killed in an automobile accident near Bryson City in April 1931. There is a plaque on a millstone about 200 ft off the trail, R, if you cross a small stream at the trail jct.) (*Deep Creek Trail* continues downstream 3.9 mi to Deep Creek Campground.) At 14.3 mi arrive at Martin's Gap (3,430) and jct R and L with *Sunkota Ridge Trail;* turn L. (*Indian Creek Trail* continues ahead 5.2 mi to rejoin *Deep Creek Trail.*) Ascend gradually on the E slope among hardwoods. Wild boars wallow in the springs. Jct with *Thomas Divide Trail,* R and L, at 19.1 mi. Turn R. At 19.5 mi leave the *Thomas Divide Trail,* turn L, and begin *Newton Bald Trail* to Newton Bald backcountry campsite #52 at 19.7 mi. Water is 150 yd, R, on a steep slope. At 20.2 mi arrive at Newton Bald ridge (5,142 ft); jct R with former *Mingus Creek Trail.* Descent for the next 4.7 mi on *Newton Bald Trail* is 2,900 ft. Cross a small stream and pass a tall hemlock grove at 22.6 mi. At 24.4 mi turn L on horse trail, and turn L again after 0.2 mi. At 24.8 mi arrive at Newfound Gap Rd and turn R (hitchhiking prohibited). Reach the parking area at 24.9 mi, opposite the entrance to Smokemont Campground. (It is 2.7 mi S to Oconaluftee Visitor Center, another 1.3 mi to the BRP, and another 1.7 mi into

Cherokee for groceries, restaurants, motels, and other services. It is 42.7 mi on the BRP to the next access of the *MST;* construction is continuing; call 919-846-9991 for an update. (*USGS Maps:* Clingmans Dome, Smokemont)

### From Bear Pen Gap (BRP mp 427.6) to NC-215 (BRP mp 423.2) (Jackson and Haywood Counties)

• LENGTH AND DIFFICULTY: 9.1 mi, easy to moderate

• TRAILS FOLLOWED: Parts of *Gage Bald/Charley Bald Trail, Buckeye Gap Trail;* described in Chapter 6

• TRAILHEAD AND DESCRIPTION: From jct of NC-215 and the BRP at Beech Gap, drive S 4.4 mi to Bear Pen Gap parking lot, L (5,560 ft). Enter the trail at the SE corner; follow old road into the Nantahala NF on the *Gage Bald/Charley Bald Trail,* and cross a streamlet at 0.4 mi. Pass through a yellow birch grove and keep L at all jeep-road jcts in a curve around Rough Butt Bald (5,925 ft) at 0.6 mi. At 1.3 mi reach an open area, by a rock, L, in goldenrod and asters (an excellent place to see deer and turkey). Turn L, go 110 ft to reenter the woods on a footpath, a new white-blazed trail for the *MST.* (A few yd ahead is Wet Camp Gap; old grassy jeep road to Gage Bald [5,574 ft] and Charley Bald area [5,520 ft] for 1.5 mi.) At 1.6 mi begin switchbacks, and enter areas of profuse wildflowers. At 2 mi enter a berry field—blueberry, blackberry, strawberry, and gooseberry. Area is scenic; fly poison, ferns, and gentians. Cross the BRP in Haywood Gap (mp 426.5) (5,225 ft) at 2.9 mi. Enter a thick mint patch, and jct with *Haywood Gap Trail,* L, after 185 ft. (A descent of 0.2 mi on *Haywood Gap Trail* leads to a spring.) Follow a handcrafted footpath through a beautiful forest of spruce, birch, rhododendron, maple, and wood sorrel with mosses and ferns on the forest floor. There are springs along the way. At 4.7 mi reach Buckeye Gap (mp 425.5), and jct with *Buckeye Gap Trail,* L and R. Turn L on an old RR grade. (Up the bank, R, it is 260 yd to Rough Butt Bald Overlook access, BRP mp 425.4.)

Make a sharp R at 5.4 mi among spruce, yellow birch, turtlehead, and ferns. At 5.7 mi cross Buckeye Creek, which cascades

L. Go 75 yd to a sharp turn R, up the bank, and ascend. (*Buckeye Gap Trail* continues ahead on an old RR grade with RR artifacts. See Chapter 3, Section 3.) Enter an open area of blueberry and blackberry patches. At 6.1 mi cross the headwaters of Buckeye Creek; ferns, birch, and rhododendron are prominent. Jct with an old trail, R, at 6.4 mi. Keep L and descend easily. Leave the foot trail at 7.1 mi and follow an old RR grade. At 7.3 mi are views of Beech Gap ahead, Mt Hardy R, and more blackberry patches on the trailside. After another 0.2 mi there are views of large cliffs on Fork Ridge, L. Cross a ravine at 7.7 mi and follow R of old RR grade, but rejoin it after 0.2 mi. Turn L sharply to follow another old RR grade. Arrive at the confluence of streams in a rocky streambed at 8.1 mi. Rock-hop and enter an area of rhododendron and fetterbush. Follow an old RR grade to a grazing field. At 8.6 mi reenter the woods, pass a spring R, and follow the old road. Reach NC-215 at 8.9 mi, turn R, up the road, and cross a bridge over cascading Bubbling Spring Branch. The *MST* continues L, up an embankment at 9.1 mi. (The parking area is up the road 200 ft, R, and 0.5 mi ahead is the BRP in Beech Gap.) This 9.1-mi part of the *MST* was designated a state trail in May 1987. (*USGS Map:* Sam Knob)

## Segment 2

### From NC-215 (BRP mp 423.2) to US-25 (BRP mp 388.8) (Haywood, Transylvania, Henderson, and Buncombe Counties)

• LENGTH AND DIFFICULTY: 61.1 mi, moderate to strenuous

• TRAILS FOLLOWED: *Art Loeb Trail, Black Mountain Trail, Buck Spring Gap Trail, Shut-in Trail;* described in Chapter 3, Section 3 and Chapter 6

• TRAILHEAD AND DESCRIPTION: At the parking area described above, descend 200 ft on NC-215 to embankment, R, and enter a rhododendron thicket and a new trail of the *MST*. At 0.5 mi cross a cascading stream in a grove of yellow birch, and after a ravine crossing begin ascent on six switchbacks. Curve around a low knob to views of Devil's Courthouse at 1 mi. At 1.5 mi a short spur, R, provides views of Devil's Courthouse. Enter a dense and beautiful conifer grove. At 2 mi jct R with a 0.1-mi spur to *Devil's Courthouse Trail* (and another 0.1 mi to a spectacular overlook). (*Devil's Courthouse Trail* descends 0.3 mi to the BRP.) At 2.2 mi jct L with *Little Sam Knob Trail.* Ahead, 0.1 mi, is a large rock outcropping, L; a climb provides splendid views of Mt Hardy and Little Sam Knob. Curve around Chestnut Bald in patches of large sweet blackberry (ripe the second week in August). Jct with the *Art Loeb Trail* at 3.2 mi. (The yellow-blazed *Art Loeb Trail* goes L 1.1 mi to FR-816 and beyond 10.9 mi to the N terminus at the Daniel Boone BSA campground.)

Turn R and descend on the *Art Loeb Trail* for the next 18 mi, a descent of 3,835 ft. At 3.6 mi cross the BRP and descend into a hardwood forest. At 5.1 mi jct with the blue-blazed *Farlow Gap Trail,* L, and at 6.1 mi arrive at an A-frame shelter. (Water is 75 yd NW of the shelter.) Ascend on switchbacks to Pilot Mtn (5,040 ft) for panoramic views at 6.8 mi. Descend on multiple switchbacks and reach Gloucester Rd (FR-475) at 9 mi. (To the E, L, it is 6.7 mi to US-276.) At 12.4 mi jct with *Butter Gap Trail,* L, and *Cedar Rock Spur Trail* ahead; continue R on the *Art Loeb Trail.* Reach the Cedar Rock A-frame shelter near a stream and other campsites at 12.6 mi. Pass *Cedar Rock Spur Trail,* L, at 14 mi, and *Cat Gap Trail,* L (formerly *Horse Cove Trail*), at 15 mi. Pass Neils Gap at 17.9 mi (where a 0.5-mi spur, L, descends to *North Slope Loop Trail*). Begin the final descent at 20 mi to the Davidson River, cross a footbridge over Joel Branch, pass through a flood plain of tall poplar and oak, and cross the Davidson River swinging bridge at 21.2 mi, the end of the *Art Loeb Trail.* To the R the *MST* continues.

(To the L, 70 yd, is a parking area. It is 0.6 mi upriver to the bridge over the Davidson River, L to the campground [seasonal hot showers, no hook-ups], and R a few yd to US-276. On US-276, L, it is 0.3 mi to the Pisgah District office [and outside public telephone], and on US-276, R, it is 1.2 mi to jct with US-64. Here are groceries, motel, laundromat, restaurant, and supply stores. On US-64/276 S toward the town of Brevard at 2.2 mi is Wash House Laundromat [corner of Osborne Rd], which has hot showers all year.)

To continue on the *MST* from the swinging bridge, turn R (on a new section of trail), cross a small stream, and turn sharply

L at 50 yd to cross US-276. Traverse a low area through hemlock, beech, and alder. At 21.6 mi pass L of a cement water box; cross Starnes Branch on a footbridge at 21.7 mi, and jct with *Starnes Branch Trail,* R and L, at 21.7 mi. (It is 0.2 mi L to the trail entrance.) Leave the conifers, ascend, enter a grazing field, and jct with the *Starnes Branch Trail* (return loop) at 21.9 mi. Reenter the woods, descend and join the *Black Mountain Trail* at 22.1 mi. (It is 0.3 mi L to the trail entrance.) Turn R and follow the *Black Mtn Trail* for the next 6.7 mi; elev increase of 1,984 ft. At 24.7 mi jct L with the orange-blazed *Pressley Cove Trail,* and jct R with *Turkey Pen Gap Trail* at 25.7 mi. Arrive at Clawhammer Mtn (4,140 ft) at 26.4 mi for superb views. Descend to *Buckhorn Gap Trail* jct, R and L, at 27.5 mi. Ascend embankment and at 27.8 mi arrive at Buckhorn Gap Shelter, R (bunk beds; a spring is nearby). Ascend to Rich Mtn where the *MST* leaves the *Black Mtn Trail* at 28.8 mi and follows a new trail down the NW slopes of Soapstone Ridge to cross the Pink Beds. (The *Black Mtn Trail* goes 1.7 mi to the Cradle of Forestry.)

Descend on an old timber road, cross a small stream at 29.5 mi, and at 30.3 mi leave the old road in a curve, L, to descend on a ridge spur. Pass through a grassy open forest; at 31.1 mi jct R and L with the orange-blazed *Pink Beds Loop Trail.* Turn L, go 75 yd, turn R off the *Pink Beds Loop Trail,* and go another 75 yd to cross a log footbridge over the South Fork of Mills River. Pass through a beautiful fern glen of the Pink Beds and cross the N side of the *Pink Beds Loop Trail* at 31.4 mi. Follow an old road through white pine, hemlock, and oak to FR-1206 at 31.9 mi. (Parking area is L 200 ft.) (To the L FR-1206 goes 1.3 mi to US-276.) Cross FR-1206 and at 32.2 mi pass R of cascades and ascend on switchbacks to jct with *Buck Spring Trail,* R and L at 32.6 mi in a hardwood forest of oak, hickory, and maple. (*Buck Spring Trail* goes L 1.1 mi to US-276.) Turn R and ascend on the *Buck Spring Trail* for 5.1 mi to the Pisgah Inn on the BRP at 37.7 mi. (Facilities here are seasonal with a restaurant, motel, campground, and svc sta, but there is an outdoor public telephone.) Go in front of the motel to a signboard and follow the 1.1-mi BRP *Buck Spring Trail* to Buck Spring Gap parking overlook at 38.8 mi. The *MST* joins the *Shut-in Trail* here and descends with it for 16.4 mi.

(The *Shut-in Trail* oscillates between the BRP boundaries and the Pisgah NF boundaries. Because you can camp in the NF and not on the BRP, call the BRP, tel: 704-259-0809, for a boundary diagram. The USGS-FS map of Dunsmore Mtn does not show the *Shut-in Trail*.) Access points on the descent (3,611 ft in elev change) are at NC-151; Elk Pasture Gap (mp 405.5) at 40.6 mi; Mills River Valley overlook (mp 404.5) at 41.8 mi; Big Ridge overlook (mp 403.6) at 42.9 mi; Stoney Bald overlook (mp 402.6) at 44.1 mi; Beaverdam Gap overlook (mp 401.7) at 45 mi; Bent Creek Gap (on Wash Creek Rd, mp 400.3) at 46.9 mi; Sleepy Gap overlook (mp 397.3) at 50.4 mi; and Walnut Cove overlook (mp 396.4) at 52.1 mi. At 55.2 mi the *MST* goes ahead and the *Shut-in Trail* turns L for 125 ft to its N terminus and parking area on Hardtimes Rd (FR-479). (It is 0.4 mi R [N] to NC-191 on Hardtimes Rd.) (Because you are outside the BRP boundary, off-the-road tent camping is possible unless otherwise designated.)

The *MST* continues 0.4 mi on a slope, with Bent Creek L, to the BRP approach ramp from NC-191 at 55.6 mi. (It is 145 yd L to FR-497, and 5 mi on NC-191, L to SW Asheville.) Turn R on the BRP approach ramp and arrive at the French Broad River bridge (BRP mp 393.6). The BRP French Broad River parking overlook [mp 393.7] is 0.1 mi. R.) Turn L and cross the scenic French Broad River bridge to the N end at 55.9 mi. Go 35 yd and turn R into an open hardwood forest. Pass under a powerline at 56 mi, enter a white pine grove but leave it at 56.5 mi. At 56.6 mi cross an old road that goes under the BRP. Ascend and descend on gentle hills, cross the BRP at 57.2 mi, and enter an oak-hickory forest. Join an old woods road and arrive at the I-26 underpass at 57.5 mi (no vehicle access to I-26). Cross the bridge, turn R into the forest at 57.6 mi. Cross a gravel road at 57.9 mi. In a mixed forest pass through wild orchids, galax, arbutus, wild ginger, and laurel. At 58.1 mi pass a man-made spring, R. Cross a number of used roads (that lead to private property) and cross a small stream at 58.7 mi. Pass through a rhododendron and laurel thicket and cross a vehicle bridge over Dingle Creek at 58.9 mi. Pass under tall oaks and white pines. Cross a gravel road at 59.9 mi (L it goes under the BRP) and other woods roads ahead. Cross a vehicle bridge over Four-mile Branch at 60.5 mi, and go under a grove of tall white pine at 60.9 mi. At 61.1 mi arrive at the US-25 bridge (BRP mp 388.8) and access ramps. (It is 2.9 mi L [N] to I-40 and S Asheville, and 16 mi R to Hendersonville.) (The *MST* is under construction for approx 7 mi from here to the Folk Art Center on the BRP.) (This section, from NC-215 to the French Broad River, was designated a state trail in September 1985.) (*USGS-FS Maps:* Sam Knob, Shining Rock, Pisgah Forest, Dunsmore Mtn, Asheville, Skyland)

### From Folk Art Center (BRP mp 382) to Rattlesnake Lodge (BRP mp 374.4) (Buncombe County)

• LENGTH AND DIFFICULTY: 9.1 mi, moderate to strenuous

• TRAILHEAD AND DESCRIPTION: At the Folk Art Center (BRP 382), which has a major display of traditional crafts of the Southern Highlands, park at the nearest parking area near the main gate. Begin the trail at the entrance gate, follow the trail sign, and parallel the BRP. Cross a bridge over Riceville Rd (SR-2002) at 0.2 mi. Cross a number of old trails and roads; pass over a water line at 0.5 mi, and cross the BRP at 0.9 mi. Descend and ascend, partly following an old woods road. On an ascent at 2.3 mi is a short spur L for scenic views of NE Asheville. Ascend on a narrow ridge, then a slope, until the mtn top at 2.8 mi in an area of laurel, hardwoods, and gentian. Descend, frequently using old logging roads, cross a streamlet at 3.7 mi, enter a laurel thicket at 4.5 mi and a wildflower patch at 4.7 mi. At 5.2 mi arrive at Craven Gap (mp 377.4) and jct with NC-694. Cross the BRP to a parking area at 5.3 mi, and at the NW corner continue on the *MST*. Ascend on a scenic rocky E slope of Rice Knob in an oak-hickory forest to encounter large banks of wildflowers such as flame azalea, wild geranium, crested dwarf iris, mtn mint, and *sedum*. At 5.9 mi jct R with a spur trail that descends 0.2 mi to Tanbark Ridge overlook (mp 376.7). At 6.4 mi cross a streamlet, and at 6.8 mi begin a descent on a ridge. Cross paved Ox Creek Rd (SR-2109) at 7 mi. (To the R it is 0.1 mi to the BRP.) Follow the footpath to the end of a ridge and descend on nine short switchbacks to Bull Gap at 7.7 mi. (To the L it is 60 yd to Ox Creek Rd.) At the former carriage entrance to

Rattlesnake Lodge, begin on the old carriage road and ascend on nine switchbacks for 0.7 mi. On a scenic route pass through rock formations and gardens of wildflowers in a hardwood forest. Reach remnants of Rattlesnake Lodge at 9.2 mi. A spring is L. Jct here with *Rattlesnake Lodge Trail*, which descends steeply, R, 0.4 mi to the BRP (mp 374.4) and a small parking area (see Chapter 6). (The *MST* continues ahead, under construction, to ascend Rocky Knob, enter Craggy Gardens and the Mt Mitchell area, and to join Segment 3 near Big Laurel Gap for approx 25 to 30 mi. Call 919-846-9991 or 704-252-6078 for a progress report.) (*USGS Maps:* Oteen, Craggy Pinnacle, Montreat)

### Segment 3

*From Ashford (US-221) to Beacon Heights (US-221 and BRP mp 305.5) (McDowell, Burke, Caldwell, Avery Counties)*

• LENGTH AND DIFFICULTY: 48.3 mi, moderate to strenuous

• TRAILS FOLLOWED: *Overmountain Victory Trail, Shortoff Mtn Trail, Table Rock Summit Trail, Table Rock Gap Trail, Upper Steels Creek Trail, Greentown Trail, Raider Camp Trail, Harper Creek Trail, North Harper Creek Trail, North Harper Creek Access Trail, Hunt-Fish Falls Trail, Lost Cove Trail, Beacon Heights Trail;* described in Chapter 3, Section 2

• TRAILHEAD AND DESCRIPTION: From the jct of US-221 and Old Linville Rd (SR-1560) in Ashford, drive 2.5 mi S on Old Linville Rd to gated FR-493, L. Follow the *Overmountain Victory Trail* sign and ascend gradually on a gold-blazed woods road to a ridgeline to cross Dobson Knob Rd at 2 mi. Descend on an old road and cross Yellow Fork at 2.5 mi in a rhododendron thicket. Cross another small stream at 3.2 mi, and jct with the gravel Kistler Memorial Highway (SR-1238) at 3.5 mi, the end of the *Overmountain Victory Trail.* Turn L to a parking area. (It is 4.1 mi R steeply down the mtn to NC-126, where with a R turn it is 7.6 mi to Nebo and US-70 jct, or a L turn 16.3 mi to Morganton.) Continue N on SR-1238 and at 4.3 mi turn R on a jeep road that leads 0.2 mi to the Pinnacle. (SR-1238 continues ahead 12.3 mi to Linville Falls.)

A spur trail, R at the Pinnacle, provides a panoramic view of Linville Gorge (E), Lake James (S), Shortoff Mtn (E), Table Rock (NE), and Dogback Mtn (N). Follow the white blaze in a hardwood forest and understory of laurel down the mtn. Turn L on an old logging road at 4.8 mi. Reach a clearcut at 5.1 mi. Follow an old logging road, cross Sandy Branch twice, 5.5 mi and 5.8 mi. Ascend to a knob and pass through patches of bristly locust. Descend, turn sharply L off the logging road at 6.6 mi, reach a road and gate to private property at 6.7 mi. Turn L and after 0.3 mi turn sharply R off the road in a descent to the Linville River (1,280 ft elev). Vegetation includes ironwood, doghobble, sycamore, hemlock, gums, and yellow root. Wade the 50-ft-wide river, turn R, and go downstream for 0.2 mi. Turn L, ascend through a rhododendron thicket, and cross a ravine at 7.5 mi. Ascend in a forest of oak, pine, laurel, and turkey beard. Jct with an old woods road at 7.7 mi; turn L. Ascend gradually to jct with a foot trail, L and R, at 8.8 mi. (The old road ahead is a longer route to the top of Shortoff Mtn, and the foot trail R is an access route from Old Wolf Pit Rd, a private access.) Turn L on *Shortoff Mtn Trail*. Scenic views of the Linville Gorge Wilderness soon begin along the precipitous W side of the mtn. A small spring is in a crevice at 9.2 mi. (Spring usually has water, but not dependable in long dry summer.) There are more scenic views, L on short spur trails. There are thick patches of Allegheny sand myrtle, chestnut oak, and blueberry. Reach the old jeep-road entrance (3,000 ft) at 9.3 mi. To the L are spectacular views of Linville Gorge, Table Rock, and Hawksbill. Follow the old jeep road, but turn L on another old woods road at 9.5 mi. Pass a water hole, L, at 9.8 mi. Reach a knob at 12.2 mi in a forest of large white pine and oak. Leave ridgecrest, turn R, and at 12.7 mi enter a bed of galax, where to the R is a 60-yd spur to an intermittent spring. Reach Chimney Gap at 13.2 mi. Ascend, steeply in spots, to the Chimneys at 13.8 mi. Pass through dense evergreens on the W side of the Chimneys at 14.1 and to scenic areas for views at 14.5 mi. Chinquapin grow here among the blueberries. Arrive at Table Rock Picnic Area at 14.9 mi. (Area has picnic tables, garbage stand, vault toilets, but no water. Day use only; no camping.)

(Access is from NC-181 in Jonas Ridge on Old Gingercake Rd [SR-1264] for 0.3 mi, L on Gingercake Acres Rd [SR-1265], which becomes FR-210 for 5.9 mi and a turn R on FR-210B for another 2.9 mi.)

Cross the parking area and follow *Table Rock Summit Trail.* Jct L with *Little Table Rock Trail* at 15.2 mi. Turn R, ascend 100 yd, and take a sharp L on *Table Rock Gap Trail. (Table Rock Summit Trail* continues the ascent of 0.4 mi to panoramic views [3,909 ft].) Follow a rocky treadway, and at 15.9 mi begin a steep descent. Reach an unmaintained road cul-de-sac at 16.1 mi, the end of the wilderness boundary. Cross the road, turn R, descend on an old logging road to gravel FR-210 at 16.3 mi. Turn R on FR-210 and go 0.1 mi to make a L turn off the road. Descend, steeply in spots, on an old woods road in rhododendron, white pine, and oak to reach gravel FR-496 at 16.8 mi. A small stream is R. (It is 5.6 mi L on FR-496 to N terminus of *Upper Steels Creek Trail* and continuing *MST.*) Turn R on FR-496 and reach a gate and parking area at 16.9 mi. (It is 35 yd ahead to FR-210, and 65 yd R on FR-210 to Table Rock Picnic Rd, FR-210B, L.) Continue on the *MST,* L, from the gate on an old jeep road over hummocks. Pines, rhododendron, and arbutus are prominent. The headwaters of Buck Creek can be heard from the L. Turn sharply R on a foot trail at 17.4 mi. Follow an erratic trail, partly on footpaths or old logging roads, up and down grades in coves, over streamlets, and over ridges for 2.2 mi to an exceptionally steep descent at 19.6 mi. Arrive at the base of the ridge and trail jct at 20 mi in an area of Devil's walking stick, white pine, and ferns. Turn L (R is a fisherman's trail downstream), and rock-hop Buck Creek. Jct with *Upper Steels Creek Trail,* R. (To the R, *Upper Steels Creek Trail* crosses the creek and follows an old 4WD route downstream for 0.2 mi to FR-228 and a parking area. From here it is 3.9 mi out to NC-181.)

Continue upstream, jointly with *Upper Steels Creek Trail,* and ascend by rapids and pools. To the R is a waterfall at 20.5 mi. Cross a drainage at 20.6 mi. Turn sharply L at 20.8 mi (easy to miss) and ascend steeply. Follow a logging road and RR grades, cross a deep chasm, and pass cascades and pools. Arrive at a beautiful flat area at 21.1 mi with campsites in fern beds and tall maple, poplar, locust, and hemlock giving shade. Enter a grazing field and follow the E edge to a FR; turn R, rock-hop Gingercake Creek, and after 70 yd rock-hop Steels Creek. Walk on an easy FR amid tall poplar, white pine, and hemlock. At 21.8 mi rock-hop Steels Creek and again at 21.9 mi. Continue on the old FR and gradually ascend to a ridge at 22.6 mi. Enter a cut in the ridge and jct with an old road, R, the *MST* route, at 22.7 mi. (Here the *Upper Steels Creek Trail* goes ahead for 120 yd to the locked gate and access with FR-496. R on FR-496 is 1.3 mi to NC-181.) Follow the *MST* on the old road and cross a scenic and high cascading tributary to Steels Creek at 22.8 mi. Reach a parking area on FR-496 at 23.2 mi; follow R on the road and pass a grassy field at 23.5 mi. Arrive at NC-181 at 24.1 mi, and cross the highway to a parking area for *Greentown Trail.*

For the next 18.2 mi the white-blazed *MST* follows trails described in detail in the Grandfather Ranger District, Chapter 3, Section 2. As a result only jct points are listed below. On the *Greenwood Trail* pass a post-gate entrance and descend to Upper Creek. At 26.5 mi jct with *Greentown Short-cut Trail,* R, near the mouth of Burnthouse Branch. At 28 mi jct with FR-198R. At 29.9 mi jct with *Raider Camp Trail,* and turn R. (To the L it is 0.2 mi to a superb view of South Harper Creek Falls.) Jct with *Phillips Creek Trail,* R, at 32.1 mi (at two large poplars with initials R.J.). Rock-hop Harper Creek at 32.4 mi and jct with *Harper Creek Trail,* R and L, at 32.5 mi. (*Harper Creek Trail,* R, has an access 1.3 mi out to Wilson Creek Rd, SR-1328.) Turn L on *Harper Creek Trail* and pass cascades and waterfalls. Rock-hop the creek twice before a jct with *North Harper Creek Trail,* R at 34.8 mi, where *Harper Creek Trail* turns L. Rock-hop the creek twice again, and jct R and L with *Persimmon Ridge Trail* at 35.3 mi. Jct with *North Harper Creek Access Trail* at 36.9 mi, and turn R on it. (*North Harper Creek Trail* continues upstream.) Arrive at FR-464 and a parking space at 37.9 mi. Turn R and follow FR-464 0.6 mi to a parking area, L, at the S trailhead of *Hunt-Fish Falls Trail* at 38.5 mi. Descend on *Hunt-Fish Falls Trail* to a beautiful area of falls and pools at 39.3 mi and a jct with *Lost Cove Trail,* R and L. Turn R and at 40.8 mi jct L with *Timber*

*Ridge Trail.* Follow Gragg Prong upstream by cascades to FR-981 (near Roseborough) and cross the bridge to a parking area, R, at 42.4 mi.

Across the road from the parking area is the S entrance to FR-192. The *MST* follows this narrow and rocky road 3.2 mi upstream, R of cascading Gragg Prong. (Jeep and 4WD are better suited for a vehicular attempt.) Hughes Ridge towers R. At Old House Gap at 45.5 mi, the road improves (to accommodate passenger vehicles coming in from FR-45). To the R is primitive FR-451, and to the L the *MST* continues on an old woods road. Ascend, and turn off, R, at 46.1 mi. Follow an old logging road 0.1 mi to a foot trail, L. Pass a natural rock shelter at 46.4 mi. At 46.5 mi are views of Beacon Heights and Grandfather Mtn. Cross two small streams in a forest of tall hemlock and oak. Cross two ravines and at 47.2 mi enter a 0.1-mi rhododendron arbor. Reach a headwaters stream of Andrews Creek at 47.4 mi under tall hemlock and cucumber trees. Ascend on switchbacks to scenic areas R at 47.9 mi and 48 mi. Pitch pine, laurel, witch hazel, and blueberries are here. At 48.1 mi jct with a wide trail; turn R (L it is 35 yd to a small parking area on Gragg Rd, SR-1513). At 48.2 mi jct with *Beacon Heights Trail.* (To the R is a large rock outcropping for panoramic views.) Continue ahead on *Beacon Heights Trail* and jct at 48.3 mi with *Tanawha Trail,* R. To the L, go 130 yd to the Beacon Heights parking area on the BRP (mp 305.3.) On the BRP, R, is a jct with US-221, and 3 mi S on US-221 into Linville are groceries, restaurant, motel, and supply stores. (This section was designated a state trail, October 1986.) (*USGS-FS Maps:* Grandfather Mtn, Ashford, Chestnut Mtn, Linville Falls)

## Segment 4

### From Beacon Heights (BRP mp 305.3) to Blowing Rock (BRP mp 291.9) (Avery, Watauga, and Caldwell Counties)

• LENGTH AND DIFFICULTY: 24.6 mi, moderate to strenuous

• TRAILS FOLLOWED: *Tanawha Trail, Boone Fork Trail, Rich Mountain Trail, Watkins Trail;* described in Chapter 6

• TRAILHEAD AND DESCRIPTION: Access to the S trailhead is at the Beacon Heights parking area (mp 305.3) (elev 4,205 ft) at the jct of the BRP and US-221. The *MST* follows the *Tanawha Trail,* an extraordinary example of trail design and construction by the NPS. It is described in detail, N to S, in Chapter 6. Therefore, only the access points and trail connections are covered below in a S to N direction. (Camping is not allowed on the *Tanawha Trail* or other BRP properties, except at Price Lake Memorial Park.) Begin at the jct of *Beacon Heights Trail* and *Tanawha Trail,* and follow the signs. (Tanawha means "fabulous hawk" in Cherokee, and the trail is marked with a feather logo.) Cross US-221 at 0.3 mi and at 0.8 mi arrive at the Stack Rock parking area (mp 304.8), L. Approach the Linn Cove parking area (mp 304.4), L, at 1.5 mi, and gently descend to an observation deck of the BRP Linn Cove Viaduct, an engineering marvel. Pass under the viaduct at 1.7 mi and cross Linn Cove Branch. At 2.7 mi arrive at the Wilson Creek overlook (mp 303.7), R. Ascend to Rough Ridge boardwalk at 3.8 mi for superb scenic views in a natural garden of turkey beard, blueberry, mtn ash, red spruce, and Allegheny sand myrtle. Descend to Rough Ridge parking area (mp 302.9), R at 4 mi. (Interpretive board is a story of Andre Michaux and plant communities.) Reach Raven Rocks overlook (mp 302.3), R at 4.7 mi, and at 5.3 mi Pilot Ridge overlook (mp 301.8), R. Jct with *Daniel Boone Scout Trail,* L, at 7.3 mi, and *Grandfather Trail Ext,* L, at 7.4 mi. (Both trails are commercial trails of Grandfather Mtn Inc, and a fee registration is required to hike them. Camping is allowed at designated sites. See Chapter 14.) Jct R with the (proposed) *Daniel Boone Scout Trail,* a 0.4-mi access route (named *Grandfather Mtn Access Trail* by the NPS) to US-221 at 7.6 mi. Cross the scenic Upper Boone Fork bridge and jct R with an access to the Boone Fork parking area (mp 299.9) and *Upper Boone Fork Trail,* which goes 0.5 mi to the Calloway Peak overlook (mp 299.7). At 9.6 mi jct with *Cold Prong Pond Trail,* R, which leads 0.2 mi to Cold Prong Pond overlook (mp 299). Continue through a mixed forest with a varied understory of rhododendron, flame azalea, and laurel, and arrive at a large pastoral area (first of 3) at 10.5 mi. Cross Holloway Rd (SR-

1559) with stiles at 11.6 mi. After a section of forest, enter the third pasture at 12.2 mi and descend gently into a forest. Reach a jct with *Boone Fork Trail* at 12.6 mi, R and L, near another stile, R. (The *Tanawha Trail* follows the *Boone Fork Trail*, R for 0.4 mi before it forks R and reaches the Price Lake parking area [mp 297.3] at 13.3 mi.)

The *MST* turns L and jointly follows the *Boone Fork Trail* 0.3 mi before they turn sharply R to leave the pasture and descend to the Bee Tree Creek headwaters. At 14.1 mi cross Bee Tree Creek for the last time and curve around the ridge R to follow upstream on Boone Fork. After a scenic route through birch and rhododendron and cascades, pass an old dam site, L at 15.1 mi. At 15.3 mi reach a huge rock formation by the river; descend to leave the *Boone Fork Trail* and rock-hop or wade Boone Fork. (The *Boone Fork Trail* continues ahead 1.1 mi to the picnic area at Price Memorial Park mp 295.5.)

Across the river ascend steeply to a flat knoll at 15.4 mi with laurel, white pine, galax, and running cedar. Follow an old, wide, and level road to old John Rd at 15.8 mi. Turn R and at 15.9 mi turn L, off the road, and into a large pine plantation (to the R is a chimney from a pioneer farmhouse.) Ascend in a mixed forest and at 16.2 mi pass L of a spring (the last on the climb to Rich Mtn) near a homestead site. Continue ascending the slope of Martin Knob and reach a pasture at the ridgeline at 16.8 mi. Turn R and arrive at Shulls Mills Rd (SR-1552) and gated fence in Martin Gap at 16.9 mi (R, on the paved road, it is 1.7 mi to BRP mp 294.6). Turn R on the road and after a few yd turn L up the embankment to follow the ridgeline. Pass through white pine and then a hardwood area with a grove of flame azalea. Reach a fence and jct with *Rich Mtn Trail*, R and L at 17.4 mi. (To the L the *Rich Mtn Trail* ascends to its W terminus at Rich Mtn summit, 4,370 ft.) Turn R on *Rich Mtn Trail* and follow the carriage road (3.2 mi to the Moses Cone Manor) into a pasture. Turn L at the first curve and descend into a forest. At 19 mi take the L fork and go under large hemlocks. Reach a drained trout lake at 19.2 mi. Cross the dam and arrive at Flannery Fork Rd (SR-1541). Turn R, but after 0.4 mi leave it, L, and ascend on the carriage road with switchbacks to another pasture. Reach the BRP at 20.6 mi, the end of *Rich Mtn Trail.* Go under the BRP (mp 294) and jointly follow *Watkins Trail.* Pass the stables, R, and access steps to the parking area of Moses Cone Memorial Park. Follow a paved carriage trail to the front of the manor, but turn sharply at the first L at 20.8 mi and descend into a forest of white pine and hemlock. Parallel the BRP and stay L of other carriage roads. At 22.2 mi keep L in a curve (the carriage road R is *Black Bottom Trail,* which connects with other carriage trails in the park). Pass L of a lake and spillway at 24 mi, cross Penley Branch in a grove of handsome oak, maple, and tall hemlock. At a private road at 24.4 mi turn R, and reach the end of *Watkins Trail* at US-221/321 at 24.6 mi. (Across the road is the New River Inn. To the R it is 1 mi to Blowing Rock; to the L it is 0.2 mi to BRP mp 291.9 jct; and ahead it is 6 mi to Boone. Both towns have groceries, restaurants, supply stores and motels. (*USGS Maps:* Grandfather Mtn, Valle Crucis, Boone)

# Appendix

Without the organizations and clubs in the state there would not be a state trails system. They are the citizen teams of researchers, planners, and workers who are concerned about the natural environment. Some of them are essential watchdogs of properties abused by federal, state, and local governments and commercial developers. In many ways they all form partnerships with government or lobby against or for issues that involve legislative action. The condition of a state's trail system is a barometer of its environmental quality. Some of the groups give purpose, maintenance, and direction to such historic routes as the *AT*, the *Bartram Trail*, the *Foothills Trail*, and more recently the *Benton MacKaye Trail*. (The latter will form a double loop from the *AT* at Springer Mtn, Georgia, to the Cherokee NF in Tennessee, cross the *AT* at Shuckstack Mtn in the GSMNP, and follow the park's east edge to Davenport Gap and jct with the *AT*.) In addition, a private equestrian club in Tryon has proposed a new trail on private property that would go from the *Foothills Trail* at Caesars Head State Park in South Carolina N to connect with the *AT* on Roan Mtn. The route would use public property on part of the *MST*. If completed, the trail would provide a long loop using the *Foothills Trail*, the *Bartram Trail*, and the *AT*.                    **754**

There are other organizations, such as the N.C. Chapter of the Sierra Club, N.C. Nature Conservancy, N.C. chapters of the Audubon Society, N.C. Recreation and Park Society, Friends of

State Parks, and the N.C. Trails Association that not only have a strong interest in trails but also in the preservation of our natural heritage and improving the quality of life. They often have led campaigns separately and collectively to save scenic rivers, protect wildlife habitats, preserve historic places, and promote wilderness areas, clean air, and water. Their work is one of vigilance. They fought to have Congress designate the South Fork of the New River a Scenic River in 1976, only to discover a decade later that this "jewel in the state's scenic crown" was a hollow victory because state and county governments had failed to acquire easements to prevent riverside developments. They won in stopping a road through what is now the Slickrock Wilderness Area (though another road, in spite of classic vigilance, was built within sight of the Joyce Kilmer Memorial Forest). In the long, often bitter, crusade to save Slickrock, Carl A. Reiche wrote, "I envisioned a thousand frustrations and a web of powerful interests and multitudinous interwoven bureaucracies that became realities." The heat of the campaign became so intense that he eventually lost faith in the USFS and the environmental groups that supported his cause.

A vigilant public is aware of the flagrant abuse by the USFS of the public trust. Sometimes under the disguise of "timber management" taxpayer money is wasted, one example being an average loss on timber sales of 60 to 85 cents per dollar in N.C. And on a number of occasions the USFS ignored the Clean Water Act, the Environmental Protection Act, and the Multiple-Use Act. An example of the latter occurred when Alan Householder in 1986 hiked the *Bartram Trail*; he met timbermen destroying nearly five miles of the trail. He asked why. "We are cutting only the trees authorized by the forest service," was the reply. There will be enough outcry from members of the Bartram Trail Society to have the slash removed, but in the process they will have to labor more to maintain it. (Nationwide, 40,000 miles of hiking trails in the USFS have disappeared in the past 40 years. Road building has been frenzied, a process one writer called the "roads to ruin.")

Some private organizations, such as the N.C. Nature Conservancy, are at work "preserving biological diversity by protecting natural lands." The Conservancy has acquired 25 areas for a total of 293,000 acres. A few of these properties have trails. One example is Nags Head Woods, whose *Sweet Gum Trail* is on a 680-acre undisturbed preserve that has not changed since the first Englishmen saw it 400 years ago. For days and hours the preserve is open to the public, call 919-441-2521 (see address under N.C. Citizens' Groups below).                    **755**

Although the USFS places trails low on its budget and its priorities, it does not mean that the trails and preservation of special areas are forgotten by the USFS staff. For example by 1988 the Pisgah and Nantahala forests had 39 special management areas (40,771 acres, including the wilderness areas). And on the state level, the N.C. Natural Heritage Program of the DNRCD is responsible for protecting natural resources and natural areas on both public and private properties. Its plan is to have "400 protected natural areas by the end of this century" on the Registry of Natural Heritage Areas. Meanwhile, the commercial forests in the state are shrinking at the rate of one million acres every ten years. (Worldwide, it is 50 acres each minute, equal to the disappearance of all of North Carolina's trees in less than one year.) To preserve our forests and trails, we have a great responsibility. One way to help is by becoming an active member (if not already) of a citizen group. "You don't have to be a hiker to love trails," said Elisabeth Hair of Charlotte.

### Carolina Mountain Club

On June 17, 1920, organized mountaineering began in North Carolina when a southern chapter of the Appalachian Mountain Club of Boston was formed tentatively in Asheville. Dr. Chase Ambler, originator of the Weeks National Forest Land Purchase Act, was the first president. Three years later, the club withdrew from the AMC and incorporated under the name of the Carolina Mountain Club (CMC) with Dr. Gaillard Tennent its first president. In 1930 the Carolina Appalachian Trail Club was formed with George Stephens as its first president, but one year later the vigorous hiking club was merged into the CMC, Inc. Stephens, like Tennent, hiked actively with the CMC for many years. He published extensive maps and guides, including *100 Favorite Trails,* a hiking guide for some of the Smokies and the Blue Ridge Mountains in the state.

During the Appalachian Trail Conference's early years, CMC's president Marcus Book was an ATC board member. He was succeeded in 1938 by Arch Nichols (1979 Honorary Member of ATC). In 1940 Nichols engaged the Rev. A. Rufus Morgan to work on the Nantahala *AT* section; Nichols later started the Tennessee Eastman Hiking Club north of Spivey's Gap, and helped to establish the Piedmont Appalachian Trail Hikers, a Greensboro-based club (see below). Other accomplishments have been the securing of the Craggy Scenic Area; the naming of Tennent Mountain; marking Mt Craige and Big Top; naming George Masa Mtn; securing the Shining Rock Wilderness Area; establishing the *Art Loeb Trail;* securing the Max Patch properties for the *AT;* and starting the Mt Pisgah to Mt Mitchell Trail System, which will become a section of the *MST.* In 1968 the CMC worked hard for the passage of the National Scenic Trail Act by the U.S. Congress and the Appalachian Trail Act of 1978, and it assisted the USFS in acquiring aerial photos of the *AT* for the Federal Register. CMC is the state's oldest trail club, and it maintains 89.7 mi of the *AT* from Davenport Gap to Spivey Gap.

• INFORMATION: Carolina Mountain Club, PO Box 68, Asheville, NC 28802, tel: 704-252-6078.

—Arch Nichols

### Nantahala Hiking Club

The Nantahala Hiking Club was founded in 1950 by the Rev. A. Rufus Morgan to assist in maintaining the *AT* in the Nantahala Mountains area. Morgan was the NHC's first president and held that position for 18 years, during which time the membership grew to over 200 and the club's program expanded to include "pleasure hiking" in northern Georgia, western North Carolina, and eastern Tennessee. As a maintaining member of the Appalachian Trail Conference, the NHC still brushes and renews blazes on 59.8 miles of the *AT* from Bly Gap at the Georgia-North Carolina state line to Wesser (US-19).

Since 1978, under an agreement with the USFS, major trail construction and maintenance have been done by the Wayah Ranger District of the Nantahala NF (since the *AT* is within its boundaries). Club members have also been active in the design, construction, and maintenance of the 81-mile *Bartram Trail,* which crosses the *AT* on Wayah Bald. The club holds its monthly meetings at the Nonah Craft House in Cartoogechaye (a few miles W of Franklin) and publishes a bimonthly bulletin.

• INFORMATION: Nantahala Hiking Club, 31 Carl Slagle Rd, Franklin, NC 28734, tel: 704-369-6820.

—Kay Coriell

### Piedmont Appalachian Trail Hikers

The Piedmont Appalachian Trail Hikers (PATH) was organized in 1965 with the assistance of Arch Nichols and the Rev. A. Rufus Morgan of Asheville, and Tom Campbell, an ATC board member and a member of the Roanoke Appalachian Trail Club. The Roanoke AT Club relinquished 16 miles of the *AT,* from US-21/52 at Walker Mountain to Groseclose, to PATH. In 1966 an additional 11 miles of the *AT* from Groseclose to VA-16 (formerly maintained by the Rev. A.J. Shoemate and his Boy Scouts of Rural Retreat) was assigned to PATH. Almost immediately a portion of the *AT* was relocated to bypass Mountain Empire Airport. Several other relocations were made, including major shift of the *AT* from Walker Mtn to Garden Mtn, which partially encircles picturesque Burkes Garden. This rerouting added 13 miles. In 1987 the Mt Rogers AT Club relinquished 8 miles of the *AT* from VA-16 to the South Fork of the Holston River at SR-670.

PATH is associated with the Jefferson NF and its personnel in the Wythe Ranger District. The two have worked together in scouting and relocating trails, selecting shelter sites, monitoring trail corridors, and updating management plans (including the one on the Beartown Wilderness, which is adjacent to the Chestnut Ridge section of the *AT*). PATH's membership includes volunteer workers from Greensboro, High Point, Winston-Salem, Reidsville, Burlington, Durham, Raleigh, and other areas, thus members drive from 100 to 225 miles for maintenance trips.

• INFORMATION: Piedmont Appalachian Trail Hikers, PO Box 945, Greensboro, NC 27402-0945, tel: 919-272-7971.

—Bill Sims

### Smoky Mountains Hiking Club

By 1924, interest in the development of National Park status for the Great Smoky Mountains had progressed, and certain members of the Knoxville YMCA decided a group for adult hikers would be a useful program. It would also "stimulate further interest in the National Park movement." In October of that year, a group of interested hikers from the Knoxville area gathered on top of Mt LeConte and formed the Smoky Mountains Hiking Club. The affiliation with the YMCA was dropped shortly, but the purpose of gaining park status for the beloved mountains was never abandoned.

The group began with three major areas of interest. The first was the construction, marking, and mapping of hiking trails. Second, the group set up a hiking program, with hikes held at least once a month. And third, the club worked to publicize the beauty and uniqueness of the Great Smokies in order to convince public officials that the area should be protected by park status. The early goals having been reached, the club now sees itself as a watchdog for the park and the *AT*, which it helped to construct. It has also been active in the campaign to have the park included under the Wilderness Act for further protection. The club maintains the *AT* from Wesser (US-19) to Davenport Gap, a distance of 97.4 mi. Mostly from the Knoxville/Oak Ridge area in Tennessee, the club members sponsor day hikes and overnight backpacking trips. There is a membership fee and the club publishes a monthly newsletter.

• INFORMATION: Smoky Mountains Hiking Club, PO Box 1454, Knoxville, TN 37901, tel: 615-693-9203.

—H. Richard Bolen

### Tennessee Eastman Recreation Club

The TERC Hiking and Canoeing Club is organized under the auspices of the Tennessee Eastman Recreation Club of the Tennessee Eastman Company, a Division of Eastman Kodak Company. Persons other than Eastman employees are also welcome at club activities.

Founded in 1946, the club now has an Eastman membership of over 500. It sponsors a program of both hiking and canoeing, with about 75 trips each year. As a member of the ATC, the club is responsible for the maintenance of 125 miles of the AT from Spivey Gap, North Carolina, to Damascus, Virginia, a section that generally follows the Tennessee-North Carolina border until Elks Park and then through Tennessee. Trail maintenance is accomplished by a system of teams within the club under cooperative agreements with the Jefferson, Cherokee, and Pisgah national forests and the Tennessee Valley Authority. These teams generally devote in excess of 2,500 hours each year to clearing, marking, rehabilitation, relocations, signs, shelters, and ensuring the accuracy of guidebook data.

• INFORMATION: TERC Hiking and Canoeing Club, PO Box 511, Kingsport, TN 37662, tel: 615-229-3771.

—S.C. Banks

## ▶ OTHER SOURCES OF INFORMATION

There are over 150 addresses of national, regional, state, and local forests, parks, allied agencies, and private organizations listed under *address* or *information* in this book's narrative. A few other allied government or citizen groups whose addresses do not appear elsewhere in the book but that are related to the subjects of this book are listed below.

### *United States Government Departments*

Department of Agriculture
Forest Service
PO Box 2417
Washington, DC 20013
(202-477-3975)

Regional Foresters #8
Suite 800,
1720 Peachtree Rd, NW
Atlanta, GA 30367

Department of Agriculture
Conservation Service
PO Box 2890
Washington, DC 20013
(202-447-4543)

Regional Biologists
Federal Center Bldg 23
Felix and Hemphill Sts
Fort Worth, TX 76115

State Field Biologist
310 New Bern Ave,
Fed Bldg
Raleigh, NC 27601
(919-856-4690)

State Conservationist
310 New Bern Ave,
Fed Bldg
Raleigh, NC 27601
(919-755-4210)

Department of the Army
Army Corps of Engineers
Pulaski Bldg, 20 Mass Ave,
NW
Washington, DC 20314
(202-272-0001)

Department of the Interior
C St, Interior Bldg
Washington, DC 20240
(202-343-1100)

Bureau of Land
Management
Eastern States
350 S Pickett St
Alexandria, VA 22304
(703-235-2833)

National Park Service
Interior Bldg
Washington, DC 20240
(202-343-4747)

Regional Director
75 Spring St SW
Atlanta, GA 30303
(404-221-5185)

US Fish and Wildlife Service
Washington, DC 20240
(202-343-4717)

Russell Fed Bldg
75 Spring St SW,
Rm 1200
Atlanta, GA 30303
(404-221-3588)

Environmental Protection
Agency
401 M St., SW
Washington, DC 20460
(202-755-2673)

Region IV
345 Courtland St NE
Atlanta, GA 30308
(404-881-4727)

Tennessee Valley Authority
400 West Summit Hill
Knoxville, TN 39702
(615-632-2101)

Migratory Bird Conservation
Commission
Interior Bldg
Washington, DC 20240
(202-653-7653)

## *Interstate Organizations (nongovernmental)*

Air Pollution Control Assoc
PO Box 2861
Pittsburgh, PA 15230
(412-621-1090)

American Camping Assoc
Bradford Woods
Martinsville, IN 46151
(317-342-8456)

American Forestry Assoc
1319 18th St, NW
Washington, DC 20036
(202-467-5810)

American Geographical
Society
156 5th Ave, Suite 600
New York, NY 10010
(212-242-0214)

American Hiking Society
1701 18th St, NW
Washington, DC 20009
(202-234-4609)

American Nature Study
Society
5581 Cold Brook Rd
Homer, NY 13077
(607-749-3655)

American Rivers Conservation Council
322 4th St, NE
Washington, DC 20002
(202-547-6900)

Appalachian Mountain Club
5 Joy St
Boston, MA 02108
(617-523-0636)

Boy Scouts of America
Southeast Region
300 Interstate N Pkwy
Atlanta, GA 30099
(404-955-2333)

Camp Fire Club of America
230 Camp Fire Rd
Chappaqua, NY 10514
(914-941-0199)

Camp Fire Inc
4601 Madison Ave
Kansas City, MO 64112
(816-756-1950)

Conservation Foundation
1717 Mass Ave, NW
Washington, DC 20036
(202-797-4300)

Darling Conservation Foundation
PO Box 657
Des Moines, IA 50503
(515-281-2371)

Defenders of Wildlife
1412 16th St, NW
Washington, DC 20036
(202-797-6800)

Ducks Unlimited Inc
1 Waterfowl Way
Long Grove, IL 60047
(312-438-4300)

Environmental Task Force
Suite 912
1346 Connecticut Ave, NW
Washington, DC 20036
(202-822-6800)

Friends of the Earth
1045 Sansome St
San Francisco, CA 94111
(415-433-7373)

Girl Scouts USA
830 3rd Ave
New York, NY 10022
(212-940-7500)

Humane Society of the US
2100 L St, NW
Washington, DC 20037
(202-452-1100)

Izaak Walton League of America
1701 N Fort Myer Dr, Suite 1100
Arlington, VA 22209
(703-528-1818)

National Audubon Society
950 Third Ave
New York, NY 14221
(212-832-3200)

National Campers and
   Hikers Assoc
7172 Transit Rd
Buffalo, NY 14221
(716-634-5433)

National Geographic Society
17th and M St, NW
Washington, DC 20036
(202-857-7000)

National Trails Council
PO Box 44172
Indianapolis, IN 46204

National Wildlife Federation
1412 16th St, NW
Washington, DC 20036
(202-797-6800)

   Region 3, Rt 15
   Box 557A
   Lexington, NC 27292
   (704-787-5364)

Nature Conservancy
Suite 800, 1800 N Kent St
Arlington, VA 22209
(703-841-5300)

Sierra Club
730 Polk St
San Francisco, CA 94109
(415-776-2211)

Student Conservation Assoc
Box 550
Charleston, NH 03603
(603-826-5206)

Trout Unlimited
501 Church St, NE
Vienna, VA 22180
(703-281-1100)

Wilderness Society
1400 I St, NW, 10th Floor
Washington, DC 20005
(202-828-6600)

### *North Carolina Citizen Groups*

Benton MacKaye Trail Assoc
NC Chapter
PO Box 53271
Atlanta, GA 30355

Carolina American Youth
   Hostels
PO Box 10766
Winston Salem, NC 27108

Carolina Bird Club Inc
PO Box 27647
Raleigh, NC 27611
(919-833-1923)

Conservation Council of NC
307 Granville Rd
Chapel Hill, NC 27514
(919-942-7935)

Friends of State Parks
4204 Randleman Rd
Greensboro, NC 27406
(919-846-9991 and 919-885-
4249))

Nags Head Woods Preserve
PO Box 1942
Kill Devil Hills, NC 27948
(919-441-2525)

National Audubon Society
950 Third Ave
New York, NY 14221
(212-832-3200)

Because the Audubon Society chapter addresses change with each new chapter, request addresses and telephone numbers from the national office above by giving your zip code.

N.C. Recreation and Park
   Society
436 N Harrington St
Raleigh, NC 27603
(919-737-3386)

N.C. Trails Association
PO Box 1033
Greensboro, NC 27402
(919-855-9399)

N.C. Wildflower Preservation
   Society
903 Raleigh Rd
Wilson, NC 27893
(919-243-3005)

N.C. Wildlife Federation
Box 10626
Raleigh, NC 27605
(919-833-1923)

Sierra Club
North Carolina Chapter
730 Polk St
San Francisco, CA 94109
(415-776-2211)

Because the Sierra Club group addresses change with each new chair, request addresses and telephone numbers from the national office above. Groups in N.C. are: Blue Ridge, Broad River, Cape Fear, Capital, Central Piedmont, Coastal, Cypress, Foothills, Headwaters, Kephart, Piedmont Plateau, Research

Triangle, Sandhills, Smoky Mountains, South Mtn, and WENOCA.

Triangle Greenways Council
PO Box 2746
Raleigh, NC 27602
(919-828-4252)

Wildlife Society, NC Chapter
Department of Forestry,
  NCSU
Raleigh, NC 27650
(919-737-3386)

## College and University Organizations

Outing Club
UNC-Asheville
One University Heights
Asheville, NC 28804-3299

Davidson Outdoors
Davidson College Union,
  Box 1780
Davidson, NC 28036

Appalachian Outdoor
  Wilderness Society
Lees-McRae College
Banner Elk, NC 28604

Outing Club & Project
  WILD
Office of Student Activities
101–3 Bryan Center
Duke University
Durham, NC 27706

Office of Outdoor Programs
Appalachian State University
Boone, NC 28607

Elon College Outing Society
Student Activities Office
Campus Box 2262
Elon College, NC 27244

UNC-CH Outing Club
Box 16, Carolina Union
  065-A
Chapel Hill, NC 27514

Intramural-Recreational
  Services
East Carolina University
204 Memorial Gymnasium
Greenville, NC 27858-4353

Venture Program, UNC-
  Charlotte
Cone University Center
Charlotte, NC 28223

Mountain Adventures Club
1000 Hickory Blvd
Caldwell Community College
& Technical Institute
Lenoir, NC 28638

Davidson County Community College Ski Club
PO Box 1287
Lexington, NC 27293-1287

Appalachian Trail and Whitewater Club
College Box 845, Louisburg College
Louisburg, NC 27549

Mars Hill College Outdoor Center
Wren College Union
Mars Hill College
Mars Hill, NC 28754

Outing Club
Pfeiffer College
Misenheimer, NC 28109

Wilderness and Conservation Club
Montreat-Anderson College
Montreat, NC 28757

Recreation Club
Mount Olive College
Mount Olive, NC 28365

Outing Club
WPCC
1001 Burkemont Avenue
Morganton, NC 28655

Outing Club
2416 Gardner, Box 7616
North Carolina State University
Raleigh, NC 27695-7616

The Explorers
Meredith College
3800 Hillsborough Street
Raleigh, NC 27611

Outing Club/Skiing Club
Student Development Office
Catawba College
Salisbury, NC 28144-2488

Outing Club/Runner's Club
Southeastern Baptist Theological Seminary
PO Box 712
Wake Forest, NC 27587

## ▶ SOURCES OF TRAIL SUPPLIES

The following stores, alphabetized by city, have a complete or partial range of supplies and equipment for hiking, backpacking, and camping.

Burney's of Albemarle Inc
Queney Mall
1000 North First Street
Albemarle, NC 28001

Burney's of Albemarle
1926 North 1st St
Albemarle, NC 28001

Kevin Young
C/O Almay, Inc
Apex, NC 27502

Bell's Traditionals
9 Kitchen Place
Asheville, NC 28803

Black Dome Mountain Shop
2 Biltmore Plaza
Asheville, NC 28803

Mountaineering South Inc
791 Merrimon Ave
Asheville, NC 28804

Daniel Boone Council
PO Box 8125
Asheville, NC 28814

Edge of the World
PO Box 1137
Banner Elk, NC 28604

Army/Navy of Boone
Double Rings Inc
206 Blowing Rock Road
Boone, NC 28607

Footsloggers
835 Faculty Street
Boone, NC 28607

New River Outfitters, Inc
Boone Mall
Boone, NC 28607

High Country, Inc
PO Box J
Bryson City, NC 28713

Nantahala Outdoor Center
US 19, Box 41
Bryson City, NC 28713

Mountain Camper #10
Factory Outlets Inc
2378 A Corporation Parkway
Burlington NC 27215

Sportsman Cove of Cary
Cary Village Mall
Cary, NC 27511

The Trail Shop Inc
405 West Franklin Street
Chapel Hill, NC 27514

Alanby, Inc
307 W Tremont Avenue
Charlotte, NC 28203

Base Camp Mountain Sports
1534 East Blvd
Charlotte, NC 28203

Bocock Stroud
900 South Kings Drive
Charlotte, NC 28204

Great Outdoor Provision
5228 East Independence
Charlotte, NC 28208

Great Outdoor Provision Co
4271 B Park Road
Charlotte, NC 28212

Jesse Brown's
4369 S Tryon Street
Charlotte, NC 28210

The Dive Shop
PO Box 877
Claremont, NC 28610

Henderson's Backpacking
   Supply
Route 2, Box 994-B
Connely Springs, NC 28612

Roger Rountree
PO Box 2865
Cullowhee, NC 28733

Eno Traders
PO Box 2751
Durham, NC 27705

River Runner's Emporium
1201 W Main Street
Durham, NC 27701

The Outpost, Inc
4933 Bragg Blvd
Fayetteville, NC 28303

Macon County Supply Co
PO Box 349
Franklin, NC 28734

The Wagon Peddler
190 Depot Street
Franklin, NC 28734

Blue Ridge Mtn Sports
844 West Lee
Greensboro, NC 27403

Blue Ridge Mtn Sports
2805 Battleground Ave
Greensboro, NC 28204

Carolina Outdoor Sports
844 West Lee Street
Greensboro, NC 27403

Omega Sports
4118 Spring Garden
Greensboro, NC 27409

Omega Sports
2443 Battleground
Greensboro, NC 27408

Omega Sports
41023 High Point
Greensboro, NC 27407

Cline-Bradley Hardware
  Store
834 Balsam Road
Hazelwood, NC 28736

Kenyon/Orion Services
PO Box 2704
Hendersonville, NC 28793

Berndt's Inc
PO Box 349
Hickory, NC 28603

Outdoor Supply Co
774 4th Street Dr, SW
Hickory, NC 28601

Southern Outdoors
Route 3, Box 156
Hickory, NC 28601

The Happy Hiker
Log Cabin on Chestnut Street
Highlands, NC 28741

Quality Hardware Inc
2639 N Main Street
High Point, NC 27262

Whetstone Surplus
2510 English Road
High Point, NC 27261

Camp Highlander
42 Dalton Road
Horse Shoe, NC 27261

Henderson's Backpacking
  Supply
PO Box 1000
Icard, NC 28666

N Main Gun Exchange
1101 N Main Street
Kannapolis, NC 28081

Ace Hardware #4389-A
Western Auto Assoc Store
101 Mulberry St NW
Lenoir, NC 28645

Mountain Camper #9
Research Triangle
Route 2, Box 409
Morrisville, NC 27560

Diamond Brand Camping
  Center
Highway 25
Naples, NC 28760

Outdoor Supply Co
112 N Main Street
Newton, NC 28658

Paddling Unlimited
6208 Yadkinville Road
Pfafftown, NC 27040

Bob's Army Surplus
1217 S Saunders Street
Raleigh, NC 27605

Carolina Outdoor Sport
2446 Wycliff Road
Raleigh, NC 27605

Great Outdoor Provisions
Cameron Village Shopping
  Center
2023 Cameron Street
Raleigh, NC 27605

Great Outdoor Provisions
Crabtree Valley Mall
4225 Glenwood Avenue
Raleigh, NC 27612

Sportsman Cove & Company
4325 Glenwood Avenue
Raleigh, NC 27612

Wild Bills Army/Navy
1210 Ridge Road
Raleigh, NC 27607

Scuba South Diving Co
222 South River Drive
Southport, NC 28461

Brenton Textile
I-40 Ind Park
Crawford Road
Statesville, NC 28677

Lanier Sporting Goods
3901 Oleander Dr
Hanover Cen
PO Box 5248
Wilmington, NC 28403

Lifetime Sports
4402 Wrightsville Avenue
Wilmington, NC 28403

Treks & Trails
442 Aquarius Drive
Wilmington, NC 28403

Bocock Stroud
140 Stratford Court
Winston-Salem, NC 27103

Bocock Stroud
501 West 4th
PO Box 3198
Winston-Salem, NC 27102

Hills & Trails Inc
527 S Stratford
Winston-Salem, NC 27103

Omega Sports
1409 Stratford Road
Winston-Salem, NC 27103

Tatum Outfitters
Marketplace Mall B-5
2101 Peters Creek Pkwy
Winston-Salem, NC 27107

Tatum Outfitters
1215 Link Road
Winston-Salem, NC 27103

# Trail Index

The trail map numbers in the text are in parentheses. Asterisks indicate trails for the handicapped. (Additionally, a number of cities have special population trails and historic trails that are paved to accommodate the handicapped.) Because the *Appalachian Trail* and the *Mountains-to-Sea Trail* connect with numerous other trails described in the book, page numbers beyond the first mention of the trail in the book are given (in italics).

# General Index

# About the Author

Allen de Hart has been hiking, designing, and constructing trails, and writing about hiking since he was a teenager in his home state of Virginia. During the past five decades he has hiked 8,400 different trails and 16,700 miles in the United States and 18 foreign countries. He completed the Appalachian Trail in 1978. De Hart is currently a professor of history in the Social and Behavioral Science Department and Director of Public Affairs at Louisburg College in Louisburg, North Carolina.